REDISCOVERING
AMERICA

REDISCOVERING
AMERICA

The Making of
Multicultural America,

1900–2000

written and edited by CARLA BLANK,
THE BEFORE COLUMBUS FOUNDATION

THREE RIVERS PRESS • NEW YORK

Published by Three Rivers Press, New York, New York
Member of the Crown Publishing Group, a division of Random House, Inc.
www.randomhouse.com

THREE RIVERS PRESS and the Tugboat design are registered trademarks of Random House, Inc.

Printed in the United States of America

Design by Leonard Henderson

Library of Congress Cataloging-in-Publication Data

Rediscovering America: The making of multicultural America, 1900–2000, written and edited by Carla Blank, the Before Columbus Foundation.
Includes bibliographical references and index.
1. United States—History—20th century—Chronology. 2. United States—History—1865—Chronology. 3. United States—Ethnic relations—Chronology. 4. Pluralism (Social sciences)—United States—History—20th century—Chronology. 5. Minorities—United States—History—20th century—Chronology. I. Blank, Carla. II. Before Columbus Foundation.
E741 .R327 2003
973.9'02'02—dc21   2002152963

ISBN 0-609-80784-6

First Edition

To
Ethel Strasser, my mother
Marcus Blank, my father
Gail Koss, Sonya Salamon, and Judith Blank-Alsup, my sisters
and
Rose Mukerji-Bergeson, my first creative arts teacher

CONTENTS

Preface by Gundars Strads viii

Introduction xii

The Nineteenth Century 1

1900–1909 9

1910–1919 55

1920–1929 99

1930–1939 133

1940–1949 171

1950–1959 217

1960–1969 259

1970–1979 319

1980–1989 361

1990–2000 399

Selected Bibliography 448

About the Contributors and Consultants 453

Acknowledgments 460

Index 462

PREFACE

TO CALL THIS BOOK A WORK OF REVISIONIST HISTORY would in turn require the concession that all historical perspectives are innately revisionist—compelled to perpetual reinterpretation. History is not a summarization of unqualified facts, but is always a matter of perspective. That perspective imminently relies as much—if not more—on omission as on inclusion, on selectivity in the guise of focus. The contemporary news media, with their constant barrage of "information-intensive" programming, similarly exhibit a selective bias as much by what they ignore as by what they choose to observe. While the willful exclusion of information might be considered as compromising journalistic or historical integrity, there are no such strictures regarding the guiltlessness of neglect. The course of history is a detective story that goes on long after the official final verdict, the decades-later revelation that the guilty were innocent after all and the guilty were those who made the judgment.

The collective worldview narrows by design, not by accident. "Our" story becomes molded into a preferred "his" story. Priorities are set, celebrities are chosen, and the cult of personality triumphs over all. However, the course of culture and civilization flows not from the deeds and events involving the anointed—although the rich and powerful may believe that their preferences affect that course—but from the contributions and innovations of a diverse population. Tributaries infuse the mainstream, despite being labeled marginal or peripheral by those taking charge of cultural accounting. Whether through revolution or renaissance or "revisionist" reflection, the story of culture is constantly being rewritten. As this book demonstrates, the power of influence and innovation lies with producers and creators of culture, not the self-appointed owners and caretakers of culture—the renegades and rebels, not the inheritors.

In 1976 a group of writers, editors, and publishers from diverse cultural and ethnic backgrounds met in Berkeley, California, to embark on a project whose goal lay beyond collaboration and collectivism to embark on a nationwide confluence of cultural exchange. More than an integrationist assembly of minority identities and viewpoints that simply sought strength in numbers, these individuals had a vision that superseded the politics of identifying a common oppressor. Intolerance and neglect were the enemy, not a particular cultural category of individuals. Although focused on contemporary American literature, the Before Columbus Foundation envisioned a multicultural society where diversity necessitated interaction and sharing in place of the appropriation and antagonism that has been the wellspring of America's culture wars and ethnic conflicts. Debating whether everyone had a right to sit at the table would seem a futile endeavor, were it not for the experience of all those who have been disenfranchised throughout American history. A multicultural perspective demands not reverse discrimination but nondiscrimination, not retribution but restitution. BCF has always embraced the perspective that the multicultural nature of American society was a given: it did not need proving, but it did require pervasive recognition, not just fine-print acknowledgment. Consciousness-raising demanded cultural awareness, through something more vigorous than detached observation or appreciative indifference. BCF has stood for correcting the sins of omission and obviating the attitude in American culture that what sells the best is the most significant. The phrase "the cream rises to the top" is the slogan of the commercial whitewash. Even a cursory view of twentieth-century music, art, literature, science, and civics reveals that the contributions to culture are not conditional upon financial success.

America most certainly manifests a multicultural civilization, or perhaps more precisely a multi-civilization culture. This perspective does not usurp the indisputable influence and roots of the Greco-Roman, Germanic, and Anglo civilizations most prevalent in American culture, but it affirms the undeniable influence of the many other civilizations and cultures without which there would be no mainstream. America is a hybrid, polyglot, multi-component stew. Not a melting pot, where everything becomes indistinct, but a recipe that cannot claim its unique flavor without all of its ingredients. The pot is full, not of homogenization, but of inclusiveness.

There was a time when the term *multicultural* demanded definition. Simple inclusion was its basic precept. However, since it came into widespread use, the word has permeated American politics, social history, popular philosophy, commerce, and technology, as well as the arts, sparking competition over its meaning and internecine wars of interpretation. Just as the struggle for civil rights incited not-so-civil realities in the years that followed, the backlash to the multicultural perspective demanded further polarization. The concept was co-opted and "multiculturalism" was turned into a movement, a power struggle, a subversion of the dominant paradigm. Fences were built and camps set up. Furthermore, there were those on both sides of the debate who considered the adversarial relationship a necessity to further their respective agendas. Nevertheless, the adjective *multicultural* still denotes a matter of perspective, one of inclusion rather than omission. In the factionalized feuding over this simple fact, the mainstream relishes the controversy that rages while it continues to flow as the mainstream. The mainstream does not want redefinition, or even explanation.

That there are many cultures in America cannot be disputed, but their contributions continue to be relegated to the margins. Inscribed on Ellis Island is America's open invitation to all the cultures of the world. However, the spirit of that welcome belies a practice of implicit categorization. Throughout American history, there has been an obsession with assigning labels to all its immigrants, color-coded name tags that assigned social rank, a pecking order of acceptance wherein contribution to society was determined by a castelike system. Mainstream culture's reins were held by the rich and powerful, and it was this culture that determined the value of contributions to its progress, its historical evolution, its concept of civilization. When we look back at all that has been written about the salience and significance of contributions made by America—whether as a civilization, a culture, a political entity, or simply a geographical confluence of peoples—there has been an inordinate amount of hierarchical relegation. There was the "mainstream" and then there were the addenda, the footnotes, the externalities, the multiethnic trivia. The Betsy Ross flag-creation myth endures beyond all contemporary urban legends, yet actual achievements by all of America's "other" contributors are relegated to the periphery, as curios and trivia questions, such as "Did you know that George Washington Carver discovered hundreds of uses for the peanut?"

It has always been the scruffy artists, the mavericks, and the divergent thinkers who have propelled culture and civilization, even if it took centuries to recognize their true importance. By virtue of our information age, we are learning and relearning the realities of ancient history as well as last week's news. What matters most is not what we think we know already, but what we have yet to learn. The critical challenge comes not from being overwhelmed, but from being underexposed.

The virtue of this book's timeline device lies in relying on indiscriminate temporal classification rather than selective ethnic categorization. As practiced by BCF in its literary programs and American Book Awards, the democratic approach places everyone on equal footing, and rejects labels and ghettoizing. There is no Black History Month, or Asian Art Annex, or Latin Quarter, or Foreign Language Supplement. This book does not show its appreciation through isolation, with ethnic partitions and cultural compartmentalization. It does not succumb to the usual inane and irrelevant debates over degrees of influence, such as whether Charlie Parker or George Gershwin had the greater or more significant impact on American music. Culture critics are adept at weighing apples and oranges and coming up with astute but pointless analysis, declaring victory for their personal preferences. Furthermore, there are countless "top one hundred" lists that are always rendered more culpable by what they leave off than by what they appreciate. The perspective of a timeline is cumulative, representing what inexorably gets added on and included in the mix. It plays no favorites, but it does play every kind of music.

Carla Blank has not only produced an

indelible and masterful work of scholarship and research, but has offered up a cure for America's cultural myopia, not simply by reminding us of what is already in our peripheral vision, but by insisting that we take a panoramic perspective. The Grand Canyon is beautiful not because of the river that runs through it, or even in spite of it. The mainstream is simply part of a greater landscape. As we grow as a civilization, we must learn how to look at ourselves, all our selves. While it may appear that many of the contributions to our American heritage have been lost in the name of establishing mainstream cultural preferences and assigning historical priorities, they are only omissions. This book vividly demonstrates just how much we can recover.

Gundars Strads

INTRODUCTION

AMERICAN CULTURE IS THE MOST DIVERSE EVER on the face of this earth; there is at least one of every kind of person here. . . . A narrow view strictly to the mainstream ignores all the tributaries that feed it. . . . From those who have been here for thousands of years to those newest immigrants, we are all contributing to American culture. We are all being translated into a new language. Ethnic "minorities" are already the majority in America and soon, the statisticians inform us, there will not even be a particular group that is the majority of all minorities. We have to be democratic. Majority rule must give way to pluralism. . . . *Everyone knows that Columbus did not "discover" America. We are all still discovering America. And we will continue to do so.*

—From the 1992 American Book Awards program

Rediscovering America is designed to provide a comprehensive historical reference for the social, political, economic, scientific, and artistic innovations of the twentieth century, reflecting the extraordinary pluralism that distinguishes contemporary American culture. By focusing on parallel innovations and changes in the arts, sciences, technology, politics, law, business, and culture, it tells the story of how we keep reinventing our uniquely diverse nation. It charts events within a timeline format, combined with specially commissioned sidebar mini-essays, excerpts of historical documents, manifestos, and black-and-white photo images. *Rediscovering America* cross-references timeline entries and sidebars, encouraging readers to track the ripple effects of events across cultures and disciplines over the last one hundred years.

At the end of the millennium we were flooded with timelines and retrospectives that reduced the twentieth century to a handful of condensed themes. With a few years' perspective, we can now look back at that most fast-moving and complex of centuries and begin to define the moments and events of true consequence. This book also provides readers with an overview of twentieth-century America that is both interdisciplinary and multicultural, and therefore more truly comprehensive than other sources. Excellent timelines are currently available that focus on single disciplines, cultures, and ethnic experiences, including science, performing arts, visual arts, women, lesbian and gay history, and Hispanic, Native American, African American, and Asian American cultures, among others. There are also many timelines that attempt to present an overview of this country's history and development, but the perspective is invariably and adamantly European American male, with information about "other" cultures included on a token basis and ghettoized in brief sidebars. Some relegate information on people of color and women into separate chapters. Even the so-called "comprehensive" guides tend to be grossly incomplete in this way, making it difficult to comprehend everyone's role in the bigger picture of simultaneous events.

Rediscovering America boldly embraces the big, messy, complicated world of the past century in a multicultural United States. Instead of offering a monocultural, hierarchical perspective (a sure way to render information obsolete in the twenty-first century), *Rediscovering America* addresses the need to give evenhanded recognition to the many differences in American experiences and viewpoints from year to year across time. It broadens the usual conceptions of American culture by consistently reflecting our country's multicultural, multiethnic, and multiracial diversity. The book addresses how we all play a part in creating our culture, helping us understand the vagaries as well as the achievements of our past, the complex nature of the present, and the immeasurable possibilities of the future.

Innovation—across subcultures and disciplines—is at the heart of the twentieth-century American experience. It is therefore the main criteria for the entries in this book. But what is innovation? My first understanding of innovation came through the experience of being a student of the great dancer and choreographer Martha Graham. In her autobiography, *Blood Memory,* she says:

The only thing we have is the now. You begin from the now, what you know, and move into the old, ancient ones that you did not know but which you find as you go along. I think you only find the past from yourself, from what you're experiencing now, what enters your life at the present moment. We don't know about the past, except as we discover it and we discover it from the now.

According to *The American Heritage Dictionary of the English Language* and Eric Partridge's *Origins,* the word originates in the Latin *innovare,* to renew; *in* = intensive + *novare,* to make new.

Therefore, the five basic dynamics qualifying events for inclusion in this timeline are

• *events that happen for the first time*—discovery, introduction, or establishment of new ideas and methods; setting precedents; creating forms that are uniquely different, without imitation

• *events that appear to be new*—perceptions that speak to novelty and modernization, an aspect of fashion (style) and timing

• *events that make a significant change or shift in direction, including a return to past values (a renewal) from what is presently established*

• *events that are new combinations of ideas and methods, hybrid forms that derive from multiple sources*

• *events in which the participants are non-traditional players*—such as African American women scientists working in the space program (NASA), Asian American writers, and Mexican American modern dancers.

Innovations—even important ones—are actually commonplace everyday events, and can be called social in nature. Regardless of whether one person ends up getting the credit (which is frequently related to who has the most legal, public relations, and business smarts—Thomas Edison being a perfect example of this), they are generally the result of more than one person's efforts—not necessarily by working in collaboration, but from the laying of a series of small incremental discoveries that together create a major shift in understanding or effect. The sense of novelty that is associated with the experience of innovations may be the result of a kind of smoke-and-mirrors effect, as anthropologist H. T. Wilson comments:

. . . innovations can be seen in retrospect to possess the sort of novelty that results from a restructuring and recombining of already existing properties and activities. Innovation as such is therefore qualitatively new only in the sense that it is more than an addition of parts which yields mere quantitative variation.

The book is organized in a classic timeline format, providing a convenient digest of facts given in short bits of text in chronological order. It is divided into chapters by decades, with each decade introduced by a member of the board of the Before Columbus Foundation, except for the 1910–1919 chapter, where board member Andrew Hope invited Alaskan history scholar Stephen W. Haycox to contribute the introduction.

Within every year, information is divided into five basic categories of focus that can be tracked across the century in parallel lines of information. The categories are Arts and Literature; Politics and Government; Science and Technology; Business and Industry; and Culture. Still another category, World Events, tracks some of the important happenings worldwide, particularly those that will have significant effects upon U.S. arts, politics, science, business, and culture.

Sidebars comprising mini-essays, features, and lists augment the information given in the timeline entries.

Mini-essays track the ups and downs of particular political and cultural movements, provide explanations of scientific theories, sketches of leaders, descriptions of important events, and discuss their connections to inventions, art forms, or other relevant information.

Features provide quotations excerpted from manifestos, interviews, or other pertinent writings.

Lists offer convenient condensed guides grouping individuals working within disciplines, titles of works, or chronologies of events.

A work of this nature can only be a work in progress. Important innovations have surely been omitted—important items continued to be found daily while the manuscript was in the editing stages, until at a certain point both time and space ran out. Some distinctions for the reader to consider:

• Change has a cyclical pattern. One of the classic patterns of change in the twentieth century is that every revolution became an academy against which there occurred another revolution. A tradition has to be established in order for innovation to follow. The times when people were working within a tradition are the times not discussed in this timeline.

• A work can be highly influential and still not be an innovation. This is a distinction that explains the omission of many extremely popular or highly regarded artists and works of visual art, theater, film, music, and dance from this timeline. This is not to say they are not important. I trust that they are well taken care of in other texts, or contexts.

• Dates of discovery and change cannot always be pegged to a particular moment in time, and generally there is a time lag between invention and practical application. Many of the century's major theories and technologies appeared in their prototypes by the 1930s, while mass distribution, explanation, or acceptance occurred sometimes as much as twenty to thirty years later. Placement of entries on this timeline is determined by the author's search for confirmed specific events that come closest to illustrating the moment of innovation. If no dated event was found, dates of patent were used for scientific and technological inventions, even though such dates fall far later than the moment of discovery. Announcements of court decisions and the signing of bills into law are other convenient markers that were used to identify moments of change. Individuals are placed in relationship to a particularly important work or discovery, with their births and deaths noted only at the first mention of their names.

It is important to note that while more innovations and changes have occurred in the last 100 years than in the entire preceding history of mankind, innovation does not necessarily equal progress. Some innovations have been beneficial to mankind while others, such as the ability to bomb civilian populations from the air, have been devastating. Vast changes in technology have permitted millions of people to enter the middle class, but those changes have also threatened the planet with pollution, eliminated societies and cultures, and caused hormonal changes in people and wildlife.

Rediscovering America is not intended to make a case for presenting the twentieth century as the American century. That attitude represents to me a superficial examination of what was probably the most dynamic century in recorded history. Even though the influence of American popular culture is the source of worldwide admiration and disdain, the cultural interchanges that took place in the twentieth century were such that no society can make that claim. For example, one of the most revolutionary attitudes toward fomenting political or social revolution came from India's independence movement leader Mahatma Gandhi. When Martin Luther King adopted Gandhi's nonviolent strategies for the civil rights movement, it transformed the American South within a decade.

The prototype and inspiration for this book was a twenty-five-page timeline that I compiled as a teaching tool for a new course at the University of California, Berkeley, "Across Disciplines: Twentieth Century Art Forms," first taught in fall 1994. The course was developed as an introduction to, and a comparative exploration of, parallel developments in

American dance, theater, performance art, writing, painting, and sculpture. In rethinking the course when it became designated as an American Cultures course (all students at UC Berkeley must take one American Cultures course in order to graduate), it seemed appropriate to present a more complete historical overview, so my timeline continued to expand. I started distributing it to my classes after noticing that even these upper-division students needed the help of a quick reference to ground them in the history of each decade. (Originally the timeline spanned the years 1871–1980 because, since the students were all born by 1980 and had lived through the subsequent years, I figured it would be more productive to spend the rest of my time preparing the lectures.) In addition, I also began asking for student input, broadening the timeline further to reflect what their generation considered important moments of change. The students' consistent interest in and reference to the timeline led me to believe that this would be a useful tool for others also, so that is when I went looking for a publisher. Crown Publishers, and in particular my editor, Christopher Jackson, was on the lookout for just such a reference, and the original twenty-five-page chronology served as the basis for creating this book.

The author accepts all responsibility for the choices of events that are discussed or omitted, since inevitably the particular choices are affected by the judgment of the author. I invite readers to send in information for inclusion in subsequent editions that they feel deserves notice. If you do so, however, please provide all pertinent facts (the who, what, where, when, and why) or sources for finding that information.

THE NINETEENTH CENTURY

BEFORE STARTING OUR TIMELINE of the twentieth century, let's quickly put it into the context of the century that preceded it. At the end of the nineteenth century, when the United States was a newly established major power, European inventions, culture, and style heavily influenced our technological developments and tastes. But here are some of the breakthroughs in various disciplines that set the stage for the twentieth century.

THE NINETEENTH CENTURY: SCIENCE

B Y THE MIDDLE OF THE NINETEENTH century, the germ theory of disease (that many diseases are caused by tiny organisms) was becoming accepted as doctors noticed that various diseases could be spread from one person to another through contamination of a water supply or unwashed hands, and that the use of antiseptics in cleaning wounds prevented infection. This breakthrough was a major contributor to lengthening average life spans for both men and women in the twentieth century. The resultant population growth provided the dynamics to force major social and cultural changes in the twentieth century by simply meeting the ever-growing needs to support those lives: the needs for food, clothing, shelter, and the accelerating expectations for a better quality of life.

Many nineteenth-century discoveries were related to understanding the nature of electricity and established the connection between electricity and magnetism, providing a foundation for the discovery of the electron and the new practical technological applications, called electronics, that have shaped much of the twentieth century, including the inventions of electric motors, electric lighting, the telegraph, telephone, and radio, besides the twentieth century invention of television.

Essential keys to the science of genetics and its investigations of DNA were discovered in the nineteenth-century plant-breeding experiments of Austrian botanist Gregor Mendel and the theory of the evolution of species by natural selection as proposed by British naturalist Charles Darwin.

Nineteenth-century scientific developments also helped shape the aesthetic and intellectual content of the twentieth century, including inventions of the typewriter and typesetting machines, still and motion picture cameras and the movie projector, the phonograph, and Chicago architect Louis Sullivan's 1891 design of the first skyscraper.

THE NINETEENTH CENTURY: LAND, DEMOGRAPHICS, CULTURE, AND LAW

THE SEEDS FOR MANY OF THE cultural changes to come were already sown by the turn of the century also. Although the U.S. Constitution had been amended and laws protecting racial equality were on the books at the end of the Civil War, by the beginning of the twentieth century these basic rights were already betrayed. Every Southern state had new laws in place that effectively disenfranchised and segregated African Americans, with Northern states allowing similar practices, if not writing them into law. In 1896 the Supreme Court legalized segregation in *Plessy v. Ferguson,* endorsing the Jim Crow era and its justification in "separate but equal" practices.

For Native peoples inhabiting the North American continent, land belonged to everyone, and could not be owned. European settlers saw these vast stretches of land as the central prized ingredient, the means to reaching the greatest potential for growth and development of wealth. This difference underlies the years of battles and the trail of treaties that mark the relationship between the U.S. government and the continent's original inhabitants, the Native Americans. At the beginning of the 1800s, most European Americans lived east of the Appalachian Mountains. Native Americans still inhabited more than 80 percent of the remaining areas of what would become the contiguous forty-eight states. As early as the 1803 purchase of the Louisiana Territory from the French for $15 million, President Thomas Jefferson was suggesting removing the native populations from their lands in that area to lands west of the Mississippi. President Andrew Jackson carried this proposal out in the 1830s, with the policy of forced removal of the so-called Five Civilized Tribes (the Chickasaw, Cherokee, Creek, Choctaw, and Seminole nations) from Alabama, Georgia,

This nineteenth-century drawing reveals the importance of the horse, railroad, and town to the running of a farm. *(Library of Congress, Prints and Photographs Division)*

Florida, Louisiana, and Mississippi to the Oklahoma Territory. By the 1880s, all the Eastern tribes had been relocated to reservations. The treaties between the federal government and the tribes, whether honored or broken, left them without the right to vote, and in every other way legally separated from and without representation in the U.S. economic and political system. The passage of the Dawes Act of 1887, or Indian Allotment Act, sealed the basic direction of federal policies toward total assimilation and removal, by dissolving the reservation system. It replaced the system of tribal landholdings by breaking them up into 160-acre, individual family subdivisions, placing the remaining "surplus lands" up for sale and settlement by whites. This law was presented as a means to "civilize" Native Americans by teaching them the system of private property and giving them twenty-five years of full participation to learn how to manage their parcels. In 1881, Native Americans possessed 155 million acres. By 1900, Native Americans had lost 95 percent of the lands they

held in 1800, holding on to only 77 million acres. In 1890, 300 Lakota people, mostly women and children, were massacred at Wounded Knee, South Dakota, by U.S. government troops during Ghost Dance religious services. All of these events would continue to echo throughout the twentieth century and beyond.

In 1819 the U.S. bought Florida from Spain for $5 million, under the Adams-Onis Treaty, which also established the borders between the Louisiana Territory and Spanish Texas. In 1821 Mexico gained its independence from Spain, and inherited the provinces north of the Rio Grande that included parts of Texas, southern Arizona, most of New Mexico, and Alta California. By 1830, 18,000 Anglo-Americans and more than 2,000 of their slaves settled in just the Texas area alone, buying land far more cheaply than they could in U.S.-held territories. By 1836, Anglo-Texans carried out armed resistance to Mexico's military rule under Antonio López de Santa Anna, and though Mexican forces wiped out Texan defenders at the battle of the Alamo, the Anglo settlers ultimately defeated the Mexican forces, declared the Republic of Texas to be independent of Mexico, and began to force Mexicans off their property. When Texas was officially annexed to the U.S. in 1846, an angered Mexican government continued to skirmish in border conflicts. These conflicts allowed the U.S. government to claim its right, under the Manifest Destiny doctrine, to invade Mexico in 1846, taking Mexico City in 1847. The Mexican government surrendered shortly thereafter, and by 1848 the two countries signed the Treaty of Guadalupe Hidalgo, which ended the war and ceded half of Mexico's lands to the U.S., including Texas, California, most of Arizona and New Mexico, and parts of Colorado, Utah, and Nevada. Mexican nationals were given one year to choose U.S. or Mexican citizenship, and

Indian women riding in a railway coach. William Henry Jackson, photographer, 1895. *(Library of Congress, Prints and Photographs Division)*

approximately 75,000 chose to become U.S. citizens. When gold was discovered in California in 1848, Anglo-American settlers flooded that territory, and many tried to take land from the Californios (Hispanic Californians). Although Congress passed the California Land Act to help them prove their land ownership, many Californios lost their land. California became a state in 1850.

Once the territory of the continental U.S. was possessed, the nation began turning its attention toward gaining territories beyond its boundaries. In 1867 the U.S. Senate agreed to buy Alaska from Russia for $7.2 million. In 1893 the U.S. marines landed in Hawaii and annexed the islands to the U.S.; by 1898 the sovereignty of the Hawaiian republic was ceded to the U.S. The Spanish-American War was declared in 1898 after the sinking of the USS *Maine* in Havana harbor, and was fought both in the Philippines and the Caribbean, where the U.S. invaded Cuba. Spain was defeated and ceded the Philippines (for a $20-million indemnity), Guam, and Puerto Rico to the U.S. under the Treaty of Paris, which was ratified by the U.S. Senate in 1899. Cuba gained its independence from Spain, but was placed under U.S. military control until 1902. In 1898 the U.S. also annexed Hawaii, Wake Island, and American Samoa. These islands became useful for U.S. military operations.

In 1890, the Bureau of the Census declared that since the country could no longer be divided into settled and unsettled lands, the American frontier was closed.

On April 10, 1899, speaking to the Hamilton Club in Chicago on "The Strenuous Life," New York's governor, Theodore Roosevelt, expressed the vision that he would follow in leading the U.S. into becoming an international superpower in the twentieth century:

> If we are to be a really great people, we must strive in good faith to play a great part in the world. We cannot avoid meeting great issues. . . . We cannot avoid the responsibilities that confront us in Hawaii, Cuba, Porto Rico, and the Philippines. All we can decide is whether we shall meet them in a way that will redound to the national credit, or whether we shall make of our dealings with these new problems a dark and shameful page in our history. To refuse to deal with them at all merely amounts to dealing with them badly. . . . We cannot sit huddled within our own borders and avow ourselves merely an assemblage of well-to-do hucksters who care nothing for what happens beyond. Such a policy would defeat even its own end; for as the nations grow to have ever wider and wider interests, and are brought into closer and closer contact, if we are to hold our own in the struggle for naval and commercial supremacy, we must build up our power without our own borders. We must build the isthmian canal, and we must grasp the points of vantage which will enable us to have our say in deciding the destiny of the oceans of the East and the West. . . . The guns that thundered off Manila and Santiago left us echoes of glory, but they also left us a legacy of duty. (From Mario R. DiNunzio, *Theodore Roosevelt: An American Mind: Selected Writings* [New York: Penguin Books, 1994, 184–89].)

Starting in the last three decades of the nineteenth century, a steady decline in rural life began in the U.S. By 1900, farming was still the dominant occupation, with 60 percent of the U.S. population living on farms or communities with populations smaller than 2,500. By the end of the twentieth century, an even larger percentage of Americans were living in the cities, and only 1.1 percent of Americans living on farms.

Historian Howard Zinn reports that

> Between the Civil War and 1900, steam and electricity replaced human muscle, iron replaced wood, and steel replaced iron (before the Bessemer process, iron was hardened into steel at the rate of three to five tons a day; now the same amount could be processed in fifteen minutes). Machines could now drive steel tools. Oil could lubricate machines and light homes, streets, factories. People and goods could move by railroad, propelled by steam along steel rails; by 1900 there were 193,000 miles of railroad. The telephone, the typewriter, and the adding machine speeded up the work of business. (Zinn, *A People's History of the United States* [New York: Harper & Row, 1980].)

By 1900, capitalists were well on the way to structuring an economy shaped like a pyramid, with a few very wealthy multimillionaires at the top. Their business practices were so commonly exploitative, even if mostly legal, that Congress felt the necessity of establishing some trade restraints. They passed the Sherman Anti-Trust Act in 1890, which declared that every contract, combination (in the form of trust or otherwise), or conspiracy in restraint of interstate or foreign trade was illegal.

A constant flow of immigrants from Europe, Asia, and Latin America helped to make all of this fortune-building possible. The rise of capitalism was creating a new enslavement for working men, women, and children, whether they were white, black, yellow, brown, immigrant, or native-born. In 1886 the American Federation of Labor (AFL) was founded as a craft union in New York, led by Samuel Gompers, an English immigrant and former cigar factory worker. By 1892 there were strikes all over the country—frequently violent insurrections that ended with the instatement of martial law, with little or no gains won for the striking workers. In one of the most notorious strikes of that year, hundreds of Pinkerton guards, hired to protect strikebreakers, were used to break up the first organized strike by 10,000 workers and their sympathizers at the Homestead Steel Mills, owned by Andrew Carnegie and managed by Henry Clay Frick. Strikers and guards suffered casualties. The governor of Pennsylvania sent in the militia to establish order. The strike leaders were charged with murder, 160 strikers were charged with lesser crimes, and finally the Strike Committee was arrested on charges of treason. All were acquitted by their juries. The strike lasted four months until the strikers agreed to return to work, defeated by strikebreakers who were often brought in by locked train, unaware of their destination.

The U.S. government, responding to intense pressure from anti-immigrant nativist groups, instituted a new policy of national controls on immigration. A series of immigration laws established various restrictions regarding admission for skilled or unskilled labor, and criteria for admission and exclusion, starting with the Chinese Exclusion Act of 1882, which suspended immigration of Chinese laborers for ten years, barred Chinese from naturalization, and provided for the deportation of Chinese who were in the U.S. illegally. (To avoid a similar ban, the Japanese government carefully screened applicants for emigration to the U.S. until 1894, limiting exit visas to healthy, literate, and at least relatively well-educated candidates, because they viewed all workers as diplomats who had a responsibility to maintain the reputation of Japan.) This act also directly influenced Korean immigration to the U.S., because the Hawaiian sugar and pineapple plantations needed to recruit workers from other countries when they could no longer recruit in China, and, fearful of increasing the Japanese population on the islands, they chose to recruit workers from Korea, which was then a protectorate of Japan. The Koreans, most of whom were Christians, were treated terribly on the plantations, and so, by the Great Depression, they migrated by the thousands from Hawaii to the U.S. mainland, mainly to California, Utah, Colorado, and Wyoming, where they sought work in copper and coal mines, and on the railroads.

Natural resources and land were not the only treasures to be found in the United States. Just as the Europeans were able to find inspiration in objects from the cultures of the Pacific Islands and Africa, some saw a rich culture here for the taking also. For one European immigrant, Antonin Dvořák, a Czech composer who was appointed director of the National Conservatory of Music in New York City in 1892, inspiration could be found in "Negro melodies," which he integrated into the writing of his Symphony No. 9, *From the New World.* He said, "The future music of this country must be founded upon what are called negro melodies. . . . There is nothing in the whole range of composition that cannot be supplied with themes from this source."

Edward Curtis documented this Cheyenne "Sun dance in progress," c. 1910. *(Library of Congress, Prints and Photographs Division, Edward S. Curtis Collection)*

1900–1909

Wounded Knee and the Turn of the Century
Gerald Vizenor

T HE MASSACRE OF THE SIOUX AT Wounded Knee in 1890 marked a moment of profound transformation in the narrative of America and its native population, who within a decade would see their numbers drop to historic lows. The story of America over the last hundred years in some ways starts here; the American story is in crucial ways the story of those who have been marginalized, attacked, destroyed, or held captive, and yet have survived to remember, bear witness, create, innovate, and contribute.

Luther Standing Bear was one of the first native students at the new federal boarding school at Carlisle, Pennsylvania. "One day when we came to school there was a lot of writing on one of the blackboards," he wrote in *My People the Sioux*. "We did not know what it meant, but our interpreter came into the room and said, 'Do you see all these marks on the blackboard? Well, each word is a white man. They are going to give each one of you one of these names by which you will hereafter be known.'"

John Rogers was born at the turn of the twentieth century on the White Earth Reservation in Minnesota, and attended the federal boarding school at Flandreau, South Dakota. "At school, if we brought in a nest or a pretty leaf, we were given much credit, and we thought we would also please Mother by bringing some to her," he wrote in *Red World and White*. "But she did not like our doing this. She would scold and correct us and tell us we were destroying something." Rogers wrote with a sense of adventure, peace, and native responsibility, in spite of the adversities of assimilation policies that he experienced on reservations. He praised his boarding school education and, at the same time, he was critical of the government.

Captain Richard Pratt, the first superintendent of the federal industrial school at Carlisle, told an annual meeting of educators, three years after the massacre at Wounded Knee, South Dakota, in 1890 that "the Indian has learned by long experience to believe somewhat that the only good white man is a dead white man, and he is just as right about it as any of us are in thinking the same of the Indian. It is only the Indian in them that ought to be killed; and it is the bad influences of the bad white man that ought to be killed too. How are these hindering, hurtful sentiments and conditions on both sides to be ended? Certainly, never by continuing the segregating policy, which gives the Indian no chance to see, know, and participate in our affairs and industries, and thus prove to himself and us that he has better stuff in him, and which prevents his learning how wrong is his conception of the truly civilized white man."

Luther Standing Bear, John Rogers, and others of their generation were the last to hear the oral stories of natural reason in their native families before the stories were recorded and translated, and they were the first to learn how to write about their memories and experiences. Charles Alexander Eastman was raised with a tribal name in the traditions of the Santee Sioux. He graduated with distinction from Dartmouth College, and earned a degree from the Boston University Medical School. He was determined to serve native communities, and

became the government physician at the Pine Ridge Reservation. A few months later, on December 29, 1890, he treated the few survivors of the Wounded Knee Massacre, in which the Seventh Cavalry had murdered hundreds of "ghost dancers" and their families. Eastman was raised to be a traditional native leader, but that natural course would not be honored in the course of history. Many Lightnings, his father, was sentenced to death in connection with the violent conflict with settlers and the Minnesota Sioux in 1862, President Abraham Lincoln commuted his sentence, and he was imprisoned for three years.

Christianity touched his father and he chose the name Jacob Eastman. Charles was about twelve years old when he and his relatives escaped the retribution of the military. His sense of a traditional native world was never the same, and his new surname, education, and marriage were revolutions in tribal and personal identities at the time. Elaine Goodale, his wife, was a teacher on the Pine Ridge Reservation. She was from Massachusetts. He was burdened with the remembrance of the horror of the massacre at Wounded Knee.

Eastman and others of his generation, the first to be educated at federal and mission boarding schools, must have been haunted in their dreams by the atrocities of the cavalry soldiers. Wounded Knee has put an emotional burden on several generations because the stories of the survivors were seldom honored in the literature and histories of dominance. *The American Heritage Dictionary,* for instance, notes in the geographic entries that Wounded Knee was the "site of the last major battle of the Indian Wars." Indeed, the massacre of unarmed men, women, and children is not the

In 1900 the U.S. census reports a population of 76.1 million, including 8.83 million African-Americans (12 percent of the total population). Native Americans total only 237,196. The average life span of a man is forty-eight years; that of a woman is fifty-one years. The average work week is 51.7 hours. Forty-two percent of the workforce is engaged in farming. Women make up 18.3 percent of the total workforce. Immigration will dramatically increase between 1901 and 1910, with slightly over 8 million people entering from Europe, slightly over 133,000 from Latin America, and approximately 323,500 entering from Asia. Ten percent of the total population is illiterate.

"last major battle." The murder of native dancers was the end of a civilization.

"Those soldiers had been sent to protect these men, women, and children who had not joined the ghost dancers, but they had shot them down without even a chance to defend themselves," wrote Luther Standing Bear in *My People the Sioux.* He had graduated from Carlisle and returned to teach at the government school on the Rosebud Reservation when he heard the horror stories of the massacre at Wounded Knee. "The very people I was following—and getting my people to follow—had no respect for motherhood, old age, or babyhood. Where was all their civilized training?"

Native American Indians have published thousands of books, stories, and poems since the nineteenth century. George Copway and Sarah Winnemucca were followed by Charles Eastman, Francis La Flesche, Gertrude Bonnin,

and countless others who wrote and published life stories, autobiographies, short stories, and novels in the twentieth century. *Wynema* by Sophia Alice Callahan, the first novel attributed to a native author, was published in 1891. Callahan, a mixed-blood Creek, was aware of federal policies, the Ghost Dance, and Wounded Knee. She "devotes most of the novel to Indian issues," wrote LaVonne Ruoff in "Justice for Indian Women," in *World Literature Today.* Callahan "also includes some strong statements about equality for women." Born in 1868, Callahan studied at the Wesleyan Female Institute in Virginia, and taught at Muskogee's Harrell International Institute and the Wealaka School. She died three years after the publication of her novel.

1900

ARTS AND LITERATURE

• Two dance forms that will come to be considered quintessentially American attain widespread popularity: the first is the cakewalk, a dance of African origin that plantation slaves mixed with imitations of the minuet, a European ballroom dance of their masters. It passes to mainstream America via minstrel shows, and has its Broadway introduction in the 1900 musical farce *The Sons of Ham,* performed by Egbert (Bert) Williams and George Walker. The cakewalk becomes an international dance craze, with contests in large arenas, circuses, and ballroom exhibitions for European royalty and salon society. The other dance is the buck and wing, a dance that puts swing into Irish jigs (in 6/8 time), reels (2/4 and 4/4), and English clog dances by combining them with an African American vernacular

chord with both new urbanites and immigrants, who feel nostalgic for former times and pre-industrialized ways. It immediately becomes a new classic of literature, the first of a fourteen-book series on the land of Oz. Baum adapts the original story for the stage in 1903, and it becomes a film classic in 1939.

A family, probably recent immigrants, living in an attic home with drying laundry, c. 1900–1910. *(Library of Congress, Prints and Photographs Division)*

dance in 4/4 time. First brought to prominence in the mid-nineteenth century by an African American dancer, William Henry Lane, aka Master Juba, and claimed to be introduced on the American popular stage in 1880 by Irish dancer James McIntyre, by 1900 it is referred to as tap dancing. Both forms are linked with the simultaneous emergence of another great American art form, jazz.

• "Lift Ev'ry Voice and Sing," the song now widely referred to as "the black national anthem," with lyrics by James Weldon Johnson (1871–1938) and music by his brother, J. Rosamond Johnson (1873–1954), is first performed by a chorus of 500 schoolchildren at a celebration of Abraham Lincoln's birthday.

• L. Frank Baum (1856–1919) publishes a "modernized fairy tale" for the twentieth century, *The Wizard of Oz*. The novel strikes a

• American-born dancer Isadora Duncan (1878–1927) finds success performing in Paris, and travels to other European cities spreading her revolutionary idea that dance can be a medium of individual expression befitting a twentieth-century art form. She chooses a language of movement that combines the natural actions of walking and running with gestures found in Greek and Renaissance art. When she dances in Boston in 1922, she inflames the conservative public with her radical movement, Bolshevik ideas, and aggravating behavior, waving her red silk scarf in confrontational indignity. Although most Americans find it hard to accept her unconventional lifestyle and emotional, spiritual art, her legacy inspires the later pioneers of a fundamentally American art form called contemporary dance or modern dance, as well as feminist reforms and progressive education theories.

• American dancer Loie Fuller (1862–1928) appears at the Paris Universal Exhibition in a theater built especially for her, where she invents the precursors of modern stage lighting design, including fitting colored glass onto electric lighting instruments to create special effects, and sculpting space with light. In 1910 she brings her magical illusions to the Metropolitan Opera House in New York City, creating fantastical images by combining her technical innovations and her unique utilization of fabric and props.

• Scott Joplin's "The Entertainer," "Elite Syncopations," and "The Ragtime Dance" are published in St. Louis by white Civil War veteran John Stark, igniting a ragtime craze that will last almost twenty years. Owning a piano at the turn of the century had become a mark of status, and the first player pianos began to be manufactured in 1897, allowing nonplayers to pump away and enjoy rolls of "piano rags." Piano ragtime, a style of left-hand-heavy bass rhythm against lively right-hand banjo- and fiddle-imitative lines, was invented by black musicians who needed to improvise for hours in houses of prostitution throughout the Midwest and Southwest. In 1903 Joplin, who never wanted to be known only as a composer of piano rags, completes the first of his two operas, *A Guest of Honor—A Ragtime Opera*, but it is never published and no copies have ever been found.

• The greatest of all jazz creators, Louis Armstrong, symbolically claims to have been born on July 4 in New Orleans. Armstrong probably was born sometime in 1898, around the same time as this new music began to emerge. Jazz, or "jass," as it was called until the mid-1920s, is based on improvising upon known melodies, including pieces of marches, church hymns, and dance music played by brass bands in New Orleans and the western territories. Similarly improvisational blues and ragtime attitudes are major contributors to the new instrumental form. In 1924, Armstrong will move to New York City to play with Fletcher Henderson and begin his period of greatest renown. He will die July 6, 1971.

• Several artists at the San Ildefonso pueblo begin experimenting with two-dimensional painting. Known as the San Ildefonso

Watercolor Movement, their works mark the beginnings of what is known as the Southwest Movement. Shortly after World War I, the watercolors are widely exhibited in New York City galleries and other mainstream art-world venues. A prestigious art journal review by E. H. Cahill of their 1922 exhibition at the Society of Independent Artists in New York says the watercolors "mark the birth of a new Art in America." The Southwest Movement will be the reigning force in Native American

Dancer Isadora Duncan creates her own form of self-expression and, along with many other artists working in other disciplines, became a catalyst for what would be called modern art. *(New York Public Library for the Performing Arts)*

painting for the next sixty years. Prominent practitioners include Api-Begay (Navajo), Woodrow Crumbo (1912–1989, Creek/Potawatomi), Velino Herrera (Zia pueblo), Fred Kabotie (1900–1986, Hopi), Crescencio Martinez (circa 1879–1918, Tewa), Pablita Velarde (b. 1918, Santa Clara), and San Ildefonso pueblo artists Julian Martinez (circa 1897–1943), Tonita Peña (1895–1949), Alfredo Montoya (b. unknown–1913), and Alfonso Roybal (Awa Tsireh) (1898–1955).

GOVERNMENT AND POLITICS

• Republican William McKinley (1843–1901) is reelected president, with Theodore Roosevelt (1858–1919), leader of the celebrated Rough Riders during the recent Spanish-American War, as his vice president. He defeats Democrat William Jennings Bryan for the second time. The election marks a turning point, signaling voters' approval for the overseas expansionist policies that both McKinley and Roosevelt advocate.

• The Foraker Act establishes a legal basis for U.S. expansion by declaring that Puerto Rico, an island protectorate, is a U.S. territory. The U.S. sets up a civilian government in which Puerto Ricans are classified as "nationals, but not citizens" of the U.S., a status they share with Native Americans. The U.S. grants itself the power to control appointments of the island's governors and top administrators, and institutes a district court to enforce U.S. laws. Samoa, an island in the south central Pacific Ocean, is also annexed as a territory by one treaty with Germany and Great Britain, who have shared protectorate status with the U.S. since 1889, and another with Samoan leaders, who have negotiated use of their harbors since 1872.

• The 1900 U.S. Census reports the Native American population at 237,000, the lowest number since contact with Europeans began. This reflects the effects over the years of European-introduced diseases, wars with European groups, intertribal wars, and the desperate poverty and malaise brought on by the loss of lands and resources through the U.S. government policy of forced allotments and "surplus land" sales to development compa-

---

Pretty soon they seen some good farmlands so they start opening up land sale. They call it "forced patent," and that's how a lot of non-Indians are buying Indian land. The Government says, 'You have five hundred acres and you don't need two hundred acres. Why don't you sell it? We'll fill out your application.' A lot of old people didn't realize that this was forced patent, and you didn't have to do it. They got around one dollar an acre, then it went up to five, ten—now it's thirty-three dollars an acre. The BIA sends the appraiser out from the Area office. He walks around the land and he looks around and says, "Well, it's worth seventeen dollars an acre." That's how we lost quite a bit of our reservation.

(SEVERT YOUNG BEAR, PORCUPINE DISTRICT CHAIRMAN, PINE RIDGE RESERVATION, IN *Voices from Wounded Knee, 1973*, EDITED BY ROBERT ANDERSON, JOANNA BROWN, JONNY LERNER, AND BARBARA LOU SHAFER [ROOSEVELTOWN, N.Y.: AKWESASNE NOTES, 1974] 10)

Japanese or Filipino laborers working on a sugar cane plantation, Oahu. (*Library of Congress, Prints and Photographs Division*)

nies. In 1900, Native Americans hold 77 million acres of tribal lands, down from the 155 million acres held in 1881, and will eventually lose more than 86 million acres.

🔲 1928, 1934

• The Organic Act is passed by the U.S. Congress and goes into effect. It establishes Hawaii as an American territory and abolishes the contract-labor system. This has an immediate effect on the employment status of Japanese, Chinese, and Portuguese plantation workers, since contract workers had no legal right to strike. The act triggers a wave of twenty strikes in its first year, with 8,000 laborers protesting the harsh and unsafe plantation work conditions. Because of the labor crisis in Hawaii and building anti-Japanese hysteria on the mainland, the Japanese and U.S. governments enter into negotiations to arrive at their first "gentleman's agreement."

• A black Congressman from North Carolina, George H. White, proposes the first anti-lynching bill to be considered in Congress. The bill is stopped in committee and never brought to a vote. This year a total of 106 blacks and nine whites are lynched. (From 1882 to 1900, there were 3,011 victims of lynching—an average of one every other day—with about 85 percent black victims.)

🔲 1921, 1935

• The Currency Act officially puts the U.S. on a gold standard, so that "all forms of money issued or coined by the U.S. shall be maintained at a parity with this standard." Now Americans can safely assume their dollars are as good as gold, although the gold dollar has actually been functioning as the standard unit of currency for two decades. Congress establishes a fixed ratio for the "price" of a dollar—one-thirty-fifth of an ounce of gold—and requires the Federal Reserve to hold gold certificates (a special kind of paper money issued by the U.S. Treasury that is backed 100 percent by gold bullion stored in Fort Knox), equal in value to at least 25 percent of all outstanding notes.

▣ 1967, 1970, 1975

SCIENCES AND TECHNOLOGY

• African American inventor Elijah McCoy applies for a patent for his graphite lubricator, an invention that saves significant time and money by allowing engines on trains and other machinery to keep moving while being lubricated. (Before McCoy's invention, machines had to be stopped for lubrication.) Although others imitate this invention, McCoy's machine is so superior that "the real McCoy" becomes an expression to identify something as the genuine article.

• Eastman Kodak introduces the Brownie, an inexpensive, small, point-and-shoot box camera. The simplicity of the camera makes it possible for the average person, even a child, to produce photographs. Kodak also starts offering to develop the film, eliminating the need to know how to operate a darkroom. Eastman Kodak's new products are a major factor in popularizing and democratizing photography, and 250,000 are sold in its first year.

• Chemist Charles Palmer invents a new process that yields gasoline from petroleum, setting up the eventual dominance of the internal combustion engine in the transportation market, over competing electric or steam-driven vehicles.

• Benjamin Holt invents the first successful track-type tractor, which can be used to plow marshy land that had previously been difficult to convert into farmland. Holt converts the tractor, known as the "Caterpillar," from steam to gasoline power in 1908, ensuring its commercial success. In World War I, the tractors will be used to tow Allied troops' military equipment, where they will inspire the British to develop the tank into a weapon that profoundly alters ground warfare tactics.

• American electrical engineer Reginald Fessenden (b. Quebec, 1866, d. U.S., 1932) transmits the spoken words "CQ," followed by a song, the reading of a verse, a violin solo, and a speech by radio waves over a distance of one mile in Brant Rock, Massachusetts. Fessenden, who is also the inventor of the AM radio, proves that wireless communication is possible, a breakthrough that will help shrink the world to the reach of any radio.

• An army commission headed by Major Walter Reed (1851–1902) in Havana, Cuba, builds on twenty years of work by Cuban-American researcher Carlos J. Finlay, to discover that yellow fever, a dreaded tropical disease, is transmitted by the bite of a species of mosquito, *Aedes aegypti*. Jesse William Lazear and James Carroll, two members of the commission who deliberately infect themselves as part of their experiments, die from the disease. By the following year, Reed establishes that a virus causes the disease, thereby making it possible to eliminate the scourge. The development of a vaccine speeds up plans for the Panama Canal and encourages the U.S. to consider taking over the project.

▣ 1904

• Russian-American chemist Moses Gomberg (1866–1947) identifies "free radicals," unstable and reactive groups of atoms with an unpaired electron. These molecules will later be found to cause increasing toxic damage when present in diseased or injured biological cells.

▣ 1969

BUSINESS

• Olds Motor Works, an automobile manufacturing plant that was established by inventor and manufacturer Ransom P. Olds in Lansing, Michigan, in 1899, becomes the first plant to begin mass-producing gasoline-driven automobiles in 1900. They introduce their Oldsmobile to the marketplace in 1901. Even though the car is fairly expensive at $650, the company sells 600 in the first year, making it the first commercially successful car built in the U.S. By 1904, almost 6,000 Oldsmobiles will have been sold, but their sales will soon take second place to Henry Ford's Model T. The success of these companies and their gasoline engines will ensure the need for a vast new petroleum market.

• In Buxton, a community located in south-central Iowa, the Consolidated Coal Company builds a progressive, integrated company mill town. The company provides an architecturally planned community with homes, schools, churches, and stores for its 5,000 racially integrated residents. Until 1914, Buxton prospers, with mine workers and their families living together peacefully. Then things begin to change due to the opening of a new mine in Consol, ten miles west, a series of disastrous fires, and a mining explosion that puts 300 people out of work. By 1918 the Buxton mines are closed. Buxton slowly vanishes, leaving only a few ruins of buildings in a southern Iowa meadow, although it is called a utopia by many, and serves as a model for other American communities.

• Puerto Rico's currency, based on the peso, is devalued and supplanted with the U.S. dollar. This, combined with the U.S. prohibition against the island entering into commercial treaties with other countries, creates an economic disaster for thousands of independent coffee farmers. U.S. sugar companies take advantage of their plight, buying up Puerto Rican lands. Between 1900 and 1901, more than 5,000 Puerto Ricans are transported by ship to Hawaii, under contract to the Hawaiian Sugar Planters Association. Most are located on Oahu, where they establish the first major Puerto Rican community outside their homeland.

• With only 3.5 percent of the U.S. workforce organized, the American Federation of Labor (AFL) is formed from 216 trade unions, giving workers a united national forum to negotiate with management for their rights and protections. At the same time, the International Ladies' Garment Workers Union (ILGWU) is founded in New York City when seven smaller unions consolidate. The ILGWU is established in an effort to end exploitative home contracts, a common system for paying women to sew piecework in their own homes. The ILGWU maintains a largely male membership (men holding the preferred jobs of cutters and pressers in the garment trade) until 1909–1910, when industry-wide strikes bring women into both membership and leadership positions.

• The U.S. manufactures one-third of the world's goods, ranking first in the world in total productivity at the beginning of the century, and also first in iron and steel production. Cotton, which was once "king," now constitutes only 17 percent of all exports. Improvements in cot-

ADVERTISING, CIRCA 1900

Kathleen Moran

In the spring of 1899, the N. W. Ayer and Sons Advertising Agency launched the first multimillion-dollar ad campaign for the National Biscuit Company. "Uneeda" biscuit ads, featuring a boy in a yellow slicker carrying a box of crackers, appeared in newspapers, magazines, posters, and painted signs throughout the U.S. Though product trademarks and slogans were not new, the "Uneeda" campaign marked the birth of national advertising culture.

The turn of the century also marked the beginning of advertising's commitment to new forms of commercial art, design, packaging, and graphics. Photo-engraving techniques were developed that permitted the reproduction of multiple color plates and high-quality halftones. By 1900, national magazines began to include full-page color ads, and advertising agencies had begun to hire gallery artists to promote their products. In the first decade of the twentieth century, Frederic Remington, Maxfield Parrish, Jessie Wilcox Smith, N. C. Wyeth, Charles Dana Gibson, James Montgomery Flagg, J. C. Leyendecker, and Norman Rockwell would create visual images that would influence the way Americans saw themselves.

ton gins and other mechanized farming equipment by several new companies encourage specialization of crops. Although 60 percent of the nation's population currently lives in rural centers, these improvements also decrease farmers' employment needs and encourage field workers to leave rural areas for industrialized cities, including what will be called the "Great Migration" of 2 million African Americans who leave the South for Northern and Midwestern cities from 1914 through the 1920s, looking for jobs and a better life.

CULTURE AND SOCIETY

• Ellis Island, the East Coast immigration receiving station in New York City's harbor, is reopened (an 1892 fire destroyed the original building the day after its opening). By 1910, more than 9 million largely poor and uneducated immigrants from Russia, Italy, and central Europe will have passed through its intimidating system of medical examinations, interviews, and literacy tests designed to keep out "undesirables," before gaining admittance to the U.S. mainland, where they will mostly settle in cities and transform American culture.
▣ 1921

• The number of Italian immigrants to America grows rapidly. At least 100,000 arrive this year, most of them from southern Italy. More than 2 million Italians will come to the U.S. in the first fourteen years of the 1900s. An estimated 75 percent of New York City's construction workers are Italian. During construction of the New York subway, Italian workers strike several times and win shorter hours and better pay.

• Cities transform into sprawling urban metropolitan areas as the century turns. Improvements in elevator technology and spi-

Most immigrants being processed through Ellis Island would have this view-point as they approached the Ellis Island Ferry House in New York's harbor. Gottscho-Schleisner, Inc., 1938. *(Library of Congress, Prints and Photographs Division)*

raling costs of land invigorate the use of sky-scrapers for commercial design, where they are considered the ultimate modern architectural expression. The Otis Elevator Company will install its first escalator in Philadelphia's Gimbel's department store in 1901. Electrical elevators make skyscraper designs more feasible since their manufacture by Otis beginning in 1889. Boston, which began operating the first U.S. subway system in 1898, also develops an electric trolley car system to replace horse-cars in 1900. This year, New York City begins construction work on their subway system, which starts operation in four years.

• The Automobile Club in New York sponsors the country's first automobile show in New York City's Madison Square Garden. In a year when about 8,000 cars are registered in the U.S., they announce a plan for a transcon-tinental roadway, advocating for automobiles as a way for individuals to access relatively cheap and easy cross-country travel. Construction on the first coast-to-coast road will not actually begin until 1913.

• Carry Nation (1846–1911) begins her anti-liquor campaign, leading a group of women through Kansas, attacking saloons and other liquor-selling establishments with a hatchet. Her advocacy for sobriety will eventually lead to Prohibition, instituted by the Eighteenth Constitutional amendment, which prohibits the "manufacture, sale or transportation of intoxicating liquors."

🎞 1919

• The influential daily Chinese-language newspaper *Chung Sai Yat Po* is founded by Ng Poon Chew and others in San Francisco. The newspaper helps create and maintain a Chinese-

This photo of Mr. Lew and his sons was taken in Chinatown, San Francisco, by Arnold Genthe between 1896 and 1906. According to Genthe, "Mr. Lew was known for his great height . . . and his great wealth. The boys are wearing very formal clothing made of satin with a black velvet overlay. The double mushroom designs on the boys' tunics are symbolic of the scepter of Buddha and long life." (*Library of Congress, Prints and Photographs Division*)

American community for Chinese cut off from their homeland by exclusion laws and isolated from the European-American community, by publishing news of Chinatown events, rental ads, and employment opportunities. It presents a community that would be unrecognizable to readers of the anti-Chinese propaganda in William Randolph Hearst's *San Francisco Chronicle*.

• The Japanese Association of America is founded in San Francisco to counter anti-Japanese discrimination. Immigrants of Japanese descent have become the most frequent targets of increasing nativist hysteria. The attacks have become especially vitriolic as Republicans, Democrats, and Populists in the California state legislature consider how to bypass a power vested only in the U.S. Congress, in order to outlaw immigration from East Asia to the state.

• Buddhism establishes its first organizational niche in the U.S. when five San Franciscans form a group known as the Dharma Sangha of Buddha. The organization will publish an English-language bimonthly, *The Light of Dharma*. Daisetz Teitaro Suzuki publishes his first book in English translation, *Ashvagosha's Discourse on the Awakening of Faith in the Matayana*. Suzuki's teaching and writings will inspire many scholars and artists who come to prominence in the 1950s and 1960s, including Alan Watts, John Cage, Allen Ginsberg, and Gary Snyder.

WORLD EVENTS

• The Boxer Uprising in China begins as a peasant-led mass movement involving spirit-possession rituals and is joined by Manchu government forces under dowager empress Tz'u-hsi. Their first aim, to expel Christian influences from China, then grows into an effort to reject all "foreign" influences. The uprising inspires an early cooperative intervention by a multinational force, the International Expedition, in which 18,000 soldiers from the U.S., Britain, France, Germany, Japan, Russia, Italy, and Austria join to suppress the hostilities. The Chinese are compelled to pay $739 million in gold and to uphold an "Open Door Policy" giving the foreign powers equal access to Chinese markets and resources. President Roosevelt sets aside the American portion of indemnities for Chinese student scholarships to American universities, which provide U.S. educations for many future leaders of the Chinese Republic.

• The World Exposition in Paris offers Europeans and Americans living in Europe a close-up view of cultures and arts from the French and English colonies of Africa, Asia, and the Pacific Islands that they consider "exotic." The U.S. displays the self-taught or "outsider" crafts of American Negroes, and John Philip Sousa introduces Europeans to the syncopated rhythms of ragtime. These exhibits will become major influences on the techniques, styles, and forms of what will soon be called Modern Art.

• German physicist Max Planck (1858–1947) presents a paper to the Berlin Physical Society that is the beginning of quantum theory or quantum mechanics. Five years later, Albert Einstein proposes a similar theory that explains the "photoelectric effect" by positing that light behaves not only as a continuous wave, but also like discrete particles.

Quantum theory will form the basis of myriad inventions including radar and lasers. Its discovery typically separates classical physics from modern physics.

• Chemists Marie (Polish-French, 1868–1934) and Pierre Curie (French, 1859–1906), coin the term *radioactivity,* the property of certain elements that causes them constantly to emit penetrating radiation. In 1903 they will share the Nobel Prize for their work. Marie, Pierre, and their daughter will all die from the effects of exposure to radiation.

• The first of six Pan-African Congresses meets in London this year that France adds to European imperialism on the African continent by taking control of the northern Sahara and Chad. Convened by African-American leader W. E. B. Du Bois and other African American and African Caribbean leaders, the congress focuses on the inequities of colonialism. Du Bois first proposes that "the problem of the twentieth century is the problem of the color line, the question as to how far differences of race, which show themselves chiefly in the color of the skin and the texture of the hair, are going to be made, hereafter, the basis of denying to over half the world the right of sharing to their utmost ability the opportunities and privileges of modern civilization." Three years later he will write a similar statement in his classic work *The Souls of Black Folk.*

• Count Ferdinand von Zeppelin's first flight in an airship, the dirigible LZ1, provides humans with a new point of view, from above the earth, and is a major contributor to the general sense that a new era is being entered.

• Sigmund Freud (b. Austria, 1856–1939), the founder of psychoanalysis, publishes *The*

Interpretation of Dreams, a breakthrough book that theorizes on where dreams originate, and how interpretation will open "the royal road to knowledge of the unconscious activities of the mind." Freud changes traditional understanding of the source of dream symbols, with his hypothesis that they are driven by basic drives in disguise, revealing hidden thoughts, emotions, and desires.

◘ 1924

1901

ARTS AND LITERATURE

• Architect Frank Lloyd Wright (1869–1959) announces his plans for creating modern American living environments in an article, "A Home in a Prairie Town," published in *The Ladies' Home Journal.* His ideal home consists of a single-family, two-story house designed on a grid system emphasizing the horizontal instead of the vertical. The design sustains traditional values by centering family life around a fireplace core. It provides open, interlocking spaces with use determined by changing individual needs, and keeps an "organic" relationship to each setting by "growing from the inside out." Wright's suggestion for neighborhood clusters, formed out of independent units, is a precursor of the "suburban ranch style," a look that will dominate home building in post–World War II communities.

◘ 1947

• Booker T. Washington (1856–1915) publishes his immensely popular autobiographical book, *Up from Slavery,* recounting his beginnings as a Southern slave, his 1881 co-founding of Tuskegee Institute as a secondary school and teacher training program that goes on to graduate thousands of professionals. The book lays out Washington's message emphasizing race pride and self-sufficiency through economic development. The book becomes the urtext of the self-help school of black political thought that continues to resonate throughout the century. Considered the principal spokesman for African Americans at this time, Washington becomes the first African American invited to dine at the White House, and both President Theodore Roosevelt and Washington receive wide criticism for the visit.

◘ 1905

SCIENCES AND TECHNOLOGY

• New oil drilling techniques invented by the Hamill brothers, co-owners in a mining speculation project with engineer Captain Anthony Lucas hit a massive oil strike at Spindletop, Texas, dubbed the "Lucas gusher." Its 200-foot tower of oil is the first indication that oil is actually under more than two-thirds of the state. The discovery transforms the Southwest, beginning the decline of the state's farming and ranching industries and changing it into a major economic center of the country.

• A spin-off discovery of photographic technology leads to X-ray treatment for breast cancer, as announced in Chicago, by Dr. J. E. Gillman.

• A chemist at Johns Hopkins Medical School, Jokichi Takamine (b. Japan, 1854–1922), isolates and purifies the first hormone, adrenaline, furthering research to understand and influence functions of the endocrine system. Dr. Takamine refuses to accept an award of "honorary" citizenship until all immigrants with Japanese ancestry are allowed to apply for citizenship.

GOVERNMENT AND POLITICS

• President William McKinley is assassinated in Buffalo, New York, by an American-born anarchist, Leon Czolgosz. (McKinley's death will lead to immigrant tests that seek to stop anarchists from entering the country.) Vice President Theodore Roosevelt is sworn in as the twenty-sixth president. Roosevelt expands the powers of the president, shaping the U.S. into a world power through American territorial dominion in the Caribbean and Pacific. He institutes domestic reforms that continue to be important, such as consumer protection through the Food and Drug Act, conservation of land and natural resources, and trust busting.

• The Alabama state constitution disenfranchises African Americans by requiring documentation proving that a person's grandfather voted, as well as literacy tests. It effectively takes away voting rights won in 1868, with passage of the Fourteenth Amendment to the U.S. Constitution. This law exemplifies the legalized practices of discrimination, segregation, and disenfranchisement that are now firmly in place throughout the South.
▣ 1957

• The Platt Amendment is passed by Congress, limiting Cuban independence before turning over the government of Cuba to the Cuban people. The U.S. has written into the 1901 Cuban constitution that Cuba must receive U.S. approval before signing treaties with other countries or borrowing money. It also gives the U.S. the right to build a naval base in Cuba.
▣ 1902

• When the Hay-Paunceforte Treaty is signed with Britain, it nullifies the Clayton-

---

DISSENTING OPINION BY SUPREME COURT JUSTICE JOHN MARSHALL HARLAN IN *DOWNES V. BIDWELL* (1901)

The idea that this country may acquire territories anywhere upon the earth, by conquest or treaty, and hold them as mere colonies or provinces, the people inhabiting them to enjoy only such rights as Congress chooses to accord to them, is wholly inconsistent with the spirit and genius as well as with the words of the Constitution.

Bulwer Treaty of 1850, and grants the U.S. sole rights to build, control, and fortify a canal across Central America. The U.S. agrees to allow all nations access to the canal for military transport and commercial shipping. The governments of Colombia, Nicaragua, and Costa Rica negotiate for the next two years, with much political and financial jockeying, about where the route should be placed. In 1902, President Roosevelt decides the Isthmus of Panama will be the favored site.

• In *Downes v. Bidwell,* one of a series of challenges known as "Insular Cases," the Supreme Court rules against a pivotal challenge to the Foraker Law, allowing U.S. colonialist expansion to continue in Puerto Rico. According to Juan Gonzalez in his *Harvest of Empire: A History of Latinos in America*, these Insular Case rulings "have provided the principal legal backing for this country's holding of colonies to the present day. They are the equivalent for Puerto Ricans of the Dred Scott Decision for African Americans."

"Boomers entering Oklahoma Territory," a drawing by Albert Richter, c. 1905, illustrates the chaotic scramble for lands that resulted from the "first come, first served" policy on Oklahoma lands purchased from the Kiowa, Apache, and Comanche. (*Library of Congress, Prints and Photographs Division*)

• Congress indefinitely extends Chinese exclusion laws that originally went into effect in 1882 under the presidency of Chester A. Arthur, barring Chinese laborers from immigrating to the U.S. In 1902, Congress renews the Chinese Exclusion Act again, but on this second renewal no expiration date is set. The law will maintain the imbalance between men and women immigrants, since most Chinese men cannot bring their wives and families to the U.S. if they are husbands or fiancées; if they are bachelors, they have to return to China to marry a Chinese woman. Because of strict miscegenation laws and a widespread feeling of racial superiority among the Chinese, most do not marry outside of their race and few Chinese Americans are born in the late 1800s and early 1900s. (The 1900 U.S. Census reports a ratio of 1,887 Chinese males to 100 Chinese females.)
▣ 1943

• In the Oklahoma Land Rush, 6,500 white homesteaders stake settlement claims on a "first come, first claimed" basis. They gobble up 64,000 square miles of land in the Oklahoma Territory, purchased for $2 million in federal cash payments to the Kiowa, Apache, and Comanche plus a 160-acre allotment for each tribal member.

• The National Bureau of Standards (now called the National Institute of Standards and Technology) is instituted, creating a resource for reference in maintaining quality controls, coordinating and setting of global standards, creating a common language to use in technical applications, and furthering innovative research in the sciences and industry.

BUSINESS AND INDUSTRY
• U.S. Steel Corporation becomes the first billion-dollar corporation when investment banker J. Pierpont Morgan (1837–1913) pays for the most expensive merger in American business history to this date. He merges several companies with his investment banking firm, including Andrew Carnegie's steel corporation located in Pittsburgh, Pennsylvania, John D. Rockefeller's iron mines located in Mesabi, Minnesota, various ore production companies, and a Great Lakes shipping line.
▣ 1906

• Andrew Carnegie (1835–1919), a Scottish-born immigrant who became a millionaire by his mid-twenties, sells his Carnegie Steel Corporation to J. P. Morgan's newly formed U.S. Steel Corporation for $225 million. He retires from business in Pittsburgh and announces he will give away his $300-million fortune to philanthropic causes. He first establishes a $4-million endowment fund for retired and disabled employees of his Carnegie Steel Corporation. Next he sets up a $1-million construction fund for three free public libraries, located where many of his workers live, in the Pittsburgh area cities of Braddock, Duquesne, and Homestead. This contribution makes the printed word accessible to anyone, serving as one of the most democratizing elements of our society, not equaled in breadth until the GI Bill. In 1902 he will found the Carnegie Institute, to promote research in the humanities and sciences. Carnegie sets a bar for responsible philanthropy that encourages other men of wealth to give back to their communities.

▣ 1944

• The new recording technology of preserving music by pressing discs displaces cylinders of recorded music that have been sold since 1890. The technology will have an immense effect on musical styles and tastes, including dictating the length of a work, the way it is performed, and how it is packaged and sold. Very few cylinder recording companies considered giving black musicians an opportunity to record on this new technology.

CULTURE AND SOCIETY

• The College Entrance Examination Board gives its first standardized basic aptitude tests by measuring math and verbal abilities; they become known as the Standard Achievement Test (SAT) in 1947. The tests are originally intended to help level the playing field for students who are not privileged to have received a prep-school education or have parents who attended college. However, over time they come under severe criticism for doing the opposite.

• One branch of the Pentecostal movement

WILLIAMS AND WALKER GO MAINSTREAM WITH THE HIT TUNE "GOOD MORNING CARRIE"

When the Columbia Record Company, established in 1899, turns down Bert A. Williams, he and George Walker approach a newly founded mainstream recording company, the Victor Talking Machine Company. They become the first black recording artists on disc, making several records for Victor, including their hit song "Good Morning Carrie." Walker does not like the sound of his voice on recordings, but Williams continues recording as a solo artist, making more than fifteen records between 1902 and 1904. When the centerpiece of his live vaudeville act, a comic monologue called "Elder Eatmore's Sermon," sells over 500,000 copies, it convinces the Victor Talking Machine Company to record more African American talent, including six records by the Dinwiddle Colored Quartet, who record traditional spirituals like "Steal Away" and "My Way Is Cloudy," and novelty songs from minstrel shows. Just before World War I, Columbia finally breaks its color-bar rule and makes a series of records by the Fisk Jubilee Singers.

begins in Topeka, Kansas, when Charles Fox Parham identifies an outbreak of "speaking in tongues," an ecstatic form of speech, as a sign of "spirit baptism."

WORLD EVENTS

• Victoria, Queen of England and the British Empire since 1837, dies at eighty-two, symbolically ending the Victorian era. The Victorian era's cultural and moral values are a major influence in the U.S. and other nations as well. Her death, and the decline of the once-powerful and global British Empire, dovetails with the rise of the U.S. as the next world superpower, both economically and culturally.

• Italian physicist Guglielmo Marconi (1874–1937), succeeds in sending the first transatlantic transmission of radio waves, by tapping the letter *S* in a Morse code signal in a telephone call from Cornwall, England, to Newfoundland, Canada (2,232 miles), proving that wireless telegraphy can be used globally.

🔲 1906

1902

ARTS AND LITERATURE

• *In Dahomey* proves to be the most commercially successful Negro musical to date, with a book by Jesse Shipp, lyrics by poet Paul Lawrence Dunbar (1872–1906), and music by Will Marion Cook (1869–1944). The first show by African Americans to open on Times Square, it then travels to London, where it plays at Buckingham Palace for the birthday of the Prince of Wales, continues on to Paris, and returns to the U.S. for a forty-week tour of major cities. *In Dahomey* serves as a prototype for the "musical," a narrative musical the-

ater form that many consider an American innovation.

🔲 1921

• Charles Ives (1874–1954), considered the grandfather of "modern" music, completes his Second Symphony, which will not be publicly performed until 1951, and works on his Third Symphony (1901–1904), which will win the Pulitzer Prize in 1947. His then-radical techniques mix polyrhythms, bi-tonal forms that he learned from his father, and quotations of fragments from conventional musical forms, such as popular marches, hymns, and patriotic music.

• Charles Alexander Eastman, a Santee Sioux graduate of Dartmouth and Boston University Medical School, and practicing medical doctor, publishes *Indian Boyhood*, the first Native American autobiography of the twentieth century. It includes Eastman's experiences as part of the first generation to be educated at federal and mission boarding schools. The book enjoys considerable popularity, and he will also publish *The Soul of the Indian* (1911) and *From the Deep Woods to Civilization* (1916).

GOVERNMENT AND POLITICS

• The U.S. practices "gunboat diplomacy" when it makes a show of force to scare the Colombian senate after they turn down a U.S. monetary offer for rights to build a canal through their Isthmus of Panama. Panama declares its independence from Colombia on November 6, 1903, and two days later the U.S. recognizes the new nation. By November 18 the U.S. signs the Hay–Bunau-Varilla Treaty with Panama. Under this treaty the U.S. agrees to a $10-million cash payment and an annual subsidy of $250,000 for permission to use 553 square miles as the Panama Canal Zone until the year 2000, when full sovereignty is to be returned to Panama. Philippe Bunau-Varilla, who has been an engineer for the Panama Canal Company and an instigator of the revolt, becomes minister of the newly formed nation. To protect their investment in building the canal, the U.S. government decides it is necessary to actively invoke the Monroe Doctrine to maintain peace in the Caribbean and Central American region.

• Military Governor Leonard Wood turns over the government of Cuba to Tomás Estrada Palma as Cuba declares its independence from the U.S.

• Congress passes the Reclamation Act, which founds the U.S. Reclamation Service, whose "mission" is to "reclaim" arid Western lands through federal water development projects. This launches the most massive civil engineering program in history, as the bureau spends billions of federal dollars to provide water and build drainage facilities to encourage irrigation in the arid western U.S. By the Great Depression, five of the largest dams in the world will be under construction, with many Native Americans and Hispanic Americans dispossessed of their lands in the process. These engineering projects will have a spectacular effect in the short term, making it possible for many cities, including Phoenix, Las Vegas, Denver, Salt Lake City, Los Angeles, and the San Francisco Bay Area to exist. By 1970, no Western river will remain free-flowing and undammed.

▣ 1976

• Oregon becomes the first state to approve' general initiatives and referendums. This gives voters a systematic way to exercise their governmental power, allowing them to introduce new legislative ideas or override existing legislation within the state. It will become a powerful tool in many states, useful for testing the waters before investing in policy debates in the national arena.

BUSINESS AND INDUSTRY

• President Theodore Roosevelt becomes known as a "trust buster" when he orders his attorney general, Philander Knox, to initiate suits to break up the Northern Securities Company, a New Jersey corporation; the Great Northern Railway Company, a Minnesota corporation; the Northern Pacific Railway Company, a Wisconsin corporation; and the holdings of various individuals including J. P. Morgan. He invokes the Sherman Antitrust Act of 1890, arguing that the mergers are in violation since their reason for being is to prevent competition between the participating companies. Roosevelt refuses to bow to pressure from J. P. Morgan to "fix it up," saying, "We don't want to fix it up, we want to stop it." The Supreme Court upholds the suits.

▣ 1904

• Two thousand sugar beet workers of Japanese and Mexican ancestry strike in Oxnard, California, and form the first successful farm worker's union. Because they are not European Americans, the American Federation of Labor (AFL) denies the workers entry to their union. However, in this same year the Federación Libre de los Trabajadores (Workers Labor Federation, or FLT) affiliates with the AFL, a reversal of their usual exclusionary policy against nonwhites.

• Recruiting through El Paso, American railroad companies, including the Southern Pacific

Railroad and the Atchison, Topeka and Santa Fe, begin hiring Mexican workers to lay tracks in California on six-month contracts. This practice will continue through the end of World War II, when these Bracero Program workers are repatriated. (The Bracero Program, an informal name for the Mexican Farm Labor Supply Program, is set up through a bilateral agreement between the governments of Mexico and the U.S. to permit Mexicans to enter the Southwest to provide manpower during labor shortages during the war. *Bracero* refers to the Spanish word *brazo,* as the workers are required to use the strength of their arms.) During World War I, Mexican workers will be brought to the Midwest to build railroads there. By 1908, approximately 16,000 Mexicans will have worked in the Southwest and West, with the peak hiring coming between 1910 and 1912.

• Cuban President Tomás Estrada Palma signs trade agreements with the U.S., reducing Cuban sugar tariffs 20 percent in an arrangement that continues until the Castro era. He also talks Washington into giving up claims on coaling and naval bases, except for Guantánamo Bay and a smaller site.

• The United Mine Workers strike, demanding a nine-hour day and wage increases, signals the beginning of a trend toward shorter workdays.

SCIENCE AND TECHNOLOGY

• Walter Sutton (1877–1918), a geneticist, establishes the basis for the chromosomal theory of heredity, by proving chromosomes come in pairs and carry the units of inherited characteristics.

• Mechanical engineer Willis Carrier (1876–1950) invents the first air conditioner for the Sackett-Wilhelms Lithographing and Publishing Company in New York, although this name will first be used in 1906 for a different device. Carrier's machine draws hot, muggy air over coils holding chilled calcium chloride brine, blowing it back into the room as cool, dry, clean air. Some credit the invention of air conditioning as one of the century's most important, for it will profoundly influence the ways and places people can live, work, study, and play. Southern cities such as Atlanta and Miami experience large population explosions as tourism and new industries develop the economies.

• Arthur Little, Harry Mork, and William Walker receive a U.S. patent for their rayon production process, which spins the synthetic textile from a man-made cellulose acetate. The fabric is called "artificial silk" until 1924, when it gains the name "rayon," as in light ray. It gives clothing and home design industries their first fiber that is not completely dependent on agricultural sources or processes, as are silk, wool, and cotton. By the end of the century, more than half the textiles produced in the U.S. will be from synthetic fibers.

CULTURE AND SOCIETY

• The Education Act places elementary and secondary schools under the control of county councils, keeping curriculum and hiring guidelines under community rather than federal standards. Although the concept of community control has merit, it also leads to differences in educational quality that, by 1954, cause the Supreme Court to rule that districts that allow schools to become racially separate are also likely to offer unequal educational opportunities to their students.

▣ 1954

WORLD EVENTS

• Georges Méliès, a French filmmaker, creates *A Trip to the Moon*, a fourteen-minute film, an adaptation of a Jules Verne novel. This is the first film to become an international sensation. Instead of presenting a series of animated photographs, as generally seen in early cinemas, it sets a precedent in the medium for using fiction plot structures. Its enchanting images of life on the moon popularize the idea that man could travel to the moon.

• Claude Debussy (1862–1918) composes his Impressionist opera *Pelléas et Melisande*, both reflecting a debt to Wagner in its use of "endless melody" and bypassing the Wagnerian Romantic bombast with understatement and powerful silences.

1903

ARTS AND LITERATURE

• W. E. B. Du Bois (1868–1919) publishes a collection of essays and short stories, *The Souls of Black Folk*, in which he urges black leaders to work for voting rights, equal civil rights, and education. He talks about how it feels to be black in a white culture, naming it as a problem of "double-consciousness." In the 1970s, Asian American and Hispanic American activists and writers will invoke this concept in their speeches and writing, describing how they experience constant reminders of their "otherness," even if they are longtime citizens of the U.S.

▣ 1968, 1969, 1974

• In this same year Du Bois coins a term, "the Talented Tenth," for an elite of African Americans who are to lift the masses toward excellence. The phrase resonates throughout the century, especially when invoked to describe the

W. E. B. DU BOIS DEFINES THE TALENTED TENTH (1903)

Can the masses of the Negro people be in any possible way more quickly raised than by the effort and example of this aristocracy of talent and character? Was there ever a nation on God's fair earth civilized from the bottom upward? Never; it is, ever was and ever will be from the top downward that culture filters. The Talented Tenth rises and pulls all that are worth the saving up to their vantage ground. This is the history of human progress; and the two historic mistakes which have hindered that progress were the thinking first that no more could ever rise save the few already risen; or second that it would better the unrisen to pull the risen down.

movers and shakers of the Harlem Renaissance in the 1920s to early 1930s.

• *The Great Train Robbery*, Edwin S. Porter's twelve-minute silent film (the longest American film so far), introduces the use of a sequential story line. It is the first example of what will become a classic American film genre, the Western, and in a scene where the barrel of a gun is pointed directly toward the audience, presents the first use of graphic violence.

• Steuben Glass Works is founded in Corning, New York. When one of the founders, Englishman Frederick Carder (1863–1963), develops new technologies for color formulas and methods of decoration that are different from those used by Louis Tiffany, they quickly take the lead in manufacturing decorative and

ASIAN AMERICANS AND THE VISUAL ARTS

Yoriko Yamaguchi

By the early 1900s, even though anti-Asian Yellow peril propaganda was strong, the rise of people's interest in Asian art can be seen in several exhibitions organized in art museums. After Tenshin Okakura's (b. Japan, 1862–1913) 1904 exhibit at the Boston Art Museum, the Metropolitan Museum of Art in New York developed its Asian Art section in 1915. Yasuo Kuniyoshi (b. Japan, 1893–1953) founded Salons of America in 1922 in New York, which gave a number of Japanese artists chances to expose their works to American audiences. *East West Art Society,* founded by Chiura Obata (b. Japan, 1885–1975) in 1922, consisted of artists of Anglo, Chinese, Italian, Japanese, and Russian descent. Perman W. Nahl, Ching Lee (b. China, 1896), Matsusaburo Hibi (1886–1947), and Yukiye Kotoku (b. Japan, 1890–1933) were included as members. Yun Gee (b. China, 1906–1963), a Northern California Modernist painter, founded an art school, the California Revolutionary Art Club, in 1926 in San Francisco.

Many Asian American artists participated in the Works Progress Administration (WPA) projects from 1933, including Yun Gee, Eitaro Ishigaki (b. Japan, 1893–1958), Takeo Terada (b. Japan, 1908), Roberto Vallangca (b. Philippines, 1907–1979), and Jade Fon Woo (b. U.S., 1911–1983). From 1942, when people of Japanese ancestry were put into internment camps, amazingly, they formed art schools in the camps immediately. In the postwar years, interaction between East and West became more intensive in the American art scene, as many European American artists and scholars traveled extensively in Asia, becoming influenced by or practitioners of the philosophies of Buddhism and Hinduism. The Metropolitan Museum of Art displayed an exhibition of contemporary Chinese paintings as early as 1948. With the rise of Abstract Expressionism, Japanese art and philosophy, especially Zen Buddhism, quickly influenced many then-contemporary artists in the U.S. including Franz Kline (b. U.S., 1910–1962) and Robert Motherwell (b. U.S., 1915–1991). The exhibition "New Japanese Abstract Calligraphy," held at the Metropolitan Museum of Art, placed examples of contemporary and traditional calligraphic art directly within the home base of the New York School. Sabro Hasegawa (b. Japan, 1906–1957) was one of the influential U.S.-based Asian artists at the time. A close friend of Hasegawa, Isamu Noguchi (b. U.S., 1904–1988) sought his artistic roots in Asia by returning to Japan for travel and research. Noguchi's ceramic works, sculptures, site-specific works, and theatrical set and furniture designs are mixtures of techniques and aesthetics of East and West. Chuang Che (b. China, 1934) saw graffiti as an American public calligraphic art and incorporated both techniques into his art works. American artist Mark Tobey (b. U.S., 1890–1976), whose work reflects an Eastern aesthetic together with Western modern painting, in turn influenced Asian artists such as Fay Chong (b. China, 1912–1973) and Frank Okada (b. U.S., 1931). Nong (b. Korea, 1930) incorporated traditional Korean art with abstract art style. An international conceptual art group, Fluxus, formed in the early 1960s, included members such as Yoko Ono (b. Japan, 1933) and Nam June Paik (b. Korea, 1932), both of whom played a major role in creating innovations that characterized Fluxus style.

When changes in immigration laws opened up quotas for Asian immigrants in 1965 and greatly increased the total population of Asians living in the U.S., it heightened the voices of artists having two cultural backgrounds into the arts also, with many Asian American artists choosing to tell their stories through their artwork. In 1994, Margo Machida (b. U.S.) curated the Asia Society's "Asia/America" exhibit, which included twenty contemporary Asian American artists, including Hung Liu (b. China, 1948), Long Nguyen (b. Vietnam, 1958), and Manuel Ocampo (b. Philippines, 1965).

functional Art Nouveau–style colored glass objects in the U.S. The migration of a cluster of skilled Norwegian glassblowers to the Corning area is another element that helps Steuben Glass Works rise to leadership in the glass-producing industry.

GOVERNMENT AND POLITICS

• Eugene V. Debs (1855–1926), who received more than 100,000 votes on the Socialist ticket in the 1900 presidential race, declares he will run again. Socialism is gathering strength in American politics as immigrants bring in new radical ideas for reform.
▣ 1950

• The United States and Colombia sign the Panama Canal Treaty with the new government of Panama, allowing construction of the Panama Canal to begin. The U.S. establishes naval bases at Guantánamo and Bahía Honda, Cuba; the U.S. sends troops to protect American interests during a revolution in the Dominican Republic.
▣ 1914

BUSINESS AND INDUSTRY

• Maggie Lena Walker (1867–1934, African American) becomes the first woman to own and operate a bank, St. Luke Penny Savings Bank in Richmond, Virginia, which later, as the largest black-owned bank in the country, will be called the Consolidated Bank and Trust Company. Her achievement allows local black people to gain a measure of economic self-reliance, by establishing loans and insurance programs that they could not receive from white banks.

• The National Women's Trade Union League is organized to fight for better working conditions and pay scales equal to those offered to men. At this time, when most women workers are excluded from union membership, they average one-third of the salary of unionized men.

• The Clifton-Morenci Mine Strike by copper miners politicizes Mexican and Mexican-American workers in Arizona and New Mexico. The strike fails after it meets strong corporate opposition and the Euro-American workers decide not to join in.

SCIENCE AND TECHNOLOGY

• Inventors Wilbur (1867–1912) and Orville Wright (1871–1948), introduce the age of air travel when their aircraft, the *Kitty Hawk,* records flying a distance of 120 feet for twelve seconds to become the first sustained heavier-than-air powered machine to fly with a pilot on board. In 1908 they develop the U.S. Army's first plane, which is successfully tested in 1909.

• The Ford Motor Company sells its first automobile, the Model A, after experimenting with internal-combustion engines for more

Orville Wright making his record soaring flight of nine minutes, forty-five seconds at Kitty Hawk, North Carolina, on October 24, 1911. *(Library of Congress, Prints and Photographs Division)*

than twenty years, paving the way for low-cost cars affordable for many Americans.

🗐 1900

• "Typhoid Mary" is discovered to be the original carrier of the disease during a U.S. epidemic.

CULTURE AND SOCIETY

• Baseball leagues play their first World Series championship in Boston, with the American League's Boston team upsetting the National League's Pittsburgh team, beginning a national event for an emerging, but still segregated, national pastime.

1904

ARTS AND LITERATURE

• Ruth St. Denis (b. Ruth Dennis, 1879–1968), traveling as a high-kicking dancer on the vaudeville circuit, has a spiritual and creative awakening of her greater destiny as a dancer upon seeing the image of an Egyptian sphinx painted on a cigar box in Buffalo, New York. This mystical experience leads her into experimenting with choreography that mixes vaudeville, ballet, and pageant styles with her interpretations of traditional dances of Asian,

Dancer Ruth St. Denis re-creates her moment of creative insight. (*New York Public Library for the Performing Arts*)

African, and Native American cultures. This eclectic movement vocabulary becomes the foundation of her modern dance training system that she passes on to future generations of dancers through her students, including Doris Humphrey, Charles Weidman, and Martha Graham.

1914

• Ma Rainey (1886–1939), who has been singing with the finest New Orleans jazz bands, such as Kid Ory, Sidney Bechet (1897–1959), and Joe "King" Oliver (1885–1938), probably first hears the blues while touring in Missouri where a young woman shares her "strange and poignant" song about a "no-good man who has left her with a broken heart." By the next year, Rainey is well on her way to earning the title "Mother of the Blues," as she tours with Will "Pa" Rainey in Tolliver's Circus and Minstrel Extravaganza, billed as "Rainey & Rainey, Assassinators of the Blues."

1912

• The East Art section of the Boston Art Museum opens, curated by Tenshin Okakura (b. Japan, 1862–1913), an important Meiji scholar and educator of Eastern aesthetics. As co-founder of the Tokyo School of Fine Arts with the American Japanologist Ernest Fenollosa in 1889 and author of *The Ideal of the East* (1903), *The Awakening of Japan* (1904), and *The Book of Tea* (1906), Okakura exerts a major influence on the synthetical tradition of American "Oriental Thought."

GOVERNMENT AND POLITICS

• Theodore Roosevelt is elected president. In his annual message to Congress, he expresses for the first time his "amendment" to the Monroe Doctrine of 1823, a foreign policy statement that becomes known as the Roosevelt "Corollary." He declares that the U.S. has the right and responsibility to intervene in the internal affairs of other nations in the western hemisphere whenever these countries are politically or economically unstable or if any other foreign power intervenes in the internal affairs of these countries. The Corollary is invoked the following year when Great Britain threatens to use force to collect debts the Dominican Republic owes them and Roosevelt places U.S. personnel in charge of

Dominican earnings until the country is no longer in danger of bankruptcy. The Corollary is resented by Latin American countries and becomes such a burdensome responsibility for the U.S. that the Department of State will disavow it in 1930. However, it sets a precedent that will guide U.S. foreign policy throughout the century, justifying interventions in other areas of the world besides the western hemisphere, regardless of what political party is in control of the White House.

• The U.S. acquires from a private French canal company the concession to build the Panama Canal. Since the U.S. has already acquired the rights to control the Canal Zone,

The President in Panama, by Clifford Kennedy Berryman, 1906. (Library of Congress, Prints and Photographs Division)

this allows the U.S. to move forward with plans for their building project. Before building actually begins, however, they must protect their workers by waging an eighteen-month "war" on malaria-carrying mosquitoes. The project is so difficult that is takes over ten years to complete construction of the 50.7-mile canal, and costs about 20,000 lives and more than $600 million. It does succeed in connecting the Atlantic with the Pacific Ocean through the Panama isthmus, so that ships will no longer need to circle the tip of South America. The canal will be considered an engineering marvel and a symbol of progress. The U.S. will continue in control of the canal zone for the rest of the century, until they hand it back to the Panamanians in 1999.

🖻 1902, 1999

• In this year, Kentucky schools are legally racially segregated; ferries are segregated in South Carolina; streetcars are segregated in Mississippi; Maryland institutes a series of Jim Crow laws; and legal disenfranchisement of African Americans is practiced in nearly every Southern state. When Berea College, an integrated Kentucky school, decides to challenge the school segregation law in *Berea College v. Commonwealth of Kentucky*, the law is upheld, first by the Court of Appeals and then, in 1908, by the U.S. Supreme Court, signaling the courts' hands-off policy on segregation.

BUSINESS AND INDUSTRY

• By this year, more than 1,000 railroad lines have consolidated into six great corporate combinations in a reorganization made possible because many states relaxed their incorporation laws at the end of the nineteenth century. These mega-mergers, most of which are controlled by Morgan and Rockefeller interests, become known as trusts. On March 4, 1904, the Supreme Court rules in a five-to-four decision that the Northern Securities Company represents an illegal merger between the Great Northern and Northern Pacific railway companies. Justice Harlan states that "the mere existence of such a combination constitutes a menace" to freedom of commerce, which is the public's right, and therefore the federal government should interfere to protect the public by stopping this unreasonable restraint of interstate trade.

CULTURE AND SOCIETY

• The U.S. government outlaws the Sun Dance, clearly violating First Amendment rights in its attempt to eradicate Native American religious expressions. As practiced by at least twenty-six Plains Indian tribes, the Sun Dance is a religious ritual that involves the total community in a week of ceremony, sacrifice, and dance. The Sun Dance goes underground disguised as Fourth of July celebrations, or evolves within Gourd Dance Society traditions, even after the Indian Reorganization Act of 1934 legalizes formerly banned religious rituals, until it is openly revived in 1950.

• The Louisiana Purchase Exposition (commonly called the St. Louis World's Fair) opens in St. Louis, Missouri, one year behind schedule; it was supposed to open as a centennial commemoration of the 1803 Louisiana Purchase. Under construction for four years, this world's fair is the largest of ten to open in the first five years of the century, with exhibits

from forty-three nations. Nineteen million people visit the fair, which President Roosevelt officially opens by pushing a gold button in Washington. The sounds of John Philip Sousa's band and American gunboats volleying salutes from the harbor embody the fair's ambition to present the U.S. as a major world power. Its dual themes, American know-how and education, are demonstrated through modern architecture that contains the latest technological innovations and open-air displays of people called "living anthropological exhibits," people from Native American tribes including Eskimo, Kwakiutl, Pawnee, Pima, Pomo, Pueblo, and Rosebud Sioux, and 1,200 Filipinos. Abusive conditions cause some Filipinos to freeze to death in a boxcar in transit to the fair, and at least three others die during their encampment on the fairgrounds. Mourning rituals, viewed by heedless white fairgoers as another performance, have to be practiced without access to the bodies, which have been removed immediately from the fairgrounds and eventually show up in the Smithsonian and other museum collections. Games also occur in connection with the fair, featuring "Anthropology Days," in which an African pygmy, an American Indian, and an Ainu from Japan compete in athletic events. New Orleans jazz great Jelly Roll Morton makes his out-of-town debut. Other major attractions are designed to showcase new consumerism, displaying automobiles, the De Forest wireless telegraphy tower system, and Westinghouse movies of its Pittsburgh foundry, along with soon-to-be classic American foods—the hamburger, iced tea, and ice-cream cones.

EXCERPT FROM PRESIDENT THEODORE ROOSEVELT'S
ADDRESS AT THE DEDICATION CEREMONIES OF THE
LOUISIANA PURCHASE EXPOSITION, APRIL 30, 1903

The history of the land comprised within the limits of the [Louisiana] Purchase is an epitome of the entire history of our people. . . . The people of these States have shown themselves mighty in war with their fellow man, and mighty in strength to tame the rugged wilderness. They could not thus have conquered the forest and the prairie, the mountain and the desert, had they not possessed the great fighting virtues, the qualities which enable a people to overcome the forces of hostile men and hostile nature. . . . The need for the pioneer virtues remains the same as ever. The peculiar frontier conditions have vanished; but the manliness and stalwart hardihood of the frontiersmen can be given even freer scope under the conditions surrounding the complex industrialism of the present day.

WORLD EVENTS

• War breaks out between Russia and Japan over control of Manchuria and the Korean Empire. It will become one of the world's largest armed conflicts ever, with automatic weapons used on a large scale for the first time. ▣ 1905

• Women from the U.S. and eight European countries meet in Berlin as the International Council of Women to write a "Declaration of Principles" calling for equality of men and women, including the right to vote, and a list of women's grievances under national laws that becomes the prototype for the Women's Suffrage platform in the U.S.

• A sacred well is uncovered in an ancient Mayan city, Chichén Itzá, by an amateur expedition led by the American consul to Mexico, Edward Thompson. The archaeological diggings uncover sophisticated tools, gold jewelry, and ornaments from an earlier millennium, many of which are illegally removed to the U.S.

1905

ARTS AND LITERATURE

• Alfred Stieglitz and fellow photographer and painter Edward Steichen (1879–1973) open the Little Galleries of the Photo-Secession, known as Gallery 291, in New York City. They exhibit photography alongside paintings, drawings, and sculptures, asserting that photography deserves to be considered as another fine art. Starting in 1908, they exhibit the works of European modernists including Paul Cézanne, Pablo Picasso, Georges Braque, Constantin Brancusi, Henri Matisse, and Auguste Rodin, introducing most of them to American audiences for the first time. Gallery 291 is the first to promote the first generation of American-born modernists, including the painter Georgia O'Keeffe (1887–1986), who is also the subject of many of Stieglitz's photographs and will become his wife. In 1914 the gallery claims to mount the first U.S. exhibit of central and west African sculpture, where it is called art rather than ethnography. After the U.S. enters World War I, Stieglitz cannot afford to continue his financial support of the gallery, which closes in 1917, but Stieglitz continues promoting new American artists through other galleries that he opens in New York City over the next two decades.

1913

• The first formal movie theater, called a "nickelodeon" because it charges a five-cent admission fee, opens near Pittsburgh, Pennsylvania. Among its first features are Edwin Porter's silent film *The Great Train Robbery* and *Potemkin,* a film in the style of a newsreel that reconstructs this year's real life mutiny by Russian sailors on the battleship *Potemkin* and the massacre by czarist troops that follows. Generally located in converted storefronts, by 1908 more than 10,000 nickelodeons are open nationwide, speeding the trend to democratize art by making an international art form easily accessible to the mass public.

• The Pekin, the first black-owned theater, is founded in Chicago by Robert Motts, and it serves as the model for establishing other black theaters in other major cities, including the Howard Theater in Washington, D.C., the Lafayette and Lincoln theaters in New York City, the New Standard and Dunbar theaters in Philadelphia, and the Booker T. Washington Theater in St. Louis.

• The Institute of Musical Art is founded by Walter Damrosch in New York City, across town from the National Conservatory that at one time was directed by the Czech composer Antonin Dvořák (1841–1904). With funding from the Augustus Juilliard Foundation, the Juilliard Graduate School is created in 1924, and in 1945 the Institute and the Graduate School join to become the Juilliard School of Music. With the addition of dance and theater departments, it becomes simply the Juilliard School, perhaps the most celebrated training institution for performing artists in the U.S.

GOVERNMENT AND POLITICS

• Theodore Roosevelt is inaugurated for a full term in January. He appoints Francis E. Leupp his Commissioner of Indian Affairs. Leupp seems to be looking for a new cultural understanding in saying, "The Indian is a natural warrior, a natural logician, a natural artist. . . . Let us not make the mistake, in the process of absorbing them, of washing out of them whatever is distinctly Indian. . . . Our proper work with him is improvement, not transformation." His views begin a slow thirty-year shift in public policy toward an acceptance of, and even respect for, Native American art, religion, and social organization.

• The U.S. Forest Service is formed under the Department of Agriculture and headed by Gifford Pinchot. It will carry through President Roosevelt's conservationist policies by designating parks and wildlife refuges on over 140 million acres of government land.

• Two hundred delegates representing radical labor and socialist organizations meet in Chicago to form the Industrial Workers of the World (IWW), popularly referred to as the "Wobblies." Leaders include Eugene V. Debs of the American Socialist Party; Daniel de Leon of the Socialist Labor Party; Mother Jones, veteran organizer of "women's armies"; Father Thomas Haggerty, a Marxist ex-priest and editor of the *Voice of Labor;* and

William D. Haywood and Charles Moyer, both representing the Western Federation of Miners. Big Bill Haywood addresses the assembly, saying, "Fellow workers, this is the Continental Congress of the working class. The aims and objects of this organization shall be to put the working class in possession of economic power . . . without regard to the capitalist masters." They organize workers in any industry without regard to sex, race, or skills, and send their leaders around the country to help strikers anywhere within the western hemisphere.

• Ricardo and Enrique Flores Magon, founders of El Partido Liberal Mexicano (PLM), a syndicalist anarchist political party (a radical movement advocating direct actions, such as strikes and sabotage, to bring government and industry under the control of labor unions), living in exile from Mexico in the southern U.S., initiate publication of the party's magazine, *Regeneración,* an early example of "border citizens" building cross-cultural bridges.

SCIENCE AND TECHNOLOGY

• J. B. Murphy develops the first prosthesis, a "replacement part" that functions as an artificial joint for a patient with an arthritic hip. Throughout the century, refinements continue being developed in surgeries for hips and other joints. By the end of the century, hip replacements achieve a success rate of 96 percent, one of the most successful of all surgeries, with most people returning to normal or near-normal activities without pain.

CULTURE AND SOCIETY

• Ellis Island reports Russian immigration increases 20 percent in this year that Czar

Nicholas II orders his troops to shoot at 100,000 workers and their families as they march on the Winter Palace in St. Petersburg to ask for better working conditions.

• W. E. B. Du Bois and journalist William Monroe Trotter call on sixty male African American leaders to form an organization that becomes known as the Niagara Movement because its first meeting is held at Niagara Falls, Canada. The group protests any denial of civil rights, calling for school integration, equal voting rights, and election of African Americans to political offices. They oppose Booker T. Washington's promotion of Protestant virtue and economic self-help through vocational training as the platform for black advancement. Lasting five years, it becomes the precursor of the NAACP and the prototype for other African

THE EIGHT PRINCIPLES OF THE NIAGARA MOVEMENT

1. Freedom of speech and criticism.
2. An unfettered and unsubsidized press.
3. Manhood suffrage.
4. The abolition of all caste distinctions based simply on race and color.
5. The recognition of the principle of human brotherhood as a practical present creed.
6. The recognition of the highest and best human training as the monopoly of no class or race.
7. The belief in the dignity of labor.
8. United effort to realize these ideals under wise and courageous leadership.

American political organizations that engage in militant advocacy of individual rights.

• The Asiatic Exclusion League, a coalition of white workers, is established in San Francisco. It lobbies for segregation of Caucasians from Asians in many jobs, campaigning to continue the existing exclusions of Chinese immigrant workers and to authorize an extension of this ban to Japanese immigrant workers as well. The Hearst papers, including its flagship, the *San Francisco Chronicle,* fan anti-Japanese hysteria by labeling Japanese immigrants "the yellow peril."

BUSINESS AND INDUSTRY

• Madame C. J. Walker (1867–1919) develops a hot iron or hair-straightening comb and conditioner, used in styling African American women's hair. She starts her business by making her products in her own kitchen and peddling them door to door. She is so successful that she buys a manufacturing plant in Indianapolis and trains women to sell her products, developing an organization and a certified training program that gives black women access to one of their best opportunities for income at that time. Madame Walker becomes known as the first woman millionaire in the U.S., although in fact her total wealth is somewhat under $1 million. Her lavish Harlem townhouse serves as a salon for artists and community leaders associated with the Harlem Renaissance.

WORLD EVENTS

• Albert Einstein (b. 1879, Germany; d. 1955, U.S.) submits his first paper, in June, on Special Relativity, "on the electrodynamics of moving bodies," postulating that light will be measured at a constant velocity by any observer whether at rest or in rapid motion. In September he submits, "Does the inertia of a body depend on its energy content?" which contains his famous equation $E = mc^2$, expressing the equivalence of mass and energy, and hinting that small amounts of mass have enormous potential energy. This will lead to the discovery of radioactivity nine years later, and lies at the heart of the devastative power of the nuclear bomb. Einstein's theory of general relativity will not be completed for another eleven years.

• In the midst of a flourishing literary renaissance and an Irish cultural revival championing a return to the Gaelic language, Sinn Fein (Gaelic for "ourselves alone"), founded in 1899 as a loose coalition of nationalist discussion clubs, is formalized as a political party. Sinn Fein preaches passive resistance to British rule for eleven years, until 1916, when its agenda changes in the wake of a harsh backlash against the organization by the British Army, which incorrectly assumes it is the cause of a week-long revolt against British rule called the Easter Uprising. Sinn Fein's membership rises as a mass expression of sympathy for imprisoned and tortured members, causing it to become the most powerful political organization in Ireland. It endorses the use of guns as a means to achieve its ends, a modern, monarchy-free Irish Republic.

• "Les Fauves" (the Wild Beasts) is an art critic's nickname for the group of young painters who wake up Paris with their vivid reds, blues, and yellows at the Paris Salon d'Automne of 1905. Including Henri Matisse (1869–1954), André Derain (1880–1954), and Georges Braque (1882–1963), they are inspired by children's paintings, Cézanne, Van Gogh, and Gauguin, as well as folk and traditional tribal arts. Other

Expressionist exhibits follow in Dresden and Munich. Matisse says, "Fauvism is not everything but it is the foundation of everything." It fosters experimentation, a basic tenet of modernism, and also the belief that painting consists only of its materials, the pigments and canvas, an expression of "something that only painting can do." After two years the movement evolves into another new art movement, Cubism.

Edward Curtis photographed this Hopi woman in a traditional "squash blossom" hair arrangement for his twenty-volume series, *The North American Indian.* (*Library of Congress, Prints and Photographs Division*)

• Japan decisively defeats Russia on land and sea. On March 13, after suffering 200,000 casualties in two weeks of fighting in the war's largest land battle, the Russian army abandons thirteen heavy guns in its frantic retreat from a battlefield in Mukden, in southern Manchuria. On May 28 the heralded Russian Baltic fleet suffers a massive defeat as the Japanese navy, led by Vice Admiral Togo, sinks twelve warships in the Strait of Tsushima. Exhausted, Japan secretly asks President Theodore Roosevelt to act as mediator between the two nations in the spring. In August, in Portsmouth, New Hampshire, Roosevelt helps negotiate a peaceful settlement. Japan is given protection over Korea, leading directly to Japan's annexation of Korea in 1910. These agreements cement Japan's entrance into the circle of the world's superpowers and will have great influence on the alignments of powers in World War II. In 1906, Roosevelt's diplomatic efforts are rewarded when he becomes the first American to win a Nobel Peace Prize.

1906

ARTS AND LITERATURE

• Upton Sinclair's (1878–1968) novel *The Jungle* is published, exposing the contaminated conditions in the Chicago stockyards and meatpacking plants, causing the public to demand changes. After President Roosevelt reads the book and confers with Sinclair, he urges Congress to pass a meat inspection law and regulatory laws for processed foods, which becomes the Pure Food and Drug Act.

• Jack London (1876–1916) writes *People of the Abyss,* warning of fascism in America and holding up socialism as an ideal.

• J. Stuart Blackton makes the first animated film, *Humorous Phases of Funny Faces.*

• Edward Curtis (1868–1952), a young photographer, wins the patronage of J. P. Morgan (1837–1913), at the urging of Theodore Roosevelt. Morgan supports Curtis, spending a million dollars over a twenty-year period, during his travels to the reservations of more than eighty Indian tribes of the Northern Plains, Southwest, and Northwest. His critics charge that Curtis creates romantic fictions, staging many of his subjects as cultural curios, pointing out how he poses many subjects in traditional dress taken from museums and private collections, when by this time native people have already largely adopted European American clothing styles. Curtis produces 40,000 glass-plate slides that he prints in soft focus with sepia tints and publishes in twenty volumes with other materials, such as transcriptions of songs and legends. The volumes are so expensive that they are only accessible to libraries and wealthy collectors, and the work does not get widespread public exposure until reprints are published in the 1960s and 1970s.

GOVERNMENT AND POLITICS

• The Pure Food and Drug Act becomes law. The law sets standards to protect the public from any food or drug that is manufactured or shipped within the U.S. It prohibits the sale of contaminated or impure foods and drugs, and requires labels to include all contents. It also institutes the Meat Inspection Act, which sets guidelines and inspects for mandatory sanitary conditions at meat-packing plants, besides organizing the Food and Drug Administration.

• The biggest Southern race riot between 1900 and 1910 occurs in September in Atlanta, Georgia, following inflammatory local press reports of a "crime wave" of rapes and murders by blacks and fabricated stories of planned aggression against whites. There is a sensational call to revive the Klan, with rewards offered for a "lynching bee." Martial law is declared as the city is paralyzed for several days, transportation stops, and factories close. Black homes are looted and burned, many are injured, and ten blacks and two whites are killed before the violence ends. In the aftermath, a biracial citizen group forms the Atlanta Civic League to work to improve social conditions and prevent future riots.

• In August, in Brownsville, Texas, a racial altercation between an African American soldier in the First Battalion of the 25th Infantry Regiment (Colored) and a European American merchant touches off an incident called the Brownsville Affair. Three companies of the 25th Infantry USCT (a seasoned all–African American unit that has seen hard duty fighting against the Great Plains Sioux and Filipino guerrillas, and has fought in Mexico and in Cuba, where they reinforced the Rough Riders storming up San Juan Hill) are alleged to have gone on a ten-minute fatal shooting rampage in Brownsville, Texas. Although there is hard evidence proving their innocence, and though they have many supporters, including Secretary of War Taft, President Roosevelt dishonorably discharges all but three of the First Battalion's 170 soldiers under pressure from a congressional investigative committee. Feeling betrayed, African American voters start shifting away from their traditional allegiance to the Republican Party. By 1908 large numbers of African Americans are voting Democratic, except for Booker T. Washington and his set, who will remain steady in their support of the Republican Party.

• California expands its anti-miscegenation law to include Mongolians (the term used as an ethnic division, including Chinese, Japanese, Koreans, Malaysians, Mongolians, Eskimos, and American Indians). Laws banning marriages between European and non-European Americans have already been enacted in many other states.

• President Roosevelt sends Secretary of Commerce and Labor Victor H. Metcalf to San Francisco when the San Francisco school board orders all children of "the Mongolian race" to be separately educated from European American students. The school board claims that sixty-three Japanese pupils, as well as Korean and Chinese pupils, are a contamination threat to other schoolchildren, as a result of overcrowded situations due to earthquake damage. Roosevelt does not want to anger the Japanese government, which maintains an active interest in how its subjects are treated abroad— even going so far as to give instructions on proper deportment in hygiene and dress to Japanese travelers at ports of departure. Secretary Metcalf finds a solution that soothes both parties: he suggests separating students out into special schools or classes on two bases, the first of which is to learn English before they join a regular classroom, in an early version of a bilingual program; the second is by setting age limits, since many of the Asian students, because of their lack of English language skills, are far older than their European American counterparts in a given grade.

• An emergency appeal to stop a state court trial ruling moves a rape-and-murder case, *State of Tennessee v. Ed Johnson,* from the U.S. District Court in Knoxville to the U.S. Supreme Court, the highest federal appellate court. Through this case, the Supreme Court gives a clear demonstration of how federal courts can intervene to protect an individual's rights, particularly when they are innocent of criminal charges or when racial prejudices influence procedures in state legal systems. Attorneys Emanuel D. Molyneaux Hewlett and Noah Walter Parden become the first African American lawyers to argue before the U.S. Supreme Court when they petition Associate Justice John Marshall Harlan to appeal an execution sentence for Tennessee state prisoner Ed Johnson based on evidence that Johnson is innocent of his rape-and-murder conviction. They present evidence that Johnson was denied a fair trial and given ineffective court-appointed trial attorneys, so that his death-by-hanging sentence violates his legal rights to "due process" and protection under the Fourteenth Amendment's equal-protection clause. Justice Harlan sets a precedent allowing federal court intervention in state court cases when he gives a temporary stay of execution to allow time for an appeal to the Supreme Court. Ed Johnson's case is never presented before the full Supreme Court, however, because a lynch mob is able to break into the Chattanooga jail, drag him out of his cell, and decide his fate. The mob hangs him from the Walnut Street Bridge across the Tennessee River, then riddles his body with bullets and leaves it with a note attached saying, "To Justice Harlan. Come get your nigger now." Witnesses to the lynching include police. Because Johnson is a federal prisoner at the time of his murder, within seven months the U.S. Justice Department accuses twenty-seven defendants of contempt of court in *U.S. v. Shipp,* the first contempt proceedings heard by the U.S. Supreme Court in its history.

🔲 1909

SCIENCE AND TECHNOLOGY

• Thaddeus Cahill invents the Dynamophone (aka the Telharmonium), the first major electronic instrument, a synthesizer that produces music by an alternating current from generators. Cahill's idea is to use his synthesizer to transmit sounds over telephone wires to restaurants, hotels, and private homes, making him the "Father of Muzak." But the Dynamophone weighs over 200 tons, and requires the laying of telephone cables that prove too delicate for all the signals (customers complain to the New York Telephone Company that their conversations are being interrupted by Rossini overtures). In 1914 Cahill has to abandon his project and declare bankruptcy.

BUSINESS AND INDUSTRY

• President Roosevelt orders the U.S. government to prohibit any further expansion of the Rockefeller Oil Trust by invoking the Sherman Antitrust Act. In 1911 the Supreme Court will finally hand down a ruling that the trust should be dissolved because, in their determination, Standard Oil engaged in "unreasonable" restraint of interstate commerce of petroleum and its products. Lawyers read the decision as favorable to "big business" in the long run, because the ruling applies only to "unreasonable" restraint of trade. Rockefeller will actually become wealthier as a result of this ruling, keeping large shares in the companies that spin off from the breakup.

• The first live radio broadcasts presidential election returns to home-rigged receivers in Pittsburgh, Pennsylvania. Westinghouse will build KDKA, the first radio station, which begins regularly scheduled broadcasting in 1920, also in Pittsburgh.

CULTURE AND SOCIETY

• The most severe earthquake in U.S. history, estimated to measure 8.3 on the Richter scale, strikes San Francisco along the San Andreas Fault. Some unpredictable results come in its aftermath of fires, providing long-run benefits for the Asian American community. Because the city's birth and immigration records are destroyed, including those in Chinatown, a bureaucratic loophole allows people in the Chinese immigrant community to claim they were born in the U.S., and are therefore U.S. citizens. Since the immigration laws allow families of citizens unrestricted entry into the U.S., any children fathered in China could now claim U.S. citizenship. A surge of "paper sons," immigrants using fake documents to claim they are American-born, or that they are the children of U.S. citizens, begins arriving in San Francisco. A State Department report notes that for all these claims to be true, "every known Chinese woman in San Francisco before the earthquake would have had to have 800 children." Also as a result of the earthquake, 10,000 Japanese Americans move into formerly European American neighborhoods, where many are greeted with acts of racial violence. Japan sends a $250,000 relief contribution, more than all other foreign contributions combined.

• African American preacher William J. Seymour guides his multiracial congregation at the Azusa Street Revival in Los Angeles into beginning the major stage of the Pentecostal movement. The Pentecostals will become a worldwide sect, recognized for its members' gift for "speaking in tongues."

• The first organization that claims it represents all American Jews, the American Jewish Committee, is established.

World Events

• India's Congress Party, a nationalist movement whose adherents are mainly Hindu, protests Britain's partition of the state of Bengal into two administrative units in 1905 because it results in a Muslim majority in the new East Bengal region. This event foretells the difficulties of maintaining unity between India's Muslim and Hindu citizens. In this same year the father of Indian independence and future leader of the Congress Party, Mohandas (later known as Mahatma) Gandhi begins to develop his method of passive resistance, called *satyagraha,* or "firmness in truth." Gandhi organizes this first nonviolent campaign in South Africa, where he practices law from 1893 to 1914, to confront racial and political persecution against the Indian immigrant community.

• Two events that are considered starting points for the influence of "primitivism" in modern art: Pablo Picasso (1881–1973), Amedeo Modigliani (1884–1920), Constantin Brancusi (1876–1957), and other Paris-based artists discover African tribal art at the Procadero Museum of Man, and also begin collecting tribal sculptures, masks, fabrics, and other objects that they display and study in their work and living spaces; a Paris show of paintings by Paul Gauguin (1848–1903) stirs up excitement because of the way he

incorporates symbols, decorative motifs, and backgrounds from the art of the Pacific island people he lived among, along with influences appropriated from other non-Western court styles, such as Egyptian, Persian, Cambodian, and Javanese.

• Finland becomes the first country in the world to give women the right to vote, when they are included with all citizens over twenty-four years of age, except those supported by the state.

• The Zionist Congress chooses Palestine, an area of the Middle East mostly occupied by Arabs at this time, as the site to form a national home, a Jewish state, for all Jews.

• China sanctions a year-long boycott of U.S.-made goods, to protest the treatment of Chinese in the U.S.

1907

Arts and Literature

• *Mr. A. Mutt,* the precursor of *Mutt and Jeff,* is published on the racing pages of the *San Francisco Chronicle.* Drawn by Bud Fisher, it is the first nonpolitical newspaper cartoon to be called a comic strip, and the first to run six days a week in the dailies rather than just appearing in Sunday supplements, as had been the practice up to this time. (Richard Felton Outcault's *The Yellow Kid,* considered by many to be the first definitive comic strip, appeared in William Randolph Hearst's *New York Journal* in 1896.) Other comic artists will soon debut, including *Happy Hooligan* by Frederick Opper (from 1900 to c. 1932), *The Kewpies* by Rose O'Neill (starting in 1905), and *Bringing Up Father* by George McManus (from 1917 to 1954). The comics' immediate success indicates that a great and popular American art form has been discovered.

• Natalie Curtis, a musician and musicologist, publishes *The Indian's Book,* a collection of Native American myths, songs, and music, documenting the movement, sound, and visual elements of performances. She is supported by President Theodore Roosevelt to "revive for the younger generation that sense of the dignity and worth of their race which is the Indians' birthright, and without which no people can progress."

• The Ziegfeld Follies is born in New York City, produced by Florenz Ziegfeld (1869–1932) to show off female finesse in extravagant musical productions that become a major ingredient of the Broadway style of entertainment.

GOVERNMENT AND POLITICS

• Oklahoma is admitted to the Union as the forty-sixth state after President Roosevelt and Congress advise against a plan, voted on by Indians and some non-Indians, to have the Indian Territory admitted as a separate state, named Sequoyah. A prohibition against alcohol is written into the state constitution.

• President Theodore Roosevelt negotiates a second "gentleman's agreement" with Japan, settling the dispute between that country and the U.S. over the Immigration Act of 1907, which blocks Japanese laborers from entering the U.S. through Hawaii, Mexico, or Canada. The U.S. agrees to block any legislation that could cause harrassment to Japanese already living in the U.S., and Japan agrees to set exit visa restrictions. Although Japanese immigration peaks in this year, with 30,200 immigrants, this agreement, which is signed

by both countries the following year and is known as the 1908 Gentleman's Agreement, will shortly curtail Japanese laborers from coming to the U.S.

• Nicaragua, led by its president, José Santos Zelaya, invades and occupies Honduras in a war against Honduras, Guatemala, and El Salvador. U.S. banana plantation owners persuade President Roosevelt to send the U.S. Marines into Honduras to safeguard their property and Americans' lives. Just as the U.S. troops are about to engage in battle with Zelaya's forces, Secretary of State Elihu Root and Mexican President Porfirio Diaz negotiate a withdrawal of the Nicaraguans. The peace talks lead to the establishment of a new entity to arbitrate conflicts in the area, the Central American Court of Justice. The U.S. government uses media to stereotype opponents as butchers and tyrants when their policies run counter to U.S. interests, creating a stereotype called "El Jefe" in Latin America.

BUSINESS AND INDUSTRY

• An economic boom ends in October, with the Panic of 1907. The panic starts with a dramatic decline in copper prices, which causes the market for copper mining stocks to fall, and which then threatens banks that have heavily underwritten the copper industry. In New York City, amid rumors that a chain of banks are in danger of failing, the Knickerbocker Trust Company, with 18,000 depositors and $67 million in deposits, is forced to suspend payments and shut its doors after a run by its depositors. Financier J. P. Morgan, whose interests would be jeopardized by a depression or panic, leads a collusion of bankers who save another large bank, the Trust Company

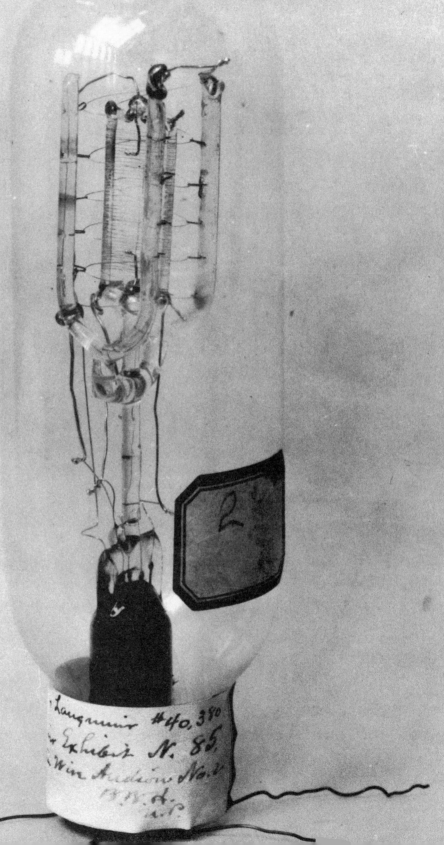

This vacuum tube (designed by Irving Langmuir, a GE research scientist and 1932 Nobel Prize winner in Chemistry), is a modification of Lee De Forest's original Triode design. His invention proves to be the foundation for powering electronic devices for the first half of the century, and is a predecessor of the transistor. *(Hall of Electrical History of the Schenectady Museum)*

of America, and smaller trusts that experience depositors' runs over the following weeks. The bankers shore up the banks by importing $100 million in European gold, secured with the help of a government loan of $6,000,000 that is hurriedly delivered to New York by Secretary of the Treasury George Cortelyou in person, and guaranteed by J. P. Morgan & Co., which becomes, in effect, the lender of last resort. The Wall Street stock market still crashes, and the resulting depression continues into 1908. These incidents, made worse because there is no central banking system for bankers to turn to in the emergency, lead to a special congressional review of the nation's entire financial system in the next decade. Their findings lay the foundation for the Federal Reserve System, which is set up in 1913.

• Canton Bank is established as the first Chinese bank in the continental United States. It will remain in business until 1926.

SCIENCE AND TECHNOLOGY

• Photographs can now be transmitted by cable. News media will employ this new technology to reproduce images of the latest breaking news stories, because they can obtain images almost instantly.

• Lee De Forest (1873–1961) invents the Triode or Audion tube, the first three-element vacuum-tube detector, a simple and inexpensive electronic device that amplifies electric signals over distance. The Audion tube makes it practical to develop far-reaching commercial radio broadcasting. Although De Forest never enjoys financial success because of technical and legal problems, his tube becomes the standard in radio sets, besides providing the base

that allows television, radar, and early computers to be developed.

• Reginald A. Fessenden and E. F. W. Alexanderson invent a high-frequency electric generator.

• Thomas Hunt Morgan (b. Kentucky, 1866–1945) begins work studying the chromosomes of fruit flies. His work leads to a basic understanding of heredity.

CULTURE AND SOCIETY

• The U.S. Immigration Commission initiates a study of immigration in this year when immigration reaches its twentieth-century peak of 1.2 million. Most of these immigrants come from countries in central and eastern Europe. They tend to settle in large cities, and the resulting population expansion and job competition spark some anti-Semitic and anti-Catholic feelings. In 1911 the commission publishes its report, which offers support to anti-immigrant factions by recommending new legislation to limit entry with quota and literacy requirements.

WORLD EVENTS

• A painting by Georges Braque (1882–1963) is rejected by the jury of the Salon d'Automne. When Henri Matisse (1859–1954), who is one of the judges, describes Braque's painting as being made up of "little cubes," he gives Cubism its name. Cubism rejects the optical realism of Impressionism. It owes much to the artists' observations of traditional arts from Africa, the Pacific Islands, and the Americas, besides non-Western court styles such as Egyptian, Persian, Cambodian, and Javanese. Cubism will involve Braque, Pablo Picasso (1881–1973), who will paint *Les Demoiselles d'Avignon* in this year,

Juan Gris (1887–1927), and others for at least the next ten years.

1908

ARTS AND LITERATURE

• A group of eight realistic painters from the U.S. exhibit their works together for the first time at the Macbeth Gallery in New York. The press calls them the Eight, as they are known until 1934, when art historians and curators Alfred Barr and Holger Cahill refer to them as the Ashcan School. Although they rarely paint ashcans and are not a school, the name sticks. The Eight believe in painting images of everyday life in the city that are usually hidden or not discussed in proper society, a kind of visual muckraking that reveals drunks in rundown bars, cleaning women, and rowdy Broadway crowds. Often cited as the first American art movement of the twentieth century, the Eight include Arthur B. Davies (1862–1928), Maurice Prendergast (1859–1924), Ernest Lawson (1873–1939), and John Sloan (1871–1951). Robert Henri (1865–1929) functions as leader and instigator of this group. The group will help organize the Armory Show in 1913, shifting Americans toward new ways of thinking about art that generally rejects any kind of realism.

• Charles Ives composes *The Unanswered Question,* a magically impressionistic work for trumpet, flutes, and strings, that introduces the innovation of "style collage," superimposing three tempos, three themes, and three contrasted harmonic idioms.

GOVERNMENT AND POLITICS

• The first conference on the conservation of natural resources is convened in Washington, D.C., by the director of the National Forest Service, Gifford Pinchot, and chaired by President Roosevelt. They will lay the groundwork for a conservation policy that will double the number of national parks.

• The forerunner of the Federal Bureau of Investigation is initiated by Attorney General Charles J. Bonaparte when he appoints an unnamed force of special agents within the Department of Justice. (In 1909 it is named the Bureau of Investigation, and it receives its present title in 1935.) They are to be the principal investigative arm of the Department of Justice, for violations of federal laws related to national banking, bankruptcy, naturalization, land fraud, antitrust crime, peonage (compulsory servitude), and neutrality violations.

• William Howard Taft (1857–1930), a Republican who is Roosevelt's secretary of war and his chosen successor, beats William Jennings Bryan to be elected twenty-seventh president. He will leave little to call a legacy during his term in office, so little that Roosevelt remarks, "Taft meant well, but he meant well feebly."

BUSINESS AND INDUSTRY

• The Model T, a touring car nicknamed "Tin Lizzy" because the body is fabricated with lightweight steel sheets, is introduced by the Ford Motor Company. Costing $850 and taking fourteen work hours to assemble, it is the first car to have left-side steering. More than 15 million will be driven over the next twenty years.

SCIENCE AND TECHNOLOGY

• American chemist Leo Baekeland (b. Belgium, 1863–1944) invents and patents Bakelite, his trade name for phenol-formaldehyde, the first insoluble plastic. Once heat and pressure

> How would you like to iron a shirt a minute? Think of standing at a mangle just above the washroom with the hot steam pouring up through the floor for ten, twelve, fourteen, and sometimes seventeen hours a day! Sometimes the floors are made of cement and then it seems as though one were standing on hot coals, and the workers are dripping with perspiration. . . . They are . . . breathing air laden with particles of soda, ammonia, and other chemicals! The Laundry Workers Union . . . in one city reduced this long day to nine hours and has increased the wages fifty percent. . . .
>
> (1909 HANDBOOK OF THE WOMEN'S TRADE UNION INDUSTRIAL LEAGUE)

have formed it, it cannot be melted or changed in shape. Bakelite, as the first of more than 2,000 synthetic plastic resins, starts a revolution in manufacturing, making possible one of the country's largest industries.

• The Hughes Tools Company develops a steel-toothed rock-drilling bit that revolutionizes oil drilling, because it allows drilling through hard rock.

CULTURE AND SOCIETY
• The rural population of the U.S. falls to 50 percent of the total population for the first time.

WORLD EVENTS
• Scottish electrical engineer A. A. Campbell Swington writes a letter in *Nature* titled "Distant Electric Vision," outlining a method that becomes the fundamental basis for modern television transmission, sixteen years before the first TV picture will be seen.

1909

ARTS AND LITERATURE
• William Christopher Handy (1873–1958), called "the father of the blues," writes "The Memphis Blues," which many people refer to as the first blues. Handy actually has just put a new set of lyrics by George Norton to one of his tunes, "Mr. Crump," that was originally about a Memphis politician. Because the blues is a new form, unfamiliar to mainstream music publishers, Handy has trouble getting it published. In 1912 two other blues tunes, "Baby Seals Blues" by Artie Matthews and "Dallas Blues" by Hart A. Wand, are published before Handy decides to publish "The Memphis Blues" himself. It quickly becomes popular around the country.

▣ 1914

GOVERNMENT AND POLITICS
• Congress authorizes a constitutional amendment initiating a federal tax on incomes, called the Income Tax Amendment, in response to dissatisfaction with excise taxes and high tariffs. It will be ratified by the states and go into effect as the Sixteenth Amendment in 1913.

• The U.S. Congress passes the first copyright law, giving copyright owners exclusive rights to perform and reproduce their own work. It also gives publishing companies that file for the right 50 percent of ownership and royalty rights. This law will provide a boon to Tin Pan Alley, because record companies will have to pay royalties to the composers and/or the publishing firms that own at least half of the copyrighted work.

• The U.S. Justice Department and the Supreme Court confront rising mob rule incidents in *U.S. v. Shipp,* finding six men guilty of lynching Ed Johnson in 1906 while he was a federal prisoner awaiting a Supreme Court decision on his appeal in a rape-and-murder case. In the first contempt proceedings heard by the U.S. Supreme Court in its history, Joseph F. Shipp, sheriff of Hamilton County, is found guilty of contempt-of-court charges for his failure to protect Johnson by unlawfully conspiring with a lynch mob. Shipp is sentenced to ninety days of imprisonment along with two other men. Another three defendants are sentenced to sixty days' imprisonment, while three other defendants are declared not guilty. This ruling, in combination with the 1906 case *State of Tennessee v. Ed Johnson,* has a ripple effect throughout the rest of the century, sets precedents that underline the power and authority of the Supreme Court, and promotes respect for the rule of law.

◫ 1906

BUSINESS AND INDUSTRY

• In McKees Rocks, Pennsylvania, the Industrial Workers of the World (IWW) lead a strike by 6,000 steel mill workers against the Pressed Steel Car Company, a subsidiary of U.S. Steel that manufactures cars for use in New York City's Hudson and Manhattan tunnels. The strikers, who work twelve hours a day for wages that can barely keep their families alive, are demanding changes in the working conditions in the mills, known as "the slaughterhouse," where at least one worker a day is said to be killed by faulty machinery. The strike turns violent, as workers fight state troopers and other armed patrols. At least five workers and three troopers are killed before the strikers win. IWW leaders continue organizing throughout the country, and although their membership never exceeds five to ten thousand at any time, they succeed in inspiring thousands throughout the country to mobilize.

• Twenty thousand New York City garment workers, consisting mostly of women and recent immigrants, go on strike for the right to unionize and to get better working conditions. The strike succeeds in producing reforms in garment shops throughout the city.

• To stop unlicensed filmmaking companies from producing motion pictures, Thomas Edison founds the Motion Picture Patents Company.

• In the Japanese strike of 1909, 7,000 Japanese plantation laborers on Oahu strike to protest a differential-wage system based on ethnicity. The American plantation owners immediately move to break the strike by hiring scabs among Koreans, Hawaiians, Chinese, and Portuguese, and by importing large numbers of Filipinos. The strike continues for four months, changing the workers' identities from Japanese into Japanese Americans: ninety-two strikers write a letter to the plantation manager on May 19 saying, "We have decided to permanently settle here, to incorporate ourselves with the body politique [*sic*] of Hawaii—to unite our destiny with that of Hawaii, sharing the prosperity and adversity of Hawaii with other citizens of Hawaii. . . ." The Japanese workers do win their demands for higher wages and an undifferentiated wage system, but they also give the owners a weapon of using workers of other nationalities to break future strikes.

◫ 1919

SCIENCE AND TECHNOLOGY

• Russian-American chemist Phoebus Levene (1869–1940) discovers that nucleic acid consists of two types of genetic materials, RNA and DNA. He will later locate the sugar ribose, the R in ribonucleic acid (RNA), in 1909, and the sugar deoxyribose, the D in deoxyribonucleic acid (DNA), in 1929.

CULTURE AND SOCIETY

• Geronimo, leader of the Chiricahua Apaches, dies at Fort Sill, Oklahoma, where he has been a prisoner of war for twenty-three years, since 1894, except for the day Teddy Roosevelt requested he ride in his inaugural parade, in 1902.

• The National Negro Committee, a biracial group, is formed by W. E. B. Du Bois and members of the Niagara Movement. Backed by forty-seven European Americans and six African Americans, they publish a "Call" in national newspapers, asking leaders "to Discuss Means for Securing Political and Civil Equality for the Negro." This group expands to include social reformer Jane Addams (1860–1935), philosopher and educator John Dewey (1859–1952), journalist Ida B. Wells-Barnett (1862–1931), social worker Henry Moscowitz, socialist humanitarian Mary White Ovington, and other prominent humanitarians and religious leaders. They found the National Association for the Advancement of Colored People (NAACP), a civil rights organization committed to social justice, holding their first conference in New York City this year. They set the basic agenda that the NAACP follows, to contest prejudicial laws, provide the public with information concerning the adverse effects of discrimination, publicize lynchings and other racial abuses, and provide legal defense that sets precedents in laws at the local, state, and federal level.

• Sigmund Freud, the Austrian founder of psychoanalysis, and his associate C. G. Jung (1874–1961), a Swiss psychiatrist, give a lecture series at Clark University in Worchester, Massachusetts. Their visit to the U.S., along with the first translation of a paper by Freud, "On the Psychical Mechanism of Hysterical Phenomena," brings international recognition to their theories and work in helping patients recognize repressed thoughts, actions, and forgotten traumas through hypnosis, interpretation of dreams, and "free association."

WORLD EVENTS

• The wireless radio is developed by Italian electrical engineer Marchese Guglielmo Marconi (1874–1937).

• After seven expeditions, Admiral Robert Edwin Peary (1856–1920) claims to have reached the North Pole. Although there are doubts he actually reached the top of the globe, he definitely did come within sixty miles of it. He is accompanied by four Inuit guides and his longtime African American assistant, Matthew Henson (1866–1955). Henson has excellent survival skills, and is fluent in the Inuit language. He is actually the first one to step on the spot they believe to be the North Pole and the one to place the American flag there. In two years the last unexplored continent, the South Pole, will be claimed too.

• The Futurist Movement is founded in Italy by painter Luigi Russolo (1885–1947) and poet Emilio Filippo Tommaso Marinetti (1876–1944), with the 1909 publication of the first of many manifestos, "The Foundation and Manifesto of Futurism." It celebrates speed, mechanization, danger, militarism, and dynamism, calling war "the world's only hygiene." The Futurists take advantage of the current wave of nationalism and colonialism sweeping Europe, and their nationalistic ideas come to Mussolini's attention, influencing the formulation of the Fascists' philosophy. The Futurist writers, visual artists, and musicians invent "synthetic" theater, using a variety style that swiftly compresses one idea after another into a series of events, carefully avoiding a story line. By 1912 the Futurists' ideas will have spread across Europe, including a Futurist art exhibit housed in Paris, and the publication of an English translation of the 1909 manifesto. Their witty, outrageous live performance style is often credited as the beginning of a new art form that continues to resurface throughout the century, carried on by the Dadaists in the 1920s, and John Cage (1912–1992) and Fluxus in the 1950s and 1960s. In the 1970s, critics will invent the term "performance art" for this genre.

🖸 1961

• German painter and printmaker Franz Marc (1880–1916) is inspired to paint horses blue after looking at the ledger drawings of Plains Indians. His work inspires the name for a movement, Der Blaue Reiter (Blue Rider), a group of Expressionist artists who publish a book by the same name in Munich with works by visual artists Wassily Kandinsky (b. Russia, 1866–1944) and Marc, with composer Arnold Schoenberg (1874–1951) writing on music.

• Romanian sculptor Constantin Brancusi (1876–1957) and Italian sculptor Amedeo Modigliani (1884–1920) begin working together in Paris over the next year, with dedication to simple, abstract forms influenced by African and

WHAT COMES AROUND GOES AROUND: GASOLINE-DRIVEN CARS VS. ELECTRICAL OR STEAM-DRIVEN CARS

At the turn of the century both electric vehicles (EV) and gasoline-driven automobiles (IC) could be found. Along with steam-driven engines, all three were being produced in equal numbers. (An EV is driven by an electric motor that uses electricity stored in batteries as fuel; an IC has an internal combustion engine that uses petroleum-based substances as fuel. EVs are quiet, have low-maintenance, and do not generate pollution, even if they are left on idle or have air conditioners. ICs are noisy, require expensive maintenance, and generate pollution that seriously affects the health of humans, plants, and the ozone layer, especially if they have air conditioners.) Thomas Edison and Henry Ford were in competition to see which type of car would prevail in the marketplace. Because the ICs could outlast and outdistance EVs, with energy storage capacity 100 times that concentrated in electric batteries, EV technology was put on the back burner, and the large manufacturing companies, such as Ford and Oldsmobile, concentrated on ICs. Recent studies by the Department of Energy show that Americans drive their private vehicles an average of 40 miles on daily trips, a distance that can easily be handled by ICs. So electrical cars are now making good economic and environmental sense to manufacturers and consumers, and manufacturers are test-marketing new models.

Asian carving styles. These forms become so essential to the new style of Modernism that the next generation of artists takes them for granted.

• Ralph Vaughan Williams (British, 1872–1958) composes *Fantasia on a Theme of Thomas Tallis,* an early example of so-called neoclassicism. Sergei Sergeyevich Prokofiev (Russian, 1891–1953) will write his *Classical Symphony* of 1918, another major contributor to that movement. As an alternative to the modernist movements of Wagner, the Impressionists, and the various folk-tune-honoring nationalist movements, neoclassicism is an attempt to reconnect with pan-European master composers of the Renaissance, Baroque, and Classical periods.

1910–1919

AMERICAN ACCULTURATION
AND THE ALASKA NATIVE BROTHERHOOD
STEPHEN W. HAYCOX

FOLLOWING THE AMERICAN CIVIL WAR, THE federal courts had decided that Indians were not citizens. The only way to fight that finding was through congressional legislation; Congress could have passed a law granting citizenship to all Natives (and eventually it did so). However, the politics of the late nineteenth and early twentieth century did not support such action. Rather, spokesmen on Indian policy were convinced that traditional Indian cultural beliefs and practices doomed them to extermination. The end would come mainly through poverty, starvation, general disadvantage, and alcoholism.

Assimilation, reformers thought, represented the only salvation, the only alternative. They set out to save Indians by separating them from their traditional environment and lives; they would bring the Indians to "civilization" and citizenship through an education and apprenticeship program. Their ideal was to make Indians the same as whites in dress, behavior, belief, and, if possible, in thought, replacing the communal structure of Indian life with economic self-sufficiency, political individualism, social mobility, and ideological independence.

The model for accomplishing this goal was the Dawes "Severalty" or General Allotment

Act of 1887. In this act Congress adopted an aggressive acculturation policy. An Indian head of household who would formally sever relations with his tribe and take up the "civilized" life would be given 160 acres of land. If in twenty years this Indian manifested the proper marks of civilization, the U.S. government would grant him citizenship. In law, the Dawes criteria of individualism and independence became the test of whether or not an Indian was "civilized" and thus ready for citizenship. Whatever they may have felt in their hearts, most Indians did not fight this policy overtly. Rather, many agreed that it represented the best future possible.

Both the missionary churches and the federal Indian school system (the Bureau of Education) set out to work with Indian leaders to prepare their people for whatever tests of citizenship might be required. In 1913, delegates from Juneau, Douglas, Sitka, Hoonah, Wrangell, and Klawock met in Juneau at the first convention of the Alaska Native Brotherhood. William Beattie, superintendent of the Southeast District of the federal Indian school system, played a facilitating role. Soon after the 1913 ANB meeting, Beattie wrote an official report of it for his superiors in Washington. "The ANB is not officially a Bureau enterprise," he wrote. "Nonetheless, I hope [the ANB] will become an active and progressive element in the general uplift and advancement of the Alaska Natives."

In the real work of this first convention, Peter Simpson, paternal spirit of the ANB and its first president, proposed four basic policies for the delegates' consideration. The first three dealt specifically with the acculturation program: abolition of aboriginal customs, education, cit-

izenship for Indians. Beattie, representing the government, approved all these policies. In an earlier report to the Commission of Education, Beattie had explained to Washington that the fact that Indians were not citizens, coupled with the destruction of the fishery upon which they depended, meant that they were slowly being squeezed out of existence. Beattie hoped that through the organization and progress of the ANB, the Indians might find redress for their dilemma. But first, anything that justified discrimination must be eliminated.

The solution, Beattie thought, was for Alaska Natives to seek citizenship under the theory of the Dawes Severalty Act, which stated that "any Native who has severed his tribal association is a citizen." Eradicating aboriginal customs was central to this approach, for Indians who continued to participate in old traditions could not be regarded as having severed relations with their tribe. Although many Tlingit and Haida Indians were well acculturated, a majority were not. Most were still illiterate, and many aspects of traditional Indian culture continued to characterize Indian life. With the missionaries and the Education Bureau teachers and officials, ANB leaders were adamant and aggressive in equating the adoption of Western practices with advancement, and Indian culture with backwardness. They dedicated the ANB particularly to the suppression of Indian language and to the elimination of the central Tlingit and Haida ritual, the potlatch.

Both the missionaries and the Bureau of Education had strongly urged this assault on the Tlingit language and the potlatch. They understood the identifying and unifying role of language in culture, and had prohibited the use of Tlingit language in the Presbyterian church

Mexican emigrating to U.S., Nuevo Laredo, Mexico, c. 1912. *(Library of Congress, Prints and Photographs Division)*

and in the government classrooms. Literacy in English was regarded as one of the principal indications of advancement, and illiteracy was an infallible mark of backwardness.

The potlatch violated the whites' commitment to Christianity and to individualism. The commemorative aspects of the ceremony, which sometimes included throwing tobacco and food into the campfire in honor of dead relations, seemed to some missionaries to constitute ancestor worship. At the same time, the goods given away by the clan leader who assumed the position of chief had been gathered from various members of the clan, thereby representing, in the white view, labor for which the laborer received no recompense. Money as well as material objects and foods already characterized potlatches among the Tlingit at the turn of the century. Often the holder of the potlatch used family resources as gifts, depriving the family of such meager financial resources as it might have. On other occasions, since the dead man's imme-

diate family had no claim on his property or on potlatch gifts given by the heir, they were sometimes left destitute. Missionaries and bureau teachers condemned these consequences of the potlatch. So did the ANB.

Subsequent conventions were aggressive in attacking aboriginal customs. Many of the speakers at the conventions were Bureau of Education personnel. According to a later report by Louis Paul, their advice left no doubt in delegates' minds that advancement meant giving up old customs and adopting modern ways. Teachers called on the Natives to be resolute and vigilant in rooting out ancient behaviors.

The notion that such a thorough change could be accomplished in a single generation was naïve, however well intentioned, a reality that the ANB itself came to recognize. Clan membership, based on kinship, often proved stronger than the forces of acculturation. That it survived attempts to eliminate it is significant, and it still exists today in syncretic form.

The U.S. population is 91,972,266, increasing 21 percent over the previous census, without including Hawaii or Alaska. Foreign-born persons account for 1.7 percent of the population. During this decade, 8.8 million immigrants enter the country, and 3,000,800 emigrate from the country. From 1910 to 1920, the total African American population of New York City, Chicago, and Detroit increases by nearly three-quarters of a million. Starting in 1916, during an eighteen-month period, the Department of Labor reports that a total of 350,000 Negroes have migrated from the South. Among the causes for this mass migration are general dissatisfaction with living conditions, the boll weevil, floods, the crop system, low wages, poor housing, poor schools, unfairness in court proceedings, and the prevalence of lynchings. The Mexican Revolution begins at the start of this decade, and during the next decade hundreds of thousands of Mexicans will flee across the border, settling in such cities as San Diego, Tucson, El Paso, San Antonio, and Laredo. Although, in this decade, exclusions for aliens entering as contract laborers totals 115,417, the Southwest will begin to be changed by Mexicans, who push economic growth in agriculture and the ranching, mining, and housing industries. According to the U.S. Department of Labor, almost 7.5 million women over ten years of age comprise 19.9 percent of the national workforce. By 1919, 16 percent of seventeen-year-olds are high school graduates and 7.7 percent of the population fourteen years of age and older is illiterate.

Some aboriginal customs were eradicated, however, and others were adapted. The ANB adapted the commemorative aspects of the pot-latch to its own purpose: today it is not uncommon on the death of an important leader for his kinsmen to make a major donation to the ANB.

In 1918, when he returned from service in World War I, Louis Paul of Wrangell joined the ANB and introduced a new notion of Indian acculturation. Having been accepted during his army service on the same terms as citizens of the country, Paul would argue that Indians already were citizens by virtue of the fourteenth amendment to the U.S. Constitution, which guarantees equal standing under the law for all persons born in the U.S. This was an important new argument for Indian citizenship. While he continued to believe in the necessity for acculturation, Louis Paul insisted that it was an Indian affair, not a white one. The Indian com-munity, and especially the ANB, could quite well direct an acculturation program on its own, he told federal officials, particularly since its members already were citizens. The Bureau of Education and the governor's office could help to ensure that Indians were not discriminated against, he told the governor, and leave to the ANB the challenge of seeing that Indians performed acceptably in society. This did not mean that the ANB was no longer willing to work with white officials; it simply changed the nature of the relationship from one of implied subordination to one of recognized equality.

1910

ARTS AND LITERATURE

• The Imagist movement begins a decade-long loose association of American and British poets. Ezra Pound (1885–1972), H. D. (Hilda

THE IMAGIST MANIFESTO

Many basic principles of twentieth-century art are succinctly set forth as a list of writing rules called the Imagist Manifesto, developed in various versions from 1910 to 1915 by a group of English and American poets and other writers. As set down in 1915, the six principles of the Imagist writers are as follows:

1. To use the language of common speech, but to employ always the exact word, not the nearly-exact, nor the merely decorative word.

2. To create new rhythms—as the expression of new moods—and not to copy old rhythms, which merely echo old moods. We do not insist upon "free-verse" as the only method of writing poetry. We fight for it as for a principle of liberty. We believe that the individuality of a poet may often be better expressed in free-verse than in conventional forms. In poetry a new cadence means a new idea.

3. To allow absolute freedom in the choice of subject. It is not good art to write badly of aeroplanes and automobiles, nor is it necessarily bad art to write well about the past. We believe passionately in the artistic value of modern life, but we wish to point out that there is nothing so uninspiring nor so old-fashioned as an aeroplane of the year 1911.

4. To present an image (hence the name "Imagist"). We are not a school of painters, but we believe that poetry should render particulars exactly and not deal in vague generalities, however magnificent and sonorous. It is for this reason that we oppose the cosmic poet, who seems to us to shirk the real difficulties of his art.

5. To produce poetry that is hard and clear, never blurred nor indefinite.

6. Finally, most of us believe that concentration is of the very essence of poetry.

   These principles are not new; they have fallen into desuetude. They are the essentials of all great poetry, indeed of all great literature.

Doolittle, 1886–1961), F. S. Flint (b. England, 1885–1960), Amy Lowell (1874–1905), William Carlos Williams (1883–1963), Carl Sandburg (1878–1967), John Gould Fletcher (1886–1950), E. E. Cummings (1894–1962), Wallace Stevens (1879–1955), Marianne Moore (1887–1972), James Joyce (b. Ireland, 1882–1941), Ford Madox Ford (b. England, 1873 [as Ford Madox Hueffer], d. France, 1939), D. H. Lawrence (b. England, 1885, d. France, 1930), and Joseph Campbell (1904–1987) are writers whose work, at least in its earliest publications, is associated with Imagism. They find inspiration by studying forms outside of the English-language tradition, including biblical Hebraic forms, medieval troubadour songs, ancient Chinese and Greek lyric poetry, American Indian dream songs, and Japanese poetry forms called *tanka* and *haiku*. By 1917 the Imagist movement dissolves, but Imagist

AFRICAN AMERICAN VISUAL ARTS: PART I
Corrine Jennings

Eighteenth Century

The earliest, mostly anonymous slave or freed artisans served at the pleasure of their masters or patrons, and most artisans labored to be of service to a white clientele. While some vital African elements survived, much was lost; most products, in metal, wood, clay or fabric, were for practical use in American plantation culture.

Nineteenth Century

Many nineteenth-century black artists were daguerreotypers and self-taught as painters. Others escaped the bigotry and racism of America through study or permanent residence abroad. Although by the end of the century black artists were winning important awards, they suffered the same slights as the black population.

Early Twentieth Century

In 1901, the question of patronage and the domination of the European aesthetic were of primary importance to the practicing black artists, who, losing their artisan stamp, were either working in Europe or hoping to journey there for additional training. In 1923, expatriate Henry Ossawa Tanner (1859–1937) was made Chevalier of the French Legion of Honor, and his career inspired and attracted other black painters to study in Europe for decades after his death. Those artists, and many others who determined to become internationally known during this period, often made the decision to avoid portraying racial subject matter.

But the first decades of the twentieth century saw the beginning of a fifty-year exodus of African Americans out of the South into the urban cities of the North, which also produced the call to black consciousness by W. E. B. Du Bois, Marcus Garvey, and Alain Locke. Papers such as the *Chicago Defender* (1905) and the *Pittsburgh Courier* (1907), and journals like the NAACP's *The Crisis* and the Urban League's *Opportunity* (1923) became vehicles for racially based art that depicted black people in a positive light. Cultural institutions like Karamu House (1915) in Cleveland provided a location for the development of African American arts and culture.

1920s

The 1920s became an intense period of activity in literature, art, and music, and though these activities were concentrated in urban centers across the country, the period became known as the Harlem Renaissance. In 1925, philosopher Alain Locke wrote "The Legacy of the Ancestral Arts," calling for black artists to look to Africa for inspiration. (This impulse continues to the present day.) Meta Vaux Warrick's *Aethiopia Awakening* and the works of Aaron Douglas (1899–1979) spoke to the era.

In 1921, James Herring formed the art department at Howard University in Washington, D.C. The Harlem branch of the New York Public Library exhibited nearly 200 paintings and sculptures assembled by Augustus

Granville Dill, whose Harlem bookstore was a mecca for young writers. The Tanner Art League at Dunbar High School in Washington, D.C., exhibited some eight-five works of art. In 1928, twenty years after Tanner showed in New York City, Archibald Motley (1891–1981) became the second black man to have a solo exhibition on Madison Avenue, at the New Gallery.

In the late 1920s, William E. Harmon presented Negro Achievement Awards, including one for art, and organized a foundation whose mission was to encourage blacks to develop an art devoid of academic or Caucasian influences. The Harmon monetary prizes assisted artists like Palmer Hayden (1893–1973) and William H. Johnson (1901–1970) to travel to Europe.

During the Harlem Renaissance, African Americans enjoyed a vogue among white collectors, and new emphasis was placed on the folk and primitive aspects of black culture. Whites generated new myths and new stereotypes of African Americans—white social critics wanted to look to blacks for a creative expressiveness not corrupted by modern civilization. When a black artist proved not to be naïve, he was often dropped by his white patron; when Aaron Douglas (1899–1979) received a grant to study at the Barnes Foundation in Philadelphia, he received a letter from patron Charlotte Mason suggesting he leave the Barnes before education destroyed his natural gifts.

1930s

During the Great Depression more African American artists than ever before received opportunities and training under the Federal Art Project (FAP) of the Works Progress Administration (WPA). Chicago's South Side Community Center, the Harlem Community Art Workshop, and the Augusta Savage Studio of Arts and Crafts offered WPA-funded art training and art teaching positions. Under the auspices of the WPA, many murals were completed in public buildings across the country. In the mid-1930s, Aaron Douglas completed the *Evolution of Negro Life* murals for the Harlem Public Library, and in 1937 Charles Alston (1907–1977), Georgette Seabrook Powell, Vertis Hayes, Sara Murrell, Selma Day, and Elba Lightfoot completed a series of murals at Harlem Hospital. In the 1930s, artists like Charles White (1918–1979), Elizabeth Catlett (b. 1915), John Wilson (b. 1922), Sargent Claude Johnson (1888–1967), and Charles Alston were inspired by the social relevance of the great Mexican muralists. In 1937 Hale Woodruff received a General Education Board grant to work with Diego Rivera on the Hotel Reforma mural in Mexico City.

In 1933, after his first one-man show, Richmond Barthé (1901–1989) exhibited a sculpture, *African Dancer,* in the second Whitney Museum Biennial that was later purchased by the museum. The 1935 exhibition of "An Art Commentary on Lynching" held at the Arthur B. Newton Gallery and the John Reed Club was the first occasion in which black and white artists showed together in a major exhibit in New York City, although the club censored the work submitted by Charles Alston. In 1936 the Museum of Modern Art presented the "African Negro Art" exhibition, and in 1936 Alain Locke installed the Beaulieu Collection of African Art at the Harlem Public Library. Opportunities for black artists were so limited by segregation that Hale Woodruff convinced Atlanta University to hold an annual juried "Exhibition of Paintings, Prints, and Sculpture by Negro Artists of America." These exhibits continued until 1970 and provided an exhibition venue for generations of black artists.

ideas continue to serve as basic tools of the Modernist tradition, across various art forms.

• *The Crisis,* the monthly magazine of the NAACP, begins publication with an initial print run of 1,000, and by 1918 its circulation reaches 18,000. With W. E. B. Du Bois as editor, it features short stories by Charles Waddell Chestnutt (1858–1932) and James Weldon Johnson, as well as poetry, reviews, cartoons, anti-lynching reports, and news of Pan-African Congresses. Most of the young writers who begin the Harlem Renaissance will first be published in *The Crisis,* including Langston Hughes (1902–1967) and Jean Toomer (1894–1967). Du Bois will resign as editor in 1934, but the magazine will continue to the present day.

• Musicologist and ethnologist Frances Densmore publishes *Chippewa Music,* her first collection of recordings and translations of Native American ceremonial chants and songs based on her fieldwork for the American Bureau of Ethnography. Various poets, including Mary Hunter Austin, Carl Sandburg, and Alice Corbin Henderson, will use Densmore's research to write "re-expressions" of Native American verse. It also inspires their own experiments to work outside of conventional rhyme and rhythm patterns, and guides their understanding of the roots and spirit of the American place, a strong concern of this time.

• Conductor James Reese Europe (1881–1919) is founder and first elected president of the Clef Club, an organization that functions partly as a union and booking agency and partly as a fraternal organization, to bring about improved working conditions for all types of African American entertainers. They are responsible for ending a long-standing practice at some establishments, which expected musicians to double as waiters and bartenders when hired to play. They purchase a building on West 53rd Street and form a symphony orchestra of up to 150 musicians. Included in their orchestration is a section of banjo players, along with the usual strings. After the first of several appearances at Carnegie Hall, on May 2, 1912, one critic comments that popular music has made its first invasion of the concert auditorium.

• California architect Bernard Maybeck (1862–1957) designs the First Church of Christ Scientist in Berkeley, a wooden building constructed with outer walls covered in brown wood shingles and windows made with lead and cut glass in the "Stick Style" that is generally considered to be his masterpiece. San Francisico Bay Area–based Maybeck and the Southern California–based brothers Charles Sumner and Henry Mather Greene, who all mix influences as diverse as Japan, the California missions, Moorish and Gothic ornamentation, and Beaux Arts classicism, will be mostly ignored from the 1920s to the 1940s, when they come to be considered pioneers of modern architecture.

GOVERNMENT AND POLITICS

• Angel Island, a 740-acre island in San Francisco Bay that had served as a military base since 1863, is transformed into Angel Island Immigration Station, a holding area for Chinese immigrants who are garrisoned in detention barracks, locked up like criminals, while waiting for permission to enter the U.S. Unlike Ellis Island, where most immigrants experience a three-to-five-hour wait, waits at Angel Island average two to seven weeks, and some 175,000 people are detained for up to

ANGEL ISLAND STORIES

While Chinese immigrants endure detention at the Angel Island Immigration Station in San Francisco Bay, they carve more than one hundred poems onto the barrack walls. Others tell their stories years later:

When we first arrived, we were told to put down our luggage and they pushed us towards the buildings. More than one hundred of us arrived. They assigned us beds and there were white women to take care of us. When we returned from the dining hall, they locked the doors behind us. Once you're locked in, they don't bother with you. It was like being in prison. Some read newspapers or books; some knitted. There was a small fenced-in area for exercising, sunning, and ball-playing. There were windows and we could see the boats arrive daily at about 9:30 or 10:00 A.M. Once a week, they allowed us to walk out to the storage shed where our luggage was kept. We could write as many letters as we wanted, but they examined our letters before mailing them. The same for letters coming in. There were good friends, but there were also those who didn't get along. There were arguments and people cried when they saw others who were fortunate enough to leave, especially those of us who had been there a long time. I must have cried a bowlful during my stay at Angel Island. Most of the women were *Sze Yup* (four districts southwest of the Pearl River Delta: Enping, Kaiping, Taishan, and Xinhu). Because I was *Lung Dou* (an area in the Zhongshan district), I couldn't understand them. We were all in the twenties, thirties, or forties; no one older. New arrivals came every two weeks—about thirty or forty. Most left after three weeks. There were about twenty or thirty appealing their cases like me. Three or four out of every ten would end up appealing. I was there the longest and always the one left behind.

—*Mrs. Chan, age twenty-three in 1939*

My father had a birth certificate on file, but he didn't use it. Instead he used a student paper since he studied at church. He paid $1,500 to a fellow villager who had reported he had four sons in order to buy entry papers for me. I came over with one of the "brothers." Another one had already been admitted into the country. When they interviewed the two younger brothers, the facts were conflicting. That's why I stayed there three and a half months. I had to appeal the decision. After leaving the village, I went to Hong Kong and stayed at a *gam saan jong* owned by people named Quan. I stayed there ten days to take care of the paperwork for passage. At that time all I knew was that *gam saan haak* (literally "traveler to the Golden Mountain," a colloquial term for an emigrant to the U.S.) who came back were always rich. They never told me about confinement on Angel Island. That's why people spent all their money to get here. They'd spend up to $1,500 to buy papers to come, thinking in a year or two they'd make it back. There were some people who were deported. I heard that some of them committed suicide aboard the ship.

—*Mr. Quan, age sixteen in 1913 (From Him Mark Lai, Genny Lim, Judy Yung, eds.,* Island: Poetry and History of Chinese Immigrants on Angel Island, 1910–1940 *[University of Washington Press, 1980].)*

From 1910 to 1940, Angel Island Immigration Station was the mandatory first stop for immigrants entering the United States from the Pacific Ocean. *(California Department of Parks and Recreation Photographic Archives)*

two years during the processing of their entry papers, which they must convince American authorities are legitimate. About 10 percent of the Chinese held at Angel Island are sent back to China on ships. By 1943, about 50,000 Chinese have been approved for entry into the U.S.

• The Mann Act (aka the "white slave" act, because it prohibits the transportation of women across state lines for immoral purposes) provides a tool for the federal government to investigate criminals who evade state laws but have no other federal violations. It is seen as discriminatory by many prominent blacks, especially after the first black heavyweight boxing champion, Jack Johnson (1878–1946), is arrested on charges of violating the act in 1912.

The act causes the first major expansion of the Federal Bureau of Investigation, which grows from around thirty agents to 300.

SCIENCE AND TECHNOLOGY

• Dr. J. B. Herrick identifies sickle-cell anemia, a hereditary blood disease that is mostly found among people of African American descent and is connected to abnormal hemoglobin in red blood cells.

CULTURE AND SOCIETY

• The first legal Filipino immigrants enter through the ports of Los Angeles and San Francisco. Since they arrive as U.S. nationals, unlike other Asians they cannot be turned away, even if they arrive with an infectious disease. In 1910, 406 Filipinos reside in the U.S., mostly concentrated in California. By 1920 the number of Filipinos in California will have increased 90 percent, where most will work in agriculture, as domestic servants, and in hotels and restaurants. Those who settle in Alaska will work in the salmon canneries.

• Japanese immigrant men begin selecting and bringing "picture brides" to the U.S., as their solution to the U.S. antimiscegenation laws. The so-called "picture bride" system involves an exchange of photographs, and is based on a traditional Japanese matchmaking method for families that live long distances from each other. In its new adaptation, Japanese bachelors in the U.S. become betrothed by an exchange of photos with a woman in Japan willing to travel to the U.S. After a stand-in for the groom goes through a wedding ceremony in Japan, the bride sets sail to meet the real groom. By 1920, more than 20,000 picture brides will enter the U.S. mainland and Hawaii, until the U.S. prohibits this practice in 1921.

• The *Pittsburgh Courier,* a major African American newspaper, is founded by attorney Robert L. Vann; the Russian American newspaper *Novoye Russkoe Slovo* begins publication in New York City; Slovenes, Serbs, and Croats publish three different newspapers in three different languages after ethnic rivalries flair in their new organization, the Yugoslav Socialist Federation.

WORLD EVENTS

• Japan annexes Korea following the murder of Japanese Prince Ito by a Korean national. This leaves Koreans who came to the U.S. between 1903 and 1905 without a homeland. Through their organization formed in 1909, the Korean National Association of North America (THK), they fight for *kwangbok,* the restoration of Korean sovereignty. With headquarters in San Francisco, they essentially become a Korean government-in-exile, representing Koreans in negotiations with the U.S. government. Japan continues its very harsh occupation of Korea until 1945.

• During the Italo-Turkish War (1911–1912), airplanes are tested in warfare for the first time, and the technology proves capable of accomplishing various military functions as reconnaissance craft, fighters, bombers, and carriers of troops, propaganda, and other materials. Airplanes offer greater speed and lower cost than land or sea operations. On October 26 warfare is staged from the air against people on the ground for the first time because the Italians want to revenge their heavy desert battleground losses against the Arabs, after the Arabs join forces with the Turks. The Italians

perform this first aerial bombing raid by leaning out of their single monoplane and dropping four Danish Haasen hand grenades that, according to a November 6 air force communiqué, have a "wonderful effect on the morale of the Arabs." Other firsts include the first night raid and the first plane to be shot down. Poet Tommaso Marinetti, founder of Futurism, is allowed to observe the explosives' devastation while flying from the safe vantage point of one-half mile above the ground. This inspires Marinetti to write *War, the Only Hygiene* (1911–1915), a manifesto that admires the "insane sculptures that our bullets carve out of the masses of our enemies," and calls this new form of war a "moral education." The technologically superior Italians claim victory, which proves to be very short as the war sets off a wave of nationalism and expansionism leading directly to World War I.

Later in 1912, during the first Balkan War that begins the destabilization of the Balkans, Bulgarians follow the Italians' example by using Bleriot monoplanes to drop canisters of explosives on Turkish-controlled Adrianople. Other colonial powers follow suit. By 1913, Spain drops shrapnel bombs on Moroccan villages; by 1915, England uses bombs against the Pathans in northwestern India, and then against the Egyptians and Afghans by 1916 and 1917 respectively. Airplanes change the art of war because their mass destruction does not distinguish between military and civilian targets, and civilian deaths begin to exceed military casualties. In World War I, Europeans begin to experience this airborne power on their own lands.

🔲 1913

• The *Plan de San Luis,* a call that starts the Mexican Revolution, is issued to overthrow the dictatorship of Porfirio Diaz, and to initiate social, political, and agrarian reforms. Before the revolution establishes the present Mexican state, there will be counterrevolutions that change the government three times over the next ten years. It will bring about the first large-scale migration to the U.S. as both poor *campesinos* and political and elite leaders become refugees traveling northward, causing major changes in the borderline states between Mexico and the U.S.

1911

ARTS AND LITERATURE

• Mary Hunter Austin, a writer whom choreographer Agnes De Mille (1909–1993) calls "the grand old lady of the Indian country . . . and foremost interpreter of Indian culture to the outer world," has a smash hit on Broadway, *The Arrow Maker*. It displays her careful research in its authentic songs, costumes, and scenery. The choreographer is Big Eagle (Winnebago Paiutes).

• Ragtime composer Scott Joplin (1868–1917) composes *Treemonisha,* an opera extolling the virtues of education for black Americans. It is briefly read in Harlem in 1916, without use of an orchestra or scenery, but because of the decline of ragtime and Joplin's growing illness, it will not receive its world premiere and first full production until sixty-one years later, on January 28, 1972, at the Atlanta Memorial Arts Center in Atlanta, Georgia. In 1974, ASCAP will place a monument on Joplin's neglected grave in Queens, New York, after the soundtrack to the movie *The Sting,* featuring Joplin's "The Entertainer," renews interest in his work.

• Historian J. A. Rogers calls ragtime the "direct predecessor of jazz" in his "Jazz at Home" essay in *The New Negro,* the anthology compiled by Alain Locke. Although it is not really a rag, when Irving Berlin (1888–1989) in 1911 publishes his song "Alexander's Ragtime Band," riding on the wave of black ragtime music's popularity, he hits the jackpot by selling a million copies in seven months, and redefines popular music in the U.S. Berlin says that "The reason American composers have done nothing highly significant is because they won't write American music," and calls syncopation the "soul of every American."

GOVERNMENT AND POLITICS

• A committee from the women's National Suffrage Association secures a formal hearing before committees from both the Senate and the House. They remind the Congress that while the Suffrage Amendment received a favorable committee report in 1892, it's not had an official report from committees in either house since 1896.

BUSINESS AND INDUSTRY

• The National Urban League on Urban Conditions is founded by an interracial coalition, assisted by Booker T. Washington. Carving out a separate function from the NAACP, the league focuses on assisting African Americans in making the transition to large urban centers after arriving from rural settings, by creating new employment opportunities in industry and community services in housing, education, and social welfare. Its name will be shortened later to the National Urban League, and it will continue to be a force for change, with headquarters in New

TIMELINE: LATINO ART, 1900s-1920s

George Vargas

1900s

- Among Mexican artists living and working in the United States were Cueva Del Rio, a Mexican-born muralist active in Washington, D.C.; Charles Albert Lopez (1869–1906), a Mexican-born sculptor who moved to New York City; and René Lopez, born in Mexico and active in Los Angeles. All were known in the international art market.
- A disciple of Courbet, Francisco Oller (b. Puerto Rico, 1833–1917) combined his realistic style with social commentary to depict the common people of the island, as seen in his famous painting *The Wake*.
- Influenced by Oller, Ramon Frade (b. Puerto Rico, 1875) stage designer, painter, and illustrator, painted *Our Daily Bread* (1904), one of the best examples of early Puerto Rican social commentary.
- Miguel Pou (b. Puerto Rico, 1880) painted traditional portraits of the upper class and landscapes while serving as director of an art academy in Ponce.
- Juan Jose Sicre (b. Cuba, 1898) was influenced by African sculpture of the Congo and Cameroon, and by the works of Rodin, Duchamp, Arp, and Brancusi. Professor of painting at San Alejandro Academy (est. 1815), he produced portraits of the famous Cuban revolutionary Jose Martí, and the French writer Victor Hugo.
- Black Cuban sculptor Ramos Blanco (b. Cuba, 1902) was known for his so-called primitive style.

1920s

- Among the new Cuban artists emerging in the 1920s, Victor Manuel García (b. Cuba, 1897) and Amelia Peláez (b. Cuba, 1896) became popular in the modern scene.
- Following the Mexican Revolution, postrevolutionary Mexico supported a massive public art program communicating new social issues and promoting cultural awareness among the common people during the 1920s and 1930s.

York and 114 affiliates across the country by the early 1990s.

• A fire at the Triangle Shirtwaist Company in New York City kills 146 women garment workers, many of whom are young Jewish women. Unable to escape because the factory doors are locked, either to hold workers at their machines or to deter them from stealing goods, the young women leap to their death from the eighth- and ninth-story windows of the burning building. This disaster becomes a symbol of the horrors of sweatshop conditions endured by garment industry workers. It sparks the creation of a city commission to make factories safer workplaces through more exacting building codes, and leads to reforms in city, state, and federal labor safety laws, although many related kinds of sweatshop conditions continue to go unchecked right up to the present day. It intensifies workers' interest in

Bodies of garment workers from the fire at the Triangle Shirtwaist Co. *(Library of Congress, Prints and Photographs Division)*

labor unions, helping the International Ladies' Garment Workers Union become one of the most powerful unions in the labor movement.

SCIENCE AND TECHNOLOGY

• The first message is sent around the world by commercial telegraph: "This message sent around the world." Its journey begins at the New York Times building in New York City at 7:00 P.M. and is received at the same station sixteen minutes later, after traveling 28,613 miles, and being relayed through stations in the Azores, Gibraltar, Bombay, the Philippines, Midway, Guam, Honolulu, and San Francisco.

CULTURE AND SOCIETY

• Ellis Island records a record 11,745 immigrants on a single day, April 17.

• The National Association Opposed to Woman's Suffrage (NAOWS) is organized by wealthy, powerful women and members of the Catholic clergy. With behind-the-scenes political support from urban political machines and Southern Congressmen, and with financial support from corporate magnates, distillers, and brewers, these anti-suffrage forces will prolong and intensify the suffragettes' battle.

• The Smith-Hughes Act is passed in Congress, establishing federal grants to support vocational training classes in public high schools, including agricultural home economics, carpentry, and business education.

• The Society of American Indians, a forerunner of "pan-Indianism" as the first multitribal institution, begins with a three-day meeting of fifty Indians in Columbus, Ohio. The group includes artists, lawyers, and doctors, such as Dr. Charles A. Eastman (Santee Sioux) and Dr. Carlos Montezuma (Yavapai-Apache) a fierce opponent of the Bureau of Indian Affairs, and Charles E. Dagenett (part Peoria Indian from Oklahoma), an official in the BIA. Until the organization dissolves in 1923, it provides a forum, through published articles and open debates, to promote Indians' educational, economic, political, and social progress.

• University of California anthropologists introduce Ishi (c. 1860–1916), the last surviving carrier of his northern California Yahi tribal culture, as a "wild" Indian "informant" that is "no fairy story—no dream of the dime museum press agent. He is a man unspotted by the world." Ishi, whose real name is not known, is called by the word for "man" in his language, as chosen by his protector, anthropologist Alfred L. Kroeber. He lives the remainder of his life in UC Berkeley's Anthropology Museum, where he shares detailed information with Kroeber and other ethnologists who come to study him or study with him. Ishi's story becomes a cautionary morality tale to question what constitutes savage and civilized behavior.

• Archaeologist and Yale University historian Hiram Bingham discovers Machu Picchu, a lost sacred city of the Incas hidden for nearly three centuries near Cuzco, Peru, 8,000 feet above sea level at the top of a ridge between two peaks of the Andes. Bingham and other archaeologists gradually piece together its history during expeditions co-sponsored by Yale University and the National Geographic Society, in its first archaeological grant. Its discovery challenges the validity of maintaining an exclusively Eurocentric focus on human history and increases the general public's recognition that the world still holds unknown secrets.

WORLD EVENTS

• When Roald Amundsen (Norwegian, 1872–1928) becomes the first explorer known to reach the South Pole, the last unexplored continent on earth has been touched by a human, and adventurers' thoughts now turn to the frontiers under the sea and out in space.

Opposition to giving women the right to vote remained very strong, as demonstrated by this storefront of the National Anti-Suffrage Association. Photo by Harris & Ewing, c. 1911. *(Library of Congress, Prints and Photographs Division)*

• *Pierrot Lunaire,* with its *sprechstimme,* a high-toned development of melodrama, is composed by Arnold Schoenberg. Many modern dance and ballet companies will compose dance works to this score.

• Italian painter Giorgio de Chirico (1888–1978) and French painter and printmaker Marc Chagall (b. Russia, 1887–1985) exhibit proto-Surrealist pictures in Paris.

• Raymond Roussel (1877–1933) turns his novel *Impressions d'Afrique* (*Impressions of Africa*) into a play. With its Rube Goldberg–like machines that perform human functions, curious nightclub acts (such as a worm that plays a zither), freaks of nature, and playful word games triggering changes in plot, it will have a great influence on Marcel Duchamp (b. France 1887–1968), showing him "the madness of the unexpected," and inaugurating the spirit of Dada.

• Physicist Heike Onnes (Dutch, 1853–1926) discovers that some metals and alloys lose all electrical resistance when kept at temperatures near absolute zero (–273.15 degrees C). Onnes's findings at his Cryogenic Laboratory at the University of Leiden lead to discoveries of superconductivity and the development of particle accelerators.

◙ 1956

1912

ARTS AND LITERATURE

• American publisher Harriet Monroe (1860–1936) founds the literary magazine *Poetry* in Chicago. It publishes the poetry and manifestos of the Imagists, carrying their beliefs to other poets who then incorporate their principles into their own work. It introduces readers to Hart Crane (1899–1932), Marianne Moore, Carl Sandburg (1878–1967), Wallace Stevens, and William Carlos Williams, among others. *Poetry* continues publishing and having wide influence in the literary community to the present day.

• Expatriated American poet Ezra Pound translates manuscripts and notes of Chinese poetry given to him by the widow of scholar and curator of the Boston Museum's Department of Far Eastern Art, Ernest Francisco Fenollosa. Pound says, "The first step of a renaissance or awakening is the importation of models for painting, sculpture, and writing. . . . It is possible that this century may find a new Greece in China. . . ."

• Mack Sennett (b. Canada, 1880–1960) founds Keystone Studio in Hollywood. He produces and directs the first of a series of Keystone Kops films, about a group of police who chase from disaster to disaster, usually making them worse. Sennett, a former burlesque clown, encourages a lowdown, slambang style of physical comedy that largely defines how comedy is delivered in early Hollywood films. He helps shape the early film work of Charles Chaplin (1889–1977), an English music-hall comic who makes thirty-five short comedies with Keystone, and Gloria Swanson (1897–1983), whom he stars in romantic comedies.

• Cartoonist John Bray develops a "cel" animation system that uses multiple layers of celluloid transparencies in each frame. Only layers containing moving images need to be changed from frame to frame. Patented in 1915, it remains the standard method to produce animation until digital technologies become available.

• "The Memphis Blues," by W. C. Handy, is the first blues song to be published. His "St. Louis Blues" will be published in 1914. Blues began as an improvised solo vocalization style whose origins are probably based in the pre-Emancipation unaccompanied "field hollers" combined with an improvised vocalization style created by Southern farmers after Emancipation. By 1920 the blues will become standardized, both harmonically and in form. This standardization will allow for secure improvised instrumental accompaniment and open the way for the twentieth-century-long dominance of the blues as the main crucible for all forms of nonclassical music, including boogie-woogie, swing, bebop, country, R&B,

rock, and even many examples of gospel music, Latin, Broadway, and reggae.

▣ 1904, 1915

• Composer Henry Cowell (1897–1965) introduces tone clusters in piano music with his compositions *The Banshee* and *Aeolian Harp,* in which groups of strings inside the piano are strummed or plucked. His eccentric explorations invent new music techniques of notation, dissonant counterpoint, chance procedures, and repetitive patterns, influenced by his studies of African, Javanese, and North and South Indian music, as well as the American traditional folk music, Irish jigs, and Chinese and Japanese music he heard in his San Francisco neighborhood while growing up. His students will include Lou Harrison, George Gershwin, and John Cage, who calls him "the open sesame for new music in America."

GOVERNMENT AND POLITICS

• Protest arises in lands controlled by U.S. imperialism, and President Taft responds with a show of force in usually brief occupations known as "gunboat diplomacy": In Honduras, U.S. Marines are sent to protect American investments during a revolt; in Cuba, the navy dispatches two armored cruisers to Havana to protect U.S. plantation owners' property against revolts of black laborers; in Nicaragua, 2,700 Marines are sent in to supervise presidential elections and to protect U.S. citizens and property against seizure by rebel forces under General Luis Mena. Except for brief periods of interruption, the marines will remain in Nicaragua until 1933. In their wake, U.S. diplomats and military commanders often become managers or partners in key industries

such as banking, sugar, fruit, railroad, mining, gas, and electric companies, making the countries poorer and less independent than before due to "dollar imperialism."

• Theodore Roosevelt's Progressive (Bull Moose) Party, running in a third-party challenge for the presidency, becomes the first national political party to adopt a woman suffrage plank.

• Democrat Woodrow Wilson (1856–1924) is elected president, with Thomas R. Marshall as his vice president, defeating the incumbent Republican president, William Howard Taft, by 42 percent of the popular vote, with the help of the third-party candidacies of Theodore Roosevelt's Bull Moose Party and Eugene V. Debs of the Socialist Party, who garners 6 percent of the popular vote (900,000 votes). Wilson's "New Freedom" program promises progressive domestic reforms to break up the big monopolies and restore competition, and to maintain neutrality in the widening European war.

• On March 13, approximately eight thousand women march from the Capitol past the White House to a building owned by the Daughters of the American Revolution (DAR) in connection with the inauguration, making the first mass suffrage demonstration. The parade takes Washington's police department by surprise. When they do not protect the women from attacks by jeering men, the women receive a surge in support for their cause, and the police chief loses his job.

• In January, New Mexico becomes the forty-seventh state to join the union, finally succeeding after being repeatedly rejected since 1850. Because California was admitted in 1850 without having a territorial period, many historians interpret this difference in treatment as due to the high percentage of Mexican American residents in New Mexico. Although their political and economic power will begin to lessen, Mexican Americans remain the largest ethnic community in the state into the 1930s.

• In February, Arizona is admitted as a state, the last of the forty-eight mainland states to join the union. With more than fourteen tribes represented on twenty reservations, Arizona has one of the largest Native American populations in the U.S., and a large Hispanic community that, at close to 20 percent of the total population, has political clout.

BUSINESS AND INDUSTRY

• In Lawrence, Massachusetts, the IWW leads the American Woolen Company's 10,000 mill workers earning an average wage of $8.76 per week in mass picketing and parades after the company, which owns four mills, cuts paychecks without notice in January. In order to keep striking, the workers, immigrants from Ireland, Russia, Italy, Syria, Poland, England, Portugal, and Lithuania, even send their children to other cities to be cared for by strangers sympathetic to the strike. The state police and militia are called up and martial law is invoked as strikers endure beatings, arrests, and imprisonment. In March the company gives in, and strikers accept raises of 5 to 11 percent, time and a quarter for overtime, and no discrimination for striking. Massachusetts passes the nation's first minimum-wage law soon afterward.

SCIENCE AND TECHNOLOGY

• Roosevelt Reservoir Dam, the largest engineering project ever undertaken in the U.S., opens seventy-six miles northeast of Phoenix, Arizona, after eight years of construction work. Considered a marvel in its day, the 3,567-foot-high composite thick arch-type dam is part of the Salt River Project, the first multipurpose project of the Reclamation Act that also includes a power plant, a reservoir, the Granite Reef Diversion Dam, and a canal irrigation system. It opens the surrounding area to increased agricultural production and urban population growth.

• The *Titanic,* a great ocean liner that everyone believes is a marvel of engineering technology, sinks on her maiden voyage across the Atlantic and 1,513 lives are lost at sea. The tragedy teaches a hard lesson about the potential fallibility of even the most sophisticated of modern innovations.

CULTURE AND SOCIETY

• The first Montessori School in the U.S. opens in Tarrytown, New York, the same year that Italian psychiatrist Maria Montessori (1870–1952) publishes *The Montessori Method,* her best-selling book, which starts a worldwide reevaluation of traditional teaching methods through her description of how she successfully taught Roman slum children to read by developing the children's individual initiative.

WORLD EVENTS

• The First Balkan War begins, a harbinger of the Great War to explode later in the decade. Bulgaria, Serbia, and Greece align against Turkey; Turkey makes alliances with Italy and Austria.

• Polish biochemist Casimir Funk (1884–1967) publishes a paper, "The Etiology of the Deficiency Diseases," that links certain diseases, such as scurvy and pellagra, to a lack of vitamins in the diet, bringing awareness to how vitamins can be preventive medicine, best achieved through eating a diet rich in various whole, unprocessed foods.

• Artists Pablo Picasso and Georges Braque invent collage, which involves gluing fragments of verbal text or physical objects taken from everyday life onto the surface of the canvas. Collage will be one of the most representative and important innovations of twentieth-century art, useful in both visual design and literature.

1913

ARTS AND LITERATURE

• The International Exhibition of Modern Art opens at the 69th Regiment Armory in New York, and then in Chicago and Boston, bringing 16,000 controversial European and American paintings and sculpture to the attention of the general public in the U.S. Known as the Armory Show, its most popular sensations include Marcel Duchamp's ready-mades and his painting *Nude Descending a Staircase,* and sculpture by Constantin Brancusi (Rumanian, 1876–1957); besides paintings by other Europeans including Odilon Redon (French, 1840–1916), Paul Cézanne (French, 1839–1906), Vincent van Gogh (Dutch, 1853–1890), Augustus John (English, 1878–1961), Wassily Kandinsky (Russian, 1866–1944), Fernand Léger (French, 1881–1955), Francis Picabia (French, 1879–1953), and Americans Marsden Hartley (1877–1943), Edward Hopper (1882–1967), Albert Ryder (1847–1917), Lionel Feininger (1871–1956), Joseph Stella (1877–1946), John Marin (1870–1953), and Stuart Davis (1894–1964).

• Edward Kennedy "Duke" Ellington (1899–1974) writes his first musical composition, "Soda Fountain Rag."

GOVERNMENT AND POLITICS

• Congress passes a Federal Reserve Act that replaces the Independent Treasury System with a Federal Reserve System, managed by a Federal Reserve Board, to oversee all credit and financial business through a network of twelve regional Federal Reserve banks. All banks are now required to join this system by depositing 6 percent of their capital in their regional bank. These funds become a new form of currency called "Treasury notes" that the government issues through Reserve banks. This allows funds to circulate in ways more adaptable to changing business conditions.

• The Sixteenth Amendment allows the institution of a graduated federal income tax. The tax rate is first set at 1 percent on individual incomes starting at $2,500 for a single man and $3,333.55 for a married man, to be deducted as withholdings from salaries at their source. It is expected to affect about a half-million people. This new source of income will make it possible for the government to decrease tariffs on imported goods, their former main source of revenues, which in turn will decrease prices on imported goods and make them more competitive with domestically produced goods.

• The Seventeenth Amendment to the Constitution is passed, changing the way the Senate is selected from its previous method of appointment by the state legislatures to its present election by popular vote. This has the effect of weakening the power of the state legislatures and increasing the power of the Senate.

• An expression of growing resentment against Japanese in California becomes law

This cartoon about New York politics demonstrates the influence of Marcel Duchamp's cubist painting *Nude Descending a Staircase,* on exhibit at the Armory Show at this time. "The rude descending on Sulzer" by Oscar Edward Cesare, 1913. *(Library of Congress, Prints and Photographs Division)*

when Governor Hiram Johnson signs the Webb Alien Land-Holding Bill into law, barring Japanese, Chinese, and other Asian aliens from owning land, leasing agricultural land for more than three years, or willing any land that they own. The Japanese do find a loophole whereby if they purchase or lease the land in the name of children born in the U.S. who are therefore U.S. citizens, they can operate the land as their legal guardians. President Wilson strongly objects when California's

anti-Japanese actions influence international relations with Japan.

• The U.S. backs a coup in Mexico by General Victoriano Huerta against liberal President Francisco Madero, even working out the details inside the new American embassy with Ambassador Henry Lane Wilson. General Huerta proves to be a brutal dictator, imprisoning many members of the previous government and assassinating ex-president Madero and his vice president, among others. Although other Western European nations decide to recognize the new government, and U.S. businessmen pressure him to do so, in 1913 the newly inaugurated President Wilson refuses to recognize Huerta's government, objecting on the basis that Huerta was not elected by the people. This represents a departure in American policy, setting a precedent for the U.S. to determine which governments are to be considered acceptable and which are not, rather than recognizing all governments as presented.

BUSINESS AND INDUSTRY

• Henry Ford (1863–1947) introduces mass-production methods to produce his Model T automobiles. He is able to reduce production costs, due to the shorter number of man-hours required to assemble each car (eventually down to 1.5 hours per car from 12.5) and his simplification of design. Production savings are passed on to customers, and as the cost of a Model T drops from $850 to as low as $310, sales shoot up rapidly. By 1925, more than 9,000 cars will roll off the Ford assembly line each day.

• The U.S. Parcel Post opens for business. In its first year, about 300 million packages will be mailed and delivered.

• In September, 11,000 mostly foreign-born

Serb, Greek, and Italian coal miners strike against the Rockefeller family–owned Colorado Fuel and Iron Corporation after one of their union organizers is murdered. They begin what will become one of the longest and most violent confrontations between labor and a corporation of this century. The company evicts the miners from the towns, and they construct tent camps in the surrounding hills, continuing to strike and picket even though the company hires the Baldwin-Felts detective agency to rough up the strikers. When strikebreakers are brought in, hundreds of protesting miners are arrested. When the strikers even endure the winter, in April 1914 the Rockefellers get the governor to call in the national guard at their expense. The guard torches the camp, burning alive eleven children and two women and killing thirteen others by gunfire, an action known as the Ludlow Massacre. The United Mine Workers send out a "Call to Arms," inducing hundreds of union miners to walk off their jobs in other parts of the state. One newspaper reports "the hills in every direction seem suddenly to be alive with men," as they cut telephone and telegraph wires, destroy mines, and explode shafts. Demonstrations are mounted all over the country to support the miners' cause, including 500 miners who picket Colorado's governor asking that the national guard officers be tried for murder, soldiers who refuse to fight the miners, and 400 nurses who volunteer to help the strikers. Only when the governor calls in federal troops does the strike wind down to its end. A congressional committee conducts an investigation, and although sixty-six people have been killed, no militiaman or mine guard is indicted. The union does not win recognition by the company.

Farmer with 1913 Model A Ford on Main Street of Sisseton, South Dakota. Photo by John Vachon, c. 1939. *(Library of Congress, Prints and Photographs Division)*

SCIENCE AND TECHNOLOGY

• Biologist Alfred Henry Sturtevant (1891–1970) discovers that genes line up in a row on chromosomes and pioneers gene mapping, showing five sex-linked genes.

• The first aerial map is made from an airplane by Lieutenant Sherman, a passenger on a nonstop cross-country flight from San Antonio to Texas City.

• Construction starts on the Lincoln Highway, U.S. 30, the first coast-to-coast paved road in the nation.

• Swedish American Gideon Sundback patents his invention for the "hookless" Plako slide fastener, the forerunner of the zipper. The idea gets its first endorsement in World War I, when the U.S. Navy uses them on their windproof flying suits. Rubber entrepreneur B. F. Goodrich coins the term "zipper" in 1922, because of the sound it makes when he zips up his rubber rain boots. By 1930 the zipper becomes a fashion statement that communicates the modernity of its wearer.

CULTURE AND SOCIETY

• Lucy Burns (1879–1966) and Alice Paul organize the Congressional Union, which will become known as the National Women's Party in 1916. They vow to engage in civil disobedience to publicize the cause of suffrage, encouraging women to participate in hunger strikes and to picket the White House.

• Three hundred thousand Russian immigrants enter the U.S. in this year, their largest yearly total for immigration.

WORLD EVENTS

• Composer Igor Stravinsky (1882–1971) creates a ballet in two acts, *Rite of Spring,* that premieres in Paris at the Theatre des Champs-Elysees. He bases the book and score on modern interpretations of Russian folktales and music. The music superimposes percussive rhythms, dissident chords, and folk melodies in complex combinations. The ballet is performed in collaboration with impresario Serge Diaghilev (1872–1929) and his Ballets Russes, with choreography by Vaslav Nijinsky (1890–1950), and costumes and scenery designed by Nicholas Roerich (1874–1947). The performance shakes up the audience so much that they yell, scream, boo, and whistle, staging a near riot in the theater. The production closes after six performances, but sets a benchmark for successful invention that artists invoke to this day. Subsequent London performances are calmly received with great acclaim. The score continues to be widely revered, with many staged reinterpretations.

• Luigi Russolo presents the first Futurist music concert, the "art of noises" at Marinetti's villa in Milan, Italy. Russolo advocates mechanized noise as a viable new form of music, "To present the musical soul of the masses, of the great factories, of the railways, of the transatlantic liners, of the battleships, of the automobiles and airplanes." He builds instruments out of wooden boxes, motors, and amplifiers, a Futurist orchestra he says is capable of producing 30,000 noises. The London *Times* reviews the concert: "Weird funnel shaped instruments . . . resembled the sounds heard in the rigging of a channel-steamer during a bad crossing, and it was perhaps unwise of the players— or should we call them the 'noisicians'?—to proceed with their second piece . . . after the pathetic cries of 'no more' which greeted them from all the excited quarters of the auditorium." 1909

• The Second Balkan War begins. Serbia invades Albania to gain an outlet to the sea; Italy and Austria oppose Serbian access to the Adriatic; Serbia and Greece go to war against Bulgaria, while Italy and Austria support Bulgaria.

1914

ARTS AND LITERATURE

• Oscar Micheaux (1884–1951), the first black film producer, founds Oscar Micheaux Pictures with studios in New York City, and makes *The Wages of Sin* and *The Broken Violin.* Designed for and distributed to black audiences, his films feature all-black casts and investigate subjects overlooked by Hollywood. In 1918 he will produce *Birthright,* the first full-length black film.

• Edward Curtis premieres his film *In the Land of the Headhunters,* in Seattle, Washington. It is a culmination of three years of collaboration with the Kwakiutl people of the Northwest coast, who live on Deer Island of the Queen Charlotte Islands. Along with a hokey Romeo-and-Juliet-derived plot, it offers glorious visions of the eagle and bear masks standing in the carved Kwakiutl boats as they move through the water, and performances of ceremonial dances, songs, and rituals. The film is a financial failure, but before it disappears until rediscovered in the 1940s, it serves as a model for Robert Flaherty's classic documentary film on Inuit life, *Nanook of the North* (1921).

• African American sculptor Meta Warrick Fuller (1877–1968), a believer in Pan-Africanism, sculpts *Aethiopia Awakening.* Critic Richard Powell says the sculpture's dramatic use of African art styles is a metaphorical embodiment of a woman "extracting herself from the mummy-like bandages that wrap the lower half of her body [that] . . . serves the representational needs . . . of successive generations of 'race' men and women."

• The Clef Club Orchestra travels to Europe, where they are heard by Irene (1894–1969) and Vernon (1887–1918) Castle, a European American ballroom dance team that is highly influential in bringing black music and dance into white cultural acceptance. The Castles hire the Clef Club leader, James Reese Europe, to play for them, along with Ford Dabney, who serves as musical arranger. While composing and conducting for the Castles, Europe introduces the saxophone, considered to be a novelty instrument at the time, making it an important component of the jazz orchestral sound. When Europe repeatedly plays a slow version of W. C.

> The Congress of the U.S. says to the people of Porto Rico [*sic*], once and for all, that they are part of the U.S. domain and will always remain there; that the legislation for independence in Porto Rico must come to a decided and permanent end.
>
> — STATEMENT BY MINNESOTA REPRESENTATIVE CLARENCE MILLER, IN THE CONGRESSIONAL RECORD, SIXTY-FOURTH CONGRESS, FIRST SESSION, MAY 5, 1916

Handy's "The Memphis Blues," as intermission music, the Castles are inspired to create a new social dance, first called the "bunny hug," that will later be called the "fox trot," after a vaudevillian named Harry Fox, who introduces it at the Ziegfeld Follies. The fox trot quickly becomes the latest worldwide ballroom dance craze, typifying the World War I era. When Europe leaves the Castles in 1915 to join the Army, Dabney takes over as musical director.

• Charles Ives finishes *Putnam's Camp,* a part of his orchestral suite *Three Places in New England,* in which he summons up a free-for-all celebration of the Fourth of July by layering campfire songs over marches.

GOVERNMENT AND POLITICS

• Congress passes the Clayton Act, giving labor organizations legislative protection needed to bargain with corporations. It grants labor the right to strike, boycott, and picket, and bars corporations from using injunctions to stop union efforts unless it is necessary to prevent "irreparable injury to property, or to a property right." The bill also exempts unions from antitrust laws, ruling that unions cannot be declared in restraint of trade. AFL leader Samuel Gompers (b. Britain, 1850–1924) calls it "labor's charter of freedom."

• The Federal Trade Commission is organized in Washington to oversee regulations on interstate commerce.

• The Puerto Rican House of Delegates asks the U.S. Congress to give the island full independence in this year, after ignoring their petitions for full self-rule and eventual statehood. Congress responds in 1917, overriding the unanimous objection of the House of Delegates by granting all Puerto Ricans U.S. citizenship under the Jones Act.

• In February, President Wilson orders a U.S. Marine invasion of the Mexican port city of Veracruz, in an effort to depose President Victoriano Huerta. By August, Huerta's federal army surrenders to the Constitutionalists, supported by the U.S. and led by Venustiano Carranza. By November, Carranza demands that the U.S. make an unconditional withdrawal of their forces.

🔲 1915

BUSINESS AND INDUSTRY

• The Panama Canal is formally opened to international shipping, providing westbound ships with a shortcut to Asian markets, and the U.S. with a bicoastal naval link. When the U.S. flag is raised over the headquarters of the Canal Commission building, it signals that the 147,000-mile Canal Zone territory is being operated under the sovereignty of the U.S., and guarantees a century of struggle for the return of sovereignty to Panama.

🔲 1999

• Henry Ford offers higher wages to all of his Ford Motor Company's 26,000 employees, including an increase in the minimum wage

from its present $2.34 per day to $5.00 per day at a time when the average wage in the industry is $2.40 per day. Ford also introduces profit sharing, in which the employees share in about one-half of the year's profits, and creates three shifts of eight hours a day instead of the present two nine-hour shifts. Although he is charged with creating an "industrial utopia," Ford is looking to increase productivity by increasing efficiency through a more rested, committed labor force, to maintain lower prices (the Model T is currently selling for $500), and to avoid threatened labor trouble. He also realizes that higher profits can yield higher demand because workers will have more money to spend. But it will take a while for the rest of the business world to catch on to his simple insight that mass production needs to be matched by mass consumption. The day after Ford makes this pronouncement, the *New York Times* runs an editorial stating that these gains will cause labor troubles at other companies because "the manufacturing industries of the country cannot follow an example which requires an eight-hour day" and wages that are "approximately double the prevailing rate." During the same year, for example, New Jersey sets the minimum wage for women at nine dollars per week.

• The first scheduled airplane service offers round-trip service between Tampa and St. Petersburg, Florida.

• The American Society of Composers, Authors, and Publishers (ASCAP) is founded in New York City, as a trade organization to monitor commercial performances of client members' compositions. They collect royalty fees from record labels and other music users such as radio stations, and distribute any income to

Opening of the Panama Canal. (*Library of Congress, Prints and Photographs Division*)

the appropriate composers, lyricists, and publishers. At its start, ASCAP functions as an "elite arm" of Tin Pan Alley, favoring established New York City music publishing firms and songwriters, and making it very difficult for outsiders, especially African Americans, to gain a foothold in the music industry.

• An increased demand for workers permits a steady influx of "temporary" Mexican farm workers, railroad laborers, and miners. More than 91,000 Mexicans travel north across the border from 1914 to 1919.

SCIENCE AND TECHNOLOGY

• Botanist George Washington Carver (1861?–1943) conducts experiments at the historically black Tuskegee Institute in Alabama, in which he shows that by alternating two crops, peanuts and sweet potatoes, farmers can restore soil fertility. In addition to proving that crop rotation increases crop production and nutrition, he conducts scientific experiments

that prove these crops can yield thousands of industrial and agricultural by-products, including soap, synthetic rubber, flour, tofu, peanut butter, and cheese. His research helps revitalize Southern farmers' lands, which have been destroyed by boll weevil plagues and overplanting of cotton, and promotes dietary and cooking practices that combat malnutrition. Although he receives many honors for his more than 500 agriculture-related inventions, Carver chooses to remain at Tuskegee from 1896 to 1943, so that he can help Southern farmers. By 1940, peanuts are second only to cotton as the largest cash crop in the South.

• Engineer Robert Hutchings Goddard (b. 1882), called the father of modern rocketry, patents a liquid fuel that allows for the development of experimental rockets.

• African American scientist and inventor Garrett Morgan (1877–1963) invents a "smoke inhalator," the Firefighter's Breathing Device, which will be the first gas mask used by

George Washington Carver in a full-length portrait, standing in field, probably at Tuskegee, holding a piece of soil. Photo by Frances Benjamin Johnston, 1906. *(Library of Congress, Prints and Photographs Division)*

soldiers in World War I, after proving its success when rescuing men trapped in a tunnel.

CULTURE AND SOCIETY

• Feminist and nurse Margaret Sanger (1879–1966), introduces the term "birth control" in her article advocating for a woman's right to contraception that appears in a radical feminist monthly magazine called *The Woman Rebel*. Although she has included no specific information on methods of birth control in the magazine, Sanger exiles herself to England to avoid prosecution after she sends the magazine

through the mails, as the magazine is in violation of postal obscenity laws as defined in the Comstock Law, which has set the standard for censorship in the U.S. since its passage in 1872. ▣ 1916

• In 1913, Leo Frank, a Jew, is found guilty of murdering Mary Phagan, an employee of a factory where he is manager, and is sentenced to death by an Atlanta, Georgia, jury. The Jewish community sees this as an anti-Semitic ruling, influenced by inflammatory press reports. Chicago lawyer Sigmund Livingston responds to the media's flagrant anti-Semitism by founding the Anti-Defamation League, under sponsorship of the Independent Order of B'nai B'rith. The Anti-Defamation League's mission is to combat prejudice against Jews in the U.S., by responding to the release of any derogatory or negative images in print, stage, and film, and to protest against hate crimes by individuals and groups within communities. In addition, they want "to put an end forever to unjust and unfair discrimination against and ridicule of any sect or body of citizens." Although the Georgia governor commutes Frank's death sentence to life imprisonment, the Anti-Defamation League's efforts cannot protect Frank from being lynched by a mob calling themselves a "vigilance committee" in August 1915.

• The NAACP sponsors a Pan-African Conference in Paris. The U.S. is represented by W. E. B. Du Bois and fifteen other delegates, the West Indies with twenty-one delegates, and the African countries by twelve delegates.

WORLD EVENTS

• A world crisis leading to World War I is precipitated when Archduke Francis Ferdinand, crown prince of Austria, is assassinated by a

Serbian revolutionary in Sarajevo this year. During the course of the war, Belgium, France, Russia, the British Empire, Serbia, Italy, Greece, Romania, Montenegro, Portugal, Japan, and the United States align as the Allies and Germany, Austro-Hungary, Turkey, and Bulgaria align as the Central Powers. The war fosters inventions of new, more efficient ways to kill—aerial bombing, poison gas, tanks, submarine-launched torpedoes, and confirms the importance and efficiency of machine guns, whose carnage will total in the millions. The war costs its incredibly high human toll because, although the military on both sides possess weapons of mass destruction, from 1914 to 1918 they are caught in a technological gap, without radio and telephone communication developed enough to effectively deploy their troops. The war also alters the geopolitical landscape of the modern world, its newly drawn borders creating many of the tensions that remain between nations and people today.

▣ 1915

1915

ARTS AND LITERATURE

• Marcel Duchamp makes his first trip to the U.S., where he lives in New York City and begins work on *The Bride Stripped Bare by Her Bachelors, Even* (aka *The Large Glass*), a verbal and visual puzzle of a painting on clear glass that may be his attempt to answer his question, "Can one make works which are not works of 'art' . . . not . . . Autobiography . . . nor . . . self-expression." He calls the painting "hilarious," continuing to work on it for the next nine years until he decides to stop, leaving it unfinished.

• New York Dada flourishes until about 1924, when Duchamp and Francis Picabia (1879–1953) arrive in New York, displaying a far greater measure of humor and madcap antics than the European contingent that begins in Zurich the next year. The New York Dada circle includes artists Man Ray (1890–1976), Marcel Duchamp, Beatrice Wood, and the Stettheimer sisters, Florine (1871–1944), Carrie, and Ettie. It centers around Alfred Stieglitz's 291 Gallery and the patrons and collectors Katherine Drier (1877–1952) and Walter (1878–1954) and Louise (1879–1953) Arensberg, who provide a fabulous setting for wild Dada gatherings at their West 67th Street salon. Members of the Arensberg circle produce magazines that reflect the Dada spirit, starting with *291,* whose first issue appears in March 1915, and including *Rongwrong,* whose title results from a printer's error for Duchamp's intended title, *Wrongwrong,* that he decides to keep.

• Edgard Varese immigrates to the U.S. from France in 1915 and tries to find new sounds for composing an "American music [that] must speak its own language, and not be the result of a certain mummified European music." He composes *Hyperprism* (1924) and *Ionization* (1929–1933), in which he uses only percussion instruments (thirty-seven of them) and two sirens.

• Ruth St. Denis and Ted Shawn (1891–1972) combine to become the parents of modern dance in America when they form Denishawn, a "School of Dancing & Related Arts," in Los Angeles. Their eclectic curriculum explores the "exotic" world dance forms, including Spanish, ballet, Oriental, Egyptian, Greek, American Indian, geisha, creative dance, Delsarte, primitive dance, German modern dance, folk dance, and stagecraft. The training opens doors that the next generation of dance innovators walks through, including among its illustrious alumni the choreographers Doris Humphrey (1895–1958), Charles Weidman (1901–1975), and their costume designer Pauline Lawrence; jazz and Broadway choreographer Jack Cole (1913–1974), choreographer Helen Tamaris (1905–1966), and Martha Graham and her musical director Louis Horst (1884–1964), all artists who will help found and shape the emerging new modern and jazz dance forms. The school supports itself with tours by the founders and their students, in which they perform everything from "myths" to the latest ballroom dance crazes, appearing in vaudeville houses as extras, and as dancers in the silent movies of D. W. Griffith (1875–1948) and Cecil B. De Mille (1881–1959). Denishawn continues operating until 1931, opening branches around the country.

• *Birth of a Nation,* a three-hour Civil War epic film directed by D. W. Griffith, is released. Based on *The Clansman,* a novel by Thomas Dixon that inspired the formation of the Ku Klux Klan, it immediately becomes a hit and a controversy. It is lauded as an artistic success for its innovative grammar of filmmaking techniques, effectively employing the close-up, long shot, fade-in, fade-out, and cross-cutting for the first time. The NAACP protests its overtly white-supremacist message. The film is also credited with inspiring the regeneration of the Klan, and helping to build the tensions that lead to the race riots in the "Red Summer" of 1919.

🔲 1919

• The plaster buildings of the Panama Pacific Exposition of 1915 exemplify and encourage the future San Francisco's leaders' desire for their city to be the capital of the new frontier, the Pacific rim. Inspired by the utopian dream first laid out by Oakland writer Joaquin Miller in his 1893 book, *The City Beautiful,* their expression takes a grandiose, ornamental, eclectic style that borrows from Greek, Roman, and French classical designs. The year after the Exposition opens, San Francisco's 500,000-square-foot City Hall is completed, becoming the permanent architectural focal point of their city plan. Topped with the tallest dome in the U.S., its lavish size and decoration dramatize the city's dream and its phoenixlike recovery from the 1906 earthquake.

GOVERNMENT AND POLITICS

• The U.S. begins its nineteen-year occupation of Haiti as 400 U.S. Marines land in Port-au-Prince to quell a revolutionary outbreak. Although U.S. troops will remain on the island until 1934, their presence does not influence positive lasting changes for the Haitian government or people.

• Off the Irish coast, a German submarine sinks the British liner *Lusitania,* a Cunard Line passenger ship traveling from New York to Liverpool. Among the 1,198 dead are 124 Americans. The Germans defend their action, pointing out they had printed a warning in New York newspapers that citizens of neutral nations should not travel on any vessel traveling into a "war zone," besides contending the vessel was carrying munitions.

• Mexican President Huerta is opposed by

Venustiano Carranza, Francisco "Pancho" Villa, and Emiliano Zapata. The U.S. also continues to press Mexican president Huerta to step down from office. When Huerta goes into exile, the U.S. formally recognizes the Venustiano Carranza's Constitutionalists as the government of Mexico, through a negotiation arranged by the Latin American Conference. However, Villa and Zapata unite against Carranza, which leads to Villa's raid on New Mexico and President Wilson's retaliation.

BUSINESS AND INDUSTRY

• Joe Hill, an IWW organizer, is convicted of killing a grocer in Salt Lake City in a robbery, and is executed by a firing squad.

• After stringing nearly 3,000 tons of telephone cable on 130,000 telephone poles across the U.S., American Telephone and Telegraph (AT&T) gives a demonstration of its new transcontinental hookup. Surrounded by officials in New York City, the telephone's inventor, Alexander Graham Bell, re-creates his original 1876 telephone conversation with Thomas A. Watson, who is in San Francisco. This time, when Bell says "Mr. Watson, come here. I want you," he hears a reply that instantly travels 2,572 miles: "It would take me a week to get to you this time." Within three months the system is in commercial operation, costing $20.70 for the first three minutes and $6.76 for each additional minute.

SCIENCE AND TECHNOLOGY

• Lee De Forest invents the oscillator, the basis of all electronic tone-generating electronic musical instruments.

CULTURE AND SOCIETY

• William Joseph Simmons reactivates the Klu Klux Klan in Atlanta in November, and the Superior Court accepts its charter in Fulton County, Georgia, in early December. Besides carrying on its tradition of targeting African Americans, the Klan now adds Jews, Catholics, and immigrants to their list of undesirables. By 1924 it has expanded out of the South to include the North and Midwest, and claims one and a half million members. Its membership will reach a peak of 5 million, and be especially influential in the state governments of Oklahoma, Indiana, California, Oregon, and Ohio.

• Suffragist Carrie Chapman Catt (1859–1947) proposes her "Winning Plan" to the National American Woman Suffrage Association (NAWSA) that will gain all women the right to vote at the federal level by 1920. She suggests that if NAWSA supports Democrats who are committed to suffrage for women and concentrates on using states that have already given their approval to women's right to vote, including Wyoming (1890), Colorado (1893), Utah (1896), and Washington (1911), those states and politicians can pressure the federal government into approval. She proves correct and on June 4, 1919, Congress passes the Nineteenth Amendment.

🄿 1920

WORLD EVENTS

• Turkish massacres of Armenians result in a large Armenian immigration to the U.S. The true number of Armenian immigrants is not known because immigration officials list them as Turks or Russians, but by the 1980s about a half-

The "Bandit Flag and Saber Captured by Troop 'B'" was probably taken from anarchists who were battling for social reforms in the southwestern U.S. and Mexico. *(By permission, Hidalgo County Historical Museum)*

million Armenians are living in the U.S., largely concentrated in California, Massachusetts, New Jersey, New York, and Chicago.

1916

ARTS AND LITERATURE

• James Van Der Zee (1886–1983) sets up a commercial photo studio in Harlem that he will continue to operate for fifty years. The style and energy communicated through his dressed-up, posed photographs of ordinary Harlem residents in the 1920s and 1930s helps to create the Jazz Age image of Harlem as a new cultural center for African American artists, writers, and musicians and their audiences.

• *Rachel*, a play by Angelina Weld Grimke (1880–1958), the first twentieth-century full-length play to be written, staged, and produced by African Americans, premieres in Washington, D.C.

• Charles Tomlinson Griffes, America's only major Impressionist composer and one of the greatest of all Impressionists, composes *The White Peacock*, a piano work that also exists in a popular orchestrated version. His equally powerful and elegant *Pleasure Dome of Kublai Khan* and his *Poem for Flute and Orchestra* are composed in 1919, one year before his death.

• The founding of Cleveland, Ohio's Karamu Theatre, by Oberlin College graduates Russell and Rowena Jelliffe, marks the probable beginning of the American regional theater movement. (*Karamu* is a Swahili word meaning "center of enjoyment" or "center of community.") It is part of a private philanthropic recreation welfare center built for both white and black poor. The respected African American actor Charles Gilpin founds a stock company within the center, known at first as the Gilpin Players. They begin producing plays concerned with African American life, as written by black

"Florence Mills, 1927," James Van Der Zee, photographer (© Donna Mussenden Van Der Zee)

and white authors. From their beginnings in a pool hall, they eventually build a million-dollar facility including three stages, a concert hall, and a children's theater wing. They are pivotal in promoting African American playwrights—during the 1930s, Langston Hughes develops and premieres many of his plays there, which remain in their repertoire.

1947

GOVERNMENT AND POLITICS

• President Woodrow Wilson's second term begins. Although he campaigns as a peace candidate, promising to mediate a peace between the warring nations, he will soon decide that it is necessary for the U.S. to join the Allied countries, stating that this war will make the world safe for democracy. He develops his peace initiative, and lays the foundation for the League of Nations, which he proposes as an organization to avoid future conflicts.

• New York City becomes the first city in the U.S. to set up legal zoning restrictions, for the purpose of relieving street congestion, when it enacts the Zoning Act of 1916. It will become a model for other cities' efforts to enhance quality of life through determining limits on growth and change.

• Fearing that Germany might find allies in the Dominican Republic, President Wilson tries to impose U.S.-trained national guard in place of the country's military, and to install his handpicked choices in official government positions. The Dominican government and people protest, even forgoing pay for six months when Wilson freezes custom revenues. Wilson sends in the U.S. Marines, beginning an eight-year occupation of the Dominican Republic by enforcing martial law, dissolving the legislature, establishing censorship, and imprisoning opponents. This occupation leaves a legacy of anger against the U.S., and a system of duties and customs laws that make the country dependent on the U.S. It also creates a national police institution, among whose trainees is a young recruit named Rafael Trujillo, who for thirty years will run one of the most infamous dictatorships in the western hemisphere.

• The U.S. National Park Service is created under the Department of the Interior—the first park system in the world to make wildlife protection a goal.

• When Mexican revolutionary General Francisco "Pancho" Villa (1879–1919) leads a raid on Columbus, New Mexico, killing nineteen people and burning the town, President Wilson responds by sending Brigadier General John J. Pershing and 6,000 men into Mexico on a "punitive expedition" against Villa. President Carranza orders his troops to attack U.S. soldiers, after more are mobilized along the border. After two years, although still having failed to capture Villa, the U.S. withdraws as its resources become absorbed by the war in Europe.

• Jeanette Rankin (1880–1973) of Montana becomes the first woman elected to represent her state in the U.S. House of Representatives. Both a Republican and a pacifist, she is elected before most women are even allowed to vote, and is also exceptional because she is the only legislator who will vote against entering both World War I and World War II.

BUSINESS AND INDUSTRY

• Industrialist John D. Rockefeller (1839–1937), CEO of Standard Oil, the corporation that controls 85 percent of domestic oil production in the U.S., becomes the world's first billionaire.

• The U.S. Senate passes a bill introducing the eight-hour workday as the industrial standard, after President Wilson promises an eight-hour workday for 400,000 rail workers and narrowly averts a nationwide strike sponsored by the railroad brotherhoods. The Senate also passes the Owen-Keating Law, which bars any company involved in interstate commerce of raw materials or goods from employing a child younger than fourteen years of age or requiring fourteen-to-sixteen-year-olds to work more than eight hours per day. The law affects about 13 percent of the textile industry workforce under the age of sixteen. But it will be over-

turned by the Supreme Court in 1916, in *Hammer v. Dagenhart,* on the grounds that Congress has exceeded its powers to regulate interstate commerce, and that it intrudes on police powers within states.

CULTURE AND SOCIETY

• W. E. B. Du Bois organizes the Amenia Conference of 1916 on the estate of NAACP leader Joel E. Spingarn, near Amenia, New York, to unify the divided factions among the leaders of the African American community. Du Bois writes a "Unity Platform," setting forth ways to achieve political freedom and endorsing the NAACP as the leading organization to represent the black movement.

• Margaret Sanger opens the first birth-control clinic in the U.S., in the Brownsville area of Brooklyn, New York. The clinic distributes woman-controlled contraceptives, especially promoting a flexible diaphragm fitted by trained medical staff, a new device that Sanger learned about while visiting a Dutch birth-control clinic in 1915. In its first nine days the clinic sees 464 clients, and on the tenth day Sanger is arrested. When she refuses to promise to stop disseminating contraceptive information, the judge sentences her to thirty days in the workhouse. The publicity engendered by her arrest brings attention and wealthy supporters to build an organization to carry through her birth-control education mission. Sanger founds the American Birth Control League in 1921 and helps organize the first world population conference in 1924. Her work is lauded by some, and vilified by others who find offense in her advocating for methods to reduce genetically transmitted mental or physical defects, including sterilization for the mentally incompetent, and in her connections with the reactionary wing of the eugenics movement that argues for limiting population growth based on race, class, or ethnicity.

🔲 1915

• Marcus Garvey (b. Jamaica, 1887–1940) arrives in New York on a fund-raising lecture tour this year, and by early 1918 has established his nationalist Universal Negro Improvement Association (UNIA) in the U.S. His program includes the Back-to-Africa Movement, promoting the idea that all people of African descent should resettle in Africa. It also fosters self-reliance by starting schools and various black cooperative self-help businesses. His most ambitious plan is the Black Star Line Steamship Corporation, which buys three ships that actually run some trade and passenger routes to the Caribbean. The company endures overwhelming management problems, however, as the ships keep breaking down. The fourth ship that is to travel to Liberia never actually comes into the company's possession, but remains entangled in litigation for a decade. UNIA membership will rise to 2 million followers in the U.S. and a total of 6 million worldwide. In the 1920s, Garvey begins displaying a banner for the "New Negro" with the colors black, representing "our race"; red, representing "our blood"; and green, for "our hope." Garvey and his organization are perceived as dangerous, and he gathers many enemies on the right and left, including both W. E. B. Du Bois and J. Edgar Hoover, head of the FBI. In 1922, Garvey will be indicted on mail fraud charges. After serving two years of a five-year term in a federal penitentiary in Atlanta, he will be pardoned by President Calvin Coolidge,

but he is deported to Jamaica as an undesirable alien. Garvey's message continues to resonate among African Americans, and his flag has been universally adopted, even appearing as the colors on the flags of Kenya and Rwanda.

WORLD EVENTS

• The Battle of Verdun, France, on the Meuse River, lasts from February 21 to December 18, where Germans employ artillery on a massive scale and use poisonous gas, costing an estimate of 550,000 French and 450,000 German lives. Soldiers in trenches have to deal routinely with endless dirt, lice, boredom, and danger. They contract trench fever and trench-foot, a rot caused by standing in deep mud and water. Many suffer from shell shock, and they must watch rats feed off the dead. Modern warfare makes it impossible for civilians to return to the comparative innocence of daily life, and their disorientation brings complex changes in the ways ordinary people live their lives.

• European Dada is officially launched at the Cabaret Voltaire in Zurich, Switzerland, by intellectuals and artists who may be draft dodgers, deserters, and refugees living in this neutral country as a haven from the awful horrors of World War I. Dada is a word selected at random, with much of its charm coming from its having many wildly different meanings in different languages. Dada practitioners intend to foment new attitudes and ideas about art, politics, and life in response to a world that is becoming absurd and unacceptable. The provocative antics at the Cabaret Voltaire will be seen as forerunners of performance art, punk, and postmodern aesthetics.

• Cubism spreads to Berlin, Paris, and New York, where Paul Strand (1890–1976), Morton Schamberg (1881–1918), and Charles Sheeler (1883–1965) apply its principles of geometric abstraction to the medium of photography.

1917

ARTS AND LITERATURE

• *Fountain* by R. Mutt (a porcelain urinal turned upside down, titled, dated 1917, and signed with large black painted letters by Marcel Duchamp) is submitted to an Independents art exhibition, the largest art show ever to be put on in the U.S. to date, with a board of directors made up of artists from various styles and camps. Since the art world in Europe is occupied by war, there is a sense that this is a chance for the U.S. to "forge the new art of the twentieth century." The show is to be a completely democratic effort: the directors decide to hang the works in alphabetical order of the artists' last names, with any artist invited to submit two works for five dollars in annual dues and a one-dollar initiation fee. But *Fountain* is rejected. Duchamp resigns from his board of directors position in protest, because it is supposed to be a no-jury, no-prize show,

"an opportunity for the artist to send in anything he chooses." Photographed by Alfred Stieglitz, the original of this "ready-made" work disappears. It becomes an art icon, helping to define the "anti-art" character put forth by the Dada Movement, and forever calling into question what can be called "art."

• Man Ray (1890–1977), an expatriate American artist living in Paris, creates his first "cliché-verre," a cross between a photograph and a print. It is made by etching lines on a glass plate and allowing light to pass through the lines, which fixes an image on photographically sensitive paper.

• The Original Dixieland Jazz Band (ODJB), a group of five young white New Orleans–based musicians, capitalizes on the growing rage for jazz. Their first hit record, "Livery Stable Blues" and "Dixieland Jass Band One-Step," is recorded for Victor Studios in New York and released on the Victor label in 1917. It sells over one million copies. The ODJB bill themselves the "Creators of Jazz," and are often cited as the starting point of the Jazz Age, in spite of numerous facts to the contrary. This represents the first example of what will be an accepted pattern of appropriation continuing throughout the century in the popular music industry.

Birth control is the first important step woman must take toward the goal of her freedom. It is the first step she must take to be man's equal. It is the first step they must both take toward human emancipation. . . . All of our problems are the result of overbreeding among the working class, and if morality is to mean anything at all to us, we must regard all the changes which tend toward the uplift and survival of the human race as moral. Knowledge of birth control is essentially moral. Its general, though prudent, practice must lead to a higher individuality and ultimately to a cleaner race.

(MARGARET SANGER, "MORALITY AND BIRTH CONTROL," FEBRUARY 1918)

GOVERNMENT AND POLITICS

• The NAACP wins a victory in the U.S. Supreme Court against segregated housing ordinances begun in 1910.

• The U.S. purchases 133 square miles of territories in the Virgin Islands from Denmark, for $25 million. Including the islands of St. Croix, St. Thomas, and St. John, the new territories will be used as strategic bases to guard the Panama Canal under the jurisdiction of the U.S. Navy. This is the last territory the U.S. will acquire in the western hemisphere.

• The U.S. enters World War I. An intensive propaganda campaign is launched to drum up support for the war effort. In February the Selective Service Act is passed, providing for the enlistment of all able-bodied men from twenty-one to thirty-one years of age by requiring them to register with their local draft boards. It also requires non-citizen Mexicans in the U.S. to register, even though they are not eligible for the draft. More than 15,000 American Indian men see active duty, with a few Choctaws serving as "code talkers," communicating in their native language, which cannot be deciphered by the enemy. In Hawaii, 29,000 *issei* (Japanese immigrant generation) and some *nisei* (first Japanese American generation born in the U.S.) register for the draft. And for the first time in American history, women officially join the military. The navy swears in 12,500 women they call "Yeomen," as clerical workers, the marine corps enlists 305 "Marinettes," and the army sends 1,000 overseas as translators, telephone operators, and ambulance drivers for the American Expeditionary Forces.

• The Espionage Act is used to imprison Americans who speak or write against the war. Nine hundred people are imprisoned. The law remains in effect to the present day.

• Congress passes the Jones Act, extending U.S. citizenship to all Puerto Ricans and decreeing English the official language of Puerto Rico. It also establishes two houses of legislature in Puerto Rico, with representatives elected by the people.

• The Smith-Hughes Act creates the Federal Board for Vocational Education, which provides states with matching funds to establish trade and agricultural schools.

BUSINESS AND INDUSTRY

• Marshall Burns Lloyd receives a patent to process wicker, a canelike material, out of twisted paper and wire. It will become popular for parlors and porches. Two years later he founds Lloyd Loom, a company that produces and sells over 10 million furniture items by 1940.

• The Radio Corporation of America (RCA) is incorporated this year. The company is formed as "a marriage of convenience" between large corporations and the federal government to develop wireless communication. The arrangement results from Assistant Navy Secretary Franklin D. Roosevelt's experiences in dealing with the confusion of wireless industry patents during the World War I government takeover of the industry, which persuades him to keep radio patents for the developing wireless industry under American control rather than selling them to the British Marconi Company, as planned by General Electric. RCA takes over the assets of the American Marconi Company, and begins to market radio equipment produced by GE and Westinghouse.

They say any artist paying six dollars may exhibit.

Mr. Richard Mutt sent in a fountain. Without discussion this article disappeared and never was exhibited. What were the grounds for refusing Mr. Mutt's fountain:—

1.   Some contended it was immoral, vulgar.

2.   Others, it was plagiarism, a plain piece of plumbing.

Now Mr. Mutt's fountain is not immoral, that is absurd, no more than a bathtub is immoral. It is a fixture that you see every day in plumbers' show windows.

Whether Mr. Mutt with his own hands made the fountain or not has no importance. He CHOSE it. He took an ordinary article of life, placed it so that its useful significance disappeared under the new title and point of view—created a new thought for that object.

As for plumbing, that is absurd. The only works of art America has given are her plumbing and her bridges.

(MARCEL DUCHAMP, "THE RICHARD MUTT CASE," *Blind Man* 2 [1917]:5)

SCIENCE AND TECHNOLOGY

• An Army Signal Corps officer, Edwin Armstrong, pioneers amplitude modulation (AM) radio in the U.S. through the development of a superheterodyne circuit.

• Clarence Birdseye observes Inuit fast-freezing food in their subzero-temperature environment during his years as a fur trader in Labrador. When he returns to New York in 1917, he replicates the process by spending seven dollars for a fan, ice, and salt, finding that he can fast-freeze food in a brine of minus 57 degrees Celsius. He continues refining the process until, in 1924, he and three partners form General Seafoods Corporation in Gloucester, Massachusetts. Their quick-frozen fish fillets are the beginning of a multibillion-dollar revolution in the food industry. By 1939, when a variety of precooked frozen food products begin being marketed under the Birds Eye label, most Americans take advantage of being able to instantly prepare almost any food at any season.

CULTURE AND SOCIETY

• The first Pulitzer Prizes are given out by Columbia University's School of Journalism. The winners include Laura E. Richards and Maude Howe Elliot, for their biography *Julia Ward Howe*.

• When war is declared on Germany, the loyalty of German Americans is questioned. Their communities become feared and targeted for hate crimes and violence. Cities change street and other place names that are German.

• The radical writer Randolph Bourne (1886–1918) publishes a series of essays in a magazine, *The Seven Arts*, opposing U.S. involvement in World War I, especially criticizing American intellectuals who support the enterprise and techniques of war. His analysis becomes a central moral guide for advocates of pacifism and nonintervention.

WORLD EVENTS

• The Russian Revolution begins with the defection of a Petrograd garrison, forcing Czar

Nicholas to abdicate. The Mensheviks, a moderate socialist group, come into power, led by Aleksandr Kerensky. His government, however, fails to remain in control of various revolutionary factions, especially when the more radical Bolshevik leaders Vladimir Lenin and Leon Trotsky return to Russia from Paris. They stage the October Revolution, occupying Petrograd (the former St. Petersburg), and establish Lenin as chairman over a Council of People's Commissars.

• Britain promises the "Holy Land of Palestine" to the Zionist Movement, as a national home for the Jewish people, in the form of a letter, the Balfour Declaration, written by Foreign Secretary Arthur J. Balfour. The letter specifies that nothing shall be done to "prejudice the civil and religious rights of the existing non-Jewish communities in Palestine, or the rights and political status enjoyed by Jews in any other country." The indigenous Arabs contend that calling the area a Jewish homeland will infringe on their rights. The declaration breaks Britain's 1914 promise to give independence to Arab lands under Ottoman rule, which included Palestine, in return for Arab support against Turkey during World War I, and leads to the Council of the League of Nations' Mandate for Palestine in 1922, which also favors the establishment of a Jewish homeland. It starts a migration of Jews from Europe that increases in the 1930s with the rise of Nazism, and which results, in 1948, in the withdrawal of the British and a declaration of the state of Israel.

• The ballet *Parade* translates Cubism into theatrical sets and costumes, and introduces the use of vernacular movement and naturalistic mime. It premieres in Paris in a production by the Ballets Russes, and is decried as an

"The rainbow!" Political cartoon on U.S. troops leaving for World War I, by Edwin Marcus, c. 1917. *(Library of Congress, Prints and Photographs Division)*

outrage. The work is a collaboration among Erik Satie (1866–1925), Pablo Picasso, Jean Cocteau (1889–1963), and Leonide Massine (1895–1979).

• Surrealism, growing out of Dada, begins to rise as an art movement. The term is coined by the French poet Guillaume Apollinaire this year in reference to his new drama, *Les Mamelles de Tiresias,* and to Picasso's *Parade* designs.

🄳 1924

• The Mexican Revolution comes to a close when President Carranza accepts the Constitution of 1917 that forms the foundation for the modern Mexican state.

1918

ARTS AND LITERATURE

• George W. Cronyn publishes *Path of the Rainbow,* the first comprehensive anthology of Native American poetry, which shows, through translations by poets and ethnologists, the wide variety of styles, themes, and forms.

• Mabel Dodge Luhan (1879–1962), heiress to a Buffalo department store fortune, transplants her Greenwich Village avant-garde literary and art salon to Taos, New Mexico, where she and her fourth husband, Tony Lujan, a local Tewa Indian, build a twenty-two-room adobe house that they name Los Gallos (for the ceramic roosters on the roof). It serves as an artists' retreat, nurturing the creative growth of many major innovators of the 1920s and 1930s, including D. H. Lawrence (1885–1930) and his wife, Frieda, who are frequent visitors; Ansel Adams (1902–1984), who changes careers from pianist to photographer; and Georgia O'Keeffe (1887–1986), who is inspired by its landscapes to do her first New Mexico painting.

• Conductor James Reese Europe is asked to form a military band as part of his army unit, which is known as the 369th Infantry Band. They are the first African American combat unit to land in France, entertaining troops and citizens in every city they visit and infecting them with the "jazz germ." The band returns to New York City at the end of the war, and makes a triumphant tour of U.S. cities until a tragic incident occurs at a Boston concert, when a percussionist, angered at Europe's strict directions, fatally stabs Europe with a knife.

• Louis B. Mayer Pictures is founded. In 1924, it will merge with the companies of Marcus Loew and Samuel Goldwyn to form Metro-Goldwyn-Mayer (MGM). United Artists is founded in 1919 by director D. W. Griffith and actors Charlie Chaplin, Douglas Fairbanks, and Mary Pickford. By the 1920s these studios, along with Paramount, Warner Brothers, RKO, and Twentieth Century Fox, institute the star and studio system, a set of industrial standards that will rule working conditions and moviemaking styles for more than thirty years. By 1920, the Hollywood studios employ 20,000 people; by 1926 they will employ 300,000.

GOVERNMENT AND POLITICS

• With the end of World War I, President Woodrow Wilson proposes "a new international order" based on "Fourteen Points," his solution to a postwar settlement. Its points include a removal of economic barriers and equality in trade; a reduction in armaments; impartial adjustment of colonial claims, giving equal weight to the interests of the colonial people; and his program to create a new world organization, called the League of Nations, which will function as a forum for nations to work together to keep the peace. In November 1919, the Senate votes 55 to 39 against ratifying the Treaty of Versailles, forcing the U.S. to sign a separate treaty with Germany.

• The U.S. government begins mass raids on and deportations of aliens.

• An amendment to the Espionage Act of 1917, called the Sedition Act of 1918, prohibits and penalizes any speech or press activities disloyal to the government. In a 1919 test cast reviewed by the Supreme Court, *Abrams v. U.S.,* Justice Oliver Wendell Holmes writes a dissenting opinion defending "free trade in ideas." This sets the precedent for First

Amendment theory and litigation, arguing that "we should be eternally vigilant against attempts to check the expression of opinions we loathe and believe to be fraught with death, unless they so imminently threaten immediate interference with the lawful and pressing purposes of the law that an immediate check is required to save the country, a defense known as a 'clear and present danger.' "

BUSINESS AND INDUSTRY

• Financier Bernard N. Baruch is appointed head of the War Industries Board by President Wilson. His job is to centralize and coordinate industrial production efforts during the war, advising the government departments on what purchases need to be made, and prices to pay for the Allied war effort in Europe.

SCIENCE AND TECHNOLOGY

• The Curtiss JN-4 fighter plane, known as the "Jenny," is the first U.S.-built warplane to fly over European battlegrounds. U.S. papers are full of the exploits of flying ace Eddie Rickenbacker, who shoots down seven German planes in one day, and the tragedies of Major Raoul Lufbery, who is shot down by a German biplane, and Frank Luke, who downs sixteen enemy planes in sixteen days, only to be gunned down when he defies orders and goes out on his own against ten German Fokkers.

• The gas-operated Brownsville automatic rifle is developed, offering a perfected version of the .30-caliber rifle, which improves shooter accuracy, as tested on a target 100 yards away.

CULTURE AND SOCIETY

• A worldwide influenza epidemic, known as the "Spanish flu," kills 548,452, according to the official death toll in the U.S., which is more than the total number of soldiers killed in both world wars, Korea, and Vietnam combined. Over the next three years it will continue to appear in waves, taking between twenty and thirty million lives around the world. The war helps to disperse the disease, with ports—Boston; Freetown, Sierra Leone; and Brest, France—causing the disease to spread around the globe. In San Francisco an ordinance requires people to wear surgical masks, and in Chicago, people who cough are not admitted to movie theaters. Other cities pass similar measures. Doctors and scientists are never able to isolate this virus, which is believed to enter through the nasal passages, and which kills more people than any other recorded epidemic in history. It finally—and mysteriously—vanishes.

• The Native American Church incorporates in Oklahoma this year, teaching a combination of traditional Indian beliefs and elements of Christianity. By the mid-1920s, it will be embroiled in a controversy over whether to legalize or outlaw its members' use of peyote, a sacred cactus plant with hallucinogenic properties that is a sacrament of the religion, and that provides a mystical all-seeing spiritual guide.

• Every state now has a compulsory education requirement.

• Daylight savings time is instituted, as a means of saving industrial fuel consumption.

• Feminist pacifists Carrie Chapman Catt and Jane Addams (1860–1935) object to wartime work by either men or women, while other feminists believe that, by assisting in the war effort, women entering the workforce for the first time will be able to lead the way for equality for all women. Women are being paid less than men for doing equal work. Many employers consider it women's patriotic duty to quit working when the men come back from the battlefields needing jobs.

WORLD EVENTS

• World War I ends with Germany's surrender. Fifty thousand American soldiers have died. There is widespread shock at the horror this war has caused, and a realization, in Europe and the U.S., that a flood of lies are behind the waste, pain, and loss to millions. Many artists work through their feelings and experiences. In film, *The Cabinet of Dr. Caligari* (1919), a madman's dream, directed by Robert Wiene, and F. W. Murnau's vampire classic *Nosferatu* (1921) are released in Germany, and *J'Accuse,* a French antiwar film by Abel Gance, is widely praised throughout Europe. Ernest Hemingway's novel *A Farewell to Arms* is published, as are John dos Passos's *1919* and Dalton Trumbo's *Johnny Got His Gun.* In poetry, T. S. Eliot's *The Waste Land* is published in 1922. In visual and performance arts, the Dadaists' experiments are at the fore. In Germany, the Worker's Party is founded this year. It will become the Nazi Party, whose aggression is one of the principal causes of the next "war to end all wars."

• Czar Nicholas and his wife and five children are executed by a firing squad in Russia.

1919

ARTS AND LITERATURE

• Angered by the carnage of the race riots and anti-Communist demonstrations that become known as "Red Summer," Claude McKay (1891–1948) writes the poem "If We Must Die."

🔲 1939

• The Theatre Guild is founded in New York as a membership society to present distinguished American and foreign noncommercial productions. By selecting the realistic plays of Eugene O'Neill, S. N. Behrman, Elmer Rice, and Robert E. Sherwood, among others, they define a naturalistic style that continues to dominate the American theater throughout the century, as this organization's mantle passes to the Group Theatre, and in turn is passed to the Actors Studio.

🔲 1935, 1947

GOVERNMENT AND POLITICS

• All Indians who serve in the armed forces (more than 10,000 enlisted) are granted full U.S. citizenship by Congress.

• The National Prohibition Act, the Eighteenth Amendment to the Constitution, which prohibits the "manufacture, sale or transportation of intoxicating liquors," is ratified on January 16, 1919, after Nebraska agrees to the measure. After the law is unsuccessfully contested in the courts, it becomes effective January 16, 1920. It proves to be impossible to enforce, spawning a whole new industry of bootlegging and establishments called "speakeasies" that sell liquor illegally. The new law makes it almost fashionable for ordinary people to break the law. It encourages the rise of organized crime, as gangsters fight each other to the death over territory, and corruption increases as politicians and police are bought off, although in ten years the federal government will make over half a million arrests. Instead of eradicating alcoholism,

Prohibition increases it. In 1933 it becomes the only constitutional amendment ever repealed.

BUSINESS AND INDUSTRY

• In Seattle, Washington, 100,000 workers bring the city to a halt in a walkout called by the Industrial Workers of the World (IWW). The general strike begins over a fight for higher wages by shipyard workers. Although the five-day strike is peaceful, the entire city is shut down except for striker-organized activities, such as their passing out free meals for everyone. Members of the IWW are jailed when the strike ends and Socialist party headquarters are raided. Tensions run high in the area, with the Seattle mayor talking of the strike as an "attempted revolution . . . for the overthrow of the industrial system." On Armistice Day in November, the American Legion passes the IWW hall carrying hoses and gas pipes, and shots are exchanged (no one is sure who fires first), resulting in the death of an American Legion parade leader and an IWW member, Wesley Everest, who is hanged by a vigilante mob after being dragged out of jail. This pattern of strikes followed by retaliations from vigilantes is repeated in many parts of the country. It leads to crackdowns against the IWW and the Socialist Party, as well as the passage of laws limiting immigration from Eastern Europe, severely cutting down Russian, Jewish, Italian, and Latin immigrant numbers.

SCIENCE AND TECHNOLOGY

• When physicist Robert A. Goddard (b. 1882) proposes that rockets will one day make

---

HOW THE BAUHAUS EMBODIED ITS AESTHETIC STYLE IN ITS EDUCATIONAL STYLE

The aim of the Bauhaus was to find a new and powerful working correlation of all the processes of artistic creation to culminate finally in a new cultural equilibrium of our visual environment. This could not be achieved by individual withdrawal into an ivory tower. Teachers and students as a working community had to become vital participants of the modern world, seeking a new synthesis of art and modern technology. Based on the study of the biological facts of human perception, the phenomena of form and space were investigated in a spirit of unbiased curiosity, to arrive at objective means with which to relate individual creative effort to a common background. One of the fundamental maxims of the Bauhaus was the demand that the teacher's own approach was never to be imposed on the student; that, on the contrary, any attempt at imitation by the student was to be ruthlessly suppressed. The stimulation received from the teacher was only to help him find his own bearings.

(WALTER GROPIUS, FROM HIS INTRODUCTION TO *The Theater of the Bauhaus*, EDITED BY WALTER GROPIUS AND ARTHUR S. WENSINGER, TRANSLATED BY ARTHUR S. WENSINGER [MIDDLETOWN, CONN.: WESLEYAN UNIVERSITY PRESS])

it possible to travel to the moon, newspapers call him the "moon man."

CULTURE AND SOCIETY

• This year becomes known as the "Red year," owing to various events. An American chapter of the Communist Party is formed in Chicago, Illinois, and the majority of its first members are Russian immigrants. Their party's motto is "Workers of the World, Unite!" The government launches a "Red scare" in which thousands of suspected subversives are deported. Sparked by a climate of racist newspaper accounts of blacks depicted as rapists and gangsters, bloody race riots flare up in twenty-five cities from April through December. This awful frequency of white-on-black violence becomes known as "Red Summer": seventy-six African Americans are lynched; black homes in white neighborhoods are burned and looted; and both blacks and whites are killed. The largest riot takes place in Chicago, beginning when an African American boy is killed because he swam over the line dividing the white swimming area of a beach from the black swimming area. The National Association for the Advancement of Colored People (NAACP) holds a conference on lynchings and publishes *Thirty Years of Lynchings in the U.S., 1889–1919*.

• The American Legion is formed in Paris at a meeting of around 1,000 delegates representing units of the American Expeditionary Force.

WORLD EVENTS

• At the Paris Peace Conference, thirty-two countries consider how to build a lasting world peace after the "Great War." Meetings start in January, with negotiations dominated by the Allied powers of the U.S., Britain, Italy, France, and sometimes Japan. As head of the U.S. delegation, President Wilson is the first U.S. president to visit Europe while in office, and the rhetoric of his Fourteen Points frames the discussion. W. E. B. Du Bois serves as an NAACP observer and *The Crisis* correspondent to the Peace Conference, investigating the treatment of 42,000 African American soldiers. He helps organize a simultaneous Pan-African Conference in Paris, discussing the fifth of Wilson's points: "a free, open-minded and absolutely impartial adjustment of all colonial claims . . . [where] the interests of the populations concerned must have equal weight with the equitable claims of the government whose title is to be determined."

The Treaty of Versailles, the conference's centerpiece, is intended to be the official agreement ending World War I. It also establishes a League of Nations "for the purpose of affording mutual guarantees of political independence and territorial integrity to great and small states alike." The treaty is signed in June by the U.S., Britain, Italy, and France against the defeated powers of Germany, Austria-Hungary, Turkey, and their allies. Germany loses 25,000 square miles to neighboring counties, conceding territories that break up its colonial empire. Other punishments include reparation payments, a ban on German rearmament, and trials for war crimes. President Wilson cannot persuade Congress to accept the treaty after his return to the U.S., however, and the U.S. never ratifies the treaty.

The conference drafts other treaties and agreements, redistributing colonies and affecting borders across Central and Eastern Europe, the Middle East, Africa, the Pacific Islands, and

Asia. Mandates, a form of trusteeship, authorize how territories are governed, as administered under the League of Nations or under powers mandated by the League. Negotiations based on colonial interests yield new national borders arranged without regard to how ethnic groups are thrown together. For example, Britain and France carve up the provinces of the Turkish Ottoman Empire, mixing Kurds, Arabs, Christians, Jews, and Armenians together, creating future powder kegs such as the new nation of Iraq, formed under an English mandate. When the Paris Peace Conference formally closes in January 1920, outstanding business is left to related conferences and councils to resolve, including the League of Nations. Many warn that the economic hardship placed on Germany will set the stage for another war. Hitler will later claim that Germany was betrayed, not defeated.

• The Weimar Republic begins in Germany, remaining in power until 1933.

• The Bauhaus, an institution for the visual arts, is founded in Weimar, Germany, by architect Walter Gropius (1883–1969). The artists who come to live and work there subscribe to the principal that "form follows function." The Bauhaus's mission is to make the arts a part of everyday life, by taking advantage of the mass-production technology of the modern age, so that functional, well-designed environments can be affordable to anyone, not just the wealthy. The architects who teach and work there, including Charles-Edouard Jeanneret Le Corbusier (Swiss-French, 1887–1965) and Ludwig Mies van der Rohe (Belgian, 1886–1969), help create what becomes known as the "international style" of architecture and interior design. It is recognizable for its use of simple geometric shapes and modern materials, such as the large areas of glass that become a popular feature of skyscraper design in the 1950s and 1960s. Artists in residence also serve as "master" tutors, helping their "apprentices" achieve fine but practical craftsmanship in the fields of architecture, planning, painting, sculpture, industrial design, and stage design. Painter Paul Klee (Swiss, 1879–1940) teaches stained-glass techniques; painter Wassily Kandinsky (Russian, 1866–1944) teaches wall painting; Marcel Breuer (Hungarian, 1902–1981) teaches interior design; painter and sculptor Oskar Schlemmer (German, 1888–1943) teaches theater production; Josef Albers (German, 1888–1976) teaches color theory and optical experimentation; painter Lyonel Feininger (American, 1871–1956) teaches painting, and designer Laszlo Moholy-Nagy (Hungarian, 1895–1946) teaches stage design. Moholy-Nagy will establish the New Bauhaus (later renamed the Institute of Design) in Chicago after the Nazis close the second location of the Bauhaus, in Berlin, in 1933. Ludwig Mies van der Rohe will establish an architecture department at the Illinois Institute of Technology, and Gropius will become chairman of the Harvard School of Architecture.

▣ 1933

1920–1929

1920–1929

ALTA

CULTURALLY, AMERICA WAS RED HOT. JAZZ was stepping out beyond the blues of the red-light districts and the gospel songs of the churches, and becoming America's premier art form. Movies were going from lurching images to believable stories with sound as well as visuals. The intellectual elite no longer had a solid lock on print culture—mom-and-pop presses appeared, and fine-art editions were being produced in people's homes. A wild westerner who loved drinking beer with cowboys started what many consider our finest—and certainly our most successful—literary magazine, *The New Yorker*, cleverly tapping the talents of outrageous and witty iconoclasts like Robert Benchley and Dorothy Parker.

The political scene was as wild as it has ever been in the U.S., with the victory of the vote for women, and the burgeoning union movement worldwide, which was being handled or mishandled in various ways by industrialists and governments. The wealth of the country had become available to people in a broader sense through the expansion of the stock market, and prosperity seemed possible in a broad social context, even while unions and bosses occasionally battled in disruptive ways. Investors discovered new ways that money itself could make money, and as middle-class people discovered investing, the stock market became almost a financial parlor game.

World War I ended our protective isolation, and American men were, for the first time, dying in large numbers in wars on foreign soil. America was ceasing to be the raw land of desperate immigrants, and forming its own culture and presence. It looks to us like a vibrant, exciting, and occasionally terrifying time.

Architecture soared upward, as people poured into a prosperous, expanding nation. How could everybody possibly fit on the island of Manhattan? Make the housing vertical! Skyscrapers matched the expansionist mood.

As the cities were being born and reborn and expanding, so were the boundaries of civil liberties, especially for American women. After eighty years of organizing, the vote was won, and women immediately formed their own national political party, the Women's Party, with Alice Paul as the first woman candidate for president.

Victorious though women had been, there were no provisions for battered or abandoned women or children, and very few opportunities for honorable and safe work. In an effort to protect themselves and their families, many joined the effort to enforce Prohibition, hoping to prevent violence within the family by preventing access to alcohol. As we now know, this did not solve the problem of alcoholism; in fact, it contributed to the expansion of the criminal class, who stepped into the situation as bootleggers, forming the base of what we now call "organized crime." Gangsters became an even larger part of the political scene than they had been for most of our history.

Europeans continued to enter America, mostly arriving on the East Coast and settling there, or heading to the Midwest. African Americans were moving beyond the borders of the South and the cities of the East, to work in shipyards and factories in the Midwest and on the West Coast. For the first time, Asian women were being allowed to immigrate, so that families were beginning to settle in the port cities of the West, where Asian men had been arriving for decades. The Native Americans who had survived the genocidal expansion of white settlers were relocated or confined to areas that had usually been shunned by the dominant white culture. The wars with Mexico and Canada were over, and the borders were

In January 1920, the population of the U.S. totals 106,000,000, showing an increase of 14.9 percent over the preceding decade. From 1920 to 1929, 4,107,000 immigrants enter the U.S. and 1,685,000 persons emigrate from the U.S. Almost 2.5 million of the immigrants come from Europe, 112,000 from Asia, about 15,000 from Africa and Oceania, and the balance from the Caribbean and from Central, South, and North America. The Native American population will begin to grow again, from its all-time low at the turn of the century. Compared to the first two decades of the century, immigration will slow considerably, owing to the "national origins quota system" established with the Immigration Act of May 26, 1924. According to U.S. Department of Labor statistics, over 8.6 million women over ten years of age comprise 20.4 percent of the labor force.

clearcut but permeable, so that there were already people of every race within our borders. Integration was a long way off, but the ingredients were there for a multicultural explosion of talent, and for the wrenching problems of race relations that have been a central part of our American story.

With the variety of cultural expression, and the astonishing outbursts of talent in every artistic field, American culture was like a small, tender, but very strong young tree. We are its branches.

1920

ARTS AND LITERATURE

• The Harlem Renaissance (a cultural movement also known as the New Negro Arts Movement) flourishes into the 1930s. The movement is centered in the Harlem district of uptown Manhattan, where writers, visual artists, and performing artists carve out new forms, hybrids inspired by references from African American folk idioms, ancient African roots, and European modernist traditions. They will help define American modernism, reaching out to make international connections by traveling and exhibiting in the Caribbean, Mexico, Europe, and Africa. This is a time when popular urban culture ascends to set a national style. The long roster of artists associated with this movement includes writers Langston Hughes (1902–1967), Zora Neale Hurston (1901?–1960), Claude McKay, Jean Toomer (1894–1967), Countee Cullen (1903–1946), James Weldon Johnson, W. E. B. Du Bois, and Alain Locke; visual artists Aaron Douglas (1900–1979), Archibald Motley (1891–1981), Johnson Hale Woodruff (1900–1980), Lois Mailou

Jones (1905–1998), Miguel Covarrubias (b. Mexico, 1904–1957), William Henry Johnson (1901–1970), and Palmer Hayden (1893–1973); sculptors Augusta Savage (1892–1962), Sargent Claude Johnson (1888–1967), Meta Vaux Warrick Fuller (1877–1968), and Richmond Barthé (1901–1989); musicians Duke Ellington (1899–1974), Bessie Smith (1898?–1937), Cab Calloway (1907–1994), and Fletcher Henderson (1897–1952); dancers Josephine Baker (1906–1975), Edna Guy, Hemsley Winfield, and the Cotton Club revue; filmmaker Oscar Micheaux (1884–1951); photographer James Van Der Zee (1886–1983), and author and photographer Carl Van Vechten (1880–1964), among others.

• Charles Ives (1874–1954), having turned to the business of selling insurance after eschewing public performances of his music since 1902, decides to print and circulate 750 copies of his *Concord Sonata* among the music community.

• On February 14, Mamie Smith (no relation to Bessie and just barely a blues singer), records "Crazy Blues," written by her manager, the African American songwriter Perry Bradford, for Okeh Records in New York City. It surprises everyone with enormous sales, opening the way for an era of African American women's hit recordings of the blues, led by Ma Rainey and Bessie Smith.

GOVERNMENT AND POLITICS

• U.S. women win the right to vote with passage of the Nineteenth Amendment, which guarantees the right to vote cannot be denied or abridged on account of sex. On August 26, 1920, after eighty years of struggle by suffragists, the required majority of two-thirds of the states is secured when Tennessee agrees under pressure from President Wilson.

• In the wake of World War I, the Russian Revolution, the rise of radical politics, and a growing immigrant population, a wave of anti-radicalism engulfs the nation. In response the Justice Department, led by Attorney General A. Mitchell Palmer, rounds up thousands of labor organizers in their headquarters, and immigrants in their private homes, in sweeps known as the "Palmer Raids," charging them with radicalism and socialism. Most of the immigrants, largely southern Europeans, are jailed and deported. Five members of the New York legislature are expelled because they are members of the Socialist Party, illustrating the extent to which Red hysteria is allowed to flourish. Although the legislators are reinstated, they are still refused permission to sit in session. One of the most tragic events involves two Italian-born radicals and immigrants, Nicola Sacco and Bartolomeo Vanzetti, who are arrested in May of this year on charges of armed robbery and murder of the paymaster at a shoe factory in Braintree, Massachusetts. Although Sacco has a solid alibi and there is much to question about the circumstantial evidence, the trial ends in a death sentence for both men. Many Americans decry the "trial by atmosphere," in which Webster Thayer, the presiding judge, is reported to have called the defendants "dagos," "anarchist bastards," and "sons of bitches." During their seven years in prison, thousands of letters of protest are sent to the governor of Massachusetts from ordinary citizens and respected leaders including Albert Einstein, Marie Curie, and Felix Frankfurter, and international demonstrations support efforts to reopen the case. The Supreme Court refuses to hear a last-minute appeal, and the two are executed in 1927.

• Congress passes the Merchant Marine Act, which transforms the wartime Shipping Board into a peacetime board, charged with selling the fleet to private owners and operating the ships that remain. The Water Power Act establishes the Federal Power Commission to regulate power plants. These acts are representative of the efficient system of management the federal government has developed, largely due to the war effort, which leads to the functioning of the country more as a single unified nation than an alliance of separate states.

BUSINESS AND INDUSTRY

• After the war has ended, corporations, in an effort to clear themselves of bank debts, begin issuing stock to the general public, opening up investment opportunities to a new market of investors that were only available to the wealthy previously. The concept of buying stocks "on margin" develops in the 1920s, in which individual investors buy stocks on credit, without having to pay cash up front. If stocks are rising, this system works fine, but if stocks are falling, the individual could be courting disaster. For most of the decade, stocks do rise, bought by small and large investors. In 1925 the market has a value of $34 billion; by 1929 this figure has almost doubled, to $64 billion.
🖬 1929

• Westinghouse receives the first commercial radio broadcasting license, and a few days later station KDKA begins broadcasting from the roof of the Westinghouse plant in Pittsburgh, Pennsylvania, sending out Harding-Cox presidential election returns that are received by an audience of amateur wireless operators whose homemade receiving sets are designed to pick up code messages. Within a few months, Westinghouse gets a major competitor in RCA, whose general manager, David Sarnoff, has the smart marketing idea to broadcast the world heavyweight boxing championship. Westinghouse quickly erects other stations at its other plants, and by the following year, hundreds of thousands of fans listen to their play-by-play description of baseball's World Series. By 1930, 46 percent of American households will own radios, and by 1990 the number will be 99 percent.

SCIENCE AND TECHNOLOGY

• The gramophone, also known as a phonograph, becomes commercially available, giving people the ability to listen to music in the comfort of their homes, and for the first time hear high-caliber performers whom they might never have had the chance to hear in live performance.

CULTURE AND SOCIETY

• The American Civil Liberties Union (ACLU) is founded by a small group of social reformers, including activist Helen Keller (1880–1968), novelist Upton Sinclair, and future Supreme Court Justice Felix Frankfurter. The ACLU works for those who have historically not been given equal protection, to see that constitutional rights granted in the Bill of Rights are consistently honored, whatever defendant's politics. Along with the NAACP (formed in 1909) and the labor unions, they begin working for what has become known as public interest law. They challenge constitutional violations and help create a body of laws to protect individuals, strengthening and maintaining First Amendment freedoms, privacy rights, and the essential ideals of fairness and equality.

• The National League of Women Voters is formed, to educate women about the political process, now that they have the right to vote.

WORLD EVENTS

• Mahatma Gandhi organizes a noncooperation protest movement in India against the British colonial rule, beginning widespread *satyagraha*, nonviolent protest and civil disobedience, a form of political action that will be a model for the civil rights movement in the U.S.

• British economist John Maynard Keynes (1883–1946) publishes *The Economic Consequences of Peace*. He causes a stir by predicting that the economic terms of the Versailles Treaty are a recipe for disaster. (Keynes resigned from the British delegation to the Versailles peace conference, in protest.) Keynes believes the huge reparation demands on Germany will ruin that country and possibly others as a result. He also disagrees with the provision demanding the Allies repay the capital and interest on their debts to each other, which he sees as another difficult burden that will be mostly in the interest of the U.S., as it will be the primary beneficiary. 🄯 1926

• The League of Nations holds its first meeting in Geneva, Switzerland.

• In Paris, Lev (Leon) Theremin, Russian, invents the Aetherophone (later called the theremin or Therminovox), one of the first electronic instruments that everyone could use. The inventor travels to the U.S. in 1927, and RCA buys a license to manufacture and sell the instrument in 1928. Its unique sound has a cult following to this day, through its use by composers, including Edgard Varese (1883–1965), and in

INDIAN IMMIGRANTS IN THE UNITED STATES

C. J. S. Wallia

The earliest immigrants from India, who arrived on the Pacific coast in 1899, were mostly Sikhs from the Punjab state. They were ex-soldiers and independent farmers who came seeking larger farms than they could have acquired in their densely populated homeland. Having very little capital, they had to work first as hired hands in Washington, Oregon, and California, where they encountered severe racial discrimination, including four brutal riots.

The British rulers of India, unlike the Chinese and Japanese governments, made absolutely no effort on behalf of their emigrants. In 1914 in Berkeley, California, Sohan Singh Bhakhna organized the Ghadr Party, a movement for armed rebellion against British colonial rule in India. Nearly 3,000 Indian immigrants, almost all of them Sikhs, returned to India, where they found little support. The British rulers hanged forty-six Ghadrites and imprisoned 194 for life.

In the first two decades of the twentieth century, several hundred Indian graduate students also arrived in the U.S. Some of them, after acquiring Ph.D. degrees, became college teachers and naturalized American citizens. In 1923, however, the Supreme Court ruled that immigrants from India, although Caucasians, were not white and as such were not eligible for American citizenship. Their naturalized status was retroactively canceled. Even more bizarre was the revocation of the citizenship of their white wives, all of whom were citizens by birth. A few years later, J. J. Singh Ahluwalia organized a tremendous lobbying effort that resulted in the Luce-Celler Bill of 1946, restoring their naturalized status and allowing a token 100 new immigrants from India.

Dalip Singh Saund came as a student to UC Berkeley in 1920, where he received a Ph.D. in mathematics, and, after running a farming business became, in 1948, the first Asian-American to be elected to the U.S. Congress. Paramahansa Yogananda came to the U.S. in 1920 and in the same year founded his Self-Realization Fellowship to teach India's ancient science and philosophy of yoga. His *Autobiography of a Yogi*, a perennial best-seller, has been translated into many languages. Among his early students were the horticulturist Luther Burbank, George Eastman (inventor of the Kodak camera), poet Edwin Markham, and symphony conductor Leopold Stokowski.

Subramaniam Chandrashekar came to the U.S. in the early 1930s, taught at the University of Chicago for six decades, and won the Nobel Prize for Physics in 1983. Recognizing his pioneering contributions to astrophysics, NASA recently named its orbiting X-ray observatory Chandra, in his honor. Hargobind Khorana came to the U.S. in the late 1940s, taught at the University of Wisconsin, and won the Nobel Prize for Medicine in 1968. His interpretation of the genetic code and analysis of its role in protein synthesis has helped spawn the biotechnology revolution. Narinder Singh Kapany came to the U.S. in 1950, founded Optics Technology in 1960, and taught as Regents' Professor of Physics at the University of California, Santa Cruz. He is popularly known as the "Father of Fiber Optics."

In 1965 immigration laws were liberalized and several hundred thousand Indians arrived. The 2000 census data indicate 1.4 million Indian immigrants.

Among the recent notable achievers are Kanwal Singh Rekhi, founder of Excelan; Vinod Khosla, co-founder of Sun Microsystems; Vinod Dham, designer of Intel's Pentium chip; Sabeer Bhatia, co-founder of hotmail.com; Jagdeep Singh, founder of Lightera.com; multibillionaire Sanjiv Sidhu, founder of i2 Technologies; and Amartya Sen, winner of the Nobel Prize for Economics in 1998. In the arts are the sitar player Ravi Shankar, the sarod player Ali Akbar Khan, the symphony conductor Zubin Mehta, the publisher Ajay Singh Mehta (president of Alfred A. Knopf), and the short-story writer Jhumpa Lahiri. With her debut book of short stories, Lahiri won the Pulitzer Prize for Fiction in 2000.

various films, such as Alfred Hitchcock's *Spellbound* (1945), and many science fiction movies, such as *The Thing* (1951), and *Mars Attacks!* (1996).

1921

ARTS AND LITERATURE

• *Shuffle Along,* a musical comedy conceived by Noble Sissle (1889–1975), a singer and lyricist, and Eubie Blake (1883–1983), a composer and musician, and actor-comedians and writers Flournoy Miller and Aubrey Lyles, opens on May 23 at the 63rd Street Theater. *Shuffle Along* breaks new ground for musicals and for black theater. It introduces the innovation of a dancing chorus line, sixteen women doing intricate, high-energy steps such as the buck-and-wing, tap air steps, soft shoe, and high kicks, so that, according to Jacqui Malone in *Steppin on the Blues,* "musical comedy took on a new and rhythmic life, and [white] chorus girls began learning to dance to jazz." The show sets a high bar of excellence, with music including "I'm Just Wild About Harry," composed by Hall Johnson and William Grant Still, and a pit orchestra that includes Still and

Johnson. The cast features many future international stars, including Florence Mills, Paul Robeson (1898–1976), Caterina Jarboro, and Josephine Baker (1906–1975), who becomes an unprecedented success in New York.

• The Department of Art is established at Howard University by painter and educator James V. Herring, and becomes an important training program for African American visual artists, teachers, and curators.

• The first large exhibit of African American art is presented at the 135th Street branch of the New York Public Library.

• Langston Hughes (1902–1967) has his first poem, "The Negro Speaks of Rivers," published in the organ of the NAACP, *The Crisis.* Hughes uses African American vernacular forms not considered poetry at the time, such as blues, works songs, and folk ballads. His belief that poetry is for the people, realized through his use of working-class speech, anticipates the return to vernacular by the 1960s Black Power poets. His readings, often backed by jazz groups, promote poetry as a multidisciplinary performance form, an approach popularized by the Beat and hip-hop generations.

• Thomas Wilfred (b. 1889, Denmark; d.

1968, Nyack, N.Y.), a pioneer in combining arts and technology, arrives in the U.S. as an early-music singer and professional lutenist, and joins a Theosophist group, becoming interested in building a color organ to illustrate the movement's spiritual principles of cosmic consciousness in the fourth dimension. Working with American architect Claude Bragdon, Wilfred invents the prototype this year for an internally programmed, self-operating console instrument for color music projections, which he calls the Clavilux, in reference to the clavicen, a 1734 instrument that used keys of a clavier to control transparent tapes illuminated by candles. "Lumia" is the name he gives to the resulting art form that involves light and motion. He composes more than fifty compositions for the Clavilux, besides adapting it to create scenic projections for theater productions. In 1930 he constructs sixteen sculpture units that he calls "Home Clavilux" or "Clavilux Junior." From 1933 to 1934 he founds and directs the Art Institute of Light at Grand Central Palace in New York City, installing a Clavilux containing four tiers of thirty-two projectors in the recital hall and presenting public recitals twice a week. Wilfred writes, "Light is the artist's sole medium of expression. He must mold it by optical means, almost as a sculptor models clay. He must add color, and finally motion, to his creation. Motion, the time dimension, demands that he must be a choreographer in space."

GOVERNMENT AND POLITICS

• Republican Warren Gamaliel Harding (1857–1923) becomes twenty-ninth president, with (John) Calvin Coolidge (1872–1933) as vice president, promising "a return to nor-

malcy" with the end of World War I. Instead, his term in office will be plagued by the first government corruption scandals of the century. Before the scandals send two of his appointees to jail, Harding has a heart attack, and does not live to complete his full term.

▣ 1923

• With the Emergency Quota Act, the government responds to anti-immigrant hysteria by designing legislation that will cut back on immigration from eastern and southern Europe and Asia. The Act establishes a national-origins quota system, setting entry limits for people of any nationality based on 3 percent of people living in the U.S. in 1910, with a total maximum of 375,000. Since Mexicans, Puerto Ricans, and other Latin Americans are exempted from the quotas, they become major sources of workers.

▣ 1920, 1922, 1924, 1927

• Winifred Huck (1882–1936) suggests that she could serve out the remainder of the unexpired congressional term of her father, William E. Mason (Republican, Illinois) due to his death. Although she is refused this honor she sets a precedent which for decades is the way most women gain entry to Congressional seats, as they complete unexpired terms of their fathers or husbands. Winifred Huck campaigns for and wins her father's old seat in 1922.

• Missouri's congressman L. C. Dyer introduces a bill making lynching a federal crime, and participation in mob murder a felony. It also says federal officers must make "reasonable efforts to prevent the killing" of citizens attacked by mobs, or be fined or imprisoned. The Rules Committee approves the bill, and it passes in the House of Representatives, but is defeated three times in the Senate by 1922.

SCIENCE AND TECHNOLOGY

• John Augustus Larson (Canadian-American, b. 1892) invents the polygraph (lie detector), which will be used as a legal tool to help prove the guilt or innocence of the accused, although results of polygraph tests are not always accepted as evidence by the courts.

CULTURE AND SOCIETY

• Sixty-four lynchings are reported this year, with only one taking place in a Northern state. Over the next three years, substantial numbers of African Americans leave the South, migrating mainly to industrialized cities of the Northeast, Midwest, and West. They move because of the increasing numbers of segregationist laws and mounting racial violence. African American veterans of World War I leave because they feel great discontent on returning to hostile Southern conditions after fighting to "make the world safe for democracy." Friends and family who move send back reports that in the North, African Americans can vote and move about with more freedom. African Americans also move because of economic hardship resulting in part from the destruction of cotton crops by a boll weevil plague, in part from the industrialization of farming techniques, which reduces the need for year-round laborers, and in part from the loss of new and old jobs to whites. Northern businesses and the railroads send recruiters promising jobs with higher pay. The Pennsylvania Railroad alone brings 12,000 workers to jobs in their yards and tracks.

• Tulsa, Oklahoma, becomes the first U.S. city to be bombed from the air, when city police drop dynamite from private planes to break up a riot in the city's African American Greenwood business district called the "Negro's Wall Street," home to 15,000 people and 191 businesses. The riot is caused by economic tension, although it is ignited by a white-owned newspaper, the *Tulsa Tribune,* which publishes an article headlined "To Lynch Negro Tonight," regarding an alleged rape incident between a black shoe-shiner and a white elevator operator. Whites invade the black district, looting and burning buildings; many of the mob are members of the Ku Klux Klan deputized by the police when a fight starts at the courthouse after the accused man is released because the alleged victim refuses to press charges. More than forty people are documented to have been shot, burned alive, or dragged to their death by cars. Most of these are black, although the actual death toll is said to be closer to 300, and more than 4,000 blacks are arrested and placed in camps where they are forced to carry ID cards. Insurance companies refuse to pay up on fire policies, on the basis of special riot exemptions. Whites take possession of most of the land, which today is the site of Oklahoma State University's Tulsa campus. The event is erased from Tulsa's official history until 1997, when the Tulsa Race Riot Commission is formed, holding hearings and recommending reparations after testimony from the riot's survivors.

WORLD EVENTS

• Adolf Hitler, an Austrian by birth, reorganizes the German Workers' Party in Bavaria into a nationalistic paramilitary party, the National Socialist German Workers' Party, known as the Nazi Party. Germany's widespread postwar unemployment aids Hitler's cause, allowing him to direct their anger through a campaign of prejudice against Jews,

A NATIONAL LEGACY OF MIGRATION

Peter A. Morrison

"In the U.S., there is more room where nobody is than where anybody is. That is what makes America what it is." Gertrude Stein's pronouncement is whimsical, but it strongly parallels the famous thesis of Frederick Jackson Turner concerning North America's western frontier. Turner suggested that the frontier was the key force shaping American intellectual style, national character, and political institutions. Whatever the limitations of his thesis in explaining the national character, Turner surely enriched the national mythology; the captivating image of the frontier as a place, but also as a process, was magnified into a legend with continuing intuitive appeal.

Turner's thesis is attractive not so much for what it tells us about the frontier of the Old West, but because it introduces the frontier concept—or perhaps fantasy—as a compelling force in North American development. One might suppose, for example, that the highly selective process of migration, in sorting both people and places according to an array of recognizable characteristics, perpetuates those characteristics in the national consciousness. One of the most deeply ingrained of these characteristics seems to be the sense that one can always "pick up and go"—not necessarily where nobody is, just "elsewhere." It may be, then, that the true safety valve for Turner's discontented Eastern masses was not the free lands of the West, but a kind of frontier of the mind—the image of an "elsewhere" with its idealized possibilities—created and sustained by a tradition of unhindered migration. Migrants may be carriers of some fundamental impulse that inspirits the whole society and continues to define the North American experience as one of freedom and opportunity through migration, whether one migrates or not. The promise embodied in that legacy induces movement for a certain few, and their movement keeps the promise alive for all.

intellectuals, homosexuals, Communists, pacifists, socialists, and liberals. He promises to revive Germany's Aryan origin myths, purified of all the impure elements.

• The Republic of Ireland becomes a free state, within the British Empire.

• Czech Playwright Karel Capek (1890–1938) adopts the Czech word *robot* to describe mechanical people in his satirical play *RUR* (Rossum's Universal Robots).

• Canadian physician Frederick Banting (1891–1941) and his assistant, Charles H. Best (American-Canadian, 1899–1978), extract insulin from the human pancreas to develop a treatment for diabetes. With their mentor, John Macleod (England, 1876–1935), they first experiment using insulin on dogs, and within a year they are able to test insulin successfully on humans. For discovering and isolating insulin, which helps diabetics metabolize glucose so that they can live normal lives, Banting, Macleod, and Best will receive a Nobel Prize in 1923.

1922

ARTS AND LITERATURE

• T. S. Eliot (1888–1965) writes *The Waste Land;* Eugene O'Neill (1888–1953) receives

Like the flow of deep ocean currents, demographic shifts have generated motion that, though gradual, is steady in direction and enduring in effect. Now as in the past, people continue to migrate for reasons that are connected with the workings of national economic and social systems. A characteristic of modern economies is the quick exploitation of newly developed resources or knowledge, a process that requires the abandonment of old enterprises along with the development of the new. Such economies depend on migration to alter the labor forces of localities more quickly than could be accomplished by natural increase. Without a tradition of migration, which moves people from areas where jobs are dwindling to places where workers are needed, U.S. economic growth would be sluggish and less efficient than it actually has been.

By the close of the millennium, the national legacy of migration assumed the global proportions of earlier eras. The abiding vision of some other place, where the past can be discounted and the future shaped at will, attracted immigrants from Latin America as well as Asia and other continents. As before, these newcomers were heavily weighted with the world's self-selected "strivers" seeking opportunities beyond what their own regions of birth had to offer. For, as a prism separates light into its constituent colors, so does migration select distinct types of individuals from wherever they originate. Passing through that prism of migration was more human ambition than anyone can measure.

(This essay includes excerpts from papers written by Peter A. Morrison, published by RAND and used with the permission of the author, and excerpts from a chapter titled "The Image of 'Elsewhere' in the American Tradition of Migration," co-authored by Peter A. Morrison and Judith P. Wheeler, which appears in William H. McNeill and Ruth S. Adams, eds., Human Migration: Patterns and Policies *[Bloomington: Indiana University Press, 1978].)*

the Pulitzer Prize for his play *Anna Christie;* the U.S. Post Office burns the first 500 copies of the first shipment of James Joyce's *Ulysses* to arrive for release in America.

• The first Southwestern Indian Arts and Crafts Exhibition, precursor to Indian Market, is held in Santa Fe. Initiated by anthropologist Edgar J. Hewitt, now director of the Museum of New Mexico, it institutionalizes the production of American Indian art as a means of economic development. Quality standards are set, with products judged for authenticity before they can be placed on sale. Prizes are given, and Fred Kabotie wins first prize. In 1923, the Indian Arts Fund is begun by a Santa Fe group of European American collectors and artists, including Mary Austin, John Sloan, Alice Corbin Henderson, and Hewitt, so that "notable art works should not be carried away by tourists and random collectors."

GOVERNMENT AND POLITICS

• When oil is discovered on the Navajo reservation, Secretary of the Interior Albert Fall (who will later be involved in the Teapot Dome scandal) tries to manipulate the illegal transfer of leasing rights for large sections of traditional Pueblo lands to European

Americans, without having tribal consent. In response, an All-Pueblo Council is formed by twenty pueblos to protest the land transfers, the first unified Pueblo entity to be assembled since the 1680 revolt against Spanish rule. When John Collier, a European American anthropologist and social reformer, visits the Pueblos and is exposed to their worldview by Taos Indian Antonio Lujan, the husband of Mabel Dodge Lujan, he believes he has found a "Red Atlantis," the model for his dream of a communal society where the individual's needs are integrated within the needs of the group. Collier helps the All-Pueblo Council organize a national opposition campaign, rallying European Americans into a new activist organization, the American Indian Defense Association, to lobby for changes in government policies. Their first fight successfully stops passage of a bill introduced by New Mexico's Senator Bursum, a crony of Secretary Fall, which would have given whites access to Pueblo lands and water rights. They obtain Secretary Fall's resignation from the Cabinet, on the basis of conflict of interest. Their campaign leads to the passage of the Pueblo Lands Act and the Reorganization Act of 1934.

🔲 1924, 1934

• Secretary of Commerce and mining engineer Herbert Hoover negotiates interstate water rights to the Colorado River, setting up policies for dividing the waters of the Colorado River in a manner that completely ignores Native American water rights. These policies, called the Colorado River Basin compact, form the basis of water politics in the West for the rest of the century. They provide the legal structure for the construction of Boulder Dam.

BUSINESS AND INDUSTRY

• Country Club Plaza, the world's first shopping center, opens in Kansas City.

• The public response to radio is enthusiastic, and by 1922 there are so many stations broadcasting around the country that Secretary of Commerce Herbert Hoover calls a conference to work out policies.

• Radio broadcasters come up with the idea of selling commercial advertising time. The first paid commercial will air this year when a realty company sponsors a program on New York City's WEAF, the Western Electric Company's station. The price is fifty dollars for ten minutes, and although many react negatively at first to this idea, radio is on its way to becoming a big business. With the introduction of commercials, the types of shows begin to change because entertainers, who had declined to offer their services for free, were now very interested in working for pay in the new medium. By the decade's end, CBS and NBC will be formed, and the Radio Corporation of America, which manufactures radio receivers and owns NBC, will be an uproariously successful stock in the booming market of the 1920s.

SCIENCE AND TECHNOLOGY

• Frigidaire designs a self-contained icebox, a cabinet that makes storage of perishable foods in the home more convenient. This invention is a transitional appliance that within the year will be replaced by a more efficient solution. It makes the first step toward changing the food buying and cooking habits of Americans, by allowing them to stock up on perishables that they can safely store in their

THE ORIGINAL SHOPPING CENTER

Kathleen Moran

J. C. Nichols was a leader in developing an integrated approach to commercial development. In 1922 he began building the Country Club Plaza in Kansas City as part of a much larger planned development of residential subdivisions. The Plaza included some 200 retail stores and 200 offices to serve the Country Club District—an area with over 10,000 upper-middle-class residents. Country Club Plaza was laid out so that there would be no distinct center or locational hierarchy. The Center was organized around a number of broad streets and irregular blocks to facilitate the flow of traffic, and included innovative plans to accommodate parking. Nichols's company designed, constructed, owned, and managed all the buildings in the Plaza, and Nichols is said to have been one of the first developers to use the term "shopping center" to describe this kind of planned and integrated commercial enterprise.

homes for some time without immediately having to can, smoke, or cook them.

🄯 1924

CULTURE AND SOCIETY

• The first edition of *Reader's Digest,* a pocket-sized magazine, is published by De Witt Wallace and Lila Acheson, his wife. Its innovative format, which cuts articles and literature into quick bits, matches the attention span of a speeded-up culture and appeals to a wide audience. The fortune they amass allows them to form a nonprofit foundation that is a major funding source for community arts projects throughout the country.

WORLD EVENTS

• King Tutankhamen's tomb is discovered in Egypt's Valley of the Kings, near Luxor. Especially remarkable because it has escaped any looting or damage over the centuries, the tomb of this boy-king, who was buried in 1325 B.C. with great artistry and display of wealth, causes a worldwide wave of Egyptomania.

• With a "March on Rome," the Fascist Party takes over in Italy, supported by factions within the clergy and the business community that are afraid of communism. The king appoints Benito Mussolini as prime minister, and grants him dictatorial powers to organize the government.

• Kemal Ataturk, the founder of modern Turkey, overthrows the last sultan and becomes the first president. He begins a modernization program that puts the country on the road to industrialization. The official role of Islam is reduced, including changing the Arabic writing form for the Turkish language to a Latin-based alphabet.

1923

ARTS AND LITERATURE

• Bessie Smith's first recordings for Columbia Records, "Downhearted Blues" and "Gulf

Coast Blues," sell more than 750,000 copies and establish her as the "Empress of the Blues." She goes on to record hit after hit during the 1920s, in sessions featuring such jazz greats as Louis Armstrong, Benny Goodman, James P. Johnson, and Jack Teagarden. In such major performances as "Nobody Knows You When You're Down and Out," "St. Louis Blues" (with Armstrong), "T'ain't Nobody's Bizness If I Do," and "Gimme a Pigfoot," Bessie serves as a model of intense and majestic singing for a generation of female jazz, blues, and even gospel singers to follow. She will die in an auto accident in 1937 just as she begins to come back after the stock market crash of 1929 and a life-long struggle with alcoholism.

• Duke Ellington forms a modest dance band in New York at the Kentucky Club on Times Square, and hones his genius on the job. With the addition of New Orleans–oriented trumpeter Bubber Miley and the great New Orleans clarinetist Sidney Bechet, the Ellington Band begins to become a historically great jazz ensemble.

• Mary Hunter Austin, poet, playwright, and essayist, publishes *The American Rhythm,* a collection of her "re-expressions" of Native American poetry. In the title essay she promotes the literary origins of American writing in Native American poetry. She argues that a sense of place is central to Americans' understanding of their cultural identity, and that Native Americans, as the first and longest residents of this place, can provide valuable keys to reading the American spirit and environment.

• African American choreographer Elida Webb sets off the international dance craze of the decade when she introduces the Charleston in *Runnin' Wild,* a New York City music and dance show. The Charleston beats out the time of complex rhythms with hand-clapping and foot-patting, a return to early black music forms that have never been heard or seen on a New York stage.

GOVERNMENT AND POLITICS

• President Warren Harding dies of a heart attack in August, and his vice president, Calvin Coolidge (1872–1933), becomes president, just as the Washington government corruption scandals are about to be revealed, including the Teapot Dome scandal in the Interior Department and other illegal practices in the Department of Justice and the Veteran's Bureau. Teapot Dome, the major scandal, starts with a transfer of oil land reserves in Teapot Dome, Wyoming, and Elk Hills, California, from the navy to the Department of the Interior's control. Secretary of the Interior Albert Fall secretly leases the lands to the Pan-American Petroleum Company and the Mammoth Oil Company after accepting bribes. Fall is convicted of fraud and will spend a year in prison, and Congress invalidates the leases, returning the lands to public control. Coolidge's management of Teapot Dome and other scandals restores public confidence in the Republican Party.

BUSINESS AND INDUSTRY

• U.S. Steel Corporation reduces the standard workday from twelve to eight hours.

• Henry Luce (1898–1967) and Briton Hadden, two young Yale graduates, form a new weekly magazine, a digest of the past week's events called *Time,* "because no publication has adapted itself to the time which busy men are able to spend on simply keeping informed." Although Hadden dies of a strep infection in 1929, Luce will form a news-gathering empire within the next ten years that also publishes *Life, Fortune,* and *Sports Illustrated.*

SCIENCE AND TECHNOLOGY

• General Motors introduces a new style of mechanical refrigeration unit, under a division called Frigidaire. Their "icebox" provides a self-contained cabinet that stores both the perishables and the machinery needed to keep them cool. It quickly has North American homes dispensing with the services of the iceman or with earlier versions of noisy, leaky iceboxes. It becomes a ubiquitous brand name, a standard appliance in almost 85 percent of American homes within the next twenty years.

• African American inventor Garrett August Morgan (1875–1963) receives a patent for an automatic traffic signal to regulate vehicles moving through city streets by a systematic raising and lowering of "go" and "stop" signs. He sells his patent to General Electric Company for $40,000. Morgan's system is eventually replaced by the system of red, yellow, and green lights in use today.

CULTURE AND SOCIETY

• Reformer John Collier becomes recognized as a white leader of the fight for Indian rights when he stops the Commissioner of Indian Affairs, Charles H. Burke, backed by conservative Christian missionary reformers, from putting through a congressional bill to suppress Indian dances and ceremonies, particularly in the Southwest, on the grounds that they are "obscene spectacles that needed to be stamped out." Collier's ideas become central to the proposed reforms that will frame the Indian Reorganization Act of 1934. President Franklin Roosevelt appoints Collier Commissioner of Indian Affairs in 1933.

WORLD EVENTS

• Composer Arnold Schoenberg (b. Austria, 1874–1941) creates his first twelve-tone work, *Five Piano Pieces, Op. 23,* which will lead a generation of classical composers toward a new way of thinking about creating melody and musical logic.

1924

ARTS AND LITERATURE

• Louis Armstrong plays for his first recording, "Everybody Loves My Baby."

• *Rhapsody in Blue,* a piano concerto composed by George Gershwin (1898–1937) with orchestration by Ferde Grofe, has its world premiere at New York's Aeolian Hall, accompanied by the Paul Whiteman Orchestra. A truly American symphonic style, infused with jazz and blues colors and practices, was thus created, with reverberations to the present day in the work of such composers as Aaron Copland, Leonard Bernstein, Miles Davis, the Beatles, and beyond.

• Fletcher Henderson (1897–1952), a classically trained pianist and New York City band leader, organizes the prototypical jazz band with the help of Don Redman's innovative arrangements and compositions centered around skillful call-and-response among the instrumental sections. Henderson lures Louis Armstrong from Chicago to join the band. In the band Louis learns to read music and returns the favor as his soloing genius serves as the model for the entire field of jazz. The great saxophonist Coleman Hawkins is also in that group.

GOVERNMENT AND POLITICS

• Acting President Calvin Coolidge (1872–1933) is elected. His laissez-faire policies toward government's role in big business gives a sense of prosperity, hiding the economic speculation that leads to the stock market crash and the Great Depression.

• The new attorney general, Harlan Fiske Stone, selects J. Edgar Hoover (1895–1972) to head the Bureau of Investigation (which officially becomes the Federal Bureau of Investigation, or FBI, in 1935). Hoover immediately institutes sweeping changes in qualifications, training, and regulations for agents and other FBI personnel. By 1926, law-enforcement agencies throughout the U.S. centralize fingerprint identification under the FBI, making it the world's largest collection. By 1932 the FBI establishes a research facility, the Technical Laboratory, where government criminologists develop surveillance tools and specialized testing equipment and gather an extensive reference collection of guns, watermarks, typefaces, automobile tire designs, and other data. In 1934, FBI agents gain the right to carry guns and make arrests, along with other expansions of federal jurisdiction during the all-out "war" against organized crime. The investigations also serve as weapons to rout out suspected espionage, subversion, and sabotage, and Hoover becomes ever more powerful and more willful in his surveillance choices. He orders investigations of Eleanor Roosevelt, Supreme Court Justice William O. Douglas, and Martin Luther King Jr., whose political views are all considerably more liberal than the extremely conservative Hoover, who continues to widen his interpretation of what constitutes an internal threat to U.S. security. The work of Hoover and the FBI becomes famous through wide coverage in print media, and depictions in radio dramas and film. Hoover remains head of the FBI until his death in 1972. In 1974, President Gerald Ford's attorney general, William Saxbe, reveals that investigations into FBI activities during the mid-to-late 1960s showed violations of the private rights of citizens. The FBI not only gathered data by illegal break-ins, tampering with mail, and wiretaps on political groups and leaders seen as suspect, but also actively disrupted their activities.

• The Indian Citizenship Act confers U.S. citizenship and voting rights on "all non-citizen Indians born within the territorial limits of the U.S." Although federal citizenship should have protected their voting rights, many states prevent Native Americans from voting, saying that the Fifteenth Amendment does not apply. Even though the Indian Citizenship Act makes Native Americans eligible to vote in national elections, a number of indigenous peoples, including the Hopi and Onondaga, informally do not acknowledge the act and continue to function as sovereign nations, including issuing their own passports.

▣ 1900

• Congress passes the Johnson-Reed Immigration Act (also known as the Chinese Exclusion Act or Quota Law), which establishes the "national origins quota system" that governs U.S. immigration policy until 1952. It reduces the total number of immigrants and fixes the number from each nation of origin. The law sets limits that favor northern Europeans and effectively bar southern and eastern Europeans. It maintains the "barred zone" known as the Asia-Pacific Triangle, excluding Asians as codified in the previous Immigration Act of 1917. One congressman states, "The necessity [for this provision] arises from the fact that we do not want to establish additional Oriental families here." It targets Japanese aliens by ruling that no alien ineligible to become a citizen can be admitted into the U.S. as an immigrant. It defines the term "immigrant" and designates all other alien entries into the U.S. as "nonimmigrant" or temporary visitors. Other quotas exclude anyone of African ancestry from entry into the U.S., but allow Canadians and Latin Americans to enter the country unrestricted. Family exemptions apply only to wives and minor children of American citizens.

• Under the authority of the Immigration Act of 1924, Congress establishes a Border Patrol as the mobile and uniformed arm of the Immigration and Naturalization Service under the Department of Justice. The Border Patrol monitors people and vehicles, particularly noting crossings on the 2,000-mile border to the south, between Mexico and the U.S., and, less rigorously, the over-3,000-mile border to the north, between Canada and the U.S.

BUSINESS AND INDUSTRY

• When Congress passes the Indian Oil Leasing Act, it entitles states to tax production on reservations, and to drop the previous ten-year limit for leases, extending them to last as long as oil is produced. An amendment to the bill directs states to use 37.5 percent of revenues for Native American education and roads. But since most tribes have no central authority to monitor the leasing revenues, and the royalties that tribes receive are lower than the state taxes for mining production on the

reservations, the tribes do not really benefit from this arrangement.

• Electronics engineer Vladimir Zworykin (b. Russia, 1889; d. U.S., 1982), working for Westinghouse, develops a camera tube called the iconoscope, the first practical television camera. By 1925, Zworykin files for a patent on a color TV system that is granted in 1928. Although technical development is slowed by World War II, after the war it booms. His iconoscope will not receive a patent until 1938.

SCIENCE AND TECHNOLOGY

• Astronomer Edwin Powell Hubble (1889–1953) observes Andromeda and other nebulae through a 100-inch reflecting telescope at the Mount Wilson Observatory in Pasadena, California. From the brightness of certain stars, he discovers that what were previously believed to be nebulae are actually other galaxies. He proposes Hubble's Law in 1929, stating that the farther an object is from the center of the universe, the greater its receding velocity. This becomes the basis of Big Bang theory, which will put the age of the Earth at approximately 13 billion years.

⬛ 1929

CULTURE AND SOCIETY

• Aimee Semple McPherson (b. Ontario, Canada, 1890–1944), one of the most celebrated Christian evangelists, becomes the first woman to own a radio station. When she builds the 500-watt station KFSG in Los Angeles, because she believes in preaching to sinners where they are—be it in a bar, the streets, or their homes—she sets a precedent for using public media as a pulpit that is followed by many other evangelists.

WORLD EVENTS

• The first Surrealist Manifesto is published in Paris by poet Andre Breton, the movement's primary theorist. Breton defines Surrealism as "Psychic automatism in its true state . . . dictated by thought, in the absence of any control exercised by reason, exempt from any aesthetic or moral concern." Surrealism's ideas, developed out of Dada, will dominate the visual and literary arts, especially in Europe, but also in Latin America and the U.S., for the next quarter-century, and lead directly to Abstract Expressionism. Artists associated with Surrealism include Joseph Cornell (U.S.), Salvador Dalí (Spain), Max Ernst (Germany-U.S.), Frida Kahlo (Mexico), René Magritte (Belgium), Matta (Chile), Meret Oppenheim (Switzerland), Pablo Picasso (Spain), and Yves Tanguy (France).

• V. I. Lenin dies, and the general secretary of the Communist Party, Joseph Stalin, gains leadership over the Soviet Union after an intraparty power struggle, especially with Leon Trotsky, who is ousted as commissar of war in 1925 and expelled from the USSR in 1929. Stalin will maintain power until his death in 1953.

1925

ARTS AND LITERATURE

• *The New Negro,* an anthology of poetry, essays, fiction, and art, edited by Howard University philosophy professor Alain Locke (1885–1954), is published. Locke's title essay serves "to register the transformations of the inner and outer life of the Negro in America that (had) so significantly taken place in the last few years." The anthology sets forth strategies and styles that will become identified with the Harlem Renaissance and the "New Negro Movement" (a term used by Booker T. Washington earlier in the century, as a metaphor for self-discovery, to mean an enlightened, politicized African American). It suggests looking to African arts and culture as a "profound and galvanizing influence" to promote racial pride and respect for traditions, and to provide another aesthetic reference besides Greece and Rome.

• Josephine Baker (1906–1975), who had come to Paris in the chorus line of Eubie Blake (1883–1983) and Noble Sissle's (1889–1975) all-black revue *Shuffle Along,* leaves the show and becomes the personification of the latest craze, *le jazz hot,* in Paris.

• The Grand Ole Opry makes its first radio broadcast as a "barn dance" on radio station WSM in Nashville.

GOVERNMENT AND POLITICS

• Dayton, Tennessee, high school science teacher John T. Scopes is arrested and convicted of teaching Charles Darwin's theory of evolution in violation of a new state law banning the teaching of theories that deny the divine creation of man as given in the Bible, called "creationism." Attorney Clarence Darrow defends Scopes with support from the American Civil Liberties Union, which sees this as a case for defending the rights of free speech. Christian fundamentalist William Jennings Bryan, former presidential candidate and secretary of state under Woodrow Wilson, acts as the state's prosecuting attorney in a ten-day trial known as the "Monkey Trial" and hyped by the press as "the trial of the century." Seesawing between serious theological debate and theatrics, this is the first trial to be broadcast to the public over the radio

Inventor Charles Jenkins inspecting the first new television receiver made for home use, 1928, by Underwood & Underwood. (*Library of Congress, Prints and Photographs Division*)

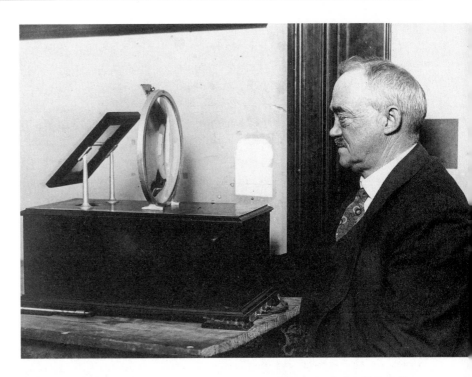

with minute-by-minute coverage. Scopes and Darrow lose, and the Tennessee state law remains in place until 1967. Although the teaching of evolution does become accepted as standard curriculum in most areas of the country, the debate between fundamentalist religious values and progressive scientific rationalism continues throughout the century.

▣ 1996, 1999

• Nellie Ross (1876?–1977), a Democrat, becomes the first woman to hold the office of governor of a state when she is inaugurated in Wyoming. She actually shares the honor by being elected on the same day that Democrat Miriam "Ma" Ferguson (1875–1961) is elected governor of Texas, but the Texas inauguration ceremony is held fifteen days after Wyoming's. Ross is completing the last two years of her husband's term as governor, after his death in 1924. She also becomes the first

woman to serve as director of the U.S. Mint, under President Franklin Roosevelt, and is the only appointee to serve throughout his entire tenure in office. Ma Ferguson runs to clear her family's name from financial corruption charges brought against her husband that resulted in his impeachment as governor. Although similar charges follow her through her two-year term, and she is not immediately reelected, she will return to the governor's office in 1932.

BUSINESS AND INDUSTRY

• The Brotherhood of Sleeping Car Porters, an all-black union, is founded by A. Philip Randolph (1889–1979), who will remain its president until 1968. The union is originally formed as a bargaining agent with the Pullman Company, which operates most of the sleeping-car facilities for the railroads.

> I am a dancer. I believe that we learn by practice. Whether it means to learn to dance by practicing dancing or to learn to live by practicing living, the principles are the same. In each it is the performance of a dedicated precise set of acts, physical or intellectual, from which comes shape of achievement, a sense of one's being, a satisfaction of spirit. One becomes in some area an athlete of God.
>
> (FROM MARTHA GRAHAM, *Blood Memory* [N.Y.: DOUBLEDAY, 1991].)

SCIENCE AND TECHNOLOGY

• A moving object is televised for the first time, to the laboratory of Charles Francis Jenkins (1867–1934) in Washington, D.C., from local radio station NOF. The telecast shows a scale-model windmill with its blades turning, and is viewed by the U.S. secretary of the navy, the director of the Bureau of Standards, and the acting secretary of commerce.

CULTURE AND SOCIETY

• The Klu Klux Klan boasts it has reached a peak membership of 4 million since its rejuvenation after World War I.

• A speculative real estate boom hits Florida, with tens of thousands flocking to buy land, even sight unseen. Although a 1926 hurricane will put a damper on the 1925 peak, Florida's culture begins to shift from this time forward, as a flood of construction begins on art-deco hotels to accommodate a growing tourist trade and retirement communities for northeasterners fleeing cold winters.

WORLD EVENTS

• Adolf Hitler's *Mein Kampf* (*My Struggle*) is published, in which Hitler lays out his plan to create a "greater Germany," including target areas for conquest, especially where ethnic Germans are currently living under the control of other nations.

• *Wozzeck,* a twelve-tone opera composed by Arnold Schoenberg's student Alban Berg, has its premiere in Berlin.

• Art deco, a machine-inspired design style used in architecture and the decorative arts, is formally introduced at L'Exposition Internationale des Arts Decoratifs et Industriels Modernes in Paris. Mixing the flourishes of art nouveau with the geometrics of Cubism, it dominates the look of the 1930s, appearing in the U.S. most famously in New York's Chrysler Building (1930) and Empire State Building (1931), and in various smaller hotels of Miami Beach and Hollywood, but its streamlined elegance is applied to kitchen appliances, furnishings, fashion, crafts, and graphics as well.

1926

ARTS AND LITERATURE

• Martha Graham makes her solo dance concert debut in New York City; three years later she founds her own modern dance company, with whom she will continue performing until 1969, at the age of seventy-six, and for whom she will choreograph 191 dance theater works, until her death in 1991. Graham collaborates with some of the century's best-known artists in related fields of music, set, and lighting design in creation of original works such as *Primitive Mysteries* (1931), *American*

Document (1938), *Appalachian Spring* (1944), *Night Journey* (1947), *Diversion of Angels* (1948), and *Acrobats of God* (1960). Graham will be known as one of the major artists of her time whose approach to her work is completely color-blind. Her company is the first and most fully integrated group of dancers on the scene, and her casting has no racial barriers.

• New Orleans–born Jelly Roll Morton (1890–1941), considered by some to be the first true jazz composer, begins a series of recordings with his New Orleans–oriented band, the Red Hot Peppers, in Chicago.

• Composer George Antheil, an expatriate American living in France, uses loud "found" sounds in his *Ballet Mécanique,* including doorbells, xylophones, and an airplane engine which is placed onstage.

GOVERNMENT AND POLITICS

• Treasury Secretary Andrew W. Mellon invokes the first use of trickle-down theory to get the economy moving and reduce the national deficit that has risen with World War I–related expenses. He lobbies Congress to pass the 1926 Revenue Act, which gives corporate tax cuts that benefit the largest corporations and income tax cuts that benefit the wealthiest Americans. As a result, the deficit is reduced and the tax cuts help produce a flood of investments in the stock market, beginning the great bull market that will end with the 1929 crash.

• Congress passes the Air Commerce Act, placing the Department of Commerce in charge of licensing aircraft and pilots. Except for subsidizing air mail, this is the first time the federal government has inserted itself into civilian aviation affairs, and is the beginning of a trend toward more federal regulation of various industries.

🖂 1926

BUSINESS AND INDUSTRY

• RCA's David Sarnoff (1891–1971) organizes the first nationwide radio network, the National Broadcasting Company (NBC). Through General Electric and Westinghouse, RCA's parent corporations, he first purchases radio station WEAF in New York, then makes it the anchor station for twenty-five stations that NBC quickly acquires across the country.

🖂 1927

SCIENCE AND TECHNOLOGY

• Warner Brothers, a Hollywood film studio, demonstrates *Don Juan,* the first motion picture using sound. The film synchronizes a music track played by the New York Philharmonic with the silent dialogue, using a sound-on-disk system called Vitaphone. Warner purchases exclusive rights to the new system, which has been developed in collaboration between AT&T, the Western Electric Company, and Bell Laboratories. In the *New York Times,* Albert Warner tells reporters that "At a phenomenally small cost, the unquestionably planned and perfected radio music program will begin a new era for moving picture patrons throughout the country."

🖂 1927

• Robert H. Goddard (1882–1945) designs and successfully launches the first liquid-fueled rocket. All previous rockets have used solid fuels that burn only in the presence of air. Motivated by his dream "to make some device which had even the *possibility* of ascending to Mars," Goddard succeeds, after twelve years of experiments on his Auburn, Massachusetts, farm, in solving the problems of how humans can travel outside Earth's atmosphere where there is no oxygen. Goddard's ten-pound rocket flies for 2.5 seconds, rising forty-one feet and traveling 184 feet. He will not live to see the realization of his dream when, starting in the late 1950s, the U.S. builds on his inventions and uses liquid fuel to launch its rockets and space shuttles for space exploration.

CULTURE AND SOCIETY

• The Spanish language newspaper *La Opinion* begins publication in Los Angeles; a portion of its shares is acquired by the *Los Angeles Times* in the late 1980s.

WORLD EVENTS

• Cambridge University economist John Maynard Keynes (1883–1946) publishes *The End of Laissez-Faire,* in which he advocates for government intervention in free-market economies. His theories, called "Keynesian economics," as presented in this book and his *General Theory of Employment, Interest, and Money* (1936), will influence U.S. government recovery policies during the Great Depression and will be adopted by many governments throughout the world.

• Russian theater director Constantin Stanislavsky (1865–1938), in his book *An Actor Prepares,* explains his acting theories and techniques as evolved at the Moscow Art Theater starting with his 1898 production of Anton Chekhov's (1860–1904) *The Seagull.* American actors and directors start picking up the "Stanislavsky Method" between 1922 and 1924, when the Moscow Art Theater tours the U.S. and Europe, and this style of stripped-down psychological realism continues to reign today in U.S. theater and film.

1927

ARTS AND LITERATURE

• Duke Ellington expands his band from five to ten musicians, and renames it the Duke Ellington Orchestra as he begins an extended engagement at the Cotton Club in Harlem.

• A new dance rage, the Lindy Hop, is born when Shorty George Snowden "breaks away" from his partner while doing the Charleston, to do some footwork on his own; this "breakaway" later evolves into the swing-out, which he says he names after Charles Lindbergh's "hop" over the Atlantic; swing dance and music will continue to reign until 1944, fueled by the big band sounds of Duke Ellington, Cab Calloway, Benny Goodman (1909–1986), Glenn Miller (1904–1944), and Count Basie (1904–1984).

• Isadora Duncan's autobiography, *My Life,* begun in 1925, is published posthumously, after she is killed instantly when her scarf becomes entangled in the rear wheel of her open touring car. In it she articulates the major influences on her development as an artist, and her beliefs about love, politics, education, and life.

• Dancer/choreographers Doris Humphrey (1895–1958) and Charles Weidman (1901–1975), past members of the Denishawn Dance Company, co-found the Humphrey-Weidman company, which continues through 1940, and their school, which remains open until 1945. They contribute to the development of contemporary modern dance, particularly through their basic principle of "fall and recovery," a theory of action encompassing both fundamental laws of movement and dramatic form that Humphrey articulates in her 1959 choreography primer, *The Art of Making Dances*.

• *The Jazz Singer* gains credit as the first "talkie" when a couple of Al Jolson's ad-libs are recorded by accident on the "silent" motion picture that uses a Vitaphone score for the music track.

▣ 1926

• Three members of the group of Native American artists known as the "Kiowa Five" are "discovered" by Susie Peters, a field matron for the Kiowa agency, while they are students of Sister Olivia Taylor (Choctaw) at a mission school in Anadarko, Oklahoma. Peters encourages them to study further with Oscar B. Jacobson, on the art faculty at the University of Oklahoma in Norman. Their style develops from the traditional Plains style that evolved into ledger-book drawings during the late nineteenth century, and from their experiences as dancers and singers. The group includes Stephen Mopope (1898–1974), Monroe Tsatoke/Tsa To Kee (1904–1937), Jack Hokeah (1902–1973), James Auchiah (1906–1975), Spencer Asah (1905–1954), and one woman, Lois Smokey/ Bougetah (1907–1981), whose work has not been as widely recognized.

• American architect and engineer Buckminster Fuller (1895–1983) champions creating designs that are characteristically modern, efficient, and economical, by converting scientific principles into industrial applications useful for humans. He designs one of the first prefabricated structures, his six-sided "Dymaxion" house, a prototype to illustrate his "energetic synergetic geometry" principles that govern the relation of parts to a whole, which he originally calls "the 4-D house" for the fourth dimension. ▣ 1947

• Jerome Kern (1885–1945), one of the great melodists in the history of popular music, opens *Showboat*, a musical depicting the plight of poor Southern blacks and white entertainers, on Broadway. With libretto and lyrics by Oscar Hammerstein II (1895–1960), its musical and psychological depth sets a standard of artistry far beyond that of the musical comedies and operettas of its day.

• Jimmy Rodgers (1924–1997), known as the "Singing Brakeman" and universally considered the father of country music, records "Blue Yodel #1" ("T for Texas"), and it sells millions of copies. His ability to "tell a story" in his lyrics, added to his blues-oriented "high lonesome" vocal style, will make him the model for country music artists for all time. Though white, his affinity for African American music is great indeed. He goes on to record many "straight" twelve-bar blues songs, and his "Blue Yodel #9" ("Standin' in the Corner") is backed by two famous jazz men, Louis Armstrong and Earl Hines.

• Photographer and painter Edward Steichen forces a public and legal discussion of the question "What is art?" when he appeals a $240 U.S. Customs import charge on his purchase of a fifty-three-inch polished bronze sculpture by Constantin Brancusi (b. Rumania, 1876–1957) called *Bird in Flight*. Although art is exempt from duty fees at this time, the customs agents rule that this work should be subject to the same tax as that levied on any manufactured item because they do not consider it art. Steichen brings expert opinions to counter that argument in court, even though he has already paid the duty.

The American Weekly, March 13, 1927, reports on the court proceedings:

Question to Steichen: "What makes you call it a bird? Does it look like a bird?"

Answer: "It does not look like a bird, but I feel it is a bird. The artist calls it a bird."

Question: "Has this picture any underlying aesthetic principle? Is it a work of art?"

Answer: "It has form and appearance. It is an object created in three dimensions by an artist. It is harmonious, and gives me a sense of pleasure and beauty. That is why I purchased it. That bird gives me the sensation of rushing."

Question to Forbes Watson, editor, *The Arts* magazine: "How does it suggest a bird?"

Answer: "There is some suggestion of form, but that is not important. It is the feeling of flight."

Question to sculptor Jacob Epstein: "Critics say it is not true to life."

Answer: "An artist uses nature . . . only as a point of departure . . . an artist is able to conceive— to make a beautiful work. . . . It pleases my sense of beauty."

Judge Wade reserves his decision until he can make up his mind whether a piece of metal, which nobody could guess the meaning of until the sculptor told them, is "art."

GOVERNMENT AND POLITICS

• Congress creates the Federal Radio Commission to regulate the new communications industry—another step toward federal regulation of what is called the private sector. 🖻 1926

BUSINESS AND INDUSTRY

• Perfection of the mechanical cotton picker in Texas reduces the need for field workers, and spurs black migration to the urban north.

SCIENCE AND TECHNOLOGY

• The first transatlantic telephone call, between the publisher of the *New York Times* and the editor of the London *Times*, establishes a new service. The call lasts three minutes and costs seventy-five dollars. The world keeps getting smaller.

• Airmail pilot Charles Lindbergh (1902–1974) succeeds in his attempt at the first solo nonstop flight to make it across the Atlantic, flying his plane, the *Spirit of St. Louis,* 3,614 miles in thirty-three and a half hours without sleeping, starting in Long Island, New York, and landing at Le Bourget Airport in Paris, where a crowd of 100,000 cheers him.

• Inventor and engineer Philo Farnsworth (1906–1971) transmits the first all-electronic television image from his San Francisco lab, by broadcasting a dollar sign to potential investors. He receives enough financial backing to file for a patent on his "television system" invention, a picture tube that electronically scans and transmits images, making commercial development of television possible. RCA keeps him from receiving earnings from the multimillion-dollar industry his invention makes feasible.

• An American Telephone & Telegraph (AT&T) team produces the first all-electronic television picture, which they demonstrate for the first time with a broadcast from Washington, D.C., by Secretary of Commerce Herbert Hoover, which is sent over 200 miles by wire, at the rate of eighteen miles a second, to an audience watching a two-by-three-inch screen in New York City. Other parts of the show include a description of the new technology by AT&T vice president J. J. Carty and others, and two comedy bits by a vaudevillian, Whippany A. Dolan, who first appears as a stage Irishman, doing a monologue in brogue, and then appears in blackface, telling jokes in "Negro dialect."

• J. A. O'Neill is issued a U.S. patent for his invention of a recording tape of powdered magnetic material, a prototype of an emerging technology that by the mid-1930s produces phonograph recordings of acceptable quality.
🎞 1949

CULTURE AND SOCIETY

• The Rose of Fraternity, a small mosque in Cedar Rapids, Iowa, that becomes known as the "Mother Mosque" because it is the first building in the U.S. constructed as a mosque, is established by leaders of the city's Islamic community.

WORLD EVENTS

• Nuclear physicist Werner Karl Heisenberg (b. Germany, 1901–1976), publishes a paper, "About the Quantum-Theoretical Reinterpretation of Kinetic and Mechanical Relationships," that posits what will come to be known as the Heisenberg Uncertainty Principle. It states that it is impossible to measure simultaneously the two characteristics, position and momentum, of a particle such as an electron, with equivalent degrees of accuracy. In the case of an electron, measuring its position requires striking it with a photon—a particle of light—thereby changing its velocity and hence its momentum. Thus one cannot observe a system without also disturbing it. At the quantum level such disturbances dramatically alter the state of systems.

• Canada and the U.S. establish diplomatic relations independently from Great Britain, and present their first diplomatic ministers in Ottawa and Washington. Later in the year, an International Peace Bridge linking Canada and the U.S. at Buffalo, New York, is opened by Vice President Charles Dawes and the Prince of Wales.
🎞 1931

1928

ARTS AND LITERATURE

• The first complete talking film is made and the first color motion pictures are shown in Rochester, New York, by photographic pioneer George Eastman (1854–1932).

• The first "talkie" animated cartoon film, *Steamboat Willie,* debuts as a sneak preview at the Colony Theater in New York, featuring Mickey Mouse as a riverboat pilot hero, and Minnie Mouse as his co-star. Mickey Mouse, who has already appeared in two silent films, is a collaborative creation, with story by Walt Disney (1901–1966) and drawings by Ub Iwerks (1901–1971). *Steamboat Willie*'s synchronized sound track, including sound effects and an orchestra playing "Turkey in the Straw," emphasizes sounds by keying them to sight gags. (It uses Pat Powers's Cinephone system, which was illegally copied from RCA's

ISLAM IN THE UNITED STATES, PART I

Dr. H. S. Hamod

At the present time, there are over 8 million Muslims in the U.S., and thousands of mosques. The growth of Islam has accelerated in recent years not only through births within Muslim families, but because of immigration and expanding conversion. Prior to the year 2000, the majority of Muslims in the U.S. were either Sunni or Shiite, with a smaller group who followed the teachings of the Honorable Elijah Muhammad as represented by Minister Louis Farrakhan. Early in 2000, at a momentous meeting in Chicago, Minister Farrakhan declared that he embraced orthodox Islam and encouraged those who followed him to embrace it as well.

Islam first came to the U.S. with the Muslims of West Africa who were brought here as slaves. As the elders were separated from their children or died off, Islam slipped away except in names that continued on in families; however, even these names became westernized (for example, Ali became Ollie, and Aliyah became Olivia). Ironically, many of the people who inherit names such as Aliyah have no idea where they came from.

The first nonslave Muslims who came to the U.S. were those who migrated from Egypt, Africa, Syria, Turkey, and what is now Lebanon, but there was no significant growth until the late 1800s. The first known mosques were set up in Ross, North Dakota; Quincy, Massachusetts; Cedar Rapids, Iowa; Detroit, Michigan; and Michigan City, Indiana. Often they were converted houses, storefronts, or churches; they served their purpose as prayer and meeting places. In 1927 the families Aossey, Igram, and Sheronick, all leaders in the Islamic group called the Rose of Fraternity, built a small mosque in Cedar Rapids, Iowa, which became known as the "Mother Mosque." There were also groups such as Asser Al Jadeed (the New Generation), in Michigan City, Indiana, and various groups in Detroit, Michigan, who met on a regular basis for prayers in rented halls. The first major central mosque in the U.S. was built in the mid-1950s in Washington, D.C. This mosque was built primarily with funding from Egypt, Turkey, and Iran. Egypt sent the architects and calligraphers, Turkey sent the tile masters, and Iran furnished the finest of Islamic rugs. Mosques were also built at locations throughout the Midwest. These buildings provided a symbol to Muslims and non-Muslims of the permanence of Islam in U.S. society. The mosques also gave Muslim leaders, such as Hassan Abraham, Abdullah Igram, and Casim Alawan, a home base from which to join interfaith conferences held in such places as Notre Dame, the University of Chicago, and the University of Iowa. Because of Islamic burial practices, many felt a need for a national Muslim cemetery; thus, in 1948, William Aossey donated substantial acreage to build such a cemetery in Cedar Rapids, Iowa.

▣ 1951

sound recording equipment.) Disney continues to employ Mickey Mouse as his laboratory in the use of color, music, special effects, and character animation. In 1929, Mickey Mouse speaks his first words ("Hot dog!") in *The Karnival Kid*. Disney accepts his first cross-promotion deal by selling a stationery company the rights to print Mickey Mouse's image on school writing tablets. Within ten years Mickey Mouse will become one of the most recognized and popular images in the world. Disney says Mickey Mouse "provided the means for expanding the organization to its present dimension and for extending the medium of cartoon animation towards new entertainment levels."

• In February, painter Archibald Motley Jr. (1891–1981) becomes the first African American artist to be given a one-man show in a New York art gallery, when the New Gallery opens a show of portraits, images of cabaret life, and voodoo rituals. The show receives a major review in the *New York Times*.

• Painter Georgia O'Keeffe (1887–1986) travels from New York City to Taos, New Mexico, because she has "used up" the subjects that brought her fame in the modernist painting establishment sponsored in the Gallery 291 of her husband, Alfred Stieglitz. She will return for annual visits until 1949, when she begins living permanently in Abiquiu, New Mexico, until her death at ninety-eight, painting abstractions of the natural and spiritual world of her adopted landscape—mountains, flowers, rocks, bleached bones, and black crosses.

GOVERNMENT AND POLITICS

• Republican presidential candidate Herbert Hoover, who says he is for continuing Prohibition and widening prosperity, benefits by taking full advantage of the new technologies of radio and film to broadcast his speeches. He defeats anti-Prohibition Democrat and Catholic Alfred E. Smith by one of the biggest popular vote margins ever recorded. The *New York Times* delivers the news of the final count instantly, flashing it to the crowd gathered in Times Square outside their building by way of a newly installed electric sign, a "zipper" of lightbulbs that wraps around the building.

• Congress establishes the Meriam Commission, an independent Institute for Government Research under the direction of Lewis Meriam, to make a comprehensive study of Native American issues. Known as the Meriam Report, but officially called *The Problem of Indian Administration,* the study recommends reforms within the BIA, criticizing how they have administered Indian affairs, suggesting the need for improvements in Indian schools, health services, and economic development, and supporting an end to seizures of Native American lands. This will become the blueprint for changes, albeit very slow ones, that will be directed by President Hoover's Indian Bureau officials within the Interior Department, and will also affect President Roosevelt's Indian "New Deal" policies.

• California adds the Public Trust Doctrine as an amendment to its state constitution, to promote reasonable and beneficial uses of water and to prohibit wasteful and unreasonable uses. It is a protective measure aimed at big farmers, land speculators, miners, and other entrepreneurs who circumvent existing water "rights" regulations, to make them technically abide by the letter of the law.

• The U.S. and fourteen other nations,

THE PUBLIC TRUST DOCTRINE

T. N. Narasimhan

When California became a state in 1859, a virgin land with abundant resources became available to an immigrant community seeking prosperity on the heels of an industrial revolution. With "manifest destiny" providing moral justification, land and resources were looked upon by the immigrants as means for material prosperity. The new state government initially encouraged unfettered private enterprise, leading to a laissez-faire economic policy. The upshot was that big farmers, land speculators, miners, and other entrepreneurs claimed "rights" for water without any feeling for responsibility. By 1878 the lack of social responsibility on the part of water manipulators became so alarming that the Constitutional Convention included Article Fourteen of its declaration, asserting that "the use of all water now appropriated, or that may hereafter be appropriated, for sale, rental, or distribution, is hereby declared to be a public use, and subject to the regulation and control of the State in the manner to be prescribed by the law."

Still, the water manipulators circumvented the law by lengthy litigations, and the courts did not care for the spirit of the law. Fifty years later, things came to a head in a major litigation in the Central Valley, between a big Central Valley landowner and an electricity generating company. The landowner insisted on her right to use of water, although in a very wasteful way. This prevented the construction of hydroelectric power plants that would have benefited a larger public. The public was outraged and enacted the amendment, forcing the courts to abide by the sprit of the law.

The real strength of the 1928 amendment surfaced in 1983 when UC Davis, Berkeley, and Stanford students took on the cause of saving Mono Lake by suing the City of Los Angeles, which was diverting water from the lake, causing it to dry up fast and imperiling its fragile ecosystem. The students and the Audubon Society invoked Public Trust Doctrine (that is, the 1928 amendment) and argued that "public benefit" included the well-being of the Mono Lake ecosystem. Los Angeles argued that Mono Lake water provided sustenance for 80,000 families. The California supreme court ruled that saving Mono Lake was a greater public benefit than providing water for 80,000 families. This ruling, empowered by the Public Trust Doctrine, is profound and balances the dollar-based economics by recognizing the value of other components of California society.

including France, Great Britain, Japan, and Italy, sign a multinational pact to outlaw war. Called the Kellogg-Briand Pact, for U.S. Secretary of State Frank B. Kellogg and French foreign minister Aristide Briand, the idea is initiated after Briand publicly proposes a bilateral pact between the U.S. and France. Kellogg is angered that Briand has not followed standard diplomatic protocol. He does not want the U.S. to enter into an alliance with France, as the country is awash in isolationist sentiment. But because the idea is taken up by peace proponents in Congress and the public, who are concerned that the U.S. has subverted the League of Nations by refusing to join, Kellogg responds with an idea for a multinational pact to outlaw war, all the while knowing it will be impossible to enforce. By the end of 1929, sixty-four nations have signed and Kellogg is awarded a Nobel Prize. However, the pact is violated by invasions of Manchuria (by Japan in 1931) and Ethiopia (by Italy in 1936), and with World War II raging by 1939, its aim has been completely destroyed.

BUSINESS AND INDUSTRY

• The last Model T rolls off the Ford Motor Company assembly line—one of 15 million built over nineteen years. In an effort to keep up with current innovations in the auto industry, Ford closes its plant for five months of refurbishment. Ford's new Model A will not, however, enjoy the unparalleled success of the Model T, perhaps due to increasing competition.

SCIENCE AND TECHNOLOGY

• Congress passes the Boulder Dam Project Act, beginning federal government involvement in the production of hydroelectric power. Starting in 1930, the Colorado River in Black Canyon, at the Arizona-Nevada border, will begin being dammed. When the project is completed six years later, it makes it possible to build and sustain large cities in the middle of the desert, such as Las Vegas. In 1947 the project will be renamed Hoover Dam, in honor of the former president.

• Chemist Waldo Semon (1898–1999), while working for B. F. Goodrich Company in its Akron, Ohio, research lab, invents vinyl by mixing polyvinyl chloride powder in a solvent and heating the mixture. It is waterproof and fire-resistant, does not conduct electricity, and

can be easily molded. But it fails to find an application until Semon's wife makes curtains out of it, inspiring its first uses as fabric for umbrellas, raincoats, and shower curtains. The company obtains a patent in 1933. Today vinyl generates a $20-billion-a-year plastics industry, surpassed only by polyethylene.

CULTURE AND SOCIETY

• Anthropologist Margaret Mead (1901–1978) publishes *Coming of Age in Samoa,* the first cultural study about women by a woman, based upon her fieldwork done while living in Samoa, an island in the western Pacific. Her method, called "participant observation," gives the book an intimacy that attracts attention and controversy. She describes finding different models for child-rearing and teaching communal responsibility for the young than are generally found in the Western cultures, observing that it is not necessary to use harsh discipline and proprietary attitudes to raise responsible and humane adults. A pioneer in the use of photography and film in field research, she continues to write about South Pacific island cultures. Her work inspires questions on many subjects, including the inevitability of gender roles and behaviors for men and women, which she observes can be very different from culture to culture. In 1949 she writes a precursor to feminist theory, *Male and Female: A Study of the Sexes in a Changing World.*

WORLD EVENTS

• Dr. Alexander Fleming (1881–1955, Scotland), a medical bacteriologist at St. Mary's Hospital Medical School in London, discovers the first antibiotic, penicillin, by accident. In 1922, Fleming discovers lysozyme, an antibacterial compound present in saliva, nasal excretions, and tears. Still studying lysozyme in 1928, he notices a blue mold contaminating and dissolving a colony of staphylococcus bacteria he is cultivating. Curious, he isolates the deadly compound, which kills only certain types of bacteria and is harmless to disease-fighting white blood cells. He names the compound "penicillin," publishes his findings, and returns to other work. Penicillin receives no further attention until 1940, when Oxford University researchers Ernst Chain and Howard Florey, studying lysozyme at the time, begin working with penicillin in an effort to prevent infection in war wounds. They are successful at producing the drug in large quantities, and it saves several thousand lives in World War II. More-powerful antibiotics follow soon, and Fleming shares the Nobel Prize for medicine with Chain and Florey in 1945.

• In his first collaboration with composer Igor Stravinsky, with a score commissioned by the U.S. Library of Congress, Russian émigré George Balanchine (1904–1983) finds a way to make ballet modern by mixing neoclassical and Africanist aesthetics in his choreography for *Apollo* (whose original title is *Apollon-Musagete*). The Paris premiere is performed by Diaghilev's Ballets Russes.

1929

ARTS AND LITERATURE

• The Museum of Modern Art (MOMA) is founded by three wealthy art collectors, Mrs. John D. Rockefeller, Mrs. Cornelius Sullivan, and Lillie P. Bliss. It opens in New York City, under the directorship of art historian Alfred H. Barr Jr. (1902–1981), whose mission is to free Americans of their provincialism by introducing them to the arts of their time. He encourages viewers to look for art in everyday life, to see factories as great architecture, and advertisements as studies in typographical design. The "story" of modernism that Barr promotes and purchases for the MOMA collection is rooted in the work of nineteenth-century western European Post-Impressionists. He will not bestow major significance on North American artists until the 1950s, starting with artists associated with Abstract Expressionism and then Pop Art styles. Barr's legacy of scholarship will continue to profoundly affect art assessment and taste in the U.S. and internationally, setting the standard for what constitutes modern masters and masterworks.

• Poet and critic Yvor Winters produces *Gyroscope*, the earliest known example of a mimeographed literary magazine, according to *A Little History of the Mimeograph Revolution* by Steven Clay and Rodney Phillips. Featuring work by Winter's Stanford University students, it presages a post–World War II nationwide explosion of "underground" poetry books and magazines, produced mainly by poets. Most will use any inexpensive means of production available, including mimeograph and photocopying, to get their work out to their own communities, although some presses carefully craft art books, using handmade paper, lithographs, and distinctive letterpress designs. By becoming their own publishers and circumventing the large, established presses, these writers will create a new, small press publishing tradition, and open up new audiences in the process.

• Laurens Hammond (b. 1895) begins building musical instruments, such as the Hammond

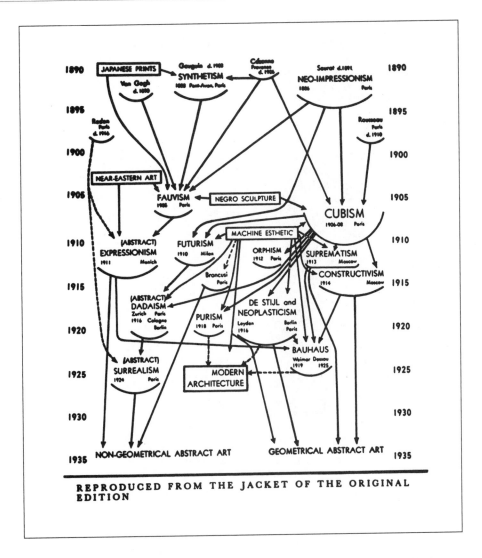

REPRODUCED FROM THE JACKET OF THE ORIGINAL
EDITION

This chart was prepared by Alfred H. Barr Jr., the first director of New York City's
Museum of Modern Art (MOMA), for the jacket of the catalog of their exhibition
"Cubism and Abstract Art," published by MOMA in 1936 and in a reprint edition for
MOMA by Arno Press in 1966. Barr's choices emphasize the role of European artists
and designers. He omits Native American and Latin American influences, and gives
barely a nod to "Negro sculpture," "Near-Eastern," and "Japanese print" influences.
This road map defines the basic layout of the museum's collection of twentieth-
century painting and sculpture, and, because of the institution's great influence, is followed by many other museums. (The Museum of Modern Art, New York)

View of Wall Street, with panicked crowds, lightning, people jumping out of buildings at the time of the 1929 stock market crash. Lithograph by James Rosenberg, 1929. *(Library of Congress, Prints and Photographs Division)*

Organ, the first commercially successful electronic instrument. Using ninety-one rotary electromagnetic disk generators driven by a synchronous motor with associated gears and tone wheels, it uses additive synthesis to create anything from simple rhythm patterns to orchestral sound arrangements. Hammond forms a company to manufacture and distribute his instruments, ensuring a steady following by developing a variety of models for professionals (popular with jazz organist Jimmy Reed and 1960s rock band musicians such as Gregg Allman and Keith Emerson) and a home organ for amateurs. He later invents the Novachord (1938), Solovox, and reverb devices.

GOVERNMENT AND POLITICS

• Herbert Hoover becomes the thirty-first president, with Charles Curtis as his vice president. He has the poor luck of being president when the stock market crashes and the Depression rages. He fails to find an effective way to turn the economy around, believing that if he helps big business, the money will "trickle down." The theory doesn't work.

BUSINESS AND INDUSTRY

• Throughout 1929, the stock market is artificially inflated, with easy credit terms and strike-it-rich stories pushing both small and large investors to speculate by buying on margin. As stock prices reach a three-year peak, it is easy to disregard various signs that the economy is weakening. The total fortunes amassed by the nation's 24,000 richest families amount to three times the total income of the 6 million poorest families, with 40 percent earning under $1,500 per year. On October 24, "Black Thursday," it is impossible to ignore the flashing signals of the dangers ahead, when the market loses $9 billion in value. Thirty billion dollars in capital disappears as the New York stock market collapses on "Black Tuesday," October 29, when the market loses $15 billion in value. Many individual investors lose fortunes in a matter of days. The crash leads directly to the Great Depression, as manufacturers close plants from lack of consumer demand, and an average of 100,000 workers are fired per week. In 1929, two million are unemployed; by 1930 four million; by 1931, eight million; and by 1932, twelve million. It will take over a decade for the economy to recover, and it will require major changes in the functions of the federal government and a changeover to a wartime economy to boot it back into health.

SCIENCE AND TECHNOLOGY

• Astronomer Edwin Powell Hubble (1889–1953) changes our concept of the cosmos when he observes that the universe is expanding, a concept already familiar to two contemporary theorists, Russian Alexander Friedmann and Belgian Georges-Henri Lemaître, who independently concluded that an expanding universe accorded with Einstein's equations. Einstein, too, considered the possibility of an expanding universe, but discarded the idea as ridiculous in favor of what he called the "cosmological constant." He would later come to call this "the greatest blunder of my life." Hubble's key observation, that the farther away an object is, the faster it is receding, becomes the signal evidence in favor of the theory of an expanding universe, and is called "Hubble's Law." It also strongly corroborates the Big Bang theory and provides a means for measuring the age, size, and future of the universe. Early estimates put the age of the universe at 2 billion years, while current thought centers around 13 billion years. A telescope named for Hubble will be launched on the space shuttle *Atlantis* in 1990.

▣ 1924, 1990

• American film producer Louis Blattner invents the "Blattnerphone," the first magnetic recorder using steel type. This prototype for the tape recorder makes it possible to secure any live sound for future reproduction. Now the voices of politicians, as well as actors, singers, and the sounds of musicians—from folk artists to the largest symphony orchestras—will be able to be captured any place and any time, and future generations will be able to experience their sound.

CULTURE AND SOCIETY

• The national origins quota, limiting immigration to a yearly maximum of 150,000, takes effect. With the beginning of the Great Depression, Mexican immigration to the U.S. almost ceases, and the number of immigrants returning to Mexico rises.

• The League of United Latin American Citizens is founded in Texas by Mexican Americans who want to do something about the limited prospects available to them in the U.S.

WORLD EVENTS

• Spanish poet Federico García Lorca (1898–1936) travels to New York and writes a new poetry collection, *Poeta en Nueva York (Poet in New York).*

To relieve the urgent food needs in an isolated mountain community in Kentucky, the Red Cross chapter took up truckloads of cornmeal. Photo by Lewis Wickes Hine. (Library of Congress, Prints and Photographs Division)

1930–1939

IMMEDIATE ANCESTORS

BOB CALLAHAN

WHEN I WAS WORKING ON *The Big Dream*, one of the "Dark Hotel" stories I'd been writing for Salon.com, I somehow slipped back into Upton Sinclair's campaign in 1934, something I didn't know a lot about. It became fascinating to me in many ways.

Sinclair ran for governor of California in 1934, and he almost won. He had won the Democratic primary, and it took an awful lot of powerful people in this state turning their backs on him, and stabbing him in the back, to keep him out of office. He fronted an organization called EPIC (End Poverty in California). And he had the idea that he would put everybody to work in a series of massive co-ops, different co-ops—that was his big idea. Apparently his idea that the state of California could sponsor its own movie-making co-op, for all the workers and writers in Hollywood, turned Hearst and the studio bosses against him, and really sank his campaign.

That's what was unique about the 1930s. Both politically and culturally it was a time of really big ideas. Because the dominating reality in everybody's life—and not just in America, we are sometimes surprised to realize—was the Depression. The Depression had enormous impact, probably more in Germany than here, because it led to Hitler in Germany. Here it led to FDR, which had a dramatically different kind of result. An extraordinary amount of poverty and panic pervaded the United States at the time, and it shook the general public's faith in the American political system, and what rose in the wreckage of that faith were radical ideas. The thirties were a period of more radical ideas than almost any other in American history.

The right wing is what I became more interested in than anything else, because it became so powerful in that decade. The crowning moment may have come in New Jersey at the end of the decade, during a meeting between the Ku Klux Klan and the German-American Bund in which they pledged a common bond against the enemies of what they felt was the white man's destiny. But there were all kinds of right-wing fascist movements in America at that time. Earlier, the Klan and other fascist movements had been largely rural in locale and operation. But now there were urban disturbances. Powerful fascist bunds existed in Oakland, California, for instance. There were brown shirts and green shirts and white shirts and silver shirts. There were little Hitler-imitation groups everywhere. And they were definitely powerful. It was a time when people were looking for new alternatives, and fascism was accepted as a viable alternative to democracy, or to capitalism, and so, of course, were socialism and Marxism. Although more is known about the left during this period, it might be the right that deserves more of our attention.

Culturally, our own immediate ancestors were beginning to assert themselves. An actual cultural front existed in that decade which clearly anticipated groups of writer- and artist-driven organizations, of the sort that the Before Columbus Foundation turned out to be in the 1970s.

The Federal Writers Project, the writers' section of the Works Progress Administration (WPA), started at about that time. The WPA put a lot of people to work; more than 6,000 writers were busy documenting the country's history through oral histories and folklore collections. It was the WPA that funded writers to put together the American Guide Series, those state guides that you still can pick up, and that remain absolutely marvelous. It was a really interesting time to be an intellectual or an artist in America. It was also the first time, I think, that you could talk about a multicultural dimension to American literature and art. It was okay to be ethnic—in fact it was almost required.

Ralph Ellison was very active, as were Conrad Aiken, Nelson Algren, Saul Bellow, Richard Wright, Zora Neale Hurston, Kenneth Rexroth, and Margaret Walker. Other great writing from the period includes *Serenade* (1937) by James Cain; *Jews Without Money* (1930) by Mike Gold; Edward Dahlberg's *Bottom Dogs* (1930); *As I Lay Dying* (1930) and *Sanctuary* (1931) by William Faulkner; Wallace Thurman's novel about the Harlem Renaissance, *Infants of the Spring* (1932); Langston Hughes's *The Ways of White Folks* (1934); Gertrude Stein's *Autobiography of Alice B. Toklas* (1933); and John Dos Passos's *U.S.A.* trilogy, published between 1930 and 1936. In 1935 Sinclair Lewis wrote a play about fascism in America, *It Can't Happen Here*—but it could, of course. Fascism was happening big-time by then.

Zora Neale Hurston's *Their Eyes Were Watching God* came out in 1937; Richard Wright's *Uncle Tom's Children* in 1938; and both John Steinbeck's *Grapes of Wrath* and Raymond Chandler's *The Big Sleep* were published in 1939; Tillie Olsen wrote *Yonnondio: From the Thirties* between 1932–1937, though it wasn't published until 1974; and maybe the most interesting, and lingering, writer of the whole period, Nathanael West, published *Miss Lonelyhearts* (1933), *A Cool Million* (1936), and *The Day of the Locust* (1939).

It was also a time when major Irish-American artists began to emerge. The big names were Eugene O'Neill and James T. Farrell, of course. But there was also the F. Scott Fitzgerald of *The Crack Up* (1936). Also a very fine and underrated writer, Ruth McKenney—who wrote *Industrial Valley* (1939), one of the first documentary novels about the strikes in Akron—and who was also married to Nathanael West. Jim Tully. Jack Conroy. Comic realists, too, like Philip Barry and Preston Sturges. It was a good time for working-class Irish writers.

Against the emergence of fascism, of course, was a countermovement of antifascism. Farrell wrote a novella called *Tommy Gallagher's Crusade*, a gem of a story about a brainless Irish kid who goes out and beats up Jewish leftists in the name of someone like Father Coughlan. It's a brilliant work of antifascism. Reading it together with Thomas Mann's novella *Mario the Magician* will put you in touch with two important writers who knew well the evil of a fascist mentality in their own times.

Irish Americans also left a stamp in the movies. There was a whole Irish Mafia, as they called it, clustered around director John Ford: Pat O'Brien, Spencer Tracy, James Cagney, and John Wayne all grew up in that world. (Wayne's real name was Marion Michael Morrison, by the way.)

Comic books started in the 1930s. Before comic books, it was all newspaper comic strips. One of our great literary heroes, Dashiell Hammett, wrote a comic strip in the 1930s called *X-9*. It was drawn by Alex Raymond, the artist who would later draw the great *Flash Gordon* strip. *Batman* and *Superman* would also come along at the end of this decade.

My America begins in the thirties. I'm a child of the New Deal, as are, I believe, all multicultural people. Right in the middle of this period you can literally see America renewing itself, going right back down to its roots to renew itself musically and artistically, and that's what makes it such an exciting decade. The line from the artists of the thirties to us is as clear as it could ever be.

1930

ARTS AND LITERATURE

• Martha Graham creates a solo, *Lamentation*, to music by Zolton Kodaly, in which she remains seated on a cube, wearing a cos-

---

In January 1930 the total U.S. population, not including Hawaii and Alaska, is 122,775,000 (an increase of 16.1 percent over the preceding U.S. Census). In this decade, more people will emigrate from the U.S. than will immigrate, owing to severe entrance restrictions. In 1930, women over ten years of age constitute 22 percent of the workforce. In 1935, average per capita personal income is $474, according to the U.S. Bureau of Economic Analysis. Unemployment figures show a huge increase over the previous decade, reflecting the devastating effects of the Great Depression: in 1930 the rate is 8.7 percent; by 1932 it reaches a high of 23.6 percent; and by 1938 it is 19 percent (U.S. Department of Labor statistics).

Martha Graham in *Lamentation.* Photo by Barbara
Morgan, 1935. *(Barbara Morgan/Timepix*
Contributors: Estate of Barbara Morgan)

Keystone, South Dakota. This face of George
Washington, an early precursor of what will
be called site-specific art, is created by twenty
jackhammers simultaneously blasting into the
mountain's rocky cliffs. Jefferson is added in
1936, Lincoln in 1937, and Theodore Roosevelt
in 1939. The sculptures are located on Lakota
Sioux land, as documented in their 1868 Fort
Laramie treaty with the U.S. government. In
1971, the American Indian Movement (AIM)
holds a demonstration at the site, to call attention to its violations: broken treaty rights and
carving on their sacred rocks the images of past
presidents who endorsed taking native land.

• Ruth Crawford Seeger composes a string
quartet that is one of the first works to employ
extended serialism, a systematic organization
of pitch, rhythm, dynamics, and articulation.

• Henry Cowell publishes *New Musical
Resources,* perhaps the first important book on
non-European compositional attitudes and
techniques.

• *Symphony of Psalms,* commissioned by
the Boston Symphony Orchestra for its fiftieth-
anniversary celebrations, is composed by Igor
Stravinsky. Among its innovations is an orchestration devoid of violins, clarinets, or violas,
and including two pianos.

• Howard University houses the first art
gallery in the U.S. to be directed and controlled
by African Americans, and among the first to
feature art by African Americans.

• John Dos Passos (1896–1970) publishes
The 42nd Parallel, the first novel of his innovative multimedia trilogy, *U.S.A.,* originally
published as three separate novels. Chrono-
logically spanning a time frame from before
World War I through 1935, he uses layout
and editing techniques usually associated with

tume of blue tricot tubing that she designs
"to indicate the tragedy that obsesses the
body," and which makes a living sculpture out
of her body. With simplicity shocking to many
at the time, this work, which is her lament
for the Spanish Civil War dead, introduces
Graham's unique approach to expressing confrontational issues and marks her emergence as
a revolutionary American dance pioneer.

• Sculptor Gutzon Borglum (1867–1941)
unveils the first of four sixty-foot-high relief portraits that will be carved into the gray granite
top of Mount Rushmore, in the Black Hills near

journalism and film to evoke the sweep of events, people, and places in what he sees as "two nations," divided between the rich and powerful and the poor and hopeless. He invents three devices: the "Newsreel," which inserts fragments of headlines, articles, slogans, mottos, popular songs, and public oratory into the text; the "Camera Eye," which shares private musings, sometimes angry, sometimes satirical, mournful, or lyrical; and twenty-seven biographical sketches of real-life public figures such as Thomas Edison, labor leader Eugene Debs, and movie star Rudolph Valentino, to further explore different kinds of success and failure and the economic and social forces that shape them. All three novels of the trilogy, also including *1919* (1932) and *The Big Money* (1936), will appear in a single volume in 1937.

GOVERNMENT AND POLITICS

• President Hoover signs the Hawley-Smoot Tariff Act, saying he is following through on his campaign promise to raise duties on most industrial and agricultural commodities. The argument behind this legislation will be stated many times throughout the rest of the century: high tariffs are a protection, necessary to keep U.S. businesses competitive against "unfair" foreign tariffs and American imports made by foreign corporations that are able to pay lower wages. However, the stiffer tariffs, which are the highest to date, generate an effect exactly opposite to what is intended. They set off trade wars as other countries impose retaliatory tariffs, depress production because of decreased demand for American-made goods, and cause unemployment to rise from 3 million to 13 million in the next two years. This prolongs the Depression in the U.S. and worldwide, and sig-

nificantly contributes to Hoover losing his bid for a second term.

SCIENCE AND TECHNOLOGY

• Vannevar Bush and co-workers at MIT develop the first analog computer, the Rockefeller Differential Analyzer, which works by the movement of gears and shafts and records information in decimal format rather than binary (0 and 1). The computer is a giant, taking up several hundred square feet of floor space, and is operated by screwdrivers and hammers instead of a keyboard. Though it can handle up to eighteen independent variables at a time and is capable of calculating lengthy sets of differential equations, it will be made obsolete by the introduction of the first electronic digital computers, the precursors of modern personal computers. One will be built between 1937–1942 by John Vincent Atanasoff and Clifford Berry at Iowa State University and another in 1939 by George Stibitz and S. B. Williams.

• The Adler Planetarium and Astronomy Museum opens in Chicago, the first in the U.S.

• Minnesota Mining and Manufacturing Company (3M) introduces a transparent cellulose tape, called Scotch Tape, which proves so useful that it becomes an instant institution in an era that necessitates thriftiness. It will survive into the present day, as a pillar of 3M's growth into an industrial giant.

• Thomas Midgley Jr. develops Freons (various nonflammable, nontoxic gaseous or liquid fluorocarbons, which are placed in production by the Kinetic Chemical Corporation in 1931. Freons will be widely used as working fluids in refrigeration and air conditioning, and as aerosol propellants. In the 1980s they will be

Unemployed queued up at a Chicago soup kitchen, by an unknown photographer *(National Archives Records of the U.S. Information Agency)*

implicated as major contributors to the depletion of ozone, the atmospheric layer that shields the Earth from harmful effects of the sun's ultraviolet rays.

• Pluto, the ninth planet of the solar system, is discovered by astronomer Clyde W. Tombaugh, working at Lowell Observatory in Flagstaff, Arizona. In the 1990s some scientists question the status of this smallest and most distant of planets, calling it an icy rock, comparable to a comet, that belongs to the Kuiper Belt just beyond our solar system.

BUSINESS AND INDUSTRY

• The Southern and Midwestern U.S. is hit by an unprecedented drought that devastates crops and family farms; unemployment exceeds 4 million.

• Hundreds of thousands of unemployed workers demonstrate in major cities throughout the country, demanding unemployment insurance. Police attack a crowd of 35,000 in New York City, and a crowd of 10,000 fights with police in Cleveland, Ohio.

• As a result of the 1929 stock market crash, more than 1,000 banks close nationwide.

CULTURE AND SOCIETY

• One year after the stock market crash that started the Great Depression, the hard times, made worse by government inaction, have begun to transform the most basic social structures, wreaking havoc on family life. Rates for marriage, divorce, and childbearing decline. Suicide and desertion rates rise. People are dispossessed of their homes, farmers watch their farms being auctioned off, former bankers sell apples in the streets, men rear young children while wives and older children go to work as domestics, if they can find a job. "Hoovervilles," shantytowns built on garbage dumps, become common, as do bread lines. Migrants roam the country, hitching rides or driving broken-down automobiles on the road, or stealing rides on freight trains in search of any kind of job.

WORLD EVENTS

• Joseph Stalin (1879–1953) emerges as the USSR's strongman, winning the power struggle that ensued after the death of Lenin in 1924 and the expulsion of Trotsky in 1929. Throughout the 1930s he continues to purge any potential military or political rivals for power, imprisoning some 12 million "enemies of the state" and executing some 7 million others. He officially becomes premier in 1941.

• Hitler's Nazi Party emerges as a major political force in Germany after the 1930 national elections, going from 12 to 107 seats out of 577 in the Reichstag, to become the country's second-largest party.

1931

ARTS AND LITERATURE

• The Exposition of Indian Tribal Arts opens in New York City and then tours North America and Europe through 1933. It is the first large-scale presentation of Native American art as art, rather than as ethnography.

• Two masterworks of modern dance that reflect growing interest in the nation's past are choreographed this year. Martha Graham premieres *Primitive Mysteries,* a three-part mass for her all-women dance company that is influenced by her observations, with her composer Louis Horst, of Southwestern Native American ceremonial dances and Mexican rituals. Doris Humphrey premieres *The Shakers,* also featuring an all-women cast. She is inspired by the religious practices of that communal sect of utopian Christians, and uses Shaker texts and hymns to present a visionary, almost trancelike service. The last concert given by Denishawn, the company where Graham and Humphrey were trained, also occurs this year.

• Hemsley Winfield organizes a company of eighteen African American dancers, who become known as the Negro Art Theatre Dance Group or the New Negro Art Dancers. They claim a showing of their work at a small New York City theater on top of the Chanin Building as the "First Negro Concert in America," although college students at Hampton Institute have been performing African American dance material since 1925. Winfield's company presents a varied program that includes suites of dances on African themes and Negro spirituals, and two Denishawn-influenced solos by Edna Guy.

• Sculptor Alexander Calder (1898–1976) exhibits the first of his hanging sculptures (named "mobiles" by Duchamp), abstract biomorphic forms that move by chance changes in air currents, which he says are inspired by "spheres of different sizes, densities, colors and volumes, floating in space, traversing clouds, sprays of water, currents of air, viscosities and odors of the greatest variety and disparity."

The first workable particle smasher, the cyclotron, is developed by Ernest Orlando Lawrence in April 1931. *(Courtesy of UC Lawrence Berkeley National Laboratory Image Library, Jean Wolslegel)*

Calder's mobiles receive immediate worldwide recognition. He also creates stationary outdoor sculptures (named "stabiles" by Hans Arp), which are generally made of welded, painted steel wire and sheet aluminum.

• Henry Cowell works with Leon Theremin to build the Rhythmicon, an instrument that can play metrical combinations of virtually unlimited complexity. With this instrument Cowell composes *Rhythmicana Concerto*.

• William Grant Still composes *Afro-American Symphony*, one of the earliest major classical works by an American black.

• Harold Clurman, Cheryl Crawford, and

Lee Strasberg (1901–1982) co-found the Group Theatre, an ensemble company of twenty-eight actors whose name reflects their egalitarian structure. Influenced by the work of Russian director Constantin Stanislavsky, they want to provide an alternative to the old-fashioned light entertainment style, such as revues and star-turn musicals, that dominate the American theater in the late 1920s. Through 1940, when the group dissolves, they produce twenty-three original, socially conscious plays "related to American life," championing the writing of Maxwell Anderson, Robert Ardrey, Sidney Kingsley, John Howard Lawson, Clifford Odets, and William Saroyan. Many of its participants, including actors Stella Adler and Morris Carnovsky, teachers Sanford Meisner and Lee Strasberg, and directors Elia Kazan and Harold Clurman, will continue to shape the look and sound of American theater for the rest of the century.

Government and Politics

• The Food and Drug Administration (FDA) is established to oversee the enforcement of laws protecting the nation's consumers from impure and unsafe drugs, cosmetics, foods, and other potentially hazardous substances, by reorganizing an agency originally set up under the 1906 Pure Food and Drug Act.

Business and Industry

• In January the President's Emergency Committee for Unemployment Relief reports that between 4 and 5 million workers are unemployed. The Ford Motor Company alone lays off 91,000 workers between the spring of 1929 and late summer of 1931.

SCIENCE AND TECHNOLOGY

• Physicist Ernest Orlando Lawrence (1901–1958) invents the first effective particle accelerator, called the "cyclotron," an "atom smasher," only five inches in diameter that can accelerate subatomic particles to a rate of 37,000 miles per second, or one-fifth the speed of light, by spinning them in circles. Built by one of Lawrence's UC Berkeley students, M. Stanley Livingston, the cyclotron is the prototype particle accelerator, and will spawn the gargantuan modern accelerators, miles in length, that allow physicists to invest particles with enough energy to bombard and disintegrate atomic nuclei so that their components can be studied. The cyclotron wins Lawrence the 1939 Nobel Prize in physics and helps develop many technologies including the electron microscope, nuclear magnetic resonance, and the atomic bomb.

• Harold C. Urey (1893–1981), a Columbia University chemist, discovers deuterium, or hydrogen-2, the isotope of hydrogen that has a nucleus of one proton and one neutron. In the following year, chemist Gilbert Newton Lewis (1875–1946) will obtain deuterium oxide, known as heavy water. These discoveries are necessary steps toward the development of the H-bomb.

• Dr. Earle Haas, a Colorado country doctor, invents the prototype for Tampax, inspired by a wife who hates sanitary pads. When the patent is approved, he forms the Tampax Corporation with another Denver doctor, Gertrude Tenderich, who makes the first products on her own sewing machine. Because of the embarrassment associated with the product, which churchmen denounce on the grounds that it could destroy the evidence of virginity and encourage masturbation, and which is mainly sold by male pharmacists, sales are slow, but pick up by 1937 when Tampax starts an advertising campaign in magazines reaching 45 million people.

CULTURE AND SOCIETY

• Nevada, looking to increase revenues, sets in motion two legal ordinances that will create new industries out of divorce and gambling, and will produce profound cultural ripple effects. By easing up on residency requirements, the state makes it possible for people to obtain "quickie" divorces, making Reno and Las Vegas the "divorce capitals of the world." (Later, other states will create more-liberal laws that will put an end to this distinction.) By legalizing gambling, they set the stage for a make-believe city of casinos that never close for gamblers who never sleep, and which will become the gambling and entertainment capital of the U.S.

• More than 114,000 Germans immigrate to the U.S. in this decade, mainly to flee increasing Nazi terrorism and anti-Semitism.

• Elijah Muhammad (b. Elijah Poole, 1897–1975) attends his first Lost-Found Nation of Islam meetings, a religious movement based on black separatism, founded by Wallace D. Fard about a year earlier in Detroit. Fard appoints Elijah Muhammad Supreme Minister in 1933, when Fard becomes a subject of government investigation because of his inflammatory messages warning of "blue-eyed devils." Muhammad adds his own message of economic self-sufficiency to Fard's mixture of various philosophies from earlier Black

LATINO ART, 1930s-1940s

Dr. George Vargas

1930s

- Impressed by the success of the Mexican Mural Movement, FDR's New Deal program builds an ambitious public art department (Public Works of Art Project) during the 1930s to support the production of American public murals and sculpture dedicated to the masses.
- Carlos Lopez (b. Cuba, 1908, prolific painter and art professor at the University of Michigan, assisted by his wife, Rhoda, produces a series of New Deal murals in Illinois and Michigan.
- Texas sculptor Octavio Medellín (b. Mexico, 1907) explores Mexican history from pre-Columbian times to the Mexican Revolution.
- Antonio García (b. Mexico, 1901) moves to San Diego, Texas, with his family, later studies at the Art Institute of Chicago. A book and magazine illustrator, he also creates New Deal murals, mostly in Goliad, Corpus Christi, and San Diego, Texas.
- Mexican American mainstream painter Edward Chavez (b. New Mexico, 1917) also produces New Deal murals in Colorado, Nebraska, Texas, and Wyoming, highlighting each state's unique cultural heritage.
- El Paso artist José Aceves (b. Mexico, 1909) paints New Deal historical murals in post offices in Texas, depicting the postal service in the frontier and life of early pioneers.
- Traveling to Detroit with her husband, Diego Rivera (b. Mexico, 1886), when he receives a mural commission from the Detroit Institute of Arts in 1932, Frida Kahlo (b. Mexico, 1907) paints a series of self-portraits based on Mexican *retablos,* attracting the attention of Surrealists in Europe. Kahlo's art influences Latin artists and feminists beginning in the 1960s.
- In the 1930s, numerous Cuban artists emerge in abstract art. Prolific and diverse, René Portocarrero (b. Cuba, 1912) receives academic training in Cuba, teaching at various schools, as well as at Havana Prison in 1940. His interests range from Spanish-Cuban baroque to Afro-Cuban fantasy, as in the expressionistic *Small Devil* of 1962. Receiving many international prizes for his works, he explores ceramics, creates fresco murals, and produces set designs.
- Minimalist Carmen Herrera (b. 1915, Cuba) is one of the first Cubans to experiment with hard-edged art when she lives in Europe, where, she claims, there is less prejudice

Muslim groups, Christian scriptures, and his own Afrocentric origin stories. The organization, which will be called the Nation of Islam, moves its headquarters to Chicago, attracting many followers who participate in their highly structured lifestyle that dictates standards for dress, diet, hygiene, and family life. By 1945 the Nation of Islam will have opened 100 temples nationwide and built a network of small businesses, restaurants, bakeries, and radio stations, besides purchasing 140 acres of Michigan farmland, all through the pooled resources of the organization.

WORLD EVENTS

- The Japanese invade Manchuria, capturing and occupying the northeastern Chinese province, thereby violating the Kellogg-Briand

against women artists. Her paintings show movement and reveal a strong architectural influence, reflecting her earlier architectural training at San Alejandro Academy. Her pure color palette is influenced by Palaez's color schemes. While Herrera frequently travels back to Cuba, she dislikes political turmoil, and therefore she resides mostly in New York during her highly successful career as an international artist.

- Surrealist painter Antonio Gattorno (b. Cuba, 1904) enrolls at the Alejandro Art Academy, then travels to Europe under a scholarship. He moves permanently to New York City in 1935, where he paints a mural in the Bacardi Company offices in the Empire State Building.
- During the 1930s in Puerto Rico, a fellowship program allows many artists to study art abroad. Among them is Rufino Silva (b. Puerto Rico, 1919), who studies at the Art Institute of Chicago (1938–1942) and later becomes an important instructor there.

1940s

- Porfirio Salinas, Mexican American self-taught painter (b. Texas, 1912), becomes popular for his landscapes of Texas featuring bluebonnets and other wildflowers. Later his

work is collected by Lyndon Baines Johnson and his wife, Lady Bird.

- In Michigan, Latina figurative artist Lola Cueto illustrates *Mexican Folk Puppets,* a book written by Roberto Lago in 1941 on the history of puppetry in Mexico from the Toltecs to modern times.
- Originally trained in political science and economics, painter Cundo Bermudez (b. Cuba, 1914) exhibits his abstract art exploring the black culture of Cuba at the Museum of Modern Art in New York in 1944. Later, fleeing the Cuban Revolution, he moves to Puerto Rico. Bermudez, though not victimized by the Cuban government, is "simply ignored."
- After studying Surrealism and Cubism in Europe, and fighting in the Spanish War, Wilfredo Lam (b. Cuba of Chinese and Afro-Cuban roots, 1902) returns home to begin a series of paintings in the early 1940s, mostly involving the Afro-Cuban gods of the Santería religion, set in a jungle environment.
- After studying art in the U.S., Madrid, and Florence, Felix Bonilla-Norat (b. Puerto Rico, 1912) opens a printmaking workshop in New York in 1946. He returns to Puerto Rico to teach printmaking techniques in San Juan in 1949, and soon begins working as an artist for the government.

Pact of 1928 and initiating hostilities that lead to World War II.

- The British Commonwealth is created by the Statute of Westminster, granting all the dominions in the British Empire, including Canada, full self-government, "equal in status, in no way subordinate to each other," although still bound by their allegiance to the English crown.

1932

ARTS AND LITERATURE

- *Black Elk Speaks: Being the Life Story of a Holy Man of the Oglala Sioux* is published. The book, as told through European American poet and writer John Neihardt, gives witness to major events, starting with Black Elk's child-

> To speak of this art recently discovered by the non-indigenous American as a "new school of painting" is a curious paradox, for it is at once America's oldest and one of her youngest arts. Oldest in the sense that the Indians have painted for centuries for themselves, and one of the youngest because only within the past few years have they been putting down their ancient truths, in modern media, for other people. . . . Here was a chance for the modern-yearning Indian young people to see how well their amazingly modern traditional motifs might unite with some of the most advanced ideas of the modern world.
>
> (DOROTHY DUNN, FROM *Modern by Tradition: American Indian Painting*
> *in the Studio Style* BY BRUCE BERNSTEIN AND W. JACKSON [1935].)

hood on the plains with the Dakota Sioux in the 1860s, where he received a mystic vision. He also experienced the Ghost Dance religion, the Wounded Knee massacre, and the Battle of the Little Bighorn, and participated in Buffalo Bill's Wild West Show. The book sells millions of copies worldwide, and remains the most widely taught work about American Indians.

• Cranbrook Academy of Art is founded in Bloomfield Hills, Michigan, by Finnish-born architect Eliel Saarinen (1873–1950) and Detroit newspaper publisher George Booth and his wife, Ellen, the only school in the U.S. solely for graduate study in design, architecture, and art at the time. Its faculty includes artist/designers whose modern slant on materials and shapes significantly influences the rest of the century's look, including designers Charles Eames (1907–1978) and Florence Knoll, sculptor Harry Bertoia (1915–1978), and architect Eero Saarinen (1910–1961), son of the founder.

• Diego Rivera (1866–1957), Mexican muralist and avowed revolutionary, receives his second one-man show, a retrospective that includes specially commissioned fresco panels at New York's Museum of Modern Art. The president of the Ford Motor Company, Edsel Ford, commissions murals on the theme of modern

industry for the Detroit Institute of Arts. By the following year, Nelson Rockefeller has commissioned a mural, to be titled *Man at the Crossroads*. Rivera starts work on the project at the seventy-story RCA Building in Rockefeller Center, until Nelson Rockefeller cancels the project and eventually destroys the work because of Rivera's inclusion of an image of V. I. Lenin. José Clemente Orozco (Mexican painter, 1883–1949) and David Alfaro Siqueiros (Mexican painter, 1896–1974), who, with Rivera, are referred to as Los Tres Grandes, are also commissioned to paint murals in the U.S. Their work inspires a mural movement throughout the U.S. that blossoms under WPA programs, so that murals will become one of the most popular public art forms, appearing on the walls of post offices and other government offices, on the sides of buildings, and on concrete road support structures.

• The Studio of the Santa Fe Indian School, a program introduced into the existing boarding school, officially opens on Sept. 9, 1932, under the direction of a non-native teacher, Dorothy Dunn (1903–1992). Students from the Sioux, Omaha, Navajo, Hopi, Zuni, and many of the Rio Grande Pueblos are encouraged to model their creative work on Dunn's archaeological

Awa Tsireh (Alfonso Roybal), *Green Corn Ceremony*, c. 1935. Painted by a member of the San Ildefonso pueblo, a graduate and teacher at the Studio of the Santa Fe Indian School, this work illustrates the balance sought in the "modern by tradition" stylistic devices promoted at the Studio school, with its realistic figures celebrating a traditional ceremony against a flat background *(The Museum of Modern Art, New York, Abby Aldrich Rockefeller Fund. © 2001 The MOMA, New York)*

research findings: design motifs found on ancient wall paintings and rock art; hide paintings on buffalo robes and tipis; sandpaintings; kiva murals; and the geometric patterns and abstract shapes in beadwork, basketry, and pottery designs. The students are asked to paint from memory and natural ability, not technical training. Essentially, Dunn helps them continue the "traditional style" of Southwestern pueblo painters of the Ildefonso school and Plains Indian artists, including those known as the Kiowa Five. Although she only directs the Studio program for five years, 1932–1937, Dunn codi-

fies a pedagogic system that becomes the model used by art departments at other Indian schools for the next twenty-five years. Her viewpoint is shared by a local community of Euro-American artists, curators, patrons, and intelligentsia with an "anti-modernist sensibility" who champion the young artists' works, claiming them as the foundation of American art.

GOVERNMENT AND POLITICS

• The Bonus Expeditionary Force (BEF), a group of more than 20,000 jobless World War I veterans and their families, builds an encamp-

Carlos Lopez, *Plymouth Trail,* a mural commissioned by the Treasury Department Public Works of Art Project (TRAP) for the Plymouth Post Office, Plymouth, Michigan, in 1938. *(George Vargas)*

ment of tarpaper shacks and takes over abandoned buildings in Washington, D.C. The veterans hold government bonus certificates that are to come due sometime in the future, but want to pressure Congress into paying them off now. When the bill to pay off the bonuses is defeated, thousands of veterans cluster in an encampment near the White House, and President Hoover directs his Army chief of staff, Douglas MacArthur (1880–1964), to evict everyone. With Major Dwight Eisenhower (1890–1969) as his aide, and George S. Patton (1885–1945) as one of his officers, General MacArthur proceeds down Pennsylvania Avenue with four troops of cavalry, four companies of infantry, a machine gun squad, and six tanks. He orders the soldiers to fire tear gas into the encampment and set the makeshift struc-

tures on fire. Men, women, and children begin running as the tear gas and fire spread throughout the encampment. Before it is over, two veterans and an eleven-week-old baby are dead, an eight-year-old boy is partially blinded by gas, two policemen have their skulls fractured, and thousands have gas-related injuries. To many people, Hoover's orders seemed like the fascist tactics being used in Europe.

• The lack of adequate measures to reorganize the economy, the deepening Depression, and the government's actions against the bonus veterans all contribute to New York's Democratic patrician governor Franklin Roosevelt (1882–1945) winning a landslide victory over incumbent President Herbert Hoover. For his first term as the thirty-second president, Roosevelt promises a "new deal" for "the forgotten man."

BUSINESS AND INDUSTRY

• Twenty thousand businesses go bankrupt and 1,616 banks fail as the Depression locks in on the country's economy. Industrial production falls by 50 percent. By 1933, approximately 15 million people, from one-fourth to one-third of the labor force, are out of work.

SCIENCE AND TECHNOLOGY

• The U.S. Public Health Service begins a forty-year syphilis experiment in Macon County, Alabama, using 300 black men as the subjects, without their knowing consent. The purpose of the experiment, known popularly as the Tuskegee Syphilis Study, is to study morbidity and mortality among untreated victims of the disease, by withholding either known or new drug therapies.

CULTURE AND SOCIETY

• The first soap operas, *One Man's Family* and *Betty and Bob,* air on NBC radio, although the genre term "soap opera" will not be coined until 1939. They are a new incarnation of melodramas whose characters endure an endless string of extraordinary events, interrupted by commercials for soap powders.

▣ 1947

1933

ARTS AND LITERATURE

• President Roosevelt establishes the Public Works of Art Project, an experimental, federally funded government program to help employ artists. The pilot program costs the government $1,312,177, gives jobs to 4,000 artists at a weekly wage varying from $26.50 to $42.50,

New York City views: "Houston Street Junk Markets IV." Photo by Samuel Herman Gottscho, March 10, 1933. *(Library of Congress, Prints and Photographs Division)*

and produces some 15,000 works. Its success leads to the formation of two agencies: the Section of Painting and Sculpture of the Treasury Department, in 1934, which is intended to provide art works for public buildings; and the Works Progress Administration, in 1935.

▣ 1935

• An experimental, progressive educational curriculum is founded by a group of educators at Black Mountain College in North Carolina. Led by John Rice Andrews, the school develops a program that attracts many artists, writers, playwrights, dancers, and musicians and scientists. Painter Josef Albers and his wife, Anni Albers, a weaver, join the school as teachers in 1933. Affiliated with the Bauhaus until just before its closure by the Nazis, they encourage more refugee colleagues to join them, including performance artist Xanti Schawinsky and musicians Stefan Wolpe and Edward Lowinsky. In 1944 a special summer arts program is added, consisting of classes, performances, exhibitions, and panels. Innovative artists of various disciplines, including John Cage and Merce Cunningham (b. 1919), Eric Bentley, David Tudor, Buckminster Fuller (1895–1983), Jasper Johns (b. 1930), Robert Rauschenberg (b. 1925), Willem de Kooning, Jacob Lawrence (1917–2000), Walter Gropius, Robert Motherwell (1915–1991), Franz Kline (1910–1962), Lyonel Feininger (b. Germany, 1871–1956), and Charles Olsen (1910–1970), are able to try out ideas together. This influential hub of creative energy lasts twenty-three years, until the school closes in 1957.

• Expatriate American writer Gertrude Stein (1874–1946) becomes a star with the publication of *The Autobiography of Alice B. Toklas,* which is full of descriptions of life with her partner and literary alter ego and the international cast of progressive artist visitors who connect at their Paris salon, including writers Ernest Hemingway (1899–1961), F. Scott Fitzgerald (1869–1940), and Ezra Pound, European visual artists Pablo Picasso, Georges Braque, and Henri Matisse, and American visual artists Charles Demuth, Arthur Dove, and Abraham Walkowitz.

• Obscenity bans are lifted on James Joyce's novel *Ulysses* (published in 1922) and Erskine Caldwell's *God's Little Acre* (published in 1933).

• Thomas A. Dorsey (1899–1933) and singer Sallie Martin create the National Convention of Gospel Choirs and Choruses, thus setting up a performance circuit allowing for the organizing and training of African American church choirs in Dorsey's highly emotional, vocally disciplined approach to choral singing. Dorsey, known in his wilder days as Ma Rainey's ragtime-trained piano accompanist "Georgia Tom," fell upon hard times in the mid-1920s. In 1929 he dedicates himself to composing only the Christian music he calls gospel songs, of which he writes over 1,000. After the unexpected deaths of his wife, Nettie, and their baby, he writes the gospel classic "Precious Lord Take My Hand" in 1932.

• Busby Berkeley (1895–1976) choreographs three hit movie musicals for Warner Brothers that chase away Depression blues with dazzling dance spectacles: *42nd Street, Gold Diggers of 1933,* and *Footlight Parade.* Instead of following the prevailing custom of filming dances from a series of angles and then splicing them together, Berkeley applies his early training as a World War I army parade director, plotting his dances as eccentric drill formations. He uses only one camera, an essential ingredient of his choreography, creating in-camera effects by alternating between close-ups, such as zooming in between a row of scissoring legs, and long shots, such as a white staircase full of platinum-haired dancers in white dresses playing violins wired to light up, and especially employing his favorite "top shot," which takes an overhead view of synchronized, kaleidoscopic patterns performed by a chorus of hundreds.

• Composer Arnold Schoenberg emigrates from Vienna to the U.S., fleeing the Nazis' campaign against the Jews.

GOVERNMENT AND POLITICS

• In the first 100 days of President Franklin D. Roosevelt's first term, he persuades Congress to give him special powers to turn the failing economy around. With a Democratic Congress to help him, Roosevelt sets about passing new laws that create new government programs, many of which will still be in place sixty years later. He ends Prohibition by getting Congress to pass the Twenty-first Amendment to the Constitution, repealing the Eighteenth Amendment. Then he pushes his "New Deal" through Congress, establishing a variety of programs. At a New York State Democratic Convention three years later, Roosevelt says, "In the spring of 1933, we faced a crisis. . . . We were against revolution. And therefore, we waged war against those conditions which make revolution—against the inequities and resentments that breed them."

• President Roosevelt implements the Good Neighbor Policy, declaring opposition to armed intervention in Latin America.

BUSINESS AND INDUSTRY

• The Civilian Conservation Corps (CCC) hires more than 120,000 out-of-work young men to build roads, bridges, cabins, culverts, trails, entrance stations, and lay water and sewage lines.

• The Tennessee Valley Authority (TVA) is an independent public corporation established by Congress that becomes a model for regional planning through its contracts with an entire rural river basin. The TVA practices flood control planning in connection with buying, building, and operating dams that also produce and sell electric power. The flood control restores farmland to productive use, and enables reforestation. The TVA is able to keep its electricity rates lower than private companies, affecting more than 40,000 cus-

tomers, many of whom had never had access to electric power in their homes before. Although fought by private companies in the courts as a threat to private enterprise, this program manages to survive.

SCIENCE AND TECHNOLOGY

• Albert Einstein immigrates to the U.S. and accepts a position at Princeton's Institute for Advanced Study, while the Nazis confiscate his property and revoke his German citizenship. With the rise of fascism, many other physicists will take refuge in the U.S. including Hans Bethe, Enrico Fermi (b. Italy, 1901–1954), Leo Szilard, Eugene Wigner (b. Hungary, 1902) and Edward Teller (b. Hungary, 1908–1993). They will all contribute to the development of atomic energy and the atomic bomb.

CULTURE AND SOCIETY

• The first drive-in movie theater is built in Camden, New Jersey.

• The Roosevelt Administration removes the standing policy establishing English as the official language of Puerto Rico.

WORLD EVENTS

• The Nazis come into power in Germany with the election of Adolf Hitler as chancellor. He proclaims the ascendancy of the Third Reich. By 1935 the Nazis pass the Nuremberg Laws, which deprive all Jews (defined as anyone with at least one Jewish grandparent) of citizenship, forbids marriage of Jews with Gentiles, and is the start of decrees that will cancel Jews' civil rights. Between 1935 and 1941, about 150,000 Jewish refugees are accepted into the U.S. However, in 1939, the SS *St. Louis,* a ship bound for Cuba, carrying 937

New Deal industrial recovery. Photomontage by Theodor Horydezak, c. 1920–1950. *(Library of Congress, Prints and Photographs Division)*

German Jewish refugees, is denied entry and returned to Germany by the U.S.

1934

ARTS AND LITERATURE

• Sierra Leone–born dancer Asadata Dafora choreographs and presents *Kykunkor, the Witch Woman,* a spectacular story ballet about a curse put upon a bridegroom, which he calls an "opera." He uses a mixed cast of Africans and African Americans in a New York City premiere, receiving great critical success. White audiences and critics remark upon seeing a new vision of Africans as humans instead of barbarians, much to the amazement of Dafora, who responded by saying "Barbarism? But there are lynchings in this country."

• Dancer and choreographer Jack Cole (1913–1974) gains attention with a polyrhythmic movement style he calls "jazz dance." Influenced by American modern dance, African-American, and East Indian dance vocabularies, the actions of different body parts can be initiated in isolation or juxtaposed against another. He creates a teaching technique, which is still present in how this style is taught today. Jazz dance becomes popular through nightclub revues, Broadway and film musicals, and television variety show productions.

• U.S. Customs bans American Henry Miller's novel *Tropic of Cancer* on charges of obscenity. Published in Paris, where Miller is living as an expatriate, it will not be published in the U.S. until 1961.

• The Native Market is opened in Sante Fe, New Mexico, providing an outlet for the Native arts being produced in federal- and state-funded projects, especially furniture and textiles. It becomes an annual event with juried competitions that attract Native American artists, dealers, and collectors from around the country.

• The American Musicological Society is founded, growing out of the New York Musicological Society, and becoming the main musical scholarly body in the U.S. The first president is Otto Kinkeldey, and founding members include the eminent scholars Gustave Reese, Joseph Schillinger, Oliver Strunk, Carl Engel, and Charles Seeger.

• Chicago-born clarinetist and band leader Benny Goodman, prodded toward jazz by record producer John Hammond, who connects

Electrification by David Stone Martin, Treasury Section of Fine Arts, 1940. *(Fine Arts Collection, General Services Administration)*

him with a body of Fletcher Henderson/Don Redman arrangements, forms a jazz band that creates a sensation among American whites for the music that will come to be called "swing." Swing band music becomes America's main dance and popular music format, launching major careers for the next decade, via radio and records, for the bands of Glenn Miller, Tommy and Jimmy Dorsey, Artie Shaw, Harry James, Duke Ellington, and Count Basie.

• George Delacorte of the Dell Publishing Company introduces "Famous Funnies," the first comic strips successfully published outside of newspapers in a book format consisting solely of comics. Distributed through department stores, the sixty-eight-page, eight-by-eleven-inch prototype for comic books sells out its first press run of 35,000 copies at ten cents per copy, and a long-standing publishing hit is born.

• In the summer after graduating from high school, Jerry Siegel (1915–1996) dreams up the essential elements of *Superman*, whose title character will become the most successful comic-book character of all time. Siegel's friend and collaborator, Joe Shuster, suggests

the character's costume of cape and leotard, and also executes the illustrations. Although they meet rejection when they try to get *Superman* syndicated as a newspaper comic strip, they find big success when, in 1938, they change it to fit the newly emerging comic-book format. For $130 cash they turn over all their rights to the Detective Comics line of National Allied Publishing, a company that will later become DC Comics, and which distributes *Superman* as its first Action Comic. Sadly, it will take most of Siegel and Shuster's lives before they or their heirs receive any more of the billions of dollars made after this first sale of the rights to their ideas.

GOVERNMENT AND POLITICS

• President Roosevelt appoints the anthropologist and longtime activist John Collier commissioner of Indian Affairs. Collier launches the "Indian New Deal," his plan to regenerate Native American communities following suggestions in the 1928 Meriam Report. He believes Native Americans need "the experience of responsible democracy," and thinks this can

Indian people didn't have any type of government that set down a law that was enforced by one guy like a chief. They were free. They made special rules, maybe, for an occasion like a hunt. They would have one of the societies within the tribe enforce those rules for as long as that hunt was going on. But no one was obligated to follow any of the leaders, and that's the way it should be now for our people.

Indian leaders were chosen by their deeds, the manner in which they acted toward their people, their generosity, and their willingness to serve their people above all else. . . . Our people didn't understand the theory of dictatorship, and the idea that all people aren't individually free and responsible for their own acts. So in order to try to explain this to our people, they made the Indian Reorganization Act.

Under the Reorganization Act, the U.S. recognizes a Tribal Government supposedly patterned after the U.S. Government—a Tribal Business Committee, or a Tribal council that has no relationship to the people. Its relationship is to the Bureau of Indian Affairs. Hence to the Federal Government . . ."

(CARTER CAMP, AIM LEADER, IN *Voices from Wounded Knee, 1973*, EDITED BY ROBERT ANDERSON, JOANNA BROWN, JONNY LERNER, AND BARBARA LOU SHAFER [ROOSEVELTTOWN, N.Y.: AKWESASNE NOTES, 1974], 11.)

be accomplished by guaranteeing the right of each Indian group to decide how to maintain its own cultural and religious liberty and the manner of control and utilization of land holdings. The Indian Reorganization Act (IRA), is drafted to revive self-government and to reform federal Indian policy, including repealing the General Allotment Act and encouraging Indian land reform policies. However, the bill that passes on June 18, 1934, does not fundamentally change the relationship between Indians and larger American society, although it does curb some of the worst abuses. The act does not receive universal approval within the Native American communities. The Klamath Crow, Fort Peck Sisseton Sioux, Turtle Mountain Chippewa, and Navajo nations reject it, and therefore become ineligible for enlarged federal

aid, with no means to negotiate improved health care or educational services. Others feel that assimilation has already gone too far and that it is too late to return to the past tribal model.

▣ 1928

• The Tydings-McDuffie Act of 1934 grants the Philippines commonwealth status, and promises independence in ten years. Although the act sounds positive, as citizens of an independent country, Filipino nationals can be reclassified as "aliens" and thus become subject to quota restrictions; the act is actually motivated by exclusionist desires to bar Filipino immigration.

▣ 1935

• With Cuba now under the dictatorship of Fulgencio Batista, the 1901 Platt Amendment, which forced protectorate limitations into Cuba's constitution, is annulled by mutual agreement. However, the U.S. continues to maintain its naval base at Guantanamo Bay. ⊡ 1901

BUSINESS AND INDUSTRY

• Between 1934 and 1937, the U.S. experiences the greatest drought in its history as dust storms blow 300 million tons of topsoil across the Midwest toward the Atlantic. Over 150,000 acres are destroyed. Entire counties in Oklahoma, north Texas, Kansas, Colorado, and Arkansas become known as the Dust Bowl. Thousands of families leave their farms, migrating west to Texas and California in search of jobs and a new life. They become known as "Okies," the people John Steinbeck (1902–1968) depicts in his novel *The Grapes of Wrath,* that Woody Guthrie (1912–1967) sings about in his songs, and that the photographers Walker Evans, Dorothea Lange, Russell Lee, and Arnold Rothstein are asked to document by the Farm Security Administration. In 1935 the federal government establishes the Soil Conservation Service, to teach farmers how to practice crop rotation (the system George Washington Carver promoted) so that the soil is renewed instead of being exhausted by each planting, and to plant trees and grasses to hold unsowed soil down.

CULTURE AND SOCIETY

• Sixty-four million pairs of nylon stockings are sold in the U.S., when they go on the market for the first time. They replace silk stockings, which are far more expensive. During World War II they are rationed, because mili-

Years of Dust by Ben Shahn. Poster for the Resettlement Administration. *(© Estate of Ben Shahn/VAGA, New York, NY, through the National Archives: FDR Library)*

tary uses for nylon take precedence over fashion, but they make an immediate comeback after the war. In the year 1990, 1.5 billion pairs are sold in the U.S.

• The Catholic Legion of Decency is founded, to let Catholics know what movies are acceptable for viewing. Their censorship code will wield a powerful influence on the film industry for decades to come.

ART SHAPED BY ITS TIME AND PLACE

Inspired by the popular newsreels of the 1930s and 1940s, photographer Walker Evans (1903-1975) champions using the camera in a straightforward documentary style, removing any manipulations that might convey the artist's personality, feelings, or politics. He is "interested in what any present time will look like as the past," seeking images that are "literate, authoritative, and transcendent." He photographs the lives of towns and people through images of their houses, factories, churches, auto graveyards, storefronts, empty streets, advertising and signs, and sharecroppers and other anonymous, down-and-out Americans, saying, "I am fascinated by man's work and the civilization that he's built. In fact, I think that's *the* interesting thing in the world, what man makes." In the late 1930s, Evans collaborates with writer James Agee (1909-1955) on a photo-essay project about tenant farmers, commissioned but never published by *Fortune* magazine, communicating a time and place through their text and images. It is published in book form in 1941 as *Let Us Now Praise Famous Men,* and Agee writes that "all of consciousness is shifted from the imagined, the revisive, to the effort to perceive simply the cruel radiance of what is. This is why the camera seems to me, next to unassisted and weaponless consciousness, the central instrument of our time."

WORLD EVENTS

• Adolf Hitler assumes the title of Fuhrer on the death of President Paul von Hindenburg, and nullifies the Treaty of Versailles by beginning to rearm Germany.

1935

ARTS AND LITERATURE

• The Works Progress Administration (WPA) is formed, under Harry Hopkins (1890–1946), to create jobs for millions of visual artists, musicians, writers, actors, dancers, and photographers; to educate art students; to expand art programs to rural areas; and to research the cultural heritage of the U.S. In a series of public-works programs involving the arts, artists of all disciplines are paid to do their work with unrestricted freedom of expression. The WPA projects offer a rare and important moment of dialogue in American art and culture, in which individual artists meet with government agencies and communities to foster experiments that will be immediately integrated into the daily lives of the community. The coming of World War II, and criticism from the press and Congress that expresses fears that subversive propaganda is being promoted through the arts projects, leads to its demise.

• The New York theater season premieres plays that explore an intensity of political consciousness new to mainstream American theater. The Group Theatre produces *Waiting for Lefty,* a one-act play about a taxi drivers' strike, written by Clifford Odets (1906–1963). Odets accurately calls it a "machine gun," causing the audience to jump to its feet and join the ending call for "Strike! Strike!" Odets also premieres *Awake and Sing* this year, a full-length play about a Jewish family living in the Bronx during the Great Depression. Maxwell Anderson (1888–1959) wins a New York

Drama Critics Circle Award for *Winterset*, his three-act play on the Sacco and Vanzetti case, where he seeks "to make tragic poetry out of the stuff" of real life events.

• *Porgy and Bess,* an opera composed by George Gershwin with libretto by DuBose Heyward and lyrics by Heyward and Ira Gershwin, premieres at the Alvin Theater in New York, and creates the first grand opera in American musical idiom.

• A year after choreographer George Balanchine (b. Russia, 1904–1983) arrives in the U.S., he establishes the School of American Ballet in New York City at the invitation of dance patron and impresario Lincoln Kirstein (1907–1966), who wants to extend the classical European tradition with an American-bred look. Within six months, Balanchine and Kirstein also form the American Ballet Company, using mostly students. Balanchine premieres *Serenade,* a dance that exemplifies the basic aspects of his artistic aesthetic: no star casting, and avoidance of guest artists, decor, scenery, and great works of music, with the main focus on pure dance— generally without the use of plot. The company goes through a reconfiguration as Ballet Caravan before taking its present name as the New York City Ballet. He modernizes ballet technique to accept turned-in coordinations and flexed feet of modern dance, unexpected combinations of steps, and shifts of accent of African-American dance; and he discards the ballerina tutu to glorify the stripped-down shape of leotards and body-revealing unitards that profoundly change the image and force of American and international ballet.

• *Your Hit Parade,* a weekly radio show, begins broadcasting, with a countdown of the ten latest and greatest tunes, innovating a for-

Maria Tallchief (b. on an Osage reservation near Fairfax, Oklahoma, 1925), one of the first principal dancers with the New York City Ballet, who helped define the long-legged, extended look that Balanchine developed in the United States, in one of the many roles he choreographed for her as Eurydice in *Orpheus,* which premiered in 1948. *(New York Public Library for the Performing Arts, courtesy George P. Lynes, II, executor, estate of George P. Lynes)*

mat that remains popular on radio stations today, and is carried over to TV. The recording industry finds it can manipulate the outcome by creating hits with under-the-counter payoffs to disk jockeys, or by pressuring stores to feature certain artists, a practice that generally favors white artists and is periodically exposed as a scandal.

• Texas-born country fiddle player/singer Bob Wills and his Texas Playboys make their first recordings for Columbia Records, thus popularizing the country swing idiom. Pat-

"Leaning on a shovel" skit from New York City production of *Sing for Your Supper,* Federal Theater Project, WPA, May 1939. By an unknown photographer. *(National Archives, Records of the Works Progress Administration)*

Printers making serigraph posters for New York City Art Project. By Rose, 1940. *(National Archives, Records of the Works Progress Administration)*

Federal Art Project Class in Harlem during the 1930s. Photographer unknown. *(Schomburg Center for Research in Black Culture, WPA Photograph Collection, Photographs and Prints Division)*

Copyists working for the Federal Music Project at the Free Library in Philadelphia, Pennsylvania, January 1936. *(National Archives, Records of the Works Progress Administration)*

terned after jazz, big-band swing added to the basic country string band, country swing, and through Wills's leadership finds novel uses for horn and rhythm sections.

• The Indian Arts and Crafts Act of 1935 promotes the production and marketing of the work of Native American artists, providing economic benefit to revitalize many tribes and officially acknowledging their important contributions to the cultural life of the nation. Under the Indian Arts and Crafts Board, funding goes to workshops that revive traditional skills of weaving, woodworking, pottery, leather, and beadwork.

GOVERNMENT AND POLITICS

• The Welch Bill, or Repatriation Act of 1935, signed by President Roosevelt, puts pressure on Filipinos living in the U.S. to leave, by offering transportation funds back to the islands for Filipinos who "volunteer" to leave the U.S. and never return. Only 2,190 people decide to relocate, as most Filipinos see this as an insult. However, when the Relief Appropriation Act of 1937 legislates public assistance preferences for U.S. citizens, and then to aliens with the right to become citizens, since Filipinos are now classified as "aliens" and are therefore not eligible for relief, many return home, and their immigration to the mainland or Hawaii significantly declines.

• The U.S. Supreme Court declares Roosevelt's "New Deal" programs in the National Recovery Act of 1933 unconstitutional in *Schechter Poultry Corp. v. U.S.,* requiring sweeping changes based on this seemingly insignificant case involving a Brooklyn poultry business charged with NRA code violations. The ruling declares that Congress has given "virtually unfettered" powers to the NRA that are "utterly

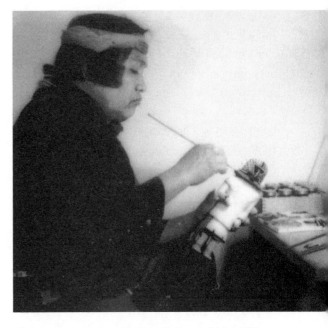

Hopi artist painting a Kachina doll, c. 1941-1942, by Dorothy F. Whiting. *(National Archives, Records of the Indian Arts and Crafts Board)*

inconsistent" with its duties, and will lead to Roosevelt's consideration of a plan to "pack" the Court with more sympathetic judges by 1937.

• The Wagner Act gives workers the right to join labor unions and collectively bargain for their rights. It also institutes the National Labor Relations Board to supervise collective bargaining.

• Congress passes the Social Security Act of 1935, a federal old-age pension for people no longer able to work, financed by a payroll tax on employees and employers. Title V provides maternal and child health services for the first time, including Aid to Families with Dependent Children. The act is amended in 1939 to provide surviving spouses with their deceased spouse's benefits, and later is amended further to provide benefits for the handicapped. The first monthly payments will start in 1942, with amounts determined at a percentage of the payroll contributions made into the system for each individual's account. Social Security is the longest-lasting government program adopted under President Roosevelt's New Deal, and perhaps the most controversial. The safety net it offers also leads to an expansion of government bureaucracy by beginning a welfare system that will eventually encompass health, through Medicare and Medicaid, and education, through Head Start.

BUSINESS AND INDUSTRY

• John L. Lewis (1880–1969) and the United Mine Workers establish the Committee for Industrial Organization, to advocate for organizing mass-production workers by their industries, such as auto, steel, and aviation, instead of by their crafts. They are expelled from the AFL and form the Congress of Industrial Organizations (CIO). By 1938 the CIO will claim a membership of 4 million. Lewis serves as its president from 1935 to 1940.

SCIENCE AND TECHNOLOGY

• Kodachrome, a color film transparency stock, is invented by Leopold Mannes and Leopold Godowsky. The film is sensitive to the three primary colors and will shortly become more popular than black and white.

• The "fluorescent lumiline lamp," a gas-filled two-foot tube that emits a bright green light, is introduced as a laboratory experiment by the General Electric Company at the annual convention of the Illuminating Engineering Society of Cincinnati, Ohio. In 1939 fluorescent lighting is launched commercially by both GE and Westinghouse. Fluorescent lighting requires less energy than standard light bulbs, a feature that increases their use in the latter part of the century.

CULTURE AND SOCIETY

• George Gallup, a statistician, establishes the American Institute of Public Opinion, which will produce the Gallup Poll, the most familiar gauge of popular opinion, whose findings are widely reported by the media.

• Alcoholics Anonymous (AA), an organization of self-professed alcoholics helping other alcoholics beat their addiction through abstinence, is founded by two men struggling against their own alcoholism, William Griffith Wilson, a New York stockbroker, and Robert Holbrook Smith, an Akron, Ohio, surgeon. AA devises meetings in which recovered alcoholics describe their experiences, provides a network where alcoholics who no longer drink help uncontrolled drinkers, and creates a "twelve step" program for members to practice, a litany that helps people stay sober based on a Christian model of confession, prayer, and redemption. By 1945, AA has 15,000 members, and by 1992, two million. AA becomes a model for programs that help their members overcome other obsessive addictions, such as drugs, sex, and food.

• Communist agitators cause the Harlem Riot, according to the white press, which start from a false rumor that an African American youth was beaten to death by police when he was caught shoplifting. But local community leaders cite more basic causes: widespread unemployment, as thousands stand around on street corners, in a situation exacerbated by the opposition of white merchants in the community to hiring African Americans; and an absence of New Deal programs directed to the Harlem community.

World Events

• Mussolini's Italian Fascist troops march into Ethiopia, and Emperor Haile Selassie calls on his people to fight for the survival of the only independent black state in Africa, while the rest of the world, including the League of Nations, does not intervene.

• The Jews of Germany lose all civil rights when Adolf Hitler signs the Nuremberg Laws, including their German citizenship as well as their right to vote, hold public office, practice a profession, or have any social interactions with non-Jews, including marriage; existing marriages between Jews and non-Jews are legally nullified. Many Jews choose to leave Germany rather than wait for the situation to inevitably worsen.

1936

Arts and Literature

• Katherine Dunham (b. 1912) receives a Rosenwald Travel Fellowship to study "Anthropology and the Dance" for eighteen months in the West Indies islands of Martinique, Jamaica, Trinidad, and Haiti. She chooses these locations for her ethnic research into ceremonial and community celebrations because the survival of African cultural connections is far stronger there than in the U.S. The materials she gathers will provide the basis for her development as a major choreographer, and she will adapt West Indian folk dance styles to fit into the worlds of nightclubs, concert dance, and film and Broadway musicals.

• Robert Johnson (1911–1938), a young Mississippi Delta blues creator, records the first of his only two sessions (twenty-nine cuts in all) in Texas for Vocalion Records. When young jazz enthusiast and producer John Hammond hears the first of these, he immediately tries to get Johnson to New York to appear on his planned "Spirituals to Swing" concerts, but it is too late; the young blues genius has died, probably violently, from a love affair gone wrong.

• Frank Lloyd Wright begins designing a private family weekend home called Fallingwater, on commission from Edgar J. Kaufmann, owner of a Pittsburgh department store. He integrates the home with its setting by creating a cantilevered structure placed over a waterfall at Bear Run in western Pennsylvania, rather than following a more conventional solution of building next to or above the stream. Considered a masterpiece of twentieth-century art today, it is completed in 1938 and the family will live there until 1963, when they place it under the care of the Western Pennsylvania Conservancy, who continue to maintain it for public viewing.

Government and Politics

• The Virgin Islands, a U.S. territory in the Caribbean, is granted the right to elect its own legislature by an act of Congress.

• President Franklin Roosevelt is elected to his second term, with John Nance Garner continuing as vice president, defeating Alf Landon by a landslide, in spite of widespread opposition from the press. The New Deal reforms succeed in breaking independent radical support, as third-party candidates such as Socialist Party nominee Norman Thomas wins only 187,000 as compared with the 881,000 he received in 1932.

BUSINESS AND INDUSTRY

• Henry Luce (1903–1967) founds *Life* magazine, a photographic news and feature weekly publication that flourishes by using "eyewitness reports," a new format of documentary photo essays that has been emerging and continues to dominate the look of popular news magazines.

◉ 1934

WORLD EVENTS

• Adolf Hitler opens the 1936 Olympic Games in Berlin. He leaves the stadium humiliated after African American Jesse Owens (1913–1980) wins four gold medals in track and long jump. Owens is one of ten African Americans who win medals in this Olympics, thereby dashing the Nazis' hopes of using the Olympics to prove their theory of Aryan racial superiority.

• The Spanish Civil War begins, presaging World War II, when army generals in the south revolt against the Popular Front government, a newly elected coalition of socialists, communists, syndicalists, and left-wing Republicans. General Francisco Franco and his fascist alliance are supported by the foreign interventions of Hitler and Mussolini. In 1937 the Lincoln Brigade, a volunteer force of about 3,000 Americans, joins the fight on the side of the Republicans against the fascists. There will be 50,000 civilian casualties on both sides of this bloody war that ends three years later, when General Franco's dictatorship begins with the surrender of Madrid in 1939.

• Germany reoccupies the Rhineland, defying the treaties of Versailles and Locarno.

• Mussolini's Italian army conquers Ethiopia, backed by Hitler. Emperor Haile Selassie flees before they capture Addis Ababa, the capital. Hitler finds encouragement in the fact that the world does not come to the aid of the Ethiopians. When the League of Nations votes to censure Italy in 1937, Italy walks out of the organization.

• The BBC starts the world's first public high-definition electronic television service in London. (There are about 2,000 television sets in use worldwide.) They stop broadcasting in the middle of a Mickey Mouse cartoon on September 1, 1939, when Britain enters World War II, and resume where they left off when the war ends, in 1945.

1937

ARTS AND LITERATURE

• John Cage (1912–1992), the first composer to focus on the use of "found" sound, presents his manifesto, *The Future of Music: Credo,* at a Seattle arts society meeting, in which he presciently outlines the necessary elements to change perceptions of what can be called music. He defines music in the twentieth century as "organization of sound," and declares his intention to include noise as part of the entire field of sounds, since "wherever we are, what we hear is mostly noise." He predicts that compositions will require the aid of electrical instruments in order to "capture and control these sounds, to use them not as sound effects, but as musical instruments." Since composers will need to look for new forms of writing their compositions, he suggests models present in percussion music, as practiced in "Oriental cultures and hot jazz," because they have found ways to represent rhythmic structure in a composition "free from the concept of a fundamental tone."

• Architect Ludwig Mies van der Rohe (b. Germany, 1886–1969) relocates the Bauhaus School in Chicago, after the Nazis close its last German-based location in Berlin in 1933. The New Bauhaus, later renamed the Institute of Design at the Illinois Institute of Technology, has a campus designed by Mies van der Rohe, and is directed by visual artist and critic Laszlo Moholy-Nagy (b. Hungary, 1895–1946). The New Bauhaus brings the Bauhaus aesthetic into prominence in the U.S., influencing all American arts, especially industrial design and architecture, where its effects can be seen in the glass-walled skyscrapers, built in the 1950s, that line New York's Park Avenue, and in the government-subsidized high-rise, low-income projects of Chicago, New York, St. Louis, and other cities.

GOVERNMENT AND POLITICS

• By suggesting that the number of judges be increased at all levels, President Roosevelt takes on the court system in general, and especially the Supreme Court, which has made many rulings that curb his legislative programs. Since the Supreme Court is currently composed solely of conservatives over sixty years of age, with six over seventy, Roosevelt devises his so-called "court-packing bill" to circumvent a constitutional amendment. The bill would give the president power to increase the nine-member Supreme Court by up to six appointments, if any of its judges over seventy refuses to retire. However, after the Court upholds some rulings favorable to New Deal legislation, especially sustaining the new social security bill, Congress only effects moderate changes.

BUSINESS AND INDUSTRY

• Drought finally ends in the U.S., but stem rust attacks the wheat crop, causing further devastation across the Midwestern and Western farm belt.

SCIENCE AND TECHNOLOGY

• The Golden Gate Bridge, a suspension bridge spanning San Francisco Bay, is opened to the public. Designed by Joseph Strauss, it is the longest suspension bridge in the world until 1964.

WORLD EVENTS

• Hitler chooses works of art that he believes are threatening to morality, including works by Paul Klee, George Grosz (b. Germany, 1893; d. U.S., 1959), Emil Nolde (German, 1867–1956), and Lyonel Feininger, displaying them publicly for one last time in Munich as the "Degenerate Art Exhibit."

1938

ARTS AND LITERATURE

• Writer and anthropologist Zora Neale Hurston's book of Negro folklore, *Tell My Horse*, is published. Using her field research in Jamaica and Haiti, she tracks how African stories survived the diaspora in the Americas, and includes an appendix of Haitian songs that are possibly the first published transcriptions of Haitian Creole.

• Katherine Dunham forms her own company, choreographing a new theatrical form of American modern dance that blends Caribbean rhythms and American technique. As a member of the Negro Unit of the Chicago branch of the Federal Theatre Project, Dunham premieres

Choreographer Katherine Dunham (c. 1945–1946) performing with her company members in *Tropical Revue,* which premiered at New York's Martin Beck Theatre in 1943. It included movement taken from religious and secular African and African American dance forms, such as the use in "Plantation Dances" of the "Cake-Walk," "Juba," "Ballin' the Jack," and "Strut." *(Dance Collection, New York Public Library of Performing Arts)*

L'Ag'Ya, inspired by her anthropological research in Martinique.

• Viola Spolin uses games to develop new techniques of improvisational theater while directing children's theater in a WPA project at Hull House in Chicago. The games, like any sport, have rules to be followed so that the director does not have to intrude by telling performers "do this" or "do that." They help performers be themselves, rather than becoming some idea of a character as in the Stanislavsky Method, and they keep performers working together, focused on what is happening at every moment. In 1939 she introduces the concept of using audience suggestions to create scenes, one of hundreds of "theater games" that in 1963 are published in Spolin's classic reference for actors, directors, teachers, and group leaders, *Improvisation for the Theater.* Her theater-games approach will help create the explosion of theater experiments in the 1950s and 1960s, both in experimental off-off Broadway companies and in comedy companies such as the Compass and Second City, besides proving useful in therapeutic work and in training workshops for business executives.

• Playwright Thornton Wilder (1897–1975) premieres his experimental drama *Our Town* on Broadway. Using little scenery to suggest its tour of life in a New England community, *Our Town* becomes the most performed American play of the century, owing to its popularity with schools, community theaters, and professional companies.

• "Primitivism in Modern Art," the first scholarly investigation of the relationship between African art and Western modern art, is published by Robert Goldwater, a New York University historian.

• Native American visual artists Stephen Mopope (Kiowa, 1989–1974), Velino Herrera (Zia Pueblo, 1902–1973), Gerald Nailor (Navajo, 1917–1952), James Auchiah (Kiowa, 1906–1975), and Woodrow Crumbo (Creek/Potawatomi, 1912–1989) are commissioned by Secretary of the Interior Harold Ickes to create murals that are a "symbol of a new day," to decorate 2,200 feet of the Department of the Interior's building in Washington, D.C.

• The Novachord, an electric keyboard instrument that simulates the sounds of many instruments, is invented by Laurens Hammond and manufactured by the Hammond Organ Company. It can sound like a harpsichord, strings, brasses, reeds, and other instruments. It is, in essence, the first synthesizer.

• Floyd Smith records "Floyd's Guitar Blues" with the Andy Kirk band. It is thought to be the first serious use of the electric guitar. Eddie Durham, trombonist and arranger for Jimmy Lunceford and Count Basie, experiments with electrically amplifying the guitar. But it is the rhythmic, harmonic, and phrasing imagination of the Texas-born Charlie Christian (1919–1942), especially as exhibited with the Benny Goodman band and sextet, that brings the instrument into world prominence.

• The Bennie Goodman Sextet (Goodman, Charlie Christian, Gene Krupa, Lionel Hampton, and Teddy Wilson, pianist) creates the first interracial jazz group.

• At Carnegie Hall, young record producer John Hammond produces "Spirituals to Swing," bringing to the straight public a host of boogie-woogie, gospel, and jazz artists of the future in an interracial format. A relative of the Vanderbilts and a determined anti-segregationist, Hammond, as a record company executive, is also responsible for the discovery of such artists as Fletcher Henderson, Billie Holiday, Bessie Smith, Count Basie, Benny Goodman, Teddy Wilson, Charlie Christian, Bob Dylan, Aretha Franklin, George Benson, and Bruce Springsteen.

GOVERNMENT AND POLITICS

• The House of Representatives creates the House Un-American Activities Committee (HUAC), ostensibly to keep watch over all such activities it considers subversive to the government, including those of Communists on the left and Nazis on the right. However, the left will soon receive its total focus.

• The Fair Labor Standards Act sets a minimum wage and a forty-hour work week, and prohibits child labor in businesses employed in interstate commerce.

BUSINESS AND INDUSTRY

• President Roosevelt recommends that Congress appropriate funding to build up the armed forces. The economy starts to take an upturn that will continue through the duration of World War II, into February 1945.

• The Allen B. DuMont Company produces the first all-electronic television in the U.S. Allen B. DuMont also forms a network, in competition with RCA.

• DuPont begins to market its first product made of nylon, a toothbrush. DuPont scientists, who have been working on developing nylon fiber for a decade, will soon be marketing many other products, such as clothing, that are made of the new material.

SCIENCE AND TECHNOLOGY

• Roy J. Plunkett, a chemist for the DuPont Company, accidentally discovers a plastic, which he calls Teflon, in the residue of refrigeration gases. Teflon will be kept secret from the general public until 1946 because of its many possible military applications, including use by the Manhattan Project.

CULTURE AND SOCIETY

• Orson Welles (1915–1985) produces and directs *The War of the Worlds*, in a radio version of the 1898 H. G. Wells novel, scripted by

Howard Koch. The verité style of the broadcast creates a panic among listeners, some of whom believe that Martians have actually landed.

WORLD EVENTS

• German scientists Otto Hahn and Fritz Strassmann, while working on splitting the uranium atom, discover that bombardment of a uranium nucleus with a slow-moving proton produces elements considerably lighter than uranium. Though they are too reticent to call their discovery fission, their work will soon lead to evidence of the fission chain reaction at the heart of the awesome power of the atomic bomb. Hahn will go on to win the Nobel Prize in physics in 1944 for his contributions in fission. ▣ 1939

• Swiss chemist Albert Hofmann, looking for a treatment for respiratory problems, synthesizes lysergic acid diethylamide (LSD) at Sandoz Laboratory in Basel. Finding that the fungus-derived compound does not work for this purpose, he shelves it until five years later, in 1943, when he accidentally absorbs some through his hands after touching the stored container and experiences "extreme activity of imagination." Three days later he deliberately ingests the LSD, discovering its hallucinogenic properties. The chemical compound will be widely used in the 1960s and 1970s.

• Ladoslao and Georg Biro, two Hungarian brothers, invent the ballpoint pen, which is introduced in the U.S. after World War II.

• Germany officially endorses acts of anti-Semitism. On *Kristallnacht*, November 9, 7,000 Jewish shops are looted and hundreds of synagogues are burned during a night of Nazi violence.

• The Munich Agreement of September 30 between Britain, Germany, France, and Italy allows for the German annexation of the Sudetenland (the border regions in Czechoslovakia of Bohemia, Moravia, and Silesia).

1939

ARTS AND LITERATURE

• The film *Gone With the Wind* is released. This screen version of the Margaret Mitchell (1900–1949) novel of the Civil War and Reconstruction period presents an early feminist protagonist and depicts slaves as loyal and docile. It becomes the most-seen movie in history. In 1940, Hattie McDaniel (1895–1952) will become the first African American to receive an Oscar, for best supporting actress for her role as Mammy in this film.

• Jazz singer Billie Holiday (1915–1959) records "Strange Fruit," a song about the lynching of blacks in the South.

• African American classical contralto Marian Anderson (1900?–1993) sings a celebrated concert to a crowd of 75,000 on the steps of the Lincoln Memorial in Washington, D.C., after being denied permission to sing at the city's Constitution Hall by the hall's owners, the Daughters of the American Revolution (DAR). Eleanor Roosevelt resigns from the DAR and, with Harold Ickes, Secretary of the Interior, helps make the arrangements for the Lincoln Memorial concert.

• Self-taught painter Anna Mary Robertson Moses (1860–1961), better known as Grandma Moses, who begins painting at the age of seventy-eight, receives her first exhibit at the Museum of Modern Art.

• Moses Asch stimulates interest in American folk and world music when he founds Disc

Records (later renamed Folkways Records) and spends the next forty years recording talents from more than forty American states, including professional singers, Native American healers, blues and jazz musicians, poets, workers, and other people in their communities. The great folklorist Alan Lomax discovers a Southern African-American ex-convict, Huddie "Leadbelly" Ledbetter (1885–1949), and Asch produces his first album, with Leadbelly singing children's songs, accompanying himself on a twelve-string guitar. He records everything Woody Guthrie (1912–1967) brings to him, including "This Land Is Your Land." Asch records Ella Jenkins, Cisco Houston, Pete Seeger (b. 1919), and the Weavers. By the late 1950s, popular mainstream musicians such as Bob Dylan, the Rolling Stones, Miles Davis, and the Grateful Dead find inspiration in the archives, which are acquired by the Smithsonian.

GOVERNMENT AND POLITICS

• Congress passes the Neutrality Act of 1939. It registers a shift in U.S. policy, by lifting an arms embargo against all belligerent nations. Prodded on by President Roosevelt, it signals favor for the Allies' cause, by allowing Britain and France to buy American weapons, as long as they carry them back home on their own ships.

BUSINESS AND INDUSTRY

• Pan American Airways begins transatlantic air service with their fleet of three Boeing Clipper seaplanes. The first flight of the first twenty-two passengers to Europe crosses the Atlantic in twenty-two hours, with two stops between Port Washington, New York, and Marseille, France. The cost is $375 each direction.

• Engineer William Hewlett (1913–2001) and manager David Packard (1912–1996), considered the "founding fathers" of Silicon Valley, start up a company to manufacture audio oscillators. Financed with a $512 capital investment from Frederick Terman, their Stanford University engineering professor, their first place of business is a garage in Palo Alto, California. Hewlet-Packard (HP) will go on to build electronic testing equipment, the first desktop calculator and handheld calculator, and will eventually become the world's leading producer of microcomputers and the largest company in the Bay Area. The relaxed, comparatively informal atmosphere and decentralized, participatory management style that they cultivate will become generally accepted as the Silicon Valley business style. The garage will be designated a state historical landmark, honored as the birthplace of Silicon Valley.

SCIENCE AND TECHNOLOGY

• FM radio is invented. Initially FM offers an alternative to the highly commercialized AM radio stations, as FM stations tailor their programming to local community interests, providing in-depth news coverage and a broader cultural focus than is available on the AM stations, besides providing an outlet for college and listener-sponsored stations, such as National Public Radio and Pacifica. However, the majority of FM stations also get taken over by commercial interests, although they generally remain targeted to programming not available on AM, such as all-classical or all-jazz music formats.

• Because of the fear that Nazi Germany might develop an atomic bomb before the U.S., physicist Leo Szilard persuades Albert Einstein to write the first of four letters to President

ALBERT EINSTEIN
OLD GROVE RD.
NASSAU POINT
PECONIC, LONG ISLAND

F. D. ROOSEVELT
PRESIDENT OF THE U.S.
WHITE HOUSE
WASHINGTON, D.C.

AUGUST 2nd, 1939

Sir:

Some recent work by E. Fermi and L. Szilard, which has been communicated to me in manuscript, leads me to expect that the element uranium may be turned into a new and important source of energy in the immediate future. Certain aspects of the situation which has arisen seem to call for watchfulness and, if necessary, quick action on the part of the Administration. I believe therefore that it is my duty to bring to your attention the following facts and recommendations:

In the course of the last four months it has been made probable—through the work of Joliot in France as well as Fermi and Szilard in America—that it may become possible to set up a nuclear chain reaction in a large mass of uranium, by which vast amounts of power and large quantities of new radium-like elements would be generated. Now it appears almost certain that this could be achieved in the immediate future.

This new phenomenon would also lead to the construction of bombs, and it is conceivable—though much less certain—that extremely powerful bombs of a new type may thus be constructed. A single bomb of this type, carried by boat and exploded in a port, might very well destroy the whole port together with some of the surrounding territory. However, such bombs might very well prove to be too heavy for transportation by air. . . .

(EXCERPT COURTESY OF ARGONNE NATIONAL LABORATORY)

Franklin D. Roosevelt concerning U.S. development of an atomic bomb. This letter initiates the largest enterprise in science history: the Manhattan Project, in which $2.2 billion will be spent and 43,000 people will be employed. The project will result in the explosion of two atomic bombs on the Japanese cities of Hiroshima and Nagasaki in 1945.

• Physicist John Dunning's (1907–1975) cyclotron at Columbia University is the first in the U.S. to split an atom, in this year when Ernest O. Lawrence wins a Nobel Prize in physics for his invention and development of the cyclotron.

• Russian-born aeronautical engineer Igor Sikorsky (1889–1972) invents and tests the

VS-300 helicopter prototype near Stratford, Connecticut. Its larger horizontal rotor and smaller vertical rotor in the tail are features that characterize future models. Production begins in 1942.

• John Atanasoff and Clifford Berry design and make the first electronic digital computer by applying Boolean algebra to computer circuitry (mathematician George Boole's [1815–1864] binary system of algebra states that mathematical equations can be presented as true or false). Atanasoff and Berry translate that principle to electric circuitry, thinking of a circuit as being either on or off. However, World War II keeps this project from developing further.

🖸 1951, 1953

• Chester Carlson takes out a patent for his "electrophotography," the technology that leads to the Xerox copying machine.

• The first disposable can for dispensing liquids under pressure is patented by Julian Seth Kahn of New York. It is first used for spraying paints, poisons, and whipped cream.

• American engineer Earl A. Thompson invents the Hydramatic drive, the precursor of the automatic transmissions that will become a standard feature of American cars.

CULTURE AND SOCIETY

• Twenty-two thousand American Nazis rally in Madison Square Garden, listening to speeches denouncing the nation's Jews for their hatred of German Nazis and National Socialism, with 1,700 policemen on duty.

• New York plays host to the 1939–1940 World's Fair, with the theme "Building the World of Tomorrow." It opens in Queens, just five months before World War II intervenes and disturbs the vision. Sixty countries and hundreds of commercial exhibitors participate in making it the biggest and most comprehensive international exhibition ever, although Germany is noticeably absent among the foreign exhibitors.

WORLD EVENTS

• World War II begins as Hitler invades Poland. Britain and the Allied powers respond by declaring war on Germany, which plans to recover German lands taken by the treaty of Versailles, including the Rhineland, Czechoslovakia, and Austria.

• The Swiss chemist Paul Muller (1899–1965) introduces dichlorodiphenyl-trichloroethane (DDT) as an effective, inexpensive pesticide. It is widely used over the next twenty years. Many insects develop a resistance to the poison, however, and it proves so toxic to the environment that it will be banned by the FDA in 1972.

• Physicists Lise Meitner (b. Vienna, Austria, 1878; d. England, 1968) and Otto Frisch (Austrian-British, b. Vienna, 1904; Meitner's nephew) interpret the uranium reactions of Otto Hahn and Fritz Strassmann as fission reactions, in which an atom of uranium is split into other, lighter elements with an enormous release of energy. Describing this reaction, they coin the term "nuclear fission" in a paper that will be sent to the journal *Nature*. The paper begins the effort to develop an atomic bomb. One year later, Hungarian-American Leo Szilard (b. Budapest, 1897; d. U.S., 1964) and Walter Zinn confirm observations first made by Hahn and Strassmann that the uranium fission reaction could be self-sustaining because of a chain reaction, the *modus operandi* of the atomic bomb.

🖸 1938

The first version of the modern electronic computer, built by theoretical physicist John Atanasoff and electric engineer Clifford Berry at Iowa State University during 1937-1942. *(Iowa State University Archives, with thanks to John McCarroll, Director of University Relations)*

New York World's Fair poster by Nembhard N. Culin, funded by the Pennsylvania Railroad, 1937. *(Library of Congress, Prints and Photographs Division)*

THE NEW YORK WORLD'S FAIR OF 1939-1940

Here the peoples of the world unite in amity and understanding, impelled by a friendly rivalry, and working toward a common purpose: to set forth their achievements of today and their contributions to the World of Tomorrow. The Fair is a force for peace in the world; for without peace the dream of a better World of Tomorrow is but a cruel and mocking illusion.

(From the official guidebook for the New York World's Fair, 1939–1940)

The "Fair of the Future" planners construct a model of American life, displaying innovative trends that are to shape the second half of the twentieth century, especially in avant-garde architectural and industrial design, new technologies in lighting, film, and color photography, and product promotion through sophisticated styles of advertising. Many "usable future" wonders of science and technology are introduced, including a transparent car by GM and transparent television by RCA; Westinghouse robots; Kodachrome and Polaroid film; fluorescent lighting; and various new cars. "Semiabstract" murals line the walls of the various halls, including the Hall of Fashions; the Building of Science, Medicine, Public Health, and Education; and buildings devoted to Electrical Products, Home Furnishings, Communications, Metals, Marine Transportation, and Consumers. The murals are painted by WPA Federal Art Project artists, including Ilya Bolotowsky (b. Russia, 1907-1981), Byron Browne (1907-1961), Stuart Davis, Willem de Kooning, Lyonel Feininger, Balcomb Greene (1904-1990), Arshile Gorky, Philip Guston (1913-1980), Rockwell Kent (1882-1971), Michael Loew, Eric Mose, Anton Refregier, and Louis Schanker, with outdoor sculptures by Augusta Savage *(The Harp)*, William Zorach (b. Lithuania, 1887-1966), and Alexander Calder's (1898-1976) "ballet of dancing water jets" fountain for Consolidated Edison's City of Light. Although TV has been in commercial development for ten years, it is introduced to the general public for the first time, with RCA, Westinghouse, and General Electric using mobile camera units to make remote broadcasts from various locations on the fairgrounds. For amusement, there is a "crystal gazing palace" designed by theater designer Norman Bel Geddes, where a nearly nude dancer performs in a room of mirrors that reflect her image "a thousandfold"; a parachute jump; a Dream of Venus pavilion by Salvador Dalí (Spain, 1904-1989); the Street of Paris, featuring Gypsy Rose Lee; and Billy Rose's Aquacade starring Olympic backstroke champion Eleanor Holm and Johnny (Tarzan) Weissmuller.

In spite of its unfortunate timing, the fair is a critical success because it presents education as entertainment, a "functional tool to prepare the individual for his or her responsibilities in a changing world and to qualify the citizen for his or her part in a democratic society."

The United States drops its second atomic bomb on Nagasaki, Japan. "Jap's eye view of A-bomb blast" (Bombing of Nagasaki) by Hiromichi Matsudo, September 12, 1946, from New York *World-Telegram and Sun* Newspaper Photograph Collection. *(Library of Congress, Prints and Photographs Division)*

1940–1949

THE 1940S

LAWRENCE DISTASI

*W*hen the forties began i was three years old. too busy roaming our block in the mostly italian

north end of bridgeport, connecticut, to have any idea that my grandpa and great aunt zi'carmela

were supposed to register for the smith act, aka the alien registration act which they probably said

va'napoli to but which would eventually fix the whereabouts of more than six hundred thousand

italian immigrants who, like them, had not yet got citizenship; and which would, shortly after pearl

harbor, cause endless wailing and trouble when my country 'tis of thee declared war on my father's

italy and all those now "enemy aliens" would have to register again including my uncle hector. who

did but whose house not ours was raided by the fbi anyway someone found out he was an enemy

alien with a radio. which my aunt ruth, her family american since before the revolution, was too,

because she married hector with the anti-immigrant provision still on the books saying that an

american woman who married a foreign man forfeited her citizenship. which she did. so in 1942

they lost their radio with shortwave like many old italians which wasn't the worst hundreds got picked up and interned and thousands in california had to move from their homes near the coast and be in by 8 at night and get arrested if they didn't. maybe that's why my father hated fdr he didn't want america at war with italy much less his own brother he loved uncle hector and italy too so when italy invaded france and fdr called it a stab in the back my father cursed and drank wine when fdr died. none of which i knew in 1942 or '44 or even years later because no one talked then or ever it was all more secret than his cold-wave formulas, a shame for fifty years.

no. but i did know about war, cousins going to war, bobby's b-29 shot down over germany never seen again and gus his brother back from africa with a cane, while in the neighborhood lots we dug trenches for war like the movies and knew my cousin marian with a bandana made bullets at remington arms but not about the bomb. no. we heard more about italy being bombed and italians begging for food and dp's wandering dazed in rags. and my mother crying when she saw, they could be her jewish relatives. and italians back from visiting the old country after the war which my father refused to believe it could be so bad he wanted to go back so bad. but never did. the war ruined the italy he had in mind. ruined the america too, the 'pre-war' one, which he always said anything 'pre-war' was good. postwar things got cheap; badly made; changed. not like before nothing but a money-making proposition hell the bomb had dropped so what was the use? trinity now meant not father son and holy ghost but the man-made fireball that changed the world.

which was what it was. changed utterly. little box houses. mothers working. war factories moving, families moving to own their own houses no we can't take care of the old lady anymore or pa either go to hell, because arguing didn't end with laughing wine anymore it ran instantly to walking out and taking sides and everyone suspect and concentration camps and annihilation. which i didn't know then either. at least not that i knew. but you could glimpse it all between features on movietone news or in school the nuns solemn about praying for the conversion of russia because there was something even worse than nazis going on they said, and though the war was over, and though the united nations flew flags on the loew's poli screen and the marshall plan helped big-eyed italians in broken buildings get food and shoes which we sent too sometimes. there was hardly a breath after d-day the postwar war started right away. not a firebomb war this time this time it was cold and silent and made people crazy suspicious again worse than before because now they could really launch a bomb to end all and not over there but right next door in new york this time hell in the g.e. plant on boston avenue near my high school this time. though in our house the important thing still was moving to a new house with not a wine cellar no a basement lab now he had to find the secret formula for the cold wave that curled ladies' hair without a heat machine. which was science, my father said, which was now the thing if you discovered something new in america now you could destroy the world or get rich. or both.

1940

ARTS AND LITERATURE

• Piet Mondrian, a Dutch painter (1872–1944), immigrates to the U.S. He provides a bridge between the Netherlands-based De Stijl Movement, who are advocates of geometric abstraction, and the growing group of U.S. painters interested in using abstract visual language.

• Martha Graham choreographs two masterpieces this year. *El Penitente* is a religious allegory that mixes the traditions of medieval passion plays with observations of pueblo dances and the religious practices of Hispanic flagellants in the American Southwest. *Letter to the World* is a forerunner of the "talking dances" that will become pervasive in the 1980s onward; it contrasts one dancer speaking the poetry of Emily Dickinson (Jean Erdman) with one dancer moving as the poet (Graham).

• The Museum of Modern Art exhibit "Twenty Centuries of Mexican Art," co-sponsored with the Mexican government, climaxes enormous popular acclaim for Mexican muralists' work, now throughout the U.S.: David Siqueiros's murals in Los Angeles; Jose Orozco's at Pomona and Dartmouth Colleges and the New School of Social Research; and Diego Rivera's at the Detroit Institute of the Arts.

• *Cabin in the Sky,* a Broadway musical, is co-choreographed by Katherine Dunham and George Balanchine. The all-black cast stars Ethel Waters and features Dunham and various members of her company.

• Richard Wright (1908–1960) publishes his novel *Native Son,* which shows a new kind of

In April 1940 the U.S. Census lists the total population of the U.S. at 131,669,000, without including Hawaii or Alaska. By 1945, 53.2 percent of housing units are owner-occupied and 46.8 percent are tenant-occupied, the first time that more homes are owned than rented. From 1941 to 1950, the census records the century's highest totals for "aliens apprehended and expelled," including 1,377,210 apprehensions and 110,849 deportations. More than 1.4 million aliens will also leave the U.S. voluntarily. The U.S. Department of Labor's 1940 report finds that women over the age of fourteen comprise 24.3 percent of the labor force, with overall unemployment at 14.6 percent. By 1944, at the height of World War II, the unemployment rate drops to 1.2 percent and rises at the end of the war, in 1945, to 3.9 percent. In 1945, average per capita personal income is $1,223 (U.S. Bureau of Economic Analysis). Of the total population fourteen years of age and older, 2.7 percent are illiterate in 1947; in 1948, 52.9 percent of seventeen-year-olds are high school graduates (U.S. Bureau of the Census).

black male character, different from the type of docile Uncle Toms as in Margaret Mitchell's novel *Gone With the Wind* (1936).

GOVERNMENT AND POLITICS

• The U.S. begins preparations for going to war. The Army Air Force is established, with Major General Henry H. Arnold as its chief. Congress passes the Naval Supply Act and the

Military Supply Act, authorizing over $30 million for defense projects. The United Service Organizations (USO) is set up to provide armed forces and defense industry personnel with social, educational, religious, and welfare services. By December, Roosevelt forms the Office of Production Management, headed by William S. Knudsen, to organize and speed up defense production.

• Native American men register for the draft for the first time in history, with the exception of Seminoles, who, because their nation remains technically at war with the U.S., refuse to register.

• Benjamin O. Davis Sr. becomes the first African American ever to reach the rank of general, and is promoted to brigadier general in the U.S. Army shortly, becoming the highest-ranking black officer in World War II. (His son, Benjamin O. Davis Jr., will become the first African American general in the air force in 1954.)

• The Smith Act, aka the Alien Registration Act, is passed by Congress. It requires all aliens to register with the government and be fingerprinted. Five million comply. It also outlaws any organizations that advocate the overthrow of the U.S. government by force or violence, and, for the first time, sanctions "guilt by association."

• President Franklin Roosevelt defeats Wendell L. Wilkie to be elected for an unprecedented third term, breaking the unwritten rule of a two-term limit that has been in practice since the days of George Washington. Henry A. Wallace is elected as his vice president. Roosevelt takes courage from this vote of confidence. In his end-of-the-year radio address to the nation, known as a "fireside chat," he calls for the U.S. to become an "arsenal of democracy."

BUSINESS AND INDUSTRY

• Although the U.S. is still in a defensive strategy, federal government contracts with industrial and research corporations to design and build planes, tanks, ships, and munitions, begin to lift the economy out of the Great Depression. In the winter of 1939–1940, the Roosevelt Administration makes a decision to support high-level research "into the explosive potential of atomic reactions." Starting with the Uranium Committee, a military-government bureaucracy that becomes part of the National Defense Research Committee (NDRC), scientists work on projects directed by orders given from the Advisory Commission of the Council of Defense. Physicists put aside their theoretical, longer-term research projects to concentrate on research projects that help the war effort. They work on radar research, and submarine, mine, and torpedo detection. By 1942, Bell Labs has over 700 scientists and engineers concentrating on military projects, and eventually 90 percent of their budget is dependent upon military contracts. Standard Oil's Development Company will also be heavily involved, as will government agencies such as the Bureau of Standards and the Department of Agriculture. Columbia, Harvard, Princeton, Cornell, Johns Hopkins, the University of Minnesota, Berkeley, the University of Chicago, and many others do research crucial to what will shortly become known as the Manhattan Project.

▣ 1942, 1945

• By this year the National Broadcasting Company (NBC), founded by David Sarnoff (1891–1971) and owned by RCA, and the Columbia Broadcasting System (CBS), owned by William S. Paley (1901–1990), have become major powers in the communication industry through their radio networks. The Mutual Broadcasting System, a smaller network, petitions the Federal Communications Commission (FCC) to restrain the power of NBC and CBS. The smaller stations charge that they are forced to give up their programming when they affiliate with their networks and are required to sign long-term contracts. In addition, CBS and NBC leave areas of the West and Middle West without any network service, and seek to impose their technical standards on the entire broadcasting industry. By 1941 the FCC brokers an agreement with all broadcasters. It favors competition, ending the five-year contract requirement, allowing stations to change their network affiliations and expanding local control over programming choices. The FCC also sets requirements for engineering standards, including the present FM radio sound and the thirty frames and 525 lines of resolution per second for televised images. During this year, NBC experiments with live television from its New York City station, airing its first commercial breaks, selling Wheaties and Procter & Gamble soap during a baseball game. Once the FCC agreement is worked out in 1941, commercial network television broadcasting is allowed to begin. Starting in July, both NBC and CBS fill fifteen hours per week with New York–based news, cartoons, and sports. NBC still maintains its lead, developing almost 150 programs with close to seventy corporate sponsors.

SCIENCE AND TECHNOLOGY

• In 1940, at a meeting of the American Philosophical Society, RCA's director of electronic development, electronics engineer Vladimir Zworykin demonstrates his newest

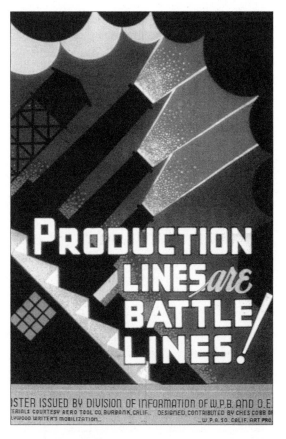

"Production Lines Are Battle Lines!" by Ches Cobb, Southern California Federal Art Project, WPA. Undated serigraph. *(National Archives, Records of the Office of Government Reports)*

invention, an electron microscope that magnifies objects to 100,000 times their size.

• Physicist John Ray Dunning (1907–1975) and a research team at Columbia University separate the isotope uranium-235, lighter and rarer than uranium-238, using a gas-diffusion process. Their experiments corroborate Niels Bohr's theory that uranium-235 is more fissionable than uranium-238. Uranium-235 will become the source of atomic energy needed to construct the first nuclear bomb.

- The term *antibiotic,* used to describe substances that kill bacteria without harming other forms of life, is coined by Russian-American microbiologist Selman Abraham Waksman (b. Russia, 1888; d. U.S., 1973).

- The first color television broadcasts are tested, using a system developed by Peter Carl Goldmark.

WORLD EVENTS

- In both France and Great Britain, pressure for political change increases as the Nazis' threat of war grows closer. In France, the government of Edouard Daladier falls, and finance minister Paul Reynaud forms a new government. In Great Britain, Winston Churchill (1871–1947) replaces Neville Chamberlain as prime minister. He gains public confidence through his unyielding opposition to Hitler and his post as chief of the Admiralty.

- Hitler invades France and signs an armistice with the fascist Vichy government under its premier, Philippe Pétain. He also invades Denmark, the Netherlands, Belgium, and Luxembourg. Mussolini and Hitler meet at the Brenner Pass, and Italy agrees to join the Axis powers against England and France.

- Russian revolutionary leader in exile Leon Trotsky is assassinated in Mexico by a Stalinist agent, while living within a community of friends centered around the artists Frieda Kahlo (1907–1954) and Diego Rivera.

1941

ARTS AND LITERATURE

- European artists Max Ernst (German painter and sculptor, 1891–1959), Andre Breton, and Andre Masson (French painter and sculptor, 1896–1987) request refuge in the U.S., bringing the ideas and techniques of Surrealism and Dada into American art salons, publications, and schools.

- Choreographer and anthropologist Katherine Dunham opens her first official training program, the Dunham School of Dance and Theatre in New York, with a curriculum offering anthropology, playwriting, languages, theater, and speech in addition to dance classes for children and adults. Over the years, the faculty includes directors Jose Ferrer and Lee Strasberg, dancers Syvilla Fort, Jose Limón, and Lavinia Williams, and anthropologist Margaret Mead. The school gives Dunham a base to develop her own dance technique. Although this school dissolves in 1955, Dunham technique evolves into a major style of dance that both maintains its own unique community and influences mainstream modern dance vocabulary.

- Orson Welles directs *Citizen Kane,* widely accepted as one of the most important commercial feature-length films ever made in the U.S. With a script co-written by Welles with Herman J. Mankiewicz, it employs a black-and-white expressionistic film-noir style to express the private motivations behind the public life of a newspaper publisher, basically following the life of the real-life newspaper publishing magnate William Randolph Hearst (1863–1951). Welles freely experiments with a fractured narrative structure that jumps back and forth in time, and with unusual camera angles and new ways to frame the action in the foreground, background, or center of the shot. Instead of editing changes in scenes by using the conventional splice, Welles is the first director to use fade and dissolve techniques as an editing tool.

• Joseph Schillinger, whose students include George Gershwin and Glenn Miller, writes *The Schillinger System of Musical Composition*. This book offers prescriptions for composition, including rhythms, pitches, and harmonies.

• Tap and ballet dancer Gene Kelly (1912–1996) makes his Broadway musical debut performing the title role of *Pal Joey*. Kelly makes an important contribution to the image of the male American dancer, choreographing and directing, on stage and on film, *Anchors Aweigh* (1943), *An American in Paris* (1951), *Singin' in the Rain* (1952), and *Brigadoon* (1954).

• Bebop is created at Minton's and other Harlem clubs, in after-hours jam sessions featuring Charlie Parker (1920–1955), Thelonious Monk (1919–1983), Dizzy Gillespie (1918–1993), Kenny Clarke (1914–1985), and others, establishing the first alternative jazz music to swing and New Orleans styles. Bebop (also called bop) features small ensembles rather than big bands (although bop big bands exist, one led by Dizzy himself), dissonances and unusual harmonies, and solo improvisations with more asymmetrically formed phrases than were customary in earlier periods.

GOVERNMENT AND POLITICS

• President Roosevelt's State of the Union address contains what he considers are the "four essential freedoms" that the people of the U.S. are dedicated to preserving: freedom of speech and expression; freedom of worship; freedom from want; freedom from fear. They will be invoked as a kind of slogan, defining the democratic reasons for fighting against the fascism of the Axis powers.

• The Lend-Lease Act is passed in March, moving the country closer to war by giving the president the go-ahead to furnish arms and war matériel to Britain, France, and other allies seen as critical to U.S. interests.

• Taking advantage of the fact that the Philippines is still a U.S. dependency, President Roosevelt nationalizes their armed forces in July, and places them under the commander of U.S. forces in the Far East, General Douglas MacArthur (1880–1964).

• On October 17 a German U-boat torpedoes the U.S. destroyer *Kearney* near Iceland, and eleven Americans are killed. On October 27, President Roosevelt tells the country that "we have been attacked, the shooting has started," but because of continuing isolationist and neutralist pressure against entering the war, he does not make a formal declaration of war.

• When Japan attacks U.S. bases in the Pacific, beginning with the aerial bombing of the Pearl Harbor naval base in Hawaii on December 7, the U.S. reacts with a formal declaration of war on the Empire of Japan. Within the week the U.S. also declares war on Germany and Italy. The day before the Japanese attack, President Roosevelt signs an executive order that leads to the development of the nuclear-fission bomb that will end the war shortly after it is dropped on Hiroshima and Nagasaki, Japan.

• Almost 400,000 Mexican Americans serve on active duty in the U.S. armed forces, with many rushing to sign up as the country enters World War II. They win proportionately more medals of honor and decorations than any other ethnic group in the U.S. during the war, and suffer proportionately more casualties. Because of their support and wartime promises of equality, returning veterans will optimistically expect equity in civilian life, but their

Pearl Harbor naval base aflame after the Japanese attack, U.S. Navy photo, 1941. *(Library of Congress, Prints and Photographs Division)*

experience will be similar to that of returning African American soldiers after World War I. 🄿 1921, 1943

• Once the U.S. has formally declared war on Japan, Italy, and Germany, U.S. military authorities use lists compiled by the FBI over the previous two years to round up community leaders such as teachers, ministers, and journalists of Italian, German, and Japanese ancestry, including citizens and noncitizens from those countries who live in the U.S. These people are detained for questioning about any activities that might constitute a fifth-column danger (engaging in sabotage, espionage, or subversion). Noncitizens are legally classified as enemy aliens.

BUSINESS AND INDUSTRY

• The Fair Employment Practices Commission (FEPC) is established by President Roosevelt's Executive Order 8802. It eliminates discrimination in employment, specifically outlawing racial discrimination in defense-industry employment, giving legal recourse to African American, Mexican American, and Asian American men and women, besides other groups who frequently experience exclusion based on race. It is issued as a result of pressure from African Americans, and leads to anticipation that this "war for democracy" will keep democracy in the workplace after the war, too.

• Penicillin, the most effective and nontoxic antibiotic, is tested on humans and produced by the U.S. pharmaceutical industry. It will save Allied troops from a venereal disease epidemic. The drug is based on Alexander Fleming's 1926 discovery of penicillin and six years of further testing conducted in England by Oxford University bacteriologist Howard Florey (b. 1898, Australia; d. 1968, England)

and German-Jewish refugee Ernst Chain (b. 1906, Berlin; d. 1979, England). Since Florey and Chain cannot find the resources in wartime Britain to begin manufacturing the drug, a cooperative arrangement is made with the U.S. The two scientists are awarded the Nobel Prize for Physiology or Medicine in 1945.

SCIENCE AND TECHNOLOGY

• Dr. Charles Drew (1904–1950), an African American hematologist, surgeon, scientist, and educator, develops a long-term preservation technique for blood plasma. This innovation becomes especially crucial to saving lives when it is adopted by the U.S. and Britain on World War II battlefields after Dr. Drew founds the first system of blood banks administered under the American Red Cross. He will die after an auto accident, when the nearest "white" hospital refuses to give him blood to save his life.

• The Office of Scientific Research and Development (OSRD) is established by President Roosevelt, with physicist Vannevar Bush (1890–1974) as chairman. The OSRD coordinates scientific and technological projects for the war and defense efforts, including radar, sonar, and the beginning of atomic bomb development. The Manhattan Engineer District, the formal coded military designation for a wartime entity known as the Manhattan Project, is formed as a section of the Army Corps of Engineers and given instructions to find numerous geographically "inaccessible" sites where different components of a project can be developed, in secret liaison with various university laboratories throughout the country. This highly secret project will lead to the development and assembly of Trinity, the code word for the first test of the atomic bomb, the most destructive weapon in history.

🎞 1945

CULTURE AND SOCIETY

• Although two-thirds of people of Japanese ancestry in the U.S. are American citizens, newspaper columnists spread wild rumors about Japanese saboteurs, and refer to Japanese Americans as "Nips," "Japs," and "yellow vermin." Henry McLemore of the Hearst papers and nationally syndicated columnist Walter Lippmann call for the evacuation of all Japanese from the West Coast to the interior of the country.

• The security goals of the Manhattan Project create a compartmentalized culture with an upward chain of command in which instructions come from the top, and workers are kept ignorant of the significance of their work, whether they are production-line workers, taught only the specific job they are to do, or high-level physicists. It will take fifty-seven years for the U.S. government to admit that the industrial processes used to make nuclear weapons exposed workers to radiation and chemical hazards from uranium, plutonium, and fluorine, leading to cancer and early death.

WORLD EVENTS

• Seventeen-thousand-year-old Paleolithic Period cave paintings are discovered by four young men in a cave in Lascaux, in the Pyrenees Mountains of southwest France. There are over 1,500 pictures using thirteen different techniques, including painting with fingers and sticks and spray-painting through hollow bone or mouth. They represent mainly animal figures, but also include signs and humans.

Thought to be connected to hunting or some other ritual, the paintings remain the earliest known examples of painting.

- The Atlantic Charter, drafted by U.S. President Roosevelt and British Prime Minister Winston Churchill in a secret meeting off the coast of Newfoundland, is signed on September 24 by fifteen anti-Axis nations, including the USSR. Listing eight goals for the world, it states that countries should "seek no aggrandizement, territorial or other," and that it is "the right of peoples to choose the form of government under which they will live." The charter brings the U.S. closer to the war and provides the beginning of a plan that will be adopted by the United Nations after the war.

1942

ARTS AND LITERATURE

- The WPA Art Project becomes the Graphic Section of the War Services Program.

- Marcel Duchamp establishes permanent residence in New York City.

- Peggy Guggenheim (1898–1979), a collector and art patron who is niece of the founder of the Guggenheim Museum, opens a gallery, Art of This Century, at 30 West 57th Street, New York City, where she will exhibit her collection and give the first solo shows to Ad Reinhardt (1913–1967), Robert Motherwell, Clyfford Still (1904–1980), Hans Hofmann (1880–1966), and Jackson Pollock before she closes it by turning it over to Betty Parsons, in 1947, and establishes a museum in a palazzo in Venice.

- Latin jazz in a form called Cubop (for "Cuban bebop") takes form with the formation of the Machito Big Band, led by Machito

(b. Havana, Cuba, 1909?; d. London, England, 1984) but mainly indebted to the arranger and trumpeter Mario Bauza, who played in the 1930s for Noble Sissle's and Chick Webb's Harlem swing bands and who played alongside Dizzy Gillespie in Cab Calloway's band. Machito's pianist, the Puerto Rican Joe Loco, is also a big contributor to the new sound.

GOVERNMENT AND POLITICS

- Congressional Bill H.R. 1844 makes it possible for Filipinos with permanent residency status to become naturalized citizens; by enlisting in the military, many others become eligible for citizenship.

- Women's military service is established when Congress passes a bill creating the Women's Auxiliary Army Corps. The bill is introduced by Representative Edith Nourse Rogers (1881–1960) in May 1941, and is passed three weeks after Pearl Harbor, with the approval of the secretary of war. By 1943, Rogers succeeds in driving through a bill that drops the auxiliary status of the women's corps. Besides the navy and army nursing corps, the army forms a women's branch called the WACS, the navy forms the WAVES, the marines the MCWR, and the Coast Guard the SPARS. Close to 350,000 women serve in the military, mostly in nursing and clerical positions, although they also engage in jobs such as weather forecasting, photography, air traffic control, cartography, motor mechanics, and computing. One thousand women fly commercial and air transport planes, and even serve as test pilots in the Women's Air Force Service Pilots corps (WASP), a feat that is barely mentioned until the 1980s.

"Getting on Evacuation Bus, Centerville, California." Photo by Dorothea Lange, 1942. (*National Archives: Still Picture Division*)

Richmond School Children: every hand up signifies a child not born in California, c. 1942. Photo by Dorothea Lange. (*Copyright the Dorothea Lange Collection, the Oakland Museum Collection, City of Oakland. Gift of Paul S. Taylor.*)

• Sixteen B-25 bombers, led by Lt. Col. James H. Doolittle, conduct the first U.S. raid on Tokyo, Japan.

• In February, Japanese submarines shell an oil refinery near Santa Barbara, California, in the first of a few incidents in which the U.S. mainland experiences an attack by Axis forces. In June, the Japanese submarines also shell the Oregon coast, and eight German saboteurs and spies are picked up as they attempt to land off the coast at New York's Long Island and Ponte Vedra Beach, Florida. The Germans are brought to trial in August, and six are electrocuted and two others imprisoned.

• California, Oregon, Washington, and Arizona are designated as military areas from which suspect peoples could be excluded, by Executive Order 9066. One month later, President Roosevelt authorizes the internment of 120,313 Japanese Americans living in those states, including 41,000 first-generation aliens *(issei)* and 72,000 second-generation citizens *(nisei)*. The majority of people are relocated to ten concentration camps placed on lands taken from the Pima and Mojave Indian reservations. The first camp is opened on May 8, 1942, in Poston, Arizona, and the last is closed in December 1947 in Crystal City, Texas. Other camps are located in Manzanar and Tule Lake, California; Gila River, Arizona; Heart Mountain, Wyoming; Amache, Colorado; Minidoka, Idaho; Topaz, Utah; and Rohwer and Jerome, Arkansas. The total loss in sales of property left behind and freezing of assets is estimated to be more than $400 million. In addition, Ellis Island and other immigration facilities are used as detention and internment stations for enemy aliens, under the authority of the Immigration and Naturalization Service.

An estimated 8,000 aliens are detained at Ellis Island, including many long-term U.S. residents who are Japanese, forbidden to become U.S. citizens according to our immigration laws.

▣ 1944, 1956, 1988

• The House Un-American Activities Committee (HUAC) promises to deliver a "Yellow Paper" implicating Japanese Americans as participants in a widespread spy ring, but the paper is never released and no Japanese Americans are convicted of spying during the war.

• Also under Executive Order 9066, 1,000–1,200 Italians, including 250–300 Italian Americans, are placed in detention centers throughout the U.S. until fall 1943, after Italy surrenders to the Allies. Besides those removed to internment camps, 600,000–700,000 other Italian Americans are placed under special restrictions, including nighttime curfews, limitations on travel beyond a five mile-radius from their homes, and confiscation of radios, cameras, and other items deemed contraband. Although their property is not seized, whole West Coast communities of farmers, fishermen, shopkeepers, and factory workers are evacuated from homes near important military bases and ordered to relocate inland.

• Documents about internment of Germans are still classified by the FBI and the Department of Justice, but hysteria is very strong against German aliens, Latin American Germans, and German Americans. From 1941 to 1945, 10,905 Germans are subjected to detention on military bases and in INS internment camps, while others experience harassment and vigilante actions. Some remain interned until as late as 1948.

THE BIRTH OF NUCLEAR ENERGY

Albert Wattenberg

On the University of Chicago campus at 56th Street and Ellis Avenue, there is a bronze plaque that reads: ON DECEMBER 2, 1942, MAN ACHIEVED HERE THE FIRST SELF-SUSTAINING CHAIN REACTION AND THEREBY INITIATED THE CONTROLLED RELEASE OF NUCLEAR ENERGY.

About forty-two people were present at that event. I was one of about two dozen young physicists who had been helping to build this first nuclear reactor. World War II broke out in December 1941. Enrico Fermi had asked me to join his group of six working at Columbia University. During 1941 the group had been testing materials and designs for a nuclear chain reaction. Szilard concentrated on getting industry to produce the exceedingly high-purity materials that were needed. The help of U.S. industries was essential to the success of the project. Fermi's group moved to Chicago in April 1942, and physicists from Chicago were added to the group. In October and November we worked around the clock, over one hundred hours a week; we were driven by the fear that we were in a race with the Nazis. On November 16 we started building the reactor. Fermi was the one who made all the detailed decisions. One evening a week, for eight weeks in October and November, he gave a wonderful set of lectures so that we all had a good understanding of what was planned. His elementary reactor theory prepared us to use the control rods to operate a nuclear reactor after it had been built.

For December 2 he planned to measure the neutron intensity for different positions of the control rod in slot 21. It took almost a half hour to measure the rate of rise of the neutron intensity and value at which it leveled off. The rod was moved out six inches at a time and the measurements were repeated for each position. Around noon Fermi announced he was hungry, and we went to lunch. After lunch, as a check on everything, Fermi repeated the measurements that we had made at the last two positions before lunch. He then moved the rod a couple more times and the intensity leveled off as expected for a reactor that was below but approaching the critical rod position. At 3:25 P.M. Fermi had the rod pulled out another foot, and announced that this would make the pile above critical, slightly more than self-sustaining. While we were watching, the neutron intensity began to increase, and he made some calculations on his little slide rule three times. Then he broke into a big smile and said the intensity would continue to rise and would not level off. After permitting the intensity to rise for twenty-five minutes, he said to put in one safety rod, and the neutron intensity dropped immediately. Not only had he achieved a self-sustaining nuclear chain reaction, but he had also shown that it could be controlled in a completely predictable way.

The event was a quantitative physics experiment. There were no explosions, no flashing lights, no cheering. But there were lots of smiles. Professor Eugene Wigner brought out a bottle of Chianti and gave it to Fermi. We all had a small drink in paper cups from the water cooler. Fermi signed his name on the raffia cover of the bottle, and it was passed around for others to sign. I hung the bottle up when I locked all the control and safety rods in the reactor. Arthur Compton, the director, telephoned James B. Conant, the civilian technical director of the project, in Washington. He said, "The Italian Navigator has safely landed, and the natives were friendly."

During World War II, Albert Wattenberg worked on the Manhattan Project in Chicago; in 1957, he was the technical adviser to President Eisenhower's "Atoms for Peace" program in Japan.

BUSINESS AND INDUSTRY

• The U.S. and Mexican governments make a bilateral agreement, the Mexican Farm Labor Supply Program, commonly known as the Bracero Program (from *brazo,* the Spanish word for "arm," referring to how workers use the strength of their arms). The program allows Mexicans to enter the Southwest to work as farm laborers, filling job vacancies caused by the employment of American workers in heavier industries for the war effort. Later this agreement is expanded to include the Midwest and extended to 1947, then to 1951, until, when it is unilaterally terminated by the U.S. in 1964, the program will have allowed nearly 5 million Mexican workers to enter.

◉ 1960, 1965, 1980

• The war economy spurs a tremendous migration out of the Southern and Midwestern farmland economies into the cities where defense jobs are becoming available. In Detroit, Michigan, jeeps replace civilian cars on the assembly line, and the Eureka Vacuum Cleaner Company produces gas masks instead of sweepers. Approximately 340,000 African Americans migrate from the Southern U.S. to California to work in the defense industry, with about 125,000 settling in the San Francisco Bay Area. Many settle in Richmond, California, building boats for the navy or loading military cargo bound for the Pacific.

• The War Manpower Commission wages a persuasive propaganda campaign to mobilize women as a "second line of defense," as many men go off to war at the same time the defense industry is creating more labor demands. They saturate the media with their invention of a heroine in blue denim coveralls with a ban-danna covering her hair, writing a patriotic popular song, "Rosie the Riveter," to tell her story. This is the first time that industry reaches out to women to solve their manpower shortages, and they are absorbed into war production work in great numbers, increasing the female labor force from 25 to 36 percent. Besides taking over traditionally male jobs like driving buses and trucks, operating gas stations, and being police officers or train conductors, women sign up for six to eight weeks of technical training to be "Rosies" by learning how to operate machine tools, study blueprints, rivet airplanes, and weld stainless steel. There are problems: the unions first fill jobs with men and place them in the senior positions; women's wages are generally lower than men's, although they are higher than in the past. After the war, many women lose their blue-collar jobs to returning veterans, particularly in the construction and aviation industries. But some formerly male white collar jobs, such as bank tellers, office clerks, and cashiers, will be completely dominated by women.

• The Johnson Publishing Company, with John Harold Johnson as CEO, begins publication of the *Negro Digest,* reprinting articles concerning African Americans in a format similar to *Reader's Digest.* The magazine's success enables the company to offer new magazines, including *Ebony* in 1945, *Tan* in 1950, and *Jet* in 1951.

SCIENCE AND TECHNOLOGY

• The beginning of the nuclear age: On December 2, Enrico Fermi (1901–1954), an Italian-born physicist, and his team achieve the first self-sustaining nuclear chain reaction in a nuclear reactor at Stagg Field, Chicago.

Chicago Pile I (CP-I), the world's first reactor. *(Argonne National Laboratory)*

Fourth annual reunion of Chicago Pile I scientists on the steps of Eckhart Hall, University of Chicago, December 2, 1946. *(Argonne National Laboratory)*

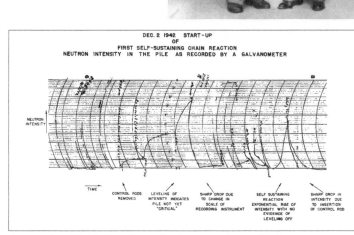

DEC. 2 1942 START-UP
OF
FIRST SELF-SUSTAINING CHAIN REACTION
NEUTRON INTENSITY IN THE PILE AS RECORDED BY A GALVANOMETER

Atomic Age "Birth Certificate." *(Argonne National Laboratory)*

The Chianti bottle Eugene Wigner brought to celebrate the first self-sustaining chain reaction, and a list of scientists present at the experiment. *(Argonne National Laboratory)*

• Magnetic recording tape is invented. It will revolutionize the recording industry by allowing musicians to create the illusion of a perfectly seamless recording event, with the aid of a sharp knife and some splicing tape, though it may in fact be an edited cut-and-paste or a layering of many "takes."

• The U.S. tests its first jet aircraft, the Bell XP-59A Airacomet, on October 1. It is built by Bell Aircraft Company, and is flown by pilot Robert M. Stanley from Muroc Dry Lake in California.

• The "Pap" test for cervical cancer, named after Greek-American physician George Nicholas Papanicolaou whose pioneering work in 1928 led to this development, is accepted as the standard test for cervical cancer.

CULTURE AND SOCIETY

• During World War II, 420 Navajo U.S. Marine recruits work in the South Pacific battle zone, on assignment to an elite group of radio cryptographers, where they encode thousands of radio messages using a secret language they create by making associations between the Navajo and military languages. At the battle of Iwo Jima, their participation is central to the Marines' victory, as they send and decode 800 messages without error during the first forty-eight hours of battle. The Navajos continue this work for the duration of the war. Perhaps because it is based on an unwritten language, the Navajo code remains among the very few military codes never deciphered. The Navajos' code work remains classified until 1968 in case it might be necessary to use the code again, but after that time the Navajo Code Talkers, as they become known, are celebrated as popular heroes. In 1982, President Reagan designates August 14 as Navajo Code Talkers Day.

🗓 1968

• All Japanese internees are required to fill out loyalty questionnaires to prove their allegiance to the U.S. government, and those who pass the test are to be allowed to serve in the U.S. Army or Navy. The two most controversial questions are "Are you willing to serve in the armed forces of the U.S. on combat duty, wherever ordered?" and "Will you swear unqualified allegiance to the U.S. of America and faithfully defend the U.S. from any or all attack by foreign or domestic forces, and forswear any form of allegiance to the Japanese emperor, or to any other foreign government, power, or organization?" Over 65,000 evacuees answer "yes" to these two questions, even though their constitutional rights have been violated, and are labeled "loyal" (33,000 *nisei* men and women serve in the U.S. armed forces during World War II, with 6,000 assigned to duty in the Pacific). Those who answer "no" become known as "No-No Boys," and are sent to Tule Lake Camp, where the most suspicious detainees are interned. John Okada (1923–1971) will write a novel, *No-No Boy,* about this experience, which will be published five years after his death. It has remained in print since that time.

• The U.S. Navy issues a new type of white cotton undershirt, which has a circular neckline and short sleeves that form a T, earning it the name "T-shirt." It is stamped with the unit or division name. By the end of the war, when returning soldiers continue to wear them, they begin to be made commercially.

WORLD EVENTS

• Adolf Hitler orders the "Final Solution to the Jewish question" at the Wannsee Conference, a meeting of Nazi leaders in Berlin, beginning the program of systematic genocide that becomes known as the Holocaust.

1943

ARTS AND LITERATURE

• Russian-American novelist and philosopher Ayn Rand (1905–1982) publishes her 747-page novel *The Fountainhead,* which first illustrates her philosophy of "Objectivism." Her worldview advocates reason determined by individual choice as the way to acquire knowledge and ensure survival, guided by an ethic of self-interest and politics based on free-market capitalism and an unchecked profit motive. The book becomes a best-seller two years after publication, and Rand's philosophy proves important to many. It is still in print at the end of the century, when Radcliffe students vote *The Fountainhead* the best book of the century.

• Choreographer and dancer Pearl Primus (b. Trinidad, 1919) makes her dance debut at the YMHA in New York this year, beginning a distinguished career combining performance, teaching, and scholarship after earning a Ph.D. in anthropology from Columbia University and doing fieldwork in the American South, the Caribbean, and Africa.

• *Oklahoma!,* a musical set in the Oklahoma Territory, with music by Richard Rodgers (1902–1979), libretto and lyrics by Oscar Hammerstein (1895–1960), and choreography by Agnes de Mille (1909–1993), premieres

March 31. A great success, it will enjoy a five-year run on Broadway. Its seamless interweaving of plot through dance and song revolutionizes the musical form.

• Maya Deren (1917–1961) opens up experimental film techniques when she writes manifestos and directs herself in her fourteen minute silent film *Meshes of the Afternoon,* made in Los Angeles as a collaboration with her husband, Czech filmmaker Alexander Hammid (b. 1910).

GOVERNMENT AND POLITICS

• The Supreme Court rules that schoolchildren should not be compelled to salute the American flag if doing so poses a religious conflict.

• The Immigration and Naturalization Act of April 29 provides the legal basis for the "Bracero Program," the importing of temporary agricultural workers from North, South, and Central America during World War II. The act of December 17, 1943, known as the Chinese Act, effectively repeals the Chinese Exclusion Acts of 1882 and 1902 by adding Chinese persons or persons of Chinese descent to the classes eligible for naturalization.

• Automatic withholding of federal income tax is signed into law in June.

BUSINESS AND INDUSTRY

• The U.S. government institutes a regimen of rationing. Beginning with a limit of three pairs of leather shoes per year per American, the list of rationed items expands to include canned goods, coffee, sugar, and meat. Civilians are required to buy these items with coupon books that use a point rationing system

U.S. Armed forces personnel with wooden clubs on the street during the Zoot Suit Riots, Los Angeles, California. *(Library of Congress, Prints and Photographs Division)*

to prove the legality of the purchase. A "black market" economy quickly accommodates anyone willing to pay more for rationed items and other goods in low supply such as gasoline, with illegal revenues amounting to $1,300,000,000 by the end of 1944.

CULTURE AND SOCIETY

• The press plays up the so-called "Zoot Suit Riots," a case of scapegoating that happens during the summer in southern California, where some newspapers are portraying Mexican Americans as foreigners. Bands of soldiers, sailors, and Marines roam through the barrios by the hundreds, looking to persecute Mexican youths dressed in their distinctive "zoot suit" style, beating them and tearing off their clothes while the police, more often than not, arrest the victims of these assaults. In actuality, with over 400,000 enlisted men at this time, Mexicans

are overrepresented in the armed forces compared to other ethnic groups.

WORLD EVENTS

• When the Allied forces invade Italy in July, Benito Mussolini's dictatorship collapses and a new government is formed by Marshal Pietro Badoglio. Mussolini is deposed by the Fascist Grand Council and placed under house arrest by King Victor Emmanuel III. The Fascist party is banned three days later. By September Premier Badoglio surrenders unconditionally to a representative of General Eisenhower. In 1945, Mussolini will be captured, tried, and executed by Italian partisans, who display his head on a rifle butt for cameras to document.

• Goebbels proclaims Berlin "free of Jews," as the Wannsee Conference's "Final Solution" is methodically carried out.

• FDR, Churchill, and Stalin hold their first

summit meeting, the Teheran Conference, from November 28 to December 1, where they discuss the projected May 1944 invasion of Europe, and continue planning for the founding of the United Nations.

1944

ARTS AND LITERATURE

• *Appalachian Spring* is choreographed by Martha Graham, with music composed by Aaron Copland (1900–1990). Using thirteen instruments, it invokes an American pioneer drama. The set is designed by Isamu Noguchi. Both the dance and its score will become American classics.

• Jerome Robbins (1918–1998), a dancer, choreographer, and director equally at home on Broadway and the concert dance stage who contributes many innovations to modern ballet and the American musical form, begins his Broadway career as a choreographer with the premiere of *On the Town,* a musical by Betty Comden and Adolph Green that is based on *Fancy Free,* his first ballet, with a story of World War II Navy men on leave. Robbins joins the New York City Ballet as associate artistic director in 1949, choreographing *The Cage, Afternoon of a Faun,* and *The Concert* in the 1950s. During the 1950s he also adapts, directs, and choreographs *Peter Pan,* creates the "Small House of Uncle Thomas" ballet in *The King and I,* and conceives, directs, and choreographs *West Side Story.*

• The San Francisco Ballet produces the first complete ballet of *The Nutcracker* in the U.S. The Christmas-theme ballet in two acts, with music by Pyotr Ilich Tchaikovsky and a libretto based on a novel by E. T. A. Hoffmann, is re-choreographed by William Christensen from the original, premiered by Lev Ivanov at Moscow's Maryinsky Theatre in 1892. *The Nutcracker* proves to be a major hit, and in less than fifty years, variations pass into every dance community in the U.S., frequently helping companies finance the rest of their year's productions. In 1954, Lew Christensen re-choreographs the ballet in an 1850s American Victorian style, the same year that George Balanchine's version premieres with the New York City Ballet. A 1980s alternative *Revolutionary Nutcracker Sweetie,* directed by the San Francisco Bay Area–based woman's dance collective, the Dance Brigade, includes hip-hoppers and a wheelchair ballet along with a Sugar Plum Fairy wielding a "Little Red Book" of Chairman Mao. In 1996, Donald Byrd premieres *The Harlem Nutcracker* at Brooklyn's Next Wave Festival, combining jazz, modern dance, and ballet vocabulary with Duke Ellington and Billy Strayhorn's arrangement of Tchaikovsky's score. This annual fantasy indulgence is probably the most frequently performed ballet in the world.

• Oakland-born writer Robert Duncan (1919–1988) publishes "The Homosexual in Society," the first discussion of homosexuality "which [includes] the frank avowal that the author [is] himself involved," in Dwight MacDonald's journal, *Politics.*

• Writers Lucien Carr, Jack Kerouac (1922–1969), and Allen Ginsberg (1926–1997) theorize about a "New Vision" in New York. They focus on three concepts: naked self-expression is the key to creativity; the artist's consciousness is expanded by derangement of the senses; art eludes conventional morality.

• Norman Granz, a young jazz fan and

Japanese American Detention Center at Manzanar, California. Photo by Dorothea Lange. *(National Archives: Still Picture Division)*

entrepreneur, organizes Jazz at the Philharmonic in Los Angeles and begins annual nationwide tours drawing huge crowds to hear such stars as Coleman Hawkins, Charlie Parker, Roy Eldridge, Dizzy Gillespie, and Lester Young.

GOVERNMENT AND POLITICS

• In June, FDR signs the Servicemen's Readjustment Act (known as the GI Bill), which provides World War II veterans with various kinds of financial aid: low-interest loans to establish homes or businesses, educational stipends to study in vocational schools and colleges plus subsistence payments of fifty to seventy-five dollars a month, unemployment benefits, and $500 for additional veterans' facilities. The GI Bill will be a major dynamic in shaping the direction of the postwar economy, allowing many people to be the first in their families to go to college and own their own home.

• President Franklin Delano Roosevelt, running against New York Republican Governor Thomas E. Dewey, is elected for an unprecedented fourth term even though he is extremely ill. Senator Harry S. Truman (1884–1972) of Missouri is elected as his vice president.

• The Supreme Court rules that voting rights

cannot be denied because of color in *Smith v. Allwright.*

• Several thousand Japanese Americans are drafted into the U.S. military from the internment camps. About 315 choose to be draft resisters. Frank Emi, who is located at Heart Mountain Camp in Wyoming, becomes a leader of the resistance movement, and serious conflicts break out in the camps between the resisters and those who believe in volunteering or accepting the draft. The draft resisters are convicted and sent to prison, although President Truman will pardon them after the war. "Go for Broke" becomes the slogan of the 442nd Regimental Combat Team, a segregated unit of *nisei* from Hawaii and the West Coast, which suffers 9,486 casualties fighting on the European battlefields and is one of the most decorated units in the history of the U.S. Army. President Truman, in recognition of their heroism, tells them, "You fought for the free nations of the world along with the rest of us. . . . You fought not only the enemy, but you fought prejudice and you won. Keep up that fight and we will continue to win to make this great republic stand for what the Constitution says it stands for: the welfare of all the people all the time."

• On July 17, at Port Chicago, a naval ammunitions depot near Sacramento, California, 320 people, including 202 African American soldiers and their white officers, are killed while loading a cargo of munitions onto navy ships. It is the worst stateside disaster of the war, and the largest man-made explosion up to that time. When the African American soldiers are ordered to go back to loading the ships, 258 refuse. Their response is out of fear, as the navy has made no changes in the conditions that led to the explosion and offers no special training to protect them in this dangerous assignment, and out of anger at the racist treatment they regularly experience from their officers, including the fact that only African Americans are assigned the loading work. The navy calls this a mutiny, convicting the soldiers on the grounds that it is against military code to refuse an order. In 1994 the navy reviews and upholds their decision on this incident, which is now known as the Port Chicago Mutiny. This incident does start a movement toward desegregation in the armed forces, which will be a factor in eventually reducing racism throughout the country.

• Segregation is practiced throughout the military, even though the War Department abolishes segregation in army posts. The army's black and white soldiers fight side by side for the first time, in December at the Battle of the Bulge, when about 2,500 African Americans volunteer to fight the Germans. After the battle is over the troops separate, returning to their segregated units.

• The Supreme Court upholds the relocation of Japanese aliens and Japanese American citizens on the grounds of national security in *Korematsu v. U.S.* On December 19, 1944, the Supreme Court rules, in *Endo v. U.S.*, that "a citizen who is concededly loyal presents no problem of espionage or sabotage. Loyalty is a matter of the heart and mind, not of race, creed or color. He who is loyal is by definition not a spy or a saboteur." As a result, on January 2, 1945, the War Department will announce that evacuation orders have been rescinded, and detainees will begin to move out of the relocation camps. The difference in the two rulings lies in the fact that, because Mitsuye Endo brought her suit while interned, she had proper grounds to challenge the legality of the law, whereas Fred Korematsu, who had resisted by going underground, did not (as in two similarly related challenges, by Minoru Yasui and Gordon Hirabayashi).

BUSINESS AND INDUSTRY

• The Puerto Rican government inaugurates Operation Bootstrap, a program that responds to increasing labor demands in the U.S. due to World War II, and encourages industrialization on the island. The program gives U.S. factories a ten-year tax exemption if they relocate from the mainland to the island. The island's agricultural economy suffers as Operation Bootstrap sets off a major migration of workers to the urban factories and to the U.S. mainland. It will continue until 1960.

SCIENCE AND TECHNOLOGY

• Bell Labs designs a radar device, the APQ-13 bombsights, produced by Western Electric, that use X-band microwaves, at a wavelength of 3 cm. These bombsights see ground-based targets clearly enough to bomb accurately through overcast and darkness. This new technology is placed on B-29 Superfortress high-altitude bombers that cruise at altitudes above 30,000 feet, providing the U.S. military with a more efficient, safer weapon because "where they can fly, they can bomb."

WORLD EVENTS

• D-Day: On June 6, the Allies land at Normandy, France, and move on to liberate Paris.

• In July, forty-four nations meet at the Bretton Woods Conference in New Hampshire, where they lay the foundation for the International Monetary Fund and International Bank for Reconstruction and Development, designing the basic international financial governing boards for the next twenty-five years.

• From August to October, at the Dumbarton Oaks Conference, the U.S., Britain, the Soviet Union, and China conceptualize ideas for an international organization to keep the peace and negotiate legal solutions after the war, drafting what becomes the basic format of the United Nations.

1945

ARTS AND LITERATURE

• Charlie Parker and Dizzy Gillespie, with sidemen Miles Davis (1926–1991), Max Roach (b. 1924), and Bud Powell (1924–1966), make classic bebop recordings for Savoy, whereupon bebop, or "bop" for short, begins to replace swing as the jazz mainstream sound. The beret and goatee of Dizzy create a major style example for hip young Americans of all races, and the "hip" slang of bop musicians (e.g., "cool," "crazy, man, crazy," and "Like . . .") makes a lasting impact on American English.

GOVERNMENT AND POLITICS

• Franklin D. Roosevelt meets with Winston Churchill and Joseph Stalin in February at Yalta, a Crimean seaside resort, to plan for the defeat of the Axis powers and provide the basis for the postwar future of Europe. The "Big Three" Allied leaders agree to divide Germany into occupied zones, and establish voting procedures for the United Nations Security Council. Roosevelt and Churchill also bargain with Stalin, gaining his agreement to declare war against Japan after the German surrender, in exchange for Russian control of parts of

Manchuria and maintaining their present status of occupation in Outer Mongolia.

• Roosevelt dies of a cerebral hemorrhage while vacationing in Warm Springs, Georgia, on April 12, and Vice President Harry S. Truman is sworn in as U.S. president.

• On May 8, one day after Germany surrenders, President Truman declares V-E Day, and lifts the nationwide directive to maintain a dim-out at night.

• June 5, the "Big Four"—the U.S., Great Britain, France, and the USSR—finalize their agreement regarding the occupation of Germany, and the boundaries of the division. These borders will remain in effect until 1989.

• The Japanese surrender Okinawa to the U.S. Army on June 21 after 160,000 Japanese and 12,500 Americans lose their lives; General Douglas MacArthur's forces recapture the Philippine Islands on July 7 after ten months of fighting and a cost of 12,000 American lives.

• President Truman authorizes dropping a plutonium-based fission bomb based on uranium-235, known as the "atomic bomb," on Japan. The official reason for the use of this new, horrific weapon is to make Japan surrender, although there is much evidence arguing that the Japanese military is already seriously considering surrender. P. M. S. Blackett, in *Fear, War, and the Bomb,* calls the bombing "the first major operation of the cold diplomatic war with Russia, dropped because the U.S. is anxious to end the Japanese front of the war before the Russians have a chance to enter the war against Japan."

• The city of Hiroshima, Japan, is bombed on August 6 with an atomic bomb. On August 9, an atomic bomb is exploded over Nagasaki, Japan. It is kept secret that this exhausts the U.S. supply of atomic bombs. Japan surrenders on August 14, and the Pacific phase of the war is over with their official signing of surrender on September 2, known as V-J Day.

BUSINESS AND INDUSTRY

• Federal defense spending has a permanent effect upon the U.S. economy, both during the war and after, setting up what is in effect a permanent war economy. This economy brings a general feeling of prosperity, demonstrating that it can provide stability and yield high corporate profits (in 1940 they totaled $6.4 billion; by 1944 they totaled $10.8 billion) even while accommodating higher wages for workers and higher prices for farmers. By providing half their market share, the federal government is largely responsible for the creation of the new industries of electronics, aerospace, and atomic energy. These industries maintain strong ties to their research laboratories in universities, promoting the buildup of suburbs in areas such as Silicon Valley, near Stanford in Palo Alto, California, and Route 126 around Boston and MIT. The government's investment in military preparedness continues on an upward spiral. Of the 1950 U.S. budget, totaling $40 billion, the military receives $12 billion. By 1955, out of a budget totaling $62 billion, the military receives $40 billion.

🔲 1950

SCIENCE AND TECHNOLOGY

• Physicist Vannevar Bush, head of the Office of Scientific Research and Development set up by President Roosevelt in 1941, delivers a forty-page report to President Truman in July titled "Science: The Endless Frontier." It urges the government to promote postwar scientific research. Bush emphasizes the need for basic

THE DECISION TO BOMB HIROSHIMA

Albert Wattenberg

In 1939, Einstein and Szilard wrote a letter to President Roosevelt that led to the atomic bomb project in the U.S. [see 1939, "The Birth of the Nuclear Era"]. On March 25, 1945, Einstein and Szilard wrote a second letter; Szilard felt that the U.S. should develop an international policy before using atomic bombs. They sent the letter to Eleanor Roosevelt, asking her to arrange a meeting with President Roosevelt. An appointment was set for May 8, 1945. President Roosevelt died on April 8, 1945. Roosevelt and the army had been setting foreign policy for the U.S. Roosevelt had never told the State Department or Vice President Truman about the atomic bomb project. Secretary of War Henry L. Stimson told Truman about the atomic bombs on the day Truman became president.

Stimson and General Groves, the director of the Manhattan Project, met secretly with President Truman on April 25, 1945. Stimson, who was one of the most thoughtful men in Washington, had been very concerned with the political and moral implications of the bomb, internationally as well as nationally, and he prepared a lengthy memo for the meeting with Truman. Stimson had consulted with James Conant and Vannevar Bush, scientific administrators, and with military advisers. The Stimson memo expressed the fears of the scientists that the U.S. could not retain its advantage indefinitely; not only Russia, but even smaller nations, could develop bombs after some years. A major immediate question was whether the U.S. should share information with other nations, and on what terms. Stimson stated that American leaders had a moral obligation and would be responsible for any disasters that might follow. As a result of the meeting of Stimson, Groves, and Truman, a committee called the Interim Committee was set up to advise Truman. It included a scientific panel to give technical input to the committee. The panel consisted of A. H. Compton, Enrico Fermi, E. O. Lawrence, and J. R. Oppenheimer, all of whom had played major roles in different parts of the Manhattan Project.

In Szilard's second attempt to get the U.S. to develop an international policy before using the atomic bombs on Japan, he used a political friend of Truman to make an appointment with Truman's secretary. Truman had anticipated the topic, and told his secretary to arrange for Szilard to see the new secretary of state, James Byrnes—a political appointment. The meeting was a disaster. Byrnes thought that the atomic bombing of Japan could be used to improve the behavior of Russia, which had already occupied Hungary and Rumania. Szilard argued that we should not use the bomb until we had developed an international policy. Szilard tried another approach to influence Truman. He prepared a petition, which was circulated among the scientists at Chicago, and I was one of those who signed the petition. At Los Alamos, Oppenheimer requested that the petition not be circulated. Compton arranged formal meetings to discuss the use of the bomb. The army objected to the meetings, so Compton set up a committee under James Franck (also a Nobel Prize winner) to prepare a report. The Franck report was sent through General Groves. He classified the report "secret," and it was not declassified until 1958.

In the late spring of 1945, the Interim Committee met for two days with the scientific panel. The scientific panel was requested to evaluate the feasibility of a demonstration of the bomb without killing people. They spent two days on the problem and were unable to develop a satisfactory plan for a convincing demonstration. Compton had been raised as a Mennonite pacifist. How could such a highly moral man agree to use the atomic bomb on Japan? He estimated that if the bomb were used, millions of Japanese lives would be saved, and it would bring a rapid end to the human suffering and tragedy of a horrible war. An understanding of Compton's thinking requires knowledge of the U.S. air campaign in the spring of 1945. On the night of March 9, 1945, General Curtis LeMay sent over Tokyo a fleet of bombers carrying incendiary bombs. They concentrated their bombing on a civilian workers' section of Tokyo and created a firestorm. About a hundred thousand Japanese died, about three-quarters of a million were wounded or badly burned, and a million people lost their homes. During the following weeks, General LeMay firebombed three other very large cities in Japan. He had plans to firebomb all major cities in Japan. He was one of the advocates of eliminating all Japanese.

That same spring, significant amounts of (weapon grade) fissionable uranium and plutonium started arriving at Los Alamos. The first atomic bomb was tested at Alamogordo, New Mexico, on July 16, 1945. On August 6, 1945, an atomic bomb was detonated over Hiroshima, Japan, and completely destroyed the city. More than 100,000 men, women, and children died in the first few days after the bomb. In the following months, about the same number died from the radiation. The stories of individuals are told in John Hersey's book *Hiroshima*.

On August 10 the Japanese offered to negotiate a conditional surrender, but James Byrnes did not report this immediately to Truman. By August 11, Truman had reconsidered dropping a second bomb. However, it was too late to stop the bombing of Nagasaki. After the bombing of Nagasaki, it was the Emperor himself who told the cabinet and military that they had to accept an unconditional surrender.

Every generation of Americans will have groups of people with strongly differing opinions on our being the first nation to use atomic bombs. In my generation there were those like my brother who luckily had lived through the deadly invasion of Normandy and who were on ships bound for an invasion of Japan. My brother and his shipmates believed that the atomic bombs had saved their lives. Some baby boomers, the children of the troops on the ships, believe they never would have been born if it were not for the atomic bombing of Japan.

research in physics, chemistry, and biology, since basic research had, by necessity, to be put aside during the war years.

• The first atomic bomb is exploded on July 16, at 5:29 A.M., at Alamogordo Air Force Base in New Mexico, a flat, semi-arid desert area near Los Alamos, by a government team of scientists headed by physicist J. Robert Oppenheimer (1904–1967). Military men, journalists, and other "distinguished visitors" are gathered there to observe the first full-scale test to detonate a nuclear fission bomb, with the code name Trinity. One of the observers, Brigadier General Thomas Farrell, calls Trinity "a justification of the several years of intensive effort by tens of thousands of people—statesmen, scientists, engineers, manufacturers, soldiers, and many others in every walk of life." Near ground zero, observers wear little goggles to protect their eyes, and are dressed in ordinary hot weather clothing. They are amazed by the intensity of the explosion, which is conservatively estimated to be in excess of the equivalent of 15,000–20,000 tons of TNT. The strength of the blast knocks several observers to the ground; eyewitness accounts mention light, heat, force, and sound. Brigadier General Leslie Groves reports to the secretary of war that the blast leaves "a crater from which all vegetation has vanished, with a diameter of 1,200 feet and a slight slope toward the center" at ground zero.

◉ 1942

• Grand Rapids, Michigan, becomes the first city in the U.S. to add fluoridation to its drinking water.

CULTURE AND SOCIETY

• In this year, when the U.S. Federal Communications Commission (FCC) sets aside twelve channels for commercial television, 5,000 homes have TV sets. In three years the number will be 1 million; by 1968, 78 million homes will have them.

• The War Brides Act of December 28 waives visa requirements and most other provisions of immigration law, to allow nationals of foreign countries who married members of the American armed services during the war to live in the U.S.

WORLD EVENTS

• On April 12, U.S. troops of the 80th Division free the survivors of the Buchenwald concentration camp. On April 30, as Russian troops enter the city, Hitler commits suicide in an underground bunker in Berlin. Germany signs an unconditional surrender near Reims, France, on May 7.

• Japan's emperor surrenders on August 14 after U.S. atomic bombs are dropped on Hiroshima (August 6) and Nagasaki (August 9). An estimated 110,000–150,000 Japanese are killed outright, and another 200,000 will die from burns and other effects of radiation within five years.

• World War II claims the lives of more than 55 million people, 20 million of whom are Russian civilians.

• The United Nations charter is signed in San Francisco by forty-seven nations. It will be ratified later in this year. The charter establishes the structure of the organization: the General Assembly, which includes all members; the Security Council, composed of five permanent members—China, France, Britain, the U.S., and the USSR—plus six rotating members; and the Secretariat, the administrative arm, headed by a secretary general.

• The League of Arab States (LAS, the Arab League) is formed in Cairo, Egypt, to strengthen communication, cultural, financial, health, social, and national relations among its member countries, which include Algeria, Bahrain, Comoros, Djibouti, Egypt, Iraq, Jordan, Kuwait, Lebanon, Libya, Mauritania, Morocco, Oman, the Palestine Liberation Organization, Qatar, Saudi Arabia, Somalia, Sudan, Syria, Tunisia, the United Arab Emirates, and Yemen.

1946

ARTS AND LITERATURE

• The term "Abstract Expressionism" is first applied to New York modernist paintings by critic Robert Coates, in a *New Yorker* review of a Hans Hofmann (b. Germany, 1880; d. U.S., 1966) exhibit at Brandt curated by Betty Parsons. (It was first used in 1919 to describe the work of Russian painter Wassily Kandinsky [Russia, 1866–1944].) Two other critics most associated with this group also coin terms: Harold Rosenberg offers "action painting" and Clement Greenberg "American style painting." Still others term the group "New York School," although Coates's term becomes the one generally used to identify a diverse group of artists experimenting with abstraction from the mid-1940s through the 1950s, including William Baziotes (1912–1963), Willem de Kooning, Adolph Gottlieb (1903–1974), Philip Guston (1913–1980), Sabro Hasegawa (b. 1906, Japan; d. 1957, U.S.), Minoru Kawabata (b. 1911, Japan), Franz Kline (1910–1962), Lee Krasner (1908–1984), Norman Lewis (1909–1979), Robert Motherwell, Barnett Newman (1905–1970), Kenzo Okada (b. Japan, 1902; d. U.S.,

1982), Jackson Pollock, Ad Reinhardt (1913–1967), Clyfford Still (1904–1980), Mark Tobey (1980–1976), and Hale A. Woodruff (1900–1980), among others.

• Buckminster Fuller applies technology and basic geometric principles to design the first of his many variations on a geodesic dome, creating a formal pattern that has become a common classic in architecture. The lacy domes, composed of a network of triangles or tetrahedrons, are both strong and light because they maintain equilibrium between tension and compression far more efficiently and economically than designs based on straight lines, cubes, squares, and rectangles. Fuller's ideas influence the military, the art world, and the world of technology and design.
🄵 1927

• Charles Eames (1907–1978) and Ray Eames (1912–1988), a husband-and-wife collaborative team, apply expensive wartime technological research to make inexpensive, innovative postwar products, notably furniture. This year they are given the first show to honor a furniture designer at the Museum of Modern Art.

GOVERNMENT AND POLITICS

• The U.S. Congress grants full independence to the Philippines on July 4, ten months after Japan's surrender. The Republic of the Philippines adopts a new constitution similar to that of the U.S. It consents to letting U.S. military bases remain, and continues trade agreements from the colonial past.

• The first Puerto Rican governor, Jesus T. Pinero, is appointed by President Truman.

• By Executive Order 9808, President Truman creates the Presidential Committee on Civil

Rights to study existing federal civil rights protections and ways to improve them.

• In *Morgan v. Commonwealth of Virginia*, Irene Morgan, an African American who refused to move from the front to the rear of a Greyhound Bus, wins a ruling that invalidates segregation on interstate buses that sets a precedent for future challenges of segregation in public facilities.

• Congress establishes the Indian Claims Commission, whereby Native tribes are able to sue the U.S. for illegally taken lands. The government acknowledges its past illegal actions, and eventually pays out $800 million to various tribes based on the market value of the land at the time it was taken, generally without figuring in interest accrued. It does not give tribes the option of regaining their old lands or buying new lands, setting a 1952 cutoff date for filing claims, after which time the tribes cannot regain their old lands. The Indian Claims Commission is followed by many more bills in the 1950s that will further the government plan to get out of the Indian business, by dissolving existing legislation that separates Indians from the rest of U.S. society.

• The U.S. Army's School of the Americas (SOA) is established at Fort Benning, Georgia, this year to help create professional military officers for Latin American countries. Called "School of the Assassins," by its critics, this secret program trains over 60,000 students to be police and military officers who use beating, murder, extortion, and other forms of torture as advanced counterinsurgency techniques. Their graduates are implicated in numerous human rights violations, including murders in Peru, El Salvador, Colombia, Guatemala, and Honduras. Famous graduates include General Raoul Cedras of Haiti, leader of a successful coup against democratically elected President Aristide; General Leopoldo Galtieri, head of the Argentine military junta responsible for killing tens of thousands in the 1980s; and Manuel Noriega, a CIA agent and the president of Panama until his ouster in 1989. In 1997, after the U.S. House of Representatives votes to close the school, the Department of Defense opens a new school at the same Fort Benning site, called the Defense Institute for Hemispheric Security Cooperation.

BUSINESS AND INDUSTRY

• The marketing of Las Vegas, Nevada, as "the entertainment capital of America" begins when gangster Bugsy Siegel opens the Flamingo, a multimillion-dollar hotel-casino in the middle of the Mojave Desert. The Flamingo is located on the Strip, a two-mile-long section of Las Vegas Boulevard that will continue sprouting ever more lavish hotel-casinos with names like the Golden Nugget and the Horseshoe. Las Vegas becomes the fastest-growing city in the U.S., surrounded by suburban communities accommodating the workers who service the tourist and gaming industry and a large population of retirees.

• Charge-It, the precursor of the credit card, is launched by the Flatbush National Bank of New York. It gives the consumer credit through a cashless payment method.

▣ 1959, 1966

SCIENCE AND TECHNOLOGY

• The Electronic Numerical Integrator and Computer (ENIAC), the first large electronic digital computer, is built by electrical engineers at the University of Pennsylvania. It weighs thirty tons, occupies a thirty-by-fifty-foot room, uses nearly 18,000 vacuum tubes, consumes 150 kilowatts to operate at full power, and requires constant vigilance to keep operating. ENIAC is able to complete very intricate calculations for ballistics tables.

CULTURE AND SOCIETY

• Pediatrician Dr. Benjamin Spock (1904–1998) publishes *The Common Sense Book of Baby and Child Care,* an advice book that revolutionizes child rearing in the U.S. by assuring parents that it is best to trust common sense, and by providing a comprehensive medical reference to help children grow from healthy infants to teenagers. Although some criticize Spock for being too permissive, the book sells over 40 million copies, goes through many revised editions, and wins him many honors.

WORLD EVENTS

• Civil war begins in China after negotiations between the U.S.-supported Kuomintang forces, led by General Chiang Kai-shek, and the Soviet-supported Communists, led by Mao Zedong, fail to result in a coalition government.

• The 1946 tribunal at Nuremberg, administered by the U.S., France, Britain, and the Soviet Union, charges twenty-four former Nazi leaders on four counts, including crimes against humanity; it is the first time "genocide" is invoked as a legal concept. Genocide will be defined by the United Nations on December 11, 1946, in General Assembly Resolution 96 (1), as "a denial of the right of existence of entire human groups, as homicide is the denial of the right to live of individual human beings; such denial of the right of existence shocks the conscience of mankind, results in great losses to humanity in the form of cultural and other contributions represented by these groups, and is contrary to moral law and the spirit and aim of the United Nations." The Nuremberg war tribunal brings in guilty verdicts against twelve Nazi defendants, sentencing them to death by hanging; seven are imprisoned, and three are acquitted. Hermann Göring, Hitler's second-in-command and chosen successor, one of those sentenced to hang, will commit suicide a few hours before the sentence is to be carried out. ▣ 1968

• Army Colonel Juan Perón (1895–1974) wins the presidency of Argentina with the help of his charismatic wife, Eva "Evita" Duarte, who helps women gain more rights, including the right to vote, and serves as unofficial head of the health and labor ministries. Perón grants himself absolute power to reorganize the country's economy. He redistributes income to workers, raising their wages and benefits, provides free medical care to the poor, and builds hospitals and schools. He nationalizes public services and creates enormous bureaucracies to regulate industries. When Eva Perón dies of cancer in 1952, Perón's popularity suffers, especially as his industrialization and economic policies move the country toward spiraling inflation. Perón issues more restraints on freedom of the press and violently purges his opposition in the universities, judiciary, and unions, until he is ousted by a revolution in 1955.

1947

ARTS AND LITERATURE

• Jackson Pollock (1914–1956) uses a "drip" painting technique, by drawing three-dimensional images in the air and letting the

A NATION SUBURBANIZED

Sonya Salamon

When the twentieth century began, the U.S. was a rural nation. Between World Wars I and II, small towns peaked in size as many left the countryside for the city. After World War II, the pent-up desire for the American dream, to own a stand-alone home with a yard, began to drive a rapid conversion of farmland to subdivisions outside major cities. The earliest of these affordable communities was the famous Levittown. By the 1970s, a population turnabout occurred as the nation grew primarily in its rural/urban fringe. For the first time since the turn of the century, rural places were gaining more population than metropolitan places. At century's end, as a consequence of the suburban "revolution," most Americans reside in metropolitan areas outside central cities. Suburbs also overtook cities as hubs for the nation's economic and commercial activities. Suburban malls replaced urban downtowns as shopping centers. More offices are outside every major city, in privately owned suburban "edge cities," such as Tyson's Corner, Virginia, than are found in urban downtowns. People live in one suburb and work in another, commuting to an office building surrounded by a parklike "campus." Major American cities are visited mainly for entertainment or cultural purposes by those who both live and work in the surrounding suburban ring. A hallmark of early-twenty-first-century political life is an agenda driven by the suburban "soccer mom."

The transformation from an urban to a suburban nation has many causes. Americans identify with the Jeffersonian agrarian ideology that defines the bulwark of democracy as farmers owning their land, and as rural life providing a morally virtuous, good life. Government policies, such as guaranteed housing loans to World War II veterans and various highway-building programs, underwrote the abandonment of central cities and the concentration of poverty there. In the past twenty-five years, farmland along the urban fringe has been gobbled up with haphazard and sprawling residential, commercial, and industrial development, in what farmers see as an irresistible tide. Rapid suburbanization has made farmers a minority in rural places, even though farming may have given a locale its agrarian identity and traditions. Farmers and small-town residents differentially foot the bill for suburbanization, with higher taxes for the new schools and the increased services that urban newcomers demand. Sprawl development has meant that poor workers, too, must travel great distances to jobs in the malls, restaurants, and businesses that provide services to suburbanites. Finding affordable suburban housing in such high-growth cities as Los Angeles, New York, Boston, Dallas, Atlanta, and Seattle means that commuting time has grown longer and longer, particularly for young families. Distance commuting has had unintended negative consequences for child-rearing and community cohesion. But Americans seem, on the whole, satisfied with suburban life.

paint fall to the canvas below, which is tacked to the floor of his studio, because "On the floor I feel nearer, more a part of the painting, since this way I can walk around it, work from the four sides and literally be in the painting. This is akin to the method of the Indian sand painters of the West." (In his early years living in the Southwest, Pollock observed the process used by the Navajo to create their sand paintings.)

• Elia Kazan (b. Constantinople, 1909), Joe Crawford, and Robert Lewis open the Actors Studio. The naturalistic technique they develop is highly influenced by the innovative training system conceived by Russian actor, director, and teacher Constantin Stanislavsky. Under the direction of Lee Strasberg (1901–1982), who directs the Actors Studio from 1951 to 1982, the Studio becomes known as a place to experiment outside the economic pressures of the professional stage, where actors perform in workshops before other actors. Known as "the method" in the U.S., the work fosters what becomes a distinctively American style of acting, best represented by the stage and film work of actors Marlon Brando (b. 1924), Paul Newman (b. 1925), Joanne Woodward, Montgomery Clift (1920–1966), Ellen Burstyn, Robert DeNiro (b. 1943), Dustin Hoffman (b. 1937), Karl Malden, Marilyn Monroe (1926–1962), Rita Moreno, Jack Nicholson (b. 1937), Al Pacino (b. 1940), Martin Sheen, Kim Stanley, Maureen Stapleton, and Rod Steiger (b. 1925), and directors Sidney Lumet, Elia Kazan, Joshua Logan (1908–1988), Harold Prince, Jose Quintero, Francis Ford Coppola (b. 1939), and many others.

• As Broadway shows become ever more expensive to produce, two new proving grounds become pivotal in developing new American plays or introducing international works, especially those experimenting with form or subject matter. One source is so close to Broadway that it is called off-Broadway, and the other is outside of New York altogether. According to the *Oxford Illustrated History of Theater*, one of the earliest theaters to mount full professional productions outside of New York, the Alley Theatre, is started as an amateur production company in Houston, Texas, this year (although Karamu Theatre, a predominately African American regional theater, opened in Cleveland in 1916 and the Pittsburgh Playhouse was formed in Pittsburgh, Pennsylvania, in 1934). The regional theater movement includes some nonprofit theaters, often affiliated with university theater training programs, such as the Yale Repertory Theater in New Haven and Arena Stage in Washington, D.C., and some commercial resident companies like the American Conservatory Theatre in San Francisco and the Guthrie in Minneapolis, Minnesota. Most tailor their performing seasons to satisfy their local communities' tastes, generally maintaining repertory from the classics and mixing in one or two contemporary works per season, although some specialize in providing safe havens for experimental works or workshopping new productions before trying a Broadway run.
🔲 1916

• Composer Milton Babbitt's *Three Compositions for Piano* serializes all aspects of pitch, rhythm, dynamics, and articulation.

• John Cage writes *Sonatas and Interludes* for "prepared piano," a technique he invents to change the piano's sound in random ways by setting small objects, such as carpenter's nails, on or between the piano strings before a performance.

• The soap opera travels from radio to television in 1947, with *A Woman to Remember*.

GOVERNMENT AND POLITICS

• Congress passes the anti-union Taft-Hartley Act over President Truman's veto. Although it allows the union shop, in which unions can negotiate contracts with employers that require newly hired workers to join unions, it outlaws the closed shop, in which unions cannot demand that employers hire only union workers. It also legalizes "right to work" laws, which allow states to prohibit union membership as a requirement of employment, establishes a Federal Mediation and Conciliation Service that can authorize imposition of sixty-day "cooling-off" periods, a time frame in which unions are not permitted to launch a strike, and permits employer lawsuits against unions for broken contracts or strike damages. Finally, it requires union leaders to file affidavits that they are not Communist Party members or forfeit their certification as bargaining agents under the National Labor Relations Act. The bill expedites the merger of the AFL and CIO, and in spite of its constraints, union membership increases from 14.6 million to 17 million from 1945 to 1952.

• Congress passes the National Security Act of 1947, which strengthens the executive branch of government's role in foreign policy by authorizing the formation of the National Security Council (NSC) to coordinate military and foreign policy under the president. It also reorganizes all military services under the National Military Establishment, which will be renamed the Department of Defense, giving them a cabinet-level secretary of defense and a presidential advisory group led by the secretaries of the army, navy, and air force, called the joint chiefs of staff. The Central Intelligence Agency (CIA) is placed under the NSC, to handle all government foreign intelligence activities, although it will also conduct domestic surveillance of activities it deems politically suspect, in violation of its charter. The Federal Bureau of Investigation (FBI) is also established out of the existing Bureau of Investigation, to handle internal intelligence activities.

• In what will become known as the Truman Doctrine, President Truman initiates the U.S. government's Cold War policy to "contain Communism." The containment concept is based on an anonymously authored article in *Foreign Affairs* magazine. (The article was actually written by George F. Kennan, a policy director in the State Department, but he signs it "X.") In the article he warns of "the domino effect," a theory that countries all over the world will fall into the hands of the Communists, as happened in the Soviet Union, unless "containment" is maintained. This policy will rule U.S. foreign policy throughout the duration of the Cold War. The first act to fight Communism and prevent the domino effect is by Truman, who requests Congress to allocate $400 million to support pro-Western governments in Greece and Turkey and, at those country's request, to send U.S. civilian and military advisers to train their soldiers. The domino effect will also be used to justify U.S. involvement in Korea and Vietnam.

• With Executive Order 9835 issued on March 22, President Truman initiates what will become known as the "Red Hunt." This program requires the Justice Department to search out any "infiltration of disloyal persons" in the U.S. government and to draw up an official list of organizations that are "totalitarian, fascist, communist, or subversive," or that have "sympathetic associations" with those organizations. By 1954, hundreds of groups' names are on this list.

• President Truman establishes the Committee on Civil Rights, headed by Charles E. Wilson, president of General Electric. In its report, "To Secure These Rights," the committee condemns racial discrimination and prejudice and proposes a bill to outlaw lynching and the establishment of a federal commission on civil rights. By 1948, President Truman, acting on these recommendations, calls for civil rights legislation covering anti-lynching laws, anti-poll-tax provisions to help black citizens gain the right to vote, and fair employment practices.

BUSINESS AND INDUSTRY

• By this year, more than twenty airlines provide service between the port of San Juan, Puerto Rico, and mainland ports of Miami and New York, facilitating the country's first big airborne migration.

SCIENCE AND TECHNOLOGY

• Willard Frank Libby (1908–1980), a University of Chicago chemist, discovers a scientific method to date the remains of what was once a living organism, using the unstable isotope carbon-14. He will win a Nobel Prize in chemistry for this radioactive carbon-14 dating technique in 1960.

• According to newspaper reports, after three days of reported sightings of flying saucers by hundreds of people in thirty-two states, a UFO (unidentified flying object) is reported to have crashed on the land of a sheep farmer near Roswell, New Mexico, killing its passengers,

who are space aliens. After carting away the debris and bodies to the Fort Worth army base in a B-52, the army initially issues a press release identifying the object as a crashed flying saucer. Within a day that statement is retracted and the object is officially redescribed as a crashed weather balloon. In 1994 the army explains the object as part of the Mogol Balloon Project, a top-secret program to monitor the atmosphere for evidence of Soviet nuclear tests. Reports of bodies are attributed to dummies, dropped from the sky during astronaut re-entry testing in the 1950s. (The army says human error in mixing events accounts for the date discrepancies.) The Roswell Incident continues to mystify some, to be rejected out of hand by others, and to provide the town of Roswell with an ongoing source of tourist income.

🖸 1961

• The Bell X-1, a rocket-powered aircraft with a fuselage shaped like a bullet, becomes the first airplane to fly faster than the speed of sound. To break the sound barrier, it reaches a speed of 700 miles per hour at an altitude of 43,000 feet, piloted by U.S. Air Force Captain Charles E. "Chuck" Yeager.

• The solid-state transistor is invented by three Bell Laboratories scientists, William Shockley (b. England, 1910), Walter Brattain (b. China, 1902), and John Bardeen (b. 1908) in December 1947. Transistors will replace vacuum tubes used in radios, TVs, radar, and computers because of their many advantages in size, speed, power consumption, reliability, and price. Shockley, Bardeen, and Brattain share a 1956 Nobel Prize in Physics for their work on semiconductors and the discovery of "the transistor effect."

🖸 1948, 1961

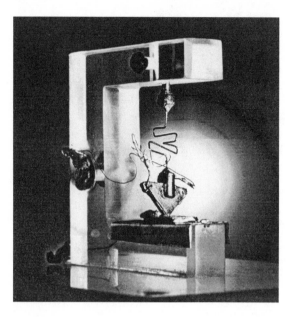

The original experimental model of an individual transistor built by John Bardeen, Walter Brattain, and William Shockley. *(Courtesy Lucent Technologies, Inc.)*

CULTURE AND SOCIETY

• Jackie Robinson (1919–1972), the first African American to sign a contract with a Major League baseball team, makes his debut playing first base for the Brooklyn Dodgers at their home site, Ebbets Field. He is named National League Rookie of the Year and leads the Dodgers to the World Series, in spite of ongoing incidents of racism by players on opposing teams, and death threats. Within two years, most major-league clubs will integrate their teams by hiring black players.

• Abraham Levitt and his sons William and Alfred buy 4,000 acres of potato farms on Long Island, thirty miles east of Manhattan, where, between 1947 and 1951, they will construct and sell a cheap, mass-produced style of suburban living that will become known as Levittown. It consists of 17,400 Cape Cod– and ranch-style homes that come in five variations, as well as seven shopping centers, fourteen playgrounds, nine swimming pools, two bowling alleys, and a town hall. By systematizing and standardizing production into twenty-seven steps, crews are able to complete a house every fifteen minutes. The basic design offers a twenty-five-by-thirty-two-foot bungalow with four and a half rooms, topped with a steeply pitched roof, placed on a poured concrete slab that allows for no basement. The completed house, including appliances, sells to World War II veterans for $7,990 with a low down payment. It receives much criticism for the seemingly stifling uniformity: early bylaws require owners to mow their lawns weekly and outlaw fences and the hanging of laundry on weekdays. Levittown will remain racially segregated until the mid-1960s, defending its discrimination clause by saying that no whites would buy in if blacks were initially allowed. It becomes the prototype for affordable housing in both Canada and the U.S.

• The American GI Forum, a civil rights organization and veterans' advocacy group, is founded by Mexican American veterans after they become outraged when a Three Rivers, Texas, funeral home refuses to bury in the city cemetery a Mexican American World War II soldier who died fighting in the Pacific. It becomes one of the largest and most influential Mexican American advocacy groups.

• The Congress of Racial Equality (CORE) tests compliance with *Morgan v. Commonwealth of Virginia*, the 1946 Supreme Court ban against segregation on interstate bus travel, by sending a group of eight black and eight

TWENTIETH-CENTURY AGRICULTURE
Claire Hope Cummings

1900–1910

- There are almost 6 million farms, with an average size of 147 acres.
- In the 1900s there are about 29 million farmers. By the year 2000 there are 1.8 million farmers.
- In 1902 the Farmer's Union, which promotes cooperatives and education for farmers, is founded.
- In 1906, Booker T. Washington of the Tuskegee Institute, Alabama, starts the "agricultural wagon," or movable farmers' school, to teach black farmers better farming methods.
- In 1910 it takes ninety minutes to produce a bushel of corn. By 2000 it takes only two minutes to produce that same bushel. In 1910 only a few hundred thousand acres are irrigated.
- By 1910 some 200,000 black farmers own over 15 million acres of land. They are politically active, through organizations such as the Colored Farmers' Alliance, which strives to address violence and discrimination by banks, suppliers, and the marketplace.
- "Canned" foods in vacuum tins appear, but advertising for prepared foods is still modest. Cooking is still an onerous chore done primarily by women. Most food is home-grown or purchased locally. Bread is still baked in 80 percent of homes.

1910–1920

- The role of federal government grows through farm legislation, and the establishment of grades and standards. Railroads move agricultural goods, and rail construction peaks at 254,000 miles. The first pesticides are applied by crop-duster aircraft to control insects in 1918, a year that also marks the first hybrid corn seed system.
- In 1913 the "Wheatland Riot" galvanizes the nation's attention on farm labor in California for the first time. The International Workers of the World organizes until violence and the riot moves the union to the Midwest, where it is successful in organizing 70,000 farm workers by 1917.
- In 1911, Crisco is developed as a butter replacement. The first self-service grocery store, Piggly-Wiggly, opens in 1916. Convenience foods like ketchup and casseroles become popular. During World War I, food is regulated.
- In 1915 the Nonpartisan League is organized, the most radical political movement in American agriculture. In 1920 the American Farm Bureau is formally organized and becomes a major political force that actively opposes labor organizing and supports agribusiness.
- In 1919, only 2 percent of farms have electricity. Commercial fertilizer use is over 6 million tons a year. By 1968, fertilizer use increases to over 40 million tons. In 1985 the USDA stops collecting fertilizer use statistics.

1920–1930

- One farmer feeds 9.8 people. Farmers still have some political power, but depressed prices bring farm purchasing power to half the average from 1910–1914. From 1920 to 1930, net migration from farm to cities is 6 million, mostly among young people under thirty-five. Trucking begins to outdistance rail as a means to transport agricultural goods.

(Continued)

- In 1920, there are more than 925,000 black-operated farms. By 2000, there are fewer than 18,500 black-operated farms.
- In 1923, congressional distribution of seeds is discontinued. Also in 1923, the now-classic tricycle row crop International Harvester, running at a few horsepower, marks the transition to machines from mules and hand labor.
- Pre-sliced "Wonder Bread" and candy bars such as Milky Way and Snickers are introduced. Milk is homogenized in 1927, and people start eating breakfast cereals like Rice Krispies.

1930-1940

- About 21.5 percent of the workforce is still farming, 34 percent of farms have telephones, and 13 percent have electricity. The average farm size is 157 acres.
- In 1930, severe drought hits the Midwest and South. The "Dust Bowl" extends over 75 percent of the country and severely affects twenty-seven states. Agricultural "adjustments" are attempted by federal legislation; these create commodity credit, price supports, and emergency aid programs. Farm income never recovers to "parity" with other employment.
- In 1935 the Soil Conservation Service is established to conserve soil fertility and prevent erosion. The "Country Life" movement promotes a "back to the land" way of life in the 1930s, led by Pulitzer Prize–winning author Louis Bromfield, who extols the virtues of farming in harmony with nature, and is an early pioneer of the "organic" farming movement, so named by J. I. Rodale, another pioneer.
- Southern cotton farmers idle land, keeping tenant farmers from farming, and causing black and white tenant farmers (sharecroppers) to form the Southern Tenants Farm Union in 1934 in Arkansas. The National Sharecroppers Fund is formed in 1943, becoming the heart of the Southern rural cooperative movement. The NSF continues its educational, organizing, and lobbying efforts, providing tools and ideas for the civil rights movement of the 1960s. The NSF also pioneers a farmer- and consumer-led food movement to develop local markets and organic farming.
- Homemaking magazines, cookbooks, and packaged prepared foods become more popular, kitchen appliances and "continuous countertops" are introduced, and vitamins begin to address nutritional deficiencies.

1940-1950

- The average farm size is 175 acres; there are over 6 million farms. Thirty-three percent of farms have electricity. The use of chemical herbicides and fertilizers accelerates in this decade.
- In 1946 the National School Lunch program begins.
- In 1940 the McDonald brothers open their first hamburger stands.
- The first precut, prepackaged meats go on sale in A&P stores, beginning the decline of meatcutting as a respected middle-class job. During the war there is food rationing, and "victory gardens" supply homes with fresh food. In 1945 the first microwave oven is introduced. Frozen foods become popular. Cake mixes are introduced in 1948.

1950–1960

- Irrigated acreage increases, from about 14.5 million acres in the 1930s to 25.5 million acres in the 1950s. One farmer feeds 15.5 people in 1950. By 1960, one farmer feeds 25.8 people. The mechanical cotton picker cuts work hours from an average of 66 per acre to 50 by 1961.
- In 1952 the typical grocery store carries over 4,000 items, up from 870 in 1928. Postwar America takes an interest in foreign foods like pizza and sukiyaki, and gobbles up anything the food industry presents, from Sugar Pops and Trix (46.6 percent sugar), to Cheez Whiz. The USDA reduces the seven basic food groups to four. The first Burger King and Kentucky Fried Chicken franchises open.

1960–1970

- Cesar Chavez starts the National Farm Workers Association in Delano, California, in 1963. In 1968 the grape boycott begins, and by the 1970s the union is negotiating labor contracts with growers.
- In 1964 the Food Stamp program begins. By the 1960s, 98.4 percent of farms have electricity, and 83 percent have phones. Bac'Os, Taster's Choice freeze-dried coffee, Tang, and Gatorade, along with diet colas, enter the American diet.
- In 1960, about 11 percent of America's farmers are black, roughly the same proportion of blacks as in the general population. By 1990, blacks represent only 1.5 percent of the nation's farmers.

1970–1980

- One farmer feeds 75.8 people in 1970. Farmers use over 40 million tons of fertilizer. In the 1970s the country's farm policy becomes "get big or get out." The average size of a farm grows to 390 acres.
- In 1975, California enacts the Agricultural Labor Relations Act, giving farm workers collective bargaining rights that they had been denied under federal law since the 1930s.
- Because of mechanization, between 1930 and 1974 at least 33 million people are "tractored off" their farms. In 1979 the American Agricultural Movement's "tractorcade" of farmers drives to Washington to lobby for higher prices, and the USDA calls for a national dialogue on the future of agriculture.
- In 1971, Frances Moore Lappé's *Diet for a Small Planet*, extolling a grain-based diet, becomes a best-selling book. Frozen yogurt, Hamburger Helper, and French food become popular.

1980–1990

- In 1980 the North Carolina Black Farmers group files suit against the USDA for institutionalized racism against black farmers. The suit is eventually settled in the late 1990s, but discrimination persists. Other minority farmers, including Hispanic and Native American farmers, follow the black farmers' example and file discrimination suits against the USDA.

(Continued)

- In 1985, musician and singer Willie Nelson holds the first "Farm Aid" concert to raise money for family farmers, as the federal government has by this time all but abandoned them in favor of supporting agribusiness with production subsidies. Farm income continues to fall as the farm economy spirals into depression and federal subsidies continue to promote production agriculture at the expense of the family farm and rural communities. The farmer's share of the food dollar drops to 20 cents or less and few farmers can make back the cost of production. Eighty-eight percent of farm operator household income comes from off-farm sources.
- In 1984 almost 20 percent of the $290 million consumers spend on food goes to "lite" and diet foods.

1990–2000

- Between 1993 and 1997 the number of mid-sized farms in the U.S. drops by 74,440, continuing the loss of family farms. The average size farm is now over 470 acres. One farmer feeds eighty-two people. In April 1993, Cesar Chavez dies.
- Agricultural research becomes privatized as universities lose public funding and turn to income from patents and partnerships with private corporations.
- The agricultural biotechnology boom revolutionizes agriculture in just a few years after its commercial introduction in the mid-1990s. Genetic engineering, a commercial technology owned and controlled by a few corporations, effectively privatize seeds through patents. Genetically engineered crops and the "pharming" of engineered animals and plants for medicines touches off storms of protests worldwide, but has not yet resulted in any effective regulation of the suspected environmental and human health risks involved.
- In 1990, Congress passes the first attempt to create a national standard for organic food. The USDA adopts a final rule for organic food in 1999.
- Some countervailing trends emerge in the 1990s: Producers and consumers reestablish sustainable, environmentally sound, family-scale farming enterprises linked directly to markets. There is enormous growth in organic food and farming, farmers' markets, urban agriculture, and gardens in schools, shelters, and jails, signaling a renewed interest in healthy food and healthy farms and hope for the future.

white "Freedom Riders," led by civil rights activist Bayard Rustin (1910–1987), on a trip through the South. Rustin is arrested in North Carolina because he refuses to move to the back of the bus, and serves twenty-two days on a chain gang. CORE's tactic becomes a model for the 1961 freedom rides and Montgomery bus boycott.

1946

World Events

- Worldwide food shortages continue in the wake of World War II.
- India and Pakistan gain independence from Britain; the partition leaves India a Hindu country under its prime minister, Jawaharlal Nehru, and Pakistan a Moslem country under its governor general, Mohammed Ali Jinnah.

• The Afrikaner Nationalist Party (ANP) wins the majority of parliamentary seats in South Africa's 1948 elections, with a platform of anticommunism, "apartheid" or racial segregation policies, and the right of self-determination for all Afrikaners, the descendents of Dutch immigrants. For the first time, South Africa has an Afrikaner prime minister, Daniel F. Malan, and an all-Afrikaner cabinet. They immediately institute apartheid, with a hierarchy of rights and restrictions for people in their four racial groups, white, black, Asian, and colored (people of mixed ancestry). Blacks are especially restricted by travel limitations, called "pass laws," which allow them into white areas only temporarily for work. In 1949 the parliament passes the Prohibition of Mixed Marriages Act. In 1950 the Population Registration Act makes the four racial categories official, and requires every man, woman, and child to be classified. Also in 1950, the ANP enacts the Suppression of Communism Act, which becomes the legal basis for creating a police state, starting with outlawing labor strikes, at a time when the country's diamond mines pay black workers seventeen cents a day.

• The United Nations establishes its permanent location in New York City, building its headquarters by the East River on land donated by John D. Rockefeller Jr. It convenes its first special session this year, after Britain decides to leave Palestine and calls upon the UN to recommend a solution to govern the area. The UN adopts a plan, endorsed by a vote of 33 to 13, that is supported by both the U.S. and the Soviet Union, to partition Palestine into Jewish and Arab states. The holy city of Jerusalem is placed under UN jurisdiction as an international zone.

1948

ARTS AND LITERATURE

• Morris Louis (1912–1962) starts making paintings with Leonard Bocour's Magna acrylic paints. But it is not until Sam Golden, who becomes a partner in his uncle's shop, Bocour Artist Colors, refines the chemistry and formulates the first acrylics for artists' use that they become a popular artists' medium. By 1949, Sam Golden is commercially producing acrylics for major artists like Morris Louis and Alfred Leslie (b. 1927). He develops the water tension breaker (Acrylic Flow Release) for Helen Frankenthaler (b. 1928), after she complains about colors not saturating or staining the canvas as oil paints would. Compared with oil paints, acrylics, which are water-based polymer paints, are odorless and quick-drying, and are more durable, maintaining their intense colors. Artists are able to experiment with new techniques and effects that could not be achieved with traditional oil-based paints because the latter dry slowly. They can be poured, thrown, dripped, and, when thinned, shot through an airbrush. By the mid-1950s, after researchers in Mexico and the U.S. develop a way to mix acrylic resins with water, artists will be able to thin the paints to create watercolor-like effects, or work on unprimed surfaces.

• Tennessee Williams (1911–1983) wins a Pulitzer Prize for his play *A Streetcar Named Desire*. Its coded use of gay slang, not generally known to audiences in 1947, offers both gay and straight audiences one of the most brilliant plays of the postwar period.

• African American master printmaker and artist Robert Blackburn (1920–2003), who

An aerial view of Levittown. (*National Archives*)

learned the art of printmaking at the WPA-funded Harlem Community Art Center, organizes the precursor of his printmaking workshop in his New York City studio this year, running it as a cooperative where artists pay a small fee to experiment with innovative art lithography techniques and materials. From 1957 to 1963, as the first master printer at Universal Limited Art Editions on Long Island, he gains fame printmaking with the rising stars of Abstract Expressionism. Starting in 1963, he directs his own printmaking workshop in New York City for the next half century, welcoming an interracial mix of students and artists in an art world not often known for such openness.

GOVERNMENT AND POLITICS

• Congress funds the Voice of America, the overseas radio broadcasting arm of the U.S. Information Agency. Besides its U.S. propaganda messages, it carries the sound of American music around the world.

• Secretary of State General George C. Marshall (1880–1959) proposes a "European Recovery Program" known as the Marshall Plan, which is passed by the U.S. Congress April 2. It eventually provides $17 billion in aid to Western European countries devastated by World War II to work against "hunger, poverty, desperation and chaos. Its purpose should be the revival of a working economy in the world so as to permit the emergence of political and social conditions in which free institutions can exist." On June 26, the Soviet Union blockades the western sector of Berlin, cutting off the city's supply line to food and fuel. The U.S. responds with an airlift that carries 2,343,000 tons of supplies on 277,000 flights through September 30, 1949. This Cold War policy, containing Communism through foreign aid, proves highly successful as Western European economic recovery is accomplished by 1952 without any defections to Communism.

• The Displaced Persons Act allows 400,000 homeless World War II refugees to settle in the U.S., subject to a quota system.

• This year marks the beginning of a twelve-year effort by various forces in Congress (especially western Republicans), known as the "termination period," to dismantle the Indian reservations. Termination means a tribe loses its federally recognized status, federal annuities, and services. Thirteen tribes are terminated (including the Menominee in Wisconsin and the Klamath in Oregon) along with 100 bands, communities, and rancherias (California Indian communities).

• The California Supreme Court rules that race-restrictive housing covenants constitute racial discrimination and denial of equal protection under the law; it also rules antimiscegenation laws are unconstitutional.

• The U.S. Supreme Court declares religious education in public schools a violation of the First Amendment.

• Incumbent Harry S. Truman is elected president, with Alben Barkley of Kentucky as vice president, defeating New York Governor Thomas E. Dewey. In July, Truman issues Executive Order 9981, to end discrimination and segregation in the armed forces "as rapidly as possible," so that all military personnel will have "equality of treatment and opportunity regardless of race, color, religion, or national origin."

BUSINESS AND INDUSTRY

• The Polaroid Land Camera goes on sale this year. Produced by the Polaroid Corporation and invented in 1947 by the company's co-founder, Edwin Herbert Land (1909–1991), the one-step camera is hailed as revolutionary because it can take, develop, and print a finished picture on a sheet of paper in one minute without needing to use a lab. The camera is the first serious challenge to Eastman Kodak Company's domination of the mass consumer photography business, and has X-ray and other technical and diagnostic applications.

SCIENCE AND TECHNOLOGY

• Hungarian American inventor Peter Goldmark (1906–1977) of CBS demonstrates his

33⅓ rpm long-playing phonograph record (LP) made of durable plastic, which offers twenty minutes of music. LPs quickly replace the far more fragile 78-rpm format that offers only five minutes of playing time, and remain the industry standard until the advent of CDs.

• Cybernetics, a new interdisciplinary science of communication, is coined and defined by MIT-based mathematician Norbert Wiener (1894–1964) in his book *Cybernetics: Control and Communication in the Animal and the Machine.* Cybernetics is a control theory used to program or predict the actions of electronic, mechanical, and biological systems (for example, a human being), especially by performing mathematical analysis on the flow of information (for example, all the processing required to catch a falling ball) in such systems. The cybernetics wave, rising in the same year as the transistor, marks a transition into a digital world of global, interactive networks, robots, and prosthetics called "cyborgs," and virtual-reality environments called "cyberspace."

• George Gamow (1904–1968), Ralph Alpher (b. 1921), and Robert Herman (1914–1997) produce research supporting the Big Bang theory on the origin of the universe. They calculate that a Big Bang, an outward explosion of the universe from an initial extremely hot, dense state, could produce quantities of hydrogen and helium that correspond to observed percentages. They also predict the existence of cosmic background radiation, a remnant from the Big Bang cosmos when the universe was too hot to allow the formation of ordinary atoms. In 1965 this radiation is discovered by Arno Penzias (German-American, b. 1933) and Robert Wilson (b. 1936) while trying to refine radio equipment.

This propaganda poster promotes the U.S. government's Marshall Plan to help restore the economy of the postwar European countries. By Reyn Dirksen, c. 1947. *(Library of Congress, Prints and Photographs Division)*

CULTURE AND SOCIETY

• Zoologist Dr. Alfred Kinsey (1894–1956) publishes a bestseller, *Sexual Behavior in the Human Male,* based on ten years spent interviewing thousands of American men. Although his research methods are generally conceded to have flaws (the informants are mostly white, male, middle-class midwesterners, and disproportionately include prisoners and sex offenders), the book shakes up commonly held assumptions about what can be considered normal human sexual acts since many behaviors thought to be perverse prove to be widely practiced (30 to 45 percent of husbands are unfaithful to their wives, 90 percent have masturbated, and one in three admits to some kind of homosexual experience).

WORLD EVENTS

• The Provisional State Council, formerly the National Council, "representing the Jewish people in Palestine and the World Zionist Movement" announces the "establishment of the Jewish State in Palestine . . . to be called the State of Israel," which is "open to immigration of Jews from all the countries of their dispersion." Skirmishes between Arabs and Jews break out immediately into a full-scale international war, the first Arab-Israeli War, which involves the armies of Egypt, Iraq, Transjordan (now Jordan), Lebanon, and Syria, with other Arab guerrilla fighters. The United Nations, with African American statesman Ralph J. Bunche (1904–1971) as its chief mediator, arranges a cease-fire to end the war. The armistice gives Israel the right to occupy 80 percent of the former Palestine, which retains an Arab population of under 200,000 after 600,000 Arabs flee to become refugees in neighboring Arab countries. These boundaries remain in place until the 1967 war. Israel's Provisional State Council organizes elections for the Knesset (parliament), which in 1949 elects Dr. Chaim Weizmann as the first president and David Ben-Gurion as first prime minister.

• Mahatma Gandhi is assassinated in New Delhi by Hindu extremists.

• Mao Zedong's Red Army pushes the Nationalist Chinese army of Chiang Kai-shek off mainland China after they lose several battles in 1948–1949. The Nationalist forces retreat to the outlying island of Formosa (now Taiwan) and set up a temporary government-in-exile in Taipei, while Mao Zedong establishes a new Chinese government on the mainland, the People's Republic of China.

• Czechoslovakia's President Edvard Beneš loses control of his democratic-style government in a coup, and is replaced by Communist leader Klement Gottwald. The new government begins Soviet-style purges and arrests, with foreign minister Jan Masaryk either a victim of murder or suicide.

• The Organization of American States (OAS) signs its charter in Bogotá, Colombia. It becomes the first regional defense bloc under the United Nations, pledging to oversee the 1947 Rio Pact, a hemispheric mutual-defense agreement, in addition to agreeing to work for mutual political, juridical, and economic stability, and promote cooperation on human rights, scientific, and educational exchanges.

• The Republic of South Korea is established, backed by the U.S., with Syngman Rhee as president. North Korea responds by establishing a People's Republic, claiming jurisdiction over both North and South Korea.

1949

ARTS AND LITERATURE

• After opening on Broadway and winning the Pulitzer Prize, *Death of a Salesman* by Arthur Miller (b. 1915) becomes the first play to be a Book-of-the-Month Club selection.

• The Artists Club, a hangout exclusively limited to New York abstract artists, is formed by Willem de Kooning, Robert Motherwell, and Philip Pavia. Moving from its first informal location to an Eighth Street site, it becomes so ingrown that the membership closes to new-comers after reaching 150, and all are required to have keys. Members share formal and informal talks (John Cage and Merce Cunningham are guest presenters) and celebrate openings together.

• The Metropolitan Museum of Art establishes its Department of American Painting and Sculpture, a measure of respect finally accorded native-born artists, although the museum's conservative tastes will find them embroiled in a controversy within one year.

• Mexican-American choreographer Jose Limón (b. Mexico, 1908; d. 1972) premieres *The Moor's Pavanne,* his signature work, at the second American Dance Festival in New London, Connecticut. A quartet set to the music of William Purcell and using Shakespeare's *Othello* as scenario, *The Moor's Pavanne* typifies the passionate theatricality Limón brings into his other dances, including *Missa Brevis, There Is a Time, The Winged,* and *The Traitor.*

• *Life* magazine asks, "Jackson Pollock: Is He the Greatest Living Painter in the U.S.?" Their cost-per-foot discussion of his painting *Number Nine,* stated in terms more usually reserved for real-estate investments, indicates the beginning of a major shift in the painting and sculpture market, from interest in works by Europeans to those by artists from the U.S., and from considering the avant garde a cultural oddity to believing in it as an investment commodity.

• Writer Jack Kerouac (1922–1969) first uses the term "Beat Generation" while talking to John Clellon Holmes.

• Toshio Mori (1910–1980), *nisei* writer, publishes *Yokohama, California,* a collection of short stories, after an eight-year delay due to World War II. This first short-story collection published by a Japanese American describes the Japanese American communities in the cities of Oakland and San Leandro before the war.

• Hank Williams (1923–1952), country music singer and songwriter of genius, debuts at the Grand Ole Opry and is forced to sing six encores. Among his classic creations are "I'm So Lonesome I Could Cry," "Your Cheatin' Heart," "Half As Much," "Jambalaya," and "Cold, Cold Heart."

GOVERNMENT AND POLITICS

• President Truman succeeds in pushing through some of his "Fair Deal" legislative objectives, carrying forward the legacy of Franklin Roosevelt's "New Deal." The National Housing Act provides cities with federal aid for slum clearance and the construction of low-income housing units for 800,000 families. An amendment to the Fair Labor Standards Act raises the minimum wage from forty-five cents to seventy-five cents per hour, and a Social Security Act extends eligibility to benefit nearly 10 million more people.

SCIENCE AND TECHNOLOGY

• African American inventor Frederick McKinley Jones (1893–1961) transforms the U.S. food transport industry by inventing the Jones Removable Cooling Unit, a practical method to refrigerate trucks.

CULTURE AND SOCIETY

• KPFA-FM, the first listener-sponsored radio station in the U.S., is founded in Berkeley, California, by Lewis Hill. With the help of Richard Moore, Eleanor McKinney, and funds contributed by John Marshall of the Rockefeller Foundation, the station, known as Pacifica Radio, becomes the first station within a network of five member-based, commercial-free radio stations and thirteen affiliate stations called the Pacifica National Radio Network. Champions of free speech, they specialize in giving coverage to political points of view generally ignored in mainstream media outlets, flourishing in Los Angeles, New York, Washington, D.C., and Houston.

WORLD EVENTS

• A military alliance known as NATO (North Atlantic Treaty Organization) is formed by twelve Western nations and ratified by the U.S. Senate, to counterbalance the alliance formed by countries of the Warsaw Pact (Bulgaria, Czechoslovakia, East Germany, Hungary, Poland, Romania, and the USSR). By 1999, after Eastern European Communist governments collapse, nineteen countries will be NATO members, including Belgium, Canada, the Czech Republic, Denmark, France, Germany, Italy, Luxembourg, Netherlands, Norway, Poland, Portugal, Spain, Turkey, the United Kingdom, and the U.S.

• The People's Republic of China is formally announced in Beijing, the new capital, with Mao Zedong as chairman and Zhou Enlai as premier and foreign minister. The U.S. does not recognize the Chinese Communist government.

• The USSR tests its first atomic bomb.

• The German Federal Republic (known as West Germany) is formally established, with its capital located in Bonn. Konrad Adenauer, founder of the Federation of Christian Democratic Parties, becomes chancellor after his party receives a majority in elections, a position he maintains for the next fourteen years.

• Apartheid (racial separation) is formally enacted in South Africa, defining all relations between white, black, Asian, and colored (mixed ancestry) groups. Although South Africa became a member of the United Nations in 1945, it refused to sign their Universal Declaration of Human Rights.

• Simone de Beauvoir (1908–1986) publishes *The Second Sex,* a groundbreaking work of feminist literature that sets in motion changes in the ways women feel about themselves. De Beauvior challenges areas of inequality with men, advocating independence for women and analyzing the social, cultural, and economic dynamics behind traditional roles women are expected to assume in society, including marriage and motherhood. It inspires the second generation of U.S. feminists when a partial English translation is published in 1953.

• George Orwell publishes *1984,* a novel that predicts a future of the world in the year of its title, although when the real-life 1984 arrives, many people will consider his "Big Brother Is Watching You" police state to have been long established.

The Seagram Building, designed by Ludwig Mies van der Rohe and Philip Johnson, demonstrates the "structural honesty" and "less is more" aesthetic of the International Style, in a 1958 night view, the year it is completed. Photo by Gottscho-Schleisner, Inc. *(Library of Congress, Prints and Photographs Division)*

1950-1959

PORTRAIT OF A NATION AS A
TEN-YEAR-OLD CHICANO, 1958
JUAN FELIPE HERRERA

Saturday.

Walking down Market Street.

"San Pancho," my mom says.

I say "San Francisco" like on TV.

I love walking in the City. The light from the sky is like a loud gold ocean. It splashes over the Woolworth's Building and bounces into my face. I smile. People peep into small storefronts. Radios and glassy purses. So many new things. "That's a picture of a Rotocycle," a man with a big hat says as he points to a photograph of a flying bicycle. A line of gray-suited men with newspapers rolled under their arms rush out of a door nearby. "President Eisenhower signs Alaska as forty-ninth state!" a newspaper boy yells out to them.

We're going to see Susan Hayward in her new movie—*I Want to Live*. I can't wait. We stay at my uncle Roberto's Victorian in the Mission District. I never knew what a Victorian was. Now I get to play with all my cousins. All day long there are voices and songs floating upstairs and falling back down stairs. Cha! Cha! Cha! Upstairs. Downstairs—Cha! Cha! Cha!

My cousin Tito says he's a "beatnik." "Soy el beatnik!" he sings in a fuzzy, wild sweater. Then he guzzles milk from the carton. Last night, at about two in the morning, he popped his head into my bunk-bed and poured his flashlight into my eyes. Then he sang out loud, "I got a girl called Boney Maroni." That's upstairs. In the afternoons, after Tito polishes his 1957 Chevy, he plays bongos out in the cement patio with his

"Persons picketing against the use of tax dollars for the development of nuclear weapons." Photo by F. Palumbo for *World-Telegram* (Library of Congress, Prints and Photographs Division)

friends. Then they listen to Cal Tjader and the Horace Silver Quintet. "Stereophonic, daddy-o!" Tito hollers to his buddies and slaps the bongos between his knees.

I love my uncle Roberto's homemade sound studio. He calls it "el Hi-Fi Room" because he has the same new machine Tito has downstairs. "Stereo recording phonograph," he reminds me. "You can hear two things from different speakers at the same time." Uncle Roberto tapes his radio show in Spanish for Radio CAFE. "You know, I started Radio CAFE in a garage in Chinatown," he tells me, and puts on his headphones and leans into a microphone. I look at all the stacks of "long play" records and reels of recording tape on his table. Uncle Roberto has posters of Pedro Infante, Cantinflas, and Maria Felix on the wall.

On Market Street. Going to see Susan Hayward with my mom, who's from another big city—Mexico City.

We stop next to Clinton's Cafeteria and buy a burger for fifteen cents in a closet-size stand-up parlor. Next to us, in another tiny booth, a man sells rubber rats tied to a long hair. "Come see the Magic Rat! Ladies and gentlemen!" he shouts out to a crowd. "See the rat slide down my hand? See the rat run up my arm? See the rat jump from one hand to the other. Jump, magic rat!" Then he shows us how the hair is wrapped to his belt and on the other end it is glued with a gumball under the rat belly. I buy one for a dollar, open the box, and look for the hair that ties everything together.

"I have an idea!" Mama says. We step into the Crystal Palace market on Eleventh Street. The Crystal Palace is my favorite place in San Pancho. It has a crystal ceiling higher than a church. Mama stops at a pie counter. She orders a lemon meringue. "Over here, Mom!" I yell, next to the roast duck. "How about a roast chicken?" she says. A man with a white cap wraps the chicken into an aluminum star. We leave and we walk one block. See? Mom points to the red plastic letters of the movie theater: *I Want to Live*, starring Susan Hayward, and *Bambi*. Across the street at the Orpheum, they are showing *Cat on a Hot Tin Roof* and *Touch of Evil*. We walk slowly into the dark.

Lights fade out.
People smoke on the side-rows
and mama gets drowsy. A black and white
newsreel comes on. Faces and words, words
about "Nehru in India."

Flashes and lights.
Big news-words about "neutrinos" and men
in doctor clothes saying there will be
"no more polio."

"U.S. launches first moon rocket!"
Another big word—
"De-se-gre-ga-tion." I say it in Spanish.
The governor of Arkansas says,
"There will be no
de-se-gre-ga-tion in my schools!"

"Sugar Ray Robinson beats Carmen Basilio!
And wins the middleweight boxing
  championship
for the fifth time!" A reporter speaks out as
he takes notes.

Mama opens the pie box slowly. "Ohio State wins the Rose Bowl football game!" another reporter says. A group of women in wavy dresses walk in front of cameras. "Today we open the doors of the Gug-gen-heim Museum in New York City." I am sweating in my flannel checkered shirt and my Levi's. The cigarette smoke makes me cough. We are sitting in the last row in the back. No one can see us. Mama pushes her right hand into the pie. She hands me a crushed and foamy sweet ball of upside-down crust. Pushes her hand into the yellow-white gel again. And giggles. We both lift our pie-hands to our mouths. "The world is changing fast," a voice says as the newsreel ends. Our hands come up to our lips. Pie first, then the chicken is next. I wash my left hand with my tongue. Mama looks at me. I look back at her in the bright flashing light. Mama knows how to walk. She teaches me so many things with every step we take. I smile at her with a lemon meringue mustache. I say, "Cool, daddy-o!"

I Want to Live
glows in hot letters on the screen.
I repeat it with my mouth full of sauce,
chicken meat, and pie.
I Want to (Live?)

1950

ARTS AND LITERATURE

• "The Irascibles" is the name given to a group of eighteen avant-garde New York artists who protest the juried competition for a forthcoming show of contemporary art at the Metropolitan Museum of Art in spring 1950. They refuse to participate because the conservative jury is "notoriously hostile to advanced art," or, in other words, is against abstract art, a style these painters share. Among the signers are the painters William Baziotes, Willem de Kooning, Robert Motherwell, Barnett New-

As of April 1950, the total U.S. resident population is 151,697,400, an increase of 14.5 percent over the preceding decade's census. This figure does not include Alaska and Hawaii. There are 1,098 aliens excluded for being subversives or anarchists, the largest total of any decade of the century. According to the U.S. Department of Labor's Monthly Labor Review, *this decade also sees 424 work stoppages involving 1,698,000 workers, totaling 30,390,000 idle days, the largest amount of work stoppages on record. In 1955, 47 percent of mothers with children under eighteen years of age are participating in the labor force, according to U.S. Department of Labor statistics. Average per capita personal income is $1,881, according to the U.S. Bureau of Economic Analysis.*

man, Jackson Pollock, Ad Reinhardt, Mark Rothko, Hedda Sterne, and Clyfford Still. Two major New York newspapers, the *Times* and the *Herald Tribune*, give the protest front-page headlines in May, and when *Life* magazine documents their action with an article and group photograph that appears in January 1951, it signals that the Abstract Expressionists have attained celebrity status.

GOVERNMENT AND POLITICS

• The National Security Council (NSC) recommends a top-secret policy, called NSC 68, of "rolling back Communist gains" throughout the world. This Cold War policy is to be accomplished by restructuring our economy to undergo a continuous, massive buildup and expansion of our military and technological capabilities, emphasizing the use of nuclear weapons.

🔲 1945

• President Truman complains of the "great wave of hysteria" sweeping the country, but over his veto, Congress passes the McCarran Act (Internal Security Act), which calls for the registration and restriction of Communists and "Communist-front" or "Communist-action" organizations. It also calls for the creation of detention camps, as an "internal" security measure, and these camps are actually prepared and will remain ready for use until the law is repealed in 1968. The Department of Justice, using its FBI division, compiles a list of hundreds of organizations that are "totalitarian, fascist, communist or subversive . . . or seeking to alter the form of government of the U.S. by unconstitutional means." Thousands of people are "purged" from federal jobs. Among the targets are homosexuals. By 1954 the list includes the Communist Party and the Ku Klux Klan, besides the Committee for the Negro in the Arts, the Nature Friends of America, the Chopin Cultural Center, the Washington Bookshop Association, the Yugoslav Seaman's Club, the Cervantes Fraternal Society, and the Committee for the Protection of the Bill of Rights. Anyone with membership or even "sympathetic association" in these organizations could be considered disloyal and therefore subject to prosecution.

• Senator Joseph McCarthy (1908–1957) of Wisconsin begins his four-year-long anti-Communist witch-hunt, from which no one is safe. At a meeting of the Women's Republican Club in Wheeling, West Virginia, he waves a fistful of papers in the air, proclaiming, "I have here in my hand a list of 205—a list of names that

were made known to the secretary of state as being members of the Communist Party and who nevertheless are still working and shaping policy in the State Department." His charges keep changing—the next day in Salt Lake City he claims to know of 57 Communists in the State Department. On the Senate floor soon afterward, he presents State Department loyalty files that are three years old, most of which belong to people no longer working for the State Department. He changes the wording in files, so that people noted as "liberal" become "communistically inclined," and an "active fellow traveler" becomes an "active Communist." He will employ similar tactics for the next few years as chairman of the Permanent Investigations Subcommittee of the Senate Committee on Government Operations, ruining careers and pitting former friends and colleagues against each other. His targets include scientists working at research centers like Los Alamos, Oak Ridge, and Lawrence Livermore Laboratories; the Voice of America, the worldwide communications voice for U.S. government propaganda; members of the literary, film, and theatrical communities; and even the past administration of President Harry Truman.

• Dillion S. Meyer, former wartime director of the Japanese American "relocation" camps, is appointed the new commissioner of the Bureau of Indian Affairs (BIA). Meyer begins to carry out the 1949 recommendations of the Hoover Commission, which advised having Native Americans "integrated economically, politically, as well as culturally" into mainstream American culture. This policy becomes officially known as the Termination Policy in 1953. By the end of this decade the Termination Policy succeeds in transforming 40 per-

CULTURAL REVOLUTION AND THE LITERARY CANON

Amiri Baraka

The 1960s Black Liberation Movement . . . the third major political upsurge by African American people in a history of continued struggle for equality and self-determination, also gave rise to an arts and cultural movement. The Black Arts Movement and, with that, the Black Theater Movement, wanted to create a poetry, a literature, which directly reflected the civil rights and black liberation movements. We wanted an art that was recognizably African American (like Duke Ellington or Billie Holiday or Charlie Parker), that was mass-oriented, a poetry for instance that could come out of the libraries into the streets where the people were. . . . A poetry that was direct, understandable, moving, and political. And lastly an art that was revolutionary, poetry that would help transform society, not merely lament or mystify the status quo.

(From Anne Waldman and Andrew Schelling, Disembodied Poetics *[Albuquerque: University of New Mexico Press, 1994].)*

cent of the Native American population into "urban Indians," as families set up residences in Chicago, Los Angeles, and other cities. At first the government assists in the relocations, providing funding for vocational education and on-the-job training. Over time, however, as many end up living in substandard housing and working at menial jobs, the urbanization movement does not achieve the government's goals. Instead of separating Native people from their tribal roots, one-third will return home to live, while others continue to maintain strong ties with the community life on their reservations, and many urban Indians will emerge as militants in the 1960s and 1970s.

🔲 1953

BUSINESS AND INDUSTRY

• African American migrant farm workers continue to dominate the migrant paths on the East Coast, the trail of farms and orchards from Maine to Florida offering seasonal jobs that become available as crops ripen for harvesting. Mexican and Mexican American workers dominate the migrant paths between Texas and the Great Lakes, the Rocky Mountain region, and the area from California to the Pacific Northwest.

SCIENCE AND TECHNOLOGY

• President Truman approves production of the hydrogen bomb by the Atomic Energy Commission.

BUSINESS AND INDUSTRY

• The Habloid Company produces the first photocopying machine.

WORLD EVENTS

• The Korean War begins on June 25 when the North Korean army invades South Korea and quickly moves south to capture Seoul, the South Korean capital. (Korea has been divided at the 38th parallel since the end of World

War II. The USSR commands the North, and the U.S. controls the South.) By June 30 the United Nations Security Council, with Soviet Russia boycotting, votes to intervene with a "police action." The UN forces are placed under the command of U.S. General Douglas MacArthur. This is the first of a series of Cold War engagements in which the non-Communist West and Communist USSR will face off on the land of a "client country." Although peace talks begin in 1951, the deadlocked struggle continues until 1953, with both sides suffering great hardships and casualties. It speeds the formation of the liberal-conservative political consensus that opposes "the rule of force," as the U.S. comes to the realization that it will have to learn to practice "mutual coexistence" with the Communists.

• *El laberinto de la soledad (Labyrinth of Solitude),* by Octavio Paz (b. Mexico, 1914), describes his interpretation of the lives of *pachucos,* the adolescents born of Mexican parents north of the Mexican border that Paz observed while living in Los Angeles during the 1940s as a Guggenheim Fellow. His view of the Hispanic cultures of Los Angeles and the Southwest—as inauthentic hybrids that lead these children to be lost souls, ashamed of their heritage—will be a source of endless discourse among Chicano intellectuals. Paz will win Mexico's first Nobel Prize for literature in 1990.

1951

ARTS AND LITERATURE

• *Dada Painters and Poets,* edited by Robert Motherwell, is published. This influential book reminds artists of how creative experiments earlier in the century, in a similar postwar period, seem very applicable today.

• Langston Hughes publishes his poem "Harlem," which begins, "What happens to a dream deferred?" It's closing words, ". . . like a raisin in the sun," will become the title of a Lorraine Hansberry (1930–1965) play in 1959. Hughes is a pivotal link between two important generations of African American writers—the writers of the Harlem Renaissance and the emerging 1960s generation of Umbra and Black Arts writers, many of whom he helps get published for the first time.

• The Living Theater collective is formed in New York City by the wife-husband team of director/actor Judith Malina (b. Germany, 1926) and designer/actor Julian Beck (1925–1985). Malina and Beck are anarchists and pacifists, who begin their work from a commitment to nonviolent revolution. They look for texts that allow actors to be real onstage, without layering a "superficial psychology" over characters, which is how they see the Method acting style dominating American theater and film. They introduce New York audiences to experimental European plays, including works by Pablo Picasso, Samuel Beckett (b. 1906, Ireland; d. 1991), and Eugene Ionesco (Romanian, born France, 1912–1994).

• Following his first one-man show at the Betty Parsons Gallery, Robert Rauschenberg creates the "white," the "red," and the "black" paintings as well as constructions that lead to what he calls his "combines," paintings that incorporate various objects, such as a stuffed goat, a bed, and tires.

GOVERNMENT AND POLITICS

• The Twenty-second Amendment to the Constitution is ratified, limiting presidents to two terms in office.

• A federal judge in New York finds Julius and Ethel Rosenberg, husband and wife, and their friend Morton Sobell guilty of selling top-secret information to the Soviet Union, including information on atomic bombs. Sobell is given a thirty-year prison sentence and the Rosenbergs are sentenced to death. Julius and Ethel Rosenberg are electrocuted at Sing Sing prison in 1953, after losing their Supreme Court appeal by a 6–3 vote, and in spite of worldwide appeals that they are not guilty as charged, but are victims of the anti-Communist hysteria that has heightened since the outbreak of the Korean War. They are the first to be condemned to death for espionage during peacetime, and the first civilians ever convicted of spying.

• The U.S. Wage Stabilization Board freezes wages and salaries to prevent inflation as the U.S. economy gears up at the beginning of the Korean War, although they are authorized to recommend fair-wage increases if labor disputes are referred for arbitration.

HELA

Christine Borland

Henrietta Lacks, a thirty-one-year-old African American woman, died of cervical cancer at Johns Hopkins Hospital, Baltimore, Maryland, in 1951. Cells from her tumor were routinely passed to the head of research of the cancer hospital before her death. They proved to be very unusual. The genetic abnormality specific to this cancer also caused the tumor cells to multiply at an astonishing rate. For the first time, human cells survived outside the body, growing in a nutrient medium. This heralded a new form of medical technology that allowed the study of cells in vitro. "HeLa," as it was code-named, became the first "cell line," an ongoing culture of cells from a common ancestor, all sharing the same genetic makeup. Over the last fifty years, H.L.'s cells have become a staple of worldwide biological research, proving invaluable in the study of human illnesses from cancer to AIDS. In 1954, "HeLa" cells were used to develop and refine the first vaccine for polio. In 1960, "HeLa" cells were sent on board the *Discover* XVII satellite to study the effects of zero gravity on the human body. In the early 1970s, when H.L.'s surviving children were contacted and asked to provide DNA samples for further research, her family discovered that their mother's cells had been cultivated for twenty years. When the cells were first cultivated in the 1950s, U.S. law did not require permission to be sought from donors or families. The family has fought for the last thirty years for recognition of their mother's contribution to science. Considering the pace of current developments in molecular biology, the case of H.L. has raised important questions regarding ownership of cell lines, and who should benefit from the products developed through their study.

(Text from Christine Borland's installation, including video, microscopic cells in culture, monitor, text, glass, and wooden shelf, "Paradise 2000" at Exit Art, New York City.)

⊡ 1980, 1995

BUSINESS AND INDUSTRY

• RCA transforms its World War II laboratories and plants into development of commercial television and experiments in color TV within forty days of the war's end. Building on the research and technology from navy-financed laboratories in Princeton, New Jersey, and a huge tube-manufacturing complex in Lancaster, Pennsylvania, production begins at RCA's Bloomington, Indiana, plant. RCA reintroduces television with its 630TS 10-inch set, selling thousands at $375 in Indianapolis before the city even has its own television station. Millions of military dollars begin pouring into other kinds of commercial laboratories, such as those involved in transistor development, an industry that by 1953–1955 will receive one-half of its development spending from military contracts. This sets up a pattern of distribution, known as "the military-industrial complex," that becomes pervasive. It allows the military and private industry to benefit mutually from war-related research, since laboratories need customers willing to pay at a higher rate to cover initial costs incurred while testing and mastering specialized technologies. After this initial investment, companies are able to commit to mass production, with a resulting lower cost to consumers.

🖻 1961

SCIENCE AND TECHNOLOGY

• Geneticist Barbara McClintock (1902–1992) shocks the scientific community with her explanation of puzzling DNA inheritance patterns found in the colors of corn, in which genes, instead of remaining fixed in their placement, change places with genes on other chromosomes during cell division. This pattern, called "jumping genes," explains how identical cells take on specialized functions (becoming bone, skin, organs, etc.), how the variety of species occurs, and how individuals and species can adapt to environmental changes over generations. McClintock receives a Nobel Prize for Physiology or Medicine in 1983 for her discovery.

• When uranium is discovered on the Navajo reservation in New Mexico and Arizona, the U.S. government hires Navajo to be the miners. Using mining methods similar to those used for mining coal, the Navajo miners work in unventilated mines, where they are not supplied with protective clothing or advised of the health dangers to themselves or their families, such as to avoid drinking radioactive water. Miners are dismissed if they get sick. Due to Cold War regulations and the defense-related nature of the nuclear industry, questions are considered unpatriotic.

• At the Nevada Test Site, about seventy-five miles northwest of Las Vegas, the U.S. begins testing atmospheric nuclear weapons developed by Hungarian-American physicist Edward Teller (b. Budapest, 1908) and a team of other atomic scientists. More than 100 aboveground nuclear devices are tested between 1951 and 1958. The radioactive fallout that results from these tests contaminates hundreds of square miles downwind, although people living in this area are not evacuated or warned.

• The Atomic Energy Commission (AEC), a government agency, sponsors an "Atoms for Peace" campaign to urge peaceful uses of atomic energy, particularly promoting it as an energy alternative to fossil fuels. Physicist Walter Henry Zinn (Canadian-American, b. Ontario, 1906) builds an experimental breeder reactor near Idaho Falls, Idaho. The next year, under AEC auspices, the Argonne National Laboratories

ISLAM IN THE UNITED STATES, PART II

Sam Hamod

In 1952, under the leadership of Hassan Abraham, Abdullah Igram, and Casim Alawan, the first national meeting of the Federation of Islamic Associations was held in Cedar Rapids, Iowa. This led to an ongoing organization that continues to this day. The purpose of this group was to build mosques and create a voice and a presence for Islam in the U.S., and to allow Muslims from throughout the U.S. and Canada to meet and communicate with one another. In their earliest stages, the mosques were built primarily by Syrians and Lebanese, as was the FIA. But as time passed, more Pakistanis, Indians, Yemenis, Palestinians, and Afghans joined their ranks. As converts have increased, the makeup of the mosques now is more diverse than ever before. However, the tensions between American-born and foreign-born Muslims from various ethnic backgrounds has become heightened since the time of Imam Khomeni of Iran. His brand of fundamentalism, which often was in conflict with Islam itself, led to excessive "covering" by women, concentrations on hell rather than on heaven and the good life God presented to humankind on Earth, and constant finger-pointing at those who questioned (in opposition to the Qur'an, which exhorts people to "read and understand"). Many American-born Muslims of Arab origin do not follow these precepts, and this conflict has caused many educated Muslims to forgo attendance at mosques because they prefer not to be involved in squabbles with the "fundamentalists" (actually, these people, while well-meaning, are more reactionaries than fundamentalists—even though the latter is the tag Western media have placed on them—because they often don't follow the fundamentals of Islam, but rather their own ethnic practices). The outcome of these conflicts is not clear; those more educated in Islam are often not allowed to speak in the mass media because they are crowded out by the reactionaries who make better press copy and make for more exciting conflict on radio and television.

Elijah Muhammad and the "Black Muslims"

In fact, many of the Muslims who followed orthodoxy were black; thus it was an error to speak of "Black Muslims" and "White Muslims." However, the American media took it upon themselves to infer that all blacks who followed Islam were followers of the Honorable Elijah Muhammad. Though his strict sense of discipline, learned from Islam, aided many African Americans in defeating their drinking and use of drugs, Muhammad overlooked the universal brotherhood that underlies Islam. Later in his life, Mr. Muhammad would allow his sons Akhbar and Warith-a-Deen (Wallace) to study Islam with Dr. Jamil Diab (a highly educated and respected Muslim Palestinian who resided in Chicago and who often spoke with Mr. Muhammad about orthodox Islam). Both of Mr. Muhammad's sons became orthodox Muslim leaders in a split with their father; however, they both came to Islam with his blessings. In fact, as he aged, he allowed his sons to go to Egypt and Saudi Arabia to study orthodox Islam and to become imams.

It was also during this time that Elijah Muhammad's follower El-Hajj Malik El-Shabazz (Malcolm X) had a difference of position with Mr. Muhammad and became more of an adherent to orthodox Islam. It was through the work of Dr. Hoballah, Dr. Shawaraby, Dr. Diab, and Mr. Hamod that Malcolm X received a visa to make the Hajj (the Muslim pilgrimage) and meet with President Gamal Abdel Nasser and other Muslim leaders in the Arab and African Muslim world. Simultaneous with these events, a group of Muslim students began meeting at the Mosque El Ameen that opened in Gary, Indiana, in 1960 and formed the Muslim Students Association. They were trying to set up an academic equivalent to the Federation of Islamic Associations. The MSA wanted to be a missionary academic group that would organize university and college students and eventually transform into ISNA (Islamic Society of North America). Many of the African Americans who followed Elijah Muhammad have broken off to follow the American Muslim Mission headed by the orthodox Warith-a-Deen Muhammad. Others follow the less orthodox, but still Muslim, Minister Louis Farrakhan. However, as time passes, with the growth of Islam in the U.S., Muslims identify more with one another than with their various groups and leaders. There are as many perspectives in Islam as there are in Christianity and Judaism, but Muslims still fit under a large umbrella with the unity of belief in the Qur'an and belief in Muhammad as a major prophet of God.

🖻 1927

builds a nuclear power station in Arco, Idaho, called the U.S. Reactor Testing Station, which uses a breeder reactor to produce electricity and more plutonium than it consumes. Nuclear power plants will prove to be a mixed blessing, but by the end of the century, nuclear power plants are generating about 17 percent of the world's energy.

• Financed by Remington Rand, engineers and physicists John Mauchly (1907–1980) and John Eckert build UNIVAC-1 (Universal Automatic Computer), the first commercial all-electronic digital computer. It stores data on magnetic tape instead of punch cards, reading 7,200 digits per second, and is so large that it fills a room. The U.S. Census installs the first UNIVAC-1 in Philadelphia.

🖻 1939, 1948, 1953, 1970

• The biological research conducted on cancer cells taken from Henrietta Lacks (1920–1951) is a harbinger for future battles over

rights to lay legal claim to living things or parts of living things.

🖻 1994

• The first transcontinental television broadcast is made from San Francisco, when President Truman addresses the nation.

CULTURE AND SOCIETY

• The Mattachine Society, a secret society to help gay men meet, is founded in Los Angeles. The name is taken from medieval court jesters who were allowed to speak the truth when they wore their masks. Their first goal, which will take twenty years to accomplish, is "to change the self-image of gay people to produce a new pride, a pride in participating in the cultural growth and social achievements of . . . the homosexual minority." A New York chapter is founded soon after.

• The first document of male gay life in America, *The Homosexual in America*, by

Donald Webster Cory, a pseudonym for Edward Sagarin, is published, arguing for removal of all laws regulating sex. At this time the American Psychiatric Association Diagnostic and Statistical Manual of Mental Health calls homosexuality a "pathologic behavior," along with "transvestism, pedophilia, fetishism, and sexual sadism (including rape, sexual assault, mutilation)." The book brings up many of the themes that have dominated the political discourse on gayness, including problems caused by discrimination, social ostracism, and the tyranny of living in the closet.
1969

• The Federation of Islamic Associations (FIA) is founded in Cedar Rapids, Iowa, by William Aossey, Mrs. Sadie Michel, Ahmed and Sammy Sheronick, and Abdullah Igram of Cedar Rapids, Iowa, Casim Alawan of Toledo, Ohio, and Hassan Abraham of South Bend, Indiana. The FIA is the first attempt to form a national Islamic society that encompasses all of the U.S. and Canada.

WORLD EVENTS

• The U.S., Australia, and New Zealand sign a Tripartite Agreement for mutual defense, a few days before a September 8 meeting in San Francisco, when forty-nine nations sign the Japanese Peace Treaty granting Japan "full sovereignty" and bringing an official end to their participation in World War II. The U.S. and Japan make a separate agreement to maintain U.S. armed forces on Japanese territory, an agreement that continues to be renewed. In April 1952, President Truman makes a formal announcement ending the state of war between the U.S. and Japan.

• University of Toronto professor Marshall McLuhan (b. Canada, 1911–1980) publishes his first book, *The Mechanical Bride: Folklore of Industrial Man*. Although his work is barely noticed at this time, McLuhan becomes a major communications theorist whose unique theories, expressed in books such as *The Gutenberg Galaxy: The Making of Typographic Man* (1962) and *Understanding Media* (1964), are sought out by businesses, politicians, and artists.

1952

ARTS AND LITERATURE

• The first "happening," a collaboration called *Untitled Event,* is organized by John Cage and performed at Black Mountain College's summer school. It demonstrates how it's possible to make a performance structure where the participants do not know exactly what will happen (although the word "happening" will be invented later by Allan Kaprow [b. 1927]). The audience is seated in the center of activities, and according to Cage, "anything that happened after that happened in the observer himself." Each performer is given a "score" that indicates time brackets where they are expected to make decisions about how to create moments of action, inaction, and silence, with no "causal" relationship between actions. Robert Rauschenberg's white paintings hang overhead, Merce Cunningham and other dancers travel through the aisles, chased by a dog, Charles Olsen and Mary Caroline Richards recite their poetry from the tops of ladders, and David Tudor plays a prepared piano. All this happens amid other elements, including Rauschenburg projecting slides and film on the ceiling and walls, old records being cranked on a hand-wound gramophone, and Cage performing a "composition with a radio."

• Ben F. Laposky composes *Electronic Abstractions,* using an analogic computer and cathode-tube oscillograph, which some art historians cite as the first computer art.

• *Invisible Man,* a novel by Ralph Ellison (1914–1994) is published and wins the National Book Award. It is a sharp departure from the naturalistic tradition of the American novel and is the most successful attempt by an American to reach the standard for the modernist novel set by James Joyce.

• Photographers Ruth Orkin and her husband, Morris Engel, direct an offbeat, independent feature film, *The Little Fugitive,* with Ray Ashley, which receives an Oscar nomination. French filmmaker François Truffaut credits this film, about a young boy who runs away to Coney Island after he is tricked into believing he has murdered his older brother, as the "seminal force" behind the French New Wave cinema.

• Lever House, New York City's first International Style skyscraper, is completed at Park Avenue and 54th Street. It follows the basic International Style formula with a blue-green tinted glass curtain wall built on a rectangular steel grid, as designed by Gordon Bunshaft, to house the offices of Skidmore, Owings & Merrill. In 1954, one of the originators of the International Style, architect Mies van der Rohe, begins to design the Seagram Building, another Park Avenue skyscraper office building, with American-born architect Philip Johnson (b. 1906). These buildings become the pervasive standard for skyscrapers in business districts throughout major cities of the U.S. and the world.

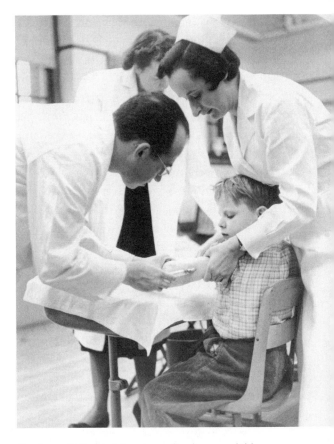

Dr. Jonas Salk administering polio shots to children, c. 1954. *(Library of Congress, Prints and Photographs Division)*

GOVERNMENT AND POLITICS

• President Truman seizes the Youngstown, Ohio, steel mills in April, to prevent a United Steelworkers strike after the steel companies reject a higher pay offer recommended by the Wage Stabilization Board. Truman calls for the government to operate the mills, using the same managers and workers, because he says a strike will harm the Korean War effort. In less than two months, the Supreme Court rules, in *Youngstown Sheet and Tube v. Sawyer,* that Truman's action violates the Constitution, as it usurps lawmaking powers rightfully belonging to Congress. Justice William O. Douglas writes: "We pay a price for our system of checks and balances. . . . Today a kindly President uses seizure power to effect a wage increase and to keep the steel furnaces in production. Yet tomorrow another President might use the same power to prevent a wage increase, to curb trade unionists, to regiment labor as oppressively as industry thinks it has been regimented by this seizure." This ruling stands with *U.S. v. Nixon* (1974) as one of the two most important limitations on presidential powers.

• Congress passes the Immigration and Nationality Act of June 27, 1952, or the McCarran-Walter Immigration and Nationality Act. It integrates the multiple laws that have governed U.S. immigration and naturalization into one comprehensive statute. It makes all races eligible for naturalization, eliminating bans on African and Asian immigration in place since 1790.

• In *McLaurin v. Oklahoma,* the Supreme Court declares that racial segregation is illegal in institutions of higher learning. When a lower court orders the University of Oklahoma Law School to admit G. W. McLaurin, an African American student, the university only complies with the letter of the law. They separate McLaurin from white students in both living and educational settings, even to the extent of making him sit in the hallway outside classrooms during lectures. The Supreme Court rules that once a student is admitted, any practice of racial segregation is illegal.

• Puerto Rico becomes a commonwealth, called Estado Libre Asociado (Free Associated State), on July 25, as the U.S. government responds to growing pressure from the United Nations and a Puerto Rican nationalist movement. In the political relationship they maintain with the U.S. to the present time, Puerto Ricans remain citizens of the U.S., with all accompanying rights except to elect senators and representatives to the U.S. Congress. Puerto Ricans are obligated to pay U.S. federal taxes and comply with military service. They may live anywhere within the U.S., and may vote in all federal elections. Under this form of colonial government, they may not conduct foreign policy, engage in foreign commerce, or otherwise act as an independent nation.

• Republican nominee Dwight D. Eisenhower (1890–1969) is elected thirty-fourth U.S. president, defeating Democratic Governor Adlai E. Stevenson of Illinois by a landslide. Richard M. Nixon becomes vice president. Fulfilling his campaign slogan of "peace and

---

I woke up this morning and I thought that one of the big differences between the art world then and now is that we knew that art could look like anything and be anything. I have to ask myself if I still think that. I hope next week's work will illustrate that this must be the case.

Art shouldn't have a concept. That's the only concept that I've ever been consistent with. I don't think I've ever deliberately done a piece that started out to be reactionary or controversial.

(Robert Rauschenberg, with Barbara Rose, *An Interview with Robert Rauschenberg* [New York: Vintage Books, 1987] 55.)

Merce Cunningham's company performs *Walkaround Time* (premiered 1968) with a set by Jasper Johns, after Marcel Duchamp's "Large Glass." "The Walk Around" was the grand finale in minstrel shows, one of the sources of the Cakewalk. Photo by James Klosty. *(Dance collection, New York Public Library of the Performing Arts)*

prosperity," Eisenhower focuses on economic development and national security measures, emphasizing containment of Communism through buildup of nuclear missiles and space exploration.

SCIENCE AND TECHNOLOGY

• On November 6, 1952, a hydrogen bomb, a thermonuclear device with a force 500 times greater than the atomic bomb that destroyed Hiroshima, is first exploded over Eniwetok Atoll, in the Marshall Islands in the South Pacific Ocean. President Eisenhower reveals the new weapon to the nation in February 1954, shortly before the U.S. detonates another hydrogen bomb at Bikini, another Marshall Island, in a test that surpasses expected magnitude.

• The Cold War intensifies as both the U.S. and the Soviet Union race to develop their first hydrogen bombs. (The Soviets explode their first thermonuclear device in 1953.) The U.S. Air Force contracts with Bell Labs to use their expertise in electronics and communications to build a network of more than fifty early-warning radar stations, as a defense against Soviet attack. The stations communicate with UHF and VHF frequencies across the northern extremes of the continent.

• Dr. Jonas Salk (1914–1995) begins public testing of a killed-virus vaccine to immunize against polio, which he has been researching since 1947 under sponsorship of the Foundation for Infantile Paralysis. He will conduct large-scale field trials in 1954, inoculating

TV DINNER (1953)

Kathleen Moran

A modest innovation to be sure, the TV dinner nonetheless represents a number of important social and technological changes that came to define the last half of the twentieth century. Swanson introduced the first ninety-eight-cent turkey dinner in December. It consisted of precooked frozen turkey and stuffing, mashed potatoes, and peas, divided into a three-compartment aluminum tray. While "frosted" food—precooked frozen entrees—had been around since the 1940s, the TV dinner was poised to take advantage of post-World War II methods of flash freezing, the spread of large suburban supermarkets, and the new consumer market for home freezers. Perhaps the most innovative aspect of the TV dinner was the package itself. Shaped like a wooden television console with a screen projection of the food, the box expressed the deepest logic of the new television age. Family dinner was moving from the kitchen table to trays facing the TV set. Indeed, a whole new room, named the family room, was built around the technology that was to dominate American leisure time up to our present day.

schoolchildren with his new polio vaccine, and the drug will be officially approved in 1955. Dr. Albert B. Sabin (1906–1993) will develop a safe live-virus oral vaccine that becomes available in the U.S. in 1960.

• G. D. Searle Laboratories develops an oral contraceptive for women that will be made available commercially in 1960.

CULTURE AND SOCIETY

• Upon his release from prison, where he has been introduced to the Muslim religion, Malcolm X (1925–1965), also known as El-Hajj Malik Al-Shabazz, joins the Black Muslims, under the leadership of Elijah Muhammad. He becomes a militant separatist and Muslim minister.

WORLD EVENTS

• King George VI dies, and his daughter Elizabeth becomes the next British monarch. Her reign will continue into the new millennium.

• The world's first accident at a nuclear power plant is caused by a technician's error at a nuclear reactor at Chalk River, Canada. The nuclear core explodes.

• In Cuba, former President Fulgencio Batista y Zaldivar regains power in a coup. He remains in power until forced to flee by Fidel Castro in 1959.

1953

• Merce Cunningham (b. 1919) forms his first dance company during the summer at Black Mountain College with a small group of dancers who have been working with him, including Carolyn Brown, Remy Charlip, Viola Farber, and Paul Taylor, with John Cage as musical director and David Tudor as company musician.

• Lawrence Ferlinghetti (b. 1919) and Peter D. Martin found City Lights, the first paperback bookstore in the U.S., in San Francisco's

North Beach area. Martin (whose idea it is) and Ferlinghetti each put $500 into the enterprise. A year later Ferlinghetti buys out Martin's interest in the store. In 1955, City Lights Press publishes its first book, Pocket Poet No. 1: Lawrence Ferlinghetti's *Pictures of the Gone World*. City Lights becomes a literary landmark, famous for publishing the works of the Beat Generation writers.

• Louis and Bebe Baron set up a private studio in New York and provide soundtracks using electronic sound scores for science fiction films like *Forbidden Planet* (1956) and *Atlantis*.

• Toledo, Ohio–born pianist Art Tatum (1909–1956), perhaps the greatest and most innovative solo pianist in the history of jazz, records over 100 solo performances for producer Norman Granz between 1953 and 1955.

GOVERNMENT AND POLITICS

• President Truman announces that the U.S. has developed a new weapon, the hydrogen bomb.

• Congress issues a joint resolution announcing their intention to free Native Americans "from Federal supervision and control and from all disabilities and limitations specially applicable to Indians," officially beginning its policy of "termination." In practice, termination means tribes experience loss of status and have to sell off lands to meet tax obligations. Thirteen tribes are terminated, comprising 3 percent of the total Native American population, including the Menominees in Wisconsin, the Klamaths in Oregon, and more than a hundred bands, communities, and rancherias (California Mission Indians), before the policy is officially ended by the Kennedy administration in 1962.

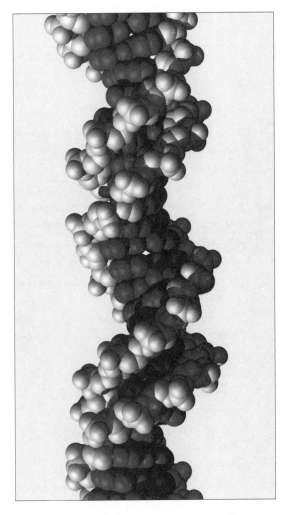

A contemporary computer representation of the structure of DNA. *(Jeramia Ory, Ph.D.)*

BUSINESS AND INDUSTRY

• Under President Eisenhower, the Office of Price Stabilization removes controls on salaries and wages in February. In March it ends controls on prices also.

SCIENCE AND TECHNOLOGY

• James Watson (b. U.S., 1928), a graduate student at England's Cambridge University,

HERNANDEZ V. STATE OF TEXAS

Marco Portales

On May 3, 1954, twelve days before the court announced its famous *Brown v. Board of Education* decision, the U.S. Supreme Court delivered another important, less-known decision stating that the exclusion of Mexican Americans from serving on Texas juries was unconstitutional. In *Hernandez v. State of Texas,* GI Forum lawyers Gus Garcia, Carlos Cadena, James de Anda, Cris Alderete, John Herrera, and Maury Maverick Jr., supported by members of the League of United Latin American Citizens (LULAC), made the following arguments on behalf of petitioner Pete Hernandez: (1) that Hernandez was found guilty of murder and sentenced to life in prison by a Texas court where county records showed that no Mexican Americans or Spanish-speaking citizens had served as jurors or jury commissioners, and that no Hispanics had even been summoned for jury duty in the last twenty-five years; (2) that Hispanic citizens denied jury duty were qualified and therefore capable of serving on juries; and (3) that such discrimination and segregation were normal practices in Jackson County, where Mexican Americans "were treated as a race, class, or group apart from all other persons." Gus Garcia contended "that such jury exclusion violated constitutional prohibition of group or class discrimination under the Fourteenth Amendment."

State of Texas attorneys countered by arguing that "because Mexican Americans were legally considered white, they could not be underrepresented as jurors in Jackson County." They claimed "that the historical absence of Spanish surnames on Jackson County jury rolls did not [by] itself prove systematic exclusion." State lawyers "surmised that the lack of Hispanic representation on Jackson County juries was merely a coincidence."

But writing for the unanimous decision of the Supreme Court's justices, Chief Earl Warren said the court was not persuaded by the state's defense: "Circumstances or chance may well decide that no persons in a certain class will serve on a particular jury or during some particular period. But it taxes our credibility to say that mere chance resulted in there being no members of this class among the over six thousand jurors called in the past twenty-five years. The result bespeaks discrimination, whether or not it was a conscious decision on the part of an individual commissioner." On these grounds, the Texas court decision against Pete Hernandez was reversed by the Supreme Court.

Hernandez v. State of Texas was significant because it was the first time that the country's highest court recognized "that Mexican Americans were indeed being treated as a class apart from the mainstream community, and that this [practice] denied them equal treatment under the law in violation of constitutional tenets." Being excluded, intentionally or not, seems to be a main feature of the Mexican American experience in the United States. (See, for example, Marco Portales, *Crowded Out Latinos: Mexican Americans in the Public Consciousness* [Philadelphia: Temple University Press, 2000].)

and biophysicist Francis Crick (b. England, 1918) elucidate the double-helix structure of deoxyribonucleic acid (DNA), the hereditary material that is passed from parent to offspring in living organisms. Using X-ray diffraction and 3-D molecular models, they discover that DNA consists of two helical strands twisted together, and in 1962 they will share the Nobel Prize in Physiology or Medicine with English scientist Maurice Wilkins for their discovery. Understanding of the structure of DNA opens the field of molecular genetics, and much later the Human Genome Project, which Dr. Watson will head for the National Institutes of Health beginning in 1988.

CULTURE AND SOCIETY

• Three events signal the contemporary sexual attitudes, practices, and awareness that are beginning to be openly acknowledged in the U.S.: Hugh Hefner's *Playboy* magazine publishes its first issue, becoming an instant success with its mix of quality erotic literature, thoughtful journalism, manly advice on how to live the good life, and a center gatefold featuring Marilyn Monroe as the first nude "Playmate of the Month." Biologist and sexual theorist Alfred Kinsey publishes the second half of the Kinsey report, *Sexual Behavior in the Human Female,* based on the case histories of 5,940 white females. It acknowledges that women engage in a wide range of sexual practices by documenting, for example, that premarital intercourse, masturbation, and homosexuality, which had been considered rare among women, are normal and prevalent behaviors. *One,* a magazine for the gay and lesbian community, starts being published by the Mattachine Society in Los Angeles. In

1958, *One* will win a case against the U.S. Post Office, setting a precedent that ensures mail service for other gay magazines.

• In San Francisco, the Chinese Six Companies, a merchants' organization, sponsors a Chinese New Year Festival, the first celebration of its kind on the U.S. mainland. The city embraces the dragon-led parade and other festivities, and it will become an annual event that encourages tourism in its North Beach area community.

WORLD EVENTS

• The signing of an armistice at Panmunjom, Korea, between United Nations forces and the North Koreans ends the Korean War, in which 25,604 Americans have been killed.

• When Premier Joseph Stalin dies after being in power since 1928, the Soviet Union starts to "thaw," by beginning to shift away from the police-state hold of the KGB (state security police), as indicated by the release of tens of thousands of political prisoners. There is a power struggle for leadership as Georgy Malenkov becomes premier, with Nikita Khrushchev appointed first secretary of the Communist Party, Vyacheslav Molotov as foreign minister, and Lavrenti Beria appointed as minister of the interior.

• Egypt becomes a republic ruled by a military junta, the Society of Free Officers, which forces King Farouk to abdicate in 1952. Colonel Gamal Abdel Nasser takes over the premiership of Egypt from General Muhammad Naguib in 1954. Nasser will become president in 1956 by referendum.

• Tito (Josip Broz) becomes president of the Federal People's Republic of Yugoslavia. With a revision of the constitution in 1963, he will

Poster: Puerto Rican independence. Poster by
Puerto Rican Solidarity Committee, c. 1965-1980.
*(Library of Congress, Prints and Photographs
Division)*

become president-for-life, maintaining peace
between the country's nationalities with his
blend of Communist economic policies and
political control mixed with relative openness
for the arts, travel, and individual enterprise.
He will rule until his death in 1980.

• In a coup d'etat in Iran, Mohammed
Mossadegh is overthrown by Iranian royalists
with the help of British and American intelligence. Mohammed Reza Shah Pahlavi is
returned to the throne, and Mohammed

Mossadegh is jailed for three years and then
held under house arrest until his death in 1967.

1954

ARTS AND LITERATURE

• The Newport Jazz Festival is founded in
Rhode Island, with the help of the tobacco-
producing Lorillard family, adding prestige,
organization, and money to the art of jazz.

• The mambo, championed by Machito in
New York and Perez Prado (b. Cuba, 1916–
1983) on the West Coast, sweeps America. A
traveling show called "The Mambo-Rhumba
Festival" tours the country and features singer
Miguelito Valdes and the bands of Pupi
Campo, Tito Puente (b. New York City, 1923),
and Joe Loco.

• Composer Edgard Varese premieres his
experimental part-electronic work, *Desert*.

• Babatunde Olatunji, a Nigerian master
drummer, records *Drums of Passion,* perhaps
the first and most influential example of
African music in the U.S. to date.

GOVERNMENT AND POLITICS

• The U.S. Supreme Court unanimously
rules that segregation of public schools is
unconstitutional in *Brown v. Board of
Education* (of Topeka, Kansas). Thurgood
Marshall (1908–1993), a young NAACP
lawyer who eventually becomes the first
African American Supreme Court justice,
argues the case. This decision overturns *Plessy
v. Ferguson*, the Court's legal sanction of segregation that had been on the books since 1896.
It marks the beginning of the end of the Jim
Crow doctrine of "separate but equal." Eleven

years after this 1954 decision, with its order for states to meet the guidelines with "all deliberate speed," more than 75 percent of the school districts in the South still remain segregated.

◻ 1965

• In *Hernandez v. Texas,* the first Mexican American discrimination case to be heard in the U.S. Supreme Court and its first case to be argued and briefed by Mexican American lawyers, the Court concedes that Hispanic Americans were not treated as equals with whites. In ruling that Pete Hernandez, a Mexican American, was denied equal protection under the law when he was convicted of murder under a jury-selection process that excluded Mexican Americans, this decision provides Hispanic Americans with a legal basis to fight against all types of discrimination, anywhere in the U.S.

• Senator Joseph McCarthy is censured by a Senate vote of 67 to 22, "for conduct . . . unbecoming a Member of the U.S. Senate," following the Army-McCarthy hearings, which last from early April to mid-June. The censure does not criticize his anti-Communist lies and abusive exaggerations, but goes after him on more minor matters: his refusal to appear before a Senate Subcommittee on Privileges and Elections; and charges that he abused an army general testifying in the Army-McCarthy hearings concerning allegations of subversive activities within the military. Senator McCarthy's lack of decorum, witnessed by millions on national television, successfully brings his four-year witch-hunt to an end.

• Four Puerto Rican Nationalists try to bring attention to their pro-independence movement by firing pistol shots randomly in the U.S.

House of Representatives. They are all arrested and jailed after wounding five representatives, and their leader, Lolita Lebron, becomes a heroine of the continuing fight against the colonial

A young Arthur Mitchell dancing. Photo by Carl Van Vechten, December 20, 1955. *(Library of Congress, Prints and Photographs Division)*

status of Puerto Rico. As a result of this incident, the FBI issues a definition of "terrorism" as an "unlawful use of force."

🖰 1999

• Operation Wetback, a government policing effort to locate and deport undocumented workers, deports 3.8 million people of Mexican descent, with few receiving a hearing. U.S. citizens of Mexican descent are also among those arrested and detained.

BUSINESS AND INDUSTRY

• RCA, which is owned by NBC, markets the first American-produced consumer color television sets, broadcasting the January 1 Rose Bowl Parade in color, even though very few people own color TV. The rest of the television industry has decided not to produce this new technology because it is too expensive to generate significant retail sales.

• The first commercial transistor radio, the Regency TR1, comes on the market. It uses four impure germanium crystals, called transistors, to turn alternating electrical current into direct electrical current, the type used by radio receivers. Although the TR1 does not become an immediate hit, within a few years hundreds of thousands of teenagers will be walking around listening to rock and roll on their transistors.

• The merger of the two largest labor unions, the AFL and CIO, into the AFL-CIO incorporates 15 million U.S. workers as members. Former head of the CIO Walter Reuther agrees to let former AFL president George Meany head the new organization. The merger occurs at the peak of organized labor's power, when the economy is flush with its postwar high level of production.

SCIENCE AND TECHNOLOGY

• The first fully transistorized computer, the Transistorized Digital Computer (TRADIC), is built for the air force by Whippany Engineers. It is able to perform "a million logical operations every second," using "700 point-contact transistors and more than 10,000 germanium crystal rectifiers in its circuits."

• Kodak releases Eastmancolor, a color film stock that is cheaper than Technicolor and can be used with standard cameras. Color in films becomes so pervasive that by 1970 it is used in 94 percent of feature films.

WORLD EVENTS

• The French are defeated at Dien Bien Phu, Vietnam, and the Indochina War is formally ended with the French–North Vietnamese Geneva Accords. The country is divided into the northern, Communist-controlled Viet Minh government under Ho Chi Minh, and the southern monarchist government under Bao Dai. Civil war begins, as does U.S. involvement in Vietnam. Bao Dai will be deposed in 1955 by his premier, Ngo Dinh Diem, and the U.S. will support Diem's regime.

1955

ARTS AND LITERATURE

• Marian Anderson (1902–1993), contralto, becomes the first African American to sing with New York City's Metropolitan Opera, when she sings in *The Masked Ball* by Verdi.

• Former Tommy Dorsey Band vocalist Frank Sinatra, now a solo act, begins to record such LP theme albums as *In the Wee Small Hours, Songs for Young Lovers,* and *Sinatra Sings of Love and Things,* most of them arranged and accompanied by Nelson Riddle and his orchestra. Sinatra brings a jazz attitude and artistic skill to the world of popular music.

• When the Compass Players opens up as a storefront theater near the University of Chicago, it provides the basis of an improvisational theater movement that will change American comedy. Started by David Shepherd, the group uses improvisational scripts (no lines are written out) and acting that changes with every performance. Participants include Mike Nichols (b. 1931), Elaine May, Andrew Duncan, Barbara Harris, Del Close, Severn Darden, Shelley Berman, Roger Bowen, and Bobbi Gordon. Group members move on after a few years, and some of the players evolve another company, called the Second City.

◫ 1938, 1959, 1963

• Dancer Arthur Mitchell (b. 1934) becomes the first black person to dance with a major ballet company, the New York City Ballet, and the first to achieve principal status in an American ballet company, which he is given by 1956.

◫ 1968

• Igor Stravinsky composes *Agon,* a twenty-minute suite, in his personal version of the twelve-tone scale. In 1957, George Balanchine choreographs *Agon,* which means "contest" in Greek, for twelve dancers of the New York City Ballet. Balanchine goes against the standard

SHOPPING MALLS

Kathleen Moran

Though various kinds of planned shopping areas and regional retail districts were built during the 1920s and 1930s, architectural historians tend to associate the development of the shopping mall with the postwar economic boom of the 1950s and with the massive migration of Americans to suburbia.

Accommodating nascent car culture became the major consideration of mall designers, but inside the malls expressed a nostalgia for the public rituals of traditional downtowns. Victor Gruen designed the first fully enclosed air-conditioned mall in Edina, Minnesota, in 1956, and his shopping center inspired mall developers to build more-compact vertical forms that were visually and climatically separate from the outside landscape. Longer operating hours, inward orientations, and new forms of spacing that encouraged browsing turned malls into worlds unto themselves, i.e., destinations. The mall came to be less a statement of urban utopianism than a form of escapism.

The activity that occurs in a shopping center has come to have its own verb—"malling"—and predictably, the mall has been the subject of artists and social critics. A mini-therapy industry has arisen to help "shopaholics," and self-help books for overspenders are sold in numerous shopping-center bookstores. The mall is the site of family bonding in Don DeLillo's *White Noise,* and a number of films are set in shopping malls. Even as some see the mall as a pathology or as living death, others find ways to use it for unconventional purposes: Teens hang out, seniors exercise in the safe, warm interiors, and people try on clothes and handle commodities that they have no intention of buying.

Rosa Parks seated toward the front of the bus in Montgomery, Alabama. UP Association photo, 1956. *(Library of Congress, Prints and Photographs Division)*

story format of classical ballet by making Stravinsky's music the subject of a modern plotless ballet with just a suggestion of an athletic contest between men and women. He reinvents ballet's movement vocabulary with his quick timing shifts contrasting with stillness and off-center body placements that have been compared to jazz and are so widely imitated that today they are part of the classical tradition.

• Dancer-choreographer Merce Cunningham and his company take their first national tour, going all the way to the West Coast on a shoe-string, traveling by bus and rented cars, and living with friends.

• A poetry reading, organized by Allen Ginsberg and emceed by Kenneth Rexroth, is held at the Six Gallery in the San Francisco Marina district on October 7. It features readings by Philip Lamantia (who reads the poems of his recently deceased friend John Hoffman), Michael McClure (b. 1932), Gary Snyder, Philip Whalen, and Ginsberg, whose first reading of *Howl* (though incomplete) galvanizes the crowd. This event marks the beginning of the San Francisco Renaissance. Jack Kerouac is in the audience and writes about the event in his novel *The Dharma Bums* (1958). Ginsberg himself suggests that writing the poem was a kind of conversion experience, a personal transformation: "I suddenly turned aside in San

Francisco . . . to follow my romantic inspiration—Hebraic-Melvillian bardic breath."

• Engineers Harry Olson and Herbert Belar invent the Electronic Music Synthesizer, aka the Olson-Belar Sound Synthesizer, while both are working for RCA. The user can program the synthesizer with a typewriter-like keyboard that punches commands into a forty-channel paper tape using binary code.

• Lejaren Hiller (1924–1992) and Leonard Isaacson compose *Illiac Suite for String Quartet*, the first piece of computer-generated music. The piece is so named because it uses a UNIVAC computer and is composed at the University of Illinois, where both men are on the faculty.

• The Columbia-Princeton Studio starts, with its beginnings in the living room of Vladimir Ussachevsky and then the apartment of Otto Luening. By 1958 they formally establish The Columbia-Princeton Electronic Music Center, Luening and Ussachevsky directing the program at Columbia, and Milton Babbitt and Roger Sessions directing the program at Princeton. They all form a group, known as the University Council for Electronic Music, which receives a Rockefeller Foundation grant of $175,000 spread over a period of five years. The grant provides technical assistants, electronic equipment, space, and materials for use by in-house and other composers free of charge, which places them in the vanguard of electronic music composition.

GOVERNMENT AND POLITICS

• When Rosa Parks (b. 1913), an African American seamstress and secretary of the Montgomery NAACP, decides to refuse to give up her seat to a white man and move to the back of a Montgomery, Alabama, city bus on December 1, the bus driver has her arrested because she is not complying with a municipal law requiring segregation on buses. Her action and arrest come to the attention of Reverend Martin Luther King Jr. (1929–1968), who, along with others, organizes a citywide bus boycott that continues for 381 days and involves over 50,000 African Americans, who cut the bus company's profits by almost two-thirds. The following year the Supreme Court rules that segregation of buses, public parks, golf courses, etc., is unconstitutional and illegal. Often cited as the spark that ignites the Civil Rights Movement, this incident leads to the formation of the Southern Christian Leadership Conference (SCLC) in 1957, and brings Reverend King to national prominence as a civil rights leader. It also revitalizes the Ku Klux Klan and White Citizen's Councils. In 1999, Rosa Parks is awarded the Congressional Gold Medal as "a living icon for freedom in America."

BUSINESS AND INDUSTRY

• Ray Kroc opens his first McDonald's fast-food restaurant in Des Plaines, Illinois, after buying the name from the owners of a San Bernardino, California, hamburger stand. The burgers cost fifteen cents, and fries are a dime. The company expands to 1,000 franchises during the 1950s and 1960s and, along with other fast-food companies, benefits from the passage of the 1956 Federal Highway Act by getting choice locations on the off-ramps of the interstate highway system. Their success has profound effects in many areas of the American economy, including labor, the American diet, and agriculture. McDonald's adapts the

WALT DISNEY'S FIRST THEME PARK

Kathleen Moran

In 1955 Walt Disney's Hollywood-inspired theme park opened its gates with live TV coverage hosted by Art Linkletter, Robert Cummings, and Ronald Reagan. Though Disneyland was a direct descendent of earlier amusement zones like Coney Island, world's fairs, and circuses, it embodied a new kind of synergy: the marriage of physical space with Hollywood imagination and television advertising. According to official biographers, Walt Disney, unhappy with plans created by architects for his new park, went to studio animators to design what amounted to a series of backlots, stage sets that allowed pedestrians to move from an old-fashioned Main Street to a medieval castle, from a jungle to the Old West. Rather than attractions like Ferris wheels and midway games, Disneyland offered a coherent and perfectly organized fantasy geography populated with figures from Disney's own films. The social significance of Disneyland (and its later and more elaborate versions in Florida, Tokyo, and Paris) lay in its ability to create corporate cross-marketing in an unprecedented form. Disney's parks became billion-dollar land-development strategies; marketing tools for Disney films and products; architectural models for themed malls, restaurants, casinos, and suburban housing projects; and alternatives to public social space.

assembly-line systems to the food industry, perfecting the use of automation and machinery so that the only skill required of workers is to respond to flashing lights and buzzers at every step of production. Their labor model becomes influential throughout the service economy: to pay minimum wage to a young, unskilled, non-union work force for jobs that offer little training. With their high turnover rate, by the end of the century, one out of eight Americans will have worked for McDonald's. Their pioneering marketing technique, to replicate their business template in franchises, is so widely copied that by May 1999 the company will open its 25,000th franchise, with restaurants in 115 countries on six continents. The McDonald's trademark will be synonymous with the phrases "the homogenization of American culture" and "the globalization of American culture."

SCIENCE AND TECHNOLOGY

• *Nautilus*, the first atomic submarine, is launched by the U.S. Navy at Groton, Connecticut, extending the U.S. nuclear arsenal into the oceans in the same year when President Eisenhower warns the world that the U.S. would be willing to use nuclear weapons in a time of war.

CULTURE AND SOCIETY

• The first Spanish-language television station to broadcast in the U.S., KCOR-TV, starts in San Antonio, Texas.

• The first formal lesbian organization, the Daughters of Bilitis, forms in San Francisco and publishes *The Ladder*. Until the mid-1970s, the Mattachine Society will be the only other prominent gay organization.

• Walt Disney opens Disneyland, a theme

Roads built under projects funded by the Federal Highway Act, a national inter-state system of highways, helped build suburban com-munities, often at the expense of long-established urban centers. This section of Interstate 43, built in 1966, removed Bronzeville, an African American neighbor-hood and commercial center of Milwaukee, Wisconsin, without a trace. *(Courtesy of John Norquist, Mayor of Milwaukee)*

park covering 160 acres in Anaheim, California, that ABC helps finance, the same year they pre-miere an after-school television program for kids called *The Mickey Mouse Club*.

WORLD EVENTS

• Winston Churchill 1874–1965 resigns as British prime minister, and is succeeded by Anthony Eden.

• The four World War II Allied powers for-mally end their occupations in East and West Germany and in Austria this year, reconfigur-ing the political alliances in postwar Europe. Following through on the Paris Agreements of October 1954, France, the U.S., and Britain end their occupation of West Germany, which is granted full independence and sovereignty, and is admitted into NATO and the Western European Union. The Soviet Union also declares East Germany a sovereign republic, and formalizes the Warsaw Pact, a mutual

defense agreement that allows the Soviets to maintain a military presence with its co-signers, Albania, Bulgaria, Czechoslovakia, East Germany, Hungary, Poland, and Roma-nia. The occupation of Austria also ends and Austria regains its sovereignty, after the Sovi-ets sign the Austrian State Treaty.

1956

ARTS AND LITERATURE

• Allen Ginsberg's *Howl and Other Poems* is published by City Lights as part of its Pocket Poets series. On March 25, Chester McPhee, from the U.S. Customs Office in San Francisco, confiscates 520 copies of the book and declares it "obscene." Customs releases the books on May 29, following a challenge by the ACLU. Three days later, publisher Lawrence Ferlinghetti and Shigeyoshi Murao, manager of City Lights bookstore, are arrested for publishing and selling obscene literature. The "Howl" trial follows. Judge Clayton Horn declares *Howl* "not obscene" and offers a criterion for obscenity. Ginsberg wins acquittal on a charge of obscenity.

- African American poet Bob Kaufman (1925–1986) begins creating *The Abomunist Manifesto* as radical, political street theater in San Francisco's North Beach area from 1956 to 1957. Created in spontaneous improvisations, including jumping on cars, the surrealistically logical political poem is first printed as a broadside from City Lights Press in 1959, and later published in Kaufman's 1965 collection, *Solitudes Crowded with Loneliness,* from New Directions Press. In April 1958, *San Francisco Chronicle* columnist Herb Caen is credited with coining the widely disseminated term "beatnik" to describe Kaufman, alluding to his association with the "beatific" aspirations of Beat Generation writers, and to his frequent beatings and arrests for disorderly conduct because, according to his wife, Eileen, the police did not approve of his wildly boisterous performance style or their interracial marriage; the suffix -*nik* is taken from Sputnik, the name of the Russian satellite that inaugurates the "space age" in November 1957.

- With the release of Elvis Presley's first hit, "Heartbreak Hotel," rock-and-roll gains worldwide market appeal through Presley's merging of a white country-western style with African American rhythm and blues.

- When Harry Belafonte brings calypso music from the Caribbean countries of Trinidad and Tobago, his recording, *Calypso,* makes the genre so popular that it becomes the first LP album to sell a million copies.

GOVERNMENT AND POLITICS

- Almost 6,000 Japanese Americans who renounced their citizenship while interned in World War II relocation camps are reinstated as U.S. citizens.

- The Interstate Highway System, the biggest public works project in American history, receives federal approval this year. Building upon programs started in the late 1930s, Congress legislates the Federal Aid Highway Act of 1956 and the Highway Revenue Act of 1956, to connect the major urban centers with a highway system designed with nationwide standards for projected traffic volumes in 1975. The expenditures are partly justified as a defense emergency measure, to provide adequate, fast routes for military vehicles, with the program named the National System of Interstate and Defense Highways. President Dwight D. Eisenhower gets Congress to make the program self-financing by crediting the newly formed Highway Trust Fund with "pay-as-you-go" revenues from federal gas and other motor-vehicle user taxes. In the next four years, 10,000 miles of the eventual 42,794 miles of highways are laid, but the project does not reach its coast-to-coast goal until the 1970s, with I-80 becoming the first completed artery going coast to coast. The Interstate Highway System changes the way Americans live, work, shop, and vacation.

SCIENCE AND TECHNOLOGY

- Transatlantic cable telephone service begins.
- The first computer programming language, FORTRAN, is invented by John Backus and his IBM team.
- The first airborne H-bomb explodes with the equivalent of 10 million tons of TNT, in a

new series of tests over Bikini Atoll in the Pacific.

• American oceanographer Bruce Charles Heezen and geologist William Ewing discover a global network of oceanic ridges, or submarine mountain chains, 60,000 km or 37,000 miles long. The only current theory to explain satisfactorily their discovery is plate tectonics, which divides the Earth's shell into twelve large "plates" and several smaller ones. The slow movement of these plates relative to one another causes the uplifting of oceanic ridge crests and earthquakes. The upwelling of magma (molten rock deep below the surface) splits the crests and causes "seafloor spreading" at the edges of the contiguous plates.

CULTURE AND SOCIETY

• Psychologist Dr. Evelyn Hooker of UCLA publishes her study for the National Institutes of Mental Health, "The Adjustment of the Male Overt Homosexual" in *The Journal of Projective Techniques*. It concludes that three standard personality tests, including Rorschach inkblot tests, given to thirty gay men and a control group of thirty straight men, prove that "gay men can be as well adjusted as straight men and some are even better adjusted than some straight men." She lays the groundwork for the American Psychiatric Association's reevaluation of its position on sexual preference and the presence of mental illness in 1973.

WORLD EVENTS

• Colonel Gamal Abdel Nasser, newly elected president of Egypt, nationalizes the Suez Canal and expels British oil and embassy officials after the U.S. and Britain withdraw

their promise of financial aid to build the proposed Aswan High Dam on the Nile River. Israel invades the Gaza Strip and the Sinai Peninsula, and occupies them. These actions lead Egypt into a war with England, France, and Israel, and a United Nations Emergency Force (UNEF) is deployed to stop the attack and remain to supervise a cease-fire, occupying the Suez Canal zone from 1957 to 1967.

1957

ARTS AND LITERATURE

• Jack Kerouac publishes *On the Road,* the prototypical novel of the Beat Generation and a siren's call for many young people to leave home and explore.

• *West Side Story,* Leonard Bernstein's musical of Puerto Rican and Italian feuding families on the streets of New York, based on Shakespeare's *Romeo and Juliet,* premieres on Broadway. The score is by Bernstein (1918–1990), the concept and choreography by Jerome Robbins (1918–1998), and lyrics by Stephen Sondheim (b. 1930). The jazz-and-mambo-infused score places dance front and center in plot development, moving the story with seamless transitions between music, dance, and speech, and establishing tragedy as a salable topic for musical theater.

• David Seville creates the singing group known as the Chipmunks by playing recordings of human voices at double speed. Electronic manipulation will not be used again in rock for about ten years.

• Miles Davis begins his collaborations with arranger-composer Gil Evans with the LP recording *Miles Ahead,* which will be followed in 1958 by *Porgy and Bess,* and in 1959 by *Sketches of Spain,* establishing cool jazz as a vessel for serious musicmaking that exhibits both sensitivity and intensity.

• Pianist Cecil Taylor opens the era of "free jazz" with his *Unit Structures* recording, featuring an improvised music with no perceivable bar lines or regular tempo.

• Max Matthews joins the acoustic research department of Bell Laboratories and begins experimenting with creating sound materials when he finds he can generate music by computers. Using his sound-generating computer program, Music I, Matthews produces the first computer music, a seventeen-second composition called *In the Silver Scale,* by Newman Guttman.

• Print art gains a revival when Tatyana Grosman opens Universal Limited Art Editions in West Islip, New York, and attracts well-known painters and sculptors to experiment with the medium's technology. Printmaking offers artists the ability to make individual or multiple editions of their works, and leads to changes in the look of paintings as artists incorporate printed components into their paintings. It also stimulates new art markets, providing artists with other sources of income, exhibition, and publication, and offering the public an enormous choice of art products that usually require less of an investment than paintings or sculpture.

GOVERNMENT AND POLITICS

• Spurred on by the Soviet Union's October 4, 1957, launch of Sputnik, the first artificial satellite to successfully orbit the Earth, President Dwight D. Eisenhower authorizes the formation of a new agency within the Department of Defense, the Advanced Research Projects Agency (ARPA). ARPA's mission is to find ways to make the U.S. the world leader in science and technology applications, especially for military purposes. Its research will have a strong focus on information technologies.

• Congress passes the Civil Rights Act of 1957, the first civil rights bill since Reconstruction, to safeguard any U.S. citizen's voting rights by setting penalties for violations of this privilege. It also creates the Civil Rights Commission to advise Congress on creating civil rights policy and laws, and to investigate and report any denial of voting rights based on color, race, creed, or national origin. The legislation is vigorously opposed, especially by South Carolina Senator Strom Thurmond, who sets a record for the longest filibuster, speaking nonstop for twenty-four hours and twenty-seven minutes.

• Arkansas Governor Orval Faubus blocks federal orders to desegregate Little Rock schools, acting in violation of the Supreme Court decision. He declares he will not protect African American students from white segregationists and calls out the Arkansas National Guard, posting them in front of Central High School's front door. In response, President Eisenhower sends 1,000 federal troops into Little Rock to enforce the federal court order. Passing in front of the white mobs, the troops escort nine African American students into the previously all-white Central High School, making it possible for them to enroll. Because crowd violence continues in front of the school, the national guard stays in Little Rock until May.

BUSINESS AND INDUSTRY

• The first commercial U.S. nuclear reactor is brought on line in Shippingport, Pennsylvania.

• One year after Jackson Pollock dies in a 1956 auto accident at the age of forty-four, sales of his paintings outperform blue-chip stocks and precious metal futures, and the prices rise 100 percent at auction. Modern art becomes a safe investment commodity.

SCIENCE AND TECHNOLOGY

• The Vanguard I rocket explodes on its launch pad at Cape Canaveral, in an attempt to launch the first American artificial satellite. In 1958, using a Jupiter C missile (derived from a military weapon), a Vanguard III launch attempt will succeed in placing a satellite in orbit. It becomes the oldest man-made object in space, which NASA expects to orbit Earth for 1,000 years.

WORLD EVENTS

• The Space Age begins with the Soviet Union's October 4 launching of a 184-pound aluminum sphere called Sputnik I (meaning "fellow traveler" in Russian). This first man-made satellite succeeds in orbiting the earth for ninety-two days and then falls out of orbit and disintegrates on its way back into Earth's atmosphere. One month later, Sputnik II, carrying a live dog, is also successfully launched, embarrassing the U.S. into realizing it does not hold the lead in the technology battlefield of the Cold War.

• In the first of many realignments among the Arab nations of the Middle East during this decade, Syria and Egypt agree to a merger, called the United Arab Republic, which Yemen joins later, re-forming the alliance into a new confederation: the United Arab State. Arab nations generally side with Egypt's President Nasser, except for Iraq and Jordan, who form a rival pro-Western alliance. These mergers will all be dissolved by 1961.

1958

ARTS AND LITERATURE

• Critic Lawrence Alloway uses the term "Pop Art" as an abbreviation of Popular Art, and it appears in print for the first time in *Architectural Design* in February of this year. Pop Art describes art using the everyday world of popular culture (what used to be called mass culture or "lowbrow") as inspiration and subject. It reacts against the "high" art concerns for pure abstraction and "highbrow" taste, and builds on the funky, junky concerns of happenings, assemblage, and environmental art that are being done around this time. Pop artists plunder consumer goods, media, advertising, packaging, comic strips, movies, television, and the celebrities that commercial products generate. New York gallery owner Leo Castelli gives two artists associated with Pop, Jasper Johns (b. 1930) and Robert Rauschenberg, their first one-man shows in 1958 and 1959 respectively. Although Pop Art does not really come onto the U.S. public's radar screen until the 1960s, its central concern with the space between art and everyday life has been evolving steadily since the 1920s.

• Composers Morton Subotnick and Ramon Sender establish the San Francisco Tape Music Center as a corporation whose mission is to experiment with any music on tape. Their Trips Festival, a kind of New Age ceremonial event, features Ken Kesey and Big Brother and the Holding Company as star attractions. By 1965 the Center receives a four-year Rockefeller Foundation grant of $50,000 per year. In order to ensure fiscal responsibility, in 1966 the Center moves to its current home on the Mills College campus in Oakland, where its name becomes the Center for Contemporary Music, and it becomes a public-access and educational studio facility.

• Max Matthews, at Bell Labs, continues to experiment with creating sound material through computers. With Joan Miller, also at Bell Labs, he creates the first widely used computer sound synthesis program, MUSICIV.

• Oscar Howe (Yankton Sioux, 1915–1983) receives a rejection for the painting he enters in the annual juried competition at the Philbrook Museum in Tulsa, Oklahoma (held from 1946 to 1979). His formal protest of this prestigious show's policy of promoting styles made popular in the 1920s and 1930s heralds a shift in Native American art practices: "Whoever said that my paintings are not in traditional Indian style has poor knowledge of Indian art indeed. There is much more to Indian art than pretty, stylized pictures. . . . Are we to be held back forever with one phase of Indian painting, with no right for individualism, dictated to as the Indian always has been, put on reservations and treated like a child, and only the White Man knows what is best for him? Now, even in Art 'You little child do what we think is best for you, nothing different.' Well I'm not going to stand for it."

GOVERNMENT AND POLITICS

• Congress funds the establishment of the National Aeronautics and Space Agency (later Administration) known as NASA, to promote space exploration, after a panel of experts recommends that the U.S. quickly launch a scientific satellite to counter the fact that the Soviet Union has beaten the U.S. into space.

BUSINESS AND INDUSTRY

• United Press and the International New Service merge to form United Press International (UPI).

• National Airlines puts two Boeing 707s into jet passenger service for the first time.

• The semiconductor industry finds a growing market in defense-industry contracts for its high-frequency transistors, switches, and other electronic components. In the rush to close the "missile gap," the manufacture of solid-state components, with weight and power consumption hundreds and thousands of times smaller than vacuum-tube counterparts, is the only real option for U.S. missiles, which have much less thrust than Soviet missiles.

SCIENCE AND TECHNOLOGY

• NASA appoints a former German rocket scientist, Wernher von Braun (1912–1977), as its chief rocket engineer, and recruits astronauts. Using the army's Jupiter C rocket, it launches Explorer I, a science satellite. This first U.S. satellite to successfully reach its orbit around the earth carries instruments to measure cosmic radiation that discover the Van Allen Belts, two regions of electromagnetic radiation 1,000 to 1,250 miles above the earth's atmosphere. These bands are responsible for the aurora borealis (the Northern Lights) and aurora australis (the Southern Lights).

• Stereophonic sound recordings are produced, giving people a sound experience that is multidimensional, and therefore closer to a "live" sound.

• The RCA Mark II synthesizer is built at Columbia-Princeton Electronic Music Center (the original version had been built for the artificial creation of human speech). The Mark II contains oscillators and noise generators. The operator has to give the synthesizer instructions on a punched paper roll to control pitch, volume, duration, and timbre. The synthesizer uses a conventional equal-tempered twelve-note scale.

• Electrical Engineer Jack Kilby (b. 1923) writes in his notebook a key inspiration leading to the monolithic integrated circuit (IC): "Extreme miniaturization of many electrical circuits could be achieved by making resistors, capacitors and transistors and diodes on a single slice of silicon." Kilby actuates his idea and builds the prototype IC for Texas Instruments from a single wafer of semiconducting material (usually germanium or silicon), effectively ending the problem of circuit miniaturization by eliminating the dependence upon wires to interconnect components. Several months later, engineer Robert Noyce (1927–1990) of Fairchild Semiconductor files a patent claim for an IC similar to Kilby's, and the companies eventually agree on a cross-licensing deal. The demand for ICs is at first strongest in the defense industry; in the rush to close the missile gap, the manufacture of miniature solid-state components is critical for the success of U.S. missiles compared to Russian missiles, which have considerably more thrust. Later, the silicon IC, or "chip," fuels the information technology boom by powering such devices as personal computers, pocket calculators, CD players, cell phones, and electronic watches.

CULTURE AND SOCIETY

• The Islamic Center is opened in Washington, D.C., initiated by Ambassador Ertegun of Turkey, father of Ahmet Ertegun of Atlantic Records fame. The land is donated by Abraham Joseph Howar (b. Mohammad Eissa Abul-Howar in Palestine) and from foreign funds in Egypt, Turkey, and Iran. Their board of directors is made up of Muslim ambassadors from around the world.

WORLD EVENTS

• The "Great Leap Forward" begins in China, a government campaign to increase agricultural and industrial output by reorganizing the entire population into communes, causing massive disruption to Chinese society.

• The European Economic Community (EEC) is established.

• Edgard Varese (1883–1965) composes *Poeme Electronique* for the Philips Pavilion at the World's Fair in Brussels. The work, for orchestra and taped sounds, is one of the first large-scale multimedia productions. It is composed specially for the site, a building designed by the architect Le Corbusier, with the assistance of Iannis Xenakis, who will also contribute *Concrete PH,* a score for burning charcoal. *Poeme Electronique* is performed on approximately 425 loudspeakers, accompanied by projected images.

1959

ARTS AND LITERATURE

• Allen Kaprow (b. 1927) presents *18 Happenings in 6 Parts,* a series of disconnected multimedia events placed in three rooms of the Reuben Gallery in New York City. The audience becomes part of the performance by moving from room to room on cue. Kaprow defines a "happening" as an "assemblage of events performed or perceived in more than one time and

Michael Kabotie (Hopi, b. 1942): "Figure with Snake." Oraibi, Arizona. *(Courtesy, National Museum of the American Indian Smithsonian Institution, Fred Harvey Collection)*

place." It becomes the term for a great variety of one-time-only environments, spectacles, or events that generally incorporate mixed media and use improvisational or chance structures.

• Writer and artist Brion Gysin (U.S., b. England, 1916–1986) tries to move writing beyond clichés and standard formal requirements such as linear time and realism, to bring it up to date with the unknown possibilities found in chance techniques influencing painting, dance, and music at this time. He experiments with a new cut-up technique, in which he cuts up words or phrases from existing prose by himself or other people, and then pastes them together randomly on paper to make a new text. Gysin works in collaboration with writer William S. Burroughs (1914–1997), whose hallucinatory novel *Naked Lunch* is published by Maurice Girodias's Olympia Press this year. One of the last books to be banned in the U.S., it extends the novel's possibilities through its horrorscape of forbidden language.

• Jose Antonio Villarreal (b. 1924) publishes *Pocho,* the first published novel written in English by a Mexican American. It tells the story of a Santa Clara, California, teenager's struggle to understand his Mexican American identity and role as a U.S. citizen.

• Lorraine Hansberry's play *A Raisin in the Sun* is the first African American woman's play to be produced on Broadway. The play captures the spirit of the times in its realistic look at the civil rights struggles, the roadblocks to success and middle-class comfort experienced by an African American family. It becomes an instant hit, a classic that is frequently performed and studied.

• *Beatitude* magazine (the title puns on "Beat") is founded by Allen Ginsberg, Bob Kaufman, John Kelly, and William Margolis. The magazine is printed at the Bread and Wine Mission in San Francisco. Its regular publication schedule ends in July 1960, but it continues to appear sporadically under various editors.

• The R. G. Davis Mime Studio and Troupe presents *Mime and Words* at the San Francisco Art Institute. This is the beginning of a performing group that will become known as the San Francisco Mime Troupe. They invent their modern agitprop (agitation and propaganda) theater by reinterpreting the fifteenth- and sixteenth-century European commedia del 'arte tradition, giving free performances of original plays on topical subjects in the parks and communities of the San Francisco Bay Area.

• The Second City, a Chicago coffeehouse cabaret theater company, opens, with a name borrowed from an A. J. Liebling profile of Chicago because it conveys their sense of being a cultural underground. Involving many former Compass players, it uses a slicker version of the old Compass improvisational comedy theater format that becomes a "show business boot camp," an ongoing comedy training school and performing institution that works as a feeder for the TV hit show *Saturday Night Live* for many alumni, including Bill Murray, John Candy, and John Belushi, and the comedy films and standup comedy explosion that follow in its wake.

• The Rockefeller Foundation sponsors a conference at the University of Arizona on the status of Indian arts. As a result, the Southwest Indian Art Project is formed to offer instruction in both traditional tribal arts and contempo-

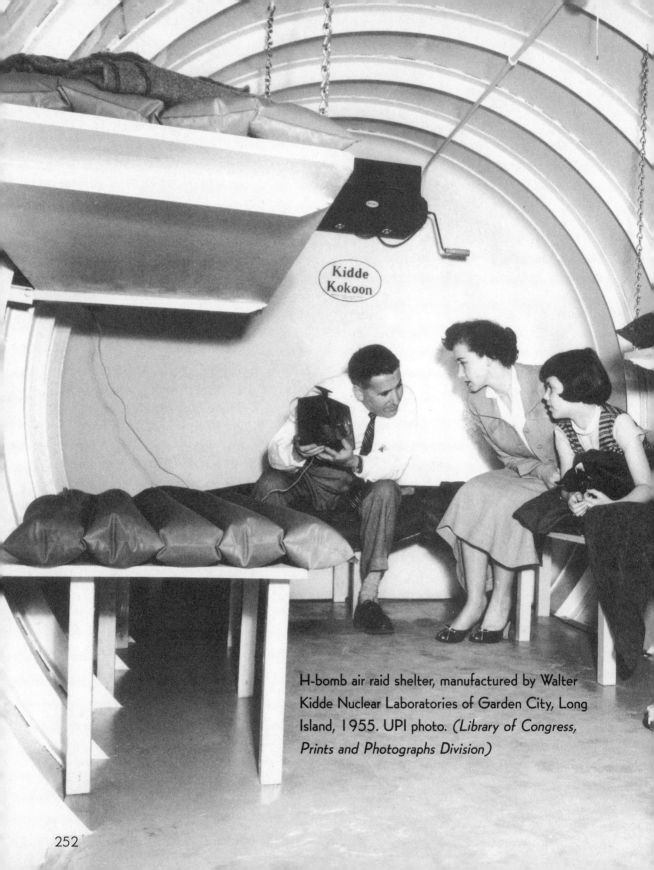

H-bomb air raid shelter, manufactured by Walter Kidde Nuclear Laboratories of Garden City, Long Island, 1955. UPI photo. (*Library of Congress, Prints and Photographs Division*)

rary fine art styles in order to "develop an individual creative consciousness [for each Indian], and to develop to the fullest his talent in art without the loss of pride in himself as an Indian." A summer program is offered in 1960 and 1961, and these programs lead to the formation of the Institute of American Indian Art in 1962.

• Ornette Coleman, an alto saxophonist from Texas, popularizes the "free jazz" concept with his Atlantic Records recordings of *The Shape of Jazz to Come* and *Change of the Century.*

• The Dave Brubeck Quartet records the album *Time Out,* which explores complex meters in a jazz context. Alto saxophonist Paul Desmond's contribution to the album *Take Five* (in 5/4 time) becomes a classic.

• The Studio for Experimental Music at the University of Illinois at Champaign-Urbana is established, under the direction of Lejaren Hiller. Composers Gordon Mumma and Robert Ashley found the Cooperative Studio for Electronic Music at the University of Michigan, in Ann Arbor.

• Miles Davis records *Kind of Blue,* with a group including saxophonist John Coltrane and pianist Bill Evans, in which he experiments with pieces based on modal scales rather than chord changes.

• Former boxer and songwriter Berry Gordy forms a new record label and production company, which he first calls Tamla, and then renames Motown, in honor of its hometown origins in Detroit, the "Motor City." Lamont Dozier and Brian and Eddie Holland, their main team of producer-songwriters, keep churning out hits that will make Motown the world's most successful African American–owned music business. Their roster of star acts includes Smokey Robinson and the Miracles, Diana Ross and the Supremes, Martha and the Vandellas, Marvin Gaye, Little Stevie Wonder, the Temptations, and, later, Gladys Knight and the Pips and the Jackson 5. By the middle of the 1960s, Motown is on top of the record industry, with 75 percent of the company's records earning a place on the national charts, and Gordy in control of everything from the recording, distribution, and management to the song publication.

GOVERNMENT AND POLITICS

• After Alaskans vote for statehood by a margin of 5 to 1, Alaska is admitted as the forty-ninth state, the largest in area in the Union, at one-fifth the size of the lower forty-eight, with indigenous peoples from the Inupiaq, Aleut/Alutiiq, Athabascan, Yup'ik, and Southeast regions.

• Hawaii is admitted as the fiftieth state. It has the greatest ethnic diversity of any state, including the indigenous Hawaiian people, the highest percentage of Asians, and the lowest percentage of whites. World War II veteran Daniel K. Inouye becomes the first Japanese American elected to the House of Representatives, where he serves two terms. In 1962, when the state elects Inouye to the Senate, they send another *nisei* Democrat, Masayuki Matsunaga, to take his seat in the House.

• The FCC creates the equal-time rule, granting all political candidates equal time on TV newscasts.

BARBIE

Kathleen Moran

Barbie, an eleven-and-a-half-inch fashion doll with a womanlike body, was introduced in 1959 by Mattel Toys founders Ruth and Elliot Handler. Along with her clothes, friends, siblings, houses, cars, makeup kits, leisure environments, and countless other spinoff products, Barbie anchored the most lucrative toy line in American history. Like all toys, she reveals a lot about the culture that produced and consumed her. For one thing, Barbie's hard-shell body was made possible by the "revolution" in toymaking that followed developments in hard vinyl production. More important, Barbie was "the first true personality doll." From the beginning, Barbie advertising depicted her not as a toy, but as a real, live teen model—with a detailed backstory, friends, glamorous adventures, and the ability to take on various roles and identities. By the late 1950s, American children were coming into their own as a marketing segment, and Barbie was among the first toys to be pitched entirely to little girls—not to parents. Ironically, Mattel Toys' Barbie expressed a timely rebellion against what Betty Friedan would identify as the feminine mystique. Instead of the nurturing and companion play associated with traditional dolls, Barbie invited children to fantasize about consumption.

BUSINESS AND INDUSTRY

• The St. Lawrence Seaway opens, giving ships access to the Midwest. This change in the transportation web causes the once-busy port city of Buffalo to go into economic decline. For the first time since the 1825 opening of the Erie Canal, the city no longer provides hub services for transfer of cargo to canal boats or railcars on the main maritime routes between the Midwestern heartland and the Eastern seacoast.

• Barbie, the most successful doll in history, debuts from Mattel this year. By 1991, 700 million Barbies will be sold worldwide.

• Xerox produces the first commercial copying machine, giving office workers and the general public a simple way to duplicate that frees them from the mess and fuss of carbon copies and purple mimeographing pages.

SCIENCE AND TECHNOLOGY

• The Atomic Energy Commission announces that the first direct conversion of energy into electricity has been achieved at the Los Alamos atomic reactor.

• When Cornell University physicists Giuseppe Cocconi and Philip Morrison publish an article in *Nature* that demonstrates the potential for using microwave radio to communicate between stars, they lay the foundation for scientific exploration of extraterrestrial life. The following year, Frank Drake, then radio astronomer at the National Radio Astronomy Observatory and current chairman of the board at the SETI Institute, conducts the first microwave search of the Milky Way galaxy for alien signals, tuning his receiver to the same spot on the radio dial favored by the Cornell physicists. In 1961, at a meeting of the Space Science Board of the National Academy of Science, he presents his Drake Equation, a research tool for estimating the greatest number of communicative civilizations in the universe using such factors as (1) the fraction of stars with planets; (2) the fraction of planets where life develops; and (3) the fraction of life-giving planets where intelligence develops. SETI (Search for Extraterrestrial Intelligence) is dominated by Russia in the 1960s and receives U.S. support from the early 1970s until 1993, when Congress cuts funding. SETI has yet to confirm the existence of extraterrestrial life.

• The U.S. government authorizes research into the effects of nuclear fallout from testing or war. To allay fears, citizens are advised to build shelters, and commercial products to protect the "nuclear family" are marketed, such as "Kidde Kokoon," an underground bomb shelter manufactured by Walter Kidde Nuclear Laboratories of Garden City, Long Island. For $3,000 it comes furnished with radio, mattresses and blankets, radiation detector, face respirator, protective apparel suit, and more.

• The "paddlewheel" satellite Explorer 6 sends back the first television pictures showing all of the Earth's 197 million square miles.

CULTURE AND SOCIETY

• Delbert Wong is appointed a judge on the Los Angeles Municipal Court, becoming the first Chinese American judge in the continental U.S.

WORLD EVENTS

• After two years of rebellion, Fidel Castro (b. 1927), leader of the Cuban Revolution, overthrows Fulgencio Batista's regime in Cuba, declaring a new Cuban republic, with Castro as President.

ABOMUNIST MANIFESTO

by Bob Kaufman

ABOMUNISTS JOIN NOTHING BUT THEIR HANDS OR LEGS, OR OTHER SAME.

ABOMUNISTS SPIT ANTI-POETRY FOR POETIC REASONS AND FRINK.

ABOMUNISTS DO NOT LOOK AT PICTURES PAINTED BY PRESIDENTS AND UNEMPLOYED PRIME MINISTERS.

IN TIMES OF NATIONAL PERIL, ABOMUNISTS, AS REALITY AMERICANS, STAND READY TO DRINK THEMSELVES TO DEATH FOR THEIR COUNTRY.

ABOMUNISTS DO NOT FEEL PAIN, NO MATTER HOW MUCH IT HURTS.

ABOMUNISTS DO NOT USE THE WORD SQUARE EXCEPT WHEN TALKING TO SQUARES.

ABOMUNISTS READ NEWSPAPERS ONLY TO ASCERTAIN THEIR ABOMINUBILITY.

ABOMUNISTS NEVER CARRY MORE THAN FIFTY DOLLARS IN DEBTS ON THEM.

ABOMUNISTS BELIEVE THAT THE SOLUTION OF PROBLEMS OF RELIGIOUS BIGOTRY IS TO HAVE A CATHOLIC CANDIDATE FOR PRESIDENT AND PROTESTANT CANDIDATE FOR POPE.

ABOMUNISTS DO NOT WRITE FOR MONEY; THEY WRITE THE MONEY ITSELF.

ABOMUNISTS BELIEVE ONLY WHAT THEY DREAM ONLY AFTER IT COMES TRUE.

ABOMUNIST CHILDREN MUST BE REARED ABOMUNIBLY.

ABOMUNIST POETS, CONFIDENT THAT THE NEW LITERARY FORM "FOOT-PRINTISM" HAS FREED THE ARTIST OF OUTMODED RESTRICTIONS, SUCH AS: THE ABILITY TO READ AND WRITE, OR THE DESIRE TO COMMUNICATE, MUST BE PREPARED TO READ THEIR WORK AT DENTAL COLLEGES, EMBALMING SCHOOLS, HOMES FOR UNWED MOTHERS, HOMES FOR WED MOTHERS, INSANE ASYLUMS, USO CANTEENS, KINDERGARTENS, AND COUNTY JAILS.

ABOMUNISTS NEVER COMPROMISE THEIR REJECTIONARY PHILOSOPHY.

ABOMUNISTS REJECT EVERYTHING EXCEPT SNOWMEN.

(As it appears in Cranial Guitar, Selected Poems by Bob Kaufman.
Edited by Gerald Nicosia. Minneapolis: Coffee House Press, 1996)

• The Chinese puppet government in Tibet brutally suppresses a revolt, burning monasteries and their ancient texts, and killing 500,000 people. Tenzin Gyatso, the Fourteenth Dalai Lama (b. 1934), the highest political and Buddhist religious leader, flees his country disguised as a Tibetan peasant. He is given political sanctuary in India. Almost 100,000 Tibetan refugees follow him into exile before the Chinese seal the border. By 1960, movement of Chinese troops into Tibet will contribute to a border war between India and China. The Dalai Lama will remain in exile, continuing to bring the world's attention to the occupation of his country. He is awarded the Nobel Peace Prize in 1989.

Ishmael Reed (left) with Malcolm X (center) and others in Buffalo, New York. *(Buffalo Criterion)*

1960–1969

MY 1960S

ISHMAEL REED

I HAD BEEN REHEARSING FOR THE sixties all my life. When I was a kid, I was alienated, rebellious, mischievous, irreverent, anti-establishment, and a bohemian who felt stifled by the provincialism of my town. Jazz musicians and boxers were my heroes and I admired people who were hip and cool. In the 1950s, hip and cool meant the same thing. We despised things that were corny.

A trip to Europe at the age of fifteen led me to challenge the education I'd received in my elementary and high schools. The African intellectuals I met in Paris provided me with a view of Africa that I wasn't able to locate in my textbooks, or in the media. While attending college in the middle fifties, I met black students who were attending historic black colleges in the south. They would spend their summers working in Buffalo factories. They were hipper than we. They recited facts about black history of which I was ignorant. They introduced us to John Coltrane and Cannonball Adderley.

One of them was Harvey Peace III, who was writing a book that was eventually published by the late Ted Wilentz's Corinth Press, *The Angry Black South*. It was all about the sit-ins at lunch counters that were being organized by black students.

I was hanging with a group of bohemians, black writers, and intellectuals that included Ted Clifton; Priscilla Thompson; Claude Walker, a musical prodigy; Carl Tillman, a writer; Ray Smith, a playwright; and Lucille Clifton, whose poetry I introduced to Langston Hughes. Some of us founded a group of players called the Buffalo Community Workshop. We performed plays by William Saroyan, Jean Anouilh, and Tennessee Williams. We were restless and wild and intent upon mocking the bourgeoisie. We attended lectures at the Socialist Workers Party. We read Colin Wilson's *The Outsider,* and "angry young men" of England like John Osborne. We felt that they were talking to us.

But the book that really influenced us was Jack Kerouac's *On the Road.* I took off for the West Coast in 1958 and began to haunt North Beach, hanging out in places like the Anxious Asp and The Place. Kerouac's way was not for me. I was still searching for answers. I remained in college until 1960, the year that I dropped out and moved into the projects, Buffalo's Talbert Mall. I began working on a newspaper that had been edited by A. J. Smitherman, who, I was later to learn, used armed self-defense in order to protect those who were about to be lynched from their fate. I had worked for Smitherman for about a year in the early 1950s. Smitherman had been the target of a vicious white mob that burned down the black section of Tulsa, Oklahoma, in 1921, killing hundreds of black people. It was during my tenure as an *Empire Star* staff correspondent that I met the man who epitomized the 1960s, the electricity, the turmoil, the daring, the promise of the 1960s. There were charismatic heroes and sheroes in those days. Patrice Lumumba, Malcolm X, Martin Luther King Jr., James Baldwin, Robert F. Kennedy, Fannie Lou Hamer, Shirley Chisholm, Flo Kennedy, Kwame Nkrumah. My friend Carl Tillman and I were standing backstage at a rally for John F. Kennedy, and at the directions of his escorts, he exited through that area instead of through the front, which was the original plan. Carl and I stood there as the lone figure walked by us. It was as though a flash of light went by. But the most fascinating figure of that period was Malcolm X.

I met Malcolm X in 1961. I was a twenty-two-year-old writer for a community newspaper called the *Empire Star.* Joe Walker, who was twenty-eight at the time, edited the newspaper. Between the two of us we wrote every issue. We got involved in racial politics and raised so much sand that the local powerful Republican newspaper said that our newspaper was written by "hatemongers"—which, given the feudalistic nature of the Buffalo establishment in those days, we took as a compliment. (Years later I received a chair at the University of Buffalo that was named after the founder of the newspaper.) I also remember the local police getting a black councilman to chew me out because I had written a story about the police using dogs to attack a group of black women. He seemed to feel that the attack was justified because the women were prostitutes.

We also had a radio show called *Buffalo Community Roundtable* on which we would interview politicians, clergymen, etc. about the issues of the day. We interviewed Malcolm X twice and after the second interview, the show was dropped because some local conservatives were offended by what they considered the angry tone of the program.

Within a year the newspaper folded. Joe Walker went to New York and got a job with the *Muhammad Speaks* newspaper. I went to New York in 1962 and saw Malcolm there on several occasions. Every time I met Malcolm X in Buffalo or New York, we had lengthy conversations. These conversations would roam over a number of subjects. Malcolm X had one of the quickest minds I've ever encountered.

Like most complex people, Malcolm X went through changes in his life. Since he was murdered while still a young man, one can only guess at what sort of politics he would have embraced had he survived. To say otherwise is to engage in pure speculation. In fact there has developed in recent years a whole industry of guessing. Some say that he would have joined forces with Martin Luther King Jr. Others say that he would have become a socialist or even a Republican conservative, the favorite image of Malcolm X promoted by the media that despised him when he was alive. And so, since there were a number of Malcolm X's, individuals and groups have seized upon that Malcolm X that promotes their own particular programs. Jealously fighting over their own version of Malcolm X. There's Malcolm Little, the child of Garveyites born in Omaha, Nebraska, on May 19, 1925. Malcolm the Roxbury zoot-suiter and jitterbug. Malcolm the Detroit hustler whose nickname was Red. Malcolm the petty criminal who overshadowed all of the other Malcolm X's in Spike Lee's ambitious movie. Malcolm the convict who became Malcolm the intellectual.

Then there is Malcolm X the ex-Muslim minister whose image has become so sanitized that one of his assassins has become a follower. There's Malcolm X who began attending Trotskyite forums after losing his place in the Muslim hierarchy. There's pre-Mecca Malcolm and post-Mecca Malcolm. There's Malik Al-Shabazz and Marshall McLuhan's electronic man who titillated white audiences with his rhetorical threats. Malcolm X, who had serious disagreements with the Christian leaders about their policy of nonviolence. Malcolm X the private person, who told novelist Paule Marshall that he wanted her to arrange an intimate gathering for him. Malcolm X the exhorter of thousands of people. Malcolm X the product, whose commercial appeal was discovered with the publication of the *Autobiography of Malcolm X,* a book that he hated and said had nothing to do with him. Malcolm X is now being used to peddle a number of products, and is so safe that the Republicans are using him to scold black men for abandoning their children when most of the children who are abandoned in this country are white. Just some of the hypocrisy and double-dealing and conniving that is being used to push a hundred-million-dollar "tough love" market, which reminds us that the U.S. bottom-line mentality is the spreading pus and rot in the American soul.

I was once criticized for saying, in the 1970s, that you couldn't criticize Malcolm X because he had become a holiday. The remark was made by an original and gifted writer whose ideology sometimes intrudes upon his sense of irony. Malcolm X was neither saint nor holiday, nor was he Satan. He was a man of extraordinary gifts, yet he was able to communicate with ordinary people. He was a man who seemed firm in his convictions, but could vacillate between sexism and feminism, anti-Semitism and philo-Semitism. It is important for young people to know that Malcolm X wasn't some sort of god beyond their grasp, but a human with human weaknesses. That his example is not residing in another dimension, but is available to all. I was able to see Malcolm X evolve from the author of a loud hate speech in 1961, delivered before an audience at Buffalo's Muslim temple, to his final days when he seemed to be moving toward an enlightened internationalism. The first words that we exchanged in a radio studio would be for me indicative of his legacy.

I had read about Malcolm X before meeting him, and asked him whether he thought that American history had been distorted, and he

Readying for nighttime surveillance of migrating moths, agricultural engineer Wayne Wolf (left) adjusts a radar dish. When initial moth flight is detected, a meteorologist will launch a constant-altitude tetroon, a tetrahedron-shaped mylar balloon that can be tracked by a chase vehicle and orbiting satellite system to measure winds that affect moth mobility. *(Agricultural Research Service, USDA)*

said, "No, American history is a cotton patch history."

For me that statement, made in 1961, contained the meaning of Malcolm X as well as his contribution. We all knew about the physical occupation that blacks lived under, but only a few understood the mental occupation, the hostile invasion of the mind that had begun with the initial kidnapping and imprisonment of African people. While there were always the ingenious types who used the Bible to subversive ends, our ancestors were instructed through biblical teachings to be good slaves. From the very first landings of African slaves, there began a campaign to obliterate African history and culture. The African American experience as depicted in the textbooks and the other apparatus of official history demeaned African American people and extolled slave traders and war criminals like Robert E. Lee and authors of genocidal Indian campaigns like Andrew Jackson and racist historians like Woodrow Wilson. It was Malcolm X who fought for a reevaluation of the African American role in American history, and he was able to defend his positions before formidable intellectual forums and a worldwide audience. If Oakland's Sarah Fabio was the mother of Black Studies, then Malcolm X is the father of modern Black Studies.

Malcolm also emphasized the importance of the extracurricular scholar, a lesson that the establishment never forgot. This is why they keep installing "new black intellectuals," even in *The Atlantic Monthly,* where some of the "theories" about black inferiority first appeared and were brought to the attention of the Reagan administration by Pat Buchanan.

Like other unruly African American historians such as James Spady, John Henrik Clarke,

and J. A. Rogers, Malcolm X had done his homework not at Yale and Harvard, but in prison. It was his invisible university. He didn't serve time, the time served him, and so while he went into prison a cootie and a petty thief, he came out a mind warrior.

The last extended conversation I had with Malcolm was in a restaurant near New York's Foley Square. I had written a poem dedicated to him, titled "Fanfare for an Avenging Angel." My friend and newspaper colleague Joe Walker had passed the poem on to Malcolm. He told me that it reminded him of the work of Virgil or Dante. He read everything, even dead white males. But like others, I had my own idea of what Malcolm X was. For me at the time in my early twenties, he was someone who was going to get even with the enemies of African Americans for the abuses they had suffered over the years.

But Malcolm X was more than that. I had underestimated the breadth of his work. I see the hip-hoppers doing the same thing. Their poster version of Malcolm X is that of someone armed, ready to do battle with his enemies. But as Jesse Jackson reminded us, those who were threatening him at the time were black. Malcolm's message is that knowledge is available to us all and that knowledge is the greatest weapon, and that if new knowledge challenges our beliefs, then those beliefs must change. He was an etymologist and an etiologist concerned about the origins of words and things. Malcolm was not a macho man but a scientist, and he knew that the most important battles have always been fought on the battleground of ideas.

Malcolm X was not the only icon I met in New York. Norman Mailer invited me to his parties. I met James Baldwin, Ralph Ellison,

As of April 1960, the total resident population is 179,323,000, including Alaska and Hawaii, showing an increase of 18.5 percent over the preceding decade. In this decade there is a large increase in immigration from the Caribbean and Central America, and African immigration almost doubles. Many immigrants are refugees. A total of 132,068 refugees, mainly from Cuba, are listed under North American entries and make up the largest group. These increases reflect the more open policy that results from passage of the 1965 Family Reunification Act. Although the prison population shows a decrease from 1960 to 1965, the rate of violators returning to prison shows a marked increase. In 1965, 3.5 percent of mothers with children under eighteen years of age are participating in the labor force. Also in 1965, per capita personal income is $2,773 (U.S. Bureau of Economic Analysis). The U.S. Census records that the white median income is nearly twice that of blacks in this decade.

John A. Williams, John O. Killens, and John Henrik Clarke. Langston Hughes was responsible for my first novel being published. I was a member of the legendary Umbra workshop, one of the most influential literary movements of the 1960s. I collaborated with white, yellow, and brown artists and writers, the beginning of my association with multicultural organizations. New York was like a lover who delivers tons of roses to your home each day and they pile up so that you don't have room to breathe, and you need a break. In 1967, I left New York for California, but have carried on a long-distance affair with the town since then. I had some bad experiences there, even tragic ones, most of which were self-inflicted, but there was more romance than not.

I entered the 1960s with hope and idealism sparked by those who set an example for us all. We thought that they would make the world a better place. John Kennedy in his television address ordering the integration of Ole Miss. We'd never heard a president talk like that. Malcolm X atop a car in Harlem as some of us stood in the crowd yelling, "We want Malcolm, we want Malcolm!" Fannie Lou Hamer on the radio, discussing her ordeal at the hands of brutal Southern police. Listening to Martin Luther King's "I Have a Dream" speech as we walked toward the trains that would take us from Washington to New York. Standing with the playwright Walter Cotton in a crowd of people as we heard that JFK had been shot. Standing at the bar at Stanley's on Avenue A, as we were told that Malcolm had been shot. Hearing of Lumumba's death, and the CIA's role in his assassination. Now my generation is fading, while a new generation takes up the struggle that began when that first Portuguese sailor injured a Nigerian and took slaves.

When I saw the film *Lumumba*, I wept. Tennessee, my youngest daughter, was shocked. She'd never seen me weep before. But I was weeping for the martyrs, for the 1960s, so maligned and denigrated by the well-fed wonks and op-ed writers. I was weeping for my shattered idealism, I was weeping for my generation's lost hope, for myself.

Maybe my daughters will be among those who move the struggle another inch. One of them was under surveillance by the University of California, Berkeley, police as a result of her participation in radical activities. It was through the agitation of her group that the University of California regents reversed their stand on affirmative action. My oldest daughter is being revived from a life of mental illness and addiction. She's attending college, completing a novel, and dedicating her life to assisting battered women. At one time, my generation were the stars; now we're grateful to be part of the supporting cast.

1960

ARTS AND LITERATURE

• Musician Robert Dunn (1929–1996) teaches his first choreography course at Merce Cunningham's studio, where he applies new ideas from music composition to dance composition. He structures discussions by asking choreographers to explain their intentions to the audience, and asks the audience to respond with information reporting whether they could see what was intended, rather than giving expression to personal opinions. (This critical approach also influences the way many contemporary journalists write on the arts.) In July 1962, after workshop pieces are shown at a concert at Judson Memorial Church in Greenwich Village, later courses move into the church's gym, which leads directly into the formation of what becomes known as the Judson Dance Theater Workshop. Judson will be regarded as a pivotal cross-disciplinary movement that advances expanded definitions and tools for dance in particular and performance in general.

• Public poetry becomes the rage as Mickey Ruskin opens his first place, the Tenth Street Coffee House, in the East Village. The Beat poets, including Allen Ginsberg, Ted Joans, Leroi Jones, Diane di Prima, Gregory Corso, and Anne Waldman, mix with a new scene that includes Diane Wakoski, Paul Blackburn, Armand Schwerner, Jerome Rothenberg, Rochelle Owens, and Jackson MacLow, who is a link between the writers and the John Cage circle of musicians and artists using chance methods. The poets start a small-press mimeo movement, interacting with a new creative generation of experimental musicians, performance artists, dancers, visual artists at the Tenth Street galleries, and playwrights who will write plays for the cafés, church lofts, and small theaters of what becomes known as Off-Off Broadway and Off-Off-Off Broadway.

• Choreographer Alvin Ailey (1931–1989) premieres *Revelations,* his signature work based on "blood memories" of his experiences growing up African American in Texas. Originally set to a suite of spirituals that are performed by a group of singers, by 1964 the musical interludes are dropped, and dance sections are added, dropped and rearranged. Ailey's unique narrative style blends traditions of modern, jazz, and African American dance, and the work is immediately embraced as a modern dance classic.

• The Society of Umbra, a collective of young African American writers, visual artists, and musicians, begins meeting for writing workshops on New York City's Lower East Side. It grows out of the area's black bohemia and, through its leader, Tom Dent, has ties to the civil rights movement. Its mentor is Harlem Renaissance poet Langston Hughes. The group includes Steve Cannon, Tom Dent, Al Hayes, Amhara Hicks, David Henderson, Calvin

Alvin Ailey and Carmen de Lavallade performing Ailey's *Roots of the Blues*, 1961. (Photo © Jack Mitchell)

Hernton, Joe Johnson, Norman Pritchard, Lennox Raphael, Ishmael Reed, Archie Shepp, Lorenzo Thomas, James Thompson, Askia M. Touré (then Rolland Snellings), Brenda Walcott, and later Barbara Christian, who is Umbra's link to the black feminist movement. Umbra is the antecedent of the Black Arts Movement and multiculturalism.

• Andy Warhol (1928–1987), who has been working as a commercial artist and graphic designer for Bonwit Teller and *Glamour* magazine since 1952, makes his first "art" comic-strip painting, *Dick Tracy*, this year. He demonstrates his practice of blurring the lines between high art, business, and commodity culture in 1961, by making blow-ups of his Dick Tracy paintings for use as a window display at Lord & Taylor, a Fifth Avenue department store in New York. He says, "When you think about it, department stores are kind of like museums."

GOVERNMENT AND POLITICS

• President Eisenhower secretly authorizes the CIA to arm and train anti-Castro Cuban exiles in Guatemala for a future invasion of Cuba.

• The Nixon-Kennedy debates are the vehicle for the first presidential election in which television plays a significant role because the TV cameras favor the youthful-looking John Kennedy (1917–1963) and harm the perspiring Richard Nixon.

• John Kennedy is elected president, with Lyndon Johnson (1908–1973) as his vice president. As the first Catholic elected to the presidency, John Kennedy's victory sends a signal that all kinds of Americans—at least, at the time, all kinds of white male Americans—can obtain positions of power.

• In May, protesters demand entrance to the House Un-American Activities Committee (HUAC) hearings in San Francisco, shouting "Abolish that committee" and singing "We Shall Not Be Moved," beginning a wave of actions, including films, that lead to the committee's loss of power.

BUSINESS AND INDUSTRY

• Satellite development heats up this year. In May, NASA negotiates with the Department of Defense to proceed with active satellite research, and by the end of the year President Eisenhower approves their leadership in communications. AT&T requests an FCC license for an experimental satellite, and by the next year has also signed cooperative agreements with NASA, building the Telstar series of communications satellites which are first launched in 1962. The U.S. launches a military Midas I satellite, replacing the U-2 espionage reconnaissance flights that have become a hot button since one of the planes was shot down flying over the central USSR. In August an aluminized plastic balloon called Echo becomes the first communications satellite to be launched. It is a simple stationary system prototype, called a synchronous orbiting satellite, that has been championed since the 1950s by John Robinson Pierce (b. 1910) as the best solution for communications. It is called Echo because when radio and TV signals are transmitted to the satellite and reflected back, they are only received by a station in view of the satellite. The U.S. also launches its first weather satellite, Tiros 1.

SCIENCE AND TECHNOLOGY

• The first operational laser is developed by physicist Theodore Maiman (b. 1927). The word *laser* is an acronym for "light amplification by stimulated emission of radiation." Maiman's device builds upon the work of Gordon Gould (a graduate student who received a 1957 patent for a laser and coined the word), and Bell Labs physicists Charles Townes and his brother-in-law Arthur Schawlow, who in 1951 built a precursor of lasers, the first "maser," which produced microwave amplification by stimulated emission of radiation. The breakthrough technology will prove useful to industry, the military, medicine, and the arts. Schawlow shares a 1981 Nobel Prize in Physics for his work in laser spectroscopy with Nicolaas Bloembergen.

▣ 1962

• Endocrinoloist Gregory Goodwin Pincus (1903–1967) develops an oral contraceptive pill for women. It is approved by the U.S. Food and Drug Administration and released on the market this year by G. D. Searle Laboratories, under the brand name Enovid. Known as "the Pill," the synthetic compound of estrogen and progesterone costs about ten dollars for one month's supply. The relative ease of this birth-control method, compared with other methods, makes it widely successful throughout the world, although it produces side-effects that can cause health problems, and later compounds will be modified. The Pill is said to give a major boost to the "Sexual Revolution" by providing women with a simple, reliable way to separate pregnancy from sexual pleasure.

• The National Institutes of Standards and Technology or NIST (formerly the U.S. Bureau of Standards) redefines the meter as 1,650,763.73 wavelengths of a particular color of light emitted by a krypton atom. Since every krypton atom in the world is the same, all labs, worldwide, can maintain their own universal standard meter.

▣ 1983

CULTURE AND SOCIETY

• In February, African American college students conduct a sit-in at the F. W. Woolworth's store in Greensboro, North Carolina, to desegregate its lunch counter after four North Carolina Agricultural and Technical State University freshmen are refused service. During the next two weeks, lunch-counter sit-ins spread to fifteen cities in five Southern states. In two months, sit-ins are organized in fifty-four cities in nine states. By the end of 1960, sixty-

Birth control poster, c. 1968. *(Library of Congress, Prints and Photographs Division)*

eight sit-ins will have occurred in thirteen states from South Carolina to Texas. Besides sit-ins, there are wade-ins at segregated beaches, read-ins at segregated libraries, kneel-ins at segregated churches, and so forth. These nonviolent demonstrations are sometimes met with great resistance, including clubs, firehoses, and gunfire. More than 140 students and fifty-eight faculty will be expelled for their participation. Of the 3,600 students arrested for their sit-in activities, 1,600 are defended by the NAACP's legal staff. As a result, eating facilities are integrated in Greensboro and 108 other Southern and border cities, as are libraries, movie theaters, beaches, and even school districts that had not been accessible to African Americans.

• A student sit-in conference at Shaw College, North Carolina, becomes the start of the Student Nonviolent Coordinating Committee (SNCC), a multiracial organization committed to working for a racially integrated society in the U.S. through direct, nonviolent confrontation.

• Bilingual education originates in Dade County, Florida, when children of Cuban immigrants fleeing the Castro regime begin flooding the public schools. Thinking that their children would be returning to Cuba, they seek a legal way to maintain fluency in Spanish, while also giving their children an opportunity to learn English.

• The 1960 census shows Mexican-Americans as the second-largest minority population in the U.S., with a count of 3,842,000. During this decade, Mexican Americans struggle to gain civil rights and shape a new political, social, and artistic identity that becomes known as the Chicano Movement. They chose to call the movement "Chicano," from a word used as a pejorative term for lower-class

Mexicans in the 1920s and slang of the 1940s and 1950s.

• An African American family initiates the first lawsuit to gain open enrollment in schools, by challenging the de facto segregation in New Rochelle, New York, schools where segregated housing patterns and gerrymandering of school board zones have resulted in all-white and all-black schools. In 1961 the court rules in favor of open enrollment.

• Del Webb opens a "retirement village" for people over fifty-two in Sun City, near Phoenix, Arizona. Two hundred seventy-two homes are sold in the first weekend. Within ten years, dozens of similar communities are located across the country.

WORLD EVENTS

• The world population reaches three billion.

• Relations between the Communist allies, China and the USSR, are seriously strained as they vie for leadership of world Communism. Their rivalry has been building up since China annexed Tibet in 1951, causing border disputes to erupt between China and India, an ally of the USSR.

• Mexico inaugurates the *Programa Nacional Fronterizo* (National Border Program), which in five years leads to the Border Industrialization Program, enabling foreign corporations to operate assembly plants, known as *maquiladoras,* on the border of Mexico and the U.S. *Maquiladoras* transform the border towns and cities of Mexico. Although they employ thousands of Mexicans, especially young women from rural areas who flood the border towns and cities of Mexico looking for work, they create new problems.

There is much exploitation of the women that goes unregulated, often with tragic results, because the cities cannot provide adequate sanitation, housing, schooling, and protections through social services.

▣ 1965, 1980

• Cuba expropriates and nationalizes all property and businesses owned by U.S. citizens, under Law 851. The U.S. government considers Cuba to be a Communist state from this ruling onward. In 1961, Premier Castro announces he is a Marxist-Leninist, two weeks after the Bay of Pigs debacle.

• Belgium holds elections and announces the formation of a newly independent Republic of the Congo, and then withdraws quickly after seventy-five years of colonial rule in which no native people have been allowed to share in running the government. Ethnic civil wars erupt immediately. The government is splintered between President Joseph Kasavubu, a figurehead for the U.S.-CIA-backed army colonel Joseph Mobutu, and Prime Minister Patrice Lumumba, head of the radical Congolese National Movement, who aligns with the USSR and tries to reestablish unity in the new nation. Lumumba is imprisoned by Mobutu's troops in 1961, and is later taken to Katanga and killed by Belgian mercenaries in the presence of Katanga's Belgian-backed leader, Moise Tshombe. The murder is hotly protested throughout the Third World and the Soviet Union, with much furor directed against the CIA, which is implicated in the murder because of then Director Allen Dulles's 1960 cable to the CIA station chief stating that Lumumba's "removal must be an urgent and prime objective and that under existing conditions this should be a high priority of our covert action." In 2002, Belgium officially apologizes for its "irrefutable part of the responsibility for the events that led to Patrice Lumumba's death."

• The Organization of Petroleum Exporting Countries (OPEC) is formed by a resolution at the Baghdad Conference to coordinate petroleum policies and stabilize international oil prices. The twelve members include Algeria, Gabon, Indonesia, Iran, Iraq, Kuwait, Libya, Nigeria, Qatar, Saudi Arabia, the United Arab Emirates, and Venezuela.

• Norwegian writer Helge Ingstad (1899–2001) and his wife, the archaeologist Ann-Stine Moe, find definitive confirmation that Vikings landed in North America on the coast of Newfoundland, 500 years before Columbus's expeditions touched ground in the western hemisphere, when they unearth remains of a Viking encampment from c. 1000 A.D.

1961

ARTS AND LITERATURE

• George Maciunas (b. Lithuania, 1931; d. U.S., 1978) makes plans to publish a magazine he calls *Fluxus,* meaning "flow" or "change." He opens the A/G Gallery in New York, where he organizes a series of "New Music" lecture-demonstrations, including what he calls "Fluxus Events," where each artist is allotted only thirty seconds to one minute to make a performance piece. Artists trained in various disciplines participate, including LaMonte Young (b. 1935), George Brecht (b. 1926), and Nam June Paik (b. Korea, 1932). Other Fluxus activities take place over the next three years at New York sites, including Yoko Ono's (b. Japan, 1933) loft, with works by Henry Flynt (b. 1940), poet Jackson MacLow (b. 1922), and composers Philip Corner and Toshi Ichiyanagi and the Audio Visual Group of Al Hansen (1927–1995) and Dick Higgins (b. 1938). It officially sponsors international concerts and festivals between 1962 and 1978, and is one of the first art circles to include significant numbers of women and artists of color, especially from Asia.

• Henry Flynt, a musician and Fluxus participant, coins the term "concept art," for art in which the materials are ideas that do not have to become physical objects, following a direction taken by Marcel Duchamp with his readymades. Artist Sol LeWitt (b. 1928) publishes "Paragraphs on Conceptual Art" in 1967, saying the "concept is the most important aspect of the [art] work," followed by his "Sentences on Conceptual Art" in 1969, where he states, "The concept of a work of art may involve the matter of the piece or the process in which it is made." These manifestos are frequently cited to explain the intention and process behind such works.

• The word "assemblage" is coined by Museum of Modern Art curators Peter Selz and William Seitz, for their "Art of Assemblage" show in New York City. The term refers to a technique for making sculptures by constructing or combining three-dimensional materials. It requires gluing or welding pieces together, similarly to the way objects are combined in a two dimensional form called "collage." Any everyday object can be transformed into an assemblage: John Chamberlain (b. 1927) crumples junk metal auto parts into abstract towers; Louisé Nevelson (1899–1988) constructs walls of recycled, painted wood furniture pieces and architectural details; Bruce Conner (b. 1933) builds secretive figures, their mysteries expressed in string, bits of cloth, and toys; and Joseph Cornell (1903–1973) constructs miniature worlds in boxes delicately filled with arrangements of recycled materials—such as toy birds, rings, wooden balls, mirrors, maps, tinsel, and images of ballerinas and movie stars—that have the magic of dreams.

• *Eat a Bowl of Tea,* by Louis Chu (1915–1970), is the first Chinese American novel published by a major press. He writes in the dialect of the "Chinamen," presenting an unexoticized male world of San Francisco's Chinatown.

• *Preface to a Twenty-Volume Suicide Note,* a collection of poetry by LeRoi Jones (b. 1934) is published, and a one-act play, *The Toilet,* is premiered in New York. In 1964, after his second book of poetry, *Dead Lecturer,* is published and he wins an Obie for the downtown production of his explosive one-act play *Dutchman,* he transforms from downtown Beat poet to "Father of the Black Arts Movement" when he goes uptown to Harlem and founds the Black Arts Theater. This revolutionary black community arts organization inspires many similar arts institutions throughout the country. In 1965 he leaves Harlem because Black Arts "got bogged down with unproductive nuts," and returns to his hometown of Newark, New Jersey, where he establishes Spirit House and creates plays with a troupe of actors called the Spirit House Movers. He signals his philosophical changes by changing his name to Ameer Baraka (meaning "blessed Prince" in his Kawaida faith, a blend of African and Islamic traditions), and then to Amiri Baraka, by which he continues to be known.

• Robert Moog meets composer Herbert A. Deutsch, and together they create a voltage-controlled synthesizer with a modular idea made possible through developments in the miniaturization of electronics. Its design is also influenced by the theremin, for which Moog has been manufacturing and selling kits since 1961, and absorption of other designs for transistorized modular synthesizers. By 1962, Moog begins to manufacture an electronic music synthesizer, called Moog, developed with Deutsch and another composer, Walter (later Wendy) Carlos. It sets the standard for analog synthesizers, although the Moog Synthesizer Company eventually loses out to other companies. It becomes commercially available in 1964.

• Robert Ashley, Gordon Mumma, and several other composers, visual artists, filmmakers, and performance artists form the Once Group in Ann Arbor, Michigan, and begin to produce Once Festivals, with programming containing elements of film, theater, dance, opera, and performance art.

• Over the next six years, composer James Tenney develops a computer program for composers, while working as a research composer in residence at Bell Labs. Over the next three years, Tenney uses his program to write *Four Stochastic Studies* (1962), *Ergodos I* (1963), *Ergodos II* (1964), and other compositions. During this same year, the first electronic music concerts at the Columbia-Princeton Studio are received with much hostility from other faculty members.

• FORTRAN-based MUSICIV is used in the generation of "Bicycle Built for Two," an arcane fact referenced in the film *2001*, when, as Hal the computer is dying, it sings its memories of originating in Max Matthews's work.

▣ 1958

• The Museum of American Folk Art (formerly the Museum of Early American Art) is founded in New York City to study and exhibit the work of "self-taught" artists or artists who create their work outside of the structure of the art world. Although the museum's original mission does not initially include twentieth-century artists, by the mid-1960s, under the direction of its curator, Herbert Waide Hemphill Jr., it makes a major shift to foster contemporary art, reflecting the growing interest in what is called "outsider art." This term basically encompasses all art made by self-taught artists, including the mentally disabled (Eddie Arning [1898–1993]), eccentric visionaries (A. G. Rizzoli [1861–1981], Sister Gertrude Morgan [1900–1980], and Henry Darger [1892–1973]), and those who used to be called "primitives" or "folk artists," such as Grandma Moses (1860–1961), William Edmondson (1870–1951), Morris Hirshfield (1872–1946), and Horace Pippin (1888–1946).

GOVERNMENT AND POLITICS

• On January 17, outgoing President Dwight Eisenhower gives a farewell address in which he warns against the dangers of the U.S. being run by the "military-industrial complex," a term coined by his speechwriter, Emmett Hughes, that remains in use.

• In his inaugural address, President Kennedy challenges the nation to "ask not what your country can do for you; ask what you can do for your country." As one of his first acts in office, President Kennedy establishes the Peace Corps, an agency that sends thousands of young people throughout the world for two years of service, working mostly as teachers or with community-based development projects. Through their work, many Peace Corps volunteers are themselves changed and return to the U.S. with a more compassionate understanding of how most of the world lives.

• In April the CIA sponsors an invasion of Cuba at the Bay of Pigs, carried out by 1,500 anti-Communist Cuban refugees who have been trained in Guatemala by the CIA and armed by the U.S. military. Within forty-eight hours, all have been captured or killed, and the invasion is defeated.

• In June the National Congress of American Indians meets in Chicago for one week. As the largest multi-tribal meeting in decades, with more than 450 delegates from ninety tribes discussing problems and proposals, it marks the beginning of a new era of pan-Indian militancy and cultural awareness. In their formal Declaration of Indian Purpose, they call for the end of "so-called termination policies" and recommend emphasis on economic development. "What we ask of America . . . is not charity, nor paternalism, even when benevolent. In short, the Indians ask for assistance, technical and financial, for the time needed, however long that may be, to regain in the America of the space age some measure of the adjustment they enjoyed as the original possessors of their native land." This call finds a response in a policy report written by the Task Force on Indian Affairs, appointed by President Kennedy's Secretary of the Interior, Stewart Udall. It agrees with the need to end the termination policy. It also calls for Indians to collaborate with the federal government to find a "new trail" to "equal citizenship and maximum self-sufficiency" for the reservations. These ideals will begin to find realization under President Johnson's

"war on poverty" and his Office of Economic Opportunity (OEO) community-action programs.

• In October, President Kennedy writes South Vietnamese President Diem: "The U.S. is determined to help Vietnam preserve its independence, protect its people against communist assassins and build a better life." By December the first U.S. military companies, including 4,000 men and thirty-two helicopters, arrive in Vietnam as "advisers" assigned to Vietnamese units. Their orders are to fire only if fired upon.

• President John F. Kennedy issues Executive Order 10925, which creates the Committee on Equal Employment Opportunity and uses the term "affirmative action" for the first time, in reference to hiring practices in federally funded projects.

🖻 1964, 1965

SCIENCE AND TECHNOLOGY

• On May 5, Alan B. Shepard Jr. becomes the first U.S. astronaut in space, on a fifteen-minute and twenty-two second suborbital flight in the Mercury spacecraft *Freedom 7*.

• African American mathematician Katherine Coleman Goble Johnson (b. 1918) works her way up from being a "human computer" (aka a number cruncher) at the National Advisory Committee on Aeronautics (NACA), the forerunner of National Aeronautics and Space Administration (NASA), to becoming a pioneer of the space era at NASA. Her computations permit NASA to compute spacecraft trajectories on the May 1961 Mercury flight and many other manned and unmanned flights, including the Apollo moon landing project, where she calculates how to get the spacecraft in lunar orbit, send its lunar lander to the Moon's surface, return it to the space-craft, and return the mission to Earth. She helps bring the Apollo 13 mission safely home in 1970, after a fuel tank explodes onboard and many systems, including the computer, are shut down. She continues working on NASA projects through the 1970s, when she becomes involved in a special project, the Earth Resources Satellite, with the mission of locating underground minerals and other essential resources.

BUSINESS AND INDUSTRY

• In the early 1960s, Justice Department investigations lead to price-fixing charges being filed in many industries, against pharmacists in Northern California, milk suppliers in Baltimore, and household movers and makers of asphalt. The most prominent price-fixing case involves a conspiracy among twenty-nine major electrical equipment firms and their executives to ensure that prices remain at high levels. Companies participating in the conspiracy include General Electric, Westinghouse Electric, Allis Chalmers Manufacturing Company, ITC Circuit Breaker Company, and Federal Pacific Electric Company. They will plead guilty or no-contest to the charges, and pay $1.9 million in fines.

• SIN, the first Spanish-language television network in the U.S., starts broadcasting, providing a U.S.-based communication link for Spanish-speaking communities.

• Bell Labs begins mass production of transistors, professional amplifiers, and suppliers.

• An industrial robot replaces humans in the workplace for the first time when General Motors installs a "Programmed Article Transfer" to unload parts from a die-casting opera-

tion. The robot is invented by George Devol and developed by Joseph Engelberger's U.S.-based company Unimation, the first in the world to sell industrial robots, computer-controlled machines that can be programmed to execute repetitive tasks or transport materials.

CULTURE AND SOCIETY

• "Freedom Rides" are organized by the biracial Congress of Racial Equality (CORE), headed by James Farmer, and later supported by the Southern Christian Leadership Conference (SCLC) to nonviolently test whether segregation practices continue to be used in bus terminals serving state and interstate travel. They are also a test to find out whether local police and the Kennedy administration will support compliance with federal laws. Seven black and six white volunteers travel together on Greyhound and Trailways buses throughout the South, beginning in Washington, D.C., on May 4, often trailed by white segregationists. Police stand by as riders are beaten and clubbed in Rock Hill, South Carolina, and a mob of 1,000 stops them in Montgomery, Alabama, injuring twenty. Attorney General Robert F. Kennedy finally responds by sending federal marshals to Alabama, and the governor of Alabama calls up the National Guard and declares martial law to restore calm. In September the Interstate Commerce Commission (ICC) forbids segregation on buses and terminal facilities used in interstate travel.

• Social critic and urban planner Jane Jacobs publishes *The Death and Life of American Cities,* in which she theorizes that American cities were more livable when they were smaller, before people fled to the suburbs and before urban renewal projects created the anonymous forms of urban sprawl that robbed cities of the particular neighborhood identities that constituted communities' souls. Her ideas inspire many reconsiderations of city planning, including the New Urbanists Movement.

WORLD EVENTS

• Yuri Gagarin, a Russian astronaut, becomes the first man in space, when he orbits the earth in *Vostok I* on April 12, preceding America's first manned space flight by three weeks.

• Amnesty International is founded in London as a grassroots activist organization dedicated to freeing prisoners of conscience, gaining fair trials for political prisoners, ending torture, political killings, and "disappearances," and abolishing the death penalty throughout the world. They monitor human rights abuses throughout the world, making their findings public through print and other media.

• The Berlin Wall is constructed by the East German government, to stop the flow of refugees to the West. The barrier stands for the next twenty-seven years as a symbol of Cold War divisions.

1962

ARTS AND LITERATURE

• Pop artists borrow from the mass media, and this year the mass media makes them stars as *Time, Life,* and *Newsweek* magazines cover pop-art events with an intensity that changes the arts into entertainment. They become part of consumer culture at the same time their work is seeing or copying the culture, a continuation of the copies-of-copies techniques and the love-hate relationship that is inherent in the work. In this year Andy Warhol (1928–1987) creates silk-screened rows of images from a photograph of actress Marilyn Monroe; Roy Lichtenstein (1923–1997) takes stereotypical images from ads and cartoons with balloon speech that he enlarges and isolates to reveal something more; Claes Oldenburg (U.S., b. Sweden, 1929) makes "symbols of our time" in his plaster sculptures and soft fabric constructions of everyday objects, collapsing masses formed as foods, typewriters, and telephones; Jasper Johns (b. 1930) and Robert Rauschenberg collage objects, maps, and newsprint images on painted surfaces; and Ed Ruscha (b. 1937) produces his first book of photographs, *Twenty-Six Gasoline Stations.*

• Off-Off Broadway flourishes downtown in New York City, in the area below 14th Street. Plays by Sam Shepard (b. 1943) are featured at Café Cino and Theater Genesis. Ellen Stewart (b. 1931) opens La Mama with plays by Rochelle Owens (b. 1936). Charles Ludlam's Theater of the Ridiculous shows camp and drag "queer theater" by Ronald Tavel and Ludlam. The Judson Poet's Theater performs plays by Frank O'Hara (1926–1966), Maria Irene Fornes (b. Cuba, 1930) and Gertrude Stein (1847–1946). Jonas Mekas (b. 1922) shows underground films by Stan Brakhage (b. 1933), Jack Smith (1932–1989), Ron Rice (1935–1964), Kenneth Anger (b. 1930), Shirley Clarke (1925–1997), Robert Frank (b. 1924), and others at Filmmakers Cinematique.

• Adrienne Kennedy (b. 1931) creates the first of her unique visions for the theater, *Funnyhouse of a Negro.* It is developed in a workshop led by playwright Edward Albee, and he produces the Obie-award-winning Off-Broadway premiere at the East End Theatre,

Room Service, a work by Yvonne Rainer structured like the game Follow the Leader, as part of "Concert # 13," at Judson Memorial Church, November 20, 1963, and set in an environment of huge welded steel pipe sculptures by Charles Ross strewn with miscellaneous "junk," such as mattresses and ladders. One of the three teams includes Carla Blank (standing figure at left) and Sally Gross (center on tire), with Rainer as leader. *(Photo by Peter Moore © Estate Peter Moore/ VAGA, New York, NY)*

New York City. The play combines Kennedy's feelings and experiences of being an African American woman, her travels in Europe and Africa, her extensive knowledge of classical literature and history, and the murder of Patrice Lumumba in the Congo.

• The East Village art world develops a dance club hangout scene called the Dom, later known as the Electric Circus, on St. Mark's

Place. Run by Stanley Tolkin, the space formerly served as the Polish National Hall. Andy Warhol rents it for what he is thinking of as an exhibit, called the "Exploding Plastic Inevitable," to house a performance by the proto-punk-rock group Velvet Underground, featuring Nico (1938–1988), Gerard Malanga (b. 1943), John Cale, and Lou Reed (b. 1944). Instead, it becomes the prototype disco envi-

AFRICAN AMERICAN VISUAL ARTS: PART 2

Corrine Jennings

1940s

"The Art of the American Negro," held at the American Exposition in Chicago, informed Locke's *The Negro in Art* (1940). Alonzo Aden, one of the organizers, then opened a gallery in Washington, D.C., with the idealistic intention of discovering and presenting new black, as well as white and international, talent. In December 1941 a major exhibition intended to reconsider the contribution of African American artists, "American Negro Art: 19th and 20th Centuries," opened at the Downtown Gallery in New York City a few days after the bombing of Pearl Harbor. Plans for future exhibitions were postponed. From this exhibition, only the work of Jacob Lawrence (1917-2000) received further support.

For the most part, the WPA was over by 1941 and artists of military age were sent to the army. Both Romare Bearden and Charles Alston trained at Fort Huachuca in Arizona. Later, along with Palmer Hayden, they created patriotic images directed to the black community. To boost morale during the war, black artists were included in "Artists for Victory" held at the Metropolitan Museum. Lawrence and Richmond Barthé were awarded prizes.

In the 1940s important exhibitions of African American art occurred under the auspices of the Pyramid Club, a black social group in Philadelphia. In New York City, Beauford Delaney (1901-1979), Hale Woodruff, and Bearden (1914-1988) held their first one-person exhibitions at white-owned galleries. In 1947, Rose Piper (b. 1917), the first black woman to exhibit solo in New York City, showed at the Roko Gallery. Poet Sterling Brown had encouraged her to "look to the blues for authenticity," and Bessie Smith inspired Piper's paintings. In 1949, Norman Lewis (1909-1979) held his first solo show at the Williard Gallery.

1950s

1950 was a pivotal year in American art history in that Abstract Expressionism, a movement also called the New York School, placed emphasis on American art rather than European. New York City became a hub of the international arts, and abstract artists were among the most favored. A number of African American artists were producing abstract work by 1950. Alston, Romare Bearden (1912-1988), Harlan Jackson (1918-1993), Norman Lewis, Heywood Bill Rivers, Thelma Johnson Street (b. 1912), and Hale Woodruff were among the first generation of American abstract artists, but their work received scant attention. Later in the decade the McCarthy era certainly affected the careers of many black artists who had looked to the American left in hope of support for progressive ideas.

In 1950 the first exhibition of contemporary African art in the U.S. was held at Howard University Gallery of Art. From the end of World War II through the 1954 Supreme Court decision, mainstream interest in black

(Continued)

277

culture waned; the white-supported all-black exhibitions ceased. A few black artists living downtown were occasionally included in the artist-run galleries that opened on 10th Street in New York City, and a few black artists managed to present solo exhibits at galleries.

1960s

Political and satirical art helped to inspire protests across the country. Artists created forums, exhibitions, and new institutions. Two generations of practicing writers, visual artists, and musicians reopened the debate regarding the role of the black artist, the nature of black art, and whether the standards applicable to it should come from critics who are not black. Well-known New York City venues, like the Martha Jackson Gallery, presented fund-raising exhibitions, especially after 1964 and the riots. Corporations like AT&T and the Port Authority of New York and New Jersey planned exhibitions of paintings by African American artists in 1967, and some museums, like the Brooklyn Museum in 1968, created traveling exhibitions.

In 1965, the Spiral artists' organization was founded. Across the U.S., other associations developed, like the Afri-Cobra Group and the National Conference of Artists. The Black Arts Repertory Theater and School, started in Harlem by poet Amiri Baraka, William White, Askia Toure, Charles and William Patterson, and other writers, visual artists, and musicians, provided a model for independent black arts organizations that developed in the remaining decades of the twentieth century.

In 1966, the First World Festival of the Arts (FESTAAC) in Dakar, Senegal was a milestone cultural event organized by poet-president Leopold Sedar Senghor that brought large numbers of African American artists to West Africa for the first time. This project initiated the globalization of African-based culture.

Black studies departments were organized in colleges and universities. New museums were established, like the Museum of African Art and the Frederick Douglass Institute in Washington, D.C., Detroit's International Afro-American Museum, Ile-Ife Museum of Afro American Art and Culture in Philadelphia, and the National Center for African American Artists in Boston. The Studio Museum in Harlem, which opened in the late 1960s, was developed after demonstrations at the Metropolitan Museum.

A 1967 exhibition, "The Evolution of the Negro Artist, 1800–1950," organized by Romare Bearden and Caroll Green Jr. at the City University of New York, attracted nearly 250,000 visitors. In this same year, Bearden, Ernest Crichlow (b. 1914), and Norman Lewis opened Cinque Gallery to support the work of younger black artists.

1970s

American colleges and universities with black studies programs employed some visual artists and suddenly, where previously blacks exhibited in churches, social halls, or black colleges, there were exhibits in academies across the country, and a few artists were offered residencies. A generation of artists looked for freedom in the way materials and tools were used. Some artists began to work with the canvas off the stretcher. Sam Gilliam (b. 1933) created paintings that were draped, and Joe Overstreet (b. 1934) suspended his geometric paintings with ropes. This was an era when black arts institutions developed and attempted to institutionalize. Some museums mounted small exhibitions of work by black artists. In the 1970s the Whitney Museum presented several such exhibitions in a small side room that was dubbed "the Kitchen."

The *Two Centuries of Black American Art* traveling exhibition and its catalog, organized by David Driskell in 1976, caused a dramatic stir throughout the U.S. In the black community, this exhibition caused great excitement and encouraged the development of privately owned black collections. The Hatch Billops Archives began producing oral histories of black art and new alternative spaces, like Kenkelaba House in New York City and the Skylight Gallery in Brooklyn's Restoration Plaza, began to offer exhibition venues. The quarterly journal the *International Review of African American Art* began publication.

The art market for black artists was still bleak. Commercial galleries represented only one or two black artists, and few black artists could live from the sales of their work.

ronment, with high-volume music, colored lights, and video projections, including a mirrored glass ball splintering light around the room, and a bar, ingredients that basically remain standard for the rest of the century. Poets Ed Sanders and Tuli Kupferberg are inspired by the same space and form the Fugs, setting their out-of-bounds scatological poetry to music.

• The Institute of American Indian Art (IAIA) is established as a college preparatory and vocational training school in Santa Fe, New Mexico, on the site of the Studio School. It provides an arts-based curriculum for the first time in a Native American educational institution, and becomes the established training ground for contemporary Indian art. Native educators design the curriculum, which takes a major departure from the traditional approaches of most Native arts programs by exposing students to contemporary, mainstream art techniques and trends, and encouraging them to find their individual style. Faculty includes sculptor Allan Houser (b.

1915, Chiricahua Apache); jeweler Charles Loloma (b. 1921, Hopi); painter Fritz Scholder (b. 1937, Luiseno), who was a student at the school; and designer and art educator Lloyd Kiva New (Cherokee) as art director. Other students include T. C. Cannon (b. 1946, Caddo), R. C. Gorman (b. 1932, Navajo), Helen Hardin (1943–1984, Santa Clara), and Dan Namingha (b. 1950, Tewa–Hopi).

• Mario Davidovsky composes *Synchronism I* for flute and tape. Like the many "synchronism" pieces that he continues to compose, it is written for live instruments and tape, and explores the synchronizing of events between the live and taped sounds.

• Composer and accordionist Pauline Oliveros becomes co-director, with Ramon Sender, of the San Francisco Tape Music Center, an experimental music lab where many of the earliest electronic works will be produced.

• In Chicago, pianist Muhal Richard Abrams founds the free jazz collective known as the Association for the Advancement of Creative

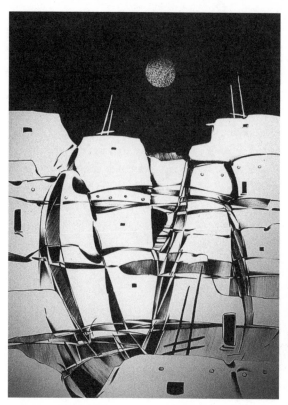

Dan Namingha (b. 1950, Hopi/Tewa), *Night Pueblo*. Black and white lithograph. Namingha is a descendant of a long line of artists, starting with his great-great-grandmother, the potter Nampeyo, and is a graduate of the Institute of American Indian Art (IAIA); his work is widely exhibited internationally. *(Courtesy, National Museum of the American Indian Smithsonian Institution)*

Musicians (AACM), with instrumentalist/composers Anthony Braxton, Leroy Jenkins, Leo Smith, and Roscoe Mitchell. Members of the group also concertize as the Art Ensemble of Chicago.

• Sea Ranch, a Sonoma County vacation resort community, is built over the next five years on ten miles of Northern California's seacoast land that was a sheep ranch.

Co-designed by an interdisciplinary team of Bay Area designers, led by architect Charles Moore (1925–1993) and landscape architect Lawrence Halprin (b. 1916), and including Donlyn Lyndon, William Turnbull, Richard Whitaker, and Joseph Esherick, it combines condominium units, single family units, golf courses, hotel, a village center, and recreation facilities. Although later developments at the site are larger, more luxurious, and intrusive in the landscape, Sea Ranch heralds a new vision of ecologically minded land planning and

Les Fetiches (1937) by African-American artist Lois Mailou Jones merged African and European influences in an innovative way. *(Courtesy of the Kenkelaba Gallery)*

community decision-making, based on what best serves the environment and the community, a prototype imitated in suburban developments throughout the country. Its signature wooden vernacular references, sometimes called "California Style," also prepares the way for acceptance of the eclectic pluralism of postmodern design.

GOVERNMENT AND POLITICS

• The U.S. Supreme Court declares mandatory prayer in public schools unconstitutional.

• James Meredith enrolls in the fall semester at the University of Mississippi as a political science student, after the Supreme Court orders the university to accept him. He is the first black student in the history of the school, a veteran of nine years in the air force, and a transfer student from Jackson State College. The riots that result from his presence require 12,000 federal troops and 200 arrests before the campus is calm enough for Meredith to go to classes. Troops will remain on campus until he graduates in 1963. Meredith is ambushed and shot at in 1966, while conducting a voter registration campaign march around the state of Mississippi, and he will appear before 15,000 people, with Martin Luther King and Stokely Carmichael, at a rally to conclude the march.

• The Kennedy administration works to gain passage of the Communications Satellite Act, inaugurating the age of global satellite communication with the formation of the Communications Satellite Corporation (COMSAT) a government-created company that incorporates as a public entity in 1963. In 1965, COMSAT launches the Early Bird, its first satellite. It serves as the U.S. signatory and is the driving force behind the creation of an international satellite organization, INTELSAT, which, by the beginning of the twenty-first century, will include 143 countries and signatories.

BUSINESS AND INDUSTRY

• The United Farm Workers Organizing Committee in California (known today as the United Farmworkers of America or UFW), organizes California agricultural laborers. Led by Cesar Chavez (1927–1993) with Dolores Huerta as vice president, over the next three years its struggles in behalf of Mexican farm workers will start with state boycotts of lettuce and grapes and then spread to a national boycott of grapes. In 1966 the union joins the AFL-CIO.

• High-fidelity (hi-fi) sound gear is commercially produced, allowing listeners to experience recordings through more than one speaker, which produces a more vibrant sound.

• Telstar 1, the first commercial communications satellite, is built by AT&T and launched into orbit by NASA on July 10. The 34½-inch sphere starts relaying the first transatlantic television images as it travels an elliptical path, from 500 to 3,500 miles above the Earth, using solar power to amplify the originating TV signals 10 billion times and beaming them back to earth. The invention sparks a huge debate over whether government or private industry should own satellite telecommunications systems. The Kennedy administration backs AT&T's bid to deliver a quick, low-orbit solution.

🖻 1963

SCIENCE AND TECHNOLOGY

• The drug thalidomide is linked to thousands of birth defects and removed from the market. Popularly prescribed in Europe since its introduction in 1957 as a sedative for sleepless-ness, tension, and nausea during pregnancy, it appeared to have no side effects on the mother. However, 12,000 malformed babies are born to mothers who take the drug, and those who sur-vive often live with truncated, flipperlike limbs and damage to eyes, ears, and internal organs. Owing to the vigilant research of a U.S. Food and Drug Administration investigator, Frances Oldham Kelsey, the drug is not approved for use in the U.S., although 1,200 doctors distribute free samples to 20,000 mothers-to-be, causing defects in about a dozen U.S. babies.

• Lasers are introduced for use in eye surgery, to repair damaged retinas and remove cataracts, turning extremely delicate operations into outpatient procedures that allow patients to go home pain-free, and often with immedi-ate restoration of normal vision.

🔲 1960

• Biologist Rachel Carson (1907–1964) publishes an environmental whistle-blower, *Silent Spring*, that brings attention to how the introduction of chemicals into food production yields a long-term chain of effects on the planet's ecosystem. Within a few weeks, Presi-dent Kennedy cites the book in ordering a review of government pesticide programs, but it takes almost a decade to establish the Environmental Protection Agency in 1970, which two years later bans DDT and other long-lasting pesticides.

• The U.S. space probe Mariner 2, the first man-made object to travel to another planet, sets a record in interplanetary communications when it beams signals 36 million miles, trans-mitting data on the temperature and atmos-phere of Venus.

This cartoon of the Cuban Missile Crisis invasion points to the "Wild West" style of brinksmanship politics that President Kennedy played in Cuba with the Russians. Political cartoon by Leslie Gilbert Illingworth, published October 24, 1962, in the *Daily Mail* (London). *(Library of Congress, Prints and Photographs Division)*

CULTURE AND SOCIETY

• Students for a Democratic Society (SDS) issues a manifesto for the New Left, called the Port Huron Statement, written by Tom Hayden and others, "bred in at least modest comfort, housed now in universities, looking uncom-fortably at the world we inherit. . . . Our work is guided by the sense that we may be the last generation in the experiment with living." It is opposed to Communism, a system it says has failed "to achieve its stated intentions of lead-ing a worldwide movement for human emanci-pation," and calls for individual responsibility in a participatory democracy, although it does not make clear how that should best be achieved.

WORLD EVENTS

• For seven days in October, the world watches events that are known as the Cuban Missile Crisis, in which U.S. President Kennedy and Premier Khrushchev of the USSR play brinkmanship politics. The U.S. sets up an arms blockade of Cuba and threatens to retaliate with nuclear weapons if the Russians do not dismantle their Cuban missile and bomber sites. Premier Fidel Castro mobilizes thousands of Cuban forces, denying the Russian presence and calling Kennedy's blockade an act of war. Negotiations move through the United Nations and other channels, until Khrushchev backs down and an agreement is reached, with the U.S. agreeing not to invade Cuba if the Soviet Union ships all its weapons back home. The U.S. continues its Cuban blockade, however.

1963

ARTS AND LITERATURE

• Andy Warhol establishes his studio, the Factory, and shoots his first film, *Sleep,* of a man sleeping for six hours. Like his other early films made in 1963–1964, including *Kiss, Eat, Haircut,* and *Blow Job,* it is shot in black and white at sixteen frames per second, rather than the normal rate of 24 frames per second, and is silent and without editing, documenting a single action or image over a long time.

• The Living Theater moves to Europe after being evicted from their 14th Street theater for nonpayment of taxes during the run of *The Brig* by Kenneth Brown, a play that criticizes the U.S. Marines prison system. Joseph Chaikin (b. 1935), a member of the company, decides to stay in New York, where he forms a new collective called the Open Theatre, whose members invent new training and performance techniques as they create new plays. The Bread and Puppet Theater is founded by Peter Schumann (b. 1934, Germany). It adapts traditional European pageant, parade, puppetry, and mime techniques to contemporary political and social protest.

• The "in" New York City artists' and writers' hangout scene shifts from the downtown West Side, where the White Horse Tavern and the Cedar Bar are located. The original Cedar Tavern—the Greenwich Village hangout for abstract expressionists, the Black Mountain New York School, pop, and Beat groups of visual and literary artists—closes. The new scene is on the East Side, where Mickey Ruskin's Max's Kansas City cabaret opens this year, in the same neighborhood as Warhol's Factory and a bit farther uptown from the Five Spot, a bar on Cooper Square, the borderline between the East and West Sides, that opens this year. It becomes the place to hear the great jazz artists Charlie Mingus (1922–1979), Sonny Rollins (b. 1930), Cecil Taylor, Thelonious Monk, and Ornette Coleman (b. 1930). It reflects the shift happening in the gallery scene, away from the high rents and older bohemians that espouse abstract expressionism, color-field paintings, and Beat and Black Mountain aesthetics, to styles named Pop, Op, minimal, earth, and conceptual art.

• Romare Bearden (1914–1988) changes from two decades of producing abstract paintings and starts producing collages, also called photomontages by art critics, to evoke "the innerness of the Negro experience." He pastes together cutouts and torn pieces of magazine photos, abstract shapes of torn and cut layers of colored paper, and sometimes pieces of his own artworks, besides mixing in areas of paint. Starting in 1964, Bearden exhibits photographically enlarged versions of these works, which he calls "Projections."

• The Art in Architecture program of the Kennedy administration's Office of General Services is launched to put art in federal buildings. This program sets a precedent for funding public art projects, such as the "percent of art" laws that are instituted in thirty-one states, requiring all construction projects using public funds to earmark one-half of one percent of each construction budget for artworks. It integrates sculpture and painting into building design, with artists and architects often becoming collaborators.

• Folksinger Joan Baez, who helped create a popular revival for the Elizabethan folk tradition, singing in Cambridge, Massachusetts, clubs since the beginning of the decade, introduces songwriter Bob Dylan (b. 1941) during her major breakthrough concert at the Newport Folk Festival in Rhode Island. Along with other members of the new generation of folk-rock singers, such as Buffy St. Marie and Judy Collins, they bring a political seriousness to their straightforward acoustic style of delivery. After five years of recording, Joan Baez gets a hit for the first time this year with a Phil Ochs ballad, "There But for Fortune." Dylan is also able to please a wide audience with his 1963 songs, keeping the radical left interested with "The Times They Are A-Changin' " and also hitting the top ten with "Blowin' in the Wind."

GOVERNMENT AND POLITICS

• The Defense Department establishes a diplomatic "hot line," a direct, encoded tele-

type line of communication linking Moscow and Washington, to avoid delays such as those experienced during the Cuban Missile Crisis.

• The first successful Hispanic political action takes place in Crystal City, Texas, where Mexican Americans make up 85 percent of the population, when five Euro-American city council members lose their elected seats to five Mexican Americans. The new council members make positive reforms, with the assistance of the Teamsters Union at the local Del Monte cannery and the Political Association of Spanish-Speaking Organizations, although they experience factionalism and resistance from the Euro-American community. Led by Jose Angel Gutierrez, they form a political party, La Raza Unita, in 1971, becoming the first U.S. city to have a Chicano third party controlling the local government. By 1981, the La Raza Unita party will have achieved its demands that the two-party system pay attention to Hispanic voters and respond to their issues, and their numbers will decline as the Democratic Party becomes more inclusive.

• The U.S. Post Office inaugurates a Zone Improvement Program, or ZIP, to speed up mail delivery. Each delivery area in the country is assigned a five digit zip code, with the first three districts indicating the district, often a city, and the last two indicating the local zone.

• The U.S.A., the USSR, and Britain are among ninety-nine nations who sign the Limited Nuclear Test Ban Treaty, which bans tests of nuclear weapons in the water, atmosphere, and outer space, but continues to permit underground testing. This is the first time any group of countries has found a way to agree on any limits regarding nuclear weapons, probably because of the development of spy satellites that make mutual inspections possible and the dangers demonstrated by the 1962 Cuban Missile Crisis.

• President John F. Kennedy is assassinated in Dallas, Texas, on November 22, while riding in a motorcade. His alleged assassin is Lee Harvey Oswald, who is also shot and killed two days later in the Dallas city jail by Jack Ruby, owner of a striptease joint. Vice President Lyndon Johnson, who is riding in another car at the time of the shooting, takes the presidential oath of office on the Dallas airfield.

SCIENCE AND TECHNOLOGY

• NASA launches Syncom II, the first geosynchronous communications satellite, meaning that its orbit matches the Earth's rotation, allowing the satellite to remain stationary above one location on the Earth's surface. It is successfully used in intercontinental communications experiments. Viewers in the U.S. watch live telecasts of the 1964 Olympic Games in Tokyo, an event for which they would otherwise have had to wait at least twelve hours, until the tapes could be transported by the fastest airplane to broadcast outlets in the U.S. ▣ 1962

• Astronomer Maarten Schmidt (Dutch-American, b. 1929, Netherlands) makes the first recognition of the farthest objects ever observed through a telescope to date. Using the five-meter Mt. Palomar telescope, Schmidt identifies a quasi-stellar radio source, called "quasar" for short, by noticing the "extraordinarily large red shift" registered in photos taken of a starlike object labeled 3C273.

CULTURE AND SOCIETY

• In June the National Guard forces Alabama's governor, George Wallace, to step aside at the door of the University of Alabama, to allow the enrollment of two black students.

• After being arrested in the spring for demonstrating against segregation in Birmingham, Alabama, Martin Luther King writes "Letter from Birmingham Jail," an open letter to eight white "liberal" Alabama clergymen. Although they had advised him to keep the civil rights battles for integration in local and federal courts, rather than in the streets where they could incite further rioting and violence, King lays out his reasons for practicing civil disobedience, because "freedom is never voluntarily given by the oppressor." King insists he "stand[s] between two opposing forces in the Negro community . . . the 'do-nothingism' of the complacent . . . [and] the hatred and despair of the black nationalist. For there is the more excellent way of love and nonviolent protest. I am grateful to God that, through the influence of the Negro church, the way of nonviolence became an integral part of our struggle."

• On June 12, Medgar Evers, the first NAACP field secretary in Mississippi, is shot while getting out of his car at home in Jackson, Mississippi, and dies of gunshot wounds. The FBI accuses a white supremacist, Byron De La Beckwith, of the murder, but it remains unsolved until 1994, when Beckwith is finally convicted of the crime. Evers's work to desegregate higher education, gain voting rights, and public accommodations for African Americans places him among the heroes and martyrs in the civil rights struggle. On Evers's burial day, President Kennedy delivers Congress a bill that is intended to guarantee equal rights in public accommodations and forbid discrimination in voting, employment, and labor unions, and in state programs receiving federal funds. It also gives the Attorney General the power to sue for enforcement of the Fourteenth and Fifteenth Amendments.

• On August 28, 250,000 people participate in the March on Washington, of which at least 60,000 of the demonstrators are white. The event shows the brilliance of its strategists, Bayard Rustin and A. Philip Randolph, who call the march as a tactic to inspire Congress to pass a proposed civil rights bill supported by President Kennedy, the strongest since Reconstruction. Martin Luther King delivers what will become his most famous address at the Lincoln Memorial, known as "I Have a Dream." The event, carried live on radio and television, solidifies King's status as leader of the civil rights movement and moral voice of the nation. President Kennedy welcomes him to the White House, just weeks before his own assassination in November, leaving newly sworn-in President Johnson to persuade Congress to pass what will become an even stronger civil rights bill.

🔲 1964

• Four African American girls are killed by a bomb explosion while attending Sunday school at the Sixteenth Street Baptist Church in Birmingham, Alabama, just eighteen days after the March on Washington. The bomb, set by pro-segregation white terrorists, is a double outrage, killing young girls in a church, and provokes a riot in which two more African American youths are killed. However, the city of Birmingham, which had gained the title of "Johannesburg of America" for its adamant and often violent refusal to comply with civil rights laws, finally accepts desegregation of the city.

WORLD EVENTS

• In June, a Buddhist monk sets fire to himself in Saigon, to protest the Diem regime, which is supported by the U.S. government.

• In June, a huge crowd roars with approval and amusement during President Kennedy's speech at the Berlin Wall in which he says "Ich bin ein Berliner." (He intends to say "I am from Berlin," but because it is a colloquial expression, it translates as "I am a jelly doughnut.") It is his expression of solidarity with a city that is isolated within the Soviet Communist bloc.

• On November 1, President Ngo Dinh Diem and his brother are executed in Saigon, after widespread protests against the Diem government by Buddhists.

• The anti-Communist Baath Party stages a coup in Baghdad, Iraq, overthrowing and later assassinating President Abdul Karem Kassim, whom the CIA considers dangerous to American interests in the Middle East. Future Iraqi President Saddam Hussein is a young Baathist activist at this time. Historian Roger Morris reports the U.S. supplies arms and the CIA supplies lists of suspected Communists and other leftists that are used in the bloodbath and repressive purges following the takeover.

🔲 1968

1964

ARTS AND LITERATURE

• Betty Friedan (b. 1921), trained as a psychologist, writes *The Feminine Mystique*, a bestseller that catapults Friedan into a leadership role in the feminist movement. Friedan writes the book after interviewing her fellow Smith College graduates at the fifteenth anniversary of their graduation, where educated women reveal their lack of fulfillment in living only through their husbands and children. She extends her research for three more years, to write a more general description of how women are supposed to limit their expectations to the inside of their homes, a message transmitted through education, the media, science, and American culture, whereas many need to find an identity outside the home. The book is criticized for not describing working-class and minority women's experiences, a criticism that will continue to plague the National Organization for Women (NOW), the feminist organization that Friedan founds and heads.

• The Organization of Young Men (OYM) a downtown political group including Calvin Hicks, A. B. Spellmen, Steve Cannon, and Amiri Baraka, moves uptown to Harlem and founds the Black Arts Repertory Theater/School (BARTS), or Black Arts as it is known, with Askia Muhammad Touré, Raymond Patterson, and Larry Neal (1937–1981), among others, developing a cultural movement and school that offers theater, art exhibits, writing workshops, martial arts, and revolutionary politics.

• The Beatles enter the U.S., topping the record charts with six hits in one year; the Rolling Stones release their first album.

GOVERNMENT AND POLITICS

• Lyndon Johnson is elected president. Under his guidance, Congress passes the Civil Rights Act of 1964, the first comprehensive civil rights legislation passed since the Civil War, which prohibits discrimination based on race, religion, national origin, color, or gender in all institutions receiving federal funds. It also establishes

the Equal Employment Opportunity Commission (EEOC) to prevent and monitor cases of job discrimination and institute affirmative-action programs. President Johnson signs the bill on July 2.

• The U.S. Congress passes the Gulf of Tonkin Resolution, which gives President Johnson the power to "take all necessary measures to . . . prevent further aggression." This escalates the Vietnam War into a large-scale U.S. military intervention that will continue for eleven more years, until 1975. One million U.S. troops are sent to Vietnam in an unsuccessful attempt to block Ho Chi Minh's North Vietnamese communist regime. The war causes the U.S. to experience its greatest antiwar movement, which helps bring the war to an end. (In August 1965, 61 percent of the American people support the war; by May 1971, 61 percent think it is wrong to be involved.)

• In April, the Freedom Democratic Party is founded in Mississippi for all Democrats, "regardless of race, creed or color." They send a delegation to the Democratic Convention in Atlantic City, headed by Fannie Lou Hamer (1917–1977), challenging the legitimacy of the all-white Mississippi Democrats by demanding their seats. They are not successful in this bid, and compromises also fall through, but they do make their point that poor blacks will no longer be intimidated from demanding their civil rights, including the right to vote.

• In September, the Warren Commission, headed by Chief Justice Earl Warren, issues its report on the assassination of President Kennedy. It concludes that Lee Harvey Oswald acted alone. However, conspiracy theories continue to circulate.

• The Office of Economic Opportunity creates an Indian desk and gives antipoverty funds directly to the tribes. This model for direct grants to tribal governments becomes the model for self-determination starting in the 1970s.

BUSINESS AND INDUSTRY

• Following precedents of his mentor, President Franklin Roosevelt, President Johnson launches a "War on Poverty" with passage of the Economic Opportunity Act (EOA). The EOA sets up the Office of Economic Opportunity (OEO), which administers various programs to help poor people, including the Job Corps, the Volunteers in Service to America (VISTA) and the Community Action Program (CAP).

SCIENCE AND TECHNOLOGY

• Gordon Moore, co-founder with Robert Noyce of the microchip goliath Intel in 1968, posits Moore's Law: the number of transistors in, and thus computational power of, integrated circuits or "chips" will double every year. In 1975 Moore updates his prediction to every two years. Intel helps prove his theory by creating the first microprocessor with 2,300 transistors in 1971, and the Pentium IV microprocessor with 42 million transistors in 2000, a doubling approximately every 2.05 years.

• Container ships are introduced, making international trade faster and easier as cargo can be handled in bulk loads, the goods transferred from ship to shore and transported by rail across the country without repacking.

• Permanent-press clothing is introduced, making it possible to wash and wear clothes without ironing them.

"I'll do the teaching around here!" Cartoon by Jim Ivey on the Free Speech Movement, UC Berkeley, published in the *San Francisco Examiner,* December 6, 1965. (*Library of Congress, Prints and Photographs Division*)

CULTURE AND SOCIETY

• The Free Speech Movement begins at the University of California, Berkeley, after almost 800 students strike, or stop attending classes. The students conduct a sit-in on the street for thirty-two hours, to prevent a police car from carrying off a student, arrested because he manned an "unauthorized" table in Sproul Plaza, to recruit volunteers and raise money for the civil rights movement in Mississippi. The movement spreads across the country, developing from its start as a student revolt against institutional monitoring of political activities on campus into general demands that administrations should exercise less control over all areas of students' lives.

• Young people from around the country go to Mississippi to help launch "Freedom Summer." In June, three civil rights workers, James Chaney, an African American from Mississippi, and Andrew Goodman and Michael Schwerner, two white volunteers from the North, are killed in Mississippi by white segregationists. Their deaths, which are widely publicized, lead to jail sentences for the sheriff, deputy sheriff, and others, and dramatically prove how inadequate protections continue to be from local and federal authorities.

• During this year and the next, urban race riots occur around the nation. The Harlem Rebellion starts in July, after a fifteen-year-old black boy is shot by an off-duty white police officer. After four nights, the riot spreads to Brooklyn's Bedford-Stuyvesant area, and is so violent that President Johnson orders the FBI to investigate its causes. In Cleveland, a riot happens after the killing of a white minister while he sits before a bulldozer to protest hiring discrimination against blacks in the construction trade. Other riots, often related to police encounters, occur in Rochester, Chicago, Philadelphia, and various cities in New Jersey. The national guard is frequently called in to restore calm. President Johnson responds by expanding the War on Poverty to fund programs fighting illiteracy, unemployment, and other conditions related to poverty. NAACP head Roy Wilkins talks of "criminal elements" in the demonstrations, airing a tactical split in the civil rights movement, between those who advocate nonviolence and those who advocate militant self-defense.

🅟 1967

• Malcolm X officially breaks away from the Nation of Islam. He travels on a pilgrimage to Mecca, announcing his conversion to orthodox Islam, and his belief in the need for brotherhood between blacks and whites. When he returns to the U.S. he forms the Organization of Afro-American Unity. He remains a militant, calling for freedom "by any means necessary," but no longer talks of separation.

• The first of two Indian occupations of Alcatraz Island in San Francisco Bay starts in late winter. Indian activists announce their intention to use the closed federal prison to establish a university, based on an 1869 Sioux treaty that granted Indians first rights to government surplus lands.

• The Episcopal Diocese of New York supports the decriminalization of homosexual acts between consenting adults, a key challenge to religious institutional viewpoints that foster anti-gay prejudices.

🅟 1968

• The first "underground" paper, the *East Village Other,* is founded by Allen Katzman, Walter Bowart, and Ishmael Reed, in New York City. It inspires "counterculture" papers to begin publishing in communities throughout the country. In San Francisco, *Open City,* an "underground" weekly, is published by John Bryan from the basement of a former stable about eight months before Max Scheer starts the *Berkeley Barb,* and the *Free Press* starts in Los Angeles. The papers report news of counterculture demonstrations against the war, and advocate for the rights of people of color, interviewing counterculture heroes (Che Guevara, Abbie Hoffman, the Black Panthers,

Allen Ginsberg, Timothy Leary, Buckminster Fuller, Marshall McLuhan, Kate Millett) and investigating its villains (President Johnson, the FBI, the CIA). They also showcase new comic art and review cutting-edge arts. They start small, with a combined circulation of 5,000 or fewer in 1965, but by 1969 the *Free Press* is selling 95,000 a week, the *Berkeley Barb* 85,000, and *The East Village Other* 65,000.

• The 1964 presidential political campaign introduces a new method of commercial advertising, in which politicians hire advertisers to create ad campaigns that employ ideological, emotionally charged visual images or buzzwords as stand-ins for substantive political discourse. Liberal Democrat Lyndon B. Johnson takes on Republican Barry Goldwater in what becomes known as the "Daisy spot." It shows a little girl picking a daisy that dissolves into a nuclear bomb explosion, implying through the images' symbolic language, without even mentioning his name, that Goldwater's extremism could erupt into World War III. That same fall, Goldwater counters with "Choice," a twenty-seven-minute commercial contrasting two American myths: the chaos of rioters, gamblers, strippers, and muggers with the uprightness of astronauts and construction workers and the patriotism of children saluting the flag. Although this commercial is considered too inflammatory and it is pulled after appearing only once or twice in California and Wisconsin, it is merely ahead of its time. Its message is studied and continues to be applied by Republicans, who succeed in winning presidencies from 1968 to 1992—except for the Carter years (1977–1981), which are a gift of the Watergate scandal—and also by Democrats.

WORLD EVENTS

• Martin Luther King Jr. receives the Nobel Peace Prize for his leadership in the nonviolent campaign against racism and segregation in the 1950s and 1960s, including his role in peacefully desegregating the bus system of Montgomery, Alabama, in 1955.

• Nikita Khrushchev is forced to retire from power in the USSR, and is replaced by Aleksei Kosygin as premier and Leonid Brezhnev as Communist Party secretary, who reinstate tight censorship and other repressive measures, and expand military and space programs.

1965

ARTS AND LITERATURE

• The first artist's video, made by performance and installation artist Nam June Paik, is shown at Café á Go-Go in New York City. An active Fluxus artist, he mixes wit in his ongoing video projects, which include large walls of complexly programmed video material, a video cello, and a video bra. Paik engineers many of the things he builds, significantly advancing the state of video technology.

• Charles Wuorinen and Harvey Sollberger, two Columbia University students, found the Group for Contemporary Music, and begin giving concerts of mainly "post-Webern serial" and electronic music at Columbia University. Wuorinen composes *Times Encomium*, and becomes the first Pulitzer Prize winner for an entirely electronic composition in 1970; Charles Dodge composes *Earth's Magnetic Field*, a great example of mapping numerical statistics into musical data.

• The term *minimalism* comes into common usage after critic Barbara Rose writes an article, "ABC Art," in *Art in America,* referring to art that has been reduced to its "minimal" essentials. The term is applied to works of painting, sculpture, music, and dance, and the style dominates the late-1960s art world. It is the first art movement of international significance pioneered by artists from the U.S. Lucinda Childs (b. 1940) and Laura Dean (b. 1945) are dancers associated with this style. Some visual artists called minimalists include Carl Andre (b. 1955), Dan Flavin (b. 1935), Donald Judd (1928–1994), Sol Lewitt (b. 1928), Brice Marden (b. 1938), Agnes Martin (b. 1912), Robert Morris (b. 1931), Dorothea Rockburne (b. 1921), Tony Smith (1912–1980) and Frank Stella (b. 1936). The term and style continues to resurface, including the variation, "post-minimalism," that appears by 1971 in *Artforum,* when critic Robert Pincus-Witten describes the more detailed and illustrative work of Eva Hesse (1936–1970) and Richard Serra (b. 1939), and returns to minimalism in the late 1980s and the beginning of the twenty-first century.

• El Teatro Campesino is founded in the Central Valley of California by Luis Valdez (b. 1940), the son of migrant Chicano farmworkers in Delano, California. It functions as a cultural voice of the United Farm Workers movement, dramatizing the struggles of the farm workers to win better working and living conditions, to gain higher wages, and to help raise funds for the UFW's fight against the huge agricultural businesses. With flatbed trucks serving as stages, they drive into the fields and barrios (neighborhoods), or into the middle of strikes, putting on bilingual *actos,* their name for their farcical style of brief, commedia-like sketches where the performers portray themselves with dialogue in the real words exchanged with the scabs in the fields every day. By 1967 the troupe splits off from the union to focus on making other kinds of theater, setting off a Chicano theater movement that includes many *teatro* groups that form throughout the Southwest.

▣ 1971

• Eldridge (Leroy) Cleaver (1935–1998), who will become a leader in the Black Panther Party and a celebrity of the New Left, publishes an autobiography in the form of a collection of letters, essays, and monologues, titled *Soul on Ice.* He confesses to the actions that put him in the U.S. penal system, describes his experiences of being black in a racist society, and details the forces that create and feed the civil rights movement. It becomes a classic document of the 1950s and 1960s in the U.S.

• The Bread and Puppet Theater, directed by Peter Schumann, begins participating in peace demonstrations and protest marches against the Vietnam War in Washington, D.C., and New York City. He rallies hundreds of volunteer operators, who march inside abstract clay masks, performing skits with giant puppets manipulated by teams using long rods to create their mimed gestures, while still others, wrapped in gray rags, create an eerie band playing home-made instruments, drums, and pipes. Their death masks, skeleton shapes, white-faced mourning puppets, and sounds become a pervasive symbol of the antiwar movement.

• In June, Bill Graham presents the San Francisco Mime Troupe in *A Minstrel Show, or Civil Rights in a Cracker Barrel,* written by Saul Landau and R. G. Davis from original, traditional, and improvised material, directed by R. G. Davis, with music by Steve Reich. It premieres at the Commedia Theatre in Palo

Alto. In November, in San Francisco, R. G. Davis is found guilty of performing in the parks without a permit, the company's major venue. However, the SF Mime Troupe continues lampooning contemporary political, environmental, social, and scientific events, in free plays presented every summer in Bay Area parks. Many actors, clowns, playwrights, and musicians will be trained in their mixing of techniques from traditional commedia del arte, brought up-to-date with its younger relatives, vaudeville and agitprop, carrying their influence into other companies' work.

• August Wilson (b. 1945) begins a cycle of ten twentieth-century history plays set in his hometown neighborhood of the Hill district in Pittsburgh, Pennsylvania, to "tell a history that has never been told," the African American historical experience from an African American point of view. He will win two Pulitzer Prizes for plays in the cycle, for *Fences* (set in the 1950s) and *Joe Turner's Come and Gone* (set in the teens), and become the first African American to have two plays on Broadway simultaneously. Other plays in the cycle include *Ma Rainey's Black Bottom* (1920s), *The Piano Lesson* (1930s), *Two Trains Running* (1960s), *Seven Guitars* (1940s), and *King Hedley II* (1980s). He will end the century with the last two plays of the cycle in progress.

GOVERNMENT AND POLITICS

• Martin Luther King Jr. of SCLC and John Lewis of SNCC lead a march, from Selma to Montgomery, Alabama on March 7, to dramatize how state-wide practices remain in place that deny the right of African Americans to vote. Governor Wallace refuses to provide the marchers with protection, and they are attacked by state troopers and sheriff's deputies wielding nightsticks, whips, and tear gas. On March 15, President Johnson calls a joint session of Congress to do something "to overcome the crippling legacy of bigotry and injustice." Five months later the Voting Rights Act of 1965 is passed. It gets rid of all qualifying tests for voter registration that relate to a person's race or color. It also legislates voter protections by promising to send federal agents to register black voters in states and districts where there is evidence of obstructions.

• Congress passes an antipollution bill that directs the Secretary of Health, Education, and Welfare to set government emission standards for maximum levels of toxic pollutants allowable in new cars, and prohibits the sale of diesel- or gasoline-powered vehicles that do not comply with the standard.

• The Department of Housing and Urban Development (HUD) is established to administer housing programs to assist in developing the nation's communities. They will oversee the Model Cities program, instituted by Congress in 1966, to rehabilitate slums and promote urban planning in "model" or demonstration cities. 📷 1966, 1968

• In *Miranda v. Arizona*, the Supreme Court expands and protects the rights of crime suspects. Its 5–4 ruling states that the Fifth Amendment guarantees protection against self-incrimination, and places the burden of proof on the prosecution, if the suspect complies with an interrogation. Accused persons must be apprised of their rights before questioning, and must be informed that their remarks may be used against them, and that they have a right to an attorney during interrogation.

• President Lyndon Johnson inaugurates his

Great Society programs, including the War on Poverty, the most sweeping set of social welfare programs enacted since President Roosevelt's New Deal. He succeeds in instituting the first national health insurance programs ever provided by the federal government, Medicaid and Medicare, which offer subsidized medical care for elderly, disabled, and indigent citizens. By 1967 he pushes through congressional approval of food stamps, VISTA, the Job Corps, and Project Head Start, a preschool program for disadvantaged children that will become a long-term success.

• The National Endowment for the Arts (NEA) and the National Endowment for the Humanities (NEH) are established with the signing of Public Law 89-209 by President Johnson, instituting the first government support of the arts since the WPA projects of the Roosevelt era. The law provides a decision-making structure for funding arts and humanities projects throughout the country. In framing these bodies, the Senate's Labor and Public Welfare Committee urges that the law provide "the fullest attention to freedom of artistic and humanistic expression. One of the artists' and humanists' great values to society is the mirror of self-examination which they raise so that society can become aware of its shortcomings as well as its strengths."

🔲 1989, 1990

• The passage of the Freedom of Information Act gives citizens greater access to public information. People can request their FBI files, and in some circles it becomes a matter of distinction to be included in their lists.

• The national origin quota system is abolished with the passage of the Immigration and Nationality Act Amendments of October 3,

1965. Also known as the Hart-Cellar Act, it amends the exclusionary McCarran-Walter Immigration and Nationality Act of 1952, by granting visas on a first-come, first-served basis and by allowing a quota of up to 20,000 entry visas per year for each independent country outside of the western hemisphere. It establishes two categories that are not subject to numerical restrictions: immediate relatives, including spouses, children, and parents of American citizens; and special immigrants, including ministers, former U.S. government employees abroad, and persons with special occupational skills or training needed in the U.S. An example that reflects the effects of this more open policy can be seen in the Korean community, where, because of a difficult economic situation in Korea, many Koreans decide to immigrate to the U.S. In 1965, 2,165 Koreans enter the U.S., and between 1965 and 1980, about 299,000 Koreans become U.S. immigrants, with the majority settling in California and New York. Many are professionals, particularly doctors. Many are also North Koreans, most of whom are practicing Christians who fled to South Korea between 1945 and 1951.

• President Johnson makes affirmative action a federal policy with Executive Order 11246, when he requires government contractors to guarantee fair hiring and employment practices for minorities. Implemented by federal agencies enforcing the Civil Rights Act of 1964 and two executive orders, affirmative action's purpose is to ensure that African Americans, other minorities, and women receive the same opportunities for education, jobs, and other resources as European American men.

🔲 1978, 1997

BUSINESS AND INDUSTRY

• Hundreds of thousands of Mexicans are forced to return to Mexico when the *bracero* program is ended in the U.S. They settle near the U.S. border, and the U.S. and Mexican governments establish the Border Industrialization Program, out of concern for leaving so many people out of work and in the hope of building up the border communities. The program allows foreign corporations to build and operate assembly plants on the border, known as *maquiladoras,* where they employ hundreds of thousands of Mexicans to do assembly work. The plan attracts multinational corporations because it increases corporate profits for many reasons: the location makes it possible to remain in close proximity to lucrative U.S. markets; the plants operate with weak unions and weak environmental regulations; and by paying workers low wages and providing poor working conditions, they cut labor costs for the assembly work, which also benefits consumers by holding down prices on goods.

▣ 1942, 1960, 1980

• September begins ten years of organizational struggle by the National Farm Organizing Committee headed by Cesar Chavez, when they join a strike initiated by Filipino grape pickers in Delano, California. Out of this strike Mexican and Mexican American pickers, who make up the majority of farm laborers, form the National Farm Workers Association (NFWA), the largest agricultural union. The strikers ask consumers to join them by participating in a national boycott of grapes. The California strike becomes a major catalyst in framing Mexican and Chicano political action and their movements for social justice.

• Lawyer Ralph Nader publishes *Unsafe at Any Speed,* an exposé of the American automobile industry, charging that the industry has emphasized profits rather than safety "for over fifty years." Among the "designed-in dangers" he reveals: owing to a badly designed rear-suspension system on the Chevrolet Corvair, which causes drivers to lose control on turns, more than one million accidents have happened over four years. When the public finds out General Motors has tried to smear Nader by hiring a detective to dig for personal dirt, he becomes a hero and GM's president has to apologize in a televised hearing. Nader launches a consumer movement known as "Nader's Raiders," to watchdog corporate practices and encourage environmental protection. New legislation inspired by the consumer protection movement includes the National Traffic and Motor Vehicle Safety Act, which, by 1968, requires cars to be equipped with front-seat shoulder belts, and the truth-in-packaging bill, which requires supermarket items to be labeled accurately, bans misleading advertising such as "jumbo ounces" or "giant half quart," and asks manufacturers to develop voluntary weight and measure standards.

SCIENCE AND TECHNOLOGY

• African American inventor Otis Boykin (1920–1982) receives the patent for a tiny electrical device that is the control unit used in cardiac pacemakers and IBM computers.

• Working independently, U.S. physicists Steven Weinberg (b. 1933) and Sheldon Lee Glashow (b. 1932), and Pakistani-British physicist Abdus Salam (b. 1926), develop the "electroweak" theory, providing a unifying explanation of both the electromagnetic and

Ralph Nader at work as a consumer advocate. Cartoon by Dennis Hermanson, March 30, 1972. *(Library of Congress, Prints and Photographs Division)*

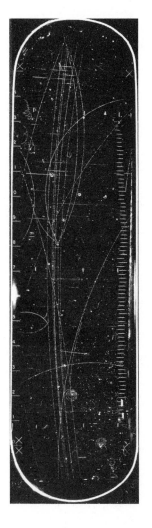

In 1953, physicist Donald Glaser invents a device he calls a "bubble chamber" to study the interactions of particles that had only been predicted in theory up to this time. Using a bubble chamber, scientists can obtain photographic images of the trails left by high-energy particles, called "particle tracks." This photograph shows a view of tracks in a seventy-two-inch Particle Detection Bubble-Chamber produced at Lawrence Berkeley National Laboratory in 1981. *(Courtesy of UC Lawrence Berkeley National Laboratory Image Library, Jean Wolslegel)*

ASK ME, I KNOW. I WAS THE TEST CASE

Earl Caldwell

I'm a journalist and, as quiet as it's kept, serious about my work. I grin a lot and try to give the impression that I'm always happy. That's the façade black folks must put up. So when I said that I wasn't going to appear before any grand jury investigating the Black Panther Party, nobody believed I was serious. Perhaps they didn't know where I'd been for the past five or six years.

I was on the balcony with Martin Luther King Jr. in 1968, and I saw him die. I saw the blood come out of his neck and stack up around his head. I watched Ralph Abernathy cradle King's head in his arms. I was there, and looked into King's eyes and watched him die. Before that I had done my time in the streets. I wasn't just in Newark or Detroit. I was on Blue Hill Avenue in Boston. I was on the west side in Dayton. I was in Cincinnati and Watts and Sacramento and Chicago and a lot of other places where black folks showed their anger and rebelled during the summer of 1967.

When I linked up with the Panthers late in 1968 on the West Coast, they called me a cop. I had to be a cop, they reasoned: *The New York Times* was not about to send a black reporter 3,000 miles just to cover them. Late one night in San Francisco they yanked an old couch away from a wall in a cramped apartment, exposing stacks of guns of every sort. I could tell my readers then to take these people seriously, and I did.

On the morning before he went into hiding and eventually slipped out of the country, I visited Eldridge Cleaver in his San Francisco home. I remember him sitting there at his typewriter with his shoes off and telling me that the time was coming when the Panthers would have to move against black journalists. Once, he explained, it hadn't made any difference what we wrote because nobody—nobody black, that is—read us. But with blacks beginning to read more, what was being written about them was becoming more important. "What good do you do anyhow?" he asked. I wrestled with the question then; it is even more difficult to answer now.

I had my first encounter with the FBI agents when I wrote about the Panthers' guns, but that time they left me alone when I assured them that all the information was available in the newspaper. Then, late in 1969, they began to interfere with my work. They wanted to pick my brain. They wanted me to slip about behind my news sources, to act like the double agents I saw on old movie reruns on TV.

It went like that for months, until one day an agent [said] that if I didn't come in and talk to them, I'd be telling what I knew in court. That's when they subpoenaed me. They asked for all of my tape recordings, notebooks, and other documents covering a period of more than fourteen months—and let me know that if I did not come in with everything, I would go to jail. As it turned out, when I did refuse to appear before the grand jury, I was found in civil contempt and sentenced to jail until I complied with the court order.

[In 1972] the case went all the way to the Supreme Court, where the initial judgment against me was upheld by a majority of the Court.

But not all of the Court misunderstood. In his dissenting opinion, Justice Douglas wrote: "A reporter is no better than his source of information. Unless he has a privilege to withhold the identity of his source, he will be the victim of governmental intrigue or aggression. If he can be summoned to testify in secret before a grand jury, his sources will dry up and the attempted exposure, the effort to enlighten the public, will be ended. If what the Court sanctions today becomes settled law, then the reporter's main function in American society will be to pass on to the public the press releases which the various departments of government issue."

(From Saturday Review's "Up Front" column, August 5, 1972; the ruling against Caldwell led to the enactment of shield laws in many states, to protect reporters' sources and information.)

weak forces, two of the four fundamental forces acting in the universe (the other two being the gravitational and strong forces). They predict that the weak force, a short-range particle force responsible for the emission of radioactivity, is governed by three previously undetected elementary particles, and in 1979 they are awarded the Nobel Prize for Physics.

CULTURE AND SOCIETY

• The most violent urban outbreak since World War II takes place in the Watts section of Los Angeles, with looting, burning of buildings, sniper fire, and attacks on whites and police by African Americans who control the streets for five days. A curfew is enforced by police, and 13,000 national guardsmen are called in to restore calm. The riot leaves thirty-four people dead, more than 1,000 injured, and 4,000 arrested. The effects of over $200 million in property damage remain long after the riot is over, as people have to travel to other parts of the city to shop for groceries and other necessities, and vacant lots remain undeveloped.

• Civil rights leader Malcolm X is assassinated in February as he is about to make a public speech to his Organization of Afro-American Unity from the stage of the Audubon Ballroom in Harlem, New York. Three men who are said to be Black Muslims are convicted of the murder, but many questions remain unanswered.

• The era of the interracial civil rights movement ends. SNCC asks whites to leave the organization and organize poor whites. Many whites join Students for a Democratic Society (SDS), where they organize anti–Vietnam War demonstrations, and in various northern cities such as Newark, Cleveland, and Chicago, they organize poor whites on causes of welfare reform and improving community housing. Women, though crucial in the day-to-day operation of the organization, are never given recognition for their work. They begin to express their need to find respect through their own movement, reacting to the truth behind such indignities as Stokely Carmichael's famous one-liner joke about Mary King's SNCC Position Paper in November 1964, discussing women's position in the organization: "The position of women in SNCC is prone!" This year, Casey Hayden, recently divorced from SDS leader Tom Hayden, and Mary King write "A Kind of Memo," a manifesto outlining many women's issues that will define the white women's feminist movement.

KWANZAA

Maulana Karenga

Kwanzaa is an African-American and Pan-African celebration of family, community, and culture. The word *Kwanzaa* comes from the Swahili *matunda ya kwanza,* which means "first fruits" and reflects the holiday's roots in harvest celebrations recorded from the earliest African history. Kwanzaa was created in 1966 in the U.S. by Maulana Karenga, an activist scholar who is currently professor and chair of the Department of Black Studies at California State University, Long Beach. Although rooted in ancient African history and culture, Kwanzaa was developed in the modern context of African American life and struggle as a reconstructed and expanded African tradition. First celebrated by members and friends of the Organization Us (meaning us African people), Kwanzaa is currently celebrated by an estimated 28 million persons throughout the world African community and on every continent in the world.

Kwanzaa begins on December 26 and continues through January 1. At the heart of this seven-day holiday are the *Nguzo Saba* (Seven Principles), which are aimed at reaffirming and strengthening family, community, and culture. These principles are *Umoja* (unity), *Kujichagulia* (self-determination), *Ujima* (collective work and responsibility), *Ujamaa* (cooperative economics), *Nia* (purpose), *Kuumba* (creativity), and *Imani* (faith). Each day of Kwanzaa is dedicated to one of the principles and is organized around activities and discussions to emphasize each principle.

Throughout Kwanzaa the people reaffirm the framework and foundation for building the good world they want and deserve to live in. And they also reaffirm the fundamental mission and meaning in human life as set forth in the sacred teaching of the ancestors, which is to bring good constantly into the world and not let any good be lost. For at the center of Kwanzaa is the emphasis on collectively cultivating, creating, harvesting, sharing, and preserving good in the world.

WORLD EVENTS

• Indonesia's President Sukarno is overthrown after the army, led by chief of staff General Suharto, crushes an attempted military coup from within Sukarno's own Indonesian Communist Party (PKI); Suharto's forces murder thousands of suspected Communists in the coup's aftermath. In 1968 Suharto becomes president and the PKI is banned.

• Upon withdrawal from the Federation of Malaysia, Singapore becomes an independent republic.

• The Palestine Liberation Organization is established this year at the urging of Egypt's President Nasser, who sees the need for an umbrella organization to unite Palestinian resistance groups. On January 1, 1965, they initiate the Palestine "revolution," whose mission is to eliminate Zionism and form a "democratic and secular" Arab state in place of Israel. Ahmad Shukeiry, Palestinian representative to the Arab League, is elected the first chairman, but by 1968, Yasser Arafat emerges as leader.

• Ferdinand E. Marcos is elected president

of the Philippines, an office he will hold through 1986.

• Fidel Castro announces that Cubans can leave the island nation if they have relatives in the U.S. He imposes a condition: Cubans already living in Florida have to come and get their relatives. All kinds of sailing craft depart from Miami, returning with relatives rejoining their families on the mainland.

▣ 1966

1966

ARTS AND LITERATURE

• Yvonne Rainer (b. 1934) choreographs *The Mind Is a Muscle, Part I* (aka *Trio A*), a four-and-one-half-minute series of unrepeated "found" movements that let go of reigning modern dance conventions of style, plot, and projection of personal expression. *Trio A* will become a primer for many dancers, and provide the basic vocabulary that trains the Grand Union, a 1970–1976 collaborative company of dancer-choreographers.

▣ 1970

• Carlene Hatcher Polite (b. 1932) publishes the first black feminist novel, *The Flagellants*. Written while living in Paris from 1964 to 1971, Polite experiments with rhythms, dialects, and other literary conventions to illustrate how issues of race, gender, and identity limit African American men and women.

• Visual artist Robert Rauschenberg and Bell Labs' engineer Billy Kluver (b. Germany, 1927) co-found Experiments in Art and Technology (EAT), a nonprofit service organization providing links between the engineering world and interested artists. They present a series of performances, Nine Evenings of Theatre and Engineering, at the 69th Regiment Armory in New York City, the site of the groundbreaking 1913 Armory Show, to showcase the results of ten months of collaborations between ten artists and thirty engineers from Bell Labs. EAT goes on to sponsor other collaborative projects in the 1970s, including the design and programming of the Pepsi-Cola pavilion at Expo '70 in Osaka, Japan, and a 1971 proposal to build a single-channel satellite television system that can be "programmed by the American people."

GOVERNMENT AND POLITICS

• President Johnson signs the Clean Waters Restoration Act, providing federal grants to fund pollution-control research and projects to clean U.S. waterways.

• Economist Dr. Robert Weaver, who first served in the Housing Authority in Washington during Franklin Roosevelt's New Deal era, becomes the first African American member of a presidential cabinet, when he is confirmed as President Johnson's secretary of the new Department of Housing and Urban Development (HUD). Economist Andrew F. Brimmer (b. 1926) becomes the first African American appointed to the Federal Reserve Board.

▣ 1964, 1968

• Edward William Brooke (b. 1919) is elected to the U.S. Senate as a Republican from Massachusetts. He serves from 1967 to 1979, the first African American to sit in the Senate in eighty-five years, since the era of Reconstruction.

• The war in Vietnam continues to escalate. For the first time, U.S. B-52s bomb the city of Hanoi and rail lines up to the Chinese border, with threats that U.S. planes will follow North Vietnamese planes into China. The buildup of

The Black Panther Party. "All Power to the People" poster by Emory, 1970. (*Library of Congress, Prints and Photographs Division*)

U.S. troops reaches a record total of 300,000 by September, and in this year 5,008 Americans are killed. The cost of waging the war is $12 billion per month. Tensions between those who oppose the war and those who defend the action also escalate. Democratic Senator William Fulbright, head of the Senate Foreign Relations committee, accuses the U.S. of "succumbing to the arrogance of power." President Johnson replies, "not arrogance but agony," and Republican senator Barry Goldwater asks Fulbright to resign for giving "aid and comfort to the enemy." Johnson calls his critics "nervous nellies." But student protests continue, with sit-ins in Chicago and New York universities, and a peace petition is handed to Vice President Hubert Humphrey with 50,000 signatures. In New York City, 20,000 peace marchers are confronted by angry pro-war activists.

• Ronald Reagan (b. 1911) is elected governor of California, where he institutes a government austerity program that makes severe cuts in funding for state welfare and education programs, including the closing of mental hospitals. In the opinion of many, these measures will seed the problem of homelessness that grows increasingly worse, plaguing the country for the rest of the century and beyond.
🄳 1980, 1999

SCIENCE AND TECHNOLOGY

• U.S. space flights rack up many firsts: two manned flights, the Gemini 10 and Agena 10, conduct the first maneuver of a docked spacecraft and the first retrieval, by Michael Collins, of an experiment from another spacecraft. On two uncrewed flights, Luna 9 conducts the first U.S. "soft" landing on the moon and transmission of lunar surface images, while Luna 10

There is a tension throughout our communities. The ghosts of that tension are Nat Turner, Martin Delaney, Booker T. Washington, Frederick Douglass, Malcolm X, Garvey, Monroe Trotter, Du Bois, Fanon, and a whole panoply of mythical heroes from Br'er Rabbit to Shine. These ghosts have left us with some very heavy questions about the realities of life for black people in America.

The movement is now faced with a serious crisis. It has postulated a theory of Black Power; and that is good. But it has failed to evolve a workable ideology. That is, a workable concept— perhaps Black Power *is* it—which can encompass many of the diverse ideological tendencies existent in the black community. This concept would have to allow for separatists and revolutionaries; and it would have to take into consideration the realities of contemporary American power, both here and abroad. The militant wing of the movement has begun to deny the patriotic assumptions of the white and Negro establishment, but it has not supported that denial with a consistent theory of social change, one that must be rooted in the history of African-Americans.

(FROM LARRY NEAL, "AND SHINE SWAM ON," IN *Black Fire: An Anthology of Afro-American Writing*, EDITED BY LEROI JONES AND LARRY NEAL [NEW YORK: WILLIAM MORROW, 1968].)

---

becomes the first to orbit the moon. AOAO 1 is the first astronomical satellite in orbit, and the first motion pictures of weather systems are sent by another satellite, ATS-1.

BUSINESS AND INDUSTRY

• Pan American World Airways makes the largest commercial aviation order to date when it signs up for $525 million worth of new Boeing 747 passenger jets to accommodate the increasing numbers of passengers desiring to travel greater distances. Known by its nickname "jumbo jet," the 747 will be the biggest of the long-range jets, and the first wide-body jetliner with two aisles. It is capable of flying over 8,000 miles, about one-third of the way around the world, without refueling. Commercial service begins in 1970.

• Office and home electronic communication is extended with the commercial introduction of Telecopier, a facsimile (fax) machine sold by Xerox. It transmits printed text and

images over telephone lines at around six minutes per page. By 1982, 350,000 machines that complete similar transmissions in around four seconds are in use in the U.S., and Intelpost, the first public international electronic facsimile service, is introduced.

CULTURE AND SOCIETY

• The Senate holds a hearing in which it issues a federal prohibition against the use of consciousness-altering drugs such as marijuana and LSD. Dr. Timothy Leary (1920–1996), a psychologist whose research on LSD at Harvard gained him a dismissal from its faculty in 1963, founds the League for Spiritual Discovery to work for legalization of LSD and marijuana as religious sacraments. He promotes a "politics of ecstasy" in which the practitioners "tune in, turn on, drop out." The first "head" shop, the Psychedelic Shop, opens on San Francisco's Haight Street, supplying the psychedelic lifestyle with mandala posters, lava lamps, strobe and black-light fixtures, and other paraphernalia for using hallucinogenic drugs.

• During this year, the concept of "Black Power!" is debated by African American civil rights organizations after Willie Ricks, a Student Nonviolent Coordinating Committee (SNCC) organizer in Alabama, uses the chant at a rally and Stokely Carmichael, the new head of SNCC, adopts it as a slogan. The Black Power! slogan is open to many interpretations. Carmichael uses it to promote black consciousness, CORE adopts it, and the NAACP rejects it. In October, Huey P. Newton and Bobby Seale found the Black Panther Party in Oakland, California. They draft a platform and program including ten demands, such as full employment, decent housing, exemption from military service for black men, freedom for all black prisoners, and provisions to build educational institutions and community organizations to promote peace in the black community. They support black people's right to self-defense against police attacks. This last, combined with their Marxist-Leninist revolutionary militant rhetoric style, precipitates harassment from local, state, and federal authorities.

• The Crusade for Justice, a Mexican American civil rights organization, is founded in Denver, Colorado, by Rodolfo "Corky" Gonzales, a former boxer. It works for better housing, jobs, and educational opportunities in Denver, besides establishing a community center with a library, classrooms, a nursery, and a gym. It sponsors the first national Chicano Youth Liberation Conference in 1969, where it drafts a document, *El Plan Espiritual de Aztlán* (The Spiritual Plan of Aztlán), calling for a radical revision of how Latinos are viewed in U.S. history, and laying

out many of the educational, economic, political, and social demands that will help define the next twenty years of the Chicano movement. Many other new organizations are formed during these years within the area they call Aztlán, the original Aztec lands ceded by the Treaty of Guadalupe Hidalgo, including La Alianza Federal de Mercedes, organized by Reies Lopez Tijerina in New Mexico, and La Raza Unida, formed by José Angel Gutierrez in Crystal City, Texas. They create independent third parties that look out for the needs of Chicanos while still participating in the U.S. election system, and succeed in getting local candidates elected to office.

• Scholar and activist Maulana Karenga invents Kwanzaa, an African American festival drawing on traditional African harvest festival rituals "to restore and reaffirm our African heritage and culture." The annual celebration lasts for seven days, from December 26 to January 1. As the years go by and it becomes widely practiced in African American communities, it also receives increasing commercial attention.

• The National Organization for Women (NOW), is founded by Betty Friedan, author of the 1963 feminist manifesto *The Feminine Mystique,* and a network of women influential in Washington government circles. Friedan serves as the first president and remains at the head of the organization until 1970. As advocates for women's civil rights, NOW's basic platform seeks to have women achieve equality "in a truly equal partnership with men."

• Dr. William H. Masters (1915–2001), a medical doctor, and Virginia E. Johnson, his co-researcher, publish *Human Sexual Response,* the first of several books that validate and popularize sexual therapy in the U.S. Although the

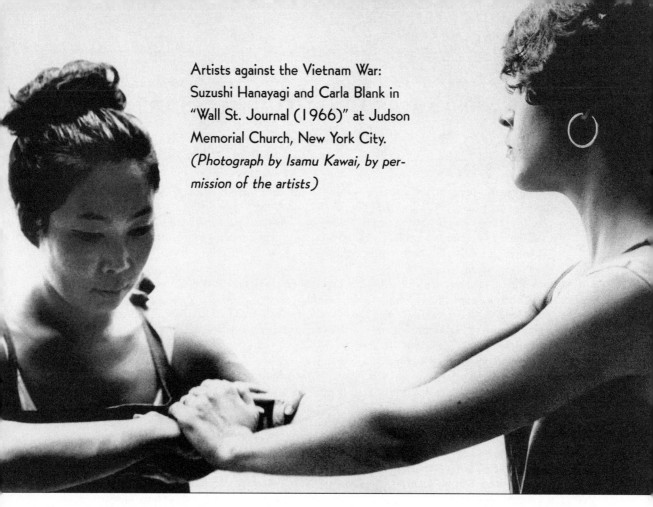

Artists against the Vietnam War: Suzushi Hanayagi and Carla Blank in "Wall St. Journal (1966)" at Judson Memorial Church, New York City. *(Photograph by Isamu Kawai, by permission of the artists)*

book is directed to an audience of doctors and other health professionals, it becomes a mainstream bestseller.

WORLD EVENTS

• Chairman Mao Zedong launches the Great Proletarian Cultural Revolution in China, calling for purges of his enemies within the Chinese Communist Party and destroying any signs of revisionism of his revolutionary programs in the culture. Mao directs a takeover of university campuses, closing schools and denouncing anti-Mao party officials, intellectuals, and technicians. He enlists 10 million university students and youths to "learn revolution by making revolution." The Red Guards emerge as the shock troops within the student groups, carrying out violent persecutions in which millions die over the next three years, before Mao's power is reestablished.

• A program is initiated to airlift Cubans to the U.S. It continues from 1966 to 1973, until it is stopped by Fidel Castro. More than 250,000 Cubans will be airlifted to the U.S., about 10 percent of the island's population.

1967

ARTS AND LITERATURE

• The arts community actively organizes their opposition to the war as 500 artists participate in Angry Arts Against the War in

LATINO AMERICAN ARTISTS, 1960s-1970s

George Vargas

1960s

- The Cuban Revolution forces artists into exile, although some of them decide to stay. Ramon Alejandro (b. Cuba, 1943) flees the political chaos in Cuba to paint in South America, exploring the spiritual realm by rendering weird-looking buildings and machines set in "dreamworld constructions." Luis Cruz Azaceta (b. Cuba, 1942) also departs Cuba in 1960 and moves to New York City, where his satirical expressionistic paintings examine contemporary issues of Latino identity, AIDS, and fascism.
- Black Cuban Juan Sosa (b. Cuba, 1941) escapes Cuba via Mariel in 1980, landing in Florida. His Afro-Cuban inspired altars have toured the world.
- Tony Mendoza (b. Cuba, 1941) also leaves Cuba during the Cuban Revolution, quitting a career in architecture to make photographic portraits of family members, Cuban celebrations, snarling cats and barking dogs and their owners.
- A great majority of artists in Puerto Rico continue to be affected by the 1950s generation of social realists, such as Myrna Baez (b. Puerto Rico, 1931), who has studied in Spain and in the U.S.
- Luis Hernandez-Cruz (b. Puerto Rico) is the first Puerto Rican artist to produce abstract prints.
- Abstract artists like Olga Albizu (b. Puerto Rico, 1924), who studied under Hans Hoffman in New York, receive harsh criticism in their attempts to discover a new expression in Puerto Rican art. Also trained in the U.S., Rafael Ferrer (b. Puerto Rico, 1933) meets with greater rejection when he first exhibits his sculptures of found objects and recycled materials (old shoes, used car parts, cast-off lumber, etc.) in his homeland.
- Known as a Destruction artist, Rafael Ortiz (b. New York City, 1934, of Puerto Rican, Mexican, and American Indian heritage) is one of the first Latino performance artists to win international attention by burning mattresses and destroying pianos.
- Chelo Gonzalez Amezcua (b. Mexico, 1903) is a self-taught artist who uses cheap, colored ballpoint pens on cardboard to create finely detailed drawings of Aztec kings, animals, and human figures.
- Among the few Mexican American women landscape painters in her time, Margaret Herrera Chavez (b. New Mexico, 1912), renders abstract landscapes of New Mexico and Latin America, Spain, and Canada.
- Luis Jimenez (b. El Paso, 1940) created some of the earliest of Chicano pop art—sculpture of Aztecs, undocumented Mexican workers, and cowboys.
- Perhaps the earliest known Chicano muralist, Antonio Bernal paints an untitled mural in 1968 on the front of Teatro Campesino's office in Del Ray, California, portraying Pancho Villa, Zapata, Cesar Chavez, and Martin Luther King Jr.
- Melesio Casas (b. El Paso, 1929) is one of the first Chicano painters involved in social commentary, and later affects the early Chicano art movement in Texas.
- Popular painter and printmaker Amado Pena Jr. (b. Laredo, 1943) helps inspire the early Chicano art movement in Kingsville, Texas, with his posters.
- Mario Castillo paints perhaps the first Chicano mural in Chicago in 1968, working with community youth to create the *Metafisica,* a unique abstract work.

- In the late 1960s and early 1970s, Latino art groups arise across the nation to produce murals and other community art forms. Artes Guadalupanos de Aztlan (New Mexico); Mujeres Muralistas, ASCO, East Los Angeles Streetscapers, "Los Four," and the Royal Chicano Air Force (California); C/S or Con Safo (Texas); MARCH (Illinois); Raza Art/Media (Michigan); Association of Hispanic Arts (New York).
- Influenced by posters and prints of Cuba and Puerto Rico, Chicano artists found Galeria de la Raza in San Francisco, La Raza Graphic Center in San Antonio, and Self Help Graphics in Los Angeles, important centers of printmaking art.
- Carmen Lomas Garza (b. Kingsville, Texas, 1948), becomes one of the best-known Chicana illustrators of children's books and prints.

1970s

- The first Chicano filmmaker who later enters the mainstream movie industry, Jesus Salvador Trevino, makes *Yo Soy Chicano* in 1972, capturing the early Chicano art and political movement.
- In Michigan, Chicano artists David Torrez (b. Michigan, 1937) of Saginaw and Jose Narezo (b. Mexico, 1945) of Grand Rapids each produce some of the earliest community murals in early 1970s.
- In 1975, Chicano artist and activist Jose G. Gonzalez (b. 1933) leads youth in Chicago in painting the mural *Raza de Oro,* inspired by Mayan mural art.
- Despite threats of censorship, Chicano artist Martin Moreno (b. Michigan, 1950) and a team of artists and youth create *Vibrations of a New Awakening* (1978), the first public mural in Adrian, Michigan, documenting Latino contributions to agriculture and industry in the state.
- Chicana artist Judith Baca (b. 1946) starts her massive mural project *The Great Wall of Los Angeles* (1976–1984), highlighting the multicultural history of California, pertaining especially to Chicanos, other people of color, and women.
- In Los Angeles, the provocative art group ASCO (meaning "nausea"), consisting of Willie Herron, Harry Gamboa Jr., Gronk, and Patssi Valdez, create the first Chicano performance and installation artworks beginning in the early 1970s, including a series of photographic stills of nonexistent movies called *No Movie.*
- Raza Art and Media (RAM) present the first Chicano and Raza art exhibition in Ann Arbor at the University of Michigan in 1975, featuring the works of Michigan artists who are joined by two key members of Con Safo (C/S) from San Antonio.
- In 1971, Paul Gonzalez (b. Mexico, 1931), a designer for the Ford Motor Company who helped to create the Mustang car, produces the first public artworks in Adrian, Michigan—an abstract water fountain sculpture called *Tlaloc,* and a copper-enamel mural.
- Latino artist Mike Rios (b. 1947) paints a billboard mural, *Homenaje de Frida Kahlo* (1978), in San Francisco.
- In San Diego, California, responding to the cultural needs of the community, Chicano artists "occupy" Chicano Park in 1975 to beautify it with mural paintings.
- In East Los Angeles, Gronk (b. Los Angeles, 1954) creates one of the first Chicano conceptual/installation/performance pieces: in *Instant Mural* (1974), ASCO members Patssi Valdez and Humberto Sandoval are taped to a wall by Gronk using a roll of cheap masking tape.

(Continued)

- California Chicana artist Yolanda Lopez (b. 1942) paints a series of feminist-inspired portraits influenced by the traditional image of the Virgen de Guadalupe in 1978, but devotees of the Virgen de Guadalupe protest against her art, claiming defamation of the holy icon.
- One of the most productive of printmakers in Chicago, Chicano labor activist and poet Carlos Cortez (b. Milwaukee, 1923) makes a series of prints unifying Mexican revolutionary activism with the IWW labor movement.
- Former member of Con Safo in San Antonio, Chicana photographer Kathy Vargas (b. 1950) shoots *Tio Gregorio y Tia Luisa* (1974) a series of photographs representing her family.

Vietnam. Fifty thousand protesters besiege the Pentagon with picketing, sit-ins, speeches, and marches, including an exorcism of the Pentagon by long-haired warlocks who "cast mighty words of white light against the demon-controlled structure," in hopes of levitating it right off the ground, an expression of "flower power" activism.

- The *Wall of Respect,* a street mural with images of black heroes including Nat Turner, Muhummad Ali, Malcolm X, Charlie Parker, and Gwendolyn Brooks, is painted on the side of a boarded-up two-story tenement building at 43rd Street and Langley Avenue in Chicago, by a group of twenty African American artists, members of the Organization for Black American Culture (OBAC, which is pronounced *obasi,* meaning "chieftain" in the Yoruba language). Some people oppose the inclusion of Martin Luther King, and argue for Stokely Carmichael instead. At times, feelings are so intense that both police and gangs feel it is necessary to guard the area. Another mural, the *Wall of Truth,* goes up across the street from the original mural, so that the whole neighborhood is enveloped. The wall becomes an undeclared landmark, stimulating a public art movement throughout the country in general, and a national black mural movement in particular.

- Richard Brautigan's (1935–1984) *Trout Fishing in America,* the first novel of the "flower child" generation to receive mainstream attention, is published by Dell.

- Electronic music successfully crosses over from the avant garde into mainstream popularity with the use of a Moog synthesizer on the album *Switched On Bach,* composed by Walter (later Wendy) Carlos. (The Moog will be patented in 1972.) Emerson, Lake, and Palmer use their "Wall of Electronics," which includes five Moog synthesizers, in live performances and recordings, including the hit "Lucky Man"; the Grateful Dead release *Anthem of the Sun,* and Frank Zappa and the Mothers of Invention release *Uncle Meat,* both albums that make extensive use of electronic manipulation; Morton Subotnick composes *Silver Apples of the Moon* (the title is from a poem by W. B. Yeats), the first electronic music work commissioned specifically for the recorded medium, and Leon Kirschner composes *String Quartet No. 3,* the first piece with electronics to win the Pulitzer Prize.

GOVERNMENT AND POLITICS

- President Johnson signs an executive order banning sex discrimination in federally connected employment, increasing awareness of

The placards in the photograph read:
陳曼麗 Man Lai Phyllis Ch...
劉珍玲 Jin Jean...
陳曼影 Man Ying Grace Chan
Wang Ngar Anita Chan
黃紹輝 Sui Fei Warren Wong
劉... Chun Yue Robert Lau

Miss April Lou, teacher at P.S. 1, Manhattan, with six Chinese children, recent arrivals from Hong Kong and Formosa, with placards giving their Chinese names, and names being entered in official school records. Photo by Fred Palumbo, 1964. *(Library of Congress, Prints and Photographs Division)*

this aspect of Title VII of the 1964 Civil Rights Act, and encouraging more-active protections in other employment sectors.

• Congress passes the Public Broadcasting Act, which allows for the creation of the non-commercial television network to be named the Public Broadcasting Service (PBS) and the non-commercial radio network National Public Radio (NPR).

• Solicitor General Thurgood Marshall becomes the first African American to serve on the U.S. Supreme Court, nominated by President Johnson and confirmed by a 69–11 majority vote of the U.S. Senate. Marshall is a pioneer in the field of public-interest law, having served as the chief of the legal team for the NAACP's Legal Defense Fund.

• Carl Stokes (1927–1996) is elected mayor of Cleveland, and Richard Hatcher (b. 1933) is elected mayor of Indianapolis. They are the first African Americans to become mayors of major American cities.

• Seeking ways to fulfill his campaign pledge to "squeeze and cut and trim" government spending, California's Governor Ronald Reagan fires 3,000 hospital mental health workers and shuts down most state-operated mental health facilities, dispersing patients into counties for local treatment. By finding a government service whose constituency does not protest, Reagan is able to save the state $20 million. However, "revolving door" mentally ill patients without a safety net often live on the streets, sometimes landing in jail or prison. Albert Vetere Lannon comments in *Fight or Be Slaves: The History of the Oakland–East Bay Labor Movement* that as a result, "homelessness became an issue for the first time since the Great Depression."

SCIENCE AND TECHNOLOGY

• R. M. Dolby invents a recording method that removes high-frequency hiss and background noise and improves fidelity. The march toward music that sounds "live" is thus given a big boost forward.

BUSINESS AND INDUSTRY

• The Federation of Southern Cooperatives is founded to "assist in the economic development of black family farmers and the rural poor across the Southern U.S.A." Through the rest of the century they will help black farmers hold on to their lands by advocating for changes in public policy, and by providing technical assistance and services related to farm management, debt restructuring, alternative crop suggestions, and marketing expertise.

CULTURE AND SOCIETY

• Militant Chicano youth form more than twenty chapters of the Brown Berets. Over the next five years they will publish a newspaper and establish a health clinic for their community. They outline a ten-point program addressing issues of housing, culture, justice, employment,

education, ethical conduct, and right to self-defense.

• The Bilingual Education Act is passed by Congress, establishing federal aid for bilingual classes. It requires schools to provide programs to aid children with limited English. By 1971, about 450 full-time or part-time teachers are hired to teach some 12,000 Hispanic children in bilingual education or "English as a second language" classes. Over the following thirty years, the seesaw battle over bilingual education, in theory and practice, is propelled almost entirely by federal legislation.

▣ 1996

• The National Organization for Women's 1967 convention drafts a new "bill of rights," calling for increased federal legislation to gain and protect equal status for women in all aspects of their participation in American society, to circumvent state laws or courts that hide behind the original language of the U.S. Constitution, which grants rights to men only. Besides supporting the Equal Rights Amendment to the Constitution, their demands include more equity in Social Security benefits and tax laws, including deductions for home and child-care expenses for working parents; more child-care centers; equal access to education and job training; funding for women in poverty; enforcement of laws banning sex discrimination in the workplace; and the rights of women to make their own reproductive decisions. Although labor unions first oppose these demands, one year later the AFL/CIO also endorses the ERA.

• The media appoint San Francisco home of the psychedelic movement's "Summer of Love," which follows a "Human Be-In," in San Francisco. They focus on author Ken

Kesey (1935–2001) and his Romantic Army of Merry Pranksters, as well as the Fillmore West music events of the Grateful Dead, Jefferson Airplane, Big Brother and the Holding Company, Country Joe and the Fish, and Janis Joplin, among others. The summer culminates in a "Death of the Hippie" ceremony in October. The East Village of New York is another center of "hip culture."

• The worst urban riots recorded in U.S. history erupt in black ghettos of the country during the so-called "hot summer." In Newark, twenty-six are killed, 1,500 injured, and 1,397 arrested in a civil disturbance that starts after police beat an African American man during a traffic arrest. It ends with "excessive and unjustified force," in the opinion of the New Jersey Governor's Select Commission, when police and national guardsman shoot indiscriminately at African Americans. In Detroit, forty-three are left dead, more than 2,000 injured, and 5,000 arrested; 1,700 stores are looted by whites as well as blacks, and 5,000 are left homeless from 1,442 fires. The overwhelming majority of those killed or injured are black civilians. Some of the other cities experiencing major riots are New York, Milwaukee, Chicago, Minneapolis, and Cambridge, Maryland. Between 1964 and 1968, racially based riots occur in 257 cities, causing 220 deaths, 8,371 injuries, 52,629 arrests, and property damage in the billions of dollars. In an effort to understand the causes and offer solutions, President Johnson asks Illinois Governor Otto Kerner to head the President's National Advisory Commission on Civil Disorders, known as the Kerner Commission. They study eight major

uprisings, thirty-three "serious but not major outbreaks, and 123 "minor" disorders. In 1968 the Kerner Commission Report is published, which cites widespread "white racism" as the cause of the riots, cautioning that the U.S. is "moving towards two societies, one black, one white, separate and unequal," and recommends job training, removal of discrimination, and overhauling the welfare system.

• Martin Luther King proposes a merger between the antiwar movement and the civil rights movement. He advocates draft evasion and calls the U.S. government the "greatest purveyor of violence in the world."

WORLD EVENTS

• At the Second Vatican Council, Pope Paul VI issues an encyclical, *Populorum Progressio* (On the Progress of Peoples), which propels the Church toward active commitment to fight oppression and help the cause of liberation in the Third World. He calls for clergy and laity to become a force for social change, especially singling out Latin America as an area of the world in need of help. This movement will become known as "liberation theology," and over the next decade at least 850 priests, nuns, and bishops living in Latin America will be tortured or jailed, or will sacrifice their lives to its cause.

• Ernesto "Che" Guevara (b. 1928, Argentina) is killed in Bolivia, where he has been living for the past year, serving as commander-in-chief of the National Liberation Army, a guerrilla organization. He is already a 1960s hero or villain in Latin America and the U.S. for his support of Marxism and guerrilla revolutionary tactics in Guatemala and in Cuba, where he helped overthrow the Batista regime with

Fidel Castro, and his death only increases his iconic stature around the world.

• After ten years of patrolling the border between Egypt and Israel, the UN's peacekeeping force withdraws in May, complying with demands of Egyptian President Gamal Abdel Nasser, who is responding to growing Arab nationalism in the region. A united Arab military command quickly mobilizes forces, blockading the Strait of Tiran, which inhibits access to the southern Israeli port of Eilat. The Six-Day War explodes between Israel and neighboring Arab nations June 5–10, when Israel strikes Syrian, Jordanian, and Egyptian air bases, virtually destroying Egypt's air force and the Arab armies. Before the UN peacekeeping forces return to supervise a cease-fire, Israel takes possession of the West Bank and Arab East Jerusalem from Jordan and the Golan Heights from Syria; retakes Gaza and the Sinai Peninsula to the east bank of the Suez Canal from Egypt; and increases its territory to four times its size at the time of the 1949 armistice. There is disagreement within Israel about whether to annex the occupied territories or to withdraw, at least partially, although a majority support the government's formal unification of East Jerusalem with the Jewish area of West Jerusalem. Arab countries are under great pressure to regain their lost territories, which include an Arab population of about 1.5 million, and these occupied areas become a major political issue after 1967. Egypt will make the first move to regain its lost territories in 1969, declaring the cease-fire void along the Suez Canal. The canal does not reopen to shipping until 1972.

• The Beatles recorded masterpiece *Sgt. Pepper's Lonely Hearts Club Band* is released,

bringing daring and sophisticated harmonies and structure to rock.

1968

ARTS AND LITERATURE

• N. Scott Momaday (Kiowa, b. 1934) wins a Pulitzer Prize for his first novel, *House Made of Dawn*.

• *Black Fire: An Anthology of Afro-American Writing*, edited by LeRoi Jones and Larry Neal, is published. It features poetry, essays, short stories, and plays by more than seventy black writers, whom Jones calls "the founding Fathers and Mothers of our nation . . . the wizards, the bards. . . ." Besides works by the editors, it includes writings of John Henrik Clarke, Harold Cruse, A. B. Spellman, Ed Bullins, Sun Ra, Stokely Carmichael, Sonia Sanchez, and Charles Patterson.

• Poet Jerome Rothenberg edits an anthology, *Technicians of the Sacred: A Range of Poetries from Africa, America, Asia, and Oceania,* which illustrates the direct and profound influences and relationships between modern poetry and what he calls "primitive and archaic" poetry from all over the world. Practices of chanting and singing texts are related to modern spoken-word styles of jazz poetry and folk rock; accounts of visions and dreams, where thinking is expressed through images rather than using logic and rules, are compared to surrealism and random poetry. The traditional function of poet as visionary or shaman in ritual and ceremony is also claimed by some modern poets, who believe they are the healers and seers of their times.

• James Broughton's (b. 1913) avant-garde film *The Bed,* made during the 1967 "Summer of Love" in San Francisco, is released and is highly successful. It represents a moment of shift in the economics and creative dynamics of the film industry, when the underground network of experimental filmmakers begins receiving support for their film work. Now, with some experimental filmmakers receiving grants from major foundations, they can make more films than before, with a wider circle of distribution.

• The first photorealist murals are painted in Venice, California. The first collective youth murals are done in Latino areas of New York City and Chicago. Works by a new generation of Chicano muralists, inspired by the Mexican Mural Movement, as well as by the Cuban Revolution, are painted in public art projects in Los Angeles, San Francisco, Houston, El Paso, Denver, and other major cities.

• Composer Terry Riley records his masterpiece *In C* on Columbia Records, creating the first major so-called "minimalist" piece.

• New York Latin pianist/composer/ arranger Eddie Palmieri records the album *Justicia* with his big band, giving salsa music an element of advanced jazz scoring. His use of big trombone sound with modal piano and horn soloing in an intensely Latino setting marks him as one of modern music's most original thinkers.

GOVERNMENT AND POLITICS

• In March, American soldiers on a search-and-destroy mission massacre between 350 and 500 civilians—women, children, and aged men—of My Lai, Vietnam, a hamlet in Quang Ngai province. The U.S. Army tries to cover up what happened, but press reports appear by 1969. Courts-martial are held against enlisted men and officers charged with war crimes, but

only one man, William Calley, will be convicted and sentenced to life in prison.

• President Johnson pushes through the Civil Rights Act of 1968, to provide freedom from discrimination in the sale, rental, or financing of housing throughout the U.S., on the basis of race, color, religion, sex, or national origin. In 1988 the act is expanded to prohibit discrimination based on disability or on familial status (presence of child under the age of eighteen or a pregnant woman). It also makes federal offenses out of actions that encourage riots.

• FBI Director J. Edgar Hoover initiates a counterintelligence program against "Black Nationalist-Hate Groups," known as COINTELPRO, to "prevent the coalition of militant black nationalist groups" or the "rise of a messiah" that might unify them. They set up more than forty field stations around the U.S., sending undercover agents into many organizations, especially targeting the Black Panthers.

• Congress sets up the Law Enforcement Assistance Administration, which funds university-level departments of criminal justice, "to study the police, courts and prisons," and improve the education of police.

• In the spring, Martin Luther King begins to connect the Vietnam War to the existence of poverty in the U.S. He helps plan a nonviolent protest, called the "Poor People's Encampment," in Washington, D.C.

• Robert F. Kennedy is assassinated on June 5 in Los Angeles, shortly after he wins the California Democratic Party's presidential primary.

• Ten thousand demonstrators stage massive protests at the Democratic Convention in Chicago, opposing the war in Vietnam, racism, and the nomination of Vice President

Hubert Humphrey as the Democratic nominee for President. A Youth International Party (Yippie) manifesto is delivered by Abbie Hoffman, Jerry Rubin, Tom Hayden, Rennie Davis, Ed Sanders, and Dave Dellinger, in which they nominate a pig for presidential candidate. Allen Ginsberg chants to calm the crowds, and Mayor Richard Daley authorizes the Chicago police to respond with violence against rock-throwing crowds. The police beat not only Yippies, but also journalists, supporters of peace candidate Eugene McCarthy, and other passers-by. Three African Americans are admitted into the Mississippi delegation, in an effort by the Democratic Party to show their support of voting rights for all citizens. The national TV coverage of all these disturbances is said to cost Humphrey the election.

• Richard Milhous Nixon (1913–1994) is elected to his first term as president, pledging he will get the U.S. out of Vietnam with a "secret plan."

BUSINESS AND INDUSTRY

• Cubicles or "systems furniture," a series of pieces that fit together like an Erector set, creating a variety of office spaces, are invented by Robert Propst, a designer for Herman Miller, Inc., a Michigan office manufacturer. The cubicles change the most common configuration of office workspaces from huge, open spaces, called "bullpens," where each worker is assigned a desk, to the ubiquitous workstations that are used by 58 percent of the nation's office workers by 1999.

SCIENCE AND TECHNOLOGY

• A U.S. House of Representatives committee reports that Lake Erie is essentially dead,

and that it will take 500 years to restore it to its World War II condition, if all polluting is stopped.

• After reviewing previously undisclosed army records indicating that lab animals fed meals irradiated with cobalt-60 developed cancer and died, Commissioner of the U.S. Food and Drug Administration James L. Goddard revokes the army's license for using cobalt-60 to sterilize food.

CULTURE AND SOCIETY

• An eight-day boycott by 3,500 Chicano high school students in Los Angeles protests the quality of education they are receiving in the public schools.

• Berkeley, California, becomes the first city to carry through full racial desegregation by busing children across town. Other cities will follow, under pressure from the Department of Health, Education and Welfare.

• The first black studies program is formally established at San Francisco State College this year. At Cornell University, black students occupy the student union, and demand an end to racism and the formation of a separate black college.

• Students close down San Francisco State College on November 19, during the Third World Strike. Their demands include an open admissions policy and the formation of a third-world studies department. Their actions reflect the rapid rise of an Asian American student movement on campuses throughout California, with focus on participation in antiwar efforts and establishment of Asian American studies programs.

• The American Indian Movement (AIM) is founded in Minneapolis by Dennis Banks

(Anishinabe), Clyde Bellencourt (Ojibwa), Mary Jane Wilson, George Mitchell, and other Indian community activists to represent Minneapolis-based Indians. The organization works to protect the traditional ways of Indian peoples, employing legal counsel to mediate cases related to treaty violations and aboriginal rights to hunting, fishing, trapping, and gathering. In its first year, AIM applies the term *genocide*, as adopted by the United Nations in 1948, to describe the experiences of indigenous American societies.

• A collective struggle by Asian American students to save the International Hotel, a central part of the San Francisco Filipino and Chinese community, will fail by 1972, following massive eviction notices issued by real estate magnate and owner Walter Shorenstein, and a mysterious fire in which three tenants die.

• Rev. Martin Luther King Jr., leader of the U.S. civil rights movement and Nobel Peace Prize winner, is assassinated in Memphis, Tennessee, where he has gone to support a strike of sanitation workers. Riots erupt in American cities after the news of his murder. One man, James Earl Ray, is convicted of his murder. In 1999 a Tennessee jury will decide that King's murder was the work of a conspiracy, not a lone assassin.

• The Women's Liberation Movement begins "consciousness raising," creating women's self-help networks, and awakens awareness about sexual harassment, pornography, and rape. Some feminists protest the annual Miss America pageant in Atlantic City, an event that brings "Women's Lib" into public consciousness. They stage guerrilla street-theater events, including one in which they burn "instruments of female torture," including high heels, nylons, garter belts, girdles, hair curlers, false eyelashes,

makeup, copies of *Playboy* and *Good House-keeping,* and—what will become the most famous item—bras.

• Hollywood's film censorship authority, the Hays Office, is abolished. As a result, the Catholic Church loses its power to influence the content of movies produced in the U.S.

WORLD EVENTS

• The Soviet Union invades Czechoslovakia with tanks and troops, blocking political and economic reforms championed by Alexander Dubcek, the leader of the Czech Communist Party.

• In France, students shut down the universities, setting up barricades in the streets of Paris against the police. Sympathetic workers join the strikers, taking over factories throughout France. Even though the government of Charles de Gaulle promises raises for workers and reorganization of the government, the voters fail to support his promises and de Gaulle resigns in 1969.

• The United Nations General Assembly approves a draft resolution to stop the spread of nuclear weapons.

• Major General Ahmed Hassan al-Bakr, a Baathist Party leader, stages another successful and violent coup in Iraq, with backing from the CIA. His second-in-command, Saddam Hussein, will succeed him as president in 1979 and remain in power into the next century.

🖻 1963

1969

ARTS AND LITERATURE

• The Dance Theater of Harlem is formed by Arthur Mitchell, a former soloist with the

New York City Ballet, in response to the assassination of Martin Luther King. He returns to the community where he was born and starts a school that develops into a major performing organization as well, and succeeds in finally dispelling the myth that African Americans cannot perform classical ballet. George Balanchine and Lincoln Kirstein, co-founders of the New York City Ballet, serve on the original board of directors.

• Starting in late 1969, New York artist activists stage a series of picket lines, sit-ins, fake docent tours, and other actions that protest the ingrained racist and sexist policies of the art-world establishment, even closing down New York museums for a day. To protest the U.S. military invasion of Cambodia, artists Carl Andre and Robert Morris organize the New York Art Strike Against War, Racism, Fascism, Sexism, and Repression in 1970. They invite artists to withdraw their work from the planned U.S. portion of the Venice Biennale, and propose an alternate exhibition at New York's School of Visual Arts. Since the group's discussions and decisions are led by white male artists, who are also the only group to be represented in the exhibit, protests manage to persuade the organizers to include women and black and Puerto Rican artists. During this protest process, women artists form Women Artists in Revolution (WAR). Faith Ringgold and her daughter, the writer Michelle Wallace, encourage black women artists to separate from WAR, and call their group Women, Students and Artists for Black Art Liberation (WSABAL). They stage protests against museums and galleries' long-standing exclusion of black women artists, suggesting that standards of selection are suspect, and should be over-

ruled in favor of an "open" policy, or a group jury process that could provide more-diverse opinions.

• Some artists disperse to far-flung communes and communities in Vermont, the Southwest, and California, where they begin doing works that by their very nature are impossible to exhibit in a museum because they can only exist in the particular places where they are made. These works are called Earth art, land art, or environmental art, because they often choose materials made of the natural elements of earth, air, fire, and water. A frequently cited archetypal work is completed this year by Michael Heizer (b. 1944). He spends one year blasting and bulldozing 240,000 tons of earth and rock at an out-of-the-way Mormon mesa, near Overton, Nevada, excavating two facing rectangular grooves, each thirty feet wide, fifty feet deep, and 100 feet long, aligned on opposite sides of the mesa. This "sculpture in reverse" implies a 1,500-foot void—the *Double Negative* of the title. His intention is to invent an "American" art that owes nothing to European sources, so his references are from Native American and Mesoamerican designs, where earth is an original source material.

• Nearly a half-million people gather on a 600-acre farm in the upstate New York village of Bethel on August 15–17 for the Woodstock Music and Arts Fair, a festival that becomes an iconic image of the 1960s. Even heavy rains do not impede "three days of peace and music" by an unprecedented assembly of major folk and rock stars, including Joan Baez, Santana, Jimi Hendrix, Janis Joplin, Sly and the Family Stone, the Who, and Crosby, Stills, Nash and Young. The dark side of drug overdoses, rapes, and violence becomes more evident at the free music festival at the Altamont Raceway in California on December 6. During the Rolling Stones' performance, a group of Hell's Angels beat and stab an eighteen-year-old black spectator to death.

• El Museo del Barrio is founded by a group of Puerto Rican parents, educators, artists, and community activists in the Spanish-speaking barrio of East Harlem on Manhattan's upper East Side, where many Puerto Ricans have settled. From its first home in a schoolroom, it will move through a series of storefront locations until it finds a permanent home at 1230 Fifth Avenue in 1977. Over the years, its mission will broaden to offer a "forum to preserve and project the cultural heritage of Puerto Ricans and all Latin Americans in the U.S."

GOVERNMENT AND POLITICS

• The trial of the Chicago Eight begins for defendants Abbie Hoffman, Jerry Rubin, Tom Hayden, Rennie Davis, David Dellinger, Lee Weiner, John Froines, and Bobby Seale, who are charged with crossing state lines to incite a riot as the aftermath of the Days of Rage at the Democratic National Convention in Chicago. Although they will be convicted in 1970, eventually all charges will be dropped. Tom Hayden says, "We were invented. We were chosen by the government to serve as scapegoats for all that they wanted to prevent happening in the 1970s."

• Congress passes the Tax Reform Act, which requires foundations to disperse a minimum of 5 percent of their endowment earnings. Foundation support shrinks.

• Richard Milhous Nixon (1913–1994) becomes the thirty-seventh president, with Spiro T. Agnew as his vice president. He fol-

lows through on his pledge to begin pulling the U.S. ground troops out of Vietnam through "Vietnamization," a policy of training and equipping the South Vietnamese to fight their own war, and increasing bombing of both North and South Vietnam. He also seeks to open diplomatic contact with the People's Republic of China and to thaw the Cold War hostilities with the Soviet Union. His administration turns a cold shoulder to antiwar protestors. When 250,000 people gather in Washington, even marching past the White House, Nixon watches a football game with a friend. Ten thousand people are teargassed at the Justice Department for protesting prosecutions of antiwar dissidents. Martha Mitchell, wife of Attorney General John Mitchell, comments, "It looked like the Russian Revolution."

SCIENCE AND TECHNOLOGY

• The Apollo 11 spacecraft is launched on July 16 to make the first landing on the Moon. Images are televised around the world of space-suited astronaut Neil Armstrong dropping onto the Sea of Tranquility's surface from the lunar module's ladder as he speaks, "That's one small step for man, one giant leap for mankind." The astronauts bounce and float in the Moon's airless, low-gravity environment, as they set up scientific experiments, take photographs, and collect lunar rock and soil samples. They return to earth on July 24, leaving behind the United States flag, forever caught in an image in which it is made to appear to fly from a pole planted in the lunar dust. The event is heralded as a major media, scientific, and political success—a symbol of infinite possibilities ahead—although many criticize the expenditure of taxes on the

Moon when there is so much poverty, disease, and other pressing needs to take care of at home.

• A human ovum is successfully fertilized in a test tube. This new procedure makes it possible for couples to become pregnant who had previously been infertile.

• The U.S. Department of Defense's Advanced Research Projects Agency funds the establishment of a computer network called ARPANET, which is a four-node network linking UCLA and Stanford's Research Institute (SRI), UC Santa Barbara (UCSB), and the University of Utah in Salt Lake City. The last letter of their first message, "login," is entered from UCLA to SRI as the system crashes, but their attempt inaugurates a success. Within the next month, other nodes are installed at UCSB and the University of Utah. This milestone enables university-based researchers to share computer resources, and is the precursor of the Internet. Within a year ARPANET hosts start using Network Control Protocol (NCP), the first host-to-host format for communication.

• The Union of Concerned Scientists (UCS) is founded by a group of students and faculty at the Massachusetts Institute of Technology (MIT) to protest the misuse of science and technology, and to encourage scientists to direct their research toward innovative applications for environmental and social problems, rather than military programs.

CULTURE AND SOCIETY

• Indians of All Tribes, a pan-Indian group, occupies Alcatraz Island in San Francisco Bay (for the second time) to draw attention to the treatment of Indians throughout the U.S. Since the prison is closed and the island has been designated as surplus land, AIM justifies its occu-

pation by citing an 1868 verbal agreement with the Sioux that granted Indians first rights to government surplus lands. They offer twenty-four dollars in glass beads as a purchase price, alluding to the purchase price the Dutch legendarily paid for Manhattan Island when they bought it from the local Native Americans in 1626. The occupation starts with fourteen activists, and grows until it involves hundreds of Indians and minority college students. They take control of the cell blocks, defying federal demands to leave the island.

• The formation of the Gay Liberation Movement is triggered by an urban riot, known as the Stonewall Rebellion, that starts after a dozen police stage a surprise raid on a gay bar, the Stonewall Inn, located in New York City's Greenwich Village. The police arrest a couple of employees and the most outrageous drag queens, on the grounds of checking for "gender-appropriate" attire. When the cops hit a cross-dressing lesbian, she hits back and the drag queens explode, setting off a four-hour riot that involves throwing of bricks and bottles, setting of fires, windows broken by barrels, and hundreds of demonstrators shouting, singing, and running through the streets. Stonewall changes the experience of growing up gay for future generations. Instead of remaining invisible, as had been the cultural norm, thousands find the pride to come out, declaring themselves gay, within the next year. Within four years, organizations including the Gay Liberation Front, Radicalesbians, the Lambda Legal Defense and Education Fund, and hundreds of others have formed.

▣ 1951

• The First Convocation of American Indian Scholars protests the ignorant or insulting treatment of Indians in children's textbooks.

• A Santa Barbara conference develops a Chicano Plan for Higher Education. A crowd of 2,000 demonstrators in Del Rio, Texas, hears the Del Rio Mexican American Manifesto to the Nation.

• Students for a Democratic Society (SDS) breaks up after its final convention, imploding from the pressures within their membership, which is splintering in increasingly separate directions. Many of the women form an autonomous new generation of feminists, and many of the men focus on the antiwar movement, while others scatter to live in communes and a small radical group goes underground to practice the outlaw tactics of the Weathermen.

• The "Second Wave" breaks from feminist organizations to form radical feminist political groups, including the Redstockings and the October 17th Movement. Over the next six years they push sexual politics as a public issue, creating a new vocabulary to fit a changed sense of self and the community of women: "the personal is political"; "sisterhood is powerful."

• Chicago police assassinate Black Panther leader Fred Hampton while he sleeps in bed, and Mark Clark, another Black Panther.

• *Sesame Street* premieres on the Public Broadcasting System, revolutionizing children's television programming by applying advertising techniques to teach preschoolers reading, writing, arithmetic, and social skills at home. The teaching is entertainingly transmitted through Muppets, puppet characters created by Jim Henson, who converse with each other and an integrated group of human friends and guest stars. *Sesame Street* becomes a twenty-five-year international success, although it has never definitively proven its educational value.

WORLD EVENTS

• Italian designer and founder of the Memphis design group, Ettore Sottsass Jr., and Perry A. King create the portable "Valentine" typewriter, an experiment that demonstrates the versatility of molded plastics, by allowing the machine to be light enough to carry anywhere, and festive enough, with its bright orange-red color, not to be associated with a work environment. It illustrates their intention of "giving souls to objects," an innovative and influential way to approach product design that also refers back to traditional practices common in many cultures.

Apollo 15 astronaut David R. Scott with the
"moon buggy" in the background. *(NASA)*

1970–1979

The Seventies: The Mapping of a Literary Asian America on a Chinese Restaurant Placemat

Shawn Wong

I N A FAIRLY SHORT PERIOD DURING 1969 and early 1970, the future of what we know about Asian American literature was forged by a series of meetings between four young Asian American writers: Frank Chin, a twenty-nine-year-old writer, former railroad worker, and Berkeley resident; Jeffery Chan, a twenty-seven-year-old Asian American Studies professor at San Francisco State University; Lawson Inada, a thirty-two-year-old English professor and poet from Southern Oregon University in Ashland; and me, a nineteen-year-old University of California, Berkeley, student and aspiring writer.

I had spent my first two years of college at San Francisco State University, studying poetry and fiction under the mentorship of Irish poet James Liddy and the renowned American writer Kay Boyle, before transferring to Berkeley. In the summer of 1969 at Berkeley, I asked myself, "Why am I the only Asian American writer I know in the world? Are there any other Asian American writers? Why has no teacher ever mentioned one in high school or college?" I was ashamed to admit that these questions came to me so late. In the middle of completing an English literature major that included mostly dead British male authors, I was hungry for contemporary literature written by authors who were alive, who wrote about issues I was interested in, and who pushed the boundaries in fiction and poetry. While I searched for the answer, I read my Chaucer, dodged tear-gas canisters, and went looking for other writers whenever Berkeley was shut down by strikes and demonstrations.

I asked my Berkeley professors for the names of Asian American writers, but they couldn't name any. I went to see my San Francisco State professor, Kay Boyle, who mentioned that one of her graduate students was Jeffery Chan, who was teaching in the Asian American Studies Department. I called Jeff and met with him. He was completing his graduate degree in creative writing at SF State, and was working on a novel titled *Auntie Tsia Lays Dying.* Jeff referred me to his friend Frank Chin, who had recently published a short story titled "Food for All His Dead."

I called Frank that same evening and introduced myself as a student at Berkeley who was interested in writing and had never met a published Chinese American writer. Chin replied, "Meet me at the Med in ten minutes. We'll talk." The Med, or Mediterranean, was a popular coffeehouse on Telegraph Avenue, just south of the university. I met my first published Chinese American author and had my first cappuccino in the same evening. A few months later, Frank and I found a book in Cody's Bookstore titled *Down at the Santa Fe Depot: 20 Fresno Poets,* an anthology edited by David Kherdian and James Baloian (Giligia Press,

1970). In the book was the poetry of Lawson Inada, a Fresno, California, native, writing about the multiracial west side of his city. Frank contacted Giligia Press and was given Inada's phone number. We contacted him, identifying ourselves as "two Chinese American writers who have read your poetry and want to meet you." It turned out that Lawson had heard of Frank when they were both at the University of Iowa at the same time, but they had never met.

Inada drove down from Ashland and met Frank and me at a publication party for Ishmael Reed's anthology *19 Necromancers From Now* (1970). Reed was publishing a chapter from Frank's unpublished novel, *A Chinese Lady Dies.* It was a significant meeting place because it forged an alliance not only between Lawson, Frank, Jeff, and me, but also between Ishmael Reed and other writers present at the party, including Al Young, Victor Hernandez Cruz, and Alex Haley. Two literary paths were constructed that evening in 1970—one headed by Ishmael Reed, who was out to define something called American multicultural writing, long before "multicultural" was the buzzword it is now; and the other path headed by Frank, Jeff, Lawson, and me, who were out to search for what we thought might be a generation of Asian American writers who came before us, hoping that those names might form an Asian American literary canon.

In 1971 we started looking, and found a lot of our own people who told us that Asian Americans didn't write. We were told there were no Asian American books. None. No histories, no novels, no collections of poetry, no published plays, and certainly no anthologies of

An Earth Day poster, using one of NASA's most evoked images of Earth, in a still very new point of view from the moon, to inspire us to care about our tiny planet and help it continue floating through the universe. *(Library of Congress, Prints and Photographs Division)*

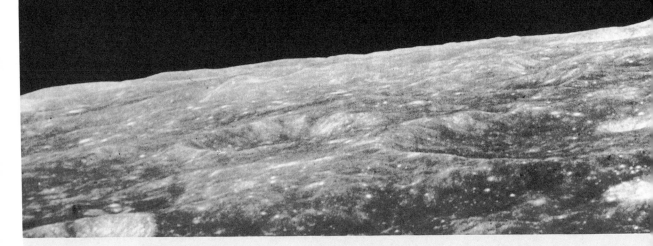

THE WHOLE
EARTH IS WATCHING

Asian American literature. They were wrong. We found that the novel *No-No Boy* by John Okada had been published in 1957 in an edition of 1,500 copies; it was *still* in print fourteen years later and still for sale for three dollars in hardcover. We found Toshio Mori's collection of short stories, *Yokohama, California* (1949) in a used-book store for twenty-five cents. We found Monica Sone's memoir, *Nisei Daughter* (1953), still in print. We found that *Eat a Bowl of Tea* (1961) by Louis Chu had been published by his friend Lyle Stuart, a publisher known more for books on gambling and sex than great Asian American literature. And we found work from writers like Hisaye Yamamoto and Wakako Yamauchi.

At the same time, a Japanese American *sansei* poet, Janice Mirikitani, became influential in gathering all the young Asian American literary voices together to read at the famous Glide Memorial Methodist Church and elsewhere around San Francisco. The voices she wanted to hear had to be tools in the fight against racism, sexism, injustice, war, and poverty across racial boundaries, across continents, and across class differences. When she called us to read our work, she was asking us to change the world. I met other young Bay Area writers at these readings, such as Jessica Hagedorn and Ntozake Shange.

At Berkeley I had studied with Jackson Burgess, who had taught both Jeff Chan and Frank Chin at different times. Lawson Inada published his first collection of poetry, *Before the War: Poems as They Happened,* in 1971. UCLA published its first issue of *Amerasia Journal* in March 1971. In the issue was an essay about Jade Snow Wong's autobiography, *Fifth Chinese Daughter* (1950), by the journal's editor, Lowell Chun-Hoon, and a poem by Ray Lou titled "A Poem for the People."

That same year, Frank, Jeff, Lawson, and I met at the Jackson Café in San Francisco's Chinatown, and mapped out on a paper placemat the table of contents for an anthology of Asian American literature. There were no college classes in Asian American literature, no teachers, no credit, and no grades. I kept writing and rewriting the introduction to our anthology, titled *Aiiieeeee!* I remember Lawson Inada writing in a letter the sentence, "We can pronounce Lillian Russell now, so we can speak for ourselves." After the four of us finished the introduction to *Aiiieeeee!,* we gave it to my professor, Kay Boyle, who read it and sent it back with pages and pages of handwritten notes. In spite of our combined youth and arrogance at believing we knew all about Asian American literature, we knew when to be students. We followed every one of Kay's suggestions for revision.

By the end of 1972 we had completed a manuscript of *Aiiieeeee!: An Anthology of Asian American Writers,* the first anthology of Asian American literature, and had started looking for a publisher, but the publishers we approached had never heard of Asian American writing and turned us down. Some of the research we had done through CARP (Combined Asian-American Resources Project) and for our anthology was published in *Asian American Authors,* a textbook edited by another one of my San Francisco State professors, Kai-yu Hsu, along with Helen Palubinskas, and published by Houghton Mifflin. It was the first Asian American literature textbook and one of the only books about Asian American literature and history in print at the time.

In 1973 the University of Washington Press reissued Carlos Bulosan's autobiography, *America Is in the Heart,* which was the first of many Asian American books the University of Washington Press would rescue from obscurity. *Farewell to Manzanar* by Jeanne Wakatsuki Houston and James D. Houston, the memoir of Jeanne Wakatsuki Houston's family's internment at the Manzanar relocation center during World War II, was published and was later made into a television movie in which Frank Chin, Lawson Inada, and I played minor characters who incited a riot in Manzanar. Most notable was Frank's line, "It's a trick, let's get out of here." Lawson's line was, "Get out of my way, white boy." And I said, "That's a lie!" We were type-cast.

Also in 1973, *Longtime Californ': A Documentary Study of an American Chinatown* was published by Victor G. and Brett de Bary Nee. The book featured oral histories of Chinese Americans, and became the first history of Chinese America from a Chinese American point of view.

Later in 1973, Frank Chin, Lawson Inada, Ishmael Reed, and I were invited to a conference held at the University of Wisconsin at Stevens Point and sponsored by the National Center for Audio Experimentation, whose director was the poet Ed Burrows. The two-week conference had no agenda and no audience, but it gathered together a remarkable group of writers, musicians, and media artists. Many of the writers hadn't published a book yet. They included Leonard Adame, Mei-mei Berssenbrugge, Americo Casiano, Leslie Marmon Silko, Melvin Dixon, Phil George, Bruce Iwasaki, Gary Soto, Simon Ortiz, Michael Harper, Karoniaktatie, Sharon Bell Mathis, Mbembe (Milton Smith), Jesus Papoleto Melendez, Javier Pacheco, Jose Antonio Parra, Ricardo Sanchez, and Joseph Bruchac. What the conference lacked in structure and direction, it made up in the understanding by all that something called "multicultural writing" was being named and identified. Every single member of that group remains to this day spiritually bound together by our shared experience in that unlikely city of Stevens Point, Wisconsin. Following the conference, we wrote letters to each other and sent our unpublished work to each other.

In 1973, Roberta Palm, a young editor at Howard University Press, contacted me because she had read that I had won a literary contest sponsored by the Council on Interracial Books for Children, and wanted to see my manuscript. In 1974, Howard University Press, in its inaugural year, issued its first ten books, among which was *Aiiieeeee!: An Anthology of Asian American Writers,* and it quickly caught the attention of book reviewers everywhere from *Rolling Stone* to *The New Yorker* to Asian community newspapers. Now almost 30 years later it continues to be lauded and reviled, often in the same essay. No matter who was praising it or who was taking exception to our definition of Asian American literature, everyone began their knowledge of Asian American literature with our anthology. It educated an audience to what Frank, Jeff, Lawson, and I were doing in our own work. *"Aiiieeeee!* named the canon," as Professor Shirley Geok-lin Lim of the University of California at Santa Barbara once said at an Asian American literature conference. The anthology has been reprinted by three other publishers since then, by the very publishers who turned us down in the years before it was published.

As of April 1970, the resident population totals 203,302,000, and, without including Hawaii and Alaska, shows an increase of 13.4 percent over the preceding decade. The number of refugees entering the country is almost double the total from the previous decade. Asian immigration and naturalization especially show a dramatic increase over the decade; Caribbean immigration almost doubles; and during this decade there is another huge increase in African immigration. Starting in 1979, the U.S. Census begins presenting statistics on drug and alcohol use by persons twelve years of age and up, stated in percentage of having ever used a substance within that year, finding: marijuana and hashish, 27.9 percent; cocaine, 8.6 percent; hallucinogens, 8.9 percent; heroin, 1.3 percent; alcohol, 88.5 percent. In 1975, 47.3 percent of mothers with children under eighteen years of age are participating in the labor force, and women over sixteen years of age make up 38.1 percent of the total labor force (U.S. Department of Labor). Per capita personal income in 1975 is $5,851 (U.S. Bureau of Economic Analysis).

In 1975, Milton Murayama published his landmark novel about Hawai'i, *All I Asking For Is My Body*. His work joined another seminal work, *Hawaii: End of the Rainbow* by Kazuo Miyamoto (1964). Also in 1975, Frank Chin and I edited an Asian American literary issue of the landmark journal *Yardbird Reader*, started by Ishmael Reed and Al Young in 1971. While mainstream American publishing was slow to recognize Asian American writing, African American presses like the Yardbird Publishing Cooperative and Howard University Press were quick to pick up on the inclusion of Asian American literature into their concept of American literature.

In 1976, Maxine Hong Kingston published *The Woman Warrior: Memoirs of a Girlhood Among Ghosts*, a nonfiction memoir, which Frank, Jeff, Lawson, and I perceived as yet another in a long line of books that portrayed China and Chinese America as products of a racist imagination—not fact, not Chinese culture, and not Chinese or Chinese American literature. Perhaps writing that it wasn't Chinese

American literature was going too far, but it was the seventies, and to make a point we had to go too far. In 1976, *Time* magazine called *The Woman Warrior* one of the greatest books of the last 200 years. We called it a fake. The good part in this history is that American publishing took note of Kingston's huge commercial success, but that's all they did. It wouldn't be until Amy Tan's *Joy Luck Club* (1989) that Asian American writers were finally published in any significant numbers by mainstream commercial publishers.

We had ended the seventies better than we had started. When Frank, Jeff, Lawson, and I were researching the existence of Asian American literature, we had run across a book by Daniel I. Okimoto, *American in Disguise* (1971). In the book, Okimoto writes:

> . . . it appears unlikely that literary figures of comparable stature to those minorities like the Jews and Blacks will emerge to articulate the nisei soul. Japanese Americans will be forced to borrow the voices of James Michener,

Jerome Charyn, and other sympathetic novelists to distill their own experience. Even if a nisei of Bernard Malamud's or James Baldwin's talent did appear, he would no doubt have little to say that John O'Hara has not already said.

Okimoto was wrong. In the introduction to *The Big Aiiieeeee!*, our sequel to *Aiiieeeee!* (1991), we described the process of finding what Okimoto and others said wasn't there: "We had to ask, inspect, corroborate, challenge, and prove the factual, textural reality of the stuff and its place in Asian universal knowledge. As we suspected, contrary to the stereotype, Chinese and Japanese immigrants were a literate people from literate civilizations whose presses, theaters, opera houses, and artistic enterprises rose as quickly as their social and political institutions. They are not few. They are not gone. They are not stupid. They were only waiting to be asked." Just as a nineteen-year-old Berkeley student had asked in 1969, "Are there any Asian American writers?"

1970

ARTS AND LITERATURE

• Owing to their activism, the routine exclusion of women artists from New York City group shows or solo exhibitions begins to change. For the first time, two African American women artists, Barbara Chase-Riboud (b. 1939) and Betye Saar (b. 1926), are included in an exhibit at the Whitney Museum, in which 4 percent of the exhibited works are by women artists; subsequent Whitney Biennial totals of women artists go up to 20–25 percent. The Los Angeles Council of Women Artists (LACWA)

protests that no women artists are included in the Los Angeles County Museum of Art (LACMA) group show, "Art & Technology," revealing that out of the fifty-three L.A. County Museum's one-artist shows, only one solo exhibition has been for a woman, the photographer Dorothea Lange. The council also serves as a network, collecting testimonials of discrimination to defend their political demands.
▣ 1969

• Sculptor Judy Chicago (b. 1939) organizes the first women's art course at Fresno State College (now California State University, Fresno), which is frequently credited as the beginning of the Feminist Art movement. The classes are for women only, and the students help create an experimental curriculum that will change how arts education is presented. The classes focus on art by and for women, challenging the entrenched European-male modernist canon long established by art schools and critics. They use an interdisciplinary approach involving consciousness raising (the structured conversation used by the women's movement), role-playing, research in women's literature, psychology, sociology, philosophy, and feminist theory to create a historical context for their thinking and art work. By the end of the year, their public performances and art exhibitions begin to interject new ways of understanding women's art forms and to redefine images and symbols used against women. Through making art about women's lives that, for example, uses the body as art, and personal, autobiographical content for subject matter, Feminist Art experiments validate various techniques and materials, including those traditionally called crafts, such as quilting, needlework and weaving, that are now commonly used by men and women artists.

• Photography, film, drawings, video, and texts become documentary tools for recording conceptual art processes and site-specific "land art" or "earthworks." They contribute different experiences for the observer, preserving one-time-only events, views of inaccessible locations, or representations of ephemeral materials and performances that can, ironically, become art objects to publish, exhibit, and sell, and are often used to finance the project or future projects. Without documentation, these works would be largely unknown.

• The Grand Union, an unconventional collective of nine New York City–based choreographers, collaborates on group improvisations that they perform at colleges and galleries throughout the U.S. over the next six years. Although its participants evolve through various configurations, they include Becky Arnold, Trisha Brown, Douglas Dunn, David Gordon, Nancy Lewis, Barbara Lloyd (Dilley), Steve Paxton, Yvonne Rainer, and Lincoln Scott.

• Visual and performing artists organize the Judson Flag Show to protest laws that limit how the American flag can be used and displayed. It includes a performance of Yvonne Rainer's *Trio A,* danced by six people dressed only in American flags that are tied like bibs around their necks. Faith Ringgold (b. 1934) exhibits her painting *Flag for the Moon: Die Nigger* (1969), which uses the flag motif to challenge racism, saying that "the flag is the only truly subversive and revolutionary abstraction one can paint." She is arrested, along with the founders of the Guerrilla Art Action Group, John Hendricks and Jean Toche, and they become known as "the Judson Three." In 1971, Ringgold is found guilty of desecrating the American flag in her paintings.

• Government funding for video is inaugurated by the New York State Council on the Arts, reflecting the growing prominence of video as an artistic medium.

• Kate Millett publishes *Sexual Politics: A Surprising Examination of Society's Most Arbitrary Folly,* her doctoral thesis, which turns into a best-seller. Taking on Sigmund Freud, she discusses ways in which the patriarchal culture makes women feel inferior, and by pointing out the misogyny and sexism in the writing of D. H. Lawrence, Henry Miller, and Norman Mailer, she formulates feminist literary criticism.

• The Bread and Puppet Theater moves to Vermont and begins presenting weekend events called the Domestic Resurrection Circus and Pageant. The Circus is performed for twenty-seven summers, mostly at the Bread and Puppet's own farm in Glover, Vermont. Each year's event is a collaboration of up to 200 men, women, and children volunteers, who are directed by Peter Schumann. Schumann and his wife always bake and hand out over 600 loaves of sourdough rye bread "because our bread and theater belong together. We want you to understand that theater is not yet an established form, not the place for commerce you think it is, where you pay to get something. Theater is different. It is more like bread, more like a necessity."

• Self-taught black teenage dancers, called "B-Boys," create breakdancing, a new competitive dance style performed by a soloist inside a ring of dancers on the streets and in the parks and dance halls of the South Bronx. It eludes mainstream notice until 1979, after police arrest the High Times breakdance crew in a New York subway, thinking they are fighting, and a *New York Post* photographer is called to cover the "riot." The kids are released after conclusively proving they are dancing, by demonstrating moves they call the "head spin," "swipe," "chin freeze," "helicopter," and "baby." Another wave of Puerto Rican dancers keeps the form evolving as an important element of the hip-hop culture of rap, graffiti tagging, DJ-ing, and MC-ing. Breaking becomes so popular, theatrical, and mainstream that it will be used to sell products on TV, and will continue to be highly visible into the 1990s.

GOVERNMENT AND POLITICS

• On April 22, the first Earth Day inaugurates the official American participation in the growing global environmental movement. Twenty million Americans celebrate the planet they live on by cleaning up beaches, roadways, city parks, and empty lots, with millions marching in New York and Washington, D.C., parades. The widespread public expression of concern for environmental damage encourages Congress to pass a National Environmental Policy Act (NEPA), requiring an environmental-impact statement for every large project funded by a federal agency, and to create the Environmental Protection Agency. Earth Day will become an annual event, a day to celebrate and care for the earth's ecology.

• The undeclared war in Vietnam escalates with the secret invasion of Cambodia by 18,000 American soldiers. After President Nixon announces the "incursion" on national TV on April 30, more than 100 student protest strikes erupt on campuses throughout the U.S., and thirty ROTC buildings are burned or bombed during the first week in May. National

guard units are called onto twenty-one campuses in sixteen states, including Kent State University in Ohio, which is one of the campuses where an ROTC building is bombed. On May 4, Governor James Rhodes calls anti–Vietnam War protesters "Brownshirts" and vows to "eradicate" them, sending the Ohio National Guard onto the Kent State campus to break up an unauthorized rally. Four students, two of whom are women, are shot and killed and at least eleven are wounded when the troops fire into the crowd after a few rocks are thrown. This tragic event marks a turning point in opposition to the war and civil disobedience throughout the U.S. On July 23 the Justice Department reports that the Ohio National Guard could have effectively dispelled the Kent State protestors with tear gas, and that the demonstration was not a riot.

This 1970 antiwar poster appropriates a news photo of a woman kneeling beside a student lying injured on the street during a riot at Kent State University. *(Library of Congress)*

• On August 20, 25,000–30,000 people, mostly Chicano, demonstrate in the National Chicano Moratorium to end the Vietnam War March, calling for resistance to the draft and social justice in the U.S., and protesting the disproportionately high number of Chicano casualties in Vietnam. A rally takes place in Laguna Park in Los Angeles, with the support of Mexican American organizations from across the Southwest. When the police use clubs and tear gas to disperse the crowds after a disturbance breaks out near the rally, three people are killed including Reuben Salazar, a *Los Angeles Times* columnist, who is accidentally killed by the police while observing the event. For the Mexican American community, Salazar's death becomes and continues to be a symbol of injustice, police brutality, and suppression of Latino civil rights.

• Native American demonstrators conduct sit-ins at the Bureau of Indian Affairs (BIA) offices throughout the U.S. They focus their demands on recognition of their rights based on treaties with the U.S. government, preservation of traditional ways, and deterrents placed on BIA abuses. Throughout the year, other actions occur: a pan-Indian coalition of fifty natives climbs up Mount Rushmore and announces a takeover; Ellis Island is occupied by Indian demonstrators, as is Fort Lawton in the state of Washington. On Thanksgiving Day, AIM stages its first national protest when it occupies the *Mayflower II* in Plymouth, Massachusetts, and declares Thanksgiving a day of national mourning. On December 15, President Nixon signs a bill formally ending the termination policy. He also returns the sacred Blue Lake and its watershed land area of 40,000 acres to the rightful owners, the Taos Indians. The returned land is part of 130,000 acres of land taken by President Theodore Roosevelt and placed under control of the U.S. Forest Service in 1906. It represents one of the few significant areas ever restored to native sovereignty.

• On August 26 a national Women's Strike for Equality commemorates the fiftieth anniversary of the day women's suffrage was ratified, gathering the largest women's demonstrations since the days of the suffrage movement, capturing media attention with teach-ins, rallies, marches, and staged events. Fifty thousand members of the second wave of feminists march down New York's Fifth Avenue. In an address by Eleanor Holmes Norton, chair of the New York City Commission on Civil Rights, she predicts that women's rights will be the movement of the 1970s, as civil rights was for the 1960s.

🖻 | 1920

• The Senate holds the first Equal Rights Amendment (ERA) hearing since 1956, for the purpose of deciding whether "equality of rights under the law shall not be denied or abridged by the U.S. or by any state on account of sex."

• Congress passes the Voting Rights Act of 1970, which includes an amendment that will protect minority voters from practices that prevent people from voting, such as gerrymandering districts (changing the boundaries) or at-large elections that require federal approval for all changes in voting procedures.

• The National Oceanic and Atmospheric Administration (NOAA) is proposed by President Nixon, evolving out of nineteenth-century agencies first established by Thomas Jefferson, and is established this year under the Department of Commerce. It includes the National Weather Service, which gathers data by continuing a tradition of a nationwide network of

10,000 volunteers who contribute to climate records by taking daily measurements from instruments as low-tech as a rain gauge, while also involving scientists, geophysicists, cartographers, engineers, pilots, and sailors. High-tech instruments such as weather and environmental satellites and supercomputers will observe, forecast, and monitor coastal, ocean, interior, and atmospheric environments.

BUSINESS AND INDUSTRY

• Grape growers finally agree to demands of the United Farm Workers, after 17 million Americans honor the grape boycott. Cesar Chavez starts another UFW strike of 7,000 farm workers, this time against the lettuce growers. When the lettuce growers sign a contract with the Teamsters, the UFW strike is expanded to include a consumer boycott of lettuce. In 1974 the new governor of California, Jerry Brown, introduces the California Agriculture Labor Relations Act, which allows elections to be held by workers. In 1979 the act helps to finally end lettuce and grape boycotts, when major California lettuce farmers sign contracts with the UFW.

• Xerox PARC is founded as a research arm for Xerox Corporation, but it actually functions as a national computer research center, the birthplace of many innovations that have become basic tools and components of computer science technology. The PARC research team's innovations make it possible to develop small interactive individual computers with various software and hardware innovations including semiconductor memory, the first drawing program, and the first page description language. The team designs the Alto, a prototype of today's PC. They also serve as a feeder, supplying the personnel that generate many Silicon Valley startup companies, including Apple Computer, Adobe Systems, and 3Com Corporation.

▣ 1972

SCIENCE AND TECHNOLOGY

• IBM introduces the floppy disk as a new way to store computer data. Inexpensive, flexible, and light enough to send through the mail, "floppies" free hard-drive space for files wanted in immediate access memory.

• Indian American biochemist Har Gobind Khorana (b. India, 1922), leader of a team of University of Wisconsin scientists, announces the first complete synthesis of an artificial gene. By 1976 this team will succeed in inserting an artificial gene into a bacterial cell, where it functions as a biologically active gene. Khorana, whose research supplies much of the groundwork for gene therapy and biotechnology, shares a 1968 Nobel Prize for Physiology or Medicine with Robert Holley (U.S.) and Marshall Nirenberg (U.S.).

• *Mariner 9*, a U.S. space probe, orbits Mars and transmits photographs of the planet and its two moons. It is the first artificial object to orbit another planet.

CULTURE AND SOCIETY

• By spring 1970, student demonstrations are happening on college campuses across the country. On May 14–15, two black students are killed and twelve wounded when police fire on a dormitory at Jackson State College, Mississippi, after demonstrations. When this tragedy does not receive the level of sympathetic demonstrations and press coverage given to the similar tragedy at Kent State University, it becomes a reference that African American scholars invoke to demonstrate ongoing patterns of disregard for experiences of African Americans and other people of color.

• A small group of immigrants from El Salvador establishes the first Salvadoran *colonias* in Los Angeles and San Francisco in 1970. They are part of a mass migration instigated by the government of Honduras, which deports over 350,000 Salvadoran banana plantation workers in 1969. The Salvadorans are the first wave of what will be a flood of undocumented Central American immigrants fleeing to the U.S. during the 1970s and 1980s, to escape the chaos of civil wars and overwhelming poverty. The Immigration and Naturalization Service (INS) puts the number of undocumented workers at 12 million, and other observers say that the number is from 3.5 to 5 million. Because of U.S. interventions in these countries, the INS refuses to acknowledge the immigrants as political refugees, although Nicaraguan immigrants are more likely to be granted political asylum once the Sandanista government is in power. In response to the people's crisis, a church-based liberation theology movement develops a grass-roots underground network in both Central America and the U.S., arranging safe passage and church asylum in the U.S. for the refugees.

🔲 1967

• The longest prison strike in U.S. history to date starts with a work stoppage at Folsom prison in California, in which 2,400 prisoners remain in their cells on a hunger strike for nineteen days before the strike is broken with harsh reprisals by prison officials.

• In 1970, San Diego State College (now University) establishes the first official women's studies program. Throughout the 1970s, stu-dents pressure universities to establish new programs focusing on the particular experiences of women, Asian American, Native American, and Latino/Chicano experiences, all of which have been omitted from degree-granting programs and academic research up to this time. Led by the formation of the African American and Black Studies program at San Francisco State University, most colleges and universities start by introducing a few courses before establishing departments that include the disciplines of literature, history, sociology, and the arts. By 1991, 250 four-year colleges have instituted some kind of black studies program, and their innovative changes trickle down to elementary grade levels, influencing hiring practices, teaching styles, and curriculum and textbook content.

🔲 1969

• Gay Pride Week is invented, in commemoration of the first anniversary of the Stonewall Rebellion. In New York City, between 5,000 and 15,000 gay militants and their supporters march from Greenwich Village to the Sheep Meadow in Central Park for a "Gay-In," waving red, green, purple, and yellow banners and shouting, "Say it loud, gay is proud!" Similar festivities are held in New York, San Francisco, Los Angeles, and Chicago. During the same month, the Gay Activists Alliance (GAA) sits in at the Manhattan office of New York's governor, Nelson Rockefeller, to make him reveal his views on homosexuality. Five members of the group are arrested and become known as the "Rockefeller Five." Four months later, three of the major Democratic and Republican candidates for U.S. senator endorse the GAA's civil rights platform, confirming the new political reality of the "homosexual vote."

WORLD EVENTS

• Dr. Salvador Allende is elected president of Chile, the first Marxist to become the freely elected head of a Western nation, despite CIA covert efforts to thwart his election, ordered directly by President Nixon. Allende's promises to redistribute land and wealth and to nationalize industries come to an end, in three years, with his assassination.

▣ 1998

• The first mass hijacking on an airplane happens this year when the Popular Front for the Liberation of Palestine seizes three passenger planes bound from Europe to the U.S. The Pan Am, TWA, and Swissair planes are blown up on the ground in Egypt and Jordan.

1971

ARTS AND LITERATURE

• The National Endowment for the Arts adds a new funding category, the "Expansion Arts and Community Cultural Program," which awards grants to communities that have not been receiving funding under the existing NEA programs, the "professionally directed community arts groups with activities involving ethnic and rural minorities."

• Walter De Maria (b. 1935) starts building a land-art work, *Lightning Field,* a grid of 400 stainless-steel poles topped by spikes, which occasionally create a theater of spectacular meteorological displays when lightning strikes on the desert terrain of Quemada, New Mexico. Commissioned by the Dia Foundation, the work is finished in 1977. Dia maintains the site and arranges tours.

• Trisha Brown (b. 1936) starts to construct dances using a process of accumulation, in which she adds one gesture or movement at a time, building movements into a pattern of repetition such as 1; 2; 1,2; 3; 1,2, 3; 4 and so on, of perhaps thirty ideas. *Accumulation,* a solo, is the first of a series of numerical pattern dances that can also be performed by groups. Also this year, following her "keen interests . . . gravity and the defiance of it," she begins making "equipment dances" by climbing into articles of clothing pinned on a rope grid hung parallel to the floor.

• Frank Chin (b. 1940), fifth-generation American, wins the East West Players playwriting contest with *The Chickencoop Chinaman.* When the play receives an Off-Broadway production at the American Place Theatre in 1972, it becomes the first Asian American play to be performed in New York City's stage history. Jack Kroll of *Newsweek* calls Chin "part Chinese Lenny Bruce, spritzing a comedy of bitter alienation, and part Number One Son, drawn to the traditional Chinese values—family, duty—which have been diluted by American Culture."

• Lawson Fusao Inada's (b. 1938) *Before the War* is published. It is the first volume of poetry by an American-born Japanese American and the first by an Asian American to be published by a major publishing house (Morrow). Inada, who was born in Fresno, California, in 1938, writes from the personal experience of being interned in Japanese American concentration camps in Arkansas and Colorado during World War II.

• Artist Chris Burden (b. 1946) receives wide media attention for his conceptual artworks, by thinking up dangerous tasks or using apparatus that test the limits of his body's endurance. In this year he performs *Shoot,*

UNTITLED

Meredith Monk

The mid-1960s in New York were heady times. In music there were two sensibilities and groups: uptown and downtown, at odds with each other. The uptown composers were either following the twelve-tone, or electronic, music tradition or the American folk-inspired music of the 1930s and 1940s. In the downtown world, music could be almost anything. There were explosive discoveries in jazz, *alleatoric* or improvised music, tape compositions, events. I was welcomed by a generation of composer/artists who had been in John Cage's composition classes at the New School. A piece of music could be the sound of someone jumping on an upright piano (on its side) until it fell apart, to the sound of sand shifting (with contact microphones underneath it), to a walk around the block noting all the sounds of the city. This "anything is possible" attitude was enormously liberating and affirming for me. When I began exploring my voice with the same intensity that I had my body, I was encouraged by the spirit of inventiveness and originality that permeated downtown New York. In school, I had developed an idiosyncratic style of movement by necessity. My technical limitations led me to find unusual ways of putting movement together. I had not thought of applying those principles to my voice until one day in 1965 when I sat at the piano vocalizing, and realized in a flash that a voice could have the same flexibility and range as the body and that I could find a vocabulary built on my possibilities of character, color, texture, gender, resonance, and ways of producing sound. I was inspired in some of the early songs by the sound environment that I lived in. New York with its grating, ever-present electric hum; things rubbing against each other; dissonances and continual complexity of events. Rock and roll was also a strong presence for me and for many other composers who were working at that time reminding us to go back to the heartbeat, raw energy, blood, fearlessness, thrust.

For me, New York is still exhilaration, thrill, vibrancy as well as irritation, exasperation, but above all laughter. I love being a part of the musical community of New York where surprising things happen constantly. I thrive on still trying to find new ways of doing things and I still believe that by sheer enthusiasm, energy and will, daring things can happen even as the possibilities in the city tighten up and shrink. We still have the most sophisticated audience in the world. My friend Daniel Nagrin, the choreographer, once said to me: "You know, Meredith, artists are the cockroaches of the world. We will always survive."

where he has a friend shoot him in the left arm; and *Five Day Locker Piece,* where he spends five days locked inside a two-by-two-by-three-foot locker. In 1972 he spends twenty-two days in an alternative art space fasting while remaining in bed; in 1973 he crawls through fifty feet of broken glass with hands held behind his back. In 1974 he has himself crucified on the hood of a Volkswagen and says, "I don't think I am trying to commit suicide. I think my art is an inquiry, which is what all art is about."

• El Teatro Campesino establishes its permanent home base in San Juan Bautista, California, where it sets up a resident company that continues exploring ways to adapt traditional Mexican performance styles to contemporary political and social themes, including the Vietnam War, racial discrimination, and life in the barrios.

▣ 1964

• John Chowning experiments with extreme vibrato to find ways to produce more interesting sounds on a computer than have been possible up to this time. He discovers an extremely economical synthesis technique, a form of frequency modulation (FM) that is licensed to Yamaha and patented in 1977, and that "can get control over a very large timbral space with a very few knobs."

• Multidisciplinary performance artist Meredith Monk (b. 1944) integrates her interests in music, dance, and theater when she premieres *Vessel: an opera epic,* her first total theater work based on the voice, using it as an instrument more than as a means of conveying text.

▣ 1983

• The Kitchen, a nonprofit institution dedicated to presenting experimental new performance, installation, and video works opens its doors on West 19th Street in Manhattan. It helps many avant-garde artists establish their careers, including performers Philip Glass, Laurie Anderson, Eric Bogosian, B. T. Jones, Karen Finley, Annie Sprinkle, and installation and video artists Cindy Sherman, Robert Longo, Jonathan Borofsky, Vito Acconci, John Sandborn, Michael Auda, and Bill Viola. In the middle of the 1990s it experiments with an Electronic Café International, using a satellite link to operate in virtual space on the Internet, connecting artists in various countries.

GOVERNMENT AND POLITICS

• The Supreme Court rules to protect women with small children from hiring-discrimination practices.

• The Supreme Court votes 9–0 to approve the use of busing in a North Carolina public school district in *Swann v. Charlotte Mecklenburg Board of Education.* The precedent setting case, of de jure segregation practice (desegregation being legal by state right under law), establishes busing as a constitutional method for desegregating schools. However, the Nixon administration counters this ruling by citing de facto segregation practices (a reality within one school district) that are beyond the court's jurisdiction, when the president warns that forcing integration in the suburbs is "counterproductive and not in the interest of better race relations," calling for federal officials to stop "forced busing" plans in Southern schools. In 1974, the Supreme Court makes its first decision against a school desegregation plan since its 1954 *Brown v. Board of Education* ruling, when busing is further compromised in a 5–4 vote passing *Milliken v. Bradley.* This ruling bars busing students across city-suburb lines in Detroit, Michigan, because the Court rules that the segregation is de facto, and therefore beyond its jurisdiction. Since Detroit's urban schools are predominantly black and the suburban schools are predominantly white, this ruling reinforces the existing segregated school situation. De facto school segregation continues to exist in other Northern states. In 1975, Federal District Court Judge W. Arthur Garrity orders Boston to implement a school integration plan that includes busing 21,000 children.

▣ 1954, 1974, 1978

• In California, Governor Ronald Reagan calls for cutbacks in the welfare rolls, beginning a trend toward welfare reforms that by the 1990s will become nationwide.

• The right to print the "Pentagon Papers," a series of articles based on a secret Pentagon study of the Vietnam War that were obtained from undisclosed sources and published by the *New York Times* and the *Washington Post,* is upheld by the Supreme Court 6–3. The majority opinion states that the government's attempt "to impose 'prior restraint' on publication of information by newspapers bears 'a heavy presumption against its constitutional validity' under the First Amendment."

• Vice President Spiro T. Agnew resigns and pleads *nolo contendere* (no contest) in a Baltimore federal court, on a charge of one count of income-tax evasion.

BUSINESS AND INDUSTRY

• In August, President Nixon orders a ninety-day freeze on wages and prices, and institutes an elaborate system of price controls that remains in place for several years, with a ceiling placed on rents, prices, wages, and salaries. Although the freeze is described as "voluntary," court injunctions and fines as high as $5,000 can be imposed for failing to comply. He does this to reduce inflation and strengthen the dollar before the 1972 election. In response to a growing trade deficit, President Nixon also sets a 10-percent tax on imports and initiates the age of floating exchange rates. He decides to stop converting foreign-held dollars to gold, unhooking the link between the dollar and gold, and the dollar and the major world currencies. Now international markets have a tool to demonstrate their opinions of a country's economic policies, because countries can decide where to set the value of the dollar in their own currencies. The dollar quickly drops in value, losing half its value in comparison with the German mark and a third against the Japanese yen. However, President Nixon says, "The time has come for exchange rates to be set straight and for the major nations to compete as equals."

🖸 1944

• On December 18, Congress approves the Alaska Native Claims Settlement Act, recognizing native claims to the area's land and resources. The legal battle is spearheaded by the Arctic Slope Native Association and the Alaska Native Federation, organizations of Native people who approve the act. They win legal title to 44 million acres, of which 76,000 acres are on Alaska's North Slope where oil has been discovered, and $962 million as compensation for relinquishing claims to nine-tenths of Alaska. (The state of Alaska received over $1 billion worth of leases from their agreements with private oil companies.) Two hundred twenty Native village and twelve regional for-profit corporations are established to divide up the land and administer distribution of the assets, of which $462.5 million will be doled out over an eleven-year period, with an additional $500 million to be invested in mineral royalties. The effects of the settlement continue to be debated, with some Natives believing that it has destroyed traditional lands and ways ordered around fishing and hunting, and others believing in the necessity of accepting change.

SCIENCE AND TECHNOLOGY

• *Apollo 15* astronauts David R. Scott and James B. Irwin take the first ride on the Moon, in their lunar rover. They travel five miles in two hours, and viewers from Earth are able to watch them collecting and evaluating rock samples.

• The Food and Drug Administration approves use of the psychopharmacological drugs lithium and L-dopa. Lithium, an element in salt form, is used to relieve symptoms of manic depression. L-dopa stimulates the brain to produce dopamine, a neurotransmitter that relieves symptoms of Parkinson's disease, an incurable nerve disorder. Although both prove to have undesirable side effects, their introduction paves the way for the widespread use of antidepressant prescription drugs.

CULTURE AND SOCIETY

• Cigarette ads are banned from U.S. television.

• In 1970, rock-and-roll great Janis Joplin (1943–1970), a white blues singer, overdosed on heroin, and Jimi Hendrix (1942–1970), master guitarist and songwriter, choked on his vomit as a result of mixing alcohol and drugs. This year Jim Morrison (1943–1971), the lead singer and writer for the Doors, dies of a drug-related heart attack. The youthful romance of "sex, drugs, and rock and roll" feels tragically over.

• New York's radical feminists stage a public *Speakout Against Rape* to bring attention to the high incidence of rape. The event brings another taboo subject out of the closet, and starts feminists working to change perceptions of individual and institutional behaviors that target women by changing accepted "customs" into crimes. Subsequent books, including *Against Our Will* (1975) by Susan Brownmiller, *The Politics of Rape* by Diana Russell (1975), *The Conspiracy of Silence: The Trauma of Incest* by

Sandra Butler (1978), and wide media attention to court cases, expose how rape victims are frequently treated as sinners or perpetrators by police, hospitals, and the courts, and heighten awareness of the universality of rape, including marital rape, date rape, and the related behaviors of incest and violence against women.

• The Native American Rights Fund, the oldest and largest Indian public-interest law firm in the U.S., is founded.

• On August 21, George Jackson, a member of the Black Panthers and author of *Soledad Brother* and *Blood in My Eye,* is killed by guards at California's San Quentin State Prison during an alleged escape attempt. His death is said to be the spark that sets off the September 9–13 revolt by 1,300 inmates at Attica State Correctional Facility, a federal maximum-security prison in upstate New York. Among prisoners' demands are "realistic rehabilitation," better medical care, a minimum wage, one shower a week, and freedom of religion. Four days of negotiations end when Governor Nelson Rockefeller calls in 500 state troopers and police. Helicopters drop pepper gas, and over 2,000 bullets are fired into the yard where hostages, inmates, and guards huddle together, killing thirty-one prisoners and nine guards. Guards violently assault the surviving prisoners with clubs in the aftermath of what is said to be the bloodiest suppression of an inmate uprising in U.S. history.

• Ed Roberts, who contracted polio in 1953, establishes the Center for Independent Living (CIL) in Berkeley, California, with associates from the Disabled Students' Program, a UC Berkeley campus group formed the previous year. In 1972, a $50,000 grant from the Rehabilitation Administration enables CIL to

POSTMODERNISM

Critical theorists seem to agree only that postmodern means "after modernism." Some critics place modernism's start in the early nineteenth century, when critic William Hazlitt labeled arts as "modern" that were made as urban, secular, industrialized societies arose. That art is now called Romanticism. Some others place it with the Futurists and Dadaists and their sense of life's absurdities that resulted from experiencing World War I, continuing through the Cold War and Abstract Expressionism. The two terms have a kind of call-and-response relationship, with postmodernism expanding modernism's principles and experiments. By the mid-1960s, the arts are becoming more inclusive, more hybrid, and more exact in process. They exhaust everything about a subject, giving images a higher resolution by appropriating the particular process or object itself, as in Andy Warhol's Campbell's Soup tin-can paintings, Brillo box constructions, and silk-screened photos of celebrities and himself; or composer Anthony Brown's performance of Duke Ellington's hybrid composition "Far East Suite," where he translates the score using the particular instruments and scales that originally served as Ellington's inspiration. Just as modernism parodied the Victorian age of ornament, postmodernism parodies modernism, breaking away from parlors, galleries, or salons full of rich or elite patrons in order to travel to deserts and fields for site-specific installations, to cheer at poetry slams, and to experiment with computers. The establishment of black, Hispanic, and Asian American studies programs reveals the populist impulse of postmodernism. Where scholars once dissected classical literature, ballet, and opera, they now also consider it worthy to investigate the dynamics of blues, jazz, rock and roll, hip-hop, advertisements, and movies. For feminism, a daughter of postmodernism, the modernist icon Sigmund Freud is considered a fraud. In fiction, the modernists' standbys of character development and plot are jettisoned, causing some critics to accuse postmodern writers of creating cartoons, especially when a modernist icon such as Karl Marx morphs into the Marx Brothers. Postmodernism becomes so fashionable by the end of the 1970s, simultaneously invoked by intellectuals, journalists, sociologists and psychologists, and the advertising and fashion industries, that hierarchical distinctions like "high" or "low" culture and art become blurred. By the 1980s, postmodern aesthetic theories are ablaze with new jargon, such as the term *deconstruction* that particularly catches both popular and scholarly attention. It posits that all forms of communication—images, writing, speech, gestures, buildings, etc.—can be considered as texts that no longer have one objective truth, but are ambiguous, shifting in meaning and open to self-reference for nations, cultures, genders, classes, races, ages, and every individual.

create a national model program, proving that people with disabilities can and should be able to live, study, and travel where they want, as independently as possible, and, if qualified, be hired regardless of their disabilities. They become an important advocate to change building codes and public access regulations, that will become standard in construction and rennovation of buildings, sidewalk curbs, subways, theaters, etc.

WORLD EVENTS

• General Idi Amin, commander of Uganda's armed forces, overthrows President Milton Obote while he is out of the country. Amin will hold absolute power for the next eight years. He destroys much of Uganda's infrastructure, accomplishing this by using the country's funds to buy arms and expand the army, placing army officers in charge of confiscated businesses taken after his 1972 expulsion of all resident Asians, which the new owners bankrupt. The Asians, mostly Indians and Pakistanis, were an envied minority who had dominated commerce and professions in the country. Amin's troops massacre 300,000 people, including many soldiers from ethnic groups in Obote's area. In 1979 Amin is driven into exile by Tanzanian troops, who stage a counterinvasion of Uganda. In 1981, Obote is returned to power.

• The new nation of Bangladesh is established when, after a brutal civil war, East Pakistan secedes from West Pakistan. Sheik Mujibur Rahman will become prime minister in 1972.

• The People's Republic of China formally joins the United Nations.

• Canada becomes the first country in the world to adopt a multiculturalism policy, called "Multiculturalism Within a Bilingual Framework," introduced by Prime Minister Pierre Trudeau to initially address French Canadians' concerns about equality with English Canadian charter groups. Within the year Trudeau advocates a more inclusive multiculturalism that acknowledges the diversity and rights of all Canadians, including aboriginal people as well as Asian, African, Latin American, and Middle Eastern immigrants, because, "We become less like others; we become less susceptible to cultural, social or political envelopment by others."

1972

ARTS AND LITERATURE

• Architect Charles Jencks is often cited for popularizing the term *postmodernism*, with his proclamation that "modernism" ends at 3:32 P.M. on July 15, 1972, in St. Louis, when three of the eleven-story towers called the Pruitt-Igoe Public Housing Project are demolished. (Designed in modernist/International style by Minoru Yamasaki [1912–1986] and George Hellmuth, Pruitt-Igoe was completed with great expense and fanfare in 1956. But owing to various complications, its stripped-down, cold high-rise design becomes so dangerous and hated by its all black inhabitants that the city dynamites the thirty remaining towers in 1973.)

• Steve Paxton (b. 1939) invents contact improvisation, a duet form of "dance sport," which, through its emphasis upon the give-and-take of weight, based upon trust, counterbalance, and support, finds new, gender-neutral solutions to partnering in dance. It takes inspiration from Asian martial arts as well as social dance, aerobics, and sports. Contact improvisation, in its recognition that anyone can dance, actively reflects countercultural beliefs in individual expression, mutual acceptance, and tolerance of differences.

• *Bless Me, Ultima,* a novel by Rudolfo Anaya (b. 1937) about a New Mexico–based village *curandera,* a folk healer, is published. Anaya, who was born in the village of

Pastura, New Mexico, sees himself as a storyteller bringing back balance and harmony by returning to the pre-Columbian literature and thought of Aztlán, the mythic homeland of the Aztecs, which corresponds to the five-state area of today's American Southwest. It sells over 300,000 copies, and continues to remain in print.

• Herbert Bayer (b. Austria, 1900; d. U.S., 1985) is commissioned by the city of Kent, Washington, to design Mill Creek Canyon Earthworks, an earth sculpture that doubles as a drainage system for the city. Bayer combines art and engineering to solve the city's problem of immoderate flows of water that are severely eroding a canyon near a residential area during periods of heavy rain, by containing excess water within an earthen ring and its surrounding moat.

• Choreographer Garth Fagan (b. 1941, Jamaica) starts a new pickup dance company he calls "Bottom of the Bucket But . . ." He is able to develop a new technique and style by training African American men and women who never thought about being dancers whom he finds in Rochester, New York, nearby the State University of New York at Brockport, where he is a professor. The company, renamed Bucket Dance Theatre, is an immediate hit in its 1978 debut at the Brooklyn Academy of Music's Dance Black America, premiering *From Before,* which is set to music by Ralph MacDonald.

• Pink Floyd's album *The Dark Side of the Moon* is released. It uses ensembles of synthesizers, and also uses tape sound collages, called concrete tracks, as interludes between tunes.

• Installation artist Adrian Piper (b. 1948) helps introduce identity politics into conceptualism when she mines her racist experiences as a light-skinned black woman from a middle-class upbringing with a private integrated school education. In a series of hand-altered black-and-white self-portraits, called "Mythic Being," she documents performance pieces made between 1972 and 1975, in which she scrambles race and gender by appearing in drag as a working-class black or Latino man with a huge Afro, dark glasses, and handlebar mustache, and to which she attaches balloon speech quotations, such as "I embody everything you most hate and fear."

• Leonard Bernstein's powerful *Mass,* juxtaposing classical, pop, and musical theater forms, opens the Kennedy Center for the Performing Arts in Washington, D.C.

GOVERNMENT AND POLITICS

• On February 17, Richard Nixon travels to China for a week, after his national security adviser, Henry Kissinger, lays the groundwork for a series of meetings with Premier Zhou Enlai and Chairman Mao Zedong. These meetings lead to an opening of trade and cultural exchange between the two nations, and the admitting of China into the United Nations (and the expelling of Taiwan).

• On June 17, during Nixon's campaign for a second term, five burglars wearing surgical gloves and possessing cameras, walkie-talkies, and electronic surveillance equipment are arrested while in the process of stealing papers from the Democratic Party's national headquarters in a Washington, D.C., office and hotel complex known as Watergate. One man, James McCord, is a retired employee of the CIA, and two others also claim ties to the CIA. This abuse of power is discovered because an African American security guard, Frank Wills, notices a tape over a lock during his regular rounds, and calls the police. A federal grand jury indicts the five burglars and two former White House aides on September 15. A long series of coverups, hush-money payoffs, and other "dirty tricks" allow Nixon to be elected to a second term by a landslide. The Democratic ticket of George McGovern and JFK's brother-in-law, Sargent Shriver, only carries Massachusetts and Washington, D.C. However, the incident, which becomes known as the "Watergate" scandal, will haunt Nixon's second term, driving him from office before his four years are served.

• Three important pieces of congressional legislation mandating equal rights for women are passed this year. The Equal Rights Amendment (ERA), stating that "equality of rights under the law shall not be denied or abridged by the U.S. or by any State on account of sex," passes both houses of Congress and is sent to the states for ratification by 1979. (The amendment requires ratification by a minimum of thirty-eight state legislatures. Although thirty states agree to comply within a year, ERA ratification stalls until 1978, when Congress grants an extension until 1982.) The Equal Employment Opportunity Act bars sex discrimination in employment; and Title IX of the 1972 Educational Amendments to the Civil Rights Act enforces sex equality in education. This last act jump-starts the whole field of women's sports by denying funds for boys and men's sports to schools that do not provide an equal amount for women's sports.

🄿 1982

• In what becomes known as *Roe v. Wade*, the Supreme Court responds to two suits, one from Texas, where all abortions are presently prohibited except to save a mother's life *(Roe v. Wade)* and one from Georgia *(Doe v. Bolton).* Anonymous women seeking abortions had brought both suits against state law-enforcement officials. The Court's 1973 decision, 7–2 in favor, stands in part on the side of a woman's right to control her own body, by granting her the inviolable right to an abortion in the first trimester of pregnancy, and at all times placing "the life and health of the mother" first. But the Court also rules that after the first thirteen weeks, state laws can regulate abortions to ensure maternal health, although the option cannot be prohibited until the last ten weeks of pregnancy. At the time the ruling is made, only four states (Alaska, Hawaii, Washington, and New York) have rulings that are in compliance, so that the laws of forty-six states become unconstitutional and have to be revised.

• The American Indian Movement (AIM) organizes the Trail of Broken Treaties Caravan, traveling from San Francisco to Washington, D.C., to bring attention to the long history of treaties that have been broken by the U.S. government. As it crosses the country the caravan grows bigger, until by the time it arrives in the nation's capital, it is a four-mile-long procession. Its participants present a twenty-point position paper to Nixon's administration representative, Assistant Secretary of the Interior Harrison Loesch. Six hundred to 800 people occupy the federal BIA building for six days, until the administration negotiates an end to the occupation two days before an election rather than risk a military action. Thirty-two AIM leaders are indicted later on charges of grand larceny and arson stemming from the occupation, and the FBI places AIM on its

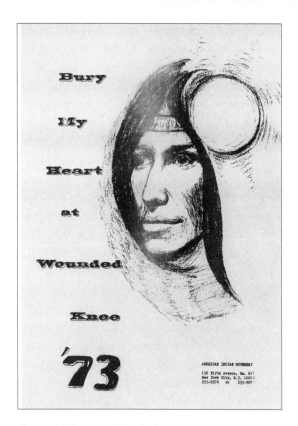

"Bury My Heart at Wounded Knee '73." Poster printed by Come Unity Press. *(Library of Congress, Prints and Photographs Division)*

counterintelligence program (COINTELPRO) watch. Indian rights are placed on the national agenda after this event.

⊡ 1973

BUSINESS AND INDUSTRY

• All U.S. airports install machines that screen passengers and their luggage at security gates before they may board an airplane, a measure instituted by the Federal Aviation Administration under the Department of Transportation to prevent possible hijackers or other terrorists from carrying weapons onto planes.

• Atari, Inc., founded by engineers Nolan Bushnell and Ted Dabney, releases the first commercially successful home version of a video game, *Hockey Pong*. By the 1980s, Atari leads a multimillion-dollar industry with their innovative gaming cartridges, two-player action, and marketing consoles that hook up to TV sets. Although Atari goes bankrupt and liquidates its inventory by 1991, owing to mismanagement and overproduction, it has contributed significantly to the popularization of video games; by the turn of the century its cartridges are collector's items.

SCIENCE AND TECHNOLOGY

• The Advanced Research Projects Agency (ARPA) is renamed the Defense Advance Research Projects Agency (DARPA) by the Department of Defense. Its purpose is to provide a secure and survivable communications mechanism for organizations engaged in defense-related research.

• Ray Tomlinson, of the Cambridge, Massachusetts, computer consulting business Bolt Beranek and Newman (BBN), develops the first electronic mail program. Known as "e-mail," it becomes a central ingredient to the success of the Internet by allowing people to write and instantly send letters without having to mail them with an envelope and stamp. Tomlinson also chooses the @ sign from the punctuation keys on his Model 33 Teletype to mean "at"; it becomes part of a new addressing system of domain names necessitated when Internet traffic gets too large to process the volume of simple computer names. Lawrence G. Roberts, director of ARPA's Information Processing Technique Office, creates the first e-mail utility program to manage files, list addresses, and selectively read, forward, and respond to messages. Used by ARPANET to send and coordinate messages across its network, e-mail catches on quickly, becoming the largest network application for the next decade.

• The Alto I, considered the first display-based, networked, interactive personal computer, is invented at Xerox Corporation's Palo Alto Research Center (known as Xerox PARC). The PARC team develops a graphical user interface that integrates the ideas of Douglas Engelbart, a mouse, a local disk drive, and a keyboard. Although the Alto itself will not become a commercially successful product, its solutions continue to be integral elements of basic PC design.

WORLD EVENTS

• Greenpeace, an international organization of environmental activists, begins to capture worldwide media attention when David McTaggart (b. Canada, 1932–2001) sails his boat *Greenpeace III* into the Mururoa atoll to protest French atmospheric atomic tests. Largely because of their tactics, France does agree to stop atmospheric testing in 1974, but maintains the right to continue underground testing. From 1976 to 1980, Greenpeace opens up offices in various European and American cities, and in New Zealand and Australia, to support their actions as "environmental commandos" in confrontational campaigns to save the whales, protect Antarctica from mining and oil drilling, end dumping of nuclear waste in oceans, and stop nuclear testing.

• The United Nations ratifies a Biological Warfare Ban Treaty to prohibit any nation from developing, acquiring, or stockpiling chemical and biological weapons while working on vaccines and other protective measures. In 1974 the U.S. ratifies the treaty, which supplements the 1925 Geneva Protocol, and it takes effect globally in 1975. In the 1990s, under the Clinton administration, the U.S. Pentagon and CIA institute secret germ-warfare research projects involving gene splicing, germ bombs, and anthrax. Rumored to push the limits of the present treaty, the research is said to be the reason the George W. Bush administration refuses to sign a stronger germ warfare treaty in 2001.

1973

ARTS AND LITERATURE

• *Yardbird Reader* and *Y'Bird* magazines are edited over the next five years in Berkeley by Ishmael Reed (b. 1938) and Al Young (b. 1939), to showcase the work of young writers. They offer new points of view by writers from a variety of backgrounds who have not generally been seen in print. The magazines are the first to publish writers of future national prominence such as Yusef Komunyakaa (b. 1947), Leslie Silko (b. 1948), Thulani Davis (as Thulani Nkabinde), Jessica Hagedorn (b. 1949), Henry Louis Gates Jr. (b. 1950), Terry McMillan (b. 1951), and Ntozake Shange (b. 1948). An excerpt from Shange's choreopoem, *for colored girls who have considered suicide / when the rainbow is enuf,* is first published in *Yardbird Reader,* and later becomes a Broadway hit. *Yardbird Reader* #3 becomes a classic because it is the first to assemble members of the emerging Asian American renaissance. *TriQuarterly* magazine designates *Yardbird Reader* as one of the most important literary magazines of the twentieth century.

GOVERNMENT AND POLITICS

• The Watergate scandals begin to be uncovered, spurred on by a combination of the rulings of Judge John J. Sirica, the investigative journalism of *Washington Post* reporters Bob Woodward and Carl Bernstein, and a Senate investigatory committee headed by Sam Ervin Jr. of North Carolina. On Dec. 8, Judge Sirica succeeds in getting President Nixon to turn over the first group of tape recordings that Nixon has revealed, on live television, were made by automatic tape recorders he secretly ordered installed in the Oval Office of the White House. The transcripts will prove that the president and his men plotted coverup strategies, committed "dirty tricks," including the Watergate break-in, made payoffs, and took illegal campaign contributions in their efforts to ensure Nixon's reelection.

• The United Nations gives the Puerto Rican people the right to decide their own future as a nation. In 1978 the UN recognizes Puerto Rico as a colony of the U.S.

• President Nixon creates the Energy Policy Office to deal with the increasing incidents of energy supply shortages. During the winter, Midwestern states close schools and factories because of shortages of heating oil. In October, when the Arab oil-producing countries place an embargo on exports to the U.S., gasoline prices rise and people panic as long lines of cars are forced to wait to fill up at service stations. President Nixon signs a bill to construct a 789-mile oil pipeline from Alaska to the lower forty-eight states that will be completed by 1980. He promotes this major undertaking as a way to make the U.S. independent of the oil cartels. He also suggests dropping the speed limit to fifty miles per hour, instituting year-round daylight savings time, and relaxing environmental standards. By 1974, a fifty-five-mile-per-hour speed limit is established nationwide, with the side effect of dramatically lowering traffic fatalities.

• When AIM leaders Russell Means and Dennis Banks return to the Pine Ridge Reservation in South Dakota after the BIA occupation in Washington, the chairman of the Pine Ridge tribal council, Richard "Dicky" Wilson, bans AIM activities. Wilson calls in federal marshals to protect the occupied BIA building and uses federal highway funds to hire a police force (called "Dickie's goons" by the demonstrators). Banks and Means are both arrested. During the winter, several hundred Oglala Sioux and their supporters from other tribes occupy Wounded Knee on the Pine Ridge for 71 days. Their action is taken at the request of Oglala traditional leaders, who charge that Wilson's tribal government is corrupt and in conspiracy with the BIA paramilitary police. The FBI, BIA police, and U.S. Marshal Service surround the occupiers during a ten-week standoff. When the U.S. Army's 82nd Airborne Division is called in, they stage a military attack in which two Indians are killed. Eventually 185 people are indicted on charges of conspiracy, burglary, civil disorder, assault, and "interfering with federal officers," generating one of the largest and most complex series of political trials in the history of the U.S. Before the occupation ends with an agreement in which "the U.S. promises to investigate the tribal government, to curb the terror on the reservation, and to reexamine the 1868 treaty." However, the agreement dissipates with a "meaningless" exchange of letters, and three years after the occupation, at least twenty Wounded Knee "sympathizers" are reported killed, and others beaten, by the so-called "goon squad."

• President Richard Nixon signs the Endangered Species Act, which offers protections for species threatened by development. In 1987 it will be used for a program that helps restore California condors, placing the last surviving vultures in protective custody at the San Diego and Los Angeles zoos.

BUSINESS AND INDUSTRY

• The Universal Product Code (UPC), the twelve-number bar-code mark that is used today on almost all marketed items, is invented by IBM and approved for use in 1973. The lines of each bar-code mark encode the manufacturer's identity and an assigned product number. A packet of Wrigley's chewing gum, with a bar code printed on the wrapper, is the first product to utilize the computerized system when it is checked out at the Marsh Supermarket in Troy, Ohio, on June 26, 1974, at 8:01 A.M. When the UPC is passed over a laser-beam scanner at the checkout counter, it transfers information concerning price, size, color, manufacture, and stock inventory into the retailer's database computer in a matter of nanoseconds. This allows businesses to keep accurate track of inventory, to manage and control stock by assessing what sells and what doesn't, so that their use of warehouse space can be maximized. Customers also benefit from a 10-percent speed-up in service and completely itemized receipts.

SCIENCE AND TECHNOLOGY

• Transmission Control Protocol/Internet Protocol (TCP/IP), an internetwork design that interprets addresses and routes computer-

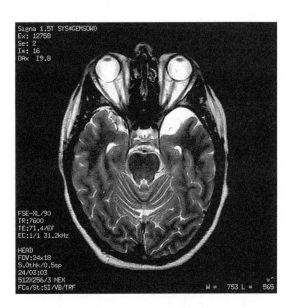

MRI image of a human brain (Kaufman, Bernadette M. [MED], *Courtesy of General Electric Medical Systems, Waukesha, Wisconsin*)

to-computer communications, is invented by Vint Cerf from Stanford and Bob Kahn from DARPA. Initially used by academic, government, and business researchers on the ARPANET, by 1983, in a refined version, it will become the standard over the Internet around the world.

• Electrical engineer Martin Cooper, a general manager of the systems division at Motorola, invents the first portable handheld cell phone and completes the first successful call, dialing from a midtown Manhattan street corner to speak into a land-phone at his main competitor, Bell Labs, which is located in New Jersey. Called the Dyna-Tac, the cell phone is packaged in a 2.5-pound unit that allows the user to dial, listen, and talk for up to thirty-five minutes before it needs recharging. Although AT&T introduced the idea of cellular communications systems in 1947, they confined its use to portable non-cellular car phones, which required installing a thirty-pound unit in a car's trunk. Cooper's idea, to make cell phones portable, is the forerunner of wireless communication, in which people can take phones anywhere.

• Medicine gains two high-tech diagnostic tools that allow physicians to see cross-sectional images of internal organs. First, Allan Cormack (b. 1924, South Africa) of Tufts University and Godfrey Hounsfield of the British company EMI introduce their computerized axial tomography (CAT) scanner, a computer-assisted X-ray machine capable of generating 3-D images of soft tissues, especially bone, for which they receive the 1979 Nobel Prize for Physiology or Medicine. Second, Raymond V. Damadian invents the nuclear magnetic resonance (NMR; also known as MRI) scanner, a device capable of higher-resolution images than CAT by using magnets instead of X rays. However, because of their lower price, traditional X rays and CAT scans are often preferred.

Culture and Society

• The National Black Feminist Organization (NBF) is founded to advocate for the concerns of African American women, which they contend are not carefully addressed by the existing feminist organizations, which speak mostly for European Americans, or the black liberation organizations, which speak mainly for African American men.

• The board of the American Psychiatric Association (APA) votes to reverse its position on homosexuality, removing it from the *Diagnostic and Statistical Manual of Mental Disorders*. They decide it is not a mental illness and cannot be considered a "sexual perver-

sion" because it does not "regularly cause emotional distress" or produce "impairment of social functioning." This ruling culminates a five-year battle by the Gay Activists Alliance, giving gays and lesbians a powerful tool to fight for their civil rights in housing, and to combat on-the-job discrimination, because the ruling also allows that there is no reason "a gay man or woman could not be just as healthy, just as effective, just as law-abiding, and just as capable of functioning as any heterosexual. . . . Furthermore . . . that laws that discriminated against them in housing or in employment were unjustified." In 1974 the membership of the APA will vote in agreement.

World Events

• The president of Chile, Dr. Salvador Allende Gossens, the first president to be elected president in a non-Communist country on a Marxist-Leninist ticket, is overthrown and killed by a military junta. Army Chief of Staff Augusto Pinochet Ugarte emerges as the new president. The junta immediately suspends the parliament, bans any political activity, and announces the arrest of 13,000 people, ending a forty-six-year era of constitutional government. A 1991 commission reports that over 2,000 people were killed by the government between 1973 and 1990, when Pinochet finally leaves office.

• An Arab oil embargo creates an energy crisis in the U.S., which also effects Europe and Japan, after Saudi Arabia, Yemen, Kuwait, and Libya go through with their promise to retaliate if the U.S. supports Israel during a three-week conflict known as the Yom Kippur War, or October War. The war involves Egypt and Syria, who attempt to win back lands occupied by Israel since the 1967 Six-Day War, including the Sinai peninsula to the Suez Canal. They surprise Israel with an invasion on October 6, the Jewish high holy day of Yom Kippur. They gain positions in the Sinai Peninsula and the Golan Heights, backed with Soviet weapons financed by Saudi Arabia and Kuwait. The U.S.-backed Israeli forces counterattack, crossing the Suez Canal into Egypt as they drive back the Arab forces. The war puts a severe economic strain on Israel, and in 1974 the Israelis agree to withdraw immediately from the west bank of the Suez Canal, and by 1982 to complete their withdrawal from the Sinai peninsula. The embargo causes oil prices to skyrocket, sets off double-digit inflation, and makes energy conservation a priority issue, at least for a while, in the nations of the West.

1974

ARTS AND LITERATURE

• Poets Allen Ginsberg, Diane di Prima, and Ann Waldman are invited by Tibetan-born Buddhist monk Chogyam Trungpa Rinpoche to establish a poetry program at the Naropa Institute, at Boulder, Colorado. With Ginsberg as the director, they establish the Jack Kerouac School of Disembodied Poetics. With their ambition to offer a crossroads between traditions of Western intellectual and critical thinking and Eastern doctrines and practices such as Buddhist and Hindu meditation, Naropa brings insights from the Beat Generation to new generations.

• Third World Communications (the Women's Collective) publishes the first anthology of Third World women writers, including Janice Mirikitani, Carol Lee Sanchez, Thulani Davis, Jessica Hagedorn, and Ntozake Shange,

who starts to develop her choreopoem *for colored girls who have considered suicide / when the rainbow is enuf* at a women's bar in Berkeley. The production will move on to New York City and eventually to Broadway by 1976.

• *Aiiieeeee!: An Anthology of Asian American Writers* is published, offering the first collection of Asian American writing edited by Asian Americans. The book includes essays, fiction, plays, autobiographies, biographies, and poetry by fourteen writers of Japanese, Chinese, and Filipino descent. The editors, Frank Chin, Jeffery Paul Chan, Lawson Fusao Inada, and Shawn Wong, also organize the first Asian American writers' conference at the Oakland Museum. *Aiiieeeee!* sparks a heated controversy in the Asian American community, with arguments over its editorial point of view, framed by its four male Asian American writers and scholars who are especially critical of early Asian American writing that is mostly by women.

• The Mellotron, an early sample player that uses tape loops, is built. Some versions play string or flute sounds, and the instrument is used in movie soundtracks.

GOVERNMENT AND POLITICS

• On January 4, President Nixon refuses to hand over the audio tapes on which he has secretly recorded all conversations in the Oval Office, and other documents subpoenaed by the Senate Watergate Committee. Seven White House officials are quickly indicted for perjury, and others, including Chief of Staff H. R. Haldeman and Attorney General Richard Kleindienst, resign in disgrace. On July 24 the Supreme Court orders Nixon to release more tapes. Included among the tapes to be turned

MODERN POWWOWS

The powwow form is constantly evolving. Today most powwows are intertribal celebrations that are open to Native and non-Native people. There are also hundreds of special song and dance styles that are separate from the pan-nation powwow tradition, but powwows are now part of the popular culture shared among many nations.

Powwows happen all over North America, in community halls and on college campuses, fairgrounds, and traditional sites in urban areas or Native reserves, generally occurring from March through early September and lasting anywhere from a few hours to a weekend. Throughout the Plains, for example, where there are more than 400 tribes, there is a powwow almost every weekend.

Although each powwow has its own characteristics, the form is structured on the circle radiating outward, circles within circles, a sacred place blessed by a spiritual leader. The drum, which includes the singers and drummers together, is placed at the center and is the heartbeat—without a drum there is no powwow. Powwows officially start with the Grand Entry, and continue with the Flag songs, Memorial songs, Veterans' songs, Intertribal songs, Contest songs, and the slower Quitting songs.

Dancers enter from the east and travel in the same direction as the sun, i.e., clockwise. They compete for prizes and recognition against other dancers, a practice that began sometime around 1920 and is largely responsible for the success of modern powwows. The categories of dance competitions include Men and Women's Traditional, Men's Grass, Men's Fancy, Women's Jingle Dress, and Women's Fancy Shawl.

Dancers wear different styles of costume according to the dance, creating multicolored wearable art regalia that are personal expressions of their lives, feelings, interests, family and tribal affiliations, and spiritual quest. Costumes can involve elaborate beadwork, quillwork, feathers, silver, leather, and appliqué. Dancers can add their own variations to the basic steps, new songs are written, and recently women began singing and playing the drums, a practice that used to be only for men.

Everything must be paid for because "when you come into the circle, you pay for a seat." Money or goods such as quilts and blankets are often given as honor prizes. People trade crafts and goods, and food is for sale. Storytelling and other demonstration events often occur outside of the dancing area. By the 1990s, competition for singers and dancers, which created the need for prize money, skyrockets with the profitability of casinos such as Schemitzun in Connecticut, which offers $25,000 for first place in just one of three categories in the drum contest, and awards five places per category.

over is one of a June 23, 1972, meeting, which becomes known as the "smoking gun." It reveals a conversation between Nixon and Haldeman, almost immediately following the Watergate break-in, where Nixon approves a plan to obstruct an FBI Watergate investigation.

• On August 9, after the House Judiciary Committee recommends that President Richard Nixon be impeached on three charges, he becomes the first U.S. president to resign from office. Vice President Gerald Ford is appointed president.

• On September 8, President Ford pardons former President Nixon of any federal crimes he may have committed while president.

• In January the U.S. Supreme Court rules that, in *Lau v. Nichols,* the San Francisco Unified School District discriminated against Kinney Lau by depriving him of meaningful participation in his schooling when he was not offered instruction that worked with his English language problem. This ruling becomes a foundation for the establishment and preservation of bilingual programs throughout the country.

• Congress passes the Equal Educational Opportunity Act of 1974, to create equality in public schools. In addition to requiring schools to provide equal facilities and access to teachers in public education, the bill also makes bilingual education programs available for Hispanic students and others who have trouble with the English language, to provide programs that help them become proficient in English.

BUSINESS AND INDUSTRY

• The Watergate scandal shakes up business-as-usual in Washington lobbying circles. Pre-Watergate, it was necessary to engage a few key players who wielded their contacts with key members of Congress in order to influence votes on legislation. The post-Watergate system changes to a professional, corporate model that involves the creation of large public-relations firms that go outside the Washington sphere of influence in order to influence the public at large. The firms apply pressure on members of Congress through a variety of approaches. They set up public-affairs think-tank services to research issues, engage in media debates, conduct polls, and generate greater support on

issues through direct-mail canvassing to the public.

SCIENCE AND TECHNOLOGY

• The U.S. space probe *Mariner 10* transmits photographs of Venus.

• The first U.S. experimental space station, Skylab, is launched. It completes a photographic series of the solar system and surveys the resources of the earth.

• Computer visionary Theodor Holm Nelson self-publishes his book *Computer Lib/Dream Machines,* which outlines his ideas for a "docuverse" or library of multimedia reference materials, foreshadowing the World Wide Web (WWW) of today. WWW is the protocol, or communication network, invented and implemented by information technologist Tim Berners-Lee in 1989 and released by CERN in 1992. He applies the term *hypertext,* coined by Nelson in 1965, to describe the formatting system that the WWW will use to allow viewers to follow links from particular words, names, or phrases on a document, by clicking the mouse, to reveal other documents with related information.

🔲 1989

1975

ARTS AND LITERATURE

• One of the first pan-tribal powwows takes place in Ann Arbor, Michigan, as a modern-day expression of Indian ways as well as a vehicle to bring back past traditions. Although there is no general agreement as to when powwows started, the practice didn't exist before the reservation system was enforced by the U.S. government, and it is usually said that the

SOUTHEAST ASIANS IN AMERICA

In the first two years after the Communist takeover, 165,000 Vietnamese refugees are admitted into the U.S. By 1985, 643,200 Vietnamese refugees will be living in the U.S. Starting in 1977, the attorney general sets a quota of 15,000 Southeast Asians per year; the quota is raised to 25,000 in 1978 and 50,000 in 1979. Although most arrive in the country on an emergency basis, many extend their temporary status as religious persecution, political repression, and severe economic measures under the Communist governments in Indochina persuade many to become permanent residents or naturalized U.S. citizens. The first refugee group, composed largely of South Vietnamese, are highly educated urbanites with professional job skills. About 50 percent are Christians. Although they often work at jobs that are not commensurate with their skills or former status, most of the first wave of Vietnamese have rebuilt careers in their fields or set up small businesses. Among the later waves of Vietnamese refugees, small-business growth increases from about 5,000 to more than 25,000 between 1982 and 1987. Later waves of refugees also include Cambodians, ethnic Chinese from Vietnam, and Laotians. These people tend to come from rural areas, have less education, fewer skills, and have had more traumatic journeys to the U.S., often arriving from refugee camps in Thailand and other first-asylum countries. Many have a difficult time adapting to U.S. culture, as they have little or no English and few survival skills applicable to life in the U.S. They often remain unemployed or hold low-paying jobs, requiring four to ten years of ongoing economic help from public assistance programs.

1870s–1880s was the beginning. Powwows experience a resurgence in the 1970s with the rise of the pan-Indian movement—a time, Vine Deloria says, "when aboriginal peoples of North America reversed the trend of four hundred years and began to rebuild their ancient customs and traditions."

• Frank Chin's play *The Year of the Dragon* receives a PBS *Theater in America* production. It is published, along with his play *The Chickencoop Chinaman*, by University of Washington Press, in 1981. The *New York Times* says the play "barges through the comfortable stereotypes of the Asian American—the quiet, hardworking contented character who keeps to himself, rarely bothering the white community . . . as a portrait of an Asian

American's struggle for identity, the play is a searing statement, a powerful cry."

GOVERNMENT AND POLITICS

• The U.S. forces quit Vietnam on April 30, two decades after their first arrival: North Vietnamese forces capture Saigon as the last Americans, eleven Marines, are evacuated by emergency helicopter airlift from the roof of the U.S. embassy, which is completely ransacked once they have left. President Duong Van Minh surrenders Saigon unconditionally to the North Vietnamese Communists. Vietnam is reunited under Communist rule, as the Democratic Republic of Vietnam, with Saigon renamed Ho Chi Minh City. On April 17, Phnom Penh, the capital city of Cambodia, falls

"The Grass Dance," a powwow dance form performed by the American Indian Dance Theatre. *(Photo © by Don Perdue)*

THE BUREAU OF RECLAMATION

T. N. Narasimhan

Among the most aggressive users of civil engineering in the world, the U.S. Bureau of Reclamation spent billions of federal dollars intercepting rivers, storing and diverting water, and "reclaiming" wetlands for agriculture. It prided itself in "making deserts bloom." While engineering had spectacular success in the short term, degradation of land and the decimation of fish and wildlife habitat began showing up by the 1950s, and by the 1970s the long-term damage of aggressive irrigation could not be overlooked anymore. The bureau underwent a remarkable metamorphosis. It concluded that it had built all the dams that it could possibly build in the West, and that from now on its mission should be one of conservation and management rather than dam-building. The change signified a recognition by engineers and water managers that the Earth is a finite planet and that long-term management of water involves a balance between science and engineering on the one hand and ecosystems, environment, and society on the other.

to Khmer Rouge troops. The U.S. embassy is closed, and Americans leave Cambodia also.

• On May 7, President Ford signs a proclamation declaring that the U.S. has come to the end "of the Vietnam era," and which terminates wartime veteran's benefits because "America is no longer at war."

• After a shoot-out at Pine Ridge, South Dakota, Leonard Peltier, a Sioux-AIM activist, is jailed and then convicted two years later for the murder of two FBI agents. Although he maintains his innocence, he remains in jail today.

• Congress passes the Voting Rights Act Amendment, extending the provisions of the original Voting Rights Act of 1965 by making the national ban on literacy tests permanent, and making bilingual ballots a requirement in certain locations, a critical change for Hispanic Americans and Asian Americans.

BUSINESS AND INDUSTRY

• The U.S. government files suit against six cigarette manufacturers for failure to adequately display health warnings.

SCIENCE AND TECHNOLOGY

• The Apollo Soyuz Test Project, the first cooperative U.S.-Soviet space mission, docks the three-man Apollo spacecraft with the two man Soviet *Soyuz 19*.

• The first personal computer, the Altair 8800, is introduced in the U.S. in the form of a $400 kit that has 256 bytes of random-access memory (RAM), a convenient storage location, and one component of a computer's processing speed. Modern personal computers have up to 1 million times more RAM.

CULTURE AND SOCIETY

• Before this year, very few Vietnamese or other Southeast Asians lived in the U.S. This changes dramatically just before the fall of Saigon as the Vietnam War comes to an end, when the first wave of Southeast Asian refugees, a group of about 86,000 South Vietnamese American employees and their dependents, arrives in the U.S.

WORLD EVENTS

• Angola and Mozambique become independent from Portugal.

• The world's population reaches 4 billion.

1976

ARTS AND LITERATURE

• The Before Columbus Foundation is founded by writers Ishmael Reed and Victor Hernandez Cruz to promote and disseminate contemporary American multicultural literature.

• *Einstein on the Beach,* a four-act opera that is a multidisciplinary collaboration by director/designer Robert Wilson (b. 1941) and composer Philip Glass (b. 1937), with choreography by Andy deGroat, and a cast of thirty-six featured performers, has its American premiere before a full house at the Metropolitan Opera in New York, following a European tour. The opera, which is four and a half hours long, is a "poetical interpretation" of Albert Einstein, in which "the person replaces the idea of plot as story." Glass and Wilson center the work around two quotations from Einstein: "The most beautiful experience one can have is the mysterious. It is the fundamental emotion that

Founders of the Before Columbus Foundation meeting in Albuquerque, New Mexico, in celebration of the Pueblo Revolt of 1680. Left to right: Simon Ortiz, David Meltzer, Ishmael Reed, Rudolfo Anaya, Victor Hernandez Cruz, Bob Callahan, Gundars Strads, and Shawn Wong. *(Courtesy of the Before Columbus Foundation, Gundars Strads)*

stands at the cradle of true art and true science"; and "In the universe, everything that happens has a reason, even it we don't know what it is." Glass goes outside Western traditions to find his hypnotic, rhythmic sound, based on repetitive-sounding phrases that actually change constantly.

• Christo (b. Bulgaria, 1935, as Christo Vladimirov Javacheff) and Jeanne Claude (b. 1935), his wife and collaborator, succeed in fulfilling their idea to create a large-scale, site-specific installation called *Running Fence* in Northern California. From April through October, a twenty-four-and-a-half-mile-long,

eighteen-foot-high nylon curtain is strung on cable that stretches like a ribbon along the coastline, fields, and farmlands of Marin and Sonoma Counties until it eventually dips into the Pacific Ocean. Costs of doing the work are covered with sales of drawings, photos, and film that document their process.

• Many artists are concerned with creating "living environments" that involve "real life" labors in order to be realized: David Ireland, a Northern California installation artist, builds an environment based on his own life when he begins renovating his own home, where he carefully integrates found objects left by previous owners and their layers of remodeling into the changes that he makes. Bonnie Sherk, another Northern California artist, locates *Farm,* which is a working farm, under the San Francisco freeway, where she gardens and grows plants, keeps animals, and presents events that are related to the environment. New York–based artist Mierle Ukeles (b. 1939) sets up an office/studio within the city's sanitation department, where she focuses public attention on all aspects of maintenance, both for private citizens in their homes and the professional workers who provide sanitation services.

• California guitarist William Ackerman founds Windham Hill Records as an acoustic-instrument exponent of the improvised impressionist-like music that will come to be called New Age music. The success of such Windham Hill artists as solo pianist George Winston and guitarist Alex De Grassi helps create a quiet boom in this field which also features the more jazz-oriented harpist Andreas Vollenweider, keyboardist Steven Halpern, and the American Indian flutist R. Carlos Nakai.

GOVERNMENT AND POLITICS

• Georgia Governor Jimmy Carter (b. 1924) defeats sitting President Gerald Ford in a close election. He is the first southerner to be elected president in a century and a half. His victory proves the power of the African American vote, which turns out with a 90-percent majority for Carter from both North and South that counterbalances the preference of southern whites for the Republican candidate Gerald Ford. Carter's vice president is Walter Mondale. He appoints many African Americans to high level positions in the administration and ambassadorial posts, including Patricia Harris as

Secretary of Housing and Urban Development and Andrew Young as ambassador to the United Nations. The U.S. will maintain peace throughout his four years in office. Carter will help Israel and Egypt come to an agreement on their first treaty, the "Framework for Peace," at the Camp David Accords.

• The U.S. Bureau of Reclamation makes a major turnaround in its water-management strategies, changing from construction projects to conservation and management after the Grand Teton Dam collapses on the Snake River in Idaho, causing a major disaster that kills eleven people and costs $1 billion in damages. The tragedy brings the concerns of politicians and environmentalists together.

BUSINESS AND INDUSTRY

• The first genetic engineering company, Genentech, Inc., founded by the UCSF's Herbert Boyer and venture capitalist Robert Swanson, is considered to represent the birth of biotechnology. It locates in South San Francisco, and recruits scientists from universities by agreeing to let them publish their work, a practice not permitted by most drug companies. In 1977, Boyer and geneticist Stanley Cohen manufacture the first human protein (somatostatin) by inserting human DNA into bacteria. This innovation, called recombinant DNA or gene splicing, produces the first human protein by splicing a gene into bacteria. In 1978 they clone human insulin, the first drug produced by genetic engineering, which Genentech licenses to Eli Lilly and Company in 1982, for treatment of diabetes. In 1985, Genentech starts to sell a human growth hormone for children whose bodies do not produce enough of the hormone. And in 1987 it receives FDA approval to mar-

THE SIDEWALK OF HIGH ART

Miguel Algarin

Nuyorican (New York + Puerto Rican) 1. Originally Puerto Rican epithet for those of Puerto Rican heritage born in New York: their Spanish was different (Spanglish), their way of dress and look were different. They were a stateless people (like most U.S. poets) until the Café became their homeland. 2. After Algarin and Pinero, a proud poet speaking New York Puerto Rican. 3. A denizen of the Nuyorican Poets Café. 4. New York's riches.

Nuyorican language is no longer the property of Puerto Ricans speaking in a blend of English and Spanish, it is now more like one of the dialects at the edges of the Roman Empire, which were once called vulgar but are now the Spanish, Italian, and Portuguese of modern Europe. . . . Gone are the days when English would remain the only means of expression for North American artists. It is clear that today alternate systems of speech are growing increasingly popular and creatively alluring. Spanish . . . is not about to disappear and in fact will continue to grow in importance as the economic relationship between the Southern and Northern hemispheres begins to equalize.

🅟 1973

ket Activase, a tissue plasminogen activator, or TPA, a drug that helps restore blood flow after heart attacks, and is credited with saving countless lives.

SCIENCE AND TECHNOLOGY

• U.S. spacecraft *Viking I* and *Viking II*, launched in 1975, make soft landings on Mars. They sample soil, wind, and atmosphere, conduct experiments to determine the existence of past or present life, and transmit images of the planet back to Earth. The missions discover volcanoes, canyons, craters, and evidence of surface water, though no signs of life.

CULTURE AND SOCIETY

• The Episcopal Church ordains its first woman priest.

WORLD EVENTS

• In Beijing, China, after Premier Zhou Enlai dies in January, and former Premier Mao Zedong dies in September, rivalries among different factions in the Communist leadership surface. The clique that is known as the Gang of Four includes Mao's widow, Jiang Qing. They are tried for crimes of the Cultural Revolution and convicted in 1981. Future premier Deng Xiaoping, who had sided with reformists in the Cultural Revolution, emerges as a power who starts China shifting away from Maoism and looking toward new economic policies. China and the U.S. establish full diplomatic relations in 1979, and by the early 1980s, China is importing Western technologies and management techniques.

• North and South Vietnam are reunited after twenty-two years of separation, and renamed the Socialist Republic of Vietnam. Saigon is renamed Ho Chi Minh City, and a Soviet naval base is housed at the former U.S. base at Cam Ranh Bay.

• A nuclear proliferation pact, to curb the spread of nuclear weapons, is signed by fifteen countries, including the U.S. and the USSR.

• VHS and Beta videocassette recorder formats are introduced by two competing Japanese companies, making distribution of both popular films and video art feasible. The formats are incompatible with each other. Although Sony's Beta format is originally the preferred professional format because of its picture quality, the Matsushita Company's aggressive marketing makes VHS into the dominant commercial format within twelve years.

1977

ARTS AND LITERATURE

• George Lucas (b. 1944) directs a science fiction thriller, *Star Wars,* a breakthrough movie for special effects that tells a classic tale of good versus evil with characters derived from theories of universal archetypes by psychiatrist Carl Jung and scholar Joseph Campbell. The movie sets box-office records, grossing almost $461 million.

• The Wooster Group, an experimental, collaborative ensemble theater company, is formed by director Elizabeth LeCompte (b. 1944) and actor Spalding Gray (b. 1941) in the SoHo area of New York City. They create a new, multidisciplinary form of contemporary theater by integrating up-to-date technologies of sound, film, and video into their productions, which are frequently based on cut-ups of preexisting scripts with materials from other sources such as poli-

tics, philosophy, television quiz shows, film, dance, and vaudeville.

• The Mission Cultural Center opens in San Francisco's Mission District, with the intent to support Latin American activism through the arts. The center hosts literary events, art exhibitions, and workshop classes open to the general community.

• The Systems Concepts Digital Synthesizer (SCDS), a music synthesizer built by Peter Samson for Stanford University's Center for Computer Research in Music and Acoustics (CCRMA), accelerates the synthesis of sound up to 1,000 times. With 256 digital oscillators to help composers shape the pitch and loudness of fundamental sound waves, the "Samson Box" is used for more than a decade.

• Hip-hop music starts being heard at parties in the Bronx, with DJ Grand Wizard Theodore, a Jamaican immigrant who uses turntables and a mixer to fuse beats with rapping over them.

GOVERNMENT AND POLITICS

• The Panama Canal Zone will be returned to Panama in the year 2000, under a new Panama Canal treaty agreement President Jimmy Carter talks Congress into signing. 🔲 1999

• The Congressional Hispanic Caucus is founded with private funding, to bring congressional attention to issues of concern to Hispanic people.

BUSINESS AND INDUSTRY

• Two new personal computers (PCs) hit the market. Apple Computer, founded the previous year by two college dropouts, entrepreneur Steven P. Jobs (b. 1955) and engineer

Stephen G. Wozniak, introduces the Apple II, a user-friendly PC encased in a professional-looking plastic molding and ready to use out of the box—no programming required. The Commodore PET, by Commodore Business Machines, comes preassembled with no connecting cables and at nearly half the price of the Apple II, though it is considerably less powerful and requires knowledge of the programming language Basic to operate.

SCIENCE AND TECHNOLOGY

• The Trans-Alaska oil pipeline opens after three years of intensive labor when the final weld is made at Pumps Station 3. Oil begins flowing through the pipeline, starting on June 20, from the North Slope oilfields in the Arctic Prudhoe Bay and arriving in refineries in Valdez on Prince William Sound on July 28. The $9.7-million pipeline supplies the U.S. with a new major source for oil whose North American location provides more protection and balance-of-power leverage, especially as the 1980s price wars take hold with the Middle Eastern oil cartels.

📖 1971

• The Voyager Interstellar Mission begins with the launching of two unmanned space probes, *Voyager 1* and *Voyager 2,* from Kennedy Space Center. The probes transmit photographs of Jupiter in 1979, Saturn in 1981, Uranus in 1986, and Neptune in 1989, completing their interplanetary mission and beginning their core objective of exploring interstellar space. The probes are expected to reach the boundary of the sun's magnetic field sometime between 2008 and 2012. They will exhaust their supplies of electrical power and propellant around the year 2020, whereupon their mission will end.

• The first functional synthetic gene is con-

structed at MIT. Its first commercial application, for human insulin, is approved in 1982.

CULTURE AND SOCIETY

• On August 4, after continuous strikes and sit-ins by community supporters, students, and the Chinese and Filipino American tenants of the "I Hotel" (International Hotel), the last building of old Manilatown, in today's financial district of San Francisco, is vacated, as tenants are forcibly carried out of their low-income rooms after an unsuccessful human blockade. The building is demolished in January 1979, and the lot remains vacant to this day. Its location is near an area transformed by the creation of a museum/convention center/arts park zone.

• The Immigration and Naturalization Service (INS) seizes more than 1 million undocumented workers this year.

WORLD EVENTS

• Egyptian President Anwar Sadat flies to Israel on a peace mission, the first Arab leader to visit the Jewish state since its founding in 1948.

1978

ARTS AND LITERATURE

• Luis Valdez writes and directs his World War II–era play, *Zoot Suit,* which is co-produced by the Center Theatre Group of Los Angeles, and plays to sold-out houses for eleven months, breaking all previous records for that theater. In March 1979 it becomes the first Chicano play to open on Broadway, and in 1981 it becomes a motion picture.

• The Nuyorican Poets Café is founded as a living-room salon in the Lower East Side apartment of Puerto Rican writer and scholar

Miguel Algarin (b. 1941) this year. Following the prize-winning success of his friend Miguel Pinero's (1947–1988) play *Short Eyes* and their coediting a mainstream publication, *The Nuyorican Poetry Anthology,* published in 1975, Algarin and Pinero rent a neighborhood Irish bar and relocate the Nuyorican. The café becomes an important showcase for poetry, music, video, visual art, and performance. According to publisher Nicolas Kanellos, Algarin and the café help "create a style and ideology that still dominates urban Hispanic writing today: working-class, unapologetic, and proud of its lack of schooling and polish. . . . Algarin helped to solidify the Nuyorican literary identity and foster its entrance into the larger world of American avant-garde poetics."

• Sam Shepard (b. 1943), a "star" of the 1960s underground art scene whose "rock and roll" plays are performed in New York's downtown cafés and theaters, gets mainstream honors when he wins a Pulitzer Prize for one of his family dramas, *Buried Child,* premiered this year at the Magic Theater in San Francisco, where, as writer-in-residence during the 1970s, he also writes *Curse of the Starving Class* and *True West.*

GOVERNMENT AND POLITICS

• California voters approve Proposition 13 by almost a 65-percent majority, a ballot initiative authored by Howard Jarvis and Paul Gann, cutting $7 billion off the amount of property tax revenue by placing a cap on local property tax rates, and ensuring a loss of $7 billion in revenues for public services. This vote anticipates a national trend that will be carried forward at the federal level by the Reagan administration, supporting cutbacks in government spending and increases in personal income through lower taxation, even if it means accepting the loss of government services. Its passage also starts a new political era in many states, whereby yes-or-no voter referenda decide policy questions, rather than legislation.

• The U.S. Supreme Court upholds the ruling of the Illinois State Supreme Court for the right of the National Socialist Party of America, aka the American Nazis, to assemble peacefully and march through Skokie, Illinois, a largely Jewish town.

• The Supreme Court rules, in *University of California Regents v. Bakke,* that Allan Bakke, a white man, has suffered illegal discrimination and must be admitted to the medical school at the University of California, Davis. Bakke contests that, owing to affirmative-action practices, he was not admitted to the school, and sues UC Davis on grounds of reverse discrimination. The ruling undermines one major legal tactic, racial quotas, that has been used for several decades as a means of leveling the playing field and creating equal opportunities for minority applicants. However, the court gives no majority opinion in this case, and five of the justices agree that race can still be considered in school admission procedures. This leaves local and federal governments little precedent on how to establish guidelines for affirmative-action programs. It also confirms that achieving racial balance in big-city public schools is extremely unlikely.
🔟 1996

SCIENCE AND TECHNOLOGY

• *Nimbus 7,* an environmental satellite, is launched. It sends back the first complete view of the hole in the Antarctic's ozone layer, the stratospheric blanket that protects life on Earth from the harmful effects of the sun's ultraviolet rays. The U.S. government bans the use of chlorofluorocarbons (CFCs) in aerosol sprays, because they are identified as ozone depleters. But manufacturers continue to use other CFCs in refrigerators, air conditioners, industrial solvents, and plastic foams.

CULTURE AND SOCIETY

• In San Francisco, Mayor George Moscone and Supervisor Harvey Milk, the city's first openly homosexual official, are shot dead in City Hall by ex-supervisor Dan White, who says he believes he is defending the city from homosexuals, pot smokers, and other threats to religion and family life.

• *The Turner Diaries,* an apocalyptic novel by Andrew Macdonald about a 1991 guerrilla war conducted by white gun-loving patriots against "the System," is published. Its conspiracy-theory plot advocates sabotage, lynching and assassination of Jews, blacks, and their white sympathizers, including the police, preachers, media, and teachers. It provides a detailed blueprint of methods to carry out white-supremacist terrorist actions. The FBI labels it "the Bible of the racist right" after copies continue to be found among the possessions of various cell groups carrying out violent attacks, including Timothy McVeigh, who is convicted and sentenced to death for carrying out the 1995 bombing of the Murrah Federal Building in Oklahoma City.

WORLD EVENTS

• A Soviet-supported rebel coup topples Afghanistan's government led by President Muhammad Daud Khan, assassinating Daud and his family. Noor Muhammad Taraki becomes the country's first Marxist president. Within a year, a fundamentalist-led rebellion against this government's efforts to centralize power will provoke the first Soviet deployment of troops since World War II.

1979

ARTS AND LITERATURE

• Judy Chicago (b. 1939) collaborates with a team of women artists for a feminist multimedia installation project, *The Dinner Party,* which receives much notice during a national tour, provoking controversy about feminist art, especially through its ceramic plates depicting vulvas labeled in honor of specific women in history. The extremely controversial work is even criticized by some feminist scholars and artists who believe that the images are too "essentialist."

• "Performance art" emerges as a popular name for live-art forms that use more than one discipline. Many women work in performance art, in some part because it is new, open territory without the baggage of having to be connected to the uptown gallery world's system of prestige and expensive price tags. However, as the form becomes accepted and the genre's definition grows broader, the practice begins to move out from its beginnings in experimental alternative spaces and outdoor sites, to appear in clubs, opera, videotape, and film. New York's East Village develops as a hub for performance-art events, with various showcases run by performance artists that flourish well into the 1980s and beyond.

• Shawn Wong (b. 1950, California) publishes his first novel, *Homebase,* which wins both the Pacific Northwest Bookseller's Award and the Washington State Governor's Writers Day Award. It is the first novel to be published by an American-born Chinese male.

GOVERNMENT AND POLITICS

• The U.S. Supreme Court upholds affirmative-action programs involving the use of quotas in unions and private businesses.

• President Jimmy Carter and Leonid Brezhnev, president of the Soviet Union, sign the Strategic Arms Limitation Treaty, known as SALT II, in Vienna on June 18, in which both countries agree to set limits on the main nuclear weapons in their arsenals, land-based intercontinental ballistic missiles (ICBMs). The U.S. Senate refuses to ratify the treaty after Soviet troops invade Afghanistan in December.

BUSINESS AND INDUSTRY

• On March 28 the nuclear power plant at Three Mile Island, near Harrisburg, Pennsylvania, begins emitting clouds of radioactive steam. After an auxiliary system that feeds water to the steam generators fails, the primary system overheats, causing pressure in the reactor to rise and a pressure-relief valve to open. A misinterpretation of instrument readings causes the radioactive core to overheat, and radioactive gases pour through the open valve. Although no one is immediately hurt and only minor amounts of radiation are released into the environment, this is the most serious nuclear accident in U.S. history to date, and leads directly to changes in how nuclear power plants are regulated. The plant at Three Mile Island is shut down permanently.

• On July 16, 1979, more than 1,100 tons of uranium mining wastes and 100 million gallons of radioactive water gush through a ruptured tailings dam at the United Nuclear Plant in Church Rock, New Mexico, contaminating the Rio Puerco, a river that provides the only water source for about 1,700 Dine Indians and their sheep and livestock. Although the Church Rock disaster is even larger than the 1979 Three Mile Island reactor meltdown, it is only part of a larger source of contamination that results from the increasing stockpiles of mill tailings throughout the Four Corners region. Los Alamos experts advise "zon[ing] of uranium mining and milling districts so as to forbid human habitation."

• U.S. Steel closes fifteen plants and mills in eight states, reducing the company's workforce by 8 percent, which means cutting 13,000 white-collar and blue-collar jobs. The company blames the pollution-control demands of the Environmental Protection Agency, which it says make the company's products uncompetitive with lower-priced imports.

• President Carter recommends, and Congress approves, a $1.5-billion loan to the Chrysler Corporation, the third-largest auto manufacturer in the U.S., when it is in danger of going belly-up because it owes so much money to private banks that it cannot borrow anymore. It is the largest federal rescue plan ever for an American company.

SCIENCE AND TECHNOLOGY

• Oracle releases the first relational database management system, a way to organize data within tables, and to view and analyze data in various ways without physically rearranging storage of the data. This is the prototype of modern databases.

CULTURE AND SOCIETY

• The Archaeological Resources Protection Act is passed, to protect archaeological sites and resources that are on public and Indian land.

WORLD EVENTS

• The Shah of Iran flees the country, and an Islamic leader, the Ayatollah Khomeini, establishes an Islamic government. On November 4, Muslim student militants seize the U.S. embassy in Teheran and take fifty-two American diplomats hostage, to humiliate the U.S. The crisis lasts 444 days, and when President Carter loses his reelection bid, many analysts point to this event as the primary cause. The crisis is resolved in secret negotiations that end in the release of all the hostages on January 20, 1980, the day of President Reagan's inauguration.

• In Nicaragua, the Sandinista Front for National Liberation (FSLN) comes into power, supported by U.S., Mexican, and Central American governments, after ousting dictator Anastasio Somoza. The Sandinistas take over lands held by the Somozas and their associates, amounting to one-fifth of the country's arable territory. By converting the seized land into state farms administrated by the Nicaraguan Agrarian Reform Institute, the Sandinistas start what will become one of Latin America's most far-reaching land-reform programs. President Jimmy Carter meets with the junta in the White House. U.S. aid to the Sandinistas will end in the Reagan administration, although the Sandinistas gain a majority of seats in the National Assembly, and their candidate, Daniel Ortega, wins the presidency in the 1984 elections.

🔲 1980, 1981

• The U.S. and the People's Republic of China resume full diplomatic relations on January 1, and the U.S. withdraws recognition of the Republic of China (ROC). Under the Taiwan Relations Act, however, the Carter administration maintains nongovernmental relations with the ROC through the American Institute in Taipei and Taiwan's coordination Council for North American Affairs.

• Afghanistan is invaded and occupied by the Soviet Union. Over the next ten years, 15,000 Soviet soldiers die fighting for what will ultimately prove a failed mission against anti-Communist Mujahedeen forces, Muslim rebel militias, who declare a *jihad,* a holy war, to liberate the country. Nearly 6 million Afghans, about one-third of the population, become refugees, fleeing to Pakistan and Iran. Amid expressions of international rebuke for the Soviet actions, more than 35,000 recruits from forty Islamic countries join Afghan Muslims between 1982 and 1992 to help bring down the pro-Communist government. Many Mujahedeen soldiers are trained and supplied under covert CIA operations, with additional aid and equipment from Saudi Arabia, Pakistan, Britain, and China, among others. One of the most active training organizations, Maktab al-Khidamat (MAK), is formed in Peshawar, Pakistan, this year by Osama bin Laden (b. 1957, Saudi Arabia) with Abdallah Azzam, spiritual leader of the Palestinian Muslim Brotherhood.

Afrika Bambaataa, a major
innovator of hip-hop culture
(Photo © Ernie Panicciolli)

1980-1989

POEM FOR THE 1980S

JOYCE CAROL THOMAS

To see everything in shifting solitude
Is to rediscover ourselves

Is to search for answers
Wondering who are we to
Snub outcasts with
Hungry hands
Begging
Outside the banks of America

Is to listen to the roof-raising hip-hopping movers
Shaking buildings
In earthquakes so forceful
Mansion windows pulse in and out
Is to hear Rap, wrapped in a cloak of striking colors,
Crashing ashore on foreign continents
Where red silk cushions tremble
At the new gospel messages erupting from
An I-will-be-heard youth

Is to witness the student asking the question
And the teacher turning and fleeing the classroom
Is to ask what about education?
Is to weep over children pushed into jails
After marching on the frontlines of battle

Is to stare unblinking at
Prisoners working for pennies an hour
Lining the pockets of pedophiles
Is to shudder at
Tots kissed by politicians in photo-ops
Is to fear the farming of children
Is to fight to make tomorrow better

Is to watch the same leaders who cut
    off the poor,
the sick, the disabled,
Apologizing for wasteful wars
Is to keep asking
Can we become more humane?

Is to behold
The privileged harvesting the crops
Of the disenfranchised
And their newly liberated wives stuffing their
    purses
Then admitting their own prejudices
What else can we do?

Is to understand women hating women
For being the trophies of abusive men
And loving them too
For raising the children, for designing
    monuments to warriors,
For finding the right mates, for inventing
    and quilting,
And voting their consciences

Is to trace the steps of
Christians and Jews and Muslims
    pulling apart
Arguing over who suffered the most
Or what to call their pain
Is to ask if the rift is a distraction
Is to catch arguments raging on TV, as silly,

as superfluous
As a squabble
Over should a toilet
Seat be left up or down
And who should raise it
And who should lower it
By folks who only a generation ago squatted
In outhouses that had no lids
Is to ask how many prayers could a writer
    pen
While time is wasting away
Is to ask can we as mixed and mixed-up
    people,
Straighten up and be more human?

Is to follow the path of the Internet
Springing from genius minds
On a tangled web where
Information spreads
Like fallout from a hydrogen bomb
Invented by scientists who would not imagine
Its consequences

Are we the Flies
Are we the Spiders
Oblivious
Living
Dancing
Grinning
Crying
Smoking, smelling like human ash trays
Alcohol-soaked and deaf to our own bodies
    talking to us
Inhaling poisons and reeling to an early grave
Driving expensive cars turning into our
    personal hearses
As smog chokes the air
And strangles oxygen from plants on the
    planet?

Is to watch gullible eyes
Patiently waiting for truth
Until the power of the pompous ebbs
And the blind begin seeing
False prophets dressing up in evil
Start murdering bodies and minds

Is to wonder
If we'll experience the gift
Writers write about, the joy Dancers dance
*   about,*
The passion Musicians sing about,
The ecstasy Artists paint about

Is to know
Spiders will
Survive
Still inventing, still writing, still singing, still
Painting, still weaving webs of praise in an
Eden set aside and sculpted by the green
*   thumb*
Of an ever-loving God

1980

ARTS AND LITERATURE

• Hip-hop, a new music style that is created by appropriating recorded songs (and other music) and editing them until the existing chorus, verse, and bridge structure are reduced to a fragment that becomes a percussive cell known as the "break," begins to move out from its origins in neighborhood street parties when the first rap albums are produced. *Super Rappin'*, demonstrating the pioneering Bronx style of performers rhyming in rhythm over a beat, is by the crew of Grandmaster Flash (born Joseph Sadler) and the Furious Five, including DJ Melle Mell (born Melvin Glover), Kid

As of April 1980 the U.S. Census reports the resident population totals 226,542,000, increasing 11.4 percent over the preceding census. Refugee admissions are double the number of the previous decade, with Asian refugee numbers nearly tripled, owing in some part to the 1980 Refugee Act, which becomes effective April 1, 1980. The U.S. Department of Labor's Bureau of Labor Statistics records that 62.1 percent of mothers with children under the age of eighteen years have jobs. The unemployment rates remain relatively high throughout the decade, starting at 7.1 percent at the beginning of the decade and reaching a high of 9.7 percent in 1982, and a low of 5.5 percent in 1988. In 1985, 61 percent of mothers with children under eighteen years of age are participating in the labor force (U.S. Department of Labor). By 1989, median family income is $35,210 for whites; $20,210 for blacks; and $23,450 for Hispanics. Per capita income is $14,000 for whites; $8,750 for blacks; and $8,390 for Hispanics.

Creole, Raheim, and Scorpio (aka Mr. Ness). Grandmaster Flash, along with Kool Herc and Afrika Bambaataa, are considered to be the first major hip-hop innovators. Bambaataa is credited with inventing various turntable techniques, including back-spinning and cutting. This year *Rapper's Delight* is recorded by the Sugar Hill Gang, a New Jersey–based crew. When the record becomes a worldwide hit by selling 10 million copies, it establishes the new style's mass appeal and ongoing potential for commercial success.

ELECTRONICS ARE MODERN FIRES

Laurie Anderson

Formerly, electronics have always been connected to storytelling. Maybe because storytelling began when people used to sit around fires and because fire is magic, compelling and dangerous. We are transfixed by its light and by its destructive power. Electronics are modern fires.

(LAURIE ANDERSON, *Stories from the Nerve Bible: A Retrospective 1972–1992* [NEW YORK: HARPERCOLLINS, 1994], 175)

• Composer Laurie Anderson premieres *U.S., Part 2* at the Orpheum Theater in New York, co-sponsored by the Kitchen, and then tours the U.S. This mixed-media work eventually totals four parts. Anderson uses projections, electronic "toys" that she discovers from "playing around with equipment," and instruments that she invents for eight hours of narrative, song, and visual tricks. With one of the songs, "O Superman," Anderson succeeds in crossing over into mainstream markets, as do other avant-garde artists around this time, including Philip Glass, Eric Bogosian (b. 1953), and Spalding Gray.

• Arte Publico, the oldest and largest publisher of Hispanic literature in the U.S., is founded and directed by Nicolas Kanellos at the University of Houston. Along with *The Americas Review* (a magazine of Hispanic literature and arts originally founded in 1973 by Dr. Kanellos as *Chicano-Riquena*), they promote the work of contemporary authors, both bilingual and monolingual English- and Spanish- speaking, including Alurista (b. Mexico City, 1947), Lorna Dee Cervantes (b. 1954, Mexican American), Sandra Cisneros (b. 1952, Mexican American), Judith Ortiz Cofer (b. 1952, Puerto Rico), Lucha Corpi (b. 1945, Mexico), Rolanda Hinojosa (b. 1929, Mexican American), Oscar Hijuelos (b. 1951, Cuban American), Nicholasa Mohr (b. 1935, Puerto Rico), Alberto Rios (b. 1951, Mexican American), Tomas Rivera (1935–1984, Mexican American), Alberto Rios (b. 1952, Mexican American), and Helena Maria Viramontes (b. 1954, Mexican American).

• The WOW (Women's One World) Café, an East Village performance space, opens in the old Electric Circus space, as an experimental venue for multimedia works by U.S. and international women artists. Lois Weaver, who, with Peggy Shaw and Holly Hughes, is one of the founders, says WOW has "a feminine aesthetic because its details are often forgotten or stepped over in male-dominated works. But little parts of our lives are as important as the big climactic events that usually make dramas."

• Barbara T. Christian (b. 1943, St. Thomas, U.S. Virgin Islands; d. 2000), professor of African American Studies at UC Berkeley, publishes her landmark study, *Black Women Novelists: The Development of a Tradition*, which is credited with nominating black women for inclusion in the U.S. literary canon. She helped establish the African American Studies Department at U.C., Berkeley in 1972, and becomes the university's first tenured African American woman (1978), first in the UC system to be promoted to full professor (1986), and first to receive the campus's Distinguished Teaching Award (1991).

GOVERNMENT AND POLITICS

• President Jimmy Carter reinstates compulsory registration for the military draft after the Soviet army invades Afghanistan.

• A U.S. commando mission to free sixty-two American hostages held by religious militants at the U.S. embassy in Tehran, Iran, fails, with President Carter taking full responsibility for the loss of several U.S. soldiers' lives when their plane crashes in the desert. The failed negotiations and commando mission will be significant factors in President Carter's defeat in his bid for a second term.

🖻 1979

• The Carter administration passes the Refugee Act of 1980, defining the term *refugee* to conform with the 1967 UN Protocol on Refugees and removing the previous limitations imposed by the standing definition of a refugee as a person fleeing from Communist persecution. This allows thousands more refugees to enter the U.S., and increases to 320,000 the annual number admitted, including many Indochinese immigrants. In its first year, 125,000 Cubans exit their country after Fidel Castro, reacting to negative press reports in April, announces that anyone who wants to leave Cuba can get an exit visa from the Peruvian embassy. Before Castro closes the port of Mariél in September, Cuban Americans from Florida operate a fleet of boats to pick up the exiles. In 1981, under the new Reagan administration, Attorney General William French Smith issues orders to hold in INS detention centers all undocumented Central American refugees applying for political asylum. Central Americans form new communities within or near the major metropolitan areas of Washington, D.C., Los

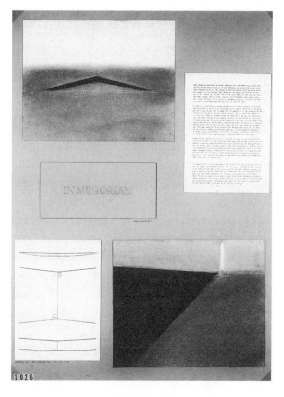

Original proposal for the Vietnam Veterans Memorial by Maya Lin (© Maya Lin, 1981, Library of Congress, Prints and Photographs Division)

Angeles, San Francisco, Chicago, Houston, and New York, and in the farmlands and small industrial towns of Florida, North Carolina, and California. Hispanic immigrants make up 40 percent of the total 6.3 million legal immigrants granted permanent residence in the 1980s.

• Ronald Reagan (b. 1911), a former movie actor and governor of California, is elected the fortieth president of the U.S. when he receives an electoral landslide victory for his first term, although half the eligible voters do not participate in the election. He is the oldest man ever elected to this office. George Bush (b. 1924) is elected his vice president. Reagan wins through an appeal to old-fashioned patriotism and "traditional" values, riding the country's rising right-wing disposition. Many disillusioned Democrats and blue-collar workers will vote Republican for the first time. His campaign slogan is "Make America Feel Good About Itself Again."

• Congress deregulates interest rates that depository institutions (savings-and-loans, credit unions, and thrift institutions) can pay on deposits, and allows the industry to offer adjustable-rate mortgages as a protection against fluctuations in the interest rate. At the same time, the government increases deposit insurance from $40,000 to $100,000 per account. This measure is supposed to protect depositors, but the thrift executives use it to attract funds, taking large risks with the money, knowing that the government will cover losses if they occur.

⊡ 1982

BUSINESS AND INDUSTRY

• Ted Turner founds the twenty-four-hour Cable News Network (CNN) in Atlanta, Georgia, the first network in the world to program solely news, and the first to broadcast nationwide on cable systems via satellite. It starts with 2 million subscribers and a $30-million budget, one-quarter of the major networks' budgets for one hour of news per day. CNN becomes a nationwide and worldwide influence, available in most hotel rooms and to anyone with a cable hookup throughout the world, so that simultaneously, viewers throughout the world share an experience of an event as it happens, where it happens, live through the lens of CNN.

• Native Americans begin to find a new source of income on tribal lands, through establishing gambling casinos, which create 120,000 jobs on reservations and an additional 160,000 spinoff jobs. This new possibility for prosperity gives Native Americans some real political clout, and helps reverse the exodus from the reservations, because they can come home to jobs. By 1983, 180 tribes are estimated to be running casino-style gambling operations on their reservations.

• Asian American immigration rises dramatically in this decade, with many choosing to become entrepreneurs. From 1982 to 1987, when the national growth rate for new business is 14 percent, Asian Americans' rate of new business growth reaches 162 percent. By 1989, 35 percent of Asian Americans earn over $50,000, making them the largest demographic group to do so.

• African Americans' educational gains this decade are not reflected in more skilled employment relative to European Americans. Thirty-three percent of black males work as professionals, managers, artisans, and in sales, as compared to 59 percent of white males; and 19 percent of black women work in these same categories, compared with 32 percent of white women. In 1985, 20.8 percent of black families earn less than $15,000, compared with 10.4 percent of white families.

• Throughout the 1980s and 1990s, Japanese industrialists and multinational corporations continue to take advantage of the *maquiladoras*, plants that operate in the border region of Mexico and the U.S., by sending greater amounts of raw materials to Mexico, where they are finished and shipped duty-free to the U.S. Many U.S. workers lose their jobs as a result, and the labor unions continue to be weakened.

⊡ 1960, 1965

CULTURE AND SOCIETY

• The U.S. Civil Rights Commission reports that nearly half of all minority children attend "racially isolated" schools. Two factors are re-creating segregation in public education: family choices of private and parochial schools and "white flight" to the suburbs, leaving inner cities with a "minority majority."

• The Bureau of Indian Affairs (BIA) estimates that one-half of the 1.5 million Native Americans counted by the national census live on or near reservations.

SCIENCE AND TECHNOLOGY

• In the landmark case *Diamond v. Chakrabarty*, the U.S. Supreme Court clears the way for the growth of the biotechnology industry when it rules, in a 5–4 decision, that new life-forms created in a laboratory can be patented. Chief Justice Warren E. Burger writes the majority opinion, stating that when General Electric scientist Ananda Chakrabarty genetically engineered bacteria that can be used at toxic spills to degrade crude oil into substances that provide food for aquatic life, it was patentable because it was "not nature's handiwork, but his own . . . [since the] relevant distinction is not between animate and inanimate things but whether living products could be seen as human-made inventions."
▣ 1951

• In 1980, physicist Luis Alvarez (b. 1911), his physicist son, Walter Alvarez, and co-workers Frank Asaro and Helen Michael help revive the catastrophic theory of history, based on their finding of an unusually high level of the heavy metal iridium in clay at a site in Italy where they are investigating the boundary between the Cretaceous and Tertiary periods,

Dr. Luis Alvarez, shown here with a hydrogen bubble chamber display, which he used to discover resonance states of elementary particles, and for which he is awarded a 1968 Nobel Prize in Physics. (Note: The catastrophe study was his 1980s work.) *(Courtesy of UC Lawrence Berkeley National Laboratory Image Library, Jean Wolslegel)*

called the K-T boundary. After comparing K-T boundary soil samples from around the world and finding the metal present, they theorize that the Earth was hit by a large asteroid or comet containing iridium at that time, causing a blanket of soot and dust to cover the planet. The resultant blockage of sunlight cooled the Earth and prevented photosynthesis. The loss of green plants at the base of the food chain, combined with the temperature change, helps explain how

Technician Christine Berry checks on futuristic peach and apple "orchards." Each dish holds tiny experimental trees grown from lab-cultured cells to which researchers have given new genes. Photo by Scott Bauer. (Agricultural Research Service, USDA)

the mass extinction of dinosaurs occurred at the end of the Cretaceous period. Debate continues as to the possible significance of this event, and whether it could be similar in effect to a catastrophe called "nuclear winter," which might result from nuclear war. Luis Alvarez will win the Nobel Prize in Physics in 1986. A pioneer in particle physics, astrophysics, geophysics, and ophthalmic and television optics, he develops most of his work at UC Berkeley, where he is an emeritus professor, and as associate director of the Lawrence Berkeley Lab.

• The Reagan administration announces

production has begun on the neutron bomb, which former President Carter had deferred throughout his term. Three months later, Reagan presents his five-point program for strengthening the military defense system. It includes building 100 B-1 bombers (also opposed by the Carter administration) and 100 MX missiles.

WORLD EVENTS

• Indira Gandhi becomes prime minister of India in a dramatic political comeback, three years after the Janata Dal party overwhelmingly won in parliamentary elections and she was driven from office.

◙ 1984

• Incoming President Reagan argues that the Soviet Union, through its Cuban connections, is using social and political issues to agitate for change in the Caribbean and Central America. Because Honduras is perceived to be threatened by the civil wars in Nicaragua and El Salvador, the U.S. establishes a military outpost there with $300 million in funding, which is used by Nicaraguan Contras. In El Salvador, José Napoleon Duarte, a reformist Christian Democrat politician, is appointed president by the ruling military junta. Civil War erupts between government forces and the leftist guerrilla groups united under the banner of the Farabundo Martí Front for National Liberation (FMLN). Government soldiers and rightist paramilitary supporters terrorize possible supporters of the FMLN. More than 1,000 civilians are assassinated per month, including Archbishop Oscar Romero, Salvadoran attorney general Mario Zamora, three American nuns, and a lay social worker, causing international expressions of outrage. The war continues

NATIVE AMERICAN VISUAL ARTISTS: 1980s AND 1990s

It is no longer possible to talk about "movements" in the arts, a fact that is as true for Native American visual artists as for the rest of the art world.

Intermedia artist, teacher, and curator Sara Bates (b. Oklahoma; Cherokee) gathers natural materials to make her works and draws on recycled materials, a reflection of her concerns for people to experience "interactive, reciprocal, sensuous" relationships to their environment.

Sculptor, mixed media constructions, performance artist, and poet Jimmie Durham (b. 1940, Arkansas; Wolf Clan Cherokee) sat on the American Indian Movement's Central Council and was a founder of the International Indian Treaty Council in the 1970s. Durham says, "I think of art as a combination of sensual and intellectual investigations in reality. The fact that governments want to control art is certainly part of the reality that art must investigate."

Painter, mixed media, lithographer, and etchings artist Harry Fonseca (b. 1946, Sacramento, California; Nisenan-Maidu/Portuguese/Hawaiian) began using the comic/ironic image of the trickster, Coyote, in 1969. He later added a female counterpart, Rose, to make "the most contemporary statements I have painted in regard to traditional beliefs and contemporary reality."

Sculptor and mixed media artist Rick Glazer-Danay (b. 1942, Coney Island, Brooklyn; New York Mohawk/White) described his work as "Coney Island baroque school."

Sculptor Bob Haozous (b. 1943, Los Angeles; Navajo/Apache/English/Spanish) is the son of sculptor and IAIA teacher Allan Houser and broke from his father's more heroic/idealized folk style of figurative sculpture to create ironic modern images that poke fun while making social commentary. In 1983 he said, "I love the land and I love people and I hope that my work symbolizes this in my own individual way."

Painter, photographer, and site-specific public art works artist Hachivi Edgar Heap of Birds (b. 1954 Wichita, Kansas; Cheyenne-Arapaho) is the great-great-grandson of an artist imprisoned at Fort Marion who was a leader of the Elk Warriors' Society, as is Heap of Birds. His works, widely exhibited by galleries and museums, have appeared on the sides of buses, park and freeway signs, and the Spectracolor billboard in Times Square. "We find it effective to challenge the white man through our use of the mass media. . . . the insurgent messages within these forms must serve as our present-day combative tactics."

Writer, photographer, painter, and first curator of the IAIA museum space that opened in Santa Fe in 1992, Rick Hill (b. 1950, Tuscarora, New York) in his Whiteman in North America series, makes documentary photographs that "look at the white man by what he leaves behind . . . photographs of decayed things" such as storefronts, old cars, and busted machines. When white viewers got angry that he was using a few photographs to describe all of white life he replied, "You're mad about what I'm saying about you, but the exact same is true the other way around. Nobody can come and study us, explain us, photograph us but us."

Printmaker and installation artist Joe Feddersen (member, Colville Federated Tribes) has collaborated on five projects with poet Elizabeth Woody (Navajo/Warm Springs/Wasco/Yakima). Their "Archives," a 1994

(Continued)

installation at the Tula Foundation in Atlanta, Georgia, addressed how stories "[are] intellectual property that belong to the individual, family, or tribal groups [that] serve the community."

Installation, video, and performance artist James Luna (b. 1950, Orange, California; Luiseno/Diegueno) is also a professional counselor, working with Indian people through a San Marcos, California, community college. "Some people only talk about the romanticized or glamorous Indians, but I want to look at the problems we're facing. I don't think I criticize other people in my work, I use myself as object."

Painter, printmaker, and sculptor Dan Namingha (b. 1950; Tewa-Hopi) comes from a long family tradition of artists, starting with his great-great grandmother, the potter Nampeyo, the first Indian artist widely known by the general public. Connected to the IAIA as both a student and teacher, he says, "Living in two cultures simultaneously as I do, I am constantly aware of the dual nature of things: night and day, past and future, then and now."

Painter, printmaker, collagist, and sculptor Frank LaPena (b. 1937, San Francisco; Wintu-Nomtipom) is a trained anthropologist with an M.A. in ethnography from California State University, Sacramento, where he presently teaches. He started exhibiting in the late 1950s. He connects past and present in his work, saying he "looks at [ancient] Chumas rock art through the eyes of an Abstract Expressionist."

Potter Diego Romero (b. Berkeley, California; Cochiti Pueblo) was raised in urban environments. His ceramic bowls, made of commercial potter's materials, mix contemporary satirical images of people, buildings, cars, and other objects with a drawing style similar to ancient pottery designed by classic Mimbres (Southwest New Mexico, 1100–1200 C.E.) and Greek cultures. Romero says, "I like the fact that they are these little cartoony, political comics on bowls and that I can make fun and comment on the history of the Pueblo people at the same time."

Glass artist Preston Singletary (b. 1964, San Francisco; Tlingit) researches traditional three-dimensional designs from his Southeast Alaskan Tlingit background in the 1990s. He says, "I'm hoping I'll be able to bring the Tlingit designs into the future. Glass is so permanent. It will never rot away like a piece of wood. The potential is there for it to be a lasting piece."

Painter, mixed media collagist, maker of drawings, and site-specific artist Jaune Quick-to-See Smith (b. 1940, Montana; Salish [Flatheads/Cree/Shosone]) layers her works with "stories" that, sometimes abstract, sometimes pictorial, are based in her concerns with landscape and political and environmental issues. She says, "When I'm in a museum, I do a compare-and-contrast kind of looking, going back and forth between modern art and Indian art, as well as other ethnic art. Eurocentrism would have us believe that there is an abrupt 'aha!' at which time white artists invented cubism, color theory, and abstract art. It's just not so."

Sculptor and potter Roxanne Swentzell (b. 1962, Taos, New Mexico; Santa Clara Pueblo) is a fifth-generation artist from a family of potters, educators, and architects. She says, "I know that I describe myself as a sculptor of human emotions. I think that the emotions get us in touch with our own centers, with ourselves. I hope others will see what I see and what I feel and what I put into my work."

Painter Kay Walking Stick (b. 1935, Syracuse, New York; Cherokee/Scottish-American) often paints diptychs, saying: "Painting, like language, is magical. It is made of the simplest ingredient: oil, pigment—which is often only refined dirt—and a support of cloth or wood. It transmogrifies into beauty, ugliness, meaning, revelation, narrative, and decoration."

Painter, printmaker, and mixed media artist Emmi Whitehorse (b. 1956, Crownpoint, New Mexico; Navajo) makes abstractions whose imagery she describes as "extremely personal." She says her "intuitive" work process is accomplished "with no top or bottom to the canvas. I have never used a paintbrush in my life."

throughout the 1980s, with millions of U.S. dollars committed to supplying weapons and military advisers to wage government battles against the FMLN.

🗓 1979

• Rhodesia becomes the independent nation Zimbabwe on April 17, after the white minority finally agrees to hold multiracial elections after all parties in a ten-year power struggle agree to a cease-fire in December 1979. Robert Mugabe, leader of the Zimbabwe African National Union (ZANU) wins the presidency by a landslide. ZANU, a black nationalist party that was instrumental in promoting the revolution that transfers power to the black majority in December 1978, begins an ambitious program to reconstruct the country, although sporadic fighting continues, especially with another black nationalist group, the Zimbabwe African People's Union (ZAPU), headed by Joshua Nkomo. President Mugabe will remain in power into the twenty-first century, after creating ZANU-PF, a one-party state with ZAPU, in a 1987 agreement with Nkomo.

• Iran and Iraq engage in open warfare that starts with a dispute over the Shatt al-Arab waterway in Southern Iraq. The war will continue for eight years, especially along the shared border, with each country launching bombing attacks against the other's cities.

Estimates of casualties in both countries range from 450,000 to 1 million. Both sides are accused of using poison gas. Iran is almost bankrupted by the war. A 1988 UN initiative will lead to a cease-fire.

🗓 1986

• A global effort to measure deforestation estimates that the Earth has lost one-fifth of its forests from preagricultural times, and predicts massive extinction of species by 2050 owing to destruction of habitats.

• The World Health Organization announces that smallpox has been eradicated worldwide, although, as recently as 1967, 2 million people died annually from the virus.

1981

ARTS AND LITERATURE

• President Ronald Reagan recommends that the National Endowment for the Arts take a budget cut of 50 percent. Congress compromises on a 10-percent cut in this year's budget, but with every year's budget discussion throughout the rest of the decade, the arts community has to learn to sell the role of culture in America.

• Maya Lin (b. 1959), a Chinese American and a Yale undergraduate, beats out 14,041 entries in a national design competition to

UNTITLED STATEMENT (1995)

Maya Lin

My work originates from a simple desire to make people aware of their surroundings—this can include not just the physical but the psychological world we live in.

This desire has led me at times to become involved in artworks that are as much politically motivated as they are aesthetically based.

I have tried in my work to respond to our current situations—communicating to an audience an idea of our time, an accounting of history—yet I would hesitate to call myself a "political artist." If anything I would prefer apolitical as a description of myself. I do not choose to overlay personal commentary upon historical facts. I am less interested in presenting my opinion than in presenting factual information—allowing the viewer the chance to come to his or her own conclusions.

The *Vietnam Veterans Memorial* is not an object inserted into the earth but a work formed from the act of cutting open the earth and polishing the earth's surface—dematerializing the stone to pure surface, creating an interface between the world of the light and the quieter world beyond the names. I saw it as part of the earth—like a geode.

(Courtesy of Maya Lin)

select a Vietnam Veterans Memorial to be located on the Mall in Washington, D.C. She proposes building a wall focused on the almost 60,000 individual U.S. citizens who died in the war, by carving their names, in the chronological order of their deaths, into a black polished granite wall that appears to rise out of an opening in the earth. Her minimalist design sparks a vigorous public debate that involves war veterans, politicians, and art experts, and eventually wins congressional approval. The wall is completed in 1982, becoming one of the most successful public sculptures of the century. President Clinton later signs legislation to allow a plaque also to be placed at the site, honoring the equal number of Vietnam veterans who died from exposure to Agent Orange, post-traumatic stress

disorder, and other causes not classified as combat wounds.

• Music Television (MTV) premieres in the U.S. on Warner Amex, the largest cable television programmer. The new outlet helps create a new popular art form, performance videos. It causes musicians to routinely consider the visual as well as aural content of their work, to supply TV's unceasing demand for new work. MTV tries a new marketing idea in television, targeting a specific audience, the 12–32 year-old age group, and it soon begins influencing fashion sales also. MTV is criticized for passing over African American performing groups, and for mainly showing male groups using scantily clad women as background props. However, MTV's quick editing style also filters into advertising and film.

GOVERNMENT AND POLITICS

• In his inaugural address, President Ronald Reagan states that he will "turn the government around" because "government is not the solution to the problem; government is the problem." He proposes to stop inflation by decreasing federal spending and deregulating U.S. industries and trade while keeping taxes at their current levels. He keeps his campaign pledges, making $48.5 billion worth of spending cuts in the 1981 federal budget by dismantling federal social programs developed over the last two decades, and turning over much of the decision-making power to individual states. Other large cuts affect mass transportation, synthetic fuel projects, and federally sponsored programs in the arts. His new economic programs puts "supply side" economics and the "trickle-down theory" into practice. The deficit is projected at $45 billion. Among his first acts are a federal hiring freeze and an increase in the military budget of $32 billion, the beginning of the largest peacetime defense buildup in U.S. history.

▣ 1966, 1981, 1999

• As former president, Jimmy Carter flies home to Georgia on President Reagan's inaugural day, the fifty-two remaining U.S. hostages, who have been held for fourteen months by the Iranian government of Ayatollah Ruhollah Khomeini, are released and flown out of Iranian airspace to neutral Algeria and then home. Reagan asks Carter to meet them.

• President Reagan extends the CIA's power, to allow spying within the U.S. borders. He also moves to support the Contras in their attempts to overthrow the revolutionary Sandinista government in Nicaragua, through military, diplomatic, and economic channels.

• President Ronald Reagan is wounded by a would-be assassin, John W. Hinckley Jr., just three months into his term. His show of bravery in recovery wins increased public support.

• Sandra Day O'Connor becomes the first woman and the 102nd person to sit on the Supreme Court. It will be twelve years before another woman sits on the court, when Ruth Bader Ginsburg is selected by President Clinton in 1993.

BUSINESS AND INDUSTRY

• IBM, the leading computer company in the world, introduces its first personal computer, with MS-DOS, its key operating system software, designed by a little-known Redmond, Washington, company called Microsoft, headed by Bill Gates. But IBM fails to acquire ownership of either the operating system or Microsoft, and ten years after this initial opportunity to create the industry standard, Microsoft and IBM will be enemies. Microsoft will become the world's largest software company, and Bill Gates the world's richest man.

• The 3M Corporation starts producing Post-it Notes, using a glue that is reusable without leaving any residue on the material it is adhering to. Research chemist Spencer Silver discovered it in 1970, and a colleague, Arthur Fry, comes up with its application in 1980. The idea is a worldwide hit, with its low-tech ability to assist in organizing homes and offices, and Post-its become a standard item, available in various shapes, sizes, and colors.

• The Jicarilla Apache Indians of New Mexico form the Jicarilla Energy Company, the first Native American–owned corporation to produce its own gas and oil. In 1982 the Oklahoma Comanche Tribe will form the

Aerial view of Seaside, Florida. *(Courtesy of Duany Plater-Zyberk & Co., Miami, Florida)*

Comanche Energy Resource Company, to produce their own oil and gas. And in Wisconsin, the Lac Courte Oreilles Band of Chipppewa Indians will gross nearly $6 million during their first year operating seven businesses, including a gas station, a supermarket, a print shop, a construction company, a bingo parlor, and a forest products business.

• American Airlines offers the first frequent-flyer program, AAdvantage Travel Awards, which within the year has 283,000 members. By 1999, 59 million Americans will take advantage of at least one airline mileage plan.

SCIENCE AND TECHNOLOGY

• Jaron Lanier, U.S. computer scientist, designs a computer-generated headset and special gloves that make it possible to experience and manipulate virtual reality.

• The AIDS virus is identified for the first time when a parasite-caused pneumonia that is serious enough to cause hospitalization is linked to five San Francisco men. In 1982 the disease is given a name, AIDS (Acquired Immune Deficiency Syndrome), by the U.S. Centers for Disease Control in Atlanta, Georgia, as a growing number of people contract the disease. The Centers for Disease Control also reports on two major conditions that are common to AIDS victims: pneumocystis and Kaposi's sarcoma. By October 1982, 665 cases have been recorded nationally. By year's end, 1,208 deaths have been reported. Millions will die worldwide in what becomes an epidemic, and many countries will cooperate to try and find a cure.

• The space shuttle with orbiter *Columbia*, otherwise known as the Space Transportation System, the U.S.'s first reusable manned spacecraft designed to transport people and cargo between Earth and orbiting spacecraft, launches

374

and successfully completes its objective of checking the overall shuttle system and making a safe descent. This is the first shuttle flight in NASA's attempt to reduce developmental costs for commercial, scientific, and military projects. Over the next twenty years, 100 space shuttle flights will take 250 people and 3 million pounds of cargo into space.

• The EPA, in a reversal, allows drums of toxic liquids to be buried in landfills.

CULTURE AND SOCIETY

• The civil war in El Salvador brings a new group of refugees to the U.S., as the Census Bureau tallies Hispanic Americans as the fastest-growing ethnic group in the U.S. The Census Bureau reports that an increasing number of blacks and Hispanics have moved to the suburbs since 1970.

• The Coalition for Better Television (CBT) is formed with the sponsorship of about 400 Christian organizations, including Reverend Jerry Falwell's Moral Majority, Reverend Donald Wildmon's National Federation for Decency, the Pro-Family Forum, Eagle Forum, American Life Lobby, and Concerned Women for America. They target television programs they deem offensive, advocating that their followers boycott the shows and their sponsor's products.

• Building begins on Seaside, Florida, the first town to be planned and designed according to New Urbanism, an alternative movement to conventional suburban development and urban renewal among city planners and architects. New Urbanists, who are also called "neo-traditionalists," advocate a more holistic approach to designing new communities or redesigning existing urban centers and towns. Andres Duany and Elizabeth Plater-Zyberk's

Dr. Mae Jemison, a medical doctor with a degree in chemical engineering, becomes the first black woman astronaut in the U.S. space program in 1987. *(National Aeronautics and Space Administration, with photo provided by the Schomburg Center for Research in Black Culture)*

Seaside design, along with their Kentlands design in Gaithersburg, Maryland (1988), and Peter Calthorpe's Laguna West in Sacramento County, California (1990), all function like traditional towns. They integrate various components of modern life—housing, work, recreation, and shopping—into mixed-use neighborhoods to successfully meet the needs of those who live and work in them. Besides encouraging public transportation to connect neighborhoods and the surrounding region, they use a measure of no more than one-quarter mile from the center to the edge of a neighborhood, to keep districts pedestrian-friendly. Their principles come to be known as "smart growth" as they prove their economic viability, as well as their living comfort. The last Seaside lot will sell for $200,000, compared with the $15,000 price ten years earlier, when they were first put on the market.

⊡ 1994

WORLD EVENTS

• Egyptian President Anwar el-Sadat, who shares a 1978 Nobel Peace Prize with Israel's Menachem Begin for their leadership in agreeing to a 1979 peace treaty between the two countries, is assassinated at a Cairo parade celebrating Egypt's success crossing the Suez in the 1973 Egypt-Israeli War. A conspiracy within the Egyptian military of Islamic fundamentalists, called the Islamic Jihad, claims responsibility. Vice President Mohammed Hosni Mubarak, a former air force chief of staff, succeeds President Sadat. The Egyptian Islamic Jihad, whose ultimate goal is to create an Islamic state, continues to orchestrate armed actions against Mubarak's government and forges alliances with other Islamic terrorist organizations.

1982

ARTS AND LITERATURE

• Bill Viola (b. 1951) makes a video-and-sound installation, *Reasons for Knocking at an Empty House*, within a year after returning to the U.S. from a cultural exchange program in Japan, where he lived with his wife, Kira Perov, and studied Zen Buddhism with master Daien Tanaka and advanced video technology at Sony Corporation's Atsugi Laboratories. His work bridges the early 1960s and 1970s video experimental works by Nam June Paik, Bruce Nauman (b. 1941), Peter Campus (b. 1937), and Vito Acconci (b. 1940). His dependence on up-to-the-minute technology, large exhibition spaces, and investment dollars is illustrative of how artists are becoming increasingly dependent on institutions to help mount projects using this form and other computer- and high-tech-driven works. In the 1980s and 1990s, video becomes an important medium for younger generations of artists, including many women and African Americans.

• African American visual artist Faith Ringgold (b. 1934) becomes one of the pioneers in using the medium of the quilt as a high art form. She calls her work feminist art, and notes that the slaves made quilts, seeing herself in their African tradition of making utilitarian objects beautiful. She receives her first solo exhibition at the Studio Museum in Harlem. In story quilts such as *Who's Afraid of Aunt Jemima* (1983), she presents political allegories, and *The Last Story Quilt* (1986) relates a story from her childhood life in Harlem.

• Alvin Singleton, innovative "classical" composer and jazz bassist, is given a premiere by the Houston Symphony Orchestra of his *A Yellow Rose Petal*.

• Digital synthesizers become commercially available, starting with Yamaha's DX7. Many U.S. composers and musicians replace their analog machines and adopt new systems of programming software by translating sounds into binary code.

• Exit Art is founded in New York City by Jeanette Ingberman and Papo as a nonprofit cultural center dedicated to transcultural, multidisciplinary explorations of contemporary art issues. They present festivals, including the Bang on a Can Festival, which has become an annual event.

GOVERNMENT AND POLITICS

• The Equal Rights Amendment (ERA) is defeated in Congress after a ten-year fight, when it fails to gain ratification in enough state legislatures by the deadline.

• President Reagan declares National Navajo Codetalkers Day to honor the Navajo World War II veterans who relayed defense information during World War II.

🔲 1942

• The Boland Amendment, introduced by Edward Boland, chairman of the House Intelligence Committee, prohibits any U.S. funding of Contra forces who are waging war against the elected Sandinistas.

🔲 1986

• Congress passes the Depository Institutions Act, which allows financial institutions to diversify their portfolios by entering new kinds of business ventures, including allowing savings-and-loan institutions to offer commercial loans. Although it is intended to strengthen the nation's savings-and-loan institutions, since one-third have lost money in the last year, it fails to consider the seriously depleted reserves of over 1,000 institutions. The relaxation of controls actually makes the situation worse when combined with the 1980 congressional deregulation of interest rates, as banks proceed to lend at levels far in excess of what is reliable, especially in the most deregulated states of Texas, California, and Florida. As a result, five hundred financial institutions fail between 1980 and 1983, when they are called upon to pay out more than their

fixed-rate mortgage portfolios can produce. Congress creates the Resolution Trust Corporation to take over the bad assets of the closed insolvent institutions.

🔲 1980, 1989

• The inspiration for the "environmental justice movement" is placed in Warren County, North Carolina, when 500 black people are arrested after lying down in front of trucks carrying PCB-contaminated soil into a landfill site built by the state for disposal of PCB-conaminated soil from fourteen North Carolina counties. Although the demonstrators, including Democratic Congressman Walter Fauntroy, Dr. Joseph Lowery of the Southern Christian Leadership Conference, and Dr. Benjamin F. Chavis Jr., are not successful in stopping the new landfill, they focus national attention on inequities in the siting of unwanted public projects.

🔲 1987

BUSINESS AND INDUSTRY

• The Bell System is finally broken up, after over 100 years of service, altering the world of telecommunications forever. American Telephone and Telegraph (AT&T) Chairman Charles Brown and Assistant Attorney General William Baxter negotiate an antitrust settlement, first brought by the U.S. Justice Department in 1974, which charges AT&T with trying to monopolize long-distance service and markets for equipment. It is the largest antitrust action since the breakup of Standard Oil in 1911. AT&T will hold on to its long-distance carriers, which in 1980 account for more than 50 percent of its $57 billion in revenues, equipment manufacturing operations, and Bell Laboratories.

• The U.S. enters the worst recession in forty years, since before World War II. Unemployment is high, as are interest rates, and the national budget deficit continues to grow to record levels.

SCIENCE AND TECHNOLOGY

• A sixty-one-year-old retired dentist, Barney Clark, receives the first total replacement of a human heart with an artificial heart in surgery at the University of Utah in Salt Lake City. William DeVries is the surgeon.

• Humulin, a genetically engineered human insulin product from Eli Lilly and Company, is the first genetically altered pharmaceutical approved for marketing by the FDA. This first commercial product of genetic engineering is used by millions of diabetics. Although this particular artificial product is obviously beneficial for people who have diabetes, its marketing raises ethical and moral questions about genetic engineering: whether it is a medically beneficial technology comparable in importance to the invention of the transistor for the information age, and whether it is capable of creating potential environmental hazards or unpredictable negative social and political consequences. By the beginning of the twenty-first century, more than 150 medical applications for genetic engineering will be developed.

• Interferon, a natural virus-fighting substance, is produced through genetic engineering by scientists in Boston.

• U.S. researcher Dana Anderson invents a holographic computer, capable of generating three-dimensional images.

CULTURE AND SOCIETY

• The Equal Employment Opportunities Commission (EEOC) establishes sexual harassment guidelines. It bans any behaviors that produce a hostile work environment, outlawing any unwanted sexual overtures or demands that seem to be, or are, made to be conditions of employment. It suggests that businesses provide workshops to sensitize employers and employees about perceptions and definitions of what constitutes sexual harassment.

• Berkeley, California, becomes the first U.S. city to offer domestic benefits to the partners of gay city employees.

WORLD EVENTS

• USSR leader Leonid Brezhnev dies and is succeeded by former head of the KGB Yuri V. Andropov. A reformer who works against institutionalized government corruption and social ills, Andropov will also die in less than two years, in February 1984, and Konstantin U. Chernenko, a old-line conservative and close associate of Brezhnev, will succeed Andropov.
🖻 1985

• Israel invades Lebanon in June, to drive out the PLO (Palestinian Liberation Organization) in response to an attempted assassination by Palestinians of the Israeli ambassador in London. Making a full-scale air and sea assault, Israeli troops surround the city of Beirut. In September the president-elect, Bashir Gemayel, a Maronite Christian, is assassinated by a car-bombing of his Christian Phalangist Party. The PLO withdraws its guerrillas from Beirut, exiting the city with one gun each, and leaving behind sophisticated heavy weaponry, including grenade launchers. The Israeli troops move in to occupy the West Beirut Muslim quarters. Bashir Gemayel's older brother, Amin Gemayel, is elected president by parliament.
🖻 1983

• World Wide Web protocols—the common set of sequences, formats, and procedures that allow computers to exchange information over the Internet—are defined at CERN, the European Laboratory for Particle Research in Geneva, Switzerland. Although this is the first stage in the eventual implementation of the World Wide Web in 1991, it is initially intended merely to foster collaboration and creativity among researchers.

1983

ARTS AND LITERATURE

• Sequential Circuits develops the Prophet 600, the first MIDI keyboard. MIDI, or "musical instrument digital interface," changes the way musicians and composers can work with electronic instruments and computers by forming a single universally compatible system that one performer can control.

GOVERNMENT AND POLITICS

• President Reagan recommends funding a ballistic-missile shield in space, the Strategic Defense Initiative, known as SDI or "Star Wars." He wants to pursue this defensive-shield idea because he believes it is the best protection for the U.S. against threats of long-range missile attacks by other countries. The proposal ignites a fierce political debate within the U.S. and among its allies, who say it will violate the Anti-Ballistic Missile Treaty of 1972 and reignite the arms race as countries develop countermeasures. Although many scientists believe there is no adequate technology available to construct the system, Reagan gains congressional funding to begin making it a reality. Reagan's dream continues receiving development funding into the twenty-first century, in spite of ongoing technological problems.

• President Reagan orders an invasion of Grenada, the most southern of the Windward Islands in the Caribbean, in an effort to thwart a Soviet-Cuban presence on the island. Stating that they need to protect American lives on the island when Prime Minister Maurice Bishop, a protégé of Cuban president Fidel Castro, is killed in a military coup on October 19, 1983, more than 1,900 U.S. Marines, with a small group of forces from the islands of Barbados, Dominica, Jamaica, St. Lucia, and St. Vincent, expel a group of Cubans and occupy the island on October 25, overthrowing a Marxist government. The United Nations denounces the U.S., calling the invasion a "flagrant violation of international law."

• President Reagan issues a proclamation that significantly increases the size of the United States, by claiming sovereignty over all living and nonliving resources in a 200-nautical mile exclusive economic zone. This territorial claim is supported by the United Nation's Law of the Sea Convention of 1982.

BUSINESS AND INDUSTRY

• General Motors and Toyota agree to a joint venture to build a new subcompact car plant in Fremont, California. As other car manufacturers make similar arrangements, it will become questionable whether it is actually possible to buy an "all-American" car.

SCIENCE AND TECHNOLOGY

• The National Institute of Standard Technologies (NIST) redefines its standard for the meter, when an atomic clock is developed, to be the distance light travels through a vacuum in 1/299,792,458 seconds.

• On January 1, TCP/IP replaces an older

host protocol known as NCP, the format or set of rules for communication that becomes the standard for the ARPA network, known as ARPANET. This is in preparation for a planned split between ARPANET, the university and laboratory research network, and MILNET, the Department of Defense's military network, used to link military sites in the U.S. The non-military network comes to be known as the Internet, and is opened to commercial use in the late 1980s.

• Sally Ride, a physicist, is selected to become the first American woman in space, and prepares to ride on the space shuttle *Challenger*.

▣ 1984, 1986

CULTURE AND SOCIETY

• A tough anti-smoking law, Proposition P, passes by a small margin in San Francisco, prohibiting people from smoking in places of business. It signals the beginning of a national change in the public's acceptance of second-hand smoke inside public spaces, with further bans soon extending to include restaurants, theaters, and commercial airlines and other forms of transportation.

• A federal commission on education reports that standardized test scores reveal a steady decline in the U.S. educational system. These findings will start a national push for emphasis on teaching "the basics," at the expense of arts, sports, counseling, and extracurricular programs in the schools.

WORLD EVENTS

• In Beirut, Lebanon, a multinational peacekeeping force of U.S. Marines, French, and Italian troops returns in September to support the Lebanese government and help maintain a

cease-fire after Christian militiamen massacre hundreds of unarmed Palestinian civilians in two West Beirut refugee camps within the Israeli area of occupation. During their stay until spring 1984, the peacekeepers are drawn into power struggles among various Lebanese factions, and the battle zone is divided by the "Green Line" into Christian and Muslim areas. Fifty people are killed in a bombing of the U.S. embassy in April, most of whom are Lebanese employed by the embassy, or visa applicants. About 250 U.S. Marines and fifty-eight French soldiers are killed in other terrorist incidents, mostly from suicide bombing attacks on military compounds. An Israeli judicial commission charges Defense Minister Ariel Sharon with "indirect responsibility" for the Palestinian massacre.

▣ 1983

1984

ARTS AND LITERATURE

• *Thriller*, the first music video featuring the narrative elements of a film, is produced by Michael Jackson.

• New York's Museum of Modern Art presents "Primitivism in 20th Century Art," a show affirming a major but rarely discussed source of modernism by placing the works of major modern vanguard artists in juxtaposition with their inspirations from African, Meso-American, Native American, Oceanic, and Eskimo objects. Subtitled "Affinity of the Tribal and the Modern," it brings up the complicated scholarly shift after World War II that changed from considering tribal works in anthropological terms and placing them in ethnology museums to seeing them as worthy of

LATINO ART IN THE 1980s

George Vargas

- Chicana expressionist Nora Mendoza (b. Texas, 1932) paints a portable mural, *Synergy,* for a funeral home in Southfield, Michigan, in 1981.
- The Museum of Modern Art in Mexico City publishes a special issue of *Artes Visuales* reporting on the state of Chicano art in the U.S., validating Chicano art as a significant international expression.
- California Chicana artist Barbara Carrasco's (b. 1955) mural *The History of L.A.: A Mexican Perspective* (1981–1983) is censored by the officials of the 1984 Summer Olympics in Los Angeles, who charge that her portrayal of Asians being discriminated against by white racists will "offend" Asian visitors.
- Successful Cuban painter Carlos Alfonzo (b. 1950) leaves Cuba with Mariel exiles, fleeing to Florida to continue his career rather than suffer censorship and/or prison.
- Sculptor Maria Brito-Avellana (b. Cuba, 1947) fled Cuba as an exile in 1961, and resettled in Florida, where she earned several degrees in art.
- Exiled, Susanna Sori (b. Cuba, 1949) moved to Chicago in 1961, traveling to India to find spiritual meaning in her life, enrolled in art schools in Chicago, Michigan, and New York, and today makes mixed-media sculpture and delicate drawings dealing with human perception, time, and motion.
- Tony Labat (b. Cuba, 1951) also left Cuba, moving to San Francisco, where he studied art. His installation pieces reveal his life in Cuba, before and after the Revolution. One of these features the great Cuban hero José Martí; another explores Afro-Cuban religion, its gods and demons.
- One of the first major touring exhibitions of Cuban artists born on the island between 1941 and 1960, *Cuba USA* is organized by Fondo del Sol Visual Arts Center (Washington), and opens in Los Angeles, St. Paul, and Chicago in 1990 and 1991.
- Chicana artist and feminist scholar Amalia Mesa-Bains constructs *An Ofrenda for Dolores del Rio* in 1984, based on the traditional Mexican altar form celebrating Día de Los Muertos.
- A member of "Los Four," Gilbert "Magu" Lujan (b. California, 1940), paints a low-rider car with Aztec Indian images.

consideration by art historians and placing them in art museums.

• Trumpeter Wynton Marsalis is the first performer to win Grammy awards in both classical and jazz music.

GOVERNMENT AND POLITICS

• Ronald Reagan wins a second term by a landslide 59 percent of the vote, against Democrat Walter Mondale and his running mate, Geraldine Ferraro (b. 1935). Ferraro is the first woman ever nominated to run for vice president by a major political party.

BUSINESS AND INDUSTRY

• Apple launches the Macintosh computer, which uses a new handheld device called a mouse, making personal computers more user-friendly machines for the general public. Since it requires almost no training to operate, students, home users, and executives can use this computer without needing to understand its inner workings. This computer and the hardware and software industry that grows around it creates the world of desktop publishing.

• Forty tons of toxic gases leak from a Union Carbide pesticide tank at a chemical plant in the city of Bhopal, India, injuring or sickening more than 500,000 people and killing 8,000 in its immediate aftermath, according to the Bhopal People's Health and Documentation Clinic. The corporation is U.S.-based and -owned, although operated by Indians. The fifteen-year-old factory is built and used under conditions that would not pass U.S. standards for materials, monitoring devices, and safety systems; however, Union Carbide says the accident is caused by a disgruntled employee. When its chairman, Warren Anderson, arrives to inspect the industrial disaster, he is arrested for "negligence and criminal corporate liability," and only released on bail after prolonged negotiations. Anderson skips bail and returns to the United States, which has refused to extradite him to India to stand trial. Union Carbide settles lawsuits amounting to $470 million in the Supreme Court of India, averaging about $90 (U.S.) per survivor and $430 per victim, with shareholders' loss at fifty cents per share. A survivors' organization places the continuing death toll at over 16,000 in 1999, as the toxic impact of the disaster continues and victims suffer slow and painful deaths. The Bhopal disaster is called the worst commercial industrial disaster in history.

🔲 1999

SCIENCE AND TECHNOLOGY

• A baboon's heart is implanted into a newborn baby, "Baby Fay," in an unsuccessful attempt to keep her alive until a human heart can be found. Surgeon William H. Clewall of the University of Colorado Health Sciences Center at Denver conducts the first successful surgery on an unborn fetus.

• Lieutenant Colonel Guion S. Bluford Jr. becomes the first African American astronaut to travel in outer space, as a member of the *Challenger* space shuttle mission, and Sally Ride (b. 1951) becomes the first woman to travel in space on the same mission.

CULTURE AND SOCIETY

• This is a key year for the Chicano cultural movement. Cultural institutions such as La Galeria de la Raza (San Diego) SPARC (Los Angeles) and La Galeria de la Raza (San Francisco) redefine themselves in relationship with the larger society—shedding separations and making multicultural alliances with other Latinos as well as blacks, Asians, feminists, and gays.

• The *Navajo Times* becomes the first daily Native American newspaper in the U.S.

• Lily Lee Chen becomes the first Chinese American woman mayor of a U.S. city, Monterey Park, California, also known as "Chinese Beverly Hills" and "Little Taipei" because of its large Chinese population. The city owes its development in great part to the financial worries of wealthy Hong Kong and Taiwanese investors concerning the impending 1997 transfer of the British colony to the People's Republic of China. Other beneficiaries of this power shift include downtown Oakland, California, which receives substantial financial investments that fund the downtown renovation, and New York's Chinatown, which will double in size between 1980 and 1990.

WORLD EVENTS

• The Soviets announce they will boycott the Los Angeles Olympics.

• India's prime minister, Indira Gandhi, is assassinated by two Sikh bodyguards, after the army attacks the Sikhs' Golden Temple in Amritsar, in the Punjab, where Sikh separatists have sought to become an independent state since the formation of India as a federal republic in 1947. One thousand people are killed in anti-Sikh riots. Her son, Rajiv Gandhi, succeeds her as prime minister.

• When Tommaso Buscetta (b. Sicily, 1929; d. 2000) decides to break the Mafia oath of silence by cooperating with Italian police, and later American prosecutors, his testimony helps to put hundreds of Mafia leaders in Italy and the U.S. behind bars, and sets off a decade of violent retribution against Italian judges, prosecutors, and local officials.

1985

ARTS AND LITERATURE

• Guerrilla Girls, an ever-changing group of activist artists who remain anonymous behind gorilla masks, act as the "conscience of the art world" by posting informational flyers and staging political actions around Manhattan's art world, exposing the galleries that exhibit no women artists and advocating for women in the art world. An African American women artists' collective called PESTS wages a similar agitprop campaign against racism and sexism in the art world.

• Marc Smith creates and hosts the Poetry Slam at the Green Mill Tavern in Chicago. It makes poetry accessible, appealing to the public through its competitive form and its offering of an open mike, with the audience in control as judges. Poetry slams spread across the country, from coast to coast, until, by the 1990s, there is a National Slam.

• HMSL (Hierarchical Music Specification Language), a widely used real-time artificial language for experimental music composition and performance, is developed at Mills College in Oakland, California, by Larry Polansky, David Rosenboom, and Phil Burke.

GOVERNMENT AND POLITICS

• EMILY's List (Early Money Is Like Yeast) is created as a women's political network to fund election campaigns to get Democratic women elected to Congress, where there are two women out of one hundred senators and twenty women out of 434 members in the House of Representatives. By 1999, in the 106th Congress, there will be nine women in the Senate and fifty-eight women in the House.

• The Philadelphia headquarters of MOVE, a radical African American activist group advocating rejection of materialism and modern technology, is bombed by the Philadelphia police on orders of Police Commissioner Gregore J. Sambor after a twenty-four-hour siege. Eleven people are killed, an entire city block of sixty-one row houses is destroyed, and 300 people are left homeless by this action. Mayor Wilson Goode appoints a commission to investigate the police operation. One of its findings is that the FBI supplied the detonation device for the bomb, which was dropped by a police helicopter onto the roof of the headquarters.

BUSINESS AND INDUSTRY

• America Online (AOL), an Internet service provider (ISP), is founded by Steven M. Case,

"HIGH" ART AND "LOW" ART

The distinctions between "high art" and "low art" continue to fade as artists mix the street sensibilities of hip-hop graffiti, billboards, advertising, and other public media forms, moving between the streets and neighborhood grassroots activism, the art galleries and late-night clubs, and the commercial world. The work is politically engaged, frequently collaborative, and energized by popular culture.

who serves as chairman and CEO. It goes public in 1992, becoming the nation's largest online information company. Known as a nonthreatening service for customers who are new to online technology, it survives various financial setbacks, merging with Netscape in 1995, a pioneering software company co-founded by Marc Andreessen in 1994. By 2000, it is serving nearly 22 million subscribers throughout the world, and merges with the nation's largest media company, Time Warner, becoming the media and technology behemoth AOL Time Warner.

◎ 2000

SCIENCE AND TECHNOLOGY

• Research and development of synfuels—alternative energy sources based on coal or oil shales—loses nearly all its funding because of a glut of petroleum on the world market.

• Seven New Jersey teenage computer whiz-kid hackers, with the tag names of Vampire, Red Barchett, Private Sector, N.J., Hack Shack, Store Manager, Treasure Chest, and Beowulf, succeed in accessing confidential computer systems of the Pentagon and AT&T, running up credit-card purchases and making free calls to Europe. The potential for a new form of terrorism comes of age.

• Construction begins on the world's largest telescope, on the peak of Mauna Kea in Hawaii. Called the Keck Observatory, its mirror will be thirty-three feet (ten meters) in diameter, and will not be cast in a single piece. The construction of the observatory causes demonstrations by native Hawaiians who see the Keck as a desecration of their holy mountain.

CULTURE AND SOCIETY

• Wilma Mankiller becomes the first woman in modern history to lead a large tribe, when she is sworn in as principal leader of the Cherokee nation.

• This year the federal government estimates that 250,000 to 300,000 people, most of whom reside in urban areas, are homeless. By 1989 the U.S. Department of Education estimates that 273,000 children are homeless, while the General Accounting Office estimates the number of homeless children at 310,000.

• Crack, a new form of cocaine, first appears on the streets of Los Angeles and New York. It is processed from cocaine powder into a crystal form and smoked rather than inhaled through the nose like powder cocaine, greatly accelerating addiction. Crack use will quickly spread to the suburbs and other cities, causing widespread problems in addiction and crime. Although in the late 1990s the federal government denies charges that they were involved, through Contra-related guns-for-drugs deals in Nicaragua, in the supply line for drugs dumped in Los Angeles, in 2002 a CIA report corroborates the charge.

STEALING THE LANGUAGE

Alicia Suskin Ostriker

Like every literary movement, contemporary women's poetry in part perpetuates and in part denounces and renounces its past. Women today tend to continue what [poet] Louise Bogan identified as the key contribution of their grandmothers to the life of American poetry: "the line of feeling." At the same time, much of their vitality derives from an explosive attempt to overcome the mental and moral confinement they identify with these grandmothers, and this effort has both thematic and formal consequences . . . a quest for autonomous self-definition . . . ; defining a personal identity . . . begin[ing] with their bodies and . . . interpret[ing] external reality through the medium of the body . . . ; expressions of rage . . . female desire . . . defin[ing] an identity which is not merely personal but communal . . . ; [with a] variety of strategies women use to subvert and overcome [an "oppressor's language" which denies them access to authoritative expression].

(FROM THE INTRODUCTION TO *Stealing the Language: The Emergence of Women's Poetry in America* BY ALICIA SUSKIN OSTRIKER. BOSTON: BEACON PRESS, 1986)

WORLD EVENTS

• The U.S. joins with other nations to impose sanctions against the Afrikaner government in South Africa, in protest of their racist policies.

• The presence of an "ozone hole" over Antarctica, an opening in the atmospheric layer that shields Earth from 99 percent of the sun's ultraviolet rays, is confirmed by satellite records. First detected by scientists in 1977, this indisputable data confirms that 2.5 percent of the Earth's ozone has disappeared in five years.
📷 1987

• When Communist Party General Secretary Konstantin Chernenko dies in March, the Kremlin picks his number-two man, Mikhail Gorbachev, to head the Soviet Union. Gorbachev introduces a restructuring of the economy and systems of government operation, called *perestroika,* and appeals for openness, called *glasnost,* to radically reconsider Soviet politics, culture, and history, condemning Stalin's reign of terror and Brezhnev's "stagnation." The easing of tensions between nations begins in earnest.
📷 1987

1986

ARTS AND LITERATURE

• Painters whose work gets noticed first as graffiti, which they "throw up" on the walls of subways and abandoned buildings with spray-can paints, include Jean-Michel Basquiat (b. 1960, Haitian/Puerto Rican American; d. 1989) whose street tag, with Al Dias, is "SAMO" (Same Old Shit); Keith Haring (1958–1990), whose "tag" signature is an image called "radiant baby"; Fab 5 Freddy (Fred Brathwaite) (b. 1957); Kenny Scharf (b. 1958); and many others who first come to prominence through their illegal "tags," the term for each artist's individual style of marker. Basquiat's first solo show in the U.S. comes in 1982 at the Annina Nosei Gallery

THE GREAT MERGER WAVE OF THE 1980s

During those "go-go" years, raiding parties of investors would search out likely targets for a "takeover." The targets were usually big but lackadaisical companies that did not run their operations with an eye on the bottom line. The raiders would then begin to buy stock in the company, usually with the help of a hefty line of credit from a cooperative bank. As soon as a raiding group succeeded in getting enough shares to exercise a controlling voice in the company's affairs, it would install a new management to complete the coup. The new management would thereupon issue very high-interest bonds, using the proceeds to pay back their indebtedness to the bank. It would also strip the company of its assets, leaving the corporate shell with massive amounts of debt that was not backed by productive assets. These so-called junk bonds then became a burden both on the company and on the incautious investors who had bought them. During these merger mania years, the total volume of corporate debt doubled, and the cost of meeting interest came to absorb 90 percent of all after-tax income of American corporations."

(From Robert Heilbroner and Lester Thurow, *Economics Explained*
[New York: Simon & Schuster, 1998], 107–8.)

in New York City. He becomes a prolific, highly sought-after painter in his short life, leaving an estate of about 900 works on paper and ninety-five paintings. In 1986, Haring opens a retail store, Haring's Pop Shop, at 292 Lafayette Street in New York City's SoHo area, where he sells inexpensive, popular items, such as T-shirts, refrigerator magnets, and buttons adorned with his "baby" tag, and cartoonlike images of barking dogs and moving stick figures. Haring wants to "reach millions of people whom I would not have reached by remaining an unknown artist. I assumed, after all, that the point of making art was to communicate and contribute to a culture" (excerpt from Keith Haring's "untitled statement," *Flash Art* 116 (March 1984): 20–28).

• Collaborative groups such as COLAB (Collaborative Projects) create new outposts of progressive art. COLAB places its 1980 exhibition, "Times Square Show," in a former massage parlor near Times Square. For one month it presents over 100 artists' conceptual art installations, political manifestos, graffiti art, and video, film, and slide projections, gaining wide media coverage for many young careers, including those of Kiki Smith (b. 1954), Nan Goldin (b. 1953), Jenny Holzer (b. 1950), Jean-Michel Basquiat, Keith Haring, Tom Otterness (b. 1952), and John Ahearn (b. 1951).

• Border Arts Workshop uses experimental art techniques and performance-derived practices to bring media attention to U.S. policies toward the southern border, to reveal human-rights violations by the U.S. Border Patrol, and to reveal distortions in media of Mexico and Mexicans. In 1986, its *End of the Line* performance seats workshop artists and friends at a huge bi-national table bisected by the borderline near the Mexican border at Tijuana. Also in 1986, the Workshop sets up an office at the

Capp Street Project in San Francisco, where its project functions as a real-life communications link between residents of the U.S., Canada, and Mexico through an 800 telephone line, fax, and mail.

- "Ultimate Breaks and Beats," an anthology of the most frequently used backbeats, drum rolls, guitar licks, and song samples, is compiled in a book by DJ Afrika Bambaataa and collector Lenny Roberts. The anthology will become a twenty-five-volume series, providing hip-hop musicians with raw materials to mix their musical collages. DJs compete with each other for the most original mixing style, but since the materials come from existing albums, some musicians invoke their rights to copyright restrictions.

- Composer Anthony Davis (b. 1951) collaborates with his cousin, writer Thulani Davis (b. 1949), on the three-act opera *X: The Life and Times of Malcolm X,* which begins as a commission from The Kitchen in 1985 and has its world premiere production at the New York City Opera this September, under the direction of Rhoda Levine. Its three acts, starting from the early life of Malcolm X in Lansing, Michigan, in 1931 and ending with his death in 1965 in Harlem, tells the story of Malcolm as an illustration of the power of individuals to transform. It incorporates musical references from blues, swing, bebop, and jazz, up to Coltrane, essential sounds from the time periods that frame Malcolm's life.

GOVERNMENT AND POLITICS

- The National Security Council violates government policy (the Boland Amendment) by taking funds made through secret sales of weapons to Iran in exchange for freeing hostages in Lebanon, and then clandestinely diverting the profits to fund the Nicaraguan Contra fighting forces. This becomes known as the Iran-Contra Affair, when the news breaks in November.

🔲 1982

- In January the Reagan Administration accuses Libyan leader Colonel Muammar el-Qaddafi of fostering international terrorist acts in his country, and imposes trade and commercial sanctions on Libya, besides ordering all U.S. citizens to leave the country. In April, 150 U.S. planes, with the support of the British Air Force, bomb two areas of Libya. These raids, aimed at military targets outside of Tripoli and Qaddafi's family living quarters in a residential area of Tripoli, kill forty civilians, including Qaddafi's infant daughter. House Republican leader Robert Michel says, "It's a new kind of war. It's a terrorist war." The U.S. action is widely protested across Europe.

- Congress passes the Immigration Reform and Control Act (IRCA or the Simpson-Mazzoli Act), offering legal status to any applicant who entered the U.S. illegally but who has continuously resided in the U.S. since January 1, 1982. The IRCA bill creates a new classification for seasonal agricultural workers, with provisions for their legalization that offers relief to undocumented Hispanics and Asians, relieving their fears of deportation and helping to stop employers' abuses of their workers' illegal status. The bill also calls for sanctions against employers who knowingly hire, recruit, or refer undocumented aliens to work in the U.S.

- Ben Nighthorse Campbell, a member of the Northern Cheyenne of Montana, is elected to the U.S. House of Representatives; John D. Waihee becomes the first native Hawaiian to be elected governor of Hawaii.

• Operation Pipeline, a federal government program under the Drug Enforcement Administration (DEA), writes the textbook on racial profiling. It instructs police departments throughout the country to train their officers to search for narcotics traffickers on major highways by singling out cars with Latinos and West Indians for extra investigation. The DEA and the Department of Transportation continue encouraging this emphasis on racial and ethnic characteristics in their descriptions of drug trade operations.

BUSINESS AND INDUSTRY

• Ivan Boesky, one of the best-known speculators in takeover stocks, pleads guilty to using illegal secret information to buy and sell stocks and securities, and receives a $100-million penalty, half of which represents his illegal profits and half as a civil penalty. Both Boesky and David Solomon, a former junk-bond trader and founder of Solomon Asset Management, reveal their illegal insider trading practices with Michael R. Milken, head of the high-yield junk-bond desk at Drexel Burnham Lambert. In 1987, Milken earns $550 million, the highest salary in history to date. He comes to symbolize the crisis, pleading guilty to six felony charges of securities fraud and conspiracy, brought by the Securities and Exchange Commission. In 1990 he is sentenced to serve ten years in jail, plus three years on probation, and to pay $600 million in fines and penalties, the largest monetary penalty to date. He serves twenty-two months in prison, and pays another $47 million in penalties after violating the terms of his parole. Since Milken has earned more than $1.1 billion at Drexel, he remains a rich man.

SCIENCE AND TECHNOLOGY

• On NASA's twenty-fifth shuttle mission, the space shuttle *Challenger* explodes in a ball of fire seventy-three seconds after takeoff from Cape Canaveral, Florida, killing all seven passengers aboard. The six astronauts include the commander, Francis R. Scobee; the pilot, Michael J. Smith; and astronauts Judith A. Resnik, Gregory B. Jarvis, African American scientist Ronald E. McNair, and Japanese American Ellison S. Onizuka. A science teacher, Christa McAuliffe, is also killed. She is the first private citizen to travel to space, invited to promote the educational aspects of the program. The accident is attributed to a malfunction in one of the solid-fuel booster rockets, caused by cold weather. The disaster causes NASA to suspend the space program to reevaluate its operations and planning.

CULTURE AND SOCIETY

• The spectacle called the Burning Man Festival is founded by two friends, Larry Harvey and Jerry James, when they build an eight-foot-high wooden man with some friends, which they ignite on June 21 on Baker Beach in San Francisco without official permits. They decide to repeat their "radical self-expression" yearly, continuing to increase the size of the wooden figure and make it more elaborate, requiring more help and resources from others. By 1990, after the "man" has become as tall as a four-story building, the event attracts hundreds of people, including the police, who insist that the man not be burned. The site is permanently moved to the Black Rock Desert, and the date changed to Labor Day weekend, where it continues as a yearly cultural event, growing ever more elaborate, especially as it is embraced by "techies" and attracts media coverage.

WORLD EVENTS

• A Soviet-designed nuclear reactor explodes in a meltdown at Chernobyl, just north of Kiev in the Ukraine, causing untold deaths and spreading a poisonous radioactive cloud that blows toward the rest of Europe and contaminates the surrounding area. It is estimated that the released radioactivity is 200 times the amount released by the atomic bombs dropped on Hiroshima and Nagasaki. Over the next fourteen years in the Ukraine itself, 4,000 cleanup workers will die, and 70,000 will be disabled by radiation. Of the Ukraine's 50 million people, about 3.4 million are considered affected by Chernobyl, including around 1.26 million children. In December 2000, Chernobyl is shut down permanently, although cleanup operations will continue to be necessary for many years.

• The International Court of Justice rules that the U.S. is in breach of international law for intervening in Nicaragua militarily and economically by their support of the Contras.

• After losing an election and U.S. support of his fight to hold on to power, former Philippine president Ferdinand Marcos goes into exile in Hawaii, and Corazon Aquino, widow of the assassinated opposition leader Benigno Aquino, is sworn into office as the new president. In 1986 the U.S. Congress approves $200 million in economic aid to stabilize the Philippine economy wrecked by the corruption of the Marcos regime.

• The Haitian National Assembly is dis-

solved and the constitution suspended as nearly thirty years of the Duvalier dynasty ends when president-for-life Jean-Claude Duvalier agrees to leave Haiti on a U.S. Air Force Jet for asylum in France.

• An *Intifadah,* or uprising, is declared by Palestinians after violence escalates in Israel and the occupied Palestinian Territories. Palestinian protests are met with Israeli police actions that lead to deaths of hundreds of demonstrators, and criticism of Israel in the UN and the U.S.

1987

ARTS AND LITERATURE

• The art world responds to the growing AIDS epidemic through the formation of two major organizations, Art Against Aids and the Names Project Memorial Quilt. Art Against AIDS raises over $5 million in its first two years through auctions of donated artworks. The Names Quilt, a commemorative artwork that grows to be the largest community art project ever known in the world, starts as a remembrance and healing made by friends, family, and lovers of those who have died from AIDS. As the epidemic continues, more people contribute three-by-six-foot panels to the project. In 1987, the 1,920-panel Memorial Quilt is displayed for the first time on the National Mall in Washington, D.C., during the National March for Lesbian and Gay Rights. As the quilt tours throughout the country in 1988, it continues to grow, gathering 6,000 panels. In 1996, the last time the quilt is displayed in its entirety, it poignantly illustrates the enormity of the epidemic as panels from every state in the

Union and twenty-eight countries cover the entire Washington Mall. By 2001, the quilt has 44,000 panels. The Names Project also raises over $3 million for AIDS organizations.

• The National Museum of Women in the Arts opens in a former Masonic Temple in Washington, D.C., established by a conservative Republican art collector, Wilhelmina Holladay, who becomes interested in creating a museum to house her private collection of women artists. The feminist art community criticizes the museum's conservative policies, which endorse avoiding artworks depicting social and political issues such as abortion and homosexuality. Some women artists fear this space will ghettoize their work, giving mainstream museums an excuse not to exhibit women's work in their spaces. However, no one wants to go on public record against the museum's formation. Holladay ignores criticism, successfully raising an endowment that establishes a very successful museum.

• *Nixon in China,* a grand opera by minimalist composer John Adams, with libretto by Alice Goodman, choreography by Mark Morris, set by Adrianne Lobel, and direction by Peter Sellars, is commissioned and performed by a consortium of presenters: the Brooklyn Academy of Music, the Houston Grand Opera Company, and the Kennedy Center. Increasingly, experimental artists are invited to work on big-budget opera productions.

GOVERNMENT AND POLITICS

• In Washington, President Reagan and Soviet leader Mikhail Gorbachev sign the first arms-control agreement between the two countries. It sets up a three-year schedule to reduce the size of both nations' nuclear arsenals, including dismantling all 1,752 Soviet and 959 American missiles with ranges of 300 to 3,400 miles. Inspectors from both countries are intended to ensure compliance. It makes no mention of Reagan's Strategic Defense Initiative (SDI) Plan, which stalled initial talks at a 1986 superpower summit in Reykjavik, Iceland.

▣ 1982

• Dr. Benjamin F. Chavis, Jr., executive director of the United Church of Christ Commission for Racial Justice, publishes their study, *Toxic Wastes and Race in the United States.* They introduce the term "environmental racism," defined as "Racial discrimination in environmental policy-making, enforcement of regulations and laws, and targeting of communities of color for toxic waste disposal and siting of polluting industries." The commission compiles a nationwide list of toxic waste facilities, identifies the census tracks where they are located, and runs four statistical analyses on their addresses to determine the relationship between the sitings and the demographic characteristics of surrounding communities. After looking at high school education, home ownership, income, and race, they find that race is the most reliable predictor as to where toxic waste dumps will be located, with three out of every five African American and Latinos residing near unregulated toxic waste sites. Their findings, as well as succeeding studies that prove economic considerations also factor into sitings, are critical to civil rights activists and environmentalists working to secure clean and healthy environments for people of color and low-income.

▣ 1981

BUSINESS AND INDUSTRY

• On October 19, the stock market experiences the worst crash since 1929, at the start of the Great Depression. The Dow drops 23 percent, falling 508.32 points to finish at 1,738.34 on a volume of 604 shares, a fall even greater than the 1929 crash that set off the Great Depression. The blame can be laid on multiple economic causes: federal spending is higher than the tax level the government is willing to set, due to Reagan's tax-cutting promises; foreign imports are far behind exports; prices are rising too quickly; and borrowing from abroad has become necessary to finance the deficit. Stock markets around the world echo the crash. But what makes this crash feel different from that of 1929 is the existence of what has come to be known as "the safety net," including federal deposit insurance, unemployment insurance, and Social Security insurance, which work as a cushion to protect against widespread destitution and financial panic.

SCIENCE AND TECHNOLOGY

• The garbage barge *Mobro,* captained by entrepreneur Lowell Harrelson, who thinks he can make a profit from methane gas produced by the rotting mess, begins a 6,000-mile, 162-day journey in search of a dumping ground for its 3,168 pounds of industrial waste. Departing from the town of Islip, Long Island, which claims it has exhausted its waste space, *Mobro* is turned away by five states and three countries before it returns home to New York, where its cargo is incinerated. The widespread media coverage alerts environmentalists and city planners to the building landfill and waste disposal problem in a nation that produces three to four pounds of trash per person per day.

CULTURE AND SOCIETY

• Treatment of women in the workforce becomes a major issue, especially with the attention given congressional hearings that include sexual harassment charges brought by Anita Hill against her former boss, Supreme Court nominee Clarence Thomas, who will receive an appointment as a Supreme Court judge.

• The Lila Wallace/Reader's Digest Fund is created. Its mission statement features funding of geographical outreach and cultural pluralism. By 1991 the fund's endowment reaches $32 million, making it the single largest private foundation supporting performing and visual arts in the U.S.

WORLD EVENTS

• The Montreal Protocols, an agreement to eliminate the use of chlorofluorocarbons (CFCs) by 2000, are signed by fifty-three industrial nations. However, countries not bound by the agreement continue production of CFCs, and CFCs produced and released in past years continue to rise into the upper atmosphere. This pollution traps reflected sunlight, raising the atmosphere's temperature and causing global warming, besides continuing to deplete the ozone layer, which intensifies the sun's ultraviolet rays and increases the occurrence of skin cancers.

🄯 1985

• Jordan releases the West Bank, an area mainly populated by Palestinians, which has been under Israeli occupation since 1967, to the Palestinians. At a meeting in Algiers in 1988, the

PNC declares the area the State of Palestine, as outlined in UN Partition Plan 181. The new state is not recognized by countries that recognize Israel, including the U.S. The UN will hold a special 1990 meeting in Geneva, so the new state's president, Yasser Arafat, can address its General Assembly on the question of Palestine, and request international protection for the Palestinian people, their property and holy places. The U.S. vetoes a Security Council motion to send a fact-finding mission to the area.

1988

ARTS AND LITERATURE

• The first National Black Arts Festival takes place in Atlanta, Georgia, featuring artists of the African diaspora, including the arts of music, theater, dance, film, literature, and the visual arts. At first scheduled to occur in alternating years with the National Black Theater Festival, it becomes an annual event that, by the beginning of the twenty-first century, attracts over 25,000 artists and audiences of over 5 million. In 1989, the National Black Theater Festival moves to its own site in Winston-Salem, North Carolina.

GOVERNMENT AND POLITICS

• On August 10, President Reagan signs the Civil Liberties Act of 1988, a law that issues a formal apology to the Japanese American community by the U.S. government, admitting that "a grave injustice" motivated by "racial prejudice, war hysteria and failure of political leadership" led to the internment of 140,000 Japanese American citizens during World War II. Twenty thousand dollars is granted as restitution to each of the surviving 60,000 Japanese

Americans internees alive on the day the bill is signed. It also creates a $1.25-billion education fund. The Aleuts of the Pribilof and Aleutian Islands are also to be compensated for their forced relocation during World War II.

• Douglas Wilder, Democrat of Virginia, is the first African American to be elected governor of a state.

• The Termination Resolution of 1953, in which 13 tribes were officially terminated, or lost federal protections and services, is officially repealed by Congress.

SCIENCE AND TECHNOLOGY

• Prozac, a synthesized fluoxetine that increases serotonin levels in the brain, receives FDA approval for use as an antidepressant in the U.S. The pill becomes wildly popular, and by 1997 there are 30 million Prozac users worldwide, with $2.56 billion received in sales.

• TAT-8, the first fiberoptic telephone cable, is laid across the Atlantic Ocean, making fiberoptic cable competitive with satellite technology for point-to-point communications used by cellular telephone systems.

CULTURE AND SOCIETY

• Thousands of undocumented aliens rush to apply for U.S. citizenship or permanent resident status, taking advantage of the U.S. government's amnesty program before the deadline is over.

• The National Education Council recommends that every school furnish counseling for students questioning their sexuality.

WORLD EVENTS

• Nicaragua plans for free elections after a cease-fire agreement is negotiated between the Sandinistas and the Contras.

• Benazir Bhutto (b. 1953) becomes prime minister of Pakistan, the first Islamic woman to hold this office.

1989

ARTS AND LITERATURE

• A frenzied art market, having shown fabulously intense and continuous growth during the 1980s, reacts to nationwide recessionary trends. Full-market and auction prices drop, galleries close, and jobs associated with the sale of art (commercial and auction) are lost.

• The National Endowment for the Arts' funding process is made the center of a massive debate over definitions of obscenity and censorship, spearheaded by Jessie Helms, the Christian Coalition, and Donald Wildmon of the American Family Association. The debate is set off by *Piss Christ,* a photograph by Andres Serrano (b. 1950) of a crucifix he placed in a container of his own urine; and depictions of gay sex acts in *X Portfolio,* a series of photographs by Robert Mapplethorpe (1946–1989) and portions of paintings by David Wojnarowicz (1954–1992). Wildmon, Helms, and the Christian Coalition solicit other members of Congress, demanding that the NEA's budget be cut back. When the Corcoran Gallery of Art in Washington, D.C., cancels a Mapplethorpe photography exhibition as a result, vigorous anti-censorship protests are waged by artists, funders, art patrons, and museum and gallery owners.

• *Tilted Arc,* a public, site-specific abstract sculpture made by Richard Serra (b. 1939) under a commission from the General Services Administration (GSA), has been installed at the Federal Plaza, a Lower Manhattan site, since

1981. Two months after its installation, 1,300 people working in buildings adjacent to the plaza petition the GSA to remove the work. It becomes the subject of years of legal and administrative battles, until it is finally dismantled and removed by the GSA in 1989. In a legal action Serra files in March 1989, he says that the removal of the sculpture "is a death blow, it's thoughtless and barbaric. The U.S. government has never before destroyed a work of art it has commissioned." After it is gone, Serra says, *"Tilted Arc* was not destroyed because the sculpture was uncivil, but because the government wanted to set a precedent in which they could demonstrate the right to censor and destroy speech."

• Congress passes the National Museum of the American Indian Act to fund the establishment of a National Museum of the American Indian housed in New York and as part of the Smithsonian complex on the Mall in Washington, D.C. The plan is to create exhibitions from the Native point of view. It also repatriates many objects from the Smithsonian's physical anthropology collection to Alaska Native villages.

GOVERNMENT AND POLITICS

• George Herbert Walker Bush (b. 1924) is inaugurated as forty-first president, with Dan Quayle as his vice president, after defeating Democrat and Massachusetts Governor Michael Dukakis by 54 percent of the popular vote.

• The National Assembly of Panama places General Manuel Noriega as head of the government, and proclaims that a state of war exists between the U.S. and Panama. After an American soldier is killed in Panama on

December 16, Noriega's government is overthrown in an invasion of Panama by 12,000 U.S. Navy, Army, Air Force, and Marine troops. General Noriega is arrested on drug-trafficking charges and taken to the U.S., where he will be imprisoned and put on trial. The Organization of American States protests the U.S. invasion.

• Army General Colin R. Powell (b. 1937) becomes the first African American chairman of the Joint Chiefs of Staff, and the youngest ever appointed to this highest military post.

BUSINESS AND INDUSTRY

• The Supreme Court rules, in *City of Richmond v. J. A. Croson Company*, that the city's hiring program is illegal in mandating that at least 30 percent "set-aside" of the city's public works funds be subcontracted to minority-owned construction firms. The Richmond plan defines "Minority Business Enterprises" as those at least 51 percent owned by "black, Spanish-speaking, Oriental, Indian, Eskimo or Aleut citizens." Their 5–4 decision is based upon the point that Richmond's plan included a corrective for ethnic populations that had not historically resided in Richmond. It refers to the definition of discrimination under the Fourteenth Amendment's Equal Protection Clause, interpreting that hiring quotas can only be legal if they are based on clear evidence that the under-representation of minorities is due to prior discrimination. The ruling adds another death knell to the use of affirmative action measures gained in the 1960s.

• President Bush signs legislation authorizing $166 billion to bail out the savings and loan industry over a ten-year period. According to Ralph Nader, the Federal bailout will eventually cost taxpayers $500 billion dollars, which will not be paid off until 2020.

🄿 1980, 1982

SCIENCE AND TECHNOLOGY

• As compact disc (CD) players, computers, digital audio tape (DAT), and other electronic devices become more accessible and affordable for many households, their increasing technological innovations inspire new art forms and applications in architecture and other design fields, film, and video. This year, computer scientist Jaron Lanier designs a computer-generated headset and special gloves that make it possible to experience and manipulate virtual reality, an advanced form of computer simulation.

• The Satellite Educational Resources Consortium begins sending educational programming to high schools in rural and other communities by way of television.

• The U.S. Department of Defense begins using an experimental network of microcomputer-based workstations that enable military personnel to practice combat situations with interactive, real-time training systems.

CULTURE AND SOCIETY

• As of this year, 66,000 deaths have resulted from the AIDS epidemic in the U.S. alone. The virus takes more lives than the Vietnam War as it spreads worldwide.

• The Civil Rights Memorial, honoring those who died fighting for equal rights, is dedicated in Montgomery, Alabama.

• After the nation's governors hold a summit conference on education, Congress establishes the National Education Goals Panel (NEGP) to set voluntary higher educational standards to be achieved by the year 2000. The NEGP is also to provide ways to monitor, measure, and report on the progress in each individual state, setting off a debate about the appropriate contents for standards and the validity of testing.

🔲 1999

WORLD EVENTS

• The USSR holds its first competitive elections since 1917, with dissident candidates winning many seats in the Supreme Soviet. Mikhail Gorbachev is elected president.

• Six weeks of student-led hunger strikes protesting for human rights and democracy take place in Tiananmen Square in central Beijing, China, following the death of a former Communist party leader, Hu Yaobang, who symbolizes political reform. Other civilians join the students in their demonstrations for a free press, more-representative government, independent labor unions, and a crackdown on corruption and inflation. In May, Deng Xiaoping and older leaders in the Politburo, the ruling political body, succeed in their calls to suppress reform, declaring martial law after a summit visit by Soviet President Gorbachev is disrupted. On June 4 the People's Liberation Army moves to retake Tiananmen Square, killing many civilians at the scene. (Chinese official records tally 200 civilians and twenty-three soldiers, while foreign estimates range from several hundred to several thousand civilians killed.) Other civilians are arrested and then executed or given long-term prison sentences. The crackdown results in a shift of leadership that continues into the twenty-first century. Jiang Zemin

becomes China's president and Communist Party general secretary, replacing party chief Zhao Ziyang, who had opposed ordering martial law. Prime Minister Li Peng, another martial-law advocate, becomes chairman of China's Parliament, the second-highest-ranking position in the Communist Party leadership. Although the U.S. institutes sanctions and protests the government actions, along with other countries throughout the world, it continues to give Chinese economic aid and trade privileges with "most favored nation" status.

• The Cold War comes to a symbolic end when East German border guards knock down parts of the Berlin Wall, and Germany is reunited for the first time since the end of World War II. Thousands of East Germans pour into West Berlin to celebrate. Throughout Eastern Europe, governments shift away from Communism and its political and economic policies.

• After forty-two years of Communist rule in Czechoslovakia, a pro-democracy movement prevails in December. This "Velvet Revolution" is headed by a loose coalition of groups called the Civic Forum, and championed by a massive student movement whose slogan is "Truth and love must prevail over lies and hatred." Their weapons are mass demonstrations in Prague's Wenceslas Square with flowers and pink-painted tanks. Playwright Vaclav Havel is elected president, and Alexander Dubcek, the former leader of the 1968 "Prague Spring" reform movement, is elected chairman of Parliament.

🔲 1968

• The Romanian Communist government of President Nicolae Ceauşescu is overthrown in a violent revolt. The president and his wife are captured, put on trial, and executed. A provisional government is organized by anti-Ceauşescu forces, with Ion Iliescu, a former Communist party official, as president. In 1990 the Communist Party is outlawed, but because no effective opposition party has emerged, Iliescu is elected president.

• In Poland, the majority of voters oppose election of Communist Party candidates and select candidates of Solidarity, an independent reformist political party, based in the trade unions, which is legalized in 1989. Solidarity wins 99 of 100 Senate seats and all the seats in the lower house they are allowed, 299 of 460, where 65 percent are reserved for the Communist Party. The parliament elects Soviet general Wojciech Jaruzelski as president, and Solidarity leader Tadeusz Mazowiecki becomes prime minister. By the following year, Solidarity will prevail and Lech Walesa, a former shipyard worker, will be elected president by 70 percent of the vote, a shift that starts in

January 1990, when the Communist Party votes to disband.

• Defeated Soviet troops evacuate Afghanistan, following acceptance of a UN-brokered agreement. After ten years of Soviet occupation and resistance by fundamentalist guerrilla fighters, called Mujahedeen, the country is left strewn with land mines, a shattered infrastructure, and most of its people living in extreme poverty. One of the most prominent Mujahedeen leaders, Osama bin Laden, forms a new international network of Muslim militants called Al-Qaeda al-Sulbah, meaning "the solid base." First headquartered with training camps in Peshawar, Pakistan, some "cells" remain in Afghanistan where fighting for control of the country continues among various Mujahedeen factions and local warlords. Other fighters trained by Al-Qaeda return to their home countries where they initiate actions against governments they consider corrupt, such as Saudi Arabia, Egypt, and Algeria, or are welcomed as heroes and assume government posts, as in the Sudan.

URBAN ENVIRONMENTALISM

Excerpts from an interview with Carl Anthony

By Ishmael Reed and Carla Blank

IR: When was the term "environmental racism" coined? Who coined that?

CA: That was a phrase coined by Ben Chavis. He used to be head of the United Church of Christ's Commission on Racial Justice. They published a report called "Toxic Waste in Race" in 1987. This study was really simple. What they basically did is they got the addresses where all the toxic waste dumps were in the country. And then they identified the census track where they were located. And then they ran four statistical analyses to determine what the relationship was between the siting of these and the demographic characteristics. They looked at high school education, home ownership, income, and race. It turned out that race was the most reliable predictor as to where these toxic waste dumps would be. Three out of four African American and Latino residents were living near uncontrolled toxic waste. But this grew out of a decade-long struggle on the part of their constituency to get the sort of established environmental groups to acknowledge the problems that black people were facing. There was a particular moment in early 1982 when 500 black people got arrested protesting outside a PCB plant in Warren, North Carolina.

IR: Are there too many people in the world?

CA: Let me just give you a little bit of arithmetic. The people in the U.S. represent 6 percent of the world's population, and use 35 percent of the world's resources. By my calculations, 35 percent of the world ought to be living here. Every one of these issues we are running up against has overlooked social dimensions. Look at global warming. The people who live in India, 800,000–900,000 people, 2 billion people in China—they're riding around on bicycles. They're not producing these CO_2 emissions that are creating global warming. But you tell the Chinese you have to sign on to protocols that say that economic development in China has to stop because of global warming while Americans riding around are causing all the CO_2 emissions. So the thing is, the polluters should pay. The simplest formula for eliminating environmental pollution is the one we all learned when we were kids—clean up behind yourselves. If you pollute, clean it up.

You have to deal with the social issues, you have to deal with economic justice, and you have to deal with racial justice. You can't just draw a line around environmental issues and say it doesn't relate. It's one thing to save the wilderness—I'm in favor of that—but let's also have some trees where the poor people live. Let's have something beautiful that they can look at. And the environmental justice movement has been focused a lot on issues of toxics. But we've been arguing that the toxics issue is both a symbol and a symptom of a much larger problem: the fact that people don't have control over their environment. People have no say over what's happening where they live. So somebody buys a piece of property and decides to build something across the street from you, you have no say over that. And this is not consistent with any sort of ecological relationship that people ought to have with their surroundings.

When my partner Jean and I were in Africa, we went around to traditional African villages. People in these villages that had nothing but mud and thatch to build with. Yet African people had an intimate relationship to their environments. When a child reached puberty, for example, the whole town came out and built a place for that child to live. And there were rituals that were built around repairing the mosque just before the rainy season. Everybody was deeply involved in this. In the U.S., we have a situation if you are tenant and you live in a housing project you don't have any say over anything. This is living in prison, not living like a human being should live. Environmental justice is not just a question of the siting of hazardous waste facilities, it's the siting of everything. Like, where do you get your food from? We have 150,000 people in S.F. today who do not meet UN standards for nutrition. Starvation. You can only go to a liquor store to buy some junk to eat because Safeway [a supermarket chain] doesn't find it convenient to be putting a Safeway in your community.

"Here" of *Still/Here* by Bill T. Jones/Arnie Zane Dance Co., 1994. (© Johan Elbers 2002, and with permission of the Bill T. Jones/Arnie Zane Dance Co.)

1990–2000

THE 1990S

MARIE ANDERSON

TOTALLY NEW TRENDS AND THE RESURGENCE of earlier concepts and patterns occur in the 1990s, a decade of major changes. America had been enjoying a booming economy, and yet there was an ever-widening gap between the "haves" and "have-nots." Many individuals were forced to work two or three jobs when previously many workers benefited from the security of long-term employment which always paid the bills.

The decade saw the rapidly increasing use of computers and the introduction of e-commerce, which took off like a rocket. The conversion of virtually all American business of any size to the use of computers for sales, research, and record-keeping was well on its way to completion by the end of the 1990s.

The cultural dominance of commercial sports and other mass entertainment became apparent. In addition to television and radio, homes now contained VCRs, CD players, and computers offering online options. Publishing became dominated by large conglomerates that gobbled up many of the smaller houses. Consolidation brought financial impacts in all parts of the industry, and many independent bookstores went by the wayside.

Large supermarkets, oil companies, and other types of chain stores also participated in mergers and acquisitions, contributing to the demise of many local mom-and-pop businesses. The telecommunications industry was opened up to competition. Many startups, however, will be unable to survive long in the capital-intense, growth-fueled telecommunications and related electronics industries.

On the health-care front, "managed care" became the new watchword signaling the end of the small, personal medical practice as we have known it. The large pharmaceutical companies continued to merge and to introduce ever more artificial drugs to sell to the public legally. On the other hand, millions of consumers began to seek alternative therapies and remedies for which they had to pay out of pocket.

The closing down of mental institutions and programs contributed to the problem of homelessness. The local shelters that existed in major urban areas such as New York and the San Francisco Bay area were not adequate to cope with the numbers of people living in the streets, many of them needing specialized care not provided to them.

The 1990s saw the growth of prison populations. More money was spent on building new prisons and housing prisoners than on rehabilitation.

The decade saw the end of smoking in offices, restaurants, schools, theaters, and other public places. Global warming and other environmental issues continued to be of concern to an increasing number of scientists and citizens. To date, however, few solutions have been implemented.

Many of those with discretionary income ignored warnings and in increasing numbers began driving gas-guzzling SUVs and using jet-skis and other "recreational toys" that were environmentally unfriendly. It was eventually acknowledged that the de-emphasis on alternative methods of transportation after the onslaught of universal auto ownership was an unforgivable error. In an attempt to solve the enormous traffic problems throughout metropolitan areas, commuter trains and ferries began to reappear.

The changes in diet over the last twenty-five years contributed to a documented 50 percent increase in the breakdown of Americans' immune systems, especially those of children. This decade saw a rise in the incidence of cancer; it is now expected that at least one in three persons will contract some form of it during their lifetimes.

Homeowners were being advised to purchase point-of-use water filtration systems, since the purity of drinking water could not be assumed. Eating fish became risky for the same reason. Because of the contamination of water and soil from pesticides and herbicides, many people began purchasing "organic" fruits and vegetables.

During the last decade of the twentieth century, Americans saw and participated in much change—some of it for the greater good. Many problems remained, however, or were excacerbated, and a great deal of work is in store for those who choose to discover and implement the solutions required for the health and welfare of the American people.

1990

ARTS AND LITERATURE

• The "Culture Wars," a popular term for controversies related to the arts and media, heat up in 1990 over issues of obscenity, freedom of expression, and artistic value. In 1990 the NEA begins requiring all organizations and individuals receiving NEA funds to sign an anti-obscenity regulation. In September the

In July 1999, the total resident population reaches 272,878,000. According to United Nations estimates, the average global life expectancy has more than doubled since 1900, when it was about thirty years. By the late 1990s, the average global life expectancy is about sixty-five years. By the late 1990s, the average life expectancy for all Americans is 76.5 years. For all American men combined it is 73.6 years, and for American women it is 79.4 years. For African American men it is 67.2 years; and for European American men it is 74.3 years. For African American women it is 74.7 years; and for European American women it is 79.9 years. Naturalization rates far surpass those of any other decade, with the majority coming from Asian, Eastern European, and African countries. Nearly two-thirds of all immigrants intend to reside in six states: California, New York, Florida, Texas, New Jersey, and Illinois. This decade also records a huge increase in numbers of aliens or "illegal immigrants" excluded or deported, largely because of the "war on drugs" and the militarization of the border. In 1990, California's non-Hispanic white population is 57 percent of the total; in 1999, for the first time since census data has been recorded in the state, the tallies indicate a shift toward increasing diversity, with the non-Hispanic white population declining to 49.8 percent of the state's total population. Among all races, 82 percent of men and 82.2 percent of women completed four years or more of high school; 26.2 percent of men and 21.7 percent of women completed four or more years of college (U.S. Census). In 1995, 69.7 percent of mothers with children under eighteen years of age are participating in the labor force (U.S. Department of Labor). Per capita personal income jumps from $18,667 in 1990 to $26,484 in 1998 (U.S. Bureau of Economic Analysis).

Independent Commission, authorized by Congress to review NEA grant procedures, reports that the NEA is "an inappropriate tribunal for the legal determination of obscenity." It recommends the NEA rescind its "obscenity pledge" requirement and authorize no legislative restrictions on the contents of art receiving federal grant funding. "Hatch-Kennedy-Pell-Kassenbaum," a bill reauthorizing NEA funding for five years, incorporates many of the commission's recommendations and those of the National Council on the Arts, including expanding the chairperson's powers and augmenting funding to state councils so that they may distribute grants to regional programs and artists. The Senate passes the bill in October, but attaches an amendment by Republican Senator Jesse Helms of North Carolina to deny funding works that denigrate religions, and a requirement that grant recipients return funding if a court rules their artwork criminally obscene. The NEA is reinstated for three years when the House and Senate reach a final compromise on October 27. The requirement to recall funds if the courts rule a work to be "criminally obscene" remains, but explicit legislative restrictions on the type of art that can be funded are eliminated. The bill does make a provision requiring the NEA to heed "general standards of decency and respect for the diverse beliefs and values of the American public" when authorizing grants.

• Guillermo Gomez Pena (b. 1955, Mexico) creates *Border Brujo*, a solo performance art-

ARTISTS' RESPONSE TO RESTRICTIONS ON GRANTS FROM THE NATIONAL ENDOWMENT FOR THE ARTS

Many artists and arts organizations, including two literary journals, the *Paris Review* and the *Gettysburg Review,* refuse to sign the NEA "obscenity" pledge, and turn down grant awards in protest of the new requirements. In July, Bella Lewitzky, director of the Bella Lewitzky Dance Company, files a suit against the NEA and its chairperson, John Frohnmayer, in Los Angeles, after turning down a $72,000 NEA grant because it requires an "obscenity pledge." *Bella Lewitzky v. John Frohnmayer* tests the constitutionality of the NEA "loyalty oath" and obscenity restrictions, which the U.S. District Court in Los Angeles finds unconstitutional in January, 1991.

An exhibit of 175 photographs by Robert Mapplethorpe (1946–1989), called "Robert Mapplethorpe: The Perfect Moment," is scheduled to open on April 7 at the Contemporary Arts Center (CAC) in Cincinnati, Ohio. The local Citizens for Community Values sends out a letter to its 16,000 members, suggesting ways to halt the show. In March the CAC, the Mapplethorpe estate, and the Robert Mapplethorpe Foundation file a suit to determine whether any of the photographs are criminally obscene according to Ohio law. On April 7, record crowds are forced to leave the museum for an hour, while Cincinnati police videotape the show as evidence that it violates "standards of decency." The museum's director, Dennis Barrie, refuses to remove the seven controversial photographs when requested by County Prosecutor Arthur Ney, and U.S. District Judge Carl Rubin blocks Cincinnati police from confiscating any photographs. Barrie and the museum are indicted on obscenity charges for exhibiting sexually explicit images that Cincinnati's Citizens for Community Values and county sheriff find "criminally obscene." On October 5, a jury takes less than two hours to find the museum and its director not guilty because the jurors "felt we had no choice. We learned that art does not have to be pretty." The same exhibition receives a citizens' action suit when it appears at Boston's Institute of Contemporary Art (ICA). The *New York Times* reports that the publicity has inflated prices the estate receives for Mapplethorpe's work, as well as income the Robert Mapplethorpe Foundation receives from licensing agreements for books, T-shirts, and posters, which will largely be donated to AIDS research, museums, and libraries. (From Philip Brookman and Debra Singer, "Chronology," in *Culture Wars: Documents from the Recent Controversies in the Arts,* edited by Richard Bolton [New York: New Press, 1992].)

Four solo performance artists, Karen Finley, John Fleck, Holly Hughes, and Tim Miller, set off a national debate when they sue the National Endowment for the Arts and its chair, John Frohnmayer. Filed in Los Angeles through the National Campaign for Freedom of Expression Legal Defense Team, the suit charges that the NEA violated the artists' constitutional rights when their grants, previously approved by peer panels, were denied by Frohnmayer in response to pressure from the conservative right, particularly protests led by Senator Jesse Helms, because the works dealt with issues of sexuality. Fleck's, Hughes's, and Miller's works are from openly gay viewpoints, while Finley's work often deals with sexual issues. The suit will wind its way through the courts, until it receives a Supreme Court ruling in 1998.

🖻 1998

work. An altar installation by Felipe Amanda serves as a set for the performance at the Sushi Performance Gallery, San Diego. In 1993 Gomez Pena collaborates with Coco Fusco and Paula Heredia on *A Couple in the Cage: A Guatinaui Odyssey.* They travel around the country portraying "specimens" from a small island off the Gulf of Mexico that are exhibited in a cage, to call up how science and popular culture, until the middle of the twentieth century, "joined together to prove the innate inferiority of non-white people." This work is conceived as a satirical comment on similar historical events, but Gomez Pena and Fusco are surprised to see people accept it as real.

• Native American artist James Luna's installation and performance work, *History of the Luiseno People: La Jolla Reservation, Xmas, 1990,* mixes fact and fiction, inspired by a Christmas tree topped with a beer can that Luna has observed on the Luiseno reservation. The performance consists mainly of Luna sitting in a room, ostensibly his home at the reservation, watching TV and drinking beer while phoning his family and friends on Christmas Eve. He says, "In my work, I'm not just criticizing the condition. I am in the condition."

• The Indian Arts and Crafts Act of 1990 is passed as an amendment to a "foreign commerce and international export" law, to "promote the development" of Native American art by putting restrictions on who can sell Indian art. Its purpose is to protect Native American artisans' markets and income, by making it illegal to display or sell fake or mass-produced Native American designs as real or "handmade" Indian crafts. It sets criminal penalties for anyone convicted of "ethnic fraud" and of "misrepresenting" a commodity as "Indian

In May, the Recording Industry Association of America unveils warning labels saying "Parental Advisory—Explicit Lyrics," a voluntary code they suggest for use on musical recordings that contain potentially controversial lyrics, especially about violence or drug use. By July, individual recording companies and artists start deciding whether to comply by placing these labels on their CDs, tapes, and albums, with restrictions on the recordings set by individual retailers.

produced." The act defines "Indian" as "any individual who is a member of an Indian tribe or . . . is certified as an Indian artist by an Indian tribe."

• The blockbuster exhibition "Chicano Art Resistance and Affirmation, 1965–1985," known as CARA, tours mainstream museums in the U.S. from 1990 to 1993, drawing record numbers of Latino and non-Latino audiences, many of whom have never before experienced Chicano culture and art.

GOVERNMENT AND POLITICS

• Congress passes the Americans with Disabilities Act, to protect the civil rights of the nation's 43 million people with disabilities. It defines a disability as "a physical or mental impairment that substantially limits one or more of the major life activities," and a disabled person as "being regarded as having such an impairment." The law aims to prevent discrimination based on a health condition that affects a person's life in a significant way. Besides profoundly changing the quality of life for disabled people, this bill also requires archi-

LATINO ART: THE 1990s AND BEYOND

Dr. George Vargas

- Representing seventeen artists, "Latino Artists: Michigan, U.S.A., Crossing Bridges," the first Michigan Latino exhibition sponsored by the U.S. Information Services to tour Europe, is well received. Large, enthusiastic crowds in eight cities in Germany view it from 1992 to 1995.

- During the 1990s, the Mexican Fine Arts Center Museum in Chicago presents annual exhibitions on the Día de Los Muertos, bringing together Latino artists and artists from Mexico to construct individual traditional and contemporary *ofrendas* or altars.

- Los Angeles Chicano filmmaker and writer Harry Gamboa Jr. (b. 1951) writes *Urban Exile* (1998), documenting his artistic and literary works, many involving the now-defunct Chicano vanguard art group ASCO.

- El Paso art teacher and popular muralist Gaspar Enriquez (b. 1942) constructs a mixed-media tableau installation, *La Rosa Dolorosa* (1995), portraying a dying Chicano gangbanger being held by his girlfriend as the Brown Madonna is unable to help—a visual protest against increasing gang violence in the U.S.

- El Paso Chicana art teacher and artist Margarita "Mago" Gandara (b. 1929, of Spanish and Mexican roots) creates a series of monumental public mosaic murals in El Paso. She receives major commissions in Juarez, Mexico, to decorate this border city.

- In Phoenix, Arizona, *A Memorial to Cesar Chavez* (a sculptural commission produced by Chicano artists Zarco Guerrero and Martin Moreno, along with Mexican architect Dalinda Jimenez) is unveiled at Cesar Chavez Plaza in 1994.

- Diana Alva, Detroit-area Chicana ceramicist and art teacher, receives an important commission from the Grosse Pointe Yacht Club to produce 200 tiles in 1996.

- Known for his murals documenting Latino military history, self-taught artist and activist Ernesto Martinez (b. El Paso, 1926) is named Artist of the Year by the state of Texas for his contributions to the development of Texan and American art in 1997. He is the first Chicano artist to receive this distinguished award.

- In Michigan, Chicana artist and feminist Nora Mendoza becomes the recipient of the prestigious Governor's Award for Outstanding Artist of the Year in 1999.

- One of the few Chicana artists working in monumental sculpture, Ambray Gonzales (b. Guam, 1956, of Mexican and Asian Pacific roots) receives a huge public art commission in 1999 from the Austin, Texas, Art in Public Places program. When completed, the limestone sculpture will decorate the city's Montoupolis Youth Center.

- Chicano art teacher and expressionist painter Vito Valdez (b. Detroit, 1952) paints the giant *Cornfield Mural* in Detroit's Mexicantown in 1998, representing Mexican farmworkers toiling in the hot sun, while protected by the Virgen de Guadalupe, who appears in the clouds above.

- Texan Chicana painter and art teacher Santa Barraza (b. Kingsville, Texas, 1951) executes *Ollin Codex Mural* at the University of Texas at San Antonio in 1997, mixing ancient Mexican cosmology with modern science to decorate the new Biosciences Building.

- In Austin, Texas, Chicano artist and early organizer of the Chicano art movement Jose Trevino (b. Austin, 1941) is shown in a retrospective exhibition, "Jose Trevino: *Raices Sin Fronteras,*" at the Mexic-Arte Museum, from October 1999 to January 2000.

- In Detroit, St. Anne's Church and the Bowen Public Branch Library sponsor one of the largest shows of Latino art in Michigan, the Tenth Annual Michigan Hispanic Artists Exhibition, in September 2000, showcasing the art of nineteen artists.

tects and city planners to incorporate design changes in future constructions, including modifications of existing public buildings and streets.

• The U.S. House of Representatives approves the Civil Rights Bill of 1990, known as a "quota" bill, that President George Bush vetoes because he says it will lead to job quotas for women and minorities. The Senate fails to override his veto by one vote.

🖻 1991

• President Bush signs the Hate Crimes Statistics Act, which orders a five-year statistical record kept on crimes with racial, ethnic, or sexual prejudice as their motivation. It is the first federal law to include the term "sexual orientation."

• Congress passes the Radiation Exposure and Compensation Act of 1990, to compensate uranium miners and their families in Arizona, Colorado, Nevada, and Utah for medical costs incurred from health problems related to their exposure to radiation during their work in the U.S. nuclear weapons program.

🖻 1995

• On August 8, 1990, President Bush tells Saddam Hussein, president of Iraq, that he has "drawn a line in the sand" that must not be crossed, six days after Hussein invades Kuwait with tanks, aircraft, and 30,000 troops, and annexes the oil-rich nation. The United Nations backs a total trade embargo against Iraq. In the next six weeks the U.S. amasses warships in the Persian Gulf, and sends more than 60,000 troops to Saudi Arabia. In September, President Bush meets with Soviet leader Mikhail Gorbachev at the Helsinki summit, where they agree to a united stand against Iraq, insisting that Iraq withdraw from Kuwait

and release their "human shield" of hostages. For the first time since 1950, the United Nations gives its sanction for military action, to be carried out by the U.S. and eleven other nations if the Iraqis do not withdraw from Kuwait by January 15, 1991.

BUSINESS AND INDUSTRY

• Cable News Network's (CNN) twenty-four-hour transmission of news coverage worldwide dominates and frames the public's understanding of what is occurring in the Persian Gulf War. The network only shows images and information released in press conferences or satellite feeds by the U.S. military information officers. The media presentations look similar to the style of high-tech video games, with their night-vision cameras that turn night scenes into a pea-green daylight haze, mock-ups to explain game plans, and repeating loops of explosions to show "successful" hits. They almost completely omit showing any of the human consequences of the exploding Scud missiles and bombs, except for exhibiting an occasional bomb crater or destroyed building.

• The U.S. economy starts a decade of expansion, the longest in its history. Presided over by Federal Reserve Chairman Alan Greenspan, his model of holding down inflation becomes a worldwide banking standard to achieve broader economic stability.

SCIENCE AND TECHNOLOGY

• The Hubble Space Telescope is launched on the space shuttle *Discovery* by NASA, allowing astronomers to probe the mysteries of time and space. Hubble is one of the largest and most complex satellites ever built. Designed to

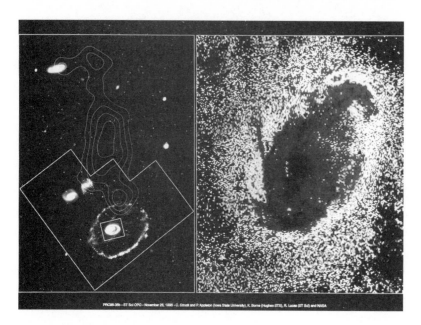

Hubble Space Telescope's images of the Cartwheel galaxy, one of four galaxies located 500 million light-years away in the constellation Sculptor. (*NASA*)

last fifteen years, the twelve-ton telescope circles the Earth in a 380-mile-high orbit. Hubble uses an eight-foot mirror, computers, imaging instruments, and pointing and control instruments to collect clearer pictures of the universe than have been possible with Earth-based telescopes. In 1994, Hubble confirms the existence of "black holes," massive stars thirty or more times larger than our sun that collapse under the force of their own gravity and pull in the space around them. (Einstein had predicted their existence in his 1915 theory of general relativity.) Hubble also detects stellar objects known as brown dwarfs, shows galaxies at the outer limits of the universe that have never been seen before, and helps calculate the age of the universe. The information being collected by Hubble will continue to inform scientists into the future.

▣ 1994, 1999

• The Department of Energy's Human Genome Project (HGP) formally begins in October. The project has two planned goals to achieve by 2005: first, to characterize an estimated 100,000 human genes (now thought to be around 30,000)—the 3 percent of human DNA interspersed between spacer "junk" sections of DNA that provide meaningful instructions for making functional proteins, the workhorses of the body; and, second, to sequence the 3.1 billion total DNA subunits, called bases, that make up the forty-six human chromosomes. The DOE's Office of Biological and Environmental Research, headed by Ari Patrinos, collaborates with the National Institutes of Health's National Human Genome Research Institute (NHGRI), headed by Francis Collins. The U.S. Human Genome Project involves researchers at laboratories and universities across the country, and coordinates an international academic consortium of nonprofit labs in at least eighteen countries. As the DNA sequences are collected, they will be posted on the Internet via the government's database GenBank, for unrestricted use by scientists. Almost immediately an ethical debate over how to control potential abuses of the HGP begins; its first topic is how to prevent medical discrimination against people with genetic predispositions to various diseases.

• Between 1990 and 1997, the average of greenhouse gas emissions increases 3.4 percent per person in the U.S.; 82 percent of these emissions result from burning fossil fuels to power our cars, heat our homes and businesses, and generate electricity. The remaining 18 percent of emissions come from methane released from landfill wastes, coal and natural gas pipelines, industrial chemicals, and other sources, such as deforestation. When atmospheric scientists compare satellite observations from 1970 and 1997, they find "direct observational evidence" that concentrations of greenhouse gases are accumulating in the Earth's atmosphere.

🖸 1992, 1998

• NASA selects electrical engineer Ellen Ochoa (b. 1958, Los Angeles) to be an astronaut in 1990. In 1993, Ochoa becomes the first Hispanic woman in space, serving as mission specialist on a Discovery Space Shuttle Mission (STS-56).

CULTURE AND SOCIETY

• The Supreme Court rules that states can outlaw religious practices (such as the use of peyote in the Native American Church, and animal sacrifice in the Santería, Candomblé, and Voodoo religions that originated in the Caribbean and South America). This is considered a major setback to First Amendment protections including religious freedom.

🖸 1979, 1993

• The Native American Graves Protection and Repatriation Act of 1990 "requires federally financed museums and institutions to compile inventories of their Indian collections and to work with tribes and Indian nations on the return of their human remains, ritual objects, and items of cultural patrimony."

• This year is the first time that Asian Americans enter the University of California at Los Angeles in greater numbers than European Americans. Asian Americans total 41 percent of the 1990 freshman class.

WORLD EVENTS

• South Africa's president, F. W. de Klerk, legalizes opposition groups including the African National Congress, the Pan African Congress, and the South African Communist Party. He also releases Nelson Mandela, international hero of the struggle against apartheid in South Africa, who has been a political prisoner for twenty-seven years. Mandela is elected deputy president of the African National Congress, and begins formal negotiations with the South African government to end apartheid.

• Namibia gains independence after being under the control of South Africa for seventy-five years, with Sam Nujoma as president.

• Jean-Bertrand Aristide, a former Catholic priest and advocate of the poor, becomes the first democratically elected president of Haiti. He will go into exile within the year, forced to flee when the Haitian military stages a successful coup.

• The Sandinista government in Nicaragua peacefully withdraws from power when its candidate, President Daniel Ortega, loses his reelection bid to Violeta Barrios de Chamorro, who becomes president.

• On October 3, East and West Germany become one nation again after being divided

Building Minnesota (1990), a public sculpture by Oklahoma-based artist Hachivi Edgar Heap of Birds, was commissioned by the Walker Art Center. The temporary installation of forty aluminum signs honored forty Dakota men who were hanged by the U.S. government for their participation in the Sioux Uprising of 1862. The signs faced the West River Parkway near downtown Minneapolis, with each man's name printed in Dakota and English. *(Photo by permission of the artist.)*

for forty-five years, since the end of World War II. United as the Federal Republic of Germany, they will use the flag, currency, and national anthem of the former West Germany. With Chancellor Helmut Kohl as head of state, Germany will have to solve how to bring the presently disparate economies and systems back into balance.

• North and South Yemen merge in May to form the Republic of Yemen. Their unified parliaments appoint President Ali Abdullah Saleh of North Yemen as president, and the secretary of the South Yemeni Socialist Party, Ali Salem Al-Baidh, as vice president.

• After Arab leaders fail to mediate a solution to Iraqi President Saddam Hussein's complaint that Kuwait is flooding the oil market and deflating oil prices, Iraq's troops invade Kuwait and take it over in August. The UN Security Council leads widespread international criticism for the action, and the U.S. moves over 60,000 troops to Saudi Arabia to defend that country from possible invasion.

• The original program for the World Wide Web, a hypertext system for publishing information on the Internet, is created by Tom Berners-Lee and Robert Cailliau for internal use at CERN, the European Laboratory for Particle Physics, a research center based near Geneva, Switzerland. Its purpose is to provide efficient information access to the international high-energy physics community. In 1992, CERN releases the World Wide Web protocols to the general public.

1991

ARTS AND LITERATURE

• Anna Deavere Smith creates and performs *Fires in the Mirror,* a one-woman play that mixes journalism and art. The play is part of a series of theater pieces that Smith started in 1982, called "On the Road," in which she builds scripts by interviewing people, editing and collaging them into a multi-voiced replay of words and actions. In *Fires in the Mirror,* Smith portrays thirty characters—involved in the violence that took place in the racially polarized Crown Heights neighborhood of Brooklyn, New York, in 1991, between a Hasidic Jewish community and a largely West Indian/African American community. Smith uses the same journalistic method to create a 1994 production, *Twilight: Los Angeles 1992,* concerning the events surrounding the Los Angeles riots. During the rest of the decade, Smith's use of a "docudrama" form influences others to mine recent history for scripts based on real words of real people in both solo and group performance works.

🖻 1997

GOVERNMENT AND POLITICS

• On January 17, United Nations forces, led by U.S. General Norman Schwarzkopf, launch a short, massive, high-tech air war, called Operation Desert Storm, to expel Iraqi soldiers from Kuwait and protect Saudi Arabian and American interests in the Persian Gulf region. During six weeks of hostilities, wave after wave of bombing blankets Iraq's capital city, Baghdad, and other targets, striking President Saddam Hussein's bunkers, intelligence services, and military targets, and destroying most of the country's infrastructure. Exactly 100 hours after sending in ground troops, President Bush announces, "Kuwait is liberated. Iraq's army is defeated.... All U.S. and coalition forces will suspend offensive combat operations." However, hostilities actually continue on both military and economic fronts throughout the rest of the decade and into the George W. Bush administration in the twenty-first century.

🖻 1999

• The U.S. Supreme Court rules that previously legally segregated schools may remain segregated if they have made a "good faith" effort to comply with court-ordered desegregation. Chief Justice William Rehnquist (b. 1924) states the majority opinion that "from the very first, federal supervision of local school systems was intended as a temporary measure to remedy past discrimination." Justice Thurgood Marshall's dissent explains that states with a history of state-imposed segregation perpetuate "the message of racial inferiority associated with segregation. Therefore such schools must be eliminated wherever feasible."

BUSINESS AND INDUSTRY

• BET (Black Entertainment Television), a cable TV station, becomes the first African American–owned company listed on the New York Stock Exchange when President Robert L. Johnson sells 4.2 million shares in an initial public offering.

🖻 1971

• Three out of four U.S. homes own VCRs, the fastest-selling domestic appliance in history, which also generates more than 4 billion cassette tape rentals in the U.S. alone.

• The Mashantucket Pequot Indians open Foxwoods gambling casino in Ledyard, Connecticut, which grows to be the single most profitable casino outside of Las Vegas. By 1995, more than 100 reservations will take advantage of the tribal governments' rights of jurisdiction over reservation lands, protected under the Indian Gaming Regulatory Act of 1988. The federal act exempts tribes from any state laws prohibiting gambling or obligations to pay state taxes. The casino revenues provide economic health to poor reservations and give Native Americans new political clout.

SCIENCE AND TECHNOLOGY

• HIV-2, a second strain of the AIDS virus originally found in West Africa, is found to be spreading.

• The U.S. tries out its high-tech weaponry systems in Iraq. It drops so-called "smart bombs" from F-117 Stealth fighter-bombers by using laser designators that lock onto targets. Unmanned U.S. Navy Prowler and Air Force Raven electronic combat aircraft scramble Iraqi radar defenses.

• Biosphere II, a quasi-scientific experiment located in the Arizona desert, places four men and four women in a hermetically sealed three-acre environment made of glass and steel, to test whether these conditions could allow humans to survive on Mars. The residents live with 3,800 plant and animal species for two years, within ecosystems simulating a rain forest, a savanna, and an ocean, but its scientific applications become questionable after various crops fail and fresh air is pumped into the oxygen-depleted dome.

Culture and Society

• Four Los Angeles police officers are indicted on March 15 for violently beating Rodney King, a black motorist, as he lay on the ground. The indictment is largely brought through the public's response to a videotape, made by a bystander testing his new camcorder, that is repeatedly aired on national TV.

🗖 1992

• The stereotype of Asian Americans as the "model minority" no longer bears out, according to economic figures gathered by the 1991 U.S. Census. A more accurate picture shows that conspicuous educational and economic differences are the norm among the now-diverse Asian American population, which includes both native-borns and immigrants among Southeast Asians, Asian Indians, and Chinese, Japanese, and Korean Americans. For

example, for every Asian American family earning a $75,000 annual income, there is another making less than $10,000 per year. Their economic difficulties are compounded by the fact that almost 90 percent have both parents present in the home, making them ineligible for programs designed for more traditional welfare models of single-parent families or families headed by teenagers.

🗖 1975

World Events

• The red flag is lowered over the Kremlin, as Soviet President Mikhail Gorbachev resigns and Russian Federation President Boris Yeltsin and the leaders of Belarus and Ukraine dissolve the United Soviet Socialist Republic and form the Commonwealth of Independent States (CIS). The former provinces joining with Russia are now the countries of Armenia, Azerbaijan, Belarus, Kazakhstan, Kyrgyzstan, Moldova, Tajikistan, Turkmenistan, Ukraine, and Uzbekistan. Estonia, Georgia, Latvia, and Lithuania abstain from participating in any formal coalition. The U.S. has to profoundly rethink how to conduct diplomacy and structure its military in light of what the Bush administration calls the "New World Order."

• The Yugoslavian confederation, including Bosnia-Herzegovina, Croatia, Slovenia, Macedonia, and Serbia, formally breaks apart after the Communist Party relinquishes total control. Ethnic animosities that had been held back under Communism ignite into a terrible bloodbath of civil war. In 1991, Serbia (a historic rival of Croatia) elects the militant Serb nationalist and Communist Party leader Slobodan Milosevic as president. Milosevic moves to block Croatia's leader, Stipe Mesic, from assuming the presidency of a new collective Yugoslavia, causing Croatia and Slovenia to secede. He is also determined to keep all ethnically Serbian areas under the control of Serbia. The Yugoslav army, dominated by Serbs, moves into both republics. Although they leave Slovenia in July, "ethnic cleansing" (involving the removal or murder of Croat civilians from Serbian-held areas) continues until January 1992, when 14,000 United Nations peacekeepers arrive to monitor a cease-fire. The Serb militias and federal forces hold one-third of Croatia, which Croatia will not win back until 1995. In 1992, after Bosnia and Herzegovina also succeed from the collective, the third successor to the name of Yugoslavia, the Socialist Federal Republic of Yugoslavia, is formed by a union of Serbia and Montenegro (which the U.S. does not formally recognize).

1995

• The world's worst man-made environmental disaster is caused by Iraqi troops, who methodically dynamite and set fire to 650 of Kuwait's oil wells during the Persian Gulf War. On November 6, the last fire is put out.

• Israel and neighboring Arab states representing the Palestinians begin the first extensive peace talks, which in 1993 will produce their first signed agreement in forty-five years.

1992

Arts and Literature

• Lincoln Center for the Performing Arts in New York creates "Jazz at Lincoln Center" under the artistic direction of leading trumpeter-composer Wynton Marsalis and producer Rob Hanrahan, giving a sense of artistic and social permanence and legitimacy to the jazz form.

Government and Politics

• Arkansas's Democratic governor, William Jefferson "Bill" Clinton (b. 1946), is elected to his first term as forty-second president, with Al Gore as his vice president. He promises to bring down the largest deficit in U.S. history, reform health care, and create new jobs. Although his health-care plans fall apart, his first term will be blessed with an era of prosperity.

• Republican Ben Nighthorse Campbell (b. 1933), a Northern Cheyenne from Colorado, is the first Native American elected to serve in the U.S. Senate.

Business and Industry

• In November, Delphi, an online information service, becomes the first U.S. gateway to the computer network that is the Internet, making it possible for the general public to access and distribute information with an ease that was never possible before.

1993

• The largest shopping mall in the U.S. opens at the seventy-eight-acre Mall of America in Minnesota. It also includes the world's largest indoor amusement park.

Science and Technology

• "Mosaic for X," or MOSAIC, becomes the first graphics-intensive World Wide Web browser, allowing any computer user access to documents throughout the Internet simply by pointing and clicking a mouse on images or highlighted text. Developed by undergraduate Marc Andreessen and seven other student programmers at the National Center for Supercomputing Applications at the University of Illinois at Champaign-Urbana, MOSAIC becomes available in 1994 as a commercial version called Navigator, through Netscape, the company Andreessen co-founds. In 1997, software development on the MOSAIC project ceases. Its declining browser market share between 1996 and 1998 will be adduced in the antitrust case against Microsoft.

CULTURE AND SOCIETY

• The quincentennial year of Christopher Columbus's landing in the Americas provokes controversy, forced into the public arena by international discussions started among intellectuals, artists, and especially Native Americans. The discussions extend to public media talk shows, school and festival exhibits, and community celebration committees. Traditional descriptions of his landing as a "discovery" of the Americas are replaced with the understanding that Columbus's landing in the Bahamas should be considered an "encounter" with a place, people, and culture already flourishing, and that it was also a crime against the ancestors of Native Americans.

• On May 2, 1992, an all-white Simi Valley, California, jury acquits four Los Angeles police officers who were televised beating Rodney King, an African American man they were arresting. Los Angeles explodes in three days of rioting that involves people from all ethnicities in the city. Fifty-eight people are killed, thousands are injured, and there is massive property damage due to fires and looting. The riot is also watched nationwide, with TV news helicopters broadcasting the crowd's actions, including the beating of a white truck driver and his eventual rescue by a black man. National guard troops are called in to patrol the city streets, and President Bush places 5,000 soldiers and marines on standby alert just outside the city.

The "L.A. Riots" spring out of heated racial tensions, immigration issues, racialized economics, and an imbalance of power in Los Angeles. While blacks are blamed for the riot, the typical arrestee is Latino, and 10 percent of the rioters are whites, as images on nationwide TV clearly show. Media commentaries inflame the situation by pointing to clashes between black rioters and Korean American merchants, although African American–owned businesses are burned as well. In the aftermath, Rodney King's question, "Can't we all just get along?" may have inspired community leaders to organize dialogues to heal relations, especially between the African American, Korean, and Latino communities of Los Angeles.

WORLD EVENTS

• The Russian Federation is formed from the nineteen republics of the former Russian Soviet Federated Socialist Republic, making it the world's largest country.

• In the Kyoto Protocol, named after the city in Japan where the treaty is negotiated and signed, delegates from industrialized nations around the world agree for the first time to set legally binding reductions in their countries' emissions of heat-trapping gases, including carbon dioxide, which is produced by the burning of fossil fuels like coal and oil, and is a major contributor to global warming and other changes in the Earth's climate. They agree to stabilize emissions at 1990 levels by 2008–2012, although many issues continue to be debated in yearly meetings between 1997 and 2000, including voluntary compliance by developing countries that are becoming increasingly industrialized. The U.S. never formally ratifies the accord or implements a reduction plan, and in 2001 the George W. Bush administration abandons the treaty altogether. The U.S. rejection receives worldwide criticism, especially since the U.S., with only 6 percent of the world's population, produces 25 percent of the globe's carbon dioxide, more than any other nation in the world.

• When CERN ends restricted access to the Internet by releasing the World Wide Web (WWW) protocols to the general public this year, the Internet is revolutionized as millions begin logging on to the World Wide Web. The prefix "www" is the hypertext system for publishing information on the Internet that also enables one to "surf" the Internet.

1993

ARTS AND LITERATURE

• Toni Morrison (b. 1931) wins the Nobel Prize for Literature, both for her own writing and for championing the development of African American literature. Morrison is author of six novels, including *The Bluest Eye* (1970); *Sula* (1974); *Song of Solomon* (1977); *Tar Baby* (1981); *Beloved* (1987), for which she won a Pulitzer Prize and an American Book Award in 1988; *Jazz* (1992), and books of essays. She is the first African American to be so honored. In accepting the award, Morrison says that it is more than a personal victory because "it says something about the evolution of African American writing, that it's no longer outside the central enterprise, that it speaks about things that matter to anyone."

• The Outsider Art Fair is presented for the first time, by Sanford L. Smith and Associates, at the Puck Building in New York. The marketing of folk art, vernacular art, self-taught or outsider art, as it is variously called, becomes one of the commercial success stories of the 1990s art world. Some of the most highly prized artists include sculptor William Edmondson (1870–1951) and painter Horace Pippin (1888–1946), both African American artists who were "discovered" during the WPA's research projects on American arts and "folkways"; Bill Traylor (1856–1947); Henry Darger (1892–1973); Nellie Mae Rowe (1900–1982); Sister Gertrude Morgan (1900–1980); the Rev. Howard Finster (b. 1915, Alabama); Achilles G. Rizzoli (1896–1981); woodcarver Herbert Singleton (b. 1945, New Orleans); and Thornton Dial Sr. (b. 1928, Alabama).

GOVERNMENT AND POLITICS

• NAFTA, the North American Free Trade Agreement, which liberalizes trade between the U.S., Mexico, and Canada by eliminating tariffs and other trade barriers, is ratified after heated debate among environmentalists, trade unions, and the government. (Negotiations begun by President George Bush are completed by President Clinton, who pushes it through Congress.)

• The FBI and the Branch Davidian sect, a religious group that lives in a compound in Waco, Texas, engage in a standoff. When the sect's compound catches fire, more than eighty members are killed, including children. The FBI is charged with mismanagement at the least, and use of pyrotechnic tear-gas canisters at the worst. "Remember Waco!" becomes an anthem of the radical right, inspiring more acts of violence, especially the bombing of the Murrah Federal Building in Oklahoma City in 1995. In 1999 the FBI will admit to its possible use of pyrotechnic tear-gas canisters.

• In an effort to avoid a definitive ruling on whether to lift the ban on homosexuals serving in the military, President Clinton and the joint chiefs of staff compromise on a "don't ask, don't tell, don't pursue" policy regarding the sexual orientation of military personnel. Congress passes legislation that, because it leaves almost all current restrictions in place, fails to end problems of discrimination in the military.

BUSINESS AND INDUSTRY

• In 1993, the U.S. White House goes online *(http://www.whitehouse.gov/)*, as does the United Nations. Business and media begin taking notice of the Internet's potential.

• One in three Americans now works at home, instead of driving to an office, recalling a common arrangement from the early 1900s when the home functioned as a workplace for garment workers who would prepare piecework in their homes. Similarly, electronic mail renews the art of correspondence, which has not had such a vogue since Victorian times. Ironically, the information age makes this possible, with its technological developments such as fax and electronic mail that allow people to be in constant communication with each other.

SCIENCE AND TECHNOLOGY

• The Environmental Protection Agency releases a report that identifies secondhand smoke as a proven carcinogen. The report supports demands for adoption of no-smoking ordinances in public buildings, restaurants, transportation, and the workplace.

• The *New England Journal of Medicine* publishes the findings of a study showing that one-third of the U.S. population uses "unconventional therapies" that are not currently being taught in U.S. medical schools. Under the label "alternative medicine," long-established medical systems such as acupuncture, chiropractic, and homeopathy are lumped together with other kinds of therapies such as massage, meditation, spiritual aids such as intercessory prayer, and forms of exercise such as Pilates, Feldenkrais, yoga, and t'ai chi. Patients are estimated to be paying about $13.7 billion, a total greater than what is being spent on hospital stays, taking it out of their own pockets, as most of these therapies are not covered under standard health insurance policies. The study reflects the beginning of a shift in what medical practices are considered acceptable. Many medical schools reassess their standard dismissal of these systems and consider introducing their students to the possibility of integrating these therapies with traditional treatments. Trial studies are started to critically assess the actual effects these treatments have on patients.

🖸 1998

• The U.S. Congress kills "Star Wars" research (the popular name for the Strategic Defense Initiative program or SDI), ten years and $30 billion after President Reagan launched the space-based satellite and missile-defense shield system. In 2000, SDI returns as a priority program of the forty-third president, George W. Bush.

CULTURE AND SOCIETY

• Dr. David Gunn is shot dead outside a Pensacola, Florida, abortion clinic by an anti-abortion protestor. This is the first assassination by anti-abortionists, and although a 1994 law makes it illegal for demonstrators to block entrances to clinics, the violence continues with more killings.

WORLD EVENTS

• In September the government of Israel and the Palestine Liberation Organization (PLO) sign a "Declaration of Principles," an agreement acknowledging their mutual recognition, at the White House. In October the PLO endorses accepting the agreement and forms the Council of the Palestinian National Authority with Yasser Arafat as president. In July 1994, President Arafat returns to Gaza and Jericho, after the last Israeli troops have left Gaza City, celebrating the end of twenty-seven years of occupation and his exile with a huge crowd of Palestinians.

Ⓟ 1996

• Terrorists bomb the basement parking garage under the twin towers of the World Trade Center, the highest buildings in Manhattan. Five people die and hundreds suffer from smoke inhalation and other injuries. This is the first of a series of violent attacks to be linked to Islamic fundamentalist militant leader Osama bin Laden and his international coalition of groups or "cells," called Al-Qaeda. In 1996, nineteen U.S. soldiers are killed and 300 wounded when a truck bomb blows up a housing complex in Saudi Arabia. In 1998, U.S. embassies in Nairobi, Kenya, and Dar es Salaam, Tanzania, are bombed, killing more than 220 people including Kenyan, Tanzanian, and U.S. employees, and injuring 4,000. The U.S. retaliates by launching seventy cruise missiles aimed at terrorist training centers in the Sudan and Afghanistan, states where bin Laden is thought to be sheltered.

The missiles kill civilians and destroy a critical pharmaceutical factory in Khartoum, Sudan, mistakenly targeted as a chemical plant. The U.S. government indicts twenty-six Al-Qaeda members in connection with the bombing, and six bin Laden associates are brought to trial and found guilty in a U.S. federal court. They state that their actions were in retaliation for U.S. support of Israel. In 2000, an explosion rocks the USS *Cole*, a navy destroyer refueling in Yemen, killing seventeen sailors. In 2001, nineteen Muslim hijackers seize four commercial passenger jets with full loads of highly combustible fuel, turning them into bombs that they crash through the upper stories of both World Trade Center towers and the Pentagon. Nearly 3,000 people, including many citizens of other nations, lose their lives in the ensuing explosions, fires, collapse of the towers, and emergency recovery efforts. Bin Laden calls the actions "defensive *jihad,*" whose "real targets were America's icons of military and economic power." President George W. Bush declares it the beginning of the "first war of the twenty-first century."

• Dr. Andras Nagy and Dr. Janet Rossant, University of Toronto scientists, report their collaboration on successfully growing an entire mouse from individual embryonic mouse stem cells. In theory, stem cells taken from a single embryo could grow into any tissue or organ. If scientists could isolate human embryonic stem cells, they could theoretically be used to grow bone marrow for cancer patients, cure diabetes by generating insulin production, or grow new skin to replace burn injuries. This research sparks debate over whether it would be ethical to use human embryonic stem cells to grow an entire human.

1994

ARTS AND LITERATURE

• The Electronic Café International conducts a technological experiment by producing a live concert that hooks up composers and musicians in three cities. Morton Subotnik plays excerpts from his *Angel Concerto* at the Kitchen in New York. By manipulating piano sounds with sensors on his hands and feet, he causes sounds to emerge from instruments at the two other sites. David Rosenboom performs *Is Art Is* live at the piano at the Electronic Café in Santa Monica, and sends it at the speed of light through a Disklavier so that it is heard as a duet with another pianist in New York City. Steina Vasulka's violin playing at Studio X in Santa Fe sets off sounds and video images at both sites across the country.

• African American choreographer Bill T. Jones (b. 1952) premieres *Still/Here,* a one-hour, forty-minute collaboration for ten dancers about "life and affirmation." The work is conceived on a large scale, costing $1.2 million, and is based on the issue of how to go on living while staring death in the face. Jones, who is HIV positive, has had to experience these issues firsthand, both in his own life and in the death of his longtime creative partner and lover, Arnie T. Zane (1948–1988). To learn how other people cope with death and survival, Jones runs fourteen "survival" workshops in eleven cities during 1993. He videotapes the sessions in which young to elderly volunteer participants articulate their thoughts about life-threatening illnesses. Jones integrates the participants' input as source material for the text and movement material of the work. Arlene Croce, a leading

dance critic, condemns the work in her article, "Discussing the Undiscussable," in *The New Yorker* magazine without attending a performance, because she believes it will be "victim art." She sets off a firestorm of debates in the art world about the role of the critic, the use of fiction and fact, and the boundaries between the arts and "real" life.

GOVERNMENT AND POLITICS

• The Florida legislature agrees to establish a $1.5-million fund to pay up to $150,000 to each survivor of the Rosewood Massacre, a January 1923 incident in the town of Rosewood in Levy County that has also been described as a white race riot and a race war. The Florida legislature also creates a $500,000 fund for reimbursement of lost property and $100,000 for college scholarships of up to $4,000 per year for descendants and other minorities. Florida's decision to make reparation payments brings up a long-simmering debate about other historical events, including slavery, that some African Americans believe also deserve reparations.

▣ 1923

• California's Proposition 187, largely funded by out-of-state supporters and used by Governor Pete Wilson as the centerpiece of his reelection campaign, is passed by 59 percent of California voters. It denies undocumented immigrants social services such as subsidized medical care, welfare, and education. It denies American citizenship to children born of illegal immigrants. It requires teachers, doctors, and other city, county, and state officials to report anyone suspected of being an illegal alien to the California attorney general and the Immigration and Naturalization Service (INS). Lawsuits are filed in state and federal courts to protest the measure as Governor Wilson issues an executive order to cut off government services to undocumented pregnant women and nursing-home patients.

• The Bureau of Justice Statistics reports that state and Federal prisons now contain more than one million inmates, the highest incarceration rate in the world.

BUSINESS AND INDUSTRY

• On January 1, the North American Free Trade Agreement (NAFTA) goes into effect, eliminating all tariffs for the next fifteen years between the U.S., Canada, and Mexico. As part of the agreement between Mexico and the U.S., 53.8 percent of U.S. imports from Mexico become duty-free, and 31 percent of imports from the U.S., excluding those imported by *maquiladoras,* are duty-free. The U.S. government extends a $6-billion line of credit to Mexico to stabilize the peso, the recently devalued currency, and to calm Mexico's NAFTA trading partners, although many manufacturing executives predict that the agreement will enhance the U.S. economy in an increasingly global economy. NAFTA is seen as a possible first step toward including the whole hemisphere in an American Common Market system similar to other international trading blocs like the European Economic Community.

• The chief executives of seven of the largest U.S. tobacco companies testify before the House Energy and Commerce Subcommittee on Health and the Environment that they do not believe cigarettes are addictive, and that evidence of health risks, including lung cancer and heart disease, is not conclusive. The hearings reveal that the companies manipulate nicotine levels in cigarettes for flavor, and that they suppress reports that prove nicotine is addictive. The hearings increase pressure on the tobacco companies to pay settlements on suits to recover monies spent on Medicaid bills for treatments of smoking-related ailments.

• The digitization of technology begins to pervade the U.S. economy: the first cyberbank, First Virtual, opens online; the first cyberstation, RT-FM, broadcasts from Interop, Las Vegas; dot-com shopping malls arrive on the Internet; and advertisements routinely include Web addresses. Marc Andreessen and Jim Clark co-found Netscape Communications, whose Navigator browser is the commercial version of Andreessen's MOSAIC. Netscape's IPO sparks the stock market trend from 1997 through 2000.

• Monsanto makes an application to the United Kingdom Advisory Committee on Novel Foods and Processes for review of the safety of glyphosate-tolerant soybeans, to grow this variety of soybeans in the U.S. It is genetically engineered to be resistant to the herbicide Roundup. In 1996 the American Soybean Association allows the genetically engineered soya to be mixed in with the conventional soybean harvest on the basis of its "substantially equivalent" ruling, which confirms, despite persistent expressions of alarm from farmers and consumer groups, that gene altering does not raise significant safety or nutritional concerns. Genetically modified crops become ubiquitous in the U.S.: by 1999, 50 percent of the total area of U.S. farmland under soybean cultivation will be planted with this herbicide-resistant variety; also in 1999, 30 percent of the U.S. corn crop will be of a pest-resistant variety, and significant percentages of cotton and grain crops will use biotech varieties also.

SCIENCE AND TECHNOLOGY

• DVD, a new digital technology for video discs and players, is introduced. DVDs resemble CDs, with more durability and storage capacity than VHS tapes. By 1999, DVDs appear in video rental stores, with sales of 45 million making up 15 percent of all video sales.

• Lou Montulli, a programmer at Netscape Communications, invents an Internet data filing system called a "persistent client state object," more commonly known as a "cookie." The system allows the Web to develop a memory that can track users' visits to Web sites, helping legitimate businesses operate more efficiently by tracking, sorting, and transferring customers' information. However, without the user being notified, it can also lead to violations of consumer privacy.

• On May 24, NASA's Hubble Space Telescope's Wide Field Planetary Camera 2 confirms the existence of black holes (a black hole is "an object that is so massive yet compact nothing can escape its gravitational pull, not even light") when it transmits an image of a huge spiral-shaped disk of hot gas at the core of an active galaxy, M87. The elliptical M87 is located 50 million light years away, in the constellation Virgo, and weighs "as much as three billion suns, but is concentrated into a space no larger than our solar system."

CULTURE AND SOCIETY

• Oregon voters narrowly approve the Death with Dignity Act, making them the first state to pass a measure legalizing physician-assisted suicide. It passes again by a 60–40-percent majority in a 1999 referendum, following a series of legal challenges. The day after this vote, the U.S. House of Representatives passes the Pain Relief Promotion Act by a vote of 271–156. This bill effectively overturns the Oregon voters' decision by making it a crime for doctors to use any federally controlled substance for the purpose of aiding suicide. Governor John A. Kitzhaber, who is himself a physician, vows to take the fight all the way to the Supreme Court, if necessary, to protect the rights of Oregon voters.

• O. J. Simpson (b. 1947), a former football star and movie actor, is charged with the murder of his wife, Nicole, and her friend Ron Goldman. He is acquitted of the charges in 1995, but in 1997 is found guilty in a civil suit brought by the victim's families. Coverage of the trials explodes across cable and network television, spawning a new media category called "infotainment," featuring heated debates between supposedly objective lawyers and expert "pundits" as they hash over the minutest details of the latest trial developments. New cable channels are formed as ratings soar with shows often programmed in time slots competing with regular news broadcasts. The new format goes looking for new tragedies or scandals to feature, using stories like the deaths of Princess Diana and John Kennedy Jr., and the investigations, trials, and impeachment proceedings related to the Clinton presidency.

WORLD EVENTS

• Mexico is shaken by increasing violence. Luis Donaldo Colosio, a top presidential candidate for the Institutional Revolutionary Party (PRI) handpicked by the current president, Carlos Salinas de Gortari, is assassinated. A masked army of 2,000 Mayan Indians, known as the Zapatista National Liberation Army, wars against the Mexican government. A series of armed guerrilla insurgencies begins in their home, Mexico's southernmost state of Chiapas, on the day the North American Free Trade Agreement (NAFTA) goes into effect. Their immediate cause is to protest PRI corruption and monopoly of power that keeps money from reaching the peasants, the indigenous population that has Mexico's highest rates of poverty, malnutrition, illiteracy, and infant mortality. Over the next seven years the Zapatista National Liberation Army continues to fight, expanding its cause to bring international attention to the mistreatment of 10 million indigenous Latin American Indians. In about a dozen days of battle, 145 Mexican army and Zapatista troops are killed in battles, hundreds die in other clashes between the rebels and government paramilitary organizations, and thousands are forced to flee their homes. In 2000, Mexico's newly elected president, Vicente Fox, will start to follow through on his election pledge to respond to the Zapatistas' demands, known as the San Andres accords, to find a resolution to the war.

• The Chunnel, a tunnel under the English Channel connecting England and France, is completed.

• The World Trade Organization (WTO) signs the Trade-Related Aspects of Intellectual Property Rights (TRIPS), an international system of statues on intellectual property rights that is to be administered by the WTO. Written by a coalition of corporations called the Intellectual Property Committee, it allows companies to access biological resources anywhere in the world without prior consent. It obligates countries to bring their patent laws into line with industrialized nations, particularly in extending the term "intellectual property" to include living organisms, without demanding that patent hold-

ers share any benefits from genetic materials with the people or country of origin.
🖻 1951

1995

ARTS AND LITERATURE

• Paul Kaiser (b. 1956) and Shelley Eshkar (b. 1970) begin working together, creating digital artworks that incorporate computer graphics and drawing. In 1997 they begin using Character Studio, an R2 computer program created by Susan Amkraut and Micharel Girard for Discreet, the multimedia division of Autodesk of San Rafael, California. This tool will perform "motion capture," a new animation technology that transposes the movement of live performers into abstract, virtual digital images. It is capable of "capturing" or making a record of "the little accidents and secondary movements that give actual movements their individual and indeed unrepeatable character," recording on cameras surrounding live moving bodies through sensors that are attached to the bodies. By 1999 they incorporate this effect into collaborations with choreographers Merce Cunningham in *BIPED* and Bill T. Jones in *Ghostcatching*.

• Philip Glass premieres his opera *The Voyage* at the Metropolitan Opera, in New York. The work explores science, space travel, and time in honor of the 500th anniversary of Columbus's voyage.

GOVERNMENT AND POLITICS

• A White House Commission on nuclear experiments reports that government-sponsored nuclear-related experiments and projects have affected indigenous peoples, particularly Alaskan Native villages near nuclear storage facilities, residents of the Marshall Islands who were exposed during the 1940s and 1950s to nuclear testing in the Pacific, and those living downwind of the fallout produced by nuclear tests in Nevada in the 1960s and 1970s.

🗓 1990

BUSINESS AND INDUSTRY

• President Clinton succeeds in arranging a $53-million international loan-guarantee package, to help Mexico stabilize its monetary and investment crisis after the Mexican government promises to institute strict austerity measures and use oil revenues as collateral for the U.S. loans.

• Amazon.com is founded by Jeffrey Bezos as an online bookstore, offering to locate any book in any language, whether in print or not. Within three years it has expanded its site to offer toys, electronic gadgets, and an auction site. Bezos is a pioneer inventor and designer of e-commerce, a champion of a new way that companies, called dot-coms, can build businesses by delivering goods, services, or content to customers who make contact through Web-based electronic transactions.

🗓 1999

• A national online newspaper network is established by major dailies as the Associated Press, a major news information service organization, announces it will distribute its articles and photographs over the World Wide Web. In addition, magazines and television news and talk shows start offering cyberspace editions. Questions regarding how to make a profit from many of these information retrieval and service Internet websites, including when to charge

viewers for access and how to maintain copyright protections, have yet to be resolved.

CULTURE AND SOCIETY

• Following an FCC ruling, a television show rating system is established and aired at the beginning of shows, to indicate whether the content contains obscenity, excessive violence, obscene language, or sexually explicit material. Context is to be given strong consideration in making rating decisions.

• The Murrah Federal Office Building in Oklahoma City is bombed in an antigovernment terrorist attack launched by U.S. citizens, killing 169 people, including nineteen young children, and damaging over 220 buildings. Initially presented as the work of Arab terrorists by the media, it turns out to be the plot of an ex-U.S. soldier, Timothy McVeigh, with ties to radical-right causes. Later McVeigh confirms that the bombing was carried out to avenge the FBI-related deaths of the Christian Branch Davidian cult, which occurred on the same date in Waco, Texas, one year earlier.

• The Alaska Native Knowledge Network is created as a component of the Alaska Rural Systemic Initiative, with the aim of legitimizing indigenous knowledge in ways that it can be recognized and utilized in the formal education process. Five years of planning, developed by a series of Elders Councils meeting from the Athabascan, Aleut, Inupiaq, and South East communities, and the Alaska Native/Rural education consortium result in the adoption of a document for culturally responsive schools.

🗓 1998

• The Million Man March/Day of Absence is initiated by Minister Louis Farrakhan of the Nation of Islam. He wants one million African

DIGITIZATION AND THE NEWS

Nancy Hicks Maynard

In much the way refrigeration changed food production and consumption, digitization potentially changes everything about the manner in which we produce and consume news. As the digital revolution marches ahead, much about the ways we define, gather, and produce news will have to change, too.

On its best days, technology improves the news. Database reporting unearths important breaches of public trust, patterns of police brutality, discriminatory lending practices for homes or cars, and inequitable application of the death penalty. For all the fluff served up, the impact of these stories provides more than equal counterweight, although they have become a smaller part of a larger, diversified information business. The trick will be to protect enterprise journalism, to create a device that distinguishes them from entertainment, e-commerce, and a host of other sins that coexist in the digital cauldron. On the other hand, digitization can impede quality. In quickening the journalistic process, layers of editing as well as production disappear. As a result, rumors are apt to make their way to the public more often.

Internet users watch more cable but less broadcast news; they read more weekly papers and specialty magazines but fewer dailies and general-interest publications. Internet users catch breaking news online or on cable; they read with less frequency but more depth. Theirs is a rhythm of attention in opposition to the current production cycles.

In media talk, convergence refers to a receiving device: the computer, television, cable box, telephone, or satellite dish. But what about convergence of function? What about the newsroom and convergence? News staffs work across media. Newspaper reporters also appear on cable news or television programs. Broadcasters write or produce stories for the Internet. Camera operators simultaneously shoot videotape for television and digital stills for publication, but both are also available for the Web site. A merged newsroom already exists in Tampa. And Bloomberg, the financial reporting company, was a pioneer in setting up a single, digital newsroom for its various Wall Street and consumer information products. MSNBC's cable network and website run convergent newsrooms in metropolitan New York and in Redmond, Washington. They support each other, as well as NBC network news and CNBC, the business network.

While digital convergence may not develop as imagined today, its effects are powerful and lasting. Best case, industry visions come true, or something approximating them will. Worst case, consumption patterns continue to change but insufficient infrastructure grows to support traditional values or providers. Preservation of journalistic standards will require content and technology to come together in a coherent way. Will they? Stay tuned.

(Nieman Reports, *Winter 2000: 11–13. Reprinted with permission from the Nieman Foundation at Harvard University.*)

American men from all over the U.S. to stand together on the Mall in Washington, D.C. On October 16, approximately one million men actually do participate. Their purpose, according to a mission statement written by a member of the executive council of the organizing committee, Dr. Maulana Karenga, from the Organization of Us, is "atonement, reconciliation, and responsibility." African American male voter registration rises after the march, giving a measurable result. In response to criticism that women are not included in the march, organizers point out that more women addressed this crowd than the 1963 March on Washington.

⬚ 1997

• Resegregation is emerging as a measurable trend in American schools, according to a Harvard University Graduate School of Education study, based on statistics from the Bureau of the Census and the federal government's National Center for Education Statistics. As was argued in the 1954 Supreme Court decision *Brown v. Board of Education,* this study finds that separate schools do not produce equal educational opportunities. The resegregated schools follow a pattern relating low academic achievement to schools with low numbers of white students and high rates of poverty. This separation of races appears as minority children make up a rapidly growing segment of school-age populations.

WORLD EVENTS

• In September, the Oslo II Agreement is signed in Washington, arranging a schedule for Israeli withdrawal from Palestinian lands in the West Bank and Gaza by 1996. On Nov. 4, Prime Minister Yitzhak Rabin is assassinated in Tel Aviv by a Jewish right-wing extremist outraged by Rabin's continuing peace negotiations with the Palestinians. Foreign Minister Shimon Peres takes over as head of the Labor government, and agrees to carry the peace plan forward.

1996

ARTS AND LITERATURE

• Another chapter in the 1990s culture wars opens when playwright August Wilson delivers his speech, "The Ground on Which I Stand," at the Theater Communications Group National Conference at Princeton University. Wilson argues the case for the necessity to continue black theater as a separate entity within the American theater community because, to his mind, it is the only way that black theater can survive and flower.

⬚ 1997

GOVERNMENT AND POLITICS

• William Jefferson Clinton is elected to a second term as president, with Al Gore continuing as vice president. During the campaign he signs bills to raise the minimum wage; ban late-term abortions; let workers take health insurance with them when they change jobs; give presidents line-item veto power; and reform federal welfare, a fulfillment of his stump-speech promise to end sixty years of "welfare as we know it." Republicans will remain in control of Congress. President Clinton appoints Madeleine Albright (b. 1937) as the first woman secretary of state.

• In February, Congress approves the Telecommunications Act of 1996, a landmark bill that affects various aspects of the related industries and the nation's economy as a whole. By

BLACK AND WHITE AND IN COLOR

Emil Guillermo

ABC just did a huge series on race. . . . The report "America in Black and White" came complete with its own manufactured facts—I mean, poll. Here's the lead: "Americans—black and white alike—overwhelmingly agree that racism is a national problem."

Wow. Racism is a national problem! Stop the presses! It would be news if everyone thought we were a "color-blind" society.

But notice the inherent racism in the very first words of the lead "Americans—black and white alike." Asians aren't American? Do we count at all? Nope. They didn't ask.

And whom do we root for? Blacks? Whites?

Imagine what ABC would have found if it had expanded its scope beyond black and white. Consider that in big cities like Los Angeles, Southeast Asians have replaced blacks as the preferred victims of discrimination. Over 40 percent live in poverty. By seeing only in black and white, ABC missed a bigger story as well as a chance to educate people on another misunderstood group—Asian Pacific Americas. We don't fit in a black-and-white model.

The American race situation is a lot more complicated than that. Old-style thinking is black and white. It won't help you in the diversity of 2000 and beyond. The world is colorized beyond even Ted Turner's wildest residual dreams.

The [report] highlighted another point: blacks and whites, the main event in the race debate, are really quite ignorant of one another. Well, here's a news flash for both groups: If they don't learn about Asians (or Latinos for that matter) anytime soon, the race situation in the U.S. is going to get a whole lot worse.

(FROM *AMOK: ESSAYS FROM AN ASIAN-AMERICAN PERSPECTIVE*
[SAN FRANCISCO: ASIAN WEEK BOOKS, 1999].)

relaxing ownership rules regulating regional cable companies, telephone companies, and radio stations, various mergers within these industries result. Mega-mergers or alliances among telephone, cable, and software companies and Hollywood studios now make it possible for one company to offer a full range of services for businesses and private homes. The act also requires new televisions be fitted with a "V-chip" to screen out violence, and increases competition among local and long-distance phone companies, pushing a major technological changeover to broadband, a new high-speed transmission system capable of transmitting large volumes of data—from e-mail to interactive TV and video-on-demand—via fiberoptic telephone lines or satellite.

[P] 1997

• California voters pass Proposition 209, the so-called Affirmative Action Initiative, that "bar[s] all preferential treatment based on race or gender in public education and employment in California." Although the ballot measure does not overrule federal regulations on hiring equity, it does dismantle most state affirmative-action programs in public employment, public education, and public contracting. It proves to have an immediate effect on faculty hiring practices across the ten-campus University of California system: When the 1995–1996 academic year, in which 35.8 percent of new hires were women, is compared with new hires of women in 1999–2000 faculty hires, the figures drop to 25.1 percent, even though 46.3 percent of graduate students and 53.7 percent of the undergraduates are women. The chill on affirmative action extends beyond California's public universities to private California institutions such as Stanford University, and to other top universities across the country, including Harvard and the Massachusetts Institute of Technology.

• California voters pass Proposition 215, which permits the use of marijuana for medicinal purposes. The measure is immediately subject to court actions and demonstrations for and against its enactment.

◎ 1999

• The Native American Rights Fund backs a lawsuit on behalf of a group of tribal members, to get an accounting of what happened to money and land held in trust for them since the 1880s, when the U.S. government broke up the tribal land ownership system and awarded 80–160-acre land allotments to individuals. These allotments were generally leased out, often to companies from the gas, oil, and timber industries. According to government estimates, the leases generated about $300 million per year in income, which should have been passed on to the descendants of the original recipients, but was instead lost through a continuing pattern of mismanagement. A 1999 finding by Federal District Court Judge Royce L. Lamberth states that the government "engaged in a shocking pattern of deception of the court" in their failure to produce records of the trust funds, and held in contempt the Secretary of Interior Bruce Babbitt, Secretary of the Treasury Robert Rubin, and Assistant Secretary of the Interior Kevin Gover.

• Congress acts on President Clinton's first-term campaign pledge to "end welfare as we know it," by passing a new welfare law that replaces the sixty-year-old federal safety net guaranteeing unlimited benefits over a lifetime. It restructures the system, setting a maximum eligibility limit of five years for benefits over a lifetime and work requirements for able-bodied adults. Nationally, welfare rolls are reduced 47 percent by 1999. Although the figures seem to show the law is a great success, critics caution that it is still not known what will happen over the long term. According to Families USA, an advocacy group that bases its figures on data from the Census Bureau and the Health Care Financing Administration, by 1997 about 675,000 people, two-thirds of whom are children, lost their health insurance coverage under Medicaid, which had been linked to welfare. And because most low-income jobs do not offer health insurance, they remain without coverage.

• A Hawaiian court rules that marriage cannot be denied to same-sex couples by state law. The judgment begins an epic battle over same-sex marriage that spawns state legislature bills in a number of states and several concurrent cases across the country.

◎ 2000

BUSINESS AND INDUSTRY

• A U.S. company launches the first commercial spy satellite.

• The Federal Trade Commission approves a merger between Time Warner and Turner broadcasting, thereby creating the world's largest media company to date.

• Under Governor Pete Wilson, California deregulates its electricity and natural gas marketplace, arguing that increased competition will decrease rates to private and commercial consumers. The deregulation comes at a time of increasing energy demands, however, caused in part by the state's growing population, the explosion of computer-related industries, and a slowdown of plans to build new power plants. By September 2000 a major Northern California supplier, Pacific Gas & Electric Company (PG&E), signals the state will be in an emergency situation, with blackouts resulting from depleted supplies and their inability to pay soaring wholesale power rates charged by out-of-state suppliers. Although the chairman of the largest U.S. energy trader, Ken Lay of Enron Corporation, says, "We didn't make the rules in California. We had nothing to do with creating the problem," federal and state investigators will prove that power sellers and traders, including Enron, Reliant, and Mirant, are guilty of illegal price manipulations and withholding energy supplies. State officials report that the $27 billion energy price tag in 2000, as compared to their 1999 fees of $7 billion, include $9 billion in overcharges. In 2001 the Federal Energy Regulatory Commission steps in to put a cap on energy prices, but ongoing effects of the deregulation significantly contribute to the state's $20 billion budget deficit by 2002.

CULTURE AND SOCIETY

• A school superintendent in western Kentucky orders pages of textbooks glued together so that grade-school children cannot read about the Big Bang theory of the origin of the universe, the principle most widely accepted in modern astronomy and cosmology, unless a version consistent with the Bible's description of Creation is also explained.
🖻 1999

• The U.S. Appeals Court upholds Proposition 209, the California ban on affirmative action.

• The New Urbanist Movement gains increased visibility this year when Disney builds the community of Celebration, on Disney World land holdings near Orlando, Florida. Although not completely true to New Urbanist design principles, it manages to mask its conventional configuration as a suburban appendage subdivision. Its mixed-use areas are designed by a collaboration of major architects, including a master plan by Robert A. M. Stern and Cooper, Robertson & Partners, a bank by Robert Venturi, a town hall, retail offices, and apartments by Philip Johnson, a post office by Michael Graves, a cinema by Cesar Pelli, a golf course by Robert Trent Jones, and a school by William Rawn.
🖻 1981

SCIENCE AND TECHNOLOGY

• At the calm 200-meter summit of the dormant volcano Mauna Kea, in Hawaii, the largest optical and infrared ground-based telescopes on the planet, including two 10-meter Keck telescopes standing eight stories and weighing 300 tons, are integrated with modern computer technology to revolutionize astronomy. The Keck mirrors are composed of 36 hexagonal segments, kept working together as a single reflective glass through computer controls. Blurring of images due to atmospheric turbulence is dramatically reduced by computers that shape deformable mirrors up to 670 times each second, to compensate for the rotation of the Earth, resulting in images ten times sharper than in the Hooker (built in 1917) and Hale (built in 1948). Native Hawaiians protest the placement of the Keck telescopes on their sacred land.

WORLD EVENTS

• The Palestinian Authority holds its first general elections, voting Yasser Arafat the president of the Executive Authority by 83 percent, and an eighty-eight-member Palestinian Legislative Council (PLC), the first steps toward establishing the Palestinian State.

🔲 1994

• On September 27 the Taliban, a fundamentalist Islamic movement whose name means "religious students" or "seekers," takes control of Kabul, the capital of Afghanistan, and displaces the ruling government headed by President Burhanuddin Rabbani. The Taliban is composed mainly of volunteers recruited from Islamic live-in schools, called madrassas, that provide religious education, food, clothing, and housing to boys and young men in Pakistan's refugee camps. The Taliban have been recipients of U.S. financial and logistical support since they fought as one of the Mujahedeen, the freedom-fighting militias, resisting Soviet occupation in 1979–1989. They remain in Afghanistan as a fighting force in the civil war that follows the Soviet retreat, declaring themselves the country's legitimate government, although ethnic minority factions continue the civil war, including a coalition of anti-Taliban forces called the Northern Alliance. The Taliban's government is established as a nonsecular state, based in their uncompromising interpretations of Islamic law as prescribed in the first century of Islam, over 1,300 years ago. This year the Taliban also agree to shelter various Islamic militant networks, including the wealthy Saudi Arabian–born Osama bin Laden and his Al-Qaeda followers. He will be accused of using Afghanistan as a training center for distributing terrorists around the world to topple the U.S. and its Middle Eastern allies. Only Pakistan, Saudi Arabia, and the United Arab Emirates officially recognize the Taliban government, and Afghanistan's United Nations representation remains with the deposed government overthrown by the Taliban.

1997

ARTS AND LITERATURE

• The Supreme Court agrees to hear the case of the NEA Four (Karen Finley, Tim Miller, John Fleck, and Holly Hughes), to decide the extent of protection granted to publicly commissioned artists under the first amendment.

• Harvard University agrees to sponsor a new six-week summer institute to serve as a laboratory for professional artists in theater, dance, film, and other fields to develop new work that might lead to public discussion on the events of our times or on ways to change society. Under the directorship of Anna Deavere Smith, with links to the W. E. B. Du Bois Institute for Afro-American Research at Harvard, the American Repertory Theater, and the John F. Kennedy School of Government, the artists will meet

AFRICAN AMERICAN VISUAL ARTS: PART 3

Corrine Jennings

1980s

In the 1980s, few black curators with any power or influence worked at the nation's museums. Many more women, including black women artists, began to exhibit after the 1980s. There were still fracture lines between the ideas of the primitive, the use of the black experience, and the belief in the European tradition.

In New York City, graffiti became a distinctly urban popular visual art movement that revolved around many black and Puerto Rican youth, including Futura 2000 (b. 1956), Les Quinones, and A-One. Most notably, self-taught Jean-Michel Basquiat (1960–1988) created a mainstream following and found opportunity for patronage that enabled his work to be preserved and at his death enter the mainstream auction market.

During the 1980s the movement identified as postmodernism encouraged many artists to abandon the formalism of European tradition. The separation between formal and folk art was obliterated. Private investors and museums began to promote southern "vernacular," or work by self-taught African American artists, through exhibits and publications. Installations, conceptual art, and performance art that combined theatrical forms, visual art, and improvisation became popular. Interdisciplinary collaborations between artists like painter Richard Mayhew (b. 1934) and musician Cecil Taylor opened ways of viewing and understanding art forms.

1990s

Black-owned galleries across the country opened in the urban areas of Atlanta, Boston, Brooklyn, Charlotte, Cleveland, Denver, Detroit, Houston, Los Angeles, New Orleans, New York City, Oakland, Philadelphia, San Diego, San Francisco, and Washington, D.C. Black art festivals and expositions were held in major cities. Books and pamphlets were published on collecting African American art. Exhibitions of work from privately owned black collections and the historic HBCU collections toured to mainstream institutions in large cities. White-owned galleries began to exhibit work of black master artists, especially those from the 1930s, to the 1950s, who were for the most part dead. The mainstream art world tried to kill off painting once and for all, and black curators accepted that as reality. The 1995 catalogue of the group exhibition, titled *Present Tense,* shows that all of the exhibiting artists have MFA degrees from mainstream institutions.

Most grants given to black artists have been government-sponsored. Some black visual artists have received grants from the MacArthur Foundation, dubbed the "genius" award. One was given to 28-year-old Kara Walker (b. 1969), an achiever of mainstream notoriety for sadomasochistic silhouettes that harked back to the coon images of the late nineteenth century minstrel tradition. Many blacks resented the control exercised by what they perceived as a hostile and ignorant curatorial juggernaut supported by the moneyed white elite; others called it end-of-the-century exhaustion, while some blacks, imported into the academies to

(Continued)

"rewrite the canon" in the 1990s, also favored this work, which led to Robert Colescott (b. 1925), whose cartoon images infuriated an earlier generation, and Kara Walker representing the U.S. at the Venice Biennale in 1997. The Tony Shafrazi Gallery gave a solo exhibition to Michael Ray Charles, another artist working with stereotypes. The success of artists who repeated the images of the old minstrel tradition to the delight of white audiences, collectors, and certain museums produced a number of artists who kept one eye on the market.

Many black artists began to use objects/elements associated with black people as emblems of black culture. Faith Ringgold (b. 1930) became well known for painted quilts. Renee Stout, in creating objects that resembled ritual objects associated with African religions, became the first African American artist to be shown at the Museum of African Art in Washington. In the 1990s artists were concerned with gender issues, with the body and with such technical issues of incorporating photography, digital technology, and objects in their work. Invitations to international exhibitions, such as in Egypt, Ecuador, and Chile, introduced other global issues into African American visual art.

Souls Grown Deep (1998), the first volume in a series of four, on so-called outsider or black folk artists, was published by another patron who maintained that "education spoils the natural gifts of black artists." In 1998, Barbara Chase-Riboud (b. 1936) installed her "Africa Rising" sculpture at the African burial ground in New York City, and became the first black woman to receive a solo exhibition at the Metropolitan Museum. Also in 1998, a Jean-Michel Basquiat painting sold for $3.3 million at Christie's auction house.

At the end of the decade, more black curators trained at mainstream colleges began to work at mainstream institutions, but in positions of little power. Black artists like Fred Wilson (b. 1954), who produced environmental installations in the 1980s, were invited to "mine the collections" of museums in order to rearrange and juxtapose objects to create dislocations of social and cultural perceptions. However, such titillating practices generally did not add much work from black artists to the permanent collections" of those institutions.

In the late 1990s, a few smaller auction houses around the nation began to auction a few works by black artists, particularly those artists handled by the white-owned galleries. Both e-Bay and a short-lived black section of the ARTNet began to sell works over the Internet. Graphic artists who produced nostalgic or heroic images of black people produced popular offset lithographs in unlimited editions for mass audiences of blacks wishing to decorate their homes with black images. By 2000, many black museums had been established, but many were devoted to the social and political history; few were devoted to the visual arts. When one of the few black museums that expressed interest in visual arts asked a black curator, trained in mainstream thinking, to develop a painting exhibit, the curator reported to a *New York Times* critic that she knew nothing about painting. Black photographers continuing documentation of the century and their communities were featured in large exhibitions and publications.

with scholars and civic leaders to gain information and ideas, asking questions such as "Can artists change society?" and "What are the responsibilities of institutions in connecting to different communities?" In 1999 the project is ended, proving useful to the artists but running into the limitations of attracting audiences that are mostly middle-aged or older and white—the general picture of theater audiences nationwide.

• Playwright August Wilson and critic Robert Brustein, artistic director of Harvard's American Repertory Theater, spark a national debate with their public conversation "On Cultural Power" at Town Hall in New York City, with Anna Deavere Smith acting as moderator. Brustein argues for an integrated "universal" American culture that prizes multiculturalism without tolerating racial hatred, without dealing with the fact that his own theater presents mostly Eurocentric work. Wilson continues to champion the position he outlined a year earlier at the Theater Communications Group meetings, arguing for the necessity of a separate black theater, although many observers are quick to note that productions of his works have largely been responsible for what integration has occurred in regional and Broadway theaters. The conversation mostly points out how complex the mix of race and culture has become in this country.

BUSINESS AND INDUSTRY

• Julia "Butterfly" Hill begins the longest "tree occupation" in North American history in October 1997, when she adopts Luna, a 200-foot-tall, 1,000-year-old redwood living in the 7,500-acre Headwaters redwood forest of Humboldt County in Northern California. Hill's feet never touch the earth for the next two years as she maintains her tree "sitting," with sponsorship by Earth First!, an environmental activist organization. Her action brings worldwide attention to her cause to protect the last forests of ancient-growth redwoods from the logging industry's saws. In December 1999, Hill climbs down from her perch after the Pacific Lumber Company agrees to preserve Luna within a 200-foot buffer zone in exchange for $50,000 raised by Hill and her many supporters. But in November 2000, Luna is found slashed by a chainsaw cut that makes it vulnerable to the frequent high winds in the area and could possibly kill the tree. The twists and turns of this story underline the difficulties of finding solutions that balance commitments to preserving the environment and the need to provide jobs to people.

• The changeover to broadband, the new high-speed data transmission system via fiber-optic telephone lines or satellite, contributes to the NASDAQ 1998–2000 stock-market boom and the subsequent 2001 bust. As an unintended consequence of the technology, local and long-distance phone companies, including satellite and wireless system operators, are surprised when they receive a low return on their broadband investment. Since, for the first time ever, there is no penalty for distance to the customer because data travels 10,000 miles or ten feet for the same basic charge, providers lose revenue as they are compelled to drop customer prices for long-distance transmission of voice and data.

SCIENCE AND TECHNOLOGY

• DVD-audio standard, a new sound format capable of delivering higher-quality sound than CD, is developed.

WORLD EVENTS

• On January 1, Hong Kong becomes a Special Administrative Region of the People's Republic of China, with the formal departure of the British colonial government, ending 156 years of British rule. Britain and China agree to the Basic Law, which includes provisions prohibiting Beijing from levying taxes, and allows Hong Kong to remain a free port, to retain its capitalist economic system and much of its legal autonomy for fifty years.

🄟 1984

• The so-called Asian financial "tiger" causes a worldwide financial fear of a domino effect when Thailand's currency collapses and the currencies of South Korea and Indonesia follow.

• The cloning of the first mammal, a sheep named Dolly, is achieved by PPL Therapeutics, a Scottish-based company. They clone a genetic twin created from a single cell retrieved from an adult sheep. In 2000, the same company succeeds in cloning a litter of five pigs at their Blacksburg, Virginia, research facility, this time genetically altering a specific gene to "humanize" the pigs' organs so they will be more acceptable to human immune systems when used in organ transplants. The research feats raise various ethical questions among scientists and others, with the general realization that if mammals such as sheep or pigs can be cloned, then one day a human can be cloned. In addition, cross-species transplantations, known as xenotransplantations, could possibly pass new contagious diseases from animal cells to people receiving transplants.

• Under the auspices of the World Trade Organization, sixty countries sign an accord to end state monopolies on telecommunications, freeing competition and foreign investments to enter local markets. With the telecommunications industry now ranking third in revenues, behind health care and banking, it signals the coming scramble for joint ventures to gain control over global markets.

1998

ARTS AND LITERATURE

• The Supreme Court upholds a 1990 congressional provision for awarding federal arts grants by a vote of 8 to 1, in *The National Endowment for the Arts v. Finley,* No. 97–371. The provision requires the NEA to take into account "general standards of decency and respect for the diverse beliefs and values of the American public." All the justices see the provision as not unconstitutionally vague, as the plaintiffs argued and the Ninth Circuit court agreed. The only dissenting opinion, by Justice David H. Souter, interprets the provision as violating the First Amendment, saying, "A statute disfavoring speech that fails to respect Americans' diverse beliefs and values is the very model of viewpoint discrimination."

🄟 1990

GOVERNMENT AND POLITICS

• The government establishes a Council on Year 2000 conversion, to oversee the changeover of computers when the year 2000 begins, and to serve as an international information clearinghouse. Since many older computers were built to record years as two digits, as in "98," they are not programmed to recognize "00" as the year 2000. The conversion effort becomes known as Y2K, and the chairman of the council, John A. Koskinen, is referred to as the Y2K Czar. This is a worldwide problem, with an urgent need to coordinate efforts internationally to prevent potential shutdowns of basic infrastructure involving banking, telecommunications, utilities, transportation, and oil and gas industries. Particular anxiety is focused on averting problems with computers that are used to run nuclear weapons and energy facilities, military installations, and air traffic control.

• On April 14 the Clinton-Gore administration announces its plan to create an "information superhighway" by deregulating communication services and widening the scope of the Internet by opening up carriers, such as television cable, to data communication. Internet 2, a consortium of industry, academic, and government groups, works to develop foundation Internet technologies. It promises to become a breeding ground for network innovations affecting the future of the Internet.

• The House of Representatives votes, along party lines, to impeach President Clinton on two charges of obstruction of justice and perjury. The senators debate whether to censure President Clinton or hold an impeachment trial.

BUSINESS AND INDUSTRY

• The *New York Times* reports that the public has a higher percentage of their assets invested in stocks than at any time since 1945, when the earliest federal data is available on record. "[W]hen all indirect stock holdings are included, stocks account for 43 percent of household financial assets, up from 39 percent in 1968, and 28 percent of total household assets, up from 26 percent in 1968."

• In April, BankAmerica, a San Francisco–based corporation, agrees to a $64-billion merger with the East Coast Nations Bank Corporation that will create the country's largest bank. This deal is eclipsed later in the year by an agreement between Citicorp and Travelers Group, Inc., two of the largest companies in the U.S., making it the largest merger in history, which, if approved, will create the largest financial services concern in the world. John S. Reed, Citicorp's CEO, says, "Frankly, we're probably talking about a restructuring of the financial services industry."

▣ 1933

SCIENCE AND TECHNOLOGY

• Alternative medicines begin being seriously discussed as possible therapies within standard medical schools and hospitals throughout the U.S. as physicians observe that many alternative treatments do work, or at least are very helpful in improving how patients feel. For example, a Center for Integrative Medicine is established at the University of Pennsylvania, within the department of psychiatry, headed by Dr. Richard Petty, a British-born psychiatrist who has trained in internal medicine, endocrinology, acupuncture, and homeopathy. The Center will introduce medical students to various forms of alternative medicine and run critical studies to research and measure their effectiveness. At Kaiser Permanente, an HMO based in Oakland, California, patients living with long-term pain are advised to consider various therapies for its management. Kaiser Permanente offers classes in meditation techniques, yoga, Feldenkrais, and bio-feedback.

▣ 1993

• The twentieth century is on record as the warmest in 600 years. The warmest years have been 1900, 1995, and 1997, according to a study released by Dr. Michael E. Mann, a climatologist at the University of Massachusetts at Amherst, with paleoclimatologists Dr. Raymond S. Bradley, also of U. Mass., and Dr. Malcolm K.

Hughes of the University of Arizona in Tucson. They make this determination through examining "proxy evidence" of climatic change in marine fossils, corals, and ancient ice, and the annual growth rings in trees.

• Nearly one out of three plant species is in danger of extinction in the U.S., and one in eight plant species is endangered worldwide, according to a study released by the Nature Conservancy, a conservation organization. Although more attention has been given to endangered species of animals, plants constitute the basis of the natural environment, converting sunlight into food, and their destruction can upset the fundamental balance necessary for nature's functioning. They also provide raw materials for medicines and genetic components needed to develop agricultural breeds of plants. Most at risk in the U.S. are 14 percent of rose species, 32 percent of lilies and irises, 29 percent of palms, 14 percent of cherry species, and many species of coniferous trees.

CULTURE AND SOCIETY

• The Alaska Standards for Culturally Responsive School are adopted by the Assembly of Alaska Native Educators. Aimed at providing educational standards for rural schools serving Native communities, these criteria shift the curriculum focus from teaching and learning about Native cultural heritage as a separate subject to teaching in and through local cultures as the foundation for all learning.
🖫 1995

• Homelessness continues to be a major problem in the U.S., according to a study released in 1998 by the U.S. Conference of Mayors. Even in a time of unprecedented economic expansion, the demand for emergency

shelter has grown every year since 1985, increasing eleven percent from 1997 to 1998, with approximately 6–7 million Americans drifting in and out of homelessness at any given time, and as many as 3 million Americans drifting in and out of homelessness at least once in any given year. (These figures do not account for those who do not use shelter systems.) The National Law Center on Homelessness and Poverty finds about 40 percent of all homeless people are families with children and 60 percent are single adults. Of the single homeless adults, 25 percent have mental illnesses and 30–35 percent are addicted to drugs or alcohol.
🖫 1966, 1980

• A Million Woman March is called, to take place on October 25 in Philadelphia's Benjamin Franklin Park. Two thousand women from all over the country actually gather, in contrast to the million men who showed up for the 1995 Million Man March. The speakers addressing the crowd include Winnie Mandela, California congresswoman Maxine Waters, Afeni Shakur, mother of slain rap star Tupac Shakur, Sister Souljah, Muhammed Ali's wife and daughter, and the wife of Louis Farrakhan.
🖫 1963, 1995

WORLD EVENTS

• A statute outlining the creation of an International Criminal Court (ICC) is drafted on July 17 by 120 nations, who vote to adopt the treaty at an international conference in Rome. Initially called for in the United Nations' 1948 Genocide Convention, the ICC is to be located in the Netherlands, where it will function as a world court to foster international accountability, and to investigate and prosecute individuals accused of human rights abuses, genocide, and war crimes. Although President Clinton declines to sign the treaty this year—bowing to opposition by Jesse Helms, the Senate's Republican Foreign Relations Committee chair, Senator John W. Warner, chairman of the Armed Services Committee, and members of the military—he authorizes endorsing it just before the December 31, 2000, deadline. The U.S. joins twenty-seven other nations in approving the ICC, including Israel and Iran, which is one-half of the total needed before the court can be formed. American support for the ICC was later withdrawn by the Bush administration.

• In October, Augusto Pinochet, the Chilean general who ruled Chile through the use of genocide, torture, and terrorism while dictator for twenty-five years after the assassination of democratically elected president Salvador Allende, is indicted in Spain for crimes committed against Spanish citizens while living in Chile. He is placed under house arrest in London, where he is residing for medical care. The U.S. government does not actively assist or participate in the rulings, although victims killed include citizens of the U.S., England, Argentina, Switzerland, Sweden, Germany, Belgium, and Luxembourg. However, Pinochet's arrest inspires a reinvestigation of connections between the U.S. government, including the CIA and other intelligence services, and his war crimes. According to *The Trial of Henry Kissinger* by journalist Christopher Hitchens, declassified U.S. government documents describe "a strategy of destabilization, kidnap and assassination, designed to provoke a military coup," with then-President Nixon's secretary of state, Henry Kissinger, acting as the "senior person concerned."

🖸 1973

Staff at the National Seed Laboratory in Fort Collins, Colorado, preserve more than 1 million samples of plant germ plasm. Here, technician Jim Bruce retrieves a seed sample from the minus-18-degree storage vault for testing. Photo by Scott Bauer. *(Agricultural Research Service, USDA)*

1999

ARTS AND LITERATURE

• The Pequot tribe opens their Mashantucket Pequot Museum and Research Center in Connecticut, which tells the story of their long pre-European presence in the area, and their terrible and bloody war with the Puritans in 1637. The

$135-million facility is endowed through their Foxwoods Resort Casino profits.

• William Bolcom's opera to a libretto by Arnold Weinstein on the American classic play by Arthur Miller, *A View from the Bridge,* premieres at the Chicago Lyric Opera Company. Bolcom is also known for his modern ragtime compositions and for his stylistic mixtures of American popular idioms with classical European practices.

• Composer Carman Moore's two-and-one-half-hour-long, multi-stylistic, multi-media *Mass for the 21st Century,* commissioned by the Lincoln Center for the Performing Arts Out-of-Doors Festival and premiered there before 10,000 people, is performed in Cape Town, South Africa, at the Parliament of the World's Religions.

GOVERNMENT AND POLITICS

• On January 7 the U.S. Senate begins its second presidential impeachment trial in the 210-year history of the country, to decide whether President Clinton should be removed from office for acts of perjury and obstruction of justice, as voted by the House of Representatives in December 1998. The chief justice of the Supreme Court, William H. Rehnquist (b. 1924), presides over the proceedings and swears in the senators to "do impartial justice." On January 12, President Clinton stops a sexual misconduct lawsuit brought by a former state of Arkansas employee, Paula Jones, by paying her an $850,000 settlement. On February 12, President Clinton is acquitted by the Senate, on a vote of 55–45 on the perjury charge. A 50–50 split blocks the obstruction-of-justice charge, with no Democrats voting to convict. Clinton tells the nation that he is "profoundly sorry."

• A federal judge approves placing a first shipment of radioactive materials and nuclear waste half a mile underground in the Waste Isolation Pilot Plant (WIPP), a specially constructed maze of fifty-five man-made nuclear-waste repository chambers that have been carved out of an ancient salt bed near Carlsbad, New Mexico. The geologic repository is designed to receive 30,000 truckloads of nuclear wastes from twenty-three military sites around the U.S. over the next thirty-five years. For twenty-five years, since 1974, opponents of this military and Energy Department plan battled to halt shipments, saying that no technology could be guaranteed to remain harmless, and that it made no sense to bury the wastes in a way that they could not be retrieved if a new technology for recycling the wastes as a resource was discovered, or if they became too hazardous to move. Nevada Governor Kenny Guinn moves to stop building a repository at Yucca Mountain, Nevada, because of the frequency of earthquakes within a fifty-mile-radius of the site. And Utah Governor Michael O. Leavitt approves legislation to halt storing radioactive waste in a commercial site on an Indian reservation.

• On October 13 the Senate rejects President Clinton's efforts to sign the Nuclear Test Ban Treaty, an agreement drafted in 1996 by forty-four nations. At present only twenty-four nations have signed on to the treaty, which cannot go into effect until ratified by all forty-four nations. This treaty will be scraped when the George W. Bush administration announces its formal withdrawal from existing arms-control agreements in December 2001.

• Congress approves legislation reconstructing the nation's financial system by removing limits that were set during the Great Depression, so that insurance companies, banks, and securities firms may now extend into each other's businesses.

• The Senate approves the Hate Crimes Prevention Act, which, for the first time in history, defines actions taken against gender, disability, and sexual orientation as hate crimes in addition to those crimes against race, national origin, culture, or religion.

• On December 14, former President Jimmy Carter symbolically hands over the Panama Canal to President Mireya Moscoso of Panama, with the words, "It's yours." The actual transfer of the canal authority occurs on December 31, as President Moscoso proclaims, "The canal is ours! . . . This territory is ours again!" The Panama Canal Commission, a U.S. government agency, is renamed the Panama Canal Authority as it becomes an independent corporation that will manage the canal.

📷 1914

• School busing ends where it began thirty years ago when a Charlotte, North Carolina, judge rules that forced integration of public schools is no longer necessary.

• The South Carolina legislature votes to relocate the Confederate flag from its current location, on top of the state house in Columbus, to a memorial to Confederate war dead, located on the state house grounds. It was installed in 1962 as a defiant gesture against the civil rights movement, and South Carolina is the last state to fly this symbolic flag. This compromise comes after the NAACP wages a vigorous campaign to remove the flag.

BUSINESS AND INDUSTRY

• A precedent to hold gunmakers liable for marketing and distributing practices is set when a federal jury in Brooklyn, New York, decides that nine gunmakers out of twenty-five are at fault in shooting deaths because their marketing and distribution practices assist illegal gun trafficking. The verdict sends gunmakers a signal that they may become subject to lawsuits similar to those against cigarette manufacturers.

• Riots break out in Seattle, where 135 world leaders, including President Clinton, have gathered for the World Trade Organization (WTO) meetings that President Clinton plans as an important step toward a global agreement on free trade. The WTO seeks to set global standards for "free market" guidelines and environmental controls. Ten thousand picketers demonstrate their concerns about globalization, asking that the agenda include setting some norms of social consciousness and responsibility for corporations to accept before practicing business as a global economy. The issues include setting environmental pollution protections, labor standards, ethical and legal guidelines to keep up with scientific research, and solutions to the growing inequality between rich and poor nations. A handful of violent incidents—followed by violent reprisals by the black-clad Seattle police—receive most of the media coverage, although the majority of protestors are peaceful. Lining the streets, their sheer numbers shut down the first day of meetings, contributing to the failure of the conference, which ultimately ends without WTO members reaching any decisions. It remains to be seen if individuals will be able to continue as an important influence in future negotiations.

• Stocks continue to rise ever higher in value online. Buyers spend 50 percent more online in the 1999 holiday season than in 1998, with 95 percent saying they will probably do so again.

Forrester Research, Inc., estimates $4 billion will be spent online during the 1999 holiday season. However, most dot-com companies record low profits in 1999. Amazon.com, one of the most recognized brand-name sites, continues to record losses, of $720 million in 1999, which they attribute to heavy investments in distribution and expenses related to startup businesses such as toys and electronics. Also in 1999, workers at Salon.com, one of the most talked about online magazines, at ValueAmerica, and at other high-profile e-commerce sites are warned of severe downsizing measures, although some dot-coms begin to make profits, such as Yahoo! and America Online, whose retail sales for the 1999 Christmas holiday season are more than double those of 1998, reaching $2.5 billion. The NASDAQ stock market, where most e-commerce sites are posted, becomes very volatile in 2000.

SCIENCE AND TECHNOLOGY

• Neurobiologist Joe Z. Tsien of Princeton University leads a team of researchers in breeding "smarter mice" by altering a gene involved in learning and memory formation. In nerve cells of a brain region called the hippocampus, this gene provides instructions for creating a cell-surface protein called NMDA that serves as a sort of docking point for glutamate, one of the most important molecules in cell-to-cell communication. The genetically altered mice, whose DNA is 98 percent identical to human DNA, are put through six different tests that they consistently perform better than normal mice. The NMDA receptor could potentially serve as a target for treating brain disorders like Alzheimer's, or even for enhancing learning and memory in healthy people.

• The Food and Drug Administration halts human gene therapy experiments at the University of Pennsylvania after the first known death related to gene therapy occurs at the facility. Jesse Gelsinger, an eighteen-year-old volunteer who suffers from a genetically induced metabolic disorder called ornithine transcarbamylase (OTC) deficiency, is participating in the medical trials despite being able to control his disorder with a combination of diet and drugs—the experiment is designed to test a treatment for babies with a fatal form of the disorder—when he dies of multiple organ failure after a severe immune reaction. The death highlights flaws in the informed-consent process, which helps patients understand procedural risks including those accompanying basic techniques such as vectors, weakened viruses that deliver corrective genes to unhealthy cells. In the case of Jesse Gelsinger, the vector is adenovirus, the common cold.

• The U.S. military introduces concrete bombs as a low-tech solution to their continued bombing of military targets located near civilian populations in Iraq. Instead of loading F-16 fighter jets with bombs containing explosives, they load them with concrete-filled bombs. The laser-guided concrete bombs are intended to destroy targets without causing "collateral damage," the military's term for civilian deaths, and their use responds to diplomatic objections to the continuing use of air strikes against Iraq. ▣ 1991

• Government studies confirm that marijuana does have medical benefits, with active ingredients that reduce pain and other symptoms related to AIDS. ▣ 1996

• The HIV virus is traced to a subspecies of chimpanzee.

• Two new elements, with atomic numbers 116 and 118, are created by scientists at the Lawrence Berkeley National Laboratory in California by dashing krypton atoms against a lead target inside a cyclotron accelerator.

CULTURE AND SOCIETY

• The Commerce Department releases *Falling Through the Net,* its report that surveys the use of powerful information tools nationwide, such as personal computers and the Internet. Using 1998 Census Bureau data, the report finds that over 40 percent of all U.S. households own computers and 25 percent have Internet access. However, there is a "digital divide" that falls "between the information-rich (whites, Asians, and Pacific Islanders, those with higher incomes, those more educated, and dual-parent households) and the information-poor (such as those who are younger, those with lower incomes and education levels, certain minorities, and those in rural areas or central cities).

• Of the 300 Native languages that were spoken before the arrival of Europeans on the North American continent, 211 are still spoken today, although, of the 175 Native languages still spoken in the U.S., only ten or fewer are currently spoken by tribal members. Many tribes now encourage reviving their languages, offering Native language courses in tribal colleges for foreign-language credit, and honoring fluent speakers as "masters" and "tribal treasures." Languages that have gone out of use are being reconstructed through study of dictionaries and written texts that were made by missionaries, and the recorded field notes and tapes of anthropologists.

• The Kansas school board votes to remove from its educational standards two mainstream theories that are basic principles of modern biology, physics, and cosmology: the origins of life through evolution; and the origin of the universe in the "Big Bang." They prefer what is referred to as the "young Earth creationist" theory, which has found ways to explain how cosmic history could have occurred in thousands of years rather than in about 15 billion years, the time span with which most modern physical scientists now agree. The board stops short of preventing teachers from presenting the mainstream scientific theories in their classrooms, permitting them to be discussed as alternative viewpoints.

🖻 1999

WORLD EVENTS

• On January 1 the euro becomes the common European currency that unites eleven countries. Transactions can be made electronically, with the actual coins and notes due to go into circulation officially by January 1, 2002, and replace each participating country's local currency by July 1, 2002. The participating countries are Austria, Belgium, the Netherlands, Finland, France, Germany, Ireland, Italy, Luxembourg, Portugal, and Spain.

• On March 12 the Eastern European nations of the Czech Republic, Poland, and Hungary join NATO. On March 24 the combined forces of NATO launch a missile and bomb attack on Serbia and Kosovo, and other targets, to punish Yugoslav leader Slobodan Milosevic's year-long assault on ethnic Albanians. On May 27 a Hague tribunal indicts Milosevic and four senior officers of war crimes in Kosovo, including charges of murder, forced deportation, and persecution.

• The United Nations sets the "Day of Six Billion," on October 12, to officially mark the

In April 2000, the total population of the U.S. is 281,422,000, a 13.2-percent gain over the last decade. The U.S. is growing at five times the rate of all other industrialized nations combined; only China and India have more people. According to the 2000 Census, the South and West account for more than three-quarters of the population increases, with Hispanic and Asian populations recording a third decade of growth. In 2000, 9.5 percent of the nation's population is foreign-born, and according to Kenneth Prewitt, director of the Census Bureau, "The twenty-first century will be the century in which we redefine ourselves as the first country in world history which is literally made up of every part of the world."

The multiracial diversity of seventy-one of the nation's 100 largest urban areas has significantly shifted, so that where in previous census counts, non-Hispanic whites constituted a majority, now no single ethnic racial group makes up a majority. (Hispanic is classified as an ethnicity, rather than as a race.) Of the most multiracial cities in the country, eight of the top ten are in California, where, for the first time ever and three years ahead of predictions, non-Hispanic whites are officially a minority, totaling 46.7 percent of the population. Black or African American Californians total 6.4 percent, Asians total 10.8 percent, and other races 3.7 percent.

California is the nation's most populous state, with a growth rate a little less than 10 percent. Its 33,871,000 people make a total greater than almost half of the other states in the Union combined. Twenty-six percent of Californians are estimated to be foreign-born, the highest percentage in the country. Forty-four percent are native Mexicans, 10 percent from other Latin American countries, and 34 percent from Asia. One-third of the nation's Hispanics live in California, and their population increase, due mainly to births rather than immigration, makes up three-quarters of the state's population growth.

Over half of the nation's 4.1 million Native Americans and Alaska Natives live in urban areas, with one in four located in California or Oklahoma. Forty percent of 1.5 million American Indians or Alaska Natives report being at least one other race. Of these, 180,940 report Latin American Indian heritage. Seventy-four percent indicate tribal membership, with the ten most populous tribal groups being Cherokee, Navajo, Latin American Indian, Choctaw, Sioux, Chippewa, Apache, Blackfeet, Iroquois, and Pueblo. The largest Alaska Native tribal group is the Eskimo, with Tlingit-Haida, Alaska Athabascan, and Aleut next in total size.

The 2000 Census finds that marriages are occurring later in life. The median age of first marriages for men rose to 26.8 years, while women's median age for first marriage is 25.1 years, both an increase of at least three years since the 1970s. Of the country's 71 million family households, single-father households with children under eighteen make up 3 percent; single-mother homes with children under eighteen comprise 7.2 percent. The number of households in which both parents raise the children increased by 6 percent during the last decade; married couples with children under eighteen make up 24 percent of all family households.

entrance of the six billionth person to Earth. Carol Bellamy, executive director of UNICEF, says that "for the majority of babies, the risks are high and the odds daunting. . . . The six billionth child will also find himself in a world where the gap between rich and poor has never been so wide." The UN chooses a boy born in Sarajevo as the person to represent this population peak.

- On December 31, Boris Yeltsin asks forgiveness for his mistakes during his time in office, resigns from the presidency of Russia, and names Vladimir Vladimirovich Putin as acting president, pending elections in March 2000, because "Russia must enter the new millennium with new politicians with new faces, with new, smart, strong, energetic people. And we who have been in power for many years already, we must go."

- A retired general, Olusegun Obasanjo, is elected the first civilian president of Nigeria in fifteen years.

- Seti Mohammed, a four-star general in the Royal Armed Forces, succeeds King Hassan II, his father, to become King Mohammed IV of Morocco.

- Politician Thabo Mbeki is elected president of South Africa in June, succeeding Nelson Mandela.

- King Abdullah II becomes the fourth ruler of the Hashemite Kingdom of Jordan, succeeding his father, King Hussein.

2000

ARTS AND LITERATURE

- The Board of Directors of the Martha Graham Center of Contemporary Dance, the umbrella organization for the Martha Graham Dance Company, a pioneering American modern-dance institution founded in 1929, suspends operations due to financial problems. Other issues involve conflicts of the board with Graham's chosen successor, Ron Protas, a nondancer who has functioned as the company's artistic director since her death in 1991. As director of the Martha Graham Trust, Protas also holds the rights to Graham's works, which gives him the power to choose which other dance companies may license performance rights. At present, only ballet companies, including the Joffrey Ballet of Chicago, have been given rights to perform Graham's choreography. This particular conflict highlights how few precedents there are in the dance world for copyright procedures, and reflects a general shift in the dance world, as modern dance companies, inheritors of a revolution that rejected ballet and split the Western dance tradition into at least two different branches, now basically merge back into one.

- Stephen King publishes *Riding the Bullet*, the first book to be exclusively distributed through the Internet. Called an e-book, the sixty-six-page, 16,000 word novella receives over half a million paid and free downloads in the first few days of availability. The effect of this new format is likened to the advent of paperbacks, further democratizing the arts and culture. Another landmark signaling the art establishment's acceptance of digital culture is the Whitney Museum's 2000 Biennial's inclusion of Internet artists' works made in and for cyberspace, positing that cyberart is the "first new art form to be introduced in the Biennial since video in 1975."

GOVERNMENT AND POLITICS

• In June, the already two-year-old antitrust case *U.S. v. Microsoft* is won by the U.S. government against Microsoft Corporation, when Federal District Judge Thomas Penfield Jackson orders Microsoft to split into two companies. Judge Jackson agrees with the Justice Department's case, finding that Microsoft did act as a "predatory" monopoly, protecting its market domain through illegal, anticompetitive means to protect its domination of the marketplace "by tying its Web browser, Internet Explorer, to Windows, the company's operating system." Lauded by some as the biggest antitrust breakup since the 1911 breakup of Standard Oil Company, others maintain the ruling is irrelevant because the market changes so quickly in the present technology-driven economy, especially since Microsoft will continue to bring further appeals to delay the breakup.

• The Clinton Administration negotiates a series of trade liberalization agreements that open up markets in China, Cuba, and Vietnam. In June, U.S.-Cuban trade and immigration policies shift into a new era as the U.S. government reconsiders lifting some parts of its forty-year embargo as a direct result of seven months of negotiations in the Elián Gonzalez custody battle, which begins in November 1999 after the six-year-old boy's mother and stepfather drown in their failed attempt to escape Cuba and gain asylum in the U.S. Elián survives by floating in an inner tube. The Cuban American relatives wage a fierce battle to keep Elián in Miami against the wishes of his natural father, Juan Miguel Gonzalez. The resultant media blitz, focused on congressional pressure and demonstrations by the family's supporters in Miami's Cuban American community, backfires as public opinion favors the child's return to his Cuban father. The negotiations reestablish contact between the governments for the first time since the Organization of American States (OAS) severed diplomatic relations and imposed a trade embargo in 1963.

• Congress agrees to grant permanent normal trade status to China. The pact improves U.S.-China relations by providing China with the same low-tariff access to U.S. markets as most other U.S. trading partners, and grants China entry into the 136-member World Trade Organization. In exchange, it opens key Chinese markets to direct foreign investment by U.S. and multinational industries, dealerships, and distribution services, including agricultural products, manufacturers of auto and heavy industrial equipment, and telecommunications, computer, software, and semiconductor firms. Although opposed by a coalition of organized labor, environmentalists, human-rights activists, and globalization opponents, pro-trade advocates argue that we cannot afford to cut off communication, either economically or politically, with more than a billion potential customers. President Clinton says the pact gives China "a chance—not a guarantee, but a chance—to build a future in the Asia Pacific region for the next fifty years very different from the last fifty." The *Wall Street Journal* calls the vote "the end of the twentieth-century struggle between communism and capitalism for dominance of the world economy. Capitalism won. With China's entry into the WTO, free markets and free trade have emerged as the unchallenged global standard for business."

• President Clinton becomes the first U.S.

FROM THE DISSENTING OPINION IN *BUSH V. GORE*

*Supreme Court Justice
John Paul Stevens*

In the interest of finality . . . the majority effectively orders the disenfranchisement of an unknown number of voters whose ballots reveal their intent—and are therefore legal votes under state law—but were for some reason rejected by ballot-counting machines. . . . Although we may never know with complete certainty the identity of the winner of this year's presidential election, the identity of the loser is perfectly clear. It is the nation's confidence in the judge as an impartial guardian of the law.

president to visit Vietnam since the end of the Vietnam War.

• During the 2000 presidential political campaign, voters engage in a new form of grassroots activism, by posting information on candidates on "home grown" Web sites, in a high-tech version of planting signs in the front yard or pasting bumper stickers on cars.

• The 2000 presidential election is not decided on election night, but remains in question for thirty-six days until a 10:00 P.M. Supreme Court decision on December 12 dramatically brings it to conclusion. In the U.S. Supreme Court ruling *Bush v. Gore*, the Court orders a stop to the manual recount of thousands of bitterly contested Florida votes. Although the Democratic Party nominee, Vice President Al Gore, wins the nationwide popular vote by a 300,000 margin, he concedes the election to the Republican Party nominee, Texas Governor George W. Bush, when the Supreme Court ruling awards Bush the electoral college vote with the Florida victory. The Court's ruling effectively leaves that state's vote count forever unknown, as many ballots will never be officially counted. The Supreme Court's 5–4 decision maintains the consistently close results of every aspect of this election: The electoral college votes tally 271 for Bush and 267 for Gore. The Senate splits fifty-fifty for the first time since 1881; the House majority goes to Republicans by only three seats. The widespread differences in voting procedures, brought to light in media discussions and court debates, lead to calls for reexamination of these systems and the institution of changes that will guarantee that every vote is counted in future elections. The U.S. Commission on Civil Rights conducts hearings in Florida, and its preliminary findings conclude that African American voters who attempted to vote in November faced discrimination, including voter intimidation, confusing ballots, and purges of eligible voters from the rolls that may constitute violations of the Voting Rights Act of 1965.

SCIENCE AND TECHNOLOGY

• Computers transition into the year 2000 without experiencing any serious mishaps, let alone the widely predicted chaos of satellites and airplanes falling out of the sky, bank systems crashing, shortages of foodstuffs and other goods, and breakdowns involving basic resources such as water, electricity, gas, and oil. The crisis prediction stems from the early days of computers, when programmers decided to save space in the precious processing and storage capacity by representing years with two digits instead of four. Over $250 billion was invested worldwide over the past two years to become "Y2K compliant," with repairs, upgrades, and contingency preparations planned by millions of computer consultants and information technology workers as they readied electronic machines to recognize and talk to each other in a year beginning with 20 rather than 19. The crisis has the side effect of getting companies to deal with neglected political and legal issues, making them reevaluate public relations, customer services, contingency planning, and questions of legal liability.

• The first fossilized dinosaur heart is found, within the ribcage of a sixty-six-million-year-old llama-sized dinosaur, *Thescelosaurus.* As announced by *Science,* the findings, by scientists at the North Carolina State University and North Carolina State Museum of Natural History, surprisingly reveal a four-chambered structure. This means the dinosaur had the heart of a warm-blooded animal, rather than the three-chambered heart of a cold-blooded animal, which until recently had been some experts' assumption. This evidence, and other recent findings made possible by increasingly sophisticated laboratory studies using computerized X-ray scans, has persuaded many experts to describe dinosaurs as fast-growing, fast-moving, warm-blooded animals. The evidence of other physical traits, such as tough hides covered with layers of soft down or feathers, and nesting behaviors make it possible to link birds, dinosaurs, and flying reptiles to a common warm-blooded ancestry.

• An intense race between the publicly funded Human Genome Project (HGP), an international consortium of scientists, and for-profit rival Celera Genomics to sequence the human genome nears completion years ahead of

---

THE HUMAN GENOME PROJECT CONFIRMS THAT RACE IS A SOCIAL CONSTRUCT

Studies of the entire human genetic sequence reveal that the world's populations are 99.9 percent identical: "I actually think that the research at the genomic level will tell us that there is no such thing as race. Race is a social identity, not a biological fact." Dr. Mildred Cho, senior research scholar at Stanford University's Center for Biomedical Ethics.

"Despite staggering population numbers, geneticists now see the human race as quite small. . . . From a geneticist's point of view, we are a very, very small species. We all descend from about 10,000 individuals in Africa a mere 5,000 generations ago. We show all the hallmarks of being a very tiny species with relatively little genetic variation." The world's 6 billion people are actually "10,000 people grown large in the blink of an eye, and therefore we're extremely closely related to each other." Dr. Eric Lander, director of the Whitehead Institute Center for Genome research in Cambridge, Massachusetts, a leading scientist working on the human genome sequencing project. (*Oakland Tribune,* February 20, 2001)

schedule. In a joint announcement in June at the White House, temporarily halting months of sometimes-bitter negotiation, Francis Collins, director of the HGP and Craig Venter, chief scientific officer of Celera, confirm that both groups have produced drafts of the genome; however, Celera's version is more advanced, at least 5 percent more complete, and is furnished at a fraction of the cost and time, owing to its proprietary shotgun-sequencing technique. The conflict over data is one of ownership: the consortium holds that human DNA sequences should be publicly owned and freely available through the website GenBank, while the Celera Group seeks private ownership for commercial purposes. Their truce is only temporary; though the two research groups agree to coordinate publication of their findings, Celera will make a preemptive submission of its research paper to the scientific journal *Science* in December. The combined historic achievement will ultimately revolutionize the way in which diseases are treated.

• The National Geophysical Data Center in Boulder, Colorado, releases a set of fourteen new three-dimensional, computer-generated relief maps of the Earth, as seen from space without cloud coverings. In addition to depicting the Earth's land surface in data six times more detailed than their 1991 version, they have for the first time been able to depict accurately the characteristics of the ocean floor by using undersea-surface topography gathered from 1970s satellite radar scans, sonar scans, and instruments lowered to the depths. These maps reveal that "Continental uplifts with their mountain ranges, plains, and depressions contrast with deep ocean basins fractured by shifting tectonic plates and massive crustal

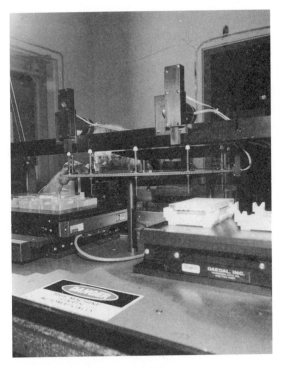

Bill Searles of the Lawrence National Lab's instrumentation group, is seen behind the Human Genome colony picking machine. When the colony picker is fully operational, the group expects it to be able to array as many as a million colonies of yeast or bacteria a year. (*Courtesy of UC Lawrence Berkeley National Laboratory Image Library, Jean Wolslegel*)

upswellings. Some of the images even show the location of fault lines that produce earthquakes."

• A new form of antibiotics synthetically replicates peptides, a naturally occurring compound that plants and humans use to resist microbe invasions. Designed by chemist Dr. Samuel H. Gellman and pharmacologist Dr. Bernard Weisblum, both researchers at the University of Wisconsin-Madison, the synthetic design is more stable than the naturally occurring compound, and different enough from it that "it could take longer for bacteria to develop resistance to drugs developed this way."

• The North Polar ice cap is found to be melting, probably for the first time in 55 million years, since the Eocene era, when open water covered the North Pole and the Earth's climate was so warm that tropical vegetation spread within both the Arctic and Antarctic circles. Although satellites have been relaying images of a steadily shrinking ice cap since the early 1990s, this new development was reported by Dr. James McCarthy, an oceanographer, director of the Museum of Comparative Zoology at Harvard University and co-head of a group expedition sponsored by the United Nations' Intergovernmental Panel on Climate Change, after the expedition observed the 90-degree north location from the deck of a Russian ice-breaker in August.

• The Environmental Protection Agency reports its findings on a protein called harpin, a "biopesticide" that offers an alternative to chemical pesticides by activating plants' natural immunities against disease and insects, saying, "For the first time in modern agriculture, growers will be able to harness the innate defense and growth systems of crops." The protein is known by its product trade name, Messenger, and comes from a bacterium that causes fire blight, a disease that attacks apple and pear trees. In 500 field trials it has proven effective against diseases caused by viruses, bacteria, and fungi, besides being effective against some insects.

• A self-replicating robot is designed and built for the first time, by two Brandeis University scientists, Hod Lipson and Jordan Pollack. By connecting a computer to a commercial plastic model-making machine, little toylike robots, using plastic cylinders and ball joints and a simple circuitry, are produced. However, their invention cannot think for itself or replicate itself, and requires humans to install a motor and a computer-programmed microchip in order to be activated.

BUSINESS AND INDUSTRY

• On March 27, Cisco Systems, a maker of equipment that routes traffic on the Internet, becomes the world's most valuable company, with a market value of $555.4 billion, bypassing Microsoft, which had been at the top of the list since September 1998. Cisco's surge, coming after they add an office telephone system to their line of computer network gear, indicates how the computer revolution has shifted. Whereas Microsoft dominated the 1980s and 1990s, with consumers hooked to their PC desktop computer system, the new demand is for faster, always-accessible connections to buy and sell goods and cut costs, which requires businesses that run the Internet, the network routers, switches, and servers.

• Eleven tribal corporations agree to commit $1 million each to underwrite a founding proposal for the Native American National Bank, the largest intertribal bank ever created, owned and controlled solely by Native Americans. Although it will make investments in non-Native-owned businesses, its primary mission is to increase wealth among all tribes by providing corporate-size loans nationwide to businesses owned by Native Americans. They seek to counter the difficulties that Native Americans have experienced historically when seeking to secure loans from mainstream commercial banks, in large part because of the banks' fears of complications from tribal law protections that do not have to recognize federal laws. It also proposes to manage new sources of capital coming into many reservations through casino revenues, and to counter the federal government's tie-up of tribal billions gained through court settlements and land lease payments. In seeking startup funds of $30 million, initial investment pledges have been made by the the the Pequots, one of the wealthiest North American tribes due to revenues received from their Foxwoods Casino in Ledyard, Connecticut; the Seminoles in Florida; the Three Affiliated Tribes of North Dakota; the Cheyenne River Sioux of South Dakota; the Grand Traverse Band of Ottawa; the Chippewa of Michigan; the Mille Lacs Band of Chippewa in Minnesota; the Ute Mountain Tribe in Colorado; the Tlingit and Haida tribes, jointly, in Alaska; the Arctic Slope Regional Corporation, representing several northern Alaska tribes; the Navajo Tribe in Utah, Arizona, and New Mexico; and the Puyallup Tribe in Washington. Four more tribes are seriously considering joining the bank, as are three commercial banks, Bank of America, Bank One, and Wells Fargo, which would benefit by fulfilling their federal requirements to invest in some minority- or community-based institutions.

• Community-sharing software programs like Napster, Macster, Gnutella, and Freenet allow Internet users to link anonymously between computers for the purpose of copying files, often digital MP3 music files, violating intellectual property copyright laws. Record companies including Sony, AOL Time Warner, Vivendi Universal, and EMI Music wage an eight-month lawsuit against Napster, resulting in a court injunction that forces Napster to filter its music index for all unauthorized copyrighted songs. However, until the record companies offer a Napster-like service at a price that makes it imprudent to risk lawsuit by infringing copyright, many believe free file-sharing software will remain popular. Freenet and other systems, which have no central file index to target, present a more formidable challenge to record companies since protecting copyrighted material would require blocking every single computer user from exploiting the software.

• The Federal Communications Commission (FCC) invites nonprofit groups to request licenses for free, low-power "microradio" stations which will broadcast up to a range of seven miles. Church groups, jazz societies, and colleges are among the institutions filing to set up community based stations, which are more in line with radio's historical mission that was intended to emphasize serving community needs.

CULTURE AND SOCIETY

• On July 1, Vermont becomes the first state to approve same-sex "civil union," after heated debate in the media and Legislature about the moral implications of such legislation. The bill adopts a state-sanctioned system that provides almost the same benefits as the state's heterosexual marriage laws, including inheritance rights and tax breaks, besides requiring a legal dissolution in family court if the couple separates. Many out-of-state gay and lesbian couples come to Vermont to officially confirm their relationships, although it is unlikely that Vermont's legal rights will be applicable in other states. The bill also provides more limited "reciprocal beneficiaries" benefits applying to blood relatives who live together, mainly regarding medical decisions and funeral arrangements.

• The 2000 Census forms include revised classifications for race, presenting 6 single race categories and 63 combinations of race categories as compared to 5 single race categories in the 1990 Census. For the first time in the history of the census, individuals are allowed to identify themselves as members of more than one race. 2.4% of the nation's total population, or 6.8 million people, identify themselves as multiracial, of which 42%, or 2.9 million are under 18 years of age.

• Preliminary Census 2000 tallies, which are not final, indicate that the country's 35.3 million Hispanic population shows a 58% growth rate since 1990 as a result of immigration and births. This number outpaces predictions, making Hispanics nearly as large a minority as African Americans nationwide. The Asian population is growing in or near big cities, also largely as a result of an influx of new immigrants, at a growth rate of from 60 percent to as much as 110 percent, with a much wider diversification outside of traditional Asian concentrations in California, Washington, and New York. The Census also shows that illegal immigration totals are at least double the estimated 6 million, making undocumented immigrants 4.6 percent of the population. The fact that illegal immigrants work at low wages possibly explains why the late-nineties economy was able to expand so far, so fast, without causing inflation.

• The top ten shrinking cities, according to 2000 population counts, are located in Eastern and Western states: Connecticut, Missouri, Indiana, Maryland, Michigan, New York, Virginia, Pennsylvania, and Ohio. "Boomburbs," a new buzzword for rapidly growing suburban cities,

are overtaking many urban centers in influence and size. According to the Fannie Mae Foundation's analysis of 2000 Census data, the boomburb regions actually match or dwarf their major metropolitan counterparts, with the top nine areas located in Arizona, California, Colorado, and Texas. Fifty-three boomburbs of over 100,000 residents are located where they are not the largest city in the area. The study states that virtually all are affluent cities containing lower-income areas and ethnically diverse residents, particularly in California.

WORLD EVENTS

• New Year, 2000, is celebrated worldwide as the end of the twentieth century and the beginning of the third millennium, although technically the twenty-first century does not officially begin until 2001. It is documented and shared through satellite video transmissions, passing from time zone to time zone, with the first sunrise of New Year's Day honored in the South Pacific, on Millennium Island of the Republic of Kiribati, the recently renamed Caroline Island, and the last at Falealupo, Samoa. (The claim that the South Pacific island is actually the site of the first sunrise of the millennium is a point of dispute, with the U.S. Naval Observatory observing that Kahuitara Point on Pitt Island in the Chatham Islands, a dependency of New Zealand, receives the earliest sunrise.) Throughout the world, beautiful moments of peace and good cheer are variously expressed with ancient rituals and the latest in technological feats. There are fire dances on the Judean Hills of Israel, a musicale at the Great Pyramid of Giza in Egypt, signal fires on the Great Wall of China, fireworks on the Eiffel Tower in Paris, flames on the Thames River in London, and thousands of people dancing in San Francisco's Embarcadero and New York City's streets as a newly designed "time ball" drops on Times Square at midnight.

• In March, Russia's Duma (parliament) ratifies the START II treaty, approving significant new cuts in Russia's nuclear weapons stockpiles, including reducing their long-range nuclear arsenal by almost half, and eliminating land-based multiple-warhead missiles. They link arms reduction to an agreement by the U.S. not to pursue a national missile defense system.

• The Dutch parliament votes to approve a set of guidelines for carrying out euthanasia, making the Netherlands the first country in the world to approve doctor-assisted suicide. Physicians must obtain a second independent doctor's opinion that the patient is facing "unremitting and unbearable suffering" before helping to carry out a voluntary patient request, and must report the cause of death as euthanasia or suicide.

• In June, North Korean President Kim Jong-il hosts a meeting with South Korean President Kim Dae Jung in Pyongyang, the capital of North Korea. This is the first official meeting between the two Koreas since they ceased a formal state of war in 1953. They agree to allow visits between families that have been separated, and to repair rail lines that have remained cut since the war. The first 100 families from North and South meet in August. Other major points of contention, such as the South Korean government's defense agreement with the U.S. allowing 37,000 U.S. troops to remain in South Korea, and North Korea's missile and possible nuclear development, are left for later negotiation. South Korean President Kim Dae Jung receives a 2000 Nobel Peace Prize for initiating and continuing to work toward reconciliation between the two countries.

• When former Coca-Cola executive and state governor Vicente Fox Quesada is elected president of Mexico, his coalition victory (an alliance between Fox's pro-business National Alliance Party and the Green-Ecology Party) upsets the world's longest-ruling party, the Institutional Revolutionary Party (PRI), which has been in power for seventy-one years.

SELECTED BIBLIOGRAPHY

Timelines and Almanacs

Bergman, Peter A. *The Chronological History of the Negro in America.* New York and Toronto: Mentor/New American Library, 1969.

Bernardo, Stephanie. *The Ethnic Almanac.* Garden City, N.Y.: Dolphin Books/Doubleday, 1981.

Brownstone, David, and Irene Frank. *Timelines of War: A Chronology of Warfare from 100,000 B.C. to the Present.* Boston: Little Brown, 1996.

Glennon, Lorraine, editor. *Our Times: The Illustrated History of the 20th Century.* Atlanta: Turner Publishing, Inc., 1995.

Hellemans, Alexander, and Bryan Bunch. *The Timetables of Science.* New York: Touchstone/Simon & Schuster, 1988.

Kanellos, Nicolas, with Cristelia Perez. *Chronology of Hispanic-American History, from Pre-Columbian Times to the Present.* Detroit and New York: Gale Research, Inc., 1995.

Kullen, Allan S., compiler. *The Peopling of America: A Timeline of Events That Helped Shape Our Nation*, 4th ed. Americans All: A National Education Program. Beltsville, Md.: The Portfolio Project, Inc., 1996.

Nies, Judith. *Native American History, A Chronology of a Culture's Vast Achievements and Their Links to World Events.* New York: Ballantine Books, 1996.

Wallechnisky, David, and Irving Wallace. *The People's Almanac Presents the 20th Century.* Woodstock and New York: Overlook Press, 1999.

Internet Timeline Sources

Burns, Kristine: Electronic Music Timeline: http://music.dartmouth.edu/~wpwem/electronmedia/music/eamhistory.html.

Chronology of the Lesbian and Gay Movement in the U.S.: http://www.glaad.org/glaad/history-month/primer/chronology.html.

Dallas Morning News, Celebrating Hispanic Heritage, "Events in Hispanic American History" www.galegroup.com/chhdmn.

Demographic data: infoplease.com.

History of Palestine/Israel: www.palestinehistory.com/time.

Hobbes's Internet Timeline: http://www.zakon.org/robert/internet/timeline.

Internet Society: History of the Internet, http://www.internetvalley.com/intval.html.

The Media History Project: Timeline 20th Century: http://www.mediahistory.com/time/.

"A Timeline of Symmetry in Physics, Chemistry, and Mathematics" (with a link to the Nobel Foundation): history.hyperjeff.net. An Audio Timeline: http://recordist.com/aeschc/docs/audio.history.timeline.html.

Other General References

Brown, Lester R., project director. *State of the World 2000.* New York and London: W. W. Norton, 2000.

Bryan, C. D. B. *The National Geographic Society: 100 Years of Adventure and Discovery.* New York: Harry N. Abrams, 1997.

Cao, Lan, and Himilee Novas. *Everything You Need to Know About Asian-American History.* New York: Plume/Penguin, 1996.

Churchill, Ward. *A Little Matter of Genocide: Holocaust and Denial in the Americas, 1492 to the Present.* San Francisco: City Lights Books, 1997.

Dent, Tom. *Southern Journey: A Return to the Civil Rights Movement.* New York: William Morrow and Company, 1997.

DuPlessis, Rachel Blau, and Ann Snitow. *The Feminist Memoir Project: Voices from Women's Liberation.* New York: Three Rivers Press, 1998.

Felder, Deborah G. *A Century of Women: The Most Influential Events in 20th Century Women's History.* New Jersey: Birch Lane Press Book / Carol Publishing Group, 1999.

Fields, Rick. *How the Swans Came to the Lake, A Narrative History of Buddhism in America,* 3rd ed. Boston and London: Shambhala, 1992.

Franklin, John Hope, and Alfred A. Moss. *From Slavery to Freedom: A History of African Americans,* 8th edition. Miller, Marilyn, and Marian Faux, project editors. New York: Alfred A. Knopf, 2000.

Gjerde, Jon, editor. *Major Problems in American Immigration and Ethnic History.* Boston and New York: Houghton Mifflin, 1998.

Gonzalez, Juan. *Harvest of Empire: A History of Latinos in America.* New York: Viking, 2000.

Hales, Peter Bacon. *Atomic Spaces: Living on the Manhattan Project.* Urbana and Chicago: University of Illinois Press, 1997.

Historical Statistics of the U.S.: Colonial Times to 1970, Parts 1 and 2, Bicentennial Editions. Bureau of the Census, 1975.

Joshi, S. T., editor. *Documents of American Prejudice: An Anthology of Writings on Race from Thomas Jefferson to David Duke.* New York: Basic Books, 1999.

Kaiser, Charles. *The Gay Metropolis, 1940–1996.* San Diego, New York, and London: Harcourt Brace, 1997.

Lindqvist, Sven. *A History of Bombing.* Translated by Linda Haverty Rugg. New York: New Press, 2001.

Litwack, Leon F., and Winthrop D. Jordan. *The United States: Becoming a World Power,* volume II, 7th ed. New Jersey: Prentice-Hall, 1991.

Loewen, James W. *Lies My Teacher Told Me: Everything Your American History Textbook Got Wrong.* New York: Touchstone / Simon and Schuster, 1996.

MacMillan, Margaret. *Paris 1919: Six Months That Changed the World.* New York: Random House, 2001.

Murolo, Priscilla, and A. B. Chitty. *From the Folks Who Brought You the Weekend: A Short, Illustrated History of Labor in the United States.* New York: New Press, 2001.

Nabokov, Peter. *Native American Testimony: A Chronicle of Indian-White Relations from Prophecy to the Present, 1492–1992,* New York: Penguin Books, 1992.

The National Data Book. *Statistical Abstract of the United States 1998,* 118th edition. U.S. Department of Commerce, Economics, and Statistics Administration, Bureau of the Census, March 1999.

New York Public Library. *American History Desk Reference.* New York: Stonesong Press / Macmillan, 1997.

Norris, Floyd, and Christine Bockelmann. *The New York Times Century of Business.* New York: McGraw-Hill, 2000.

Petroski, Henry. *Remaking the Work: Adventures in Engineering.* New York: Vintage Books, 1997.

Prashad, Vijay. *The Karma of Brown Folk.* Minnesota: University of Minnesota Press, 2000.

Quinones, Juan Gomez. *Chicano Politics: Reality and Promise, 1940–1990.* Albuquerque: University of New Mexico Press, 1990.

Rifkin, Jeremy. *The Biotech Century: Harnessing the Gene and Remaking the World.* New York: Jeremy P. Tarcher / Putnam, 1998.

Riordan, Michael, and Lillian Hoddeson. *Crystal Fire: The Invention of the Transistor and the Birth of the Information Age.* New York and London: W. W. Norton, 1997.

Rosen, Ruth. *The World Split Open: How the Modern Women's Movement Changed America.* New York: Viking, 2000.

Scientific American. Science Desk Reference. New York: John Wiley and Sons, Inc., 1999.

Siegel, Marvin, editor. *The Last Word: The New York Times Book of Obituaries and Farewells, A Celebration of Unusual Lives.* New York: Quill / William Morrow, 1997.

Stavans, Ilan. *The Hispanic Condition: Reflections on Culture and Identity in America.* New York: HarperCollins, 1995.

Suplee, Curt. *Physics in the 20th Century.* New York: Harry N. Abrams, in association with the American Physical Society and the American Institute of Physics, 1999.

Trefil, James. *101 Things You Don't Know About Science and No One Else Does Either.* Boston and New York: Houghton Mifflin, 1996.

Weatherford, Doris. *American Women's History: An A to Z of People, Organizations, Issues, and*

Events. New York: Prentice Hall General Reference, 1994.

Zia, Helen. *Asian American Dreams: The Emergence of an American People.* New York: Farrar, Straus, and Giroux, 2000.

Zinn, Howard. *A People's History of the United States, 1492–Present,* revised and updated edition. New York: Harper Perennial, 2003.

Arts and Literature

Algarin, Miguel, and Bob Holman, editors. *Aloud: Voices from the Nuyorican Poets Café.* New York: A John Macrae Book/Henry Holt, 1997.

Allen, Paula Gunn, editor. *Voice of the Turtle: American Indian Literature, 1900–1970.* New York: Ballantine Books, 1994.

Andrews, William, Frances Smith Foster, and Trudier Harris, editors. *The Oxford Companion to African American Literature.* Foreword by Henry Louis Gates, Jr. New York and Oxford, England: Oxford University Press, 1997.

Baym, Nina, general editor. *The Norton Anthology of American Literature,* 5th edition. New York and London: W. W. Norton, 1998.

Bearden, Romare, and Harry Henderson. *A History of African-American Artists, from 1792 to the Present.* New York: Pantheon Books, 1993.

Blain, Virginia, Patricia Clements, and Isobel Grundy, editors. *The Feminist Companion to Literature in English.* New Haven and London: Yale University Press, 1990.

Bourdon, David. *Designing the Earth: The Human Impulse to Shape Nature.* New York: Harry N. Abrams, 1995.

Broude, Norma, and Mary D. Garrard, editors. *The Power of Feminist Art: The American Movement of the 1970s, History and Impact.* New York: Harry N. Abrams, 1994.

Brown, Wesley, and Amy Ling, editors. *Imagining America: Stories from the Promised Land.* New York: Persea Books, 1991.

Bustard, Bruce I. *A New Deal for the Arts.* Washington, D.C.: National Archives and Records Administration, in association with the University of Washington Press, 1997.

Chadabe, Joel. *Electric Sound: The Past and Promise of Electronic Music.* Prentice-Hall College Division, 1996.

Chan, Jeffery, Paul Chan, Frank Chin, Lawson Fusao Inada, and Shawn Wong, editors. *The Big Aiieeeee!: An Anthology of Chinese American and Japanese American Literature.* New York: Meridian / Penguin, 1991.

Cheung, King-Kok, editor. *An Interethnic Companion to Asian American Literature.* Cambridge, England: Cambridge University Press, 1997.

Coleman, Janet. *The Compass: The Improvisation Theatre That Revolutionized American Comedy.* Chicago: University of Chicago Press, 1990.

De Oliveira, Nicolas, Nicola Oxley, and Michael Petry, with texts by Michael Archer. *Installation Art.* London: Thames and Hudson, 1994. U.S. edition: Smithsonian Institution Press.

Drain, Richard, editor. *Twentieth-Century Theatre: A Sourcebook.* London and New York: Routledge, 1995.

Gaspar De Alba, Alicia. *Chicano Art: Inside/ Outside the Master's House—Cultural Politics and the Cara Exhibition.* Austin: University of Texas Press, 1998.

Gates, Henry Louis, Jr., and Nellie Y. McKay, general editors. *The Norton Anthology of African American Literature.* New York and London: W. W. Norton, 1997.

Goldberg, Roselee. *Performance Art, From Futurism to the Present,* revised and expanded edition. New York: Thames and Hudson, 1979, 1988, and 2001.

Gonzalez, Ray, editor. *Currents from the Dancing River: Contemporary Latino Fiction, Nonfiction, and Poetry.* New York: Harcourt Brace, 1994.

Gottschild, Brenda Dixon. *Digging the Africanist Presence in American Performance, Dance, and Other Contexts.* Westport, Conn., and London: Greenwood Press, 1996.

Hagedorn, Jessica, editor. *Charlie Chan Is Dead: An Anthology of Contemporary Asian American Fiction.* Introduction by Elaine Kim. New York: Penguin Books, 1993.

Harjo, Joy, and Gloria Bird, editors. *Contemporary Native Women's Writings of North America.* New York and London: W. W. Norton, 1997.

Harrison, Charles, and Paul Wood, editors. *Art in Theory, 1900–2000: An Anthology of Changing Ideas.* Oxford, England, and Cambridge, Mass.: Blackwell Publishers, 2003.

Haskell, Barbara. *The American Century: Art and Culture, 1900–1950*. New York and London: Whitney Museum of American Art, in association with W. W. Norton, 1999.

Hongo, Garrett, editor. *The Open Boat: Poems from Asian America*. New York: Anchor/Doubleday, 1993.

Huxley, Michael, and Noel Witts, editors. *The Twentieth-Century Performance Reader*. London and New York: Routledge, 1996.

Kanellos, Nicolas, editor. *Hispanic American Literature: A Brief Introduction and Anthology*. New York: HarperCollins College Publishers, 1995.

———. *A History of Hispanic Theatre in the United States: Origins to 1940*. Austin: University of Texas Press, 1990.

———. *Herencia: An Anthology of Hispanic Literature of the United States*. New York: Oxford University Press, 2002.

Kardon, Janet, editor. *Revivals! Diverse Traditions, 1920–1945: The History of Twentieth-Century American Craft*. New York: Harry N. Abrams, with the American Craft Museum, 1994.

Lacy, Suzanne, editor. *Mapping the Terrain: New Genre Public Art*. Seattle: Bay Press, 1995

Ling, Amy, editor. *Yellow Light: The Flowering of Asian American Arts*. Philadelphia: Temple University Press, 1999.

Lippard, Lucy R. *Mixed Blessings: New Art in a Multicultural America*. New York: New Press, 2000.

Osumare, Halifu, *Black Choreographers Moving*. Berkeley, Calif.: Expansion Arts Services, 1991.

Patton, Sharon F. *African-American Art*. Oxford, England, and New York: Oxford University Press, 1998.

Phillips, J.J., Ishmael Reed, Gundars Strads, and Shawn Wong, editors. *The Before Columbus Foundation Fiction Anthology: Selections from the American Book Awards, 1980–1990*. New York and London: W. W. Norton, 1992.

———. *The Before Columbus Foundation Poetry Anthology: Selections from the American Book Awards, 1980–1990*. New York and London: W. W. Norton, 1992.

Phillips, Lisa. *The American Century: Art and Culture, 1950–2000*. New York and London: Whitney Museum of American Art, with W. W. Norton, 1999.

Powell, Richard J. *Black Art and Culture in the 20th Century*. London: Thames and Hudson, 1997.

Powell, Richard, and Jock Reynolds. *American Art from Historically Black Colleges and Universities*. Andover, Mass.: Addison Gallery of American Art; New York: The Studio Museum of Harlem, 1999.

Reed, Ishmael, editor. *From Totems to Hip-Hop: A Multicultural Anthology of Poetry Across the Americas, 1900–2002*. New York: Thunder's Mouth Press, 2003.

Rush, Michael. *New Media in Late 20th-Century Art*. New York: Thames and Hudson, Inc., 1999.

Rushing, W. Jackson III, editor. *Native American Art in the Twentieth Century: Makers, Meanings, Histories*. London and New York: Routledge, 1999.

Rushing, W. Jackson. *Native American Art and the New York Avant Garde: A History of Cultural Primitivism*. Austin: University of Texas Press, 1995.

Spatz, Ronald, executive editor. *Alaska Native Writers: Storytellers and Orators*. Anchorage: University of Alaska, 1999.

Stiles, Kristine, and Peter Selz, editors. *Theories and Documents of Contemporary Art: A Sourcebook of Artists' Writings*. Berkeley and Los Angeles: University of California Press, 1996.

Summers, Claude J., editor. *The Gay and Lesbian Literary Heritage*. New York: Henry Holt Reference, 1995.

Tambini, Michael. *The Look of the Century*. New York: DK Publishing, in association with the Cooper-Hewitt National Design Museum, Smithsonian Institution, 1996.

Vizenor, Gerald, editor. *Native American Literature: A Brief Introduction and Anthology*. New York: HarperCollins College Publishers, 1995.

Wallis, Brian, Marianne Weems, and Philip Yenawine, editors. *Art Matters: How the Culture Wars Changed America*. New York and London: New York University Press, 1999.

Wechsler, Jeffrey. *Asian Traditions/Modern Expressions*. New York and New Jersey: Harry N. Abrams, in association with the Jane Voorhees Zimmerli Art Museum, Rutgers, the State University of New Jersey, 1997.

Whiffen, Marcus. *American Architecture Since 1780: A Guide to the Styles,* revised edition. Cambridge, Mass., and London: MIT Press, 1993.

Wong, Shawn, editor. *Asian American Literature: A Brief Introduction and Anthology.* New York: HarperCollins College Publishers, 1996.

Young, Al, editor. *African American Literature: A Brief Introduction and Anthology.* New York: HarperCollins College Publishers, 1996.

Miguel Algarin is a poet whose collection, *Love Is Hard Work,* received an American Book Award. He is a founder of the Nuyorican Poets Cafe, located on the Lower East Side of New York City, and has won an Obie for his work in theater. He is editor of *Aloud!,* a poetry anthology, and *Action!,* a collection of plays produced at the Nuyorican Poets Cafe. He served as a consultant on literature and contributed an essay on Nuyorican culture.

alta, born in 1942 in Nevada, is founder and publisher of the first feminist publishing house in America, Shameless Hussy Press, which flourished from 1969 to 1989. She has written fourteen books of poetry and true stories and is currently involved with classical piano, which she uses as a healing art form since receiving a diagnosis of multiple sclerosis in 1981. She is a member of the board of directors of the Before Columbus Foundation and contributed the introduction to the 1920–1929 chapter.

Marie Anderson has been a teacher, entrepreneur, food and wine aficionada, health and diet consultant, artist's representative, and a printing and label design consultant. She is a member of the board of directors of the Before Columbus Foundation and contributed the introduction to the 1990–2000 chapter, besides being a consultant on American foods and diet.

Carl Anthony is an architect who is presently program officer on community development at the Ford Foundation. He founded and served as executive director of the Urban Habitat Program and as convenor of the Bay Area Alliance for Sustainable Development, and was president of the Earth Island Institute. He contributed an essay on urban environmentalism, based on an interview with Ishmael Reed. He served as a consultant on urban environmentalism.

Karin Bacon served as festival director for New York City in the 1960s and 1970s, where she originated citywide celebrations, such as Fourth of July in Lower Manhattan and New Year's Eve in Central Park, which became annual traditions. Now heading her own company, she creates large-scale events for cities, cultural institutions, corporations, and private clients. She served as a consultant on festivals and other community events.

Calvin Beale is a senior demographer at the Economic Research Service in the U.S. Department of Agriculture. His work has focused on the trends and characteristics of the population of rural and small-town America. He served as a consultant on demographics, especially interpretations of the twentieth century's U.S. Census reports.

Kristine Burns is director of electronic music studies in the School of Music at Florida International University. Her electronic music timeline, which appears online at *http://music. dartmouth.edu/~wowem/electronmedia/music/ eamhistory.html,* was the basis for many of the electronic music entries.

Earl Caldwell is an award-winning journalist who has written for the *New York Times* and New York's *Daily News.* He contributed an essay on his experiences in covering Martin Luther King and the Black Panthers.

Bob Callahan is the founding editor of *Callahan's Irish Quarterly* and edited *The Big Book of American Irish Culture* (Viking Penguin). In recent years he created, and continues to write, *The Dark Hotel,* which appeared at Salon.com from 1998 to Election Day 2000. He is a past president and member of the board of the Before Columbus Foundation and contributed the introduction to the 1930–1939 chapter.

Emery Castle is professor emeritus of the Department of Agricultural and Resource Economics, Oregon State University. He is also a fellow of the American Agricultural Economic Association, the American Association for the Advancement of Science, and the American Academy of Arts and Sciences. He was a consultant on markets and information technology.

Claire Hope Cummings is a lawyer and journalist. She is food and farming editor on KPFA, Pacific Radio's flagship station in Berkeley, California, and appears weekly on KPFA as an interviewer and commentator. She is a Kellogg Food and Society Policy Fellow, has practiced environmental and native land rights law for twenty years, and was a staff attorney for the U.S. Department of Agriculture from 1980 to 1984. She contributed a timeline on agriculture.

Lawrence DiStasi is a member of the comparative literature program at University of California, Berkeley, and a member of the board of directors of the Before Columbus Foundation. He is author of *Dream Streets: The Big Book of Italian American Culture* and *Mal Occhio: The Underside of Vision.* DiStasi is project director for *Una Storia Segreta,* a traveling exhibit about the Italian American evacuation and internment during World War II, and has recently edited a book by the same name. He contributed the 1940 to 1949 introduction and resources on Italian Americans.

Sam Hamod, Ph.D., is former director of the Islamic Center, Washington, D.C.; professor at Princeton, Michigan, Iowa, and Howard universities; editor and publisher of *Third World News* (Washington, D.C.); and a poet with ten volumes of poetry, including *Dying with the Wrong Name, The Arab Poems,* and *The Muslim Poems.* He is included in the anthologies *Unsettling America: Ethnic Poetry in the U.S.* and *Grapeleaves: 100 Years of Arab American Poetry.* He is published in *Konch, Stand, Poetry, Centennial Review, Tri Quarterly,* and other journals. He contributed essays on Arab Americans and was a consultant on the Middle East and U.S. policies in that region of the world.

Gary Handman is head of the Media Resources Center in the Moffitt Library of the University of California, Berkeley. He contributed technology information and research guidance in the arts and media.

Stephen W. Haycox is professor of history at the University of Alaska, Anchorage, where he has taught since 1970. An American cultural historian, he has published widely on Alaska, particularly on Native history. He edited *An Alaska Anthology: Interpreting the Past* (University of Washington Press, 1996), and his history of Alaska, *Alaska: An American Colony*, was published by the University of Washington Press in 2002.

Hillel Heinstein graduated from Cornell University in 1999, where he studied biology and science journalism. Since then, he has worked as an engineer for a successful Internet retailer and is currently pursuing a career in writing. He lives in Berkeley, California, and was a research assistant and contributor to science entries.

Juan Felipe Herrera is a poet and professor of Chicano and Latin American studies at California State University, Fresno. His recent projects include books for children *(The Upside Down Boy)* and young adults *(Crashboomlove).* He lives with his soul partner, the artist Margarita Luna Robles. Herrera is a member of the board of directors of the Before Columbus Foundation, and contributed the introduction to the 1950–1959 chapter.

Lillian Hoddesin is a historian of solid state physics and professor of science and technology history at the University of Illinois. She coauthored *Crystal Fire: The Invention of the Transistor and the Birth of the Information Age.* She served as a consultant on the history of transistors.

Andrew Hope III is of Xaastanch/Tlingit/ Sik'nax.ádi clan/Wolf moiety/X'aan Hít/Red Clay House ancestry. Currently residing in Juneau, Alaska, Hope is a member of the Sitka Tribe of Alaska, a poet, a coeditor of *Will the Time Ever Come?: A Tlingit Source Book,* and the southeast regional coordinator for the Alaska Rural Systemic Initiative. A past president and member of the board of directors of the Before Columbus Foundation, he served as a consultant on Alaska and Native Americans.

Corrine Jennings is cofounder of Kenkelaba House, a not-for-profit arts organization located on the Lower East Side of New York City. In more than thirty years it has evolved into a complex of artists' studios and housing units and an extensive literary and visual archive. It also houses the Kenkelaba and Wilmer Jennings galleries, which primarily exhibit nonwhite artists. She served as a consultant on the visual arts and contributed an essay on African American visual arts, based on interviews by Ishmael Reed.

Katherine Kadish is a painter and graphic artist who served as a consultant on the visual arts.

Bob Kaufman was born in 1925 in New Orleans of Martiniquais, African American, and Jewish parentage and worked as a merchant seaman and labor organizer before becoming a street poet. Often identified as a jazz poet and a major influence on the black consciousness movement, he was central to the Beat movement, although he has been called its "unsung patriarch" because his name is still frequently omitted from roll calls of Beat writers. City Lights Books first published *The Abomunist Manifesto* as a broadside in 1959, and it was included in the first of his eight poetry collections, *Solitudes Crowded with Loneliness* (New Directions, 1965). Other collections include *Golden Sardines* (City Lights Books, 1967) and *The Ancient Rain: Poems 1956–1978* (New Directions, 1981). Kaufman died in San Francisco in 1986.

Roger Malina is an astrophysicist and publisher of *Leonardo*, the journal of the International Society of the Arts, Sciences and Technology. He served as a consultant on scientific innovations, and collaborations in the arts, science, and technology.

Nancy Hicks Maynard is president of Maynard Partners, Inc., a consulting company. She is the former co-owner and publisher of the *Oakland Tribune* (California) and covered domestic policy for the *New York Times* in New York and Washington, and education for the *New York Post*. She recently published *Mega Media: How Market Forces Are Transforming News*. She was a consultant on media and contributed an essay to this book.

Meredith Monk is a composer, singer, choreographer, filmmaker, and performance artist. A recipient of a MacArthur "genius" award and many other honors, she has recorded music including *Songs from the Hill* (Wergo Records, 1979), *Dolmen Music* (ECM New Series,

1981), *Do You Be* (ECM New Series, 1987), *Facing North* (ECM New Series), and *Volcano Songs* (ECM New Series, 1997). Monk contributed an essay to this project.

Carman Moore is a composer, musician, and music critic. His commissioned orchestral works include *Wildfire and Fieldsongs* for the New York Philharmonic, Pierre Boulez conducting; *Gospel Fuse* for the San Francisco Symphony, Seiji Ozawa conducting; and *Hit: A Concerto for Percussion and Orchestra* for the Rochester Philharmonic, Isaiah Jackson conducting. Moore and his ensemble, Skymusic, are artists-in-residence at the Cathedral of St. John the Divine in New York City. A frequent collaborator with Ishmael Reed, their "gospera," *Gethsemane Park*, premiered at Berkeley's Black Repertory Theater in 1998. Moore served as general music consultant to this project, contributing and editing music entries throughout the book.

Kathleen Moran teaches in the American Studies Program at the University of California, Berkeley. She contributed timeline entries on popular culture.

H. Ford Morrison is an architect and urban planner who was a consultant on architecture.

Peter A. Morrison is the founding director of RAND Corporation's Population Research Center. His principal interests are applications of demographic analysis in tracking socioeconomic trends and envisioning their consequences for public policy and business. He has taught at the RAND Graduate School and lectures periodically at universities. Dr. Morrison has served as adviser to the National Academy of Sciences, the National Science Foundation, the Committee for Economic Development, NIH, the Congressional Research Service, the Bureau of the Census, the California Governor's Council on Growth Management, and United Way. He has testified before subcommittees of the U.S. Senate and House of Representatives and made presentations to the National Science Board, National League of Cities, and Quadrennial Review of Military Compensation. He contributed an essay on migration.

T. N. Narasimhan is a hydrogeologist and a member of the engineering and natural resources faculties at the University of California, Berkeley. He contributed two essays on water rights to this book.

Joe Overstreet is a painter, sculptor, and cofounder of the Kenkelaba House, a New York City not-for-profit arts organization focused on supporting African American arts, who served as a consultant on the visual arts.

Maggi Payne is a composer, recording engineer, and head of the Center for Contemporary Music at Mills College in Oakland, California. She served as a consultant on music history and audio technology.

Kathryn A. Pimpan is a graduate student in sociology at University of California, Berkeley. Her research centers on information technology, consumption, and commodification. She contributed information for the demographic data boxes that appear in each chapter, and immigration legislation.

Marco Portales is a professor of English at Texas A&M University and author of *Crowding Out Latinos*. He contributed an essay and served as a general consultant on Latino resources.

Ishmael Reed is a poet, novelist, essayist, playwright, filmmaker, and lecturer. His numerous books have been compiled in *The Reed Reader* (Basic Books, 2000). Reed has edited many journals and collections, including *From Totems to Hip-Hop: A Multicultural Anthology of Poetry Across the Americas, 1900–2002* (Thunder's Mouth Press, 2003), *MultiAmerica: Essays on Cultural Wars and Cultural Peace* (Viking, 1997), the four-volume Literary Mosaic Series for HarperCollins (1995–1996), and the online magazines *Konch* and *Vibes,* available at *www.ishmaelreedpub.com*. His plays include *The Preacher and the Rapper, Mother Hubbard,* and *The C Above C Above High C*. Reed is a founder of the Before Columbus Foundation and present president of its board of directors. He served as a general consultant on this project, besides contributing the introduction to the 1960–1969 chapter.

Allan J. Ryan holds a Ph.D. in anthropology from the University of British Columbia and is the author of *The Trickster Shift: Humour and Irony in Contemporary Native Art* (UBC Press, 1999). He currently has an endowed chair in Aboriginal art and culture at Carleton University in Ottawa, Canada, and served as a consultant on Native American art.

Sonya Salamon is an anthropologist and professor of community studies in the department of human and community development, University of Illinois, Urbana-Champaign, and president of

457

the Rural Sociological Society (2001–2002). She is the author of two books, *Prairie Patrimony: Family, Farming, and Community in the Midwest* (University of North Carolina Press, 1992), and *Newcomers to Old Towns: Suburbanization of the Heartlands* (University of Chicago Press, 2003). She served as a consultant on family and rural life and contributed an essay on suburbanization.

Gundars Strads is executive director of the Before Columbus Foundation and editor of UC Berkeley's *California Management Review* from the Haas School of Business. He is a coeditor of the *Before Columbus Foundation Fiction/Poetry Anthology: Selections from the American Book Awards, 1980–1990,* two volumes of contemporary American multicultural poetry and fiction (W. W. Norton, 1992). He served as a general consultant and contributed the preface.

Joyce Carol Thomas is a poet, novelist, and playwright, known for writing books and plays for the entire family. She is the recipient of many literary book honors, including the National Book Award and the American Book Award for *Marked by Fire,* which was adapted into the Broadway-bound musical *Abyssinia.* In March 2001, she received the Arrell Gibson Lifetime Achievement Award as well as the Oklahoma Book Award for the body of her work. Other recent 2000 and 2001 publications include her poetry collection for all ages, *A Mother's Heart, A Daughter's Love: Hush Songs: A Collection of African-American Lullabies,* and her debut adult novel, *House of Light* (Hyperion). A member of the board of

directors of the Before Columbus Foundation, she wrote the 1980–1989 chapter introduction.

Margaret Porter Troupe was director of the recently closed Porter Troupe Gallery in San Diego, California. She served as a visual arts consultant.

George Vargas is an artist, art historian, and writer in art history, racial, and ethnic studies, receiving his B.F.A, M.A., and Ph.D. from the University of Michigan. His writing appears in *Chicano Renaissance: Contemporary Trends* (University of Arizona Press, 2000). His forthcoming book, *Contemporary Mexican American Art: New Art of the Americas,* documents contemporary Mexican American art and will be published by University of Texas Press. His artwork is represented in various private collections, including that of the late great musician Tito Puente. Along with Martin Moreno, Vargas painted a mural (titled *CitySpirit*) for the Hubbard Richard Agency in Detroit's Mexican Town. The mural is still standing after twenty years and most recently was restored by Detroit artist Vito Valdez. His Latino art timelines appear throughout this book.

Gerald Vizenor is professor of American studies and Native American literature at the University of California, Berkeley. His most recent books include *Manifest Manners, Fugitive Poses,* and a novel, *Chancers.* Vizenor edited the *Native American Literature* volume of the Harper-Collins Literary Mosaic Series. He served as a member of the board of directors of the Before Columbus Foundation and contributed the introduction to the 1900–1909 chapter.

C. J. S. Wallia, Ph.D., teaches in the publishing and editing department of University of California, Berkeley and is the publisher of the *IndiaStar Review of Books (http://www. indiastar.com)*. He contributed an essay on Indians in the U.S.

Albert Wattenberg, a physicist, worked on the Manhattan Project in Chicago during World War II. In 1957 he was the technical adviser to President Eisenhower's "Atoms for Peace" program in Japan. He is professor emeritus of physics at the University of Illinois at Urbana-Champaign. He served as a science consultant and contributed two essays.

Shawn Wong is the author of the novels *Homebase* (Reed & Cannon, 1979; reprinted by Plume/New American Library, 1990) and *American Knees* (Simon and Schuster, 1995; Scribner paperback, 1996). Wong also co-wrote the screenplay for *American Knees* for Celestial Pictures. He is the editor or coeditor of several anthologies of Asian American literature, including *Aiiieeeee! An Anthology of Asian American Writers* (Howard University Press, 1974; reprinted in four different editions by three different publishers in the twenty-five-year history of the book). Wong also coedited *The Big Aiiieeeee! An Anthology of Chinese American and Japanese American Literature* (Meridian/NAL, 1991) and *Literary Mosaic: Asian American Literature* (HarperCollins, 1995). He is coeditor of the *Before Columbus Foundation Fiction/Poetry Anthology: Selections from the American Book Awards, 1980–1990,* two volumes of contemporary American multicultural poetry and fiction (Norton, 1992). Wong is currently head of the English department at the University of Washington, Seattle. A past president and member of the board of directors of the Before Columbus, Foundation, he contributed the introduction to the 1970–1979 chapter.

Marnie Thomas Wood is a professor in the department of theater, dance, and performance studies at the University of California, Berkeley. She was a member of the Martha Graham Dance Company, and with her late husband, David Wood, she was honored by the San Francisco Bay Area's dance community with an Isadora Duncan Lifetime Achievement Award. She served as a contributor to the dance entries throughout this book.

Yoriko Yamamoto works in the education program of Yerba Buena Center for the Arts in San Francisco. She contributed research and an essay on Asian American visual arts.

ACKNOWLEDGMENTS

This book would have been nearly impossible to assemble without the help of many people. First of all I want to thank the board of directors of the Before Columbus Foundation for giving their imprimatur to this book, which involved their willingness to provide me with research materials, editorial suggestions, and best of all, their writing. At the time of this writing, they are alta, Rudolfo Anaya, Marie Anderson, Bob Callahan, Victor Hernandez Cruz, Lawrence DiStasi, Andrew Hope, Juan Felipe Herrera, David Meltzer, Simon Ortiz, Ishmael Reed, Gundars Strads, Joyce Carol Thomas, Kate Trueblood, Gerald Vizenor, and Shawn Wong.

Also essential to making this book were my colleagues at the University of California, Berkeley, especially the group of scholars from various departments who are associated with the American Cultures Program, with special thanks to Mitch Breitweiser, who headed the program at the time this book was begun, and its administrator, Ron Choy. Their summer fellowships and research resources were invaluable to me in thinking through the structure of the book and putting me in touch with scholars from disciplines throughout the campus community. Great thanks to Donald McQuade, who got the course started; Kathleen Moran, assistant director of Berkeley's American Studies Program and former director of the Interdisciplinary Studies programs, who encouraged me to teach the course and write the book; Corliss Lee, UC Berkeley Librarian; and Gary Handman, Head of Media Resources Center, who generously introduced me to online research. Also, my thanks to four semesters of Berkeley students, whose questions started me working on a timeline that became this book, and who called my attention to events they thought were important enough to be included in the chronology.

Great thanks to sidebar contributors who also acted as consultants on images and information in the ongoing timeline: Marco Portales, professor of English, Texas A&M University; anthropology professor Sonya Salamon, University of Illinois, Champaign-Urbana; and physicist Al Wattenberg.

And grateful thanks to consultants in particular disciplines:

Music: Maggi Payne, Center for Contemporary Music, Mills College, who got me started on researching this subject and led me to Dr. Kristine Burns, director of electronic music studies, Florida International University, who contributed much of the electronic music information; and especially to composer, music writer, and critic Carman Moore, who acted as a general music editor and contributed information, especially on the classical and jazz traditions.

Visual arts: Kathleen Kadish, Corinne Jennings, Joe Overstreet, Margaret Porter-Troupe, and Kate Hirson.

Performing arts: Marnie Thomas Wood, professor, University of California Department of Theater, Dance, and Performance Studies, on dance; public events artist Karin Bacon.

Science: Roger Malina, astronomer and editor of *Leonardo,* who also connected me with artists and scientists bridging the disciplines of the arts, sciences, and technology; science historian Lillian Hoddeson from the University of Illinois, Champaign-Urbana; physicist Myron Salamon, head of the physics department at University of Illinois, Champaign-Urbana; and the late retired metallurgist, Alexander Strasser.

Research assistants: Nora Danielson, Hillel Heinstein, N. Trisha Lagaso, Kathleen Pimpan, Reliang Tsang, and Yoriko Yamamoto.

Others who helped in so many ways—talking through concepts for the design and contents of the book, giving feedback on the manuscript, helping choose images, and giving technical assistance: Lynda Banks, Rose and Clarence Bergeson, Nancy Hicks Maynard, Linda Cristol Young, and my editor, Christopher Jackson, who believed in this book from the start.

Finally I want to thank my family, Tennessee Reed and Ishmael Reed, for all their help in finding research materials, clipping newspapers, and generally being patient with my total immersion for months into years on end.

INDEX

Abernathy, Ralph, 296
Abomunist Manifesto, The, 244, 256
Abortion, 339, 414
Abrams, Muhal Richard, 279
Abrams v. U.S., 92
Abstract Expressionism, 197, 220
Acheson, Lila, 111
Ackerman, William, 352
ACLU. *See* American Civil Liberties Union
Acrylics, 209
Activase, 353
Actors Studio, 201
Adams, John, 390
Adenauer, Konrad, 215
Adler Planetarium and Astronomy
    Museum, 137
Adrenaline, 22
Advertising, 18, 110
Aerial map, 75
Aerosol can, 167
Aetherophone, 103
Affirmative action, 273, 287, 293, 356,
    358, 394, 423–24, 425
Afghanistan, 357, 358, 359, 365, 396,
    415, 426
AFL. *See* American Federation of Labor
AFL-CIO merger, 238
Africa, 21
African Americans:
    Amenia Conference, 86
    art, 60–61, 125, 277–79, 280, 306, 383,
        427–28
    in baseball, 204
    Black Power, 301, 302
    Brownsville Affair, 41
    Brown v. Board of Education, 236, 422
    civil rights, 198, 203, 241, 285–86
    dance, 139, 313–14, 338
    disenfranchisement in Alabama, 23
    educational gains, 366
    farmers, 308
    first black astronaut in space, 382
    first black chairman of Joint Chiefs of
        Staff, 394
    first black elected governor, 392
    first black mayors, 307
    first black on Supreme Court, 307
    first black-owned bank, 31
    first black-owned theater, 37
    first black producer, 76
    first black recording artists, 25
    first blacks in government positions, 299
    first black studies program, 312
    first black to dance with major ballet
        company, 239
    first black to reach rank of general, 174
    first black to sing at Metropolitan
        Opera, 238
    first black woman astronaut, 375
    first interracial jazz group, 163
    first successful black musical, 26
    founding of NAACP, 51
    Garvey's work, 87
    Greenwood (Okla.) riot, 107
    hair products for, 39
    integration, 281, 285, 333
    Kwanzaa, 298, 302
    migration from South, 107, 184
    Niagara Movement, 38
    Plessy v. Ferguson, 3, 236
    proposed anti-lynching bill, 15
    race riots, 41, 289, 297, 309, 412, 416
    segregation, 34, 204, 230, 236–37, 241,
        246, 268–69, 274, 333, 422
    student demonstrations, 329–30
    "Talented Tenth," 29
    theater, 292, 429
    voting rights, 23, 292
    women, 344, 364, 383
Agee, James, 154
Agnew, Spiro, 315, 334
Agon, 239–40
Agriculture, 205–8
AIDS (acquired immune deficiency syn-
    drome), 374, 389, 394, 409, 416, 436
Aid to Families with Dependent Children,
    157
*Aiiieeeee!: An Anthology of Asian
    American Writers,* 322, 323, 345
Ailey, Alvin, 265, 266
AIM. *See* American Indian Movement
Air Commerce Act, 119
Air conditioning, 28
Airlines, 165, 203, 248, 301, 374
Airplanes, 31, 32, 65, 78, 122, 186, 203,
    331
Air raid shelters, 252, 255
Airships, 21
Alabama, 23, 274, 285
Alaska, 5, 254, 334, 342, 355, 420, 432
Alaska Native Brotherhood, 56–58
Alaska Native Knowledge Network, 420
Al-Bakr, Ahmed Hassan, 313
Albania, 76
Albee, Edward, 275
Albright, Madeleine, 422
Alcatraz Island, 289, 316
Alcoholics Anonymous, 158
Alcoholism, 100
Aleuts, 392
Alexanderson, E. F. W., 47
"Alexander's Ragtime Band," 66

Algarin, Miguel, 353, 356
Alien registration, 174
Allen B. DuMont Company, 163
Allende Gossens, Salvador, 331, 344, 433
Alloway, Lawrence, 247
Alpher, Ralph, 212
Al-Qaeda, 396, 415, 426
Altair 8800 computer, 350
Altamont festival (Calif.), 315
Alternative medicine, 414, 431
Alto computer, 329, 341
Alvarez, Luis, 367, 368
Alvarez, Walter, 367
Amanda, Felipe, 403
Amazon.com, 420, 436
American Airlines, 374
American Civil Liberties Union (ACLU),
    103
American Federation of Labor (AFL), 7,
    17, 27, 202, 238
American flag, 187, 326
American Indian Defense Association, 110
American Indian Movement (AIM),
    312–13, 316, 339, 342
American Indians. *See* Native Americans
American Jewish Committee, 44
American Legion, 96
American Musicological Society, 150
American Psychiatric Association, 344
American Society of Composers (ASCAP),
    78–79
Americans with Disabilities Act, 403
American Telephone and Telegraph
    (AT&T), 83, 123, 267, 281, 377
American Woolen Company, 72
America Online (AOL), 383–84, 436
Amin, Idi, 337
Amnesty International, 275
Amundsen, Roald, 69
Anaya, Rudolfo, 337–38
Anderson, Dana, 378
Anderson, Laurie, 364
Anderson, Marian, 164, 238
Anderson, Maxwell, 154
Anderson, Warren, 382
Andre, Carl, 314
Andreessen, Marc, 384, 411, 417
Andropov, Yuri, 378
Angel Island, 62–64
Angola, 350
Anna Christie, 109
Antheil, George, 119
Anthony, Carl, 396–97
Antibiotics, 176, 443–44
Anti-Defamation League, 80
Anti-Semitism, 80, 164

Antiseptics, 2
AOL. *See* America Online
Apartheid, 209, 215, 407
Apollinaire, Guillaume, 91
Apollo 11 spacecraft, 315
Apollo Soyuz Test Project, 350
Appalachian Spring, 189
Apple Computer, 354–55, 381
Aquino, Corazon, 389
Arab-Israeli War, 213
Arafat, Yasser, 298, 392, 415, 426
Archaeological Resources Protection Act, 359
Architecture, 22, 62, 82, 97, 100, 216, 229
Argentina, 199
Argonne National Laboratory, 225
Aristide, Jean-Bertrand, 407
Arizona, 72
Arkansas, 246
Armed forces, 89, 163, 173–74, 177, 180, 191, 211, 365, 394, 414
Armenian massacre, 83
Arms control, 358, 390, 447
Armstrong, Edwin, 90
Armstrong, Louis, 13, 113
Armstrong, Neil, 315
Arnold, Henry H., 173
ARPANET computer network, 316, 341, 343, 380
Arrow Maker, The, 66
Art:
    Abstract Expressionism, 197, 220
    acrylics, 209
    African American, 60–61, 125, 277–79, 280, 306, 383, 427–28
    Armory Show, 48, 73
    Ashcan School, 48
    Asian American, 30–31, 33
    Bauhaus, 95, 97, 161
    collage, 73, 283–84
    computer, 229, 419
    conceptual, 271, 326, 331–32
    Cubism, 47, 88
    Dada, 81, 88
    Der Blaue Reiter, 52
    and engineering, 299
    experimental, 386
    Fauvism, 39–40
    founding of MOMA, 128
    graffiti, 385
    "high" and "low," 384
    Latino, 67, 142–43, 173, 304–6, 381, 403, 404
    minimalism, 290–91
    modernism, 52, 380
    Native American, 109, 121, 139, 144–45, 162, 248, 250, 251, 253, 279, 369–71, 403
    outsider, 272, 413
    pop, 247, 275
    primitivism, 44, 162, 380
    printmaking, 209–10, 246
    progressive, 386
    protection of publicly commissioned, 426
    protesters, 303, 306, 314
    Public Works of Art Project, 146, 147

Rauschenberg on, 230
recession in market, 393
Southwest Movement, 13
Surrealism, 91, 116
women in, 314, 325, 357, 364, 383, 390
See also Sculpture; *specific artists*
Art Against AIDS, 389
Art deco, 118
Arte Publico, 364
Arthur, Chester A., 24
Artificial heart, 378
Art in Architecture program, 284
Artists Club (N.Y.), 213
Arts. *See* Fine arts; *specific fields*
Asaro, Frank, 367
ASCAP. *See* American Society of Composers
Asch, Moses, 164, 165
Ashcan School, 48
Ashley, Robert, 272
Asian Americans:
    in arts, 30–31, 33
    immigration, 7, 24, 31, 45, 64, 100, 114–15, 187, 230, 366
    as "model minority," 410
    population, 446
    in San Francisco schools, 42
    student movement, 312
    at University of California, 407
    Webb Alien Land-Holding Bill, 74
    writers, 319–20, 322–25, 341, 345
Asiatic Exclusion League, 39
Assemblage, 271
Association for the Advancement of Creative Musicians, 279–80
Aswan High Dam, 245
AT&T. *See* American Telephone and Telegraph
Atanasoff, John, 167
Atari, Inc., 340
Ataturk, Kemal, 111
Atlanta (Ga.), 41
Atlantic Charter, 180
Atom, 166
Atomic bomb, 165–66, 167, 170, 193, 194–96, 215, 224
Atomic Energy Commission, 225, 255
Atomic number 116, 437
Atomic number 118, 437
Attica State Correctional Facility, 335
Audion tube, 47
Austin, Mary Hunter, 66, 112
Australia, 228
Austria, 45
Autobiography of Alice B. Toklas, The (Stein), 148
Automobiles:
    Chrysler Corporation loans, 358
    emission standards, 292
    exposé of, 294
    first show, 19
    gasoline-driven vs. electrical/steam-driven, 52–53
    Hydramatic drive, 167
    Model A, 31, 75, 127
    Model T, 17, 48, 74, 78, 127
    Oldsmobile, 17
Aztlán, 302, 338

Babbitt, Milton, 201
"Baby Fay," 382
Badoglio, Pietro, 188
Baekeland, Leo, 48
Baez, Joan, 284
Baghdad (Iraq), 409
Bakelite, 48–49
Baker, Josephine, 116
Bakke, Allan, 356
Balanchine, George, 128, 155, 173, 239–40, 314
Balfour Declaration, 91
Balkan Wars, 65, 72, 76
Ballet, 76, 91, 128, 150, 155, 189, 239–40, 314, 439
Ballpoint pen, 164
Bambaataa, Afrika, 360, 387
Bangladesh, 337
Banks, Dennis, 312, 342
Banks and banking:
    Federal Reserve, 73
    first black-owned bank, 31
    in Great Depression, 138, 147
    largest bank in history, 431
    largest Native American bank, 444–45
    Panic of 1907, 45, 47
Banting, Frederick, 108
Bao Dai, 238
Baraka, Amiri, 222, 271
Barbie doll, 254, 255
Bardeen, John, 203
Barkley, Alben, 211
Baron, Louis and Bebe, 233
Barr, Alfred, 48, 128, 129
Barrie, Dennis, 402
Baruch, Bernard, 93
Baseball, 32, 204
Basquiat, Jean-Michel, 385
Batista, Fulgencio, 152, 255
Battle of the Bulge, 191
Battle of Verdun, 87
Bauhaus School, 95, 97, 161
Baum, L. Frank, 12
Baxter, William, 377
Bayer, Herbert, 338
Bay of Pigs invasion, 273
Bearden, Romare, 283–84
Beat Generation, 214, 244, 245, 265, 345
Beatitude magazine, 251
Beatles, 287, 310
Beattie, William, 56
Bebop music, 177, 192
Beck, Julian, 223
Bed, The (film), 310–11
Before Columbus Foundation, 350, 351
Begin, Menachem, 376
Beirut (Lebanon), 380
Belafonte, Harry, 244
Belar, Herbert, 241
Belarus, 410
Bell, Alexander Graham, 83
Bellamy, Carol, 439
Bell Laboratories, 174, 192, 231, 246, 248, 274, 299, 377
Benchley, Robert, 99
Beneš, Edvard, 213
Bengal (India), 44
Ben-Gurion, David, 213

Berea College, 34
Berg, Alban, 118
Berkeley, Busby, 148
Berkeley (Calif.), 312, 378
Berlin, Irving, 66
Berlin (Ger.), 188, 211, 286
Berlin Wall, 275, 395
Berners-Lee, Tom, 408
Bernstein, Carl, 342
Bernstein, Leonard, 245, 338
Berry, Clifford, 167
Best, Charles H., 108
BET (Black Entertainment Television), 409
Bezos, Jeffrey, 420
Bhopal (India), 382
Bhutto, Benazir, 393
BIA. See Bureau of Indian Affairs
Big Bang theory, 115, 131, 212, 425, 437
Bilingual education, 269, 308, 347
Bingham, Hiram, 69
Bin Laden, Osama, 359, 396, 415, 426
Biological weapons, 341
Biopesticide, 444
Biosphere II, 410
Biotechnology, 352, 367
Bird in Flight, 121–22
Birdseye, Clarence, 90
Birmingham (Ala.), 286
Biro, Ladoslao and Georg, 164
Birth control, 80, 86, 88, 232, 268
Birth defects, 281–82
Birth of a Nation (movie), 82
Bishop, Maurice, 379
Black Arts, 271, 287
Blackburn, Robert, 209–10
Black Elk Speaks (Neihardt), 143–44
Blackett, P. M. S., 193
Black Fire (Jones and Neal), 310
Black holes, 406, 418
Black market, 188
Black Mountain College, 147–48, 228, 232
Black Muslims, 226–27, 232
Black Panther Party, 296, 300, 302, 311, 317
Black Power, 301, 302
Blacks. See African Americans
Black Star Line Steamship Corporation, 87
Blackton, J. Stuart, 41
Black Women Novelists (Christian), 364
Blattnerphone, 131
Bless Me, Ultima (Anaya), 337–38
Blood plasma, 179
Blues music, 49, 70, 101, 111–12
Bluford, Guion Jr., 382
Boesky, Ivan, 388
Bogan, Louise, 385
Bohr, Niels, 175
Boland Amendment, 377, 387
Bolcom, William, 434
Bombsights, 192
Bonaparte, Charles J., 48
Bonus Expeditionary Force, 145–46
Boolean algebra, 167
"Boomburbs," 446
Border Arts Workshop, 386
Border Industrialization Program, 294

Border Patrol, 115, 386
Borglum, Gutzon, 136
Borland, Christine, 224
Bosnia-Herzegovina, 410–11
Boston (Mass.), 19
Boston Art Museum, 33
Boulder Dam, 110, 127
Bourne, Randolph, 90
Boxer Uprising, 20–21
Boyer, Herbert, 352
Boykin, Otis, 294
Bracero Program, 28, 184, 187, 294
Branch Davidian sect, 413, 420
Brancusi, Constantin, 44, 52, 73, 121
Braque, Georges, 47, 73
Brattain, Walter, 203
Brautigan, Richard, 306
Bray, John, 70
Bread and Puppet Theater, 283, 291, 326
Breast cancer, 22
Breeder reactor, 225, 227
Breton, Andre, 116, 176
Bretton Woods Conference, 192
Brezhnev, Leonid, 358, 378, 385
Brimmer, Andrew F., 299
Britain. See Great Britain
Broadband transmission, 429
Broadcasting industry, 174–75
Brooke, Edward William, 299
Brotherhood of Sleeping Car Porters, 117
Broughton, James, 310
Brown, Charles, 377
Brown, Jerry, 329
Brown, Trisha, 331
Brown Berets, 308
Brownmiller, Susan, 335
Brownsville Affair, 41
Brownsville automatic rifle, 93
Brown v. Board of Education, 236, 422
Brustein, Robert, 429
Bryan, John, 289
Bryan, William Jennings, 48, 116
Bubble chamber, 295
Buchenwald concentration camp, 196
Bucket Dance Theatre, 338
Buddhism, 226
Building Minnesota, 408
Bunau-Varilla, Philippe, 27
Bunche, Ralph, 213
Burden, Chris, 331–32
Bureau of Indian Affairs (BIA), 125, 221, 328, 339, 342
Bureau of Reclamation, 349, 352
Buried Child, 356
Burke, Charles H., 113
Burning Man Festival, 388–89
Burns, Lucy, 76
Burroughs, William, 251
Buscetta, Tommaso, 383
Buses. See Public transportation
Bush, George Herbert Walker, 365, 393, 405, 409, 413
Bush, George W., 441
Bush, Vannevar, 137, 179, 193, 194
Bush v. Gore, 441
Bushnell, Nolan, 340
Busing, 333, 435
Buxton (Iowa), 17

Cabin in the Sky, 173
Caen, Herb, 244
Cage, John, 160, 201, 228, 229, 265, 332
Cahill, E. H., 13
Cahill, Holger, 48
Cahill, Thaddeus, 43
Cailliau, Robert, 408
Calder, Alexander, 139–40
Caldwell, Earl, 296–97
Caldwell, Erskine, 148
California, 5, 42, 73–74, 125, 126, 133, 184, 307, 329, 334, 356, 416–17, 423–24, 425, 438
Callahan, Sophia Alice, 11
Calley, William, 311
Cambodia, 314, 327, 348, 350
Camera, 16, 211
Campbell, Ben Nighthorse, 387, 411
Camp David Accords, 352
Canada, 123, 337, 413, 417
Cancer, 224, 227, 400
Canton Bank, 47
Capek, Karel, 108
Capitalism, 6
Carbon dioxide, 412–13
Carbon-14 dating, 203
Carder, Frederick, 29
Carlsbad (N.M.), 434
Carlson, Chester, 167
Carmichael, Stokely, 297, 302
Carnegie, Andrew, 7, 24, 25
Carnegie Institute, 25
Carnegie Steel Corporation, 25
Carr, Robert, 189
Carranza, Venustiano, 78, 83, 86, 91
Carrier, Willis, 28
Carroll, James, 16
Cars. See Automobiles
Carson, Rachel, 282
Carter, Jimmy, 352, 354, 358, 359, 365, 373, 435
Carver, George Washington, 79, 80
Case, Steven M., 383
Castelli, Leo, 247
Castle, Irene and Vernon, 77
Castro, Fidel, 232, 255, 270, 283, 299, 303, 310, 365
Catastrophic theory, 367–68
Catholic Church, 309, 313
Catholic Legion of Decency, 153
CAT scan, 344
Catt, Carrie Chapman, 83, 93
Cave paintings, 179
CBS. See Columbia Broadcasting System
Ceauşescu, Nicolae, 395–96
Celera Genomics, 442–43
Cell phone, 343–44, 392
Censorship, 313
Center for Independent Living, 335
Central America, 330, 365, 368
Central Intelligence Agency (CIA), 202, 270, 273, 338, 373
Cerf, Vint, 343
CERN (European Laboratory for Particle Research), 379, 408, 413
CFCs. See Chlorofluorocarbons
Chagall, Marc, 69
Chaikin, Joseph, 283

Chain, Ernst, 128, 179
Chakrabarty, Ananda, 367
Challenger space shuttle, 380, 382, 388
Chamberlain, John, 271
Chamorro, Violetta Barrios de, 407
Chan, Jeffrey, 319, 320, 345
Chandrashekar, Subramanyam, 104
Chaney, James, 289
Chaplin, Charles, 70
Chase-Riboud, Barbara, 325
Chavez, Cesar, 207, 208, 281, 294, 329
Chavis, Benjamin F. Jr., 390
Chen, Lily Lee, 382
Chernenko, Konstantin, 378, 385
Chernobyl (Ukraine), 389
Chiang Kai-shek, 199
Chicago, Judy, 325, 357
Chicago (Ill.), 312
Chicago Eight, 315
Chicano Plan for Higher Education, 317
Chicanos. *See* Mexican Americans
Chichén Itzá, 36
Chickencoop Chinaman, The, 331, 348
Children, 199, 293
Chile, 331, 344, 433
Chin, Frank, 319, 320, 323, 331, 345, 348
China, 20–21, 44, 199, 213, 215, 249, 269, 303, 315, 337, 338–39, 353, 359, 395, 429–30, 440
Chinese Americans, 19–20, 39, 43, 62–64, 255, 271, 323, 324, 382
Chinese Exclusion Acts, 7, 24, 114, 187
Chinese New Year, 235
Chipmunks (singing group), 245
Chippewa Music, 62
Chips. *See* Integrated circuits
Chlorofluorocarbons (CFCs), 357, 391
Cho, Mildred, 442
Choral singing, 148
Chowning, John, 333
Christian, Barbara T., 364
Christian, Charlie, 163
Christian Coalition, 393
Christo (Christo Vladimirov Javacheff), 351
Chromosomes, 28, 47, 406
Chrysler Corporation, 358
Chu, Louis, 271, 322
Chung Sai Yat Po, 19
Chunnel, 419
Churchill, Winston, 176, 180, 188, 192, 243
Church Rock (N.M.), 358
CIA. *See* Central Intelligence Agency
Cigarettes, 335, 350, 417
CIO. *See* Congress of Industrial Organizations
Cisco Systems, 444
Cities, 6, 18, 100, 274–75, 292, 375, 446
Citizen Kane (movie), 176
City Lights bookstore, 232–33, 243
City Lights Press, 233
Civilian Conservation Corps, 149
Civil Liberties Act, 392
Civil rights, 197–98, 203, 204, 241, 285–86, 302
Civil Rights Act (1957), 246
Civil Rights Act (1964), 287, 293, 307

Civil Rights Act (1968), 311
Civil Rights Bill (1990), 405
Civil Rights Memorial (Montgomery, Ala.), 394
Clark, Barney, 378
Clark, Mark, 317
Claude, Jeanne, 351
Clavilux, 106
Clayton Act, 77
Clayton-Bulwer Treaty, 23
"Clear and present danger," 93
Cleaver, Eldridge, 291, 296
Clef Club, 62, 77
Cleveland (Ohio), 307
Clewall, William H., 382
Clifton-Morenci Mine Strike, 31
Climate, 400, 412, 431–32, 444
Clinton, William Jefferson "Bill," 372, 411, 413, 414, 420, 422, 424, 431, 433, 434, 435, 440
Cloning, 430
Clurman, Harold, 140
CNN (Cable News Network), 366, 405
Coalition for Better Television, 375
Coates, Robert, 197
Cocconi, Giuseppe, 255
Cohen, Stanley, 352
Cold War, 202, 211, 220, 231, 315, 395
Cole, Jack, 150
Cole (USS), 415
Coleman, Ornette, 253
Collage, 73, 283–84
Collective bargaining, 157
Colleges. *See* Universities and colleges; *specific schools*
Collier, John, 110, 113, 151
Collins, Francis, 406, 443
Collins, Michael, 300
Colonialism, 21
Colorado Fuel and Iron Corporation, 75
Colorado River, 110
Colosio, Luis Donaldo, 418
Columbia Broadcasting System (CBS), 174–75
Columbus, Christopher, 412
Comic books, 135
Comic strips, 44, 135, 151
Coming of Age in Samoa (Mead), 127
Commedia dell 'arte, 251, 291–92
Commodore Business Machines, 355
Communications satellites, 267, 281, 285
Communism, 202, 211, 220, 221, 269, 282
Communist Party, 96, 221
Company towns, 17
Compass Players, 239
Compton, A. H., 194–95
Computers:
    ARPANET, 316, 341, 343, 380
    first analog, 137
    first art generated by, 229
    first commercial all-electronic digital, 227
    first electronic digital, 167, 168
    first fully transistorized, 238
    first large electronic digital, 198–99
    graphics, 419
    hackers, 384

holographic, 378
for military personnel, 394
mouse, 381
music generated by, 241, 246, 248, 272
personal, 329, 341, 350, 354–55, 373, 437
relief maps generated by, 443
sounds on, 333
Y2K predictions, 430–31, 441–42
See also Internet
COMSAT (Communications Satellite Corporation), 281
Conant, James, 194
Conceptual art, 271, 326, 331–32
Concrete bombs, 436
Confederate flag, 435
Congo, Republic of the, 270
Congressional Hispanic Caucus, 354
Congress of Industrial Organizations (CIO), 158, 202, 238
Congress of Racial Equality (CORE), 204, 208, 274, 302
Conner, Bruce, 271
Consolidated Coal Company, 17
Container ships, 288
Contraception. *See* Birth control
Contras, 377, 387, 389, 392
Cookie (data filing system), 418
Coolidge, Calvin, 106, 112, 114
Cooper, Martin, 343–44
Copland, Aaron, 189
Copying machine, 167, 222, 255
Copyright, 49, 445
CORE. *See* Congress of Racial Equality
Cortelyou, George, 47
Cormack, Allan, 344
Cornell, Joseph, 271
Cornell University, 312
Corporations, 102, 119
Cotton, 17, 122
Counterculture newspapers, 289–90
Country Club Plaza (Kansas City), 110, 111
Country music, 121, 155, 157
Cowell, Henry, 71, 136, 140
Crack cocaine, 384
Cranbrook Academy of Art, 144
Crawford, Cheryl, 140
Crawford, Joe, 201
Credit, 198
Crick, Francis, 235
Criminal justice, 311
Crisis, The, 62, 96, 105
Croatia, 410–11
Croce, Arlene, 416
Cronyn, George W., 92
Crop rotation, 79
Crusade for Justice, 302
Cruz, Victor Hernandez, 350, 351
Crystal City (Tex.), 284, 302
Cuba, 5, 23, 27, 28, 71, 152–53, 232, 255, 270, 273, 299, 303, 304, 365, 440
Cuban missile crisis, 282, 283
Cubism, 47, 88
Culture wars, 400, 422
Cummings, Claire Hope, 205
Cunningham, Merce, 231, 232, 240, 265

Curie, Marie and Pierre, 21
Currency, 15–16, 17, 430, 437
Currency Act, 15
Curtis, Charles, 130
Curtis, Edward, 41, 77
Curtis, Natalie, 45
Curtiss JN-4 fighter plane, 93
Cybernetics, 212
Cyclotron, 140, 141, 166
Czechoslovakia, 213, 313, 395
Czech Republic, 437
Czolgosz, Leon, 23

Dabney, Ted, 340
Dada Movement, 70, 81, 87, 88, 94
Dada Painters and Poets (Motherwell), 223
Dafora, Asadata, 150
"Daisy spot," 290
Daladier, Edouard, 176
Dalai Lama, 256
Daley, Richard, 312
Damrosch, Walter, 37
Dams, 27, 72, 352
Dance:
    African American, 139, 313–14, 338
    ballet, 76, 91, 128, 150, 155, 189, 239–40, 314
    breakdancing, 326–27
    buck and wing, 11–12
    cakewalk, 11, 231
    Charleston, 112
    contact improvisation, 337
    Denishawn, 81–82, 139
    fox trot, 77
    group improvisation, 326
    jazz dance, 150
    Lindy Hop, 120
    mambo, 236
    modern, 120–21, 139, 161–62
    in numerical pattern, 331
    powwow, 349
    West Indian, 159
    See also specific dancers and choreographers
Dance Theater of Harlem, 313
Darrow, Clarence, 116–17
Darwin, Charles, 2, 116
Database management, 358
Daud Khan, Muhammad, 357
Daughters of the American Revolution (DAR), 164
Dave Brubeck Quartet, 253
Davidovsky, Mario, 279
Davis, Anthony, 387
Davis, Benjamin O. Sr., 174
Davis, Miles, 245, 253
Davis, Rennie, 312, 315
Davis, R. G., 291–92
Davis, Thulani, 387
Dawes Severalty Act, 4, 55–56
Daylight savings time, 93
D-Day, 192
DDT (pesticide), 167, 282
Death of a Salesman, 213
De Beauvoir, Simone, 215
Debs, Eugene V, 31, 71
Debussy, Claude, 29

De Chirico, Giorgio, 69
De facto segregation, 333
Defense Advance Research Projects Agency, 340
Defense spending, 193
De Forest, Lee, 46, 47, 83
Deforestation, 371, 407
De Gaulle, Charles, 313
De jure segregation, 333
De Klerk, F. W., 407
De Kooning, Willem, 213
De La Beckwith, Byron, 285
Delacorte, George, 151
Dellinger, David, 312, 315
Deloria, Vine, 348
De Maria, Walter, 331
Democratic National Convention (Chicago), 311–12, 315
Deng Xiaoping, 353, 395
Densmore, Frances, 62
Dent, Tom, 265
Department of Defense, 202, 284, 380, 394
Department of Energy, 52
Department of Housing and Urban Development (HUD), 292, 299
Department of Justice, 48
Deposit insurance, 366
Der Blaue Reiter, 52
Deregulation, 425
Deren, Maya, 187
Detroit (Mich.), 309
Deuterium, 141
Deutsch, Herbert A., 271
Devol, George, 274
Dharma Sangha of Buddha, 20
Diabetes, 108, 352, 378
Diamond v. Chakrabarty, 367
Diaz, Porfirio, 45, 66
Diem, Ngo Dinh, 238, 273, 286
Diet, 400
Dinner Party, The, 357
Dinosaurs, 442
Di Prima, Diane, 345
Disabled, 335–36, 403, 405
Disco, 276, 279
Disc Records, 164–65
Discrimination, 178, 211, 234, 237, 287, 306
Disney, Walt, 123, 125, 242
Disneyland (Anaheim, Calif.), 242–43
Disney World (Orlando, Fla.), 425
Displaced Persons Act, 211
Divorce, 141
DNA (deoxyribonucleic acid), 2, 51, 225, 235, 352, 406, 443
Doe v. Bolton, 339
Dolby sound, 308
Domestic Resurrection Circus and Pageant, 326
Dominican Republic, 33–34, 85
Domino effect, 202, 430
Doolittle, James H., 182
Dorsey, Thomas A., 148
Dos Passos, John, 136–37
Dot.com companies, 420, 436
Douglas, William O., 230, 297
Downes v. Bidwell, 23

Draft resisters, 191
Drake, Frank, 255
Dreams, 22
Drew, Charles, 179
Drexel Burnham Lambert, 388
Drought, 138, 153, 161
Drug trafficking, 388
Duany, Andres, 375
Duarte, José Napoleon, 368
Dubcek, Alexander, 313
Du Bois, W. E. B., 21, 29, 38, 51, 62, 80, 86, 96
Duchamp, Marcel, 70, 73, 81, 88, 90, 180, 271
Due process, 42
Dulles, Allen, 270
Dumbarton Oaks Conference, 192
Duncan, Isadora, 12, 120
Duncan, Robert, 189
Dunham, Katherine, 159, 161–62, 173, 176
Dunham School of Dance and Theatre, 176
Dunn, Dorothy, 144–45
Dunn, Robert, 265
Dunning, John, 166, 175
DuPont (co.), 163
Dust Bowl, 153
Duvalier, Jean-Claude, 389
DVDs, 418, 429
Dvořák, Antonin, 7, 37
Dyer, L. C., 106
Dylan, Bob, 284
Dynamophone, 43

Eames, Charles and Ray, 197
Earth Day, 321, 327
Earthquake, 43
Easter Uprising, 39
Eastman, Charles Alexander, 10, 11, 26, 68
Eastman, George, 123
Eastman, Jacob, 10
Eastman Kodak Company, 16, 211, 238
Eat a Bowl of Tea (Chu), 271, 322
Eckert, John, 227
Economy:
    digitization of, 417
    expansion, 405
    and federal defense spending, 193
    Great Depression, 130–31, 147
    Keynes's views, 103, 120
    Panic of 1907, 45, 47
    price controls, 334
    Reagan's programs, 373
    Soviet, 385
    trickle-down theory, 119
    War on Poverty, 288, 289, 293
    in World War II, 184
    See also Stock market
Eden, Anthony, 243
Edison, Thomas, 50, 52
Education:
    African American, 366
    bilingual, 269, 308, 347
    Black Mountain College curriculum, 147–48
    busing for desegregation, 333, 435

Chicano, 312
community control, 28
compulsory, 93
decline in test scores, 380
desegregation, 312, 333
religious, 211
in San Francisco, 42, 347
school prayer, 281
segregation in public schools, 236–37,
246, 367, 409, 422
sex equality in, 339
standards for rural schools, 432
televised in rural communities, 394
vocational, 89
voluntary standards for, 395
EEOC. *See* Equal Employment
Opportunity Commission
Egypt, 235, 245, 247, 310, 344, 345, 376
Einstein, Albert, 21, 39, 131, 149, 165–66,
194, 350–51
Einstein on the Beach (opera), 350–51
Eisenhower, Dwight D., 230–31, 244, 246,
267, 272
Electric Circus (N.Y.), 276
Electric generator, 47
Electricity, 2, 255, 425
Electronic Café International, 416
Electronics, 2, 394
Electron microscope, 175
Electroweak theory, 294, 297
Elevator, 19
Eli Lilly and Company, 352, 378
Eliot, T. S., 108
Elizabeth (queen), 232
Ellington, Duke, 73, 112, 120, 336
Ellis Island, 18, 19, 68, 328
Ellison, Ralph, 229
El Museo del Barrio, 315
El Partido Liberal Mexicano, 38
El Salvador, 330, 368, 375
El Teatro Campesino, 291, 332–33
E-mail, 340–41, 414
Emergency Quota Act, 106
Emerson, Lake, and Palmer, 306
Emi, Frank, 191
EMILY's List, 383
Emission standards, 292
Employment, 178
Endangered Species Act, 343
Endo v. U.S., 191
Engel, Morris, 229
Engelberger, Joseph, 274
Engineering, 299
ENIAC computer, 198–99
Enron Corporation, 425
Environment, 282, 327, 341, 400
Environmental racism, 390
Equal Educational Opportunity Act, 347
Equal Employment Opportunity
Commission (EEOC), 287, 378
Equal Rights Amendment (ERA), 308,
328, 339, 377
Equal-time rule, 254
ERA. *See* Equal Rights Amendment
Ernst, Max, 176
Ervin, Sam, 342
Eshkar, Shelley, 419
Espionage, 178, 224

Espionage Act, 89
Ethiopia, 127, 159, 160
Europe, James Reese, 62, 77, 92
European Economic Community (EEC),
249
Evans, Gil, 245
Evans, Walker, 154
Evers, Medgar, 285
Evolution, 2, 116–17, 437
Ewing, William, 245
Exit Art, 376
Extinct species, 432
Extraterrestrial life, 255
Eye surgery, 282

Factory (N.Y. studio), 283
Fagan, Garth, 338
Fair Deal, 214
Fair Employment Practices Commission,
178
Fall, Albert, 109, 110, 112
Fallingwater (Pa.), 159
Fard, Wallace D., 141
Farmer, James, 274
Farming, 6, 18, 79, 205–8
Farm workers, 27, 281, 291, 294, 329
Farnsworth, Philo, 122
Farouk (king), 235
Farrakhan, Louis, 420
Farrell, Thomas, 196
Fascism, 40, 52, 111, 135, 188
Faubus, Orval, 246
Fauvism, 39–40
Fax machine, 301, 414
FBI. *See* Federal Bureau of Investigation
FCC. *See* Federal Communications
Commission
Federal Aid Highway Act, 244
Federal Bureau of Investigation (FBI), 48,
114, 202, 413
Federal Communications Commission
(FCC), 175, 196, 254, 267, 445
Federal Highway Act, 241, 243
Federal Power Commission, 102
Federal Radio Commission, 122
Federal Reserve System, 47, 73, 299
Federal Trade Commission, 78
Feminine Mystique, The (Friedan), 286–87
Feminism. *See* Women
Fenollosa, Ernest Francisco, 70
Ferguson, Miriam "Ma," 117
Ferlinghetti, Lawrence, 232–33, 243
Fermi, Enrico, 166, 183, 184
Ferraro, Geraldine, 381
Fessenden, Reginald, 16, 47
Fiberoptic cable, 392, 429
Film, 158, 238
Films. *See* Movies; *specific movies and
moviemakers*
Fine arts, 33, 293, 426, 430
Finland, 44
Finlay, Carlos J., 16
Fires in the Mirror, 408
First Church of Christ Scientist (Berkeley,
Calif.), 62
Fisher, Bud, 44
Fisk Jubilee Singers, 25
Fission, 164, 167

Five Civilized Tribes, 3
Flags, 187, 326, 435
Flamingo hotel (Las Vegas), 198
Fleming, Alexander, 127–28, 178
Floppy disk, 329
Florey, Howard, 128, 178–79
Florida, 4, 118, 416, 441
Fluorescent lighting, 158
Fluoridation, 196
"Fluxus Events," 270
Flynt, Henry, 271
FM radio, 165, 175
Folsom prison (Calif.), 330
Food and Drug Administration (FDA), 140
Foraker Act, 14, 23
Ford, Gerald, 346–47, 350, 352
Ford, Henry, 17, 52, 74, 78
Ford Motor Company, 31, 48, 78, 127,
140
Foreign policy, 33–34, 202
Forest Service, 37
FORTRAN programming language, 244,
272
42nd Parallel, The (Dos Passos), 136–37
Fountain, 88, 90
Fountainhead, The (Rand), 187
Fourteen Points, 92, 96
Fox, Vicente, 419, 447
Foxwoods Resort Casino (Conn.), 409,
434, 445
France, 176, 238, 313, 341
Franchises, 242
Francis Ferdinand (archduke), 80
Franco, Francisco, 160
Frank, Leo, 80
Freedom of Information Act, 293
Freedom Rides, 208, 274
Free radicals, 16
Free Speech Movement, 288
Freons, 137–38
Frequent flyer programs, 374
Freud, Sigmund, 21–22, 51, 326
Frick, Henry Clay, 7
Friedan, Betty, 286–87, 302
Frigidaire, 110, 113
Frisch, Otto, 167
Frohnmayer, John, 402
Froines, John, 315
Frozen food, 90, 232
Fry, Arthur, 373
Fugs, 279
Fulbright, William, 300
Fuller, Buckminster, 121, 197
Fuller, Loie, 12
Fuller, Meta Warrick, 77
Funk, Casimir, 72
Furniture, 197, 312
Fusco, Coco, 403
Futurist Movement, 51–52, 76

Gagarin, Yuri, 275
Gallery 291 (N.Y.), 36–37, 81
Gallup Poll, 158
Gambling casinos, 366
Gamow, George, 212
Gandhi, Indira, 368, 383
Gandhi, Mahatma, 44, 103
Gandhi, Rajiv, 383

Gang of Four, 353
Gann, Paul, 356
García Lorca, Federico, 131
Garner, John Nance, 159
Garrity, W. Arthur, 333
Garvey, Marcus, 87
Gas masks, 79–80, 184
Gasoline, 16
Gas production, 373–74
Gates, Bill, 373
Gauguin, Paul, 44
Gay community. *See* Homosexuality
Gay Pride Week, 330
Gaza Strip, 245, 310
G. D. Searle Laboratories, 232, 268
Gellman, Samuel H., 443
Gelsinger, Jesse, 436
Gemayel, Amin, 378
Gemayel, Bashir, 378
Gene mapping, 75
Genentech, Inc., 352
General Electric, 113, 158
General Motors, 113, 274, 294, 379
General Seafoods Corporation, 90
Gene splicing, 352
Gene therapy, 437
Genetically modified crops, 417
Genetic engineering, 378
Genetics, 2, 329, 355
Genocide, 199, 313
Geodesic dome, 197
George VI (king), 232
German-American Bund, 134
Germany, 94, 97, 103, 107–8, 118, 133,
    139, 149, 154, 159, 160, 164, 167,
    177, 215, 243, 395, 407–8
Germ theory, 2
Germ warfare, 341
Geronimo, 51
Gershwin, George, 113, 155
GI Bill (Servicemen's Readjustment Act),
    190
Gillespie, Dizzy, 192
Gillman, J. E., 22
Gilpin, Charles, 84
Ginsberg, Allen, 189, 240, 243–44, 251,
    312, 345
Glaser, Donald, 295
Glashow, Sheldon Lee, 294
Glass, Philip, 350–51, 419
Global warming, 400, 412, 431–32, 444
Goddard, Robert Hutchings, 79, 95,
    119–20
Godowsky, Leopold, 158
God's Little Acre (Caldwell), 148
Golan Heights, 345
Gold, 5, 15–16, 47
Golden, Sam, 209
Golden Gate Bridge, 161
Goldmark, Peter, 176, 211
Goldwater, Barry, 290, 300
Goldwater, Robert, 162
Gomberg, Moses, 16
Gomez Pena, Guillermo, 401, 403
Gompers, Samuel, 7, 78
Gone With the Wind (movie), 164
Gonzales, Rodolfo "Corky," 302
Gonzalez, Elián, 440

Gonzalez, Juan, 23
Goodale, Elaine, 10
Goode, Wilson, 383
Goodman, Andrew, 289
Goodman, Benny, 150–51, 163
"Good Morning Carrie," 25
Good Neighbor Policy, 149
Gorbachev, Mikhail, 385, 390, 395, 405,
    410
Gordy, Berry, 253
Gore, Al, 422, 441
Gottwald, Klement, 213
Gould, Gordon, 268
Graffiti, 385
Graham, Bill, 291
Graham, Martha, 118–19, 135–36, 139,
    173, 189, 439
Grandma Moses (Anna Mary Robertson
    Moses), 164
Grand Ole Opry, 116, 214
Grand Rapids (Mich.), 196
Grand Teton Dam, 352
Granz, Norman, 189, 233
Grapes, 281, 294, 329
Graphite lubricator, 16
Gray, Spalding, 354
Great Britain, 91, 103, 176, 243
Great Depression, 130–31, 133, 147
Great Migration, 18
Great Northern Railway Company, 27, 35
Great Society, 293
Great Train Robbery, The (movie), 29, 37
Greenhouse gases, 407
Greenpeace, 341
Greensboro (N.C.), 268, 269
Greenspan, Alan, 405
Grenada, 379
Griffes, Charles Tomlinson, 84
Griffith, D. W., 82, 92
Grimke, Angelina Weld, 84
Gris, Juan, 48
Gropius, Walter, 95, 97
Grosman, Tatyana, 246
Group for Contemporary Music, 290
Group Theatre, 140, 154
Groves, Leslie, 196
Gruen, Victor, 239
Guerrilla Girls, 383
Guevara, Ernesto "Che," 309
Guggenheim, Peggy, 180
Guillermo, Emil, 423
Guinn, Kenny, 434
Guitar, 163
Gulf of Tonkin Resolution, 287
Gunboat diplomacy, 26, 71
Gunn, David, 414
Guns, 435
Guthrie, Woody, 165
Gutierrez, Jose Angel, 284, 302
Gyroscope magazine, 128
Gysin, Brion, 251

Haas, Earle, 141
Habloid Company, 222
Hadden, Briton, 112
Hahn, Otto, 164, 167
Haida people, 56
Haiti, 82, 389, 407

Haldeman, H. R., 345, 346
Hamer, Fannie Lou, 287
Hammerstein, Oscar, 187
Hammond, John, 150, 159, 163
Hammond, Laurens, 128, 163
Hamod, Sam, 226
Hampton, Fred, 317
Handicapped. *See* Disabled
Handy, W. C., 49, 70
Hansberry, Lorraine, 223, 251
Harding, Warren Gamaliel, 106, 112
Haring, Keith, 385–86
Harlan, John Marshall, 23, 35, 42
Harlem (N.Y.), 84
Harlem Rebellion, 289
Harlem Renaissance, 101, 116, 223
Harlem Riot, 158
Harpin, 444
Harrelson, Lowell, 391
Harris, Patricia, 352
Hart-Cellar Act, 293
Harvard University, 426
Harvey, Larry, 388
Hatch-Kennedy-Pell-Kassenbaum bill, 401
Hatcher, Richard, 307
Hate Crimes Prevention Act, 435
Hate Crimes Statistics Act, 405
Havel, Vaclav, 395
Hawaii, 5, 7, 15, 17, 50, 254, 387, 424,
    425–26
Hawkins, Coleman, 113
Hawley-Smoot Tariff Act, 137
Hay–Bunau-Varilla Treaty, 26
Hay-Paunceforte Treaty, 23
Hayden, Tom, 282, 312, 315
Haywood, Big Bill, 38
Head Start program, 293
Health care, 400
Hearst, William Randolph, 20, 176
Heart transplant, 382
Heezen, Bruce Charles, 245
Hefner, Hugh, 235
Heisenberg Uncertainty Principle, 123
Heizer, Michael, 314
Helicopter, 167
Helms, Jesse, 393, 401, 433
Henderson, Fletcher, 113
Hendrix, Jimi, 335
Henson, Jim, 317
Henson, Matthew, 51
Heredia, Paula, 403
Heredity, 28, 47
Herman, Robert, 212
Hernandez v. State of Texas, 234, 237
Herrera, Carmen, 142–43
Herrick, J. B., 64
Herring, James V., 105
Hewitt, Edgar J., 109
Hewlett, Emanuel D. Molyneaux, 42
Hewlett Packard, 165
High-fidelity sound, 281
Highways. *See* Roads
Highway Trust Fund, 244
Hijacking, 331, 340
Hill, Anita, 391
Hill, Joe, 83
Hill, Julia "Butterfly," 429
Hill, Lewis, 214

Hiller, Lejaren, 241, 253
Hinckley, John W. Jr., 373
Hip-hop music, 354, 363, 387
Hip replacement, 38
Hiroshima (Japan), 193, 194–95, 196
Hispanic population, 446
Hitler, Adolf, 107–8, 118, 133, 139, 149, 154, 159, 160, 161, 167, 176, 187
Ho Chi Minh, 238, 287
Hoffman, Abbie, 312, 315
Hofmann, Albert, 164
Holiday, Billie, 164
Holladay, Wilhelmina, 390
Holmes, Oliver Wendell, 92
Holocaust, 187
Holt, Benjamin, 16
Homebase (Wong), 357
Homelessness, 384, 400, 432
Homestead Steel Mill strike, 7
Homosexuality, 227–28, 235, 245, 289, 316, 330, 344, 357, 378, 414
Honduras, 45, 71, 330, 368
Hong Kong, 429–30
Hooker, Evelyn, 245
Hoover, Herbert, 110, 123, 125, 130, 137, 146
Hoover, J. Edgar, 114, 311
Hoover Dam, 127
Hopkins, Harry, 154
Hormones, 22
Horn, Clayton, 244
Hostage crisis (Iran), 359, 365, 373
Hot line, 284
Hounsfield, Godfrey, 344
House Un-American Activities Committee (HUAC), 163, 182, 267
Housing, 204, 211, 214, 292
Houston, Jeanne Wakatsuki, 323
Howard University, 105, 136
Howard University Press, 323
Howe, Oscar, 248
Howl (Ginsberg), 240, 243–44
HUAC. *See* House Un-American Activities Committee
Hubble, Edwin Powell, 115, 131
Hubble's Law, 131
Hubble Space Telescope, 405–6, 418
Huck, Winifred, 106
HUD. *See* Department of Housing and Urban Development
Huerta, Dolores, 281
Huerta, Victoriano, 74, 78, 82–83
Hughes, Emmett, 272
Hughes, Langston, 105, 223, 265
Hughes Tool Company, 49
Human Genome Project, 406–7, 442–43
Human growth hormone, 352
Human rights, 198, 275, 395
Human Sexual Response (Masters and Johnson), 302
Humphrey, Doris, 120–21, 139
Humphrey, Hubert, 300, 312
Hungary, 437
Hurston, Zora Neale, 161
Hussein, Saddam, 286, 313, 405, 408
Hu Yaobang, 395
Hydramatic drive, 167

Hydrogen bomb, 222, 231, 233, 244–45
Hypertext, 347, 408, 413

IBM, 329, 343, 373
Icebox, 110–11, 113
Ickes, Harold, 162, 164
Imagism, 58–59, 70
Immigration:
    African, 230
    Angel Island, 62–64
    Armenian, 83
    Asian, 7, 24, 31, 45, 64, 100, 114–15, 187, 230, 366
    Central American, 330, 365, 375
    Ellis Island, 18, 19
    Emergency Quota Act, 106
    faked documents, 43
    Filipino, 64, 152, 157, 180
    German, 141
    Immigration Commission 1907 study of, 47
    Indian, 104–5
    Indochinese, 365
    Italian, 18
    Korean, 293
    Mexican, 131
    quota system, 114–15, 293
    and rise of capitalism, 6
    Russian, 38, 76
    undocumented aliens, 355, 387, 392, 416–17
    Vietnamese, 348, 350
    War Brides Act, 196
Immigration Reform and Control Act (IRCA). *See* Simpson-Mazzoli Act
Impeachment, 434
Impressions d'Afrique (Roussel), 69
Inada, Lawson, 319, 322, 323, 331, 345
Income tax, 49, 73, 119
In Dahomey, 26
India, 44, 103, 208, 368, 382, 383
Indian Allotment Act. *See* Dawes Severalty Act
Indianapolis (Ind.), 307
Indian Boyhood (Eastman), 26
Indian Citizenship Act, 114
Indian Oil Leasing Act, 115
Indian Reorganization Act, 110, 113, 152
Indians, American. *See* Native Americans
Indian's Book, The (Curtis), 45
Indonesia, 298, 430
Industrial waste, 391
Industrial Workers of the World (IWW), 37–38, 50, 72, 95
Ingberman, Jeanette, 376
Ingstad, Helge, 270
Insider trading, 388
Institute of Musical Art, 37
Insular Cases, 23
Insulin, 108, 352, 355, 378
Integrated circuits, 249, 288
Intel (co.), 288
Intellectual property rights, 419, 445
Interest rates, 366, 377, 378
Interferon, 378
International Bank for Reconstruction and Development, 192
International Criminal Court, 432–33

International Hotel (San Francisco), 313, 355
International Ladies' Garment Workers Union (ILGWU), 17, 68
International Monetary Fund, 192
Internet, 380
    Amazon.com, 420
    AOL, 383–84
    Cisco Systems, 444
    community-sharing software programs, 445
    "cookie," 418
    Delphi, 411
    "digital divide," 437
    e-mail, 340–41
    increased use of, 414, 417, 431
    MOSAIC, 411–12, 417
    online news, 420, 421
    original program for World Wide Web, 408
    releasing of World Wide Web protocols, 413
    Stephen King's e-book, 439
    TCP/IP, 343
Internment, 182, 190, 191, 323, 392
Interpretation of Dreams, The (Freud), 21–22
Interstate Highway System, 244
In the Land of the Headhunters (movie), 77
Intifadah, 389
Invisible Man (Ellison), 229
Iran, 236, 359, 365, 371, 373, 387
Iran-Contra Affair, 387
Iraq, 286, 313, 371, 405, 408, 409, 410, 411
Ireland, 39, 108
Ireland, David, 351
Irish-Americans, 135
Irrigation, 27
Irwin, James B., 334
Isaacson, Leonard, 241
Ishi (American Indian), 69
Islam, 123, 124, 226, 228, 249
Islamic Jihad, 376
Israel, 213, 245, 310, 344–45, 355, 376, 378, 389, 391, 411, 415, 422
Italian Americans, 182
Italo-Turkish War, 65
Italy, 111, 176, 177, 182, 188, 383
Ives, Charles, 26, 48, 101
IWW. *See* Industrial Workers of the World

Jack Kerouac School of Disembodied Poetics, 345
Jackson, Andrew, 3
Jackson, George, 335
Jackson, Michael, 380
Jackson, Thomas Penfield, 440
Jackson State College, 329
Jacobs, Jane, 274
Jacobson, Oscar B., 121
James, Jerry, 388
Japan, 7, 36, 40, 45, 65, 177, 193, 196, 228
Japanese Americans, 20, 22, 39, 42, 50, 64, 73–74, 179, 181, 182, 186, 190, 191, 214, 244, 331, 392

Jaruzelski, Wojciech, 396
Jarvis, Howard, 356
Jazz, 13, 77, 88, 92, 112, 113, 119, 189–90, 233, 236, 253, 279, 411
Jazz Singer, The (movie), 121
Jefferson, Thomas, 3, 328
Jemison, Mae, 375
Jencks, Charles, 337
Jenkins, Charles, 117, 118
Jennings, Corrine, 277
Jet aircraft, 186
Jews, 44, 80, 149, 159, 187, 188
Jiang Zemin, 395
Job Corps, 288, 293
Jobs, Steven, 354
Johns, Jasper, 247, 275
Johnson, Ed, 42, 50
Johnson, Hiram, 74
Johnson, Jack, 64
Johnson, Katherine Coleman Goble, 273
Johnson, Lyndon B., 267, 285, 288, 289, 290, 292–93, 300, 306, 307, 311
Johnson, Philip, 216, 229
Johnson, Robert, 159
Johnson, Robert L., 409
Johnson, Virginia, 302
Johnson Publishing Company, 184
Johnson-Reed Immigration Act, 114
Joint Chiefs of Staff, 394
Jones, Bill T., 416
Jones, Frederick McKinley, 214
Jones, LeRoi, 271, 310
Jones, Paula, 434
Jones Act, 89
Joplin, Scott, 13, 66
Jordan, 391, 439
Joyce, James, 109, 148
Judson Dance Theater Workshop, 265
Judson Flag Show, 326
Juilliard School of Music, 37
Jung, C. G., 51
Jungle, The (Sinclair), 40
Jupiter (planet), 355
Juries, 234, 237

Kahlo, Frida, 142, 176
Kahn, Bob, 343
Kahn, Julian Seth, 167
Kaiser, Paul, 419
Kanellos, Nicolas, 356, 364
Kansas, 437
Kapany, Narinder Singh, 104
Kaprow, Allen, 249
Karamu Theatre, 84
Karenga, Maulana, 298, 302, 422
Kasavubu, Joseph, 270
Kassim, Abdul Karem, 286
Kaufman, Bob, 244, 256
Kazan, Elia, 201
Kearney (ship), 177
Kellogg-Briand Pact, 126–27, 142–43
Kelly, Gene, 177
Kennan, George F., 202
Kennedy, Adrienne, 275–76
Kennedy, John F., 267, 272, 273, 282, 283, 285, 286, 287
Kennedy, Robert F., 274, 311
Kent (Wash.), 338

Kent State University, 327
Kentucky, 34, 132, 425
Kenya, 415
Kerensky, Aleksandr, 91
Kern, Jerome, 121
Kerner Commission, 309
Kerouac, Jack, 189, 214, 240, 245, 260
Kesey, Ken, 308–9
Keynes, John Maynard, 103, 120
Keystone Studio, 70
Khomeini, Ayatollah, 359, 373
Khorana, Har Gobind, 329
Khrushchev, Nikita, 235, 283, 290
Kilby, Jack, 249
Kim Dae Jung, 447
Kim Jong-il, 447
King, Martin Luther Jr., 241, 285, 286, 290, 292, 296, 309, 311, 313, 314
King, Mary, 297
King, Perry A., 317
King, Rodney, 410, 412
King, Stephen, 439
Kingston, Maxine Hong, 324
Kinsey, Alfred, 212, 235
Kiowa Five, 121
Kirstein, Lincoln, 155, 314
Kissinger, Henry, 338, 433
Kitzhaber, John A., 418
Kleindienst, Richard, 345
Kluver, Billy, 299
Knickerbocker Trust Company, 45
Knox, Philander, 27
Knudsen, William, 174
Kodachrome film, 158
Kohl, Helmut, 408
Korea, 7, 36, 40, 65, 213, 293, 447
Korean War, 222–23, 229, 235
Korematsu v. U.S., 191, 192
Koskinen, John A., 430
Kosovo, 437
Kosygin, Aleksei, 290
Kroc, Ray, 241
Kroeber, Alfred L., 69
K-T boundary, 367
Ku Klux Klan, 82, 83, 107, 118, 134, 241
Kuwait, 371, 408, 409, 411
Kwakiutl people, 77
Kwanzaa, 298, 302
Kyoto Protocol, 412

Labor:
    Clayton Act, 77
    collective bargaining, 157
    contract workers, 15
    eight-hour workday, 78, 86
    Fair Labor Standards Act, 163
    farm workers, 27, 281, 291, 294, 329
    founding of AFL, 7, 17
    founding of ILGWU, 17
    founding of IWW, 37–38
    merger of AFL-CIO, 238
    migrant, 79, 222
    quotas in unions, 358
    right-to-work laws, 202
    salaries and wages, 31, 94, 224, 229–30, 233, 334
    Triangle Shirtwaist Company fire, 67–68
    union shop, 202

    women's, 31, 49, 94, 308, 333, 339
    work-at-home operations, 414
    See also Minimum wage; Strikes
Lacks, Henrietta, 224, 227
La Galeria de la Raza, 382
Lake Erie, 312
Lakota people, 4
Lamberth, Royce L., 424
Land:
    Alaska Native Claims Settlement Act, 334
    California Land Act, 5
    Native American, 3–4, 14–15, 24, 27, 109–10, 198, 328, 334, 424
    Oklahoma Land Rush, 24
    Reclamation Act, 27
    Webb Alien Land-Holding Bill, 74
Land, Edwin Herbert, 211
Landfills, 375, 377, 407
Lane, William Henry (Master Juba), 12
Lange, Dorothea, 155
Langmuir, Irving, 46
Lanier, Jaron, 374, 394
La Opinion, 120
Laposky, Ben, 229
La Raza Unita, 284, 302
Larson, John Augustus, 107
Lascaux cave (France), 179
Lasers, 267–68, 282
Las Vegas (Nev.), 198
Latin America, 34, 149, 198, 309
Latino art, 67, 142–43, 173, 304–6, 381, 403, 404
Lau v. Nichols, 347
Law of the Sea Convention, 379
Lawrence, Ernest O., 141, 166
Lawrence (Mass.), 72
Lay, Ken, 425
Lazear, Jesse William, 16
L-dopa, 335
League of Arab States, 197
League of Nations, 92, 96–97, 103
Leary, Timothy, 301
Leavitt, Michael, 434
Lebanon, 378, 380, 387
Lebron, Lolita, 237
LeCompte, Elizabeth, 354
Ledbetter, Huddie "Leadbelly," 165
LeMay, Curtis, 195
Lend-Lease Act, 177
Lenin, Vladimir, 91, 116
Lesbians, 242, 344
Lettuce, 281, 329
Leupp, Francis E., 37
Levene, Phoebus, 50
Lever House (N.Y.), 229
Levittown (N.Y.), 204, 210
Lewis, Gilbert Newton, 141
Lewis, John, 292
Lewis, John L., 158
Lewis, Robert, 201
Lewitzky, Bella, 402
Libby, Willard Frank, 203
Liberation theology, 309
Libya, 387
Lichtenstein, Roy, 275
Life expectancy, 401
Life magazine, 160

"Lift Ev'ry Voice and Sing," 12
Lightning Field, 331
Lila Wallace/Reader's Digest Fund, 391
Limón, Jose, 214
Lin, Maya, 365, 371–72
Lincoln, Abraham, 10
Lincoln Center (N.Y.), 411
Lindbergh, Charles, 120, 122
Li Peng, 395
Lippmann, Walter, 179
Lipson, Hod, 444
Liquor, 19, 94–95
Lithium, 335
Little, Arthur, 28
Little Fugitive, The (movie), 229
Little Rock (Ark.), 246
Livingston, M. Stanley, 141
Livingston, Sigmund, 80
Living Theater, 223, 283
Lloyd, Marshall Burns, 89
Locke, Alain, 116
London, Jack, 40
Los Angeles County Museum of Art, 325
Los Angeles police, 410, 412
Los Gallos (Taos, N.M.), 92
Louis, Morris, 209
Louisiana Purchase Exposition, 35–36
Loyalty, 186, 191
LSD (drug), 164, 301
Lucas, George, 354
Luce, Henry, 112, 160
Ludlow Massacre, 75
Lufbery, Raoul, 93
Lujan, Mabel Dodge, 92, 110
Lujan, Tony, 92, 110
Luke, Frank, 93
Lumumba, Patrice, 270
Luna, James, 403
Luna (redwood tree), 429
Lusitania (ship), 82
Lynching, 15, 41, 42, 50, 106, 203
Lysozyme, 127–28

MacArthur, Douglas, 177, 193, 223
Machu Picchu (Peru), 69
Macdonald, Andrew, 357
Machito Big Band, 180
Macintosh computer, 381–82
Maciunas, George, 270
Macleod, John, 108
Madero, Francisco, 74
Mafia, 383
Magnetic recording tape, 186
Magnetism, 2
Magon, Ricardo and Enrique Flores, 38
Maiman, Theodore, 267
Maine (USS), 5
Malaria, 34
Malcolm X, 232, 258, 260–61, 263, 289, 297, 387
Malenkov, Georgy, 235
Malina, Judith, 223
Mall of America (Minn.), 411
Malls. *See* Shopping centers
Managed care, 400
Manchuria, 36, 40, 127, 142
Mandela, Nelson, 407

Manhattan Project, 166, 179
Manifest Destiny, 5
Mankiller, Wilma, 384
Mann Act, 64
Mannes, Leopold, 158
Manufacturing, 17
Mao Zedong, 199, 213, 215, 303, 338
Mapplethorpe, Robert, 393, 402
Maps, 75, 443
Maquiladoras, 294, 366, 417
Marc, Franz, 52
March on Washington, 286
Marconi, Guglielmo, 26, 51
Marcos, Ferdinand, 298–99, 389
Mariél boatlift, 365
Marijuana, 301, 424, 436
Mariner 2 space probe, 282
Mariner 9 space probe, 329
Mariner 10 space probe, 347
Marinetti, Tommaso, 51, 65, 76
Marriage, 424, 445
Mars (planet), 353, 410
Marsalis, Wynton, 381, 411
Marshall, Thomas R., 71
Marshall, Thurgood, 236, 307, 409
Marshall Plan, 211, 212
Martha Graham Dance Company, 439
Martin, Peter D., 232–33
Martin, Sallie, 148
Mason, William E., 106
Mass for the 21st Century, 434
Masson, Andre, 176
Mass production, 17
Masters, William, 302
Matisse, Henri, 47
Mattachine Society, 227, 242
Matthews, Max, 246, 248
Mauchly, John, 227
Max's Kansas City (N.Y.), 283
Maybeck, Bernard, 62
Maynard, Nancy Hicks, 421
Mazowiecki, Tadeusz, 396
McAuliffe, Christa, 388
McCarran Act, 221
McCarran-Walter Immigration and Nationality Act, 230, 293
McCarthy, Eugene, 312
McCarthy, James, 444
McCarthy, Joseph, 221, 237
McClintock, Barbara, 225
McCord, James, 338
McCoy, Elijah, 16
McDonald's restaurants, 241–42
McGovern, George, 339
McIntyre, James, 12
McKay, Claude, 94
McKinley, William, 14, 23
McLaurin v. Oklahoma, 230
McLemore, Henry, 179
McLuhan, Marshall, 228
McPhee, Chester, 243
McPherson, Aimee Semple, 115
McTaggart, David, 341
McVeigh, Timothy, 357, 420
Mead, Margaret, 127
Means, Russell, 342
Meany, George, 238
Meat Inspection Act, 41

Mein Kampf (Hitler), 118
Meitner, Lise, 167
Méliès, Georges, 29
Mellon, Andrew, 119
Mellotron, 345
Mena, Luis, 71
Mendel, Gregor, 2
Mental health, 307–8, 400
Merchant Marine Act, 102
Meredith, James, 281
Mergers, 27, 34–35, 386, 431
Meriam Report, 125, 151
Mesic, Stipe, 410
Metcalf, Victor H., 42
Meter (measurement), 268, 379
Methane gas, 391, 407
Metro-Goldwyn-Mayer (MGM), 92
Metropolitan Museum of Art, 214
Metropolitan Opera, 238
Mexican Americans, 31, 131, 177, 188, 204, 223, 234, 237, 238, 269, 284, 302, 308
Mexican Revolution, 58, 65–66, 91
Mexico, 4–5, 74, 78, 82–83, 91, 269, 294, 366, 386, 413, 417, 418–19, 420, 447
Meyer, Dillion S., 221
Michael, Helen, 367
Micheaux, Oscar, 76
Mickey Mouse, 123, 125
Microprocessors, 288
Microsoft, 373, 440, 444
Midgley, Thomas Jr., 137
MIDI keyboard, 379
Mies van der Rohe, Ludwig, 161, 216, 229
Migrant workers, 79, 222
Migration, 108–9
Military. *See* Armed forces
Military-industrial complex, 225, 272
Military Supply Act, 174
Milk, Harvey, 357
Milken, Michael, 388
Mill Creek Canyon Earthworks, 338
Miller, Arthur, 213
Miller, Henry, 150
Miller, Joan, 248
Miller, Joaquin, 82
Millett, Kate, 326
Milliken v. Bradley, 333
Million Man March, 420, 422
Million Woman March, 432
MILNET computer network, 380
Milosevic, Slobodan, 410, 437
Minh, Duong Van, 348
Minimalism, 290–91
Minimum wage, 78, 163, 214
Mining, 225, 405
Minority-owned businesses, 394
Miranda v. Arizona, 292
Mirikitani, Janice, 322
Miscegenation, 24, 42, 64, 211
Miss America, 313
Missiles, 248, 358, 379, 390
Mission Cultural Center (San Francisco), 354
Mississippi, 287, 289
Mitchell, Arthur, 237, 239, 313–14
Mobro (barge), 391

Mobutu, Joseph, 270
Model Cities program, 292
Modernism, 52, 380
Modigliani, Amedeo, 44, 52
Moe, Ann-Stine, 270
Moholy-Nagy, Laszlo, 161
Momaday, N. Scott, 310
Mondale, Walter, 352, 381
Mondrian, Piet, 173
Money. See Currency
Monk, Meredith, 332, 333
Monroe, Harriet, 70
Monroe, Marilyn, 235, 275
Monroe Doctrine, 27, 33
Monsanto (co.), 417
Monterey Park (Calif.), 382
Montessori schools, 72
Montgomery (Ala.), 290
Montreal Protocols, 391
Montulli, Lou, 418
Moog, Robert, 271
Moog synthesizer, 272, 306
Moon landing, 315–16, 318, 334–35
Moore, Carman, 434
Moore, Gordon, 288
Moran, Kathleen, 18, 232, 239, 254
Morgan, Garrett, 79, 113
Morgan, J. P., 24, 25, 27, 35, 41, 45, 47
Morgan, Thomas Hunt, 47
Morgan v. Commonwealth of Virginia, 198, 204
Mori, Toshio, 214
Mork, Harry, 28
Mormon Mesa (Nev.), 314
Morocco, 439
Morris, Robert, 314
Morrison, Jim, 335
Morrison, Peter A., 108
Morrison, Philip, 255
Morrison, Toni, 413
Mortgages, 366
Morton, Jelly Roll, 35, 119
MOSAIC (Internet browser), 411–12, 417
Moscone, George, 357
Moscoso, Mireya, 435
Mosques, 123, 124
Mosquitoes, 16, 34
Mossadegh, Mohammed, 236
Motherwell, Robert, 213, 223
Motion Picture Patents Company, 50
Motley, Archibald Jr., 125
Motown, 253–54
Motts, Robert, 37
Mount Rushmore (S.D.), 136, 328
MOVE (activist group), 383
Movies:
    animated, 41, 70, 123
    Busby Berkeley musicals, 148
    drive-in theaters, 149
    first black-owned theater, 37
    first black producer, 76
    first formal theater, 37
    first international sensation, 29
    first with sound, 119, 121, 123
    first Western, 29
    Hays Office, 313
    Keystone Kops films, 70
    soundtrack, 233

star/studio system, 92
    See also specific movies and movie-makers
Mozambique, 350
Mr. A. Mutt (comic strip), 44
MRI (magnetic resonance imaging), 344
MTV (Music Television), 372
Mubarak, Mohammed Hosni, 376
Mugabe, Robert, 371
Muhammad, Elijah, 141, 226–27, 232
Muller, Paul, 167
Multiculturalism, 337, 429
Multinational corporations, 294, 366
Mumma, Gordon, 272
Munich Agreement, 164
Muppets (puppets), 317
Murals, 144, 162, 173, 311
Murao, Shigeyoshi, 243
Murphy, J. B., 38
Murrah Federal Office Building (Oklahoma City), 413, 420
Museum of American Folk Art, 272
Museum of Modern Art (MOMA), 128, 129, 173, 380
Music:
    African, 236
    bebop, 177, 192
    blues, 49, 70, 101, 111–12
    Cage on, 160–61
    choral singing, 148
    Clef Club, 62
    computer-generated, 241, 246, 248, 272
    controversial lyrics, 403
    country, 121, 155, 157
    Cubop, 180
    Dvořák on, 7
    Dynamophone, 43
    electronic, 241, 290, 306, 379
    experimental composition, 383
    first black recording artists, 25
    Futurist concert, 76
    hip-hop, 354, 363, 387
    jazz, 13, 77, 88, 92, 112, 113, 119, 189–90, 233, 236, 253, 279, 411
    Juilliard School, 37
    Meredith Monk on, 332
    Napster, 445
    neoclassicism, 52
    New Age, 352
    piano compositions, 71, 84
    ragtime, 13, 21, 66
    recording technology, 25
    royalties, 49, 78–79
    salsa, 311
    swing, 151
    synthesizers, 241, 248–49, 272, 306, 354, 376
    on tape, 247
Muslims. See Islam
Mussolini, Benito, 111, 159, 160, 176, 188
Mutt, Richard, 88, 90
Mutual Broadcasting System, 175
My Lai (Vietnam), 311

NAACP. See National Association for the Advancement of Colored People
Nader, Ralph, 294, 295, 394

NAFTA (North American Free Trade Agreement), 413, 417, 419
Nagasaki (Japan), 170, 193, 196
Nagy, Andras, 415
Naked Lunch (Burroughs), 251
Names Project Memorial Quilt, 389–90
Namibia, 407
Namingha, Dan, 280
Napster, 445
Narasimhan, T. N., 126, 349
Naropa Institute, 345
NASA. See National Aeronautics and Space Administration
Nasser, Gamal Abdel, 235, 245, 247, 298, 310
Nation, Carry, 19
National Aeronautics and Space Administration (NASA), 248, 267, 273–74, 285
National Airlines, 248
National Association for the Advancement of Colored People (NAACP), 51, 62, 80, 86, 89, 302
National Black Arts Festival, 392
National Black Feminist Organization, 344
National Black Theater Festival, 392
National Broadcasting Company (NBC), 119, 174–75
National Bureau of Standards, 24
National Endowment for the Arts (NEA), 293, 331, 371, 393, 400–401, 402, 426, 430
National Endowment for the Humanities, 293
National Farm Workers Association, 294
National League of Women, 103
National Museum of the American Indian, 393
National Museum of Women in the Arts, 390
National Negro Committee, 51
National Oceanic and Atmospheric Administration, 328
National Organization for Women (NOW), 287, 302, 308
National Park Service, 85
National Public Radio, 307
National Security Act, 202
National Security Council (NSC), 202, 220, 387
National Urban League, 66–67
National Weather Service, 328–29
National Women's Trade Union League, 31
Nation of Islam, 141
Native American Church, 93
Native American Graves Protection and Repatriation Act, 407
Native American National Bank, 444–45
Native American Rights Fund, 335
Native Americans:
    acculturation, 55–58
    American Indian Movement, 312–13, 316, 339, 342
    antipoverty funds for, 287
    art, 109, 121, 139, 144–45, 162, 248, 250, 251–253, 279, 369–71, 403
    Black Elk Speaks (Neihardt), 143–44
    in children's textbooks, 316

citizenship, 94, 114
code talkers, 89, 186, 377
Collier's work for, 113, 151
controversy over Columbus, 412
first daily newspaper, 382
first to serve in Senate, 411
gambling casinos, 366, 409
land, 3–4, 14–15, 24, 27, 109–10, 198, 328, 424
languages, 437
largest intertribal bank, 444–45
Leupp on, 37
Meriam Report, 125, 151
occupation of Alcatraz Island, 289, 316
photographs of, 41
poetry, 92, 112
population, 11, 14, 100
potlatch, 56–57, 58
powwows, 346, 347–48, 349
production of own gas and oil, 373–74
reservations, 4, 211, 367
schools in Native communities, 432
Society of American Indians, 68
Sun Dance, 8, 35
"termination" policy, 211, 221–22, 233, 273, 328, 392
Trail of Broken Treaties Caravan, 339
twentieth century writings, 11
water rights, 110
Wounded Knee (S.D.) incident, 4, 9–11, 342–43
Native Market (Santa Fe, N.M.), 150
Native Son (Wright), 173
NATO (North Atlantic Treaty Organization), 215, 437
Natural gas, 425
Natural resources, 48
Nautilus (submarine), 242
Navajo people, 186, 225, 377
Navajo Times, 382
Naval Supply Act, 174
Nazism, 94, 149, 164, 176, 187, 356
NBC. *See* National Broadcasting Company
NEA. *See* National Endowment for the Arts
Neal, Larry, 310
Negro Digest, 184
Neihardt, John, 143
Nelson, Theodor Holm, 347
Neptune (planet), 355
Netherlands, 447
Netscape, 384, 412, 417, 418
Neutrality Act, 165
Neutron bomb, 368
Nevada, 141
Nevelson, Louise, 271
Newark (N.J.), 309
New Deal, 149, 157, 158, 159, 214
New Mexico, 71–72, 85–86
New Negro, The (Locke), 116
Newport Folk Festival, 284
Newport Jazz Festival, 236
New Rochelle (N.Y.), 269
Newspapers, 19, 289–90, 382, 420
News reportage, 366, 405, 421
Newton, Huey, 302
New Urbanism, 375–76, 425
New York City, 19, 85, 283

New Yorker, The, 99
New York Public Library, 105
New Zealand, 228
Niagara Movement, 38, 51
Nicaragua, 45, 71, 330, 359, 368, 373, 377, 387, 389, 392, 407
Nicholas II (czar), 38, 90–91, 94
Nichols, J. C., 111
Nigeria, 439
Nile River, 245
1984 (Orwell), 215
Nixon, Richard M., 230, 267, 312, 315, 327, 334, 338–39, 342, 343, 345–47
Nixon in China (opera), 390
Nkomo, Joshua, 371
NMDA receptor, 436
No-No Boy (Okada), 322
Noriega, Manuel, 393–94
North America, 270
North American Free Trade Agreement. *See* NAFTA
North Atlantic Treaty Organization. *See* NATO
North Carolina, 333
Northern Pacific Railway Company, 27, 35
Northern Securities Company, 27
North Korea, 213, 293, 447
North Polar ice cap, 444
North Pole, 51
Norton, Eleanor Holmes, 328
Norton, George, 49
Novachord, 163
Novoye Russkoe Slovo, 65
NOW. *See* National Organization for Women
Noyce, Robert, 249, 288
NSC. *See* National Security Council
Nuclear accidents, 358, 389
Nuclear energy, 167, 183, 184–85, 225, 232, 246
Nuclear Test Ban Treaty, 434
Nuclear testing, 341, 419–20
Nuclear waste, 434
Nuclear weapons, 175, 177, 218, 220, 225, 284–85, 313, 354, 405, 447
Nuclear winter, 368
Nucleic acid, 50
Nujoma, Sam, 407
Nuremberg Laws, 159
Nuremberg war trials, 199
Nutcracker, The, 189
Nuyorican, 353
Nuyorican Poets Café, 353, 355–56
N. W. Ayer and Sons, 18
Nylon, 153, 163

Oakland (Calif.), 134
OAS. *See* Organization of American States
Obasanjo, Olusegun, 439
Obote, Milton, 337
Obscenity, 148, 150, 243–44, 393, 400–401, 402
Oceanic ridges, 245
Ochoa, Ellen, 407
O'Connor, Sandra Day, 373
October Revolution, 91
Odets, Clifford, 154

Office of Production Management, 174
Office of Scientific Research and Development, 179
Oil. *See* Petroleum
Okada, John, 186, 322
Okakura, Tenshin, 33
O'Keeffe, Georgia, 36, 125
Okimoto, Daniel, 324–25
Okinawa, 193
Oklahoma, 24, 45
Oklahoma!, 187
Olatunji, Babatunde, 236
Oldenburg, Claes, 275
Olds, Ransom P., 17
Olds Motor Works, 17
Oliveros, Pauline, 279
Olson, Harry, 241
Olympic Games, 160, 285, 383
Once Festivals, 272
O'Neill, Eugene, 108
O'Neill, J. A., 123
One magazine, 235
Onis Treaty, 4
Onnes, Heike, 70
On the Road (Kerouac), 245, 260
On the Town, 189
OPEC. *See* Organization of Petroleum Exporting Countries
Open City, 289
Open Theatre, 283
Operation Bootstrap, 192
Operation Desert Storm, 409
Operation Pipeline, 388
Operation Wetback, 238
Oppenheimer, J. Robert, 196
Oracle (co.), 358
Oral contraceptives, 232, 268
Oregon, 27, 418
Organ (musical instrument), 130
Organic Act, 15
Organization of American States (OAS), 213
Organization of Petroleum Exporting Countries (OPEC), 270
Original Dixieland Jazz Band, 88
Orkin, Ruth, 229
Ortega, Daniel, 359, 407
Orwell, George, 215
Oscillator, 83
Oswald, Lee Harvey, 285, 287
Otis Elevator Company, 19
Our Town, 162
Owen-Keating Law, 86
Owens, Jesse, 160
Ozone layer, 356–57, 385

Pacifica Radio, 215
Pacific Gas & Electric Company, 425
Paik, Nam June, 290
Pakistan, 208, 393
Palestine, 44, 91, 213
Palestine Liberation Organization (PLO), 298, 378, 415
Palestinians, 389, 391–92, 422, 426
Paley, William S., 174, 411
Palm, Roberta, 323
Palma, Tomás Estrada, 27, 28
Palmer, Charles, 16

Palmer Raids, 102
Palmieri, Eddie, 311
Pan-African Conference, 80, 96
Pan-African Congresses, 21
Panama, 393–94, 435
Panama Canal, 23–24, 26–27, 31, 34, 78, 89, 354, 435
Panama Pacific Exposition, 82
Pan American Airways, 165, 301
Papo, 376
Pap test, 186
Parcel Post, 74
Parden, Noah Walter, 42
Paris Peace Conference (1919–20), 96–97
Parker, Charlie, 192
Parker, Dorothy, 99
Parkinson's disease, 335
Parks, Rosa, 240, 241
Particle tracks, 295
Patrinos, Ari, 406
Paul, Alice, 76, 100
Paul, Louis, 57, 58
Paul VI (pope), 309
Pavia, Philip, 214
Paxton, Steve, 337
Paz, Octavio, 223
PCB-contaminated soil, 377
PCs. See Personal computers
Peace Corps, 272–73
Pearl Harbor, 177, 178
Peary, Robert Edwin, 51
Pellagra, 72–73
Pelléas et Melisande (opera), 29
Peltier, Leonard, 350
Penicillin, 127–28, 178
Pentagon Papers, 334
Pentecostal movement, 25–26, 44
People of the Abyss (London), 40
Pequot Museum and Research Center, 433
Peres, Shimon, 422
Performance art, 228, 249, 251, 270, 272, 357, 386, 401, 403
Permanent-press clothing, 288
Perón, Eva, 199
Perón, Juan, 199
Pershing, John J., 86
Personal computers (PCs), 329, 341, 350, 354–55, 373, 437
Pesticides, 167, 282, 382, 444
Pétain, Philippe, 176
Peters, Susie, 121
Petroleum:
  gasoline from, 16
  glut of, 384
  Indian Oil Leasing Act, 115
  Lucas gusher, 22
  on Native American land, 109–10
  Native American production of, 373–74
  OPEC, 270
  shortages, 342, 344
  Teapot Dome scandal, 112
  trans-Alaska pipeline, 342, 355
Petty, Richard, 431
Peyote, 93
Phagan, Mary, 80
Pharmaceuticals, 400
Philanthropy, 25

Philadelphia (Pa.), 383
Philippines, 152, 177, 193, 197, 299, 389
Phonograph, 103, 123
Phonograph record, 212
Photoelectric effect, 21
Photography, 16, 36, 41, 47, 84, 88, 154
Physician-assisted suicide, 418, 447
Physics, 21
Piano, 13
Picabia, Francis, 81
Picasso, Pablo, 44, 47, 73
"Picture bride" system, 64
Pierce, John Robinson, 267
Pinchot, Gifford, 37, 48
Pincus, Gregory Goodwin, 268
Pine Ridge Reservation (S.D.), 342, 350
Pinero, Jesus T., 197
Pinero, Miguel, 356
Pink Floyd, 338
Pinochet Ugarte, Augusto, 344, 433
Piper, Adrian, 338
Pittsburgh Courier, 65
Planck, Max, 21
Planetarium, 137
Plants, 432
Plastics, 48, 163, 317
Plater-Zyberk, Elizabeth, 375
Plate tectonics, 245
Platt Amendment, 23, 152
Playboy magazine, 235
Plessy v. Ferguson, 3, 236
PLO. See Palestine Liberation Organization
Plunkett, Roy J., 163
Pluto (planet), 138
Pocho (Villarreal), 251
Poeme Electronique, 249
Poetry, 58–59, 70, 92, 105, 112, 222, 240, 265, 271, 310, 331, 345, 383, 385
Poetry magazine, 70
Poland, 167, 396, 437
Polaroid Land Camera, 211
Police, 410, 412
Polio, 231–32
Polite, Carlene Hatcher, 299
Political campaigns, 290
Pollack, Jordan, 444
Pollock, Jackson, 199, 201, 214, 247
Pollution, 292, 299, 312, 358
Polygraph, 107
Pop art, 247, 275
Population, 269, 437–39, 446
Porgy and Bess (opera), 155
Portales, Marco, 234
Port Chicago Mutiny, 191
Porter, Edwin S., 29, 37
Port Huron Statement, 282
Portocarrero, René, 142
Portugal, 350
Post-it Notes, 373
Postmodernism, 336, 337
Potemkin (movie), 37
Pound, Ezra, 70
Powell, Colin, 394
Powwows, 346, 347–48, 349
Pratt, Richard, 10
Prayer, 281
Presidential terms, 223

Presley, Elvis, 244
Pressed Steel Car Company, 50
Price controls, 334
Price-fixing, 274
Primitivism, 44, 162, 380
Primus, Pearl, 187
Printmaking, 209–10, 246
Prisons, 400, 417
Profit sharing, 78
Prohibition, 94–95, 100, 125, 149
Prokofiev, Sergei Sergeyevich, 52
Property tax, 356
Propst, Robert, 312
Prostheses, 38
Protas, Ron, 439
Prozac, 392
Pruitt-Igoe Public Housing Project (St. Louis), 337
Psychedelic drugs, 301–2
Public Broadcasting Service (PBS), 307
Public relations, 347
Public transportation, 198, 204, 240, 241, 274
Public Trust Doctrine, 126
Pueblo Lands Act, 110
Puerto Rico, 14, 17, 23, 77, 78, 149, 192, 197, 203, 230, 236, 237–38, 315, 342
Pulitzer Prize, 90
Pullman Company, 117
Pure Food and Drug Act, 40, 41
Putin, Vladimir, 439

Qaddafi, Muammar el-, 387
Quantum theory, 21
Quasars, 285
Quayle, Dan, 393
Quilting, 376

Rabin, Itzhak, 422
Race, 446
Race riots, 41, 289, 297, 309, 412, 416
Rachel, 84
Racial profiling, 388
Racism, 423
Radar, 192, 262
Radiation Exposure and Compensation Act, 405
Radicalism, 102
Radio:
  AM, 16, 90
  Federal Radio Commission, 122
  Fessenden's work, 16
  first commercial license, 102
  first commercial transistor, 238
  first listener-sponsored, 214–15
  first live broadcasts, 43, 103
  first soap operas, 147
  first woman to own a station, 115
  FM, 165, 175
  Marconi's work, 51
  "microradio" stations, 445
  public response to, 110
  Voice of America, 211
Radioactivity, 21, 225, 389, 434
Radio Corporation of America (RCA), 89, 103, 122, 225, 238
Ragtime music, 13, 21, 66
Rahman, Mujibur, 337

Railroads, 27–28, 34–35
Rainer, Yvonne, 299, 326
Rainey, Ma, 33, 101
Raisin in the Sun, A, 251
Rand, Ayn, 187
Randolph, A. Philip, 117, 286
Rankin, Jeanette, 86
Rape, 335
Rationing, 187–88
Rauschenberg, Robert, 223, 230, 247, 275, 299
Ray, James Earl, 313
Ray, Man, 88
Rayon, 28
RCA. *See* Radio Corporation of America
Reader's Digest, 111
Reagan, Ronald, 300, 307–8, 334, 359, 365, 368, 371, 373, 377, 379, 381, 390, 391, 392, 414
Recession, 377
Reclamation Act, 27
Recombinant DNA, 352
"Red Hunt," 202–3
"Red" hysteria, 102
Redwood trees, 429
Reed, Ishmael, 320, 341, 350, 351, 396–97
Reed, Walter, 16
Refrigerated trucks, 214
Refugees, 365
Rehnquist, William, 409, 434
Religion, 407
Research, 174, 193, 196, 340
Retirement villages, 269
Reuther, Walter, 238
Reverse discrimination, 356
Reynaud, Paul, 176
Rhapsody in Blue, 113
Rhee, Syngman, 213
Rhodesia, 371
Rhodes, James, 327
Rhythmicon, 140
Richmond (Va.), 394
Rickenbacker, Eddie, 93
Ricks, Willie, 302
Ride, Sally, 380, 382
Riding the Bullet (King), 439
Riley, Terry, 311
Ringgold, Faith, 314, 326, 376
Rinpoche, Chogyam Trungpa, 345
Rio Pact, 213
Rite of Spring, The 76
Rivera, Diego, 142, 144, 173, 176
RNA (ribonucleic acid), 51
Roads, 75, 241, 243, 244
Robbins, Jerome, 189
Roberts, Ed, 335
Roberts, Lawrence G., 340
Roberts, Lenny, 387
Robinson, Jackie, 204
Robots, 108, 274, 444
Rock and roll, 244
Rockefeller, John D., 24, 35, 86
Rockefeller, Nelson, 144, 330, 335
Rockefeller Oil Trust, 43
Rocketry, 79, 95, 119–20
Rodgers, Jimmy, 121
Rodgers, Richard, 187

Roe v. Wade, 339
Rogers, Edith Nourse, 180
Rogers, J. A., 66
Rogers, John, 9, 10
Rolling Stones, 287
Romania, 395–96
Roosevelt, Eleanor, 164
Roosevelt, Franklin D., 133
  Atlantic Charter, 180
  authorization of internment camps, 182
  court packing, 161
  death, 193
  first term election, 146
  "four freedoms," 177
  fourth term election, 190
  letters from Einstein, 165–66
  New Deal, 149, 157, 158, 159, 214
  and radio patents, 89
  second term election, 159
  Teheran Conference, 188–89
  third term election, 174
  Yalta Conference, 192
Roosevelt, Theodore, 71, 328
  appointment of Leupp, 37
  and Booker T. Washington, 22
  Corollary to Monroe Doctrine, 33–34
  expanded powers as president, 23
  "gentleman's agreement" with Japan, 45
  at Louisiana Purchase Exposition, 35, 36
  as negotiator between Japan and Russia, 40
  as "trust buster," 27, 43
  on U.S. as international superpower, 5–6
  as vice president, 14
Roosevelt Reservoir Dam, 72
Root, Elihu, 45
Rose, Barbara, 290
Rose of Fraternity, 123, 124
Rosenberg, Julius and Ethel, 224
Rosenboom, David, 416
Rosewood Massacre, 416
Ross, Nellie, 117
Rossant, Janet, 415
Roswell (N.M.), 203
Rothenberg, Jerome, 310
Roundup (herbicide), 417
Roussel, Raymond, 69
Royalties, 49, 78
Rubin, Carl, 402
Rubin, Jerry, 312, 315
Running Fence, 351
Rural areas, 6, 49
Ruscha, Ed, 275
Ruskin, Mickey, 265, 283
Russell, Diana, 335
Russia, 36, 38, 40, 90–91, 410, 412, 439, 447
Russolo, Luigi, 51, 76
Rustin, Bayard, 208, 286

Saar, Betye, 325
Saarinen, Eliel, 144
Sabin, Albert, 232
Sacco, Nicola, 102
Sadat, Anwar el-, 355, 376
St. Denis, Ruth, 32–33, 81
St. Lawrence Seaway, 255

St. Louis (ship), 149–50
St. Louis World's Fair. *See* Louisiana Purchase Exposition
Salam, Abdus, 294
Salamon, Sonya, 200
Salaries. *See* Labor; Minimum wage
Salazar, Reuben, 328
Saleh, Ali Abdullah, 408
Salk, Jonas, 231
SALT II. *See* Strategic Arms Limitation Treaty
Sambor, Gregore J., 383
Same-sex marriage, 424, 445
Samoa, 14, 127
Samson, Peter, 354
Sanders, Ed, 312
San Diego State College, 330
Sandinistas, 359, 373, 377, 392, 407
Sanford L. Smith and Associates, 413
San Francisco (Calif.), 19–20, 42, 43, 82, 235, 308, 347, 357, 380
San Francisco Chronicle, 20, 39
San Francisco Mime Troupe, 251, 291–92
San Francisco State College, 312
San Francisco Tape Music Center, 279
Sanger, Margaret, 80, 86, 88
San Ildefonso Watercolor Movement, 13
San Quentin State Prison, 335
Santa Anna, Antonio López de, 4–5
Sarnoff, David, 103, 119, 174
Satellites, 247, 248, 255, 267, 281, 285, 425
SATs (Standard Achievement Tests), 25
Saturn (planet), 355
Saudi Arabia, 408, 409
Saund, Dalip Singh, 104
Savings-and-loan institutions, 377, 394
Saxbe, William, 114
Saxophone, 77
Schawlow, Arthur, 268
Schechter Poultry Corp. v. U.S., 157
Scheer, Max, 289
Schillinger, Joseph, 177
Schmidt, Martin, 285
Schoenberg, Arnold, 69, 113, 118, 148
Schools. *See* Education
Schumann, Peter, 283, 291, 326
Schwarzkopf, Norman, 409
Schwerner, Michael, 289
Science, 2, 316
SCLC. *See* Southern Christian Leadership Conference
Scopes, John T., 116–17
Scotch Tape, 137
Scott, David R., 318, 334
Sculpture, 77, 136, 139–40, 271, 369, 393, 408
Scurvy, 72–73
SDI. *See* Strategic Defense Initiative
SDS. *See* Students for a Democratic Society
Seagram Building (N.Y.), 216, 229
Seale, Bobby, 302, 315
Sea Ranch (Calif.), 280–81
Seaside (Fla.), 374, 375–76
Seattle (Wash.), 95
Second City, 251
Second Sex, The (de Beauvoir), 215
Securities fraud, 388

Sedition Act of 1918, 92
Seeger, Ruth Crawford, 136
Segregation, 34, 191, 198, 204, 211, 230, 236–37, 241, 246, 268–69, 274, 333, 367, 409, 422
Seitz, William, 271
Selassie, Haile, 159, 160
Selective Service Act, 89
Self-incrimination, 292
Selz, Peter, 271
Semiconductors, 248
Semon, Waldo, 127
Senate (U.S.), 73, 237, 411
Sender, Ramon, 247, 279
Sennett, Mack, 70
Serbia, 76, 410–11, 437
Serra, Richard, 393
Serrano, Andres, 393
Sesame Street, 317
Seville, David, 245
Sex discrimination, 306–7, 308, 333, 339
Sexual harassment, 378, 391
Sexuality, 212–13, 235, 302, 392
Sexual Politics (Millett), 326
Seymour, William J., 43
Shah Pahlavi, Mohammed Reza, 236, 359
Shange, Ntozake, 345
Sharon, Ariel, 380
Shawn, Ted, 81
Shepard, Alan B. Jr., 273
Shepard, Sam, 356
Shepherd, David, 239
Sherk, Bonnie, 352
Sherman Antitrust Act, 6, 27, 43
Shipp, Joseph F., 50
Shockley, William, 203
Shopping centers, 110, 111, 239, 411
Shorenstein, Walter, 313
Short Eyes, 356
Showboat, 121
Shriver, Sargent, 339
Shuffle Along, 105, 116
Shukeiry, Ahmad, 298
Sickle-cell anemia, 64
Siegel, Bugsy, 198
Siegel, Jerry, 151
Sikorsky, Igor, 166
Silent Spring (Carson), 282
Silver, Spencer, 373
Simmons, William Joseph, 83
Simpson, O. J., 418
Simpson, Peter, 56
Simpson-Mazzoli Act, 387
Sinai Peninsula, 245, 310, 345
Sinatra, Frank, 238–39
Sinclair, Upton, 40, 133
Singapore, 298
Singleton, Alvin, 376
Sinn Fein, 39
Sirica, John J., 342
Sit-ins, 268–69
Six-Day War, 310, 345
Skokie (Ill.), 356
Skylab, 347
Skyscrapers, 2, 19, 100, 216, 229
Slovenia, 411
Smallpox, 371
Smart bombs, 410

Smith, Alfred E., 125
Smith, Anna Deavere, 408–9, 426
Smith, Bessie, 111
Smith, Floyd, 163
Smith, Mamie, 101
Smith, Marc, 383
Smith, William French, 365
Smith Act, 174
Smith-Hughes Act, 68, 89
Smoking, 380, 400, 414, 417
SNCC. See Student Nonviolent Coordinating Committee
Soap operas, 147, 202
Sobell, Morton, 224
Socialism, 40, 102
Social Security, 157–58
Social structures, 138–39
Society of American Indians, 68
Society of Umbra, 265
Sollberger, Harvey, 290
Solomon, David, 388
Somatostatin, 352
Somoza, Anastasio, 359
Sottsass, Ettore Jr., 317
Souls of Black Folk, The (Du Bois), 29
Sound barrier, 203
Sousa, John Philip, 21, 35
South Africa, 209, 215, 385, 407, 439
South Carolina, 435
Southern Christian Leadership Conference (SCLC), 241, 274
South Korea, 213, 293, 430, 447
South Pole, 69
Southwest Movement, 13
Soviet Union, 116, 211, 215, 231, 235, 243, 269, 283, 290, 315, 357, 358, 359, 368, 378, 385, 395, 396
Soybeans, 417
Space exploration, 247, 248, 273–74, 275, 300–301, 315–16, 318, 334–35, 347, 350, 353, 355
Space shuttle, 374–75, 380, 382, 388
Spanish-American War, 5
Spanish Civil War, 160
Spanish flu, 93
Spanish-language television, 242, 274
Special Relativity, 39
Spock, Benjamin, 199
Spolin, Viola, 162
Sports, 339
Sputnik, 246, 247
Stalin, Joseph, 116, 139, 188, 192, 235, 385
Standard Oil, 43
Standing Bear, Luther, 9, 10, 11
Stanislavsky Method, 120, 140, 162, 201
Stark, John, 13
Star Wars (movie), 354
State of Tennessee v. Ed Johnson, 42, 50
Steamboat Willie (animated film), 123
Steelworkers, 7, 50, 229, 358
Steichen, Edward, 36, 121–22
Stein, Gertrude, 108, 148
Stem cells, 415
Stereophonic sound, 248
Steuben Glass Works, 29, 31
Stevens, John Paul, 441
Stieglitz, Alfred, 36–37, 81

Still, William Grant, 140
Still/Here, 416
Stimson, Henry L., 194
Stock market, 47, 99–100, 102, 130, 391, 429, 431, 435
Stokes, Carl, 307
Stone, Harlan Fiske, 114
Stonewall Rebellion, 316, 330
Strasberg, Lee, 140, 201
Strassmann, Fritz, 164, 167
Strategic Arms Limitation Treaty (SALT II), 358
Strategic Defense Initiative (SDI), 379, 414
Stravinsky, Igor, 76, 128, 136, 239, 240
Streetcar Named Desire, A, 209
Strikes:
    Clifton-Morenci, 31
    garment workers', 50
    Homestead, 7
    Japanese of 1909, 50
    mill workers', 72
    shipyard workers', 95
    steelworkers', 7, 50, 229
    United Mine Workers, 28, 75
Student Nonviolent Coordinating Committee (SNCC), 269, 297, 302
Students for a Democratic Society (SDS), 282, 297, 317
Studio for Experimental Music, 253
Studio of the Santa Fe Indian School, 144
Sturtevant, Alfred Henry, 75
Subotnick, Morton, 247, 416
Suburbia, 200, 274, 367, 375, 446
Subways, 19
Sudan, 415
Suez Canal, 245, 310, 345
Sugar, 28
Suicide, 418, 447
Sukarno, President, 298
Sullivan, Louis, 2
Summer of Love, 308, 310–11
Sun City (Ariz.), 269
Sundback, Gideon, 75
Superconductivity, 70
Superman (comic strip), 151
Supreme Court, 42, 50, 161, 307, 373
Surrealism, 91, 116
Sutton, Walter, 28
Suzuki, Daisetz Teitaro, 20
Swann v. Charlotte Mecklenburg Board of Education, 333
Swanson, Robert, 352
Swing music, 151
Swington, A. A. Campbell, 49
Synthesizers, 241, 248–49, 272, 306, 354, 376
Syphilis, 147
Syria, 247, 310, 344
Szilard, Leo, 165–66, 167, 194

Taft, William Howard, 48, 71
Taft-Hartley Act, 202
Taiwan, 359
Takamine, Jokichi, 22
Taliban, 426
Tampax, 141
Tan, Amy, 324
Tanzania, 415

Taraki, Noor Muhammad, 357
Tariffs, 137, 413, 417
Tatum, Art, 233
Tax Reform Act, 315
Taylor, Cecil, 246
TCP/IP. *See* Transmission Control
    Protocol/Internet Protocol
Teapot Dome scandal, 112
Technicians of the Sacred (Rothenberg),
    310
Teflon, 163
Teheran Conference, 189
Telecommunications, 422–23, 430
Telegraphy, 26, 68
Telephone, 83, 122, 244, 343–44, 377,
    392
Telescope, 384, 405–6, 418, 425–26
Television:
    BBC service in London, 160
    Coalition for Better Television, 375
    color, 176, 225, 238
    Farnsworth's work, 122
    first all-electronic in U.S., 163
    first all-electronic picture, 123
    first commercials, 175
    first telecast, 117, 118
    first transcontinental broadcast, 227
    increasing use of, 196
    MTV, 372
    rating system, 420
    RCA, 225
    Spanish-language, 242, 274
    Swington's vision, 49
    V-chip, 423
    Zworykin's work, 115
Teller, Edward, 225
Telstar communications satellites, 267, 281
Tenderich, Gertrude, 141
Tennessee, 102, 117
Tennessee Valley Authority (TVA), 149
Tenney, James, 272
Tenth Street galleries (N.Y.), 265
Terman, Frederick, 165
Terrorism, 340, 415
Test tube babies, 316
Texas, 4–5, 117, 234, 237
Thailand, 430
Thalidomide, 281–82
Thayer, Webster, 102
Theater:
    African American, 292, 429
    breakthroughs of *Shuffle Along,* 105,
        116
    commedia del 'arte, 251, 291–92
    first successful black musical, 26
    founding of Theatre Guild, 94
    improvisational, 162, 239, 251
    multidisciplinary, 354
    off-off Broadway, 275
    regional, 84, 201
    street, 244
    Ziegfeld Follies, 45
    See also specific plays and playwrights
Theremin, Lev, 103
Third World Communications, 345
Thomas, Clarence, 391
Thompson, Earl A., 167
Thompson, Edward, 36

369th Infantry Band, 92
3M Corporation, 373
Three Mile Island (Pa.), 358
Thriller (video), 380
Thurmond, Strom, 246
Tiananmen Square demonstrations, 395
Tibet, 256
Tijerina, Reies Lopez, 302
Time magazine, 112
Time Warner, 384, 425
Titanic (ship), 72
Tilted Arc, 393
Tito (Josip Broz), 235–26
Tlingit people, 56, 57
Togo, Vice Admiral, 40
Tokyo (Japan), 182
Tombaugh, Clyde W., 138
Tomlinson, Ray, 340
Townes, Charles, 268
Toxic waste, 377, 390
Toyota Motor Company, 379
Tractors, 16
Trade, 413, 417, 440
Traffic signal, 113
Trans-Alaska oil pipeline, 342, 355
Transistors, 203, 204, 238, 248, 274,
    288
Transmission Control Protocol/Internet
    Protocol (TCP/IP), 343, 379
Treasury notes, 73
Treaty of Guadalupe Hidalgo, 5, 302
Treaty of Versailles, 92, 96, 103, 154
Treemonisha (opera), 66
Triangle Shirtwaist Company, 67–68
Trip to the Moon, A (movie), 29
Tropic of Cancer (Miller), 150
Trotsky, Leon, 91, 116, 176
Trotter, William Monroe, 38
Trudeau, Pierre, 311
Truman, Harry S., 190, 191, 193, 194,
    195, 202–3, 211, 214, 221, 228,
    229
Truman Doctrine, 202
Trust Company of America, 45, 47
T-shirt, 186
Tshombe, Moise, 270
Tsien, Joe Z., 436
Tulsa (Okla.), 107
Turkey, 83, 111
Turner, Frederick Jackson, 108
Turner, Ted, 366
Turner broadcasting, 425
Turner Diaries, The (Macdonald), 357
Tuskegee Institute, 22, 79
Tuskegee Syphilis Study, 147
Tutankhamen (king), 111
TV dinners, 232
Twenty-first century, 446–47
Tydings-McDuffie Act, 152
"Typhoid Mary," 32
Tz'u-hsi (empress), 21

Udall, Stewart, 273
UFOs (unidentified flying objects), 203
Uganda, 337
Ukeles, Mierle, 352
Ukraine, 389, 410
Ulysses (Joyce), 109, 148

Unemployment, 138, 140, 377
Unimation (co.), 274
Union Carbide, 382
Union of Concerned Scientists, 316
Unions. *See* Labor; Strikes; *specific unions*
United Arab Republic, 247
United Arab States, 247
United Artists, 92
United Farm Workers, 281, 291, 329
United Mine Workers, 28, 75, 158
United Nations, 189, 192, 196, 209, 213,
    313, 337, 338, 342
United Press International (UPI), 248
UNIVAC computer, 227
Universal Negro Improvement Association,
    87
Universal Product Code, 343
Universe, 131, 212, 425, 437
Universities and colleges, 230, 312, 330
University Council for Electronic Music,
    241
University of California (Berkeley), 288
University of California (Davis), 356
University of California (Los Angeles), 407
University of California system, 242
University of Mississippi, 281
University of Oklahoma, 230
University of Washington Press, 323, 348
University of Wisconsin, 323
Unsafe at Any Speed (Nader), 294
Up from Slavery (Washington), 22
Uranium, 167, 225, 358
Uranium-235, 175
Uranus (planet), 355
Urey, Harold C., 141
USO (United Service Organizations), 174
USSR. *See* Soviet Union
U.S. Steel Corporation, 24, 25, 50, 112,
    229, 358
U.S. v. Microsoft, 440
U.S. v. Shipp, 43, 50

Vacuum tube, 46, 47
Valdez, Luis, 291, 355
"Valentine" typewriter, 317
Van Allen Belts, 248
Van Der Zee, James, 84
Vann, Robert L., 65
Vanzetti, Bartolomeo, 102
Varese, Edgard, 81, 236, 249
Vargas, George, 67, 142, 304, 381, 404
VCRs. *See* Videocassette recorders
Venice Biennale, 314
Venter, Craig, 443
Venus (planet), 282, 347
Vermont, 445
Victor Emmanuel III (king), 188
Victoria (queen), 26
Victor Talking Machine Company, 25
Videocassette recorders (VCRs), 354, 409
Video games, 340
Videos, 290, 326, 372, 376, 380
Vietnam, 238, 273, 286, 353–54, 440, 441
Vietnam Veterans Memorial (Washington,
    D.C.), 365, 372
Vietnam War, 287, 291, 297, 299–300,
    303, 306, 311, 315, 327–28, 334,
    348, 350

Vikings, 270
Viking spacecraft, 353
Villa, Francisco "Pancho," 83, 85–86
Villarreal, Jose Antonio, 251
Vinyl, 127
Viola, Bill, 376
Virgin Islands, 89, 159
Virtual reality, 374, 394
VISTA (Volunteers in Service to America), 288, 293
Vitaphone, 119, 121
Voice of America, 211
Von Braun, Wernher, 248
von Zeppelin, Ferdinand, 21
Voting rights:
  of African Americans, 23, 292
  in Finland, 44
  of Native Americans, 114
  in Oregon, 27
  Smith v. Allwright, 190–91
  women's, 66, 68, 71, 76, 83, 100, 101, 328
Voting Rights Act (1965), 292, 350
Voting Rights Act (1970), 328
Voyager space probes, 355

Waco (Tex.) standoff, 413
Wages. *See* Labor; Minimum wage
Wagner Act, 157
Waide, Herbert, 272
Waihee, John D., 387
Waiting for Lefty, 154
Waksman, Selman Abraham, 176
Waldman, Ann, 345
Walesa, Lech, 396
Walker, George, 25
Walker, Madame C. J., 39
Walker, Maggie Lena, 31
Walker, William, 28
Wallace, De Witt, 111
Wallace, George, 285, 292
Wallace, Henry A., 174
Wallace, Michelle, 314
Wallia, C. J. S., 104
Wall of Respect (Chicago), 306
Wall of Truth (Chicago), 306
War Brides Act, 196
Warfare, 65, 126–27
Warhol, Andy, 267, 275, 276, 283, 336
War Industries Board, 93
Warner, John W., 433
Warner Brothers, 119
War of the Worlds, The (radio show), 163–64
War on Poverty, 289, 293
Warren Commission, 287
Warren County (N.C.), 377
Warsaw Pact, 243
War, the Only Hygiene (Marinetti), 65
Washington, Booker T., 22, 38, 41, 66, 116
Waste Isolation Pilot Plant, 434
Waste Land, The (Eliot), 108
Water, 110, 125, 126, 196, 299, 338, 349, 352, 400
Watergate affair, 338–39, 342, 345–47
Watson, James, 233, 235
Watson, Thomas A., 83

Watts (Los Angeles), 297
Weather, 328–29
Weaver, Lois, 364
Weaver, Robert, 299
Webb, Elida, 112
Weidman, Charles, 120
Weinberg, Steven, 294
Weiner, Lee, 315
Weisblum, Bernard, 443
Weizmann, Chaim, 213
Welch Bill, 157
Welfare reform, 334, 424
Welles, Orson, 163, 176
West Bank, 391
Westinghouse Corporation, 102–3, 158
West Side Story, 245
White, Dan, 357
White, George H., 15
White supremacists, 357
Wicker, 89
Wiener, Norbert, 212
Wilder, Douglas, 392
Wilder, Thornton, 162
Wildmon, Donald, 393
Wilfred, Thomas, 105–6
Wilkins, Maurice, 235
Wilkins, Roy, 289
Williams, Bert A., 25
Williams, Hank, 214
Williams, Ralph Vaughan, 52
Williams, Tennessee, 209
Wills, Bob, 155, 157
Wilson, August, 292, 422, 429
Wilson, Charles E., 203
Wilson, Henry Lane, 74
Wilson, Pete, 416–17, 425
Wilson, Richard "Dicky," 342
Wilson, Robert, 350
Wilson, Woodrow, 71, 74, 78, 85, 86, 92, 96, 102
Windham Hill Records, 352
Winfield, Hemsley, 139
Winters, Yvor, 128
Wizard of Oz, The (Baum), 12
Wojnarowicz, David, 393
Woman Warrior, The (Kingston), 324
Women:
  African American, 344, 364, 383
  in armed forces, 180
  in arts, 314, 325, 357, 364, 383, 390
  Chinese American, 382
  Declaration of Principles, 36
  EMILY's List, 383
  Equal Rights Amendment, 308, 328, 339, 377
  feminism, 286–87, 297, 299, 313, 317, 328, 335
  first American in space, 380
  first in House of Representatives, 86
  first millionaire in U.S., 39
  first priest, 353
  first on Supreme Court, 373
  first to own and operate a bank, 31
  first women's studies program, 330
  immigration of Asian, 100
  pay scales, 31, 94
  poetry, 385

as "second line of defense" in World War II, 184
  sexuality, 235
  suffrage, 66, 68, 71, 76, 83, 100, 101, 328
  Third World writers, 345
  voting rights in Finland, 44
  in workplace, 49, 308, 333, 339
Women Artists in Revolution, 314
Women's Liberation Movement, 313
Wong, Delbert, 255
Wong, Shawn, 319–20, 322, 323, 345, 357
Wood, Leonard, 27
Woodstock (N.Y.), 314
Woodward, Bob, 342
Wooster Group, 354
Works Progress Administration (WPA), 134, 154, 180, 413
World Exposition (Paris), 21
World's Fair (Brussels), 249
World's Fair (N.Y.), 167, 168, 169
World Trade Center (N.Y.), 415
World Trade Organization (WTO), 419, 435, 440
World War I, 80–81, 87, 89, 90, 94, 96, 100
World War II, 167, 173–74, 177–78, 180–82, 184, 191–96, 228
World Wide Web, 347, 378, 408, 411–12, 413, 417, 418, 420
Wounded Knee (S.D.), 4, 9–11, 342–43
WOW Café (N.Y.), 364
Wozniak, Stephen, 354–55
Wozzeck (opera), 118
WPA. *See* Works Progress Administration
Wright, Frank Lloyd, 22, 159
Wright, Richard, 173
Wright Brothers, 31, 32
WTO. *See* World Trade Organization
Wuorinen, Charles, 290
Wynema (Callahan), 11
Wyoming, 117

Xerox Corporation, 255, 301, 329, 341
X: The Life and Times of Malcolm X (opera), 387

Yahi people, 69
Yalta Conference, 192
Yardbird Reader magazine, 341
Y'Bird magazine, 341
Yeager, Charles "Chuck," 203
Year of the Dragon, The, 348
Yellow fever, 16
Yeltsin, Boris, 410, 439
Yemen, 408, 415
Yippies (Youth International Party), 312
Yogananda, Paramahansa, 104
Yom Kippur War, 344–45
Young, Al, 341
Young, Andrew, 352
Youngstown Sheet and Tube v. Sawyer, 229–30
Your Hit Parade, 155
Yucca Mountain (Nev.), 434
Yugoslavia, 235–36, 410–11

Zane, Arnie, T., 416
Zapata, Emiliano, 83
Zapatista National Liberation Army, 418–19
Zelaya, José Santos, 45
Zhao Ziyang, 395

Zhou Enlai, 215, 338, 353
Ziegfeld Follies, 45
Zimbabwe, 371
Zinn, Henry, 225
Zinn, Walter, 167
Zionism, 91, 213, 298

ZIP codes, 284
Zipper, 75–76
Zoning, 85
Zoot Suit, 355
Zoot Suit Riot, 188
Zworykin, Vladimir, 115, 175

ABOUT THE AUTHOR

Carla Blank developed and taught a University of California, Berkeley, American Cultures lecture course, "Across Disciplines: 20th Century Art Forms," from 1994 to 1999 for the Center for Theater Arts and Interdisciplinary Studies Departments (now called the Department of Theater, Dance, and Performance Studies). Teaching materials for the course led to the creation of this book. She is coauthor, with Jody Roberts, of *Live OnStage!,* an anthology of performing arts techniques and styles available in teacher resource and student editions (Dale Seymour Publications, a Pearson education imprint, 1997). North Carolina, Tennessee, Mississippi, and Idaho have adopted it for middle-school use statewide. Blank has also been a performer, director, and teacher of dance and theater for over thirty-five years, especially devoting her time to youth and community arts performance projects. She lives in Oakland, California, with her family of writers, Ishmael Reed and Tennessee Reed.